BLACK JOURNALS
OF THE
UNITED STATES

BLACK JOURNALS
OF THE
UNITED STATES

Walter C. Daniel

Historical Guides to the World's Periodicals and Newspapers

Greenwood Press
Westport, Connecticut • London, England

Library of Congress Cataloging in Publication Data

Daniel, Walter C.
    Black journals of the United States.

    (Historical guides to the world's periodicals and
newspapers)
    Bibliography: p.
    Includes index.
    1. Afro-American periodicals—History.   I. Title.
II. Series.
PN4882.5.D36   051   81-13440
ISBN 0-313-20704-6 (lib. bdg.)   AACR2

Library of Congress Catalog Card Number: 81-13440
ISBN: 0-313-20704-6

First published in 1982

Greenwood Press
A division of Congressional Information Service, Inc.
88 Post Road West
Westport, Connecticut 06881

Printed in the United States of America

10 9 8 7 6 5 4 3 2 1

Contents

Acknowledgments

Many persons assisted me in compiling this work.

The editorial department of Greenwood Press expressed interest in my first proposal, which I presented to them nearly four years ago. Cynthia Harris, editor, reference books, at Greenwood, has been patient, demanding, and instructive. My association with her over these many months has fashioned a book considerably different from what I seemed to be producing earlier in the process.

Contributors have been cooperative, and I believe the experience has been enriching for them. I am grateful to all of them: Brian Joseph Benson, Noel Heermance, Charles Holmes, Addison Reed, Mark Reger, and Arvarh Strickland.

Persons associated with libraries across the country have helped me at the Library of Congress, New York Public Library, University of Illinois at Champaign, University of Texas at Austin, University of New Mexico, Bowling Green State University, Kansas State University, and the University of California at Los Angeles and at Berkeley. The Moreland-Spingarn Research Center magazine library at Howard University has been the most helpful single source.

My friends at Lincoln University of Missouri simply opened the full resources of Inman Page Library there to me. Robert Huffman of the Elmer Ellis Library at the University of Missouri-Columbia took particular interest in my work.

Richard Wallace, associate provost for research and graduate studies at the University of Missouri-Columbia, cheerfully made small financial grants to me whenever possible.

I am grateful to all those persons.

Preparing the manuscript for the publisher is a monumental task, the scope of which often deceives one who becomes euphoric as he completes the research on a book. The people who assisted me in typing, checking a multitude of notes and references, and keeping the production moving forward have played an important part in the completed project.

Victor Errante and Scott Cytron, students of mine, helped with early drafts. Mark Reger, teaching fellow in the English department at the University of Missouri-Columbia with me, worked throughout most of one summer on clerical and editorial duties.

David Long, my associate in the College of General Studies, devoted most of his days and many nights for the last month of our work, helping to bring the full manuscript to the publisher. His help was indispensable.

My wife and David Long's wife merit my thanks for their cooperation and understanding.

Black Journals needed to be compiled. My associates on the project and I hope we did a creditable job for scholarship in American culture.

Introduction

The Afro-American press began with *Freedom's Journal*, founded in 1827 in New York City. Although this publication appeared regularly for little more than one year in its original form, it set the pattern for a black American press. John Russwurm and Samuel Cornish, its founders, established the journal as a medium of expression for news about activities among Afro-Americans and as an editorial defense against attacks that the *Daily Press* of New York City was making against free blacks in that city. That pattern of content which Russwurm and Cornish established, together with creative writing, has remained essentially the material of the Afro-American press.

Most scholarly works on communications media among blacks in America focus on the weekly newspaper. Little research has been done on the black magazine. It is a common misconception that early black journals were totally abolitionist papers. Recent research shows clearly that the *Anglo-African Magazine* (1859-1861) followed the pattern of the traditional American national magazine. The same was the case with the *A. M. E. Church Review* (1884-present) and to a large extent with *Douglass' Monthly* (1859-1893), although all the antebellum black periodicals spoke out strongly against slavery.

Most black magazines have been published during the twentieth century. Few of them have been included in the several periodical indexes. Use of their contents has been made difficult by this omission. *Black Journals* makes available historical and descriptive profiles of more than 100 Afro-American periodicals—excluding newspapers—published between 1827 and the 1980s.

Previously, three important works have provided some portions of this kind of research material. Two doctoral dissertations, Dorothy Deloris Boone's "Historical Review and a Bibliography of Selected Negro Magazines, 1910-1969" (University of Michigan, 1970), and Mary Fair Burks' "Survey of Black Literary Magazines in the United States: 1859-1940" (Columbia University Teachers College, 1975), have enhanced research in this area. Abby Arthur Johnson and Ronald Maberry Johnson's *Propaganda and Aesthetics: The Literary Politics of Afro-American Magazines in the Twentieth Century* is a seminal work on the relationship between literary and political little magazines during the Harlem

Renaissance period. *Black Journals of the United States* enlarges upon these three important pieces of scholarship.

Profiles have been chosen on the basis of available periodicals and a mix of those that seem to reflect the broad scope of the black American experience from 1827 to the 1980s. They are arranged alphabetically to facilitate easy access. An asterisk (*) has been used in each profile the first time a title of another periodical included in the text appears.

All entries include a historical essay providing information on the periodical's development and editorial policies, and the people who played a role in that development. In addition, they include two sections in which data on Information Sources and Publication History are listed in tabular form for easy reference. The section on Information Sources gives bibliographic information, index sources, and location sources. The section on Publication History lists title changes, volume and issue data, publisher and place of publication, editors, and circulation figures.

Finally, the work concludes with two appendixes: a chronology giving both the significant events in black history and the journals' founding dates, and a listing of journals by geographical location.

PROFILES
OF BLACK
JOURNALS

——— A ———

ABBOTT'S MONTHLY

One month before the stock market crash—September 1929—Robert S. Abbott began publication of *Abbott's Monthly* magazine with a first issue of 50,000 copies.[1] The journal enjoyed an enthusiastic reception, largely owing to the wide audience Abbott's *Chicago Defender* had already gained. That newspaper had revolutionized black journalism. It enlarged upon services earlier newspapers had provided: championing black causes, highlighting black accomplishments, and reporting on news items of general and particular interest to blacks. Its vitality lay in its overt appeal to the masses of black people, North and South.[2] Abbott recalled that his stepfather had told him many years earlier in Savannah, Georgia, that a good newspaper is one of the best instruments of service and one of the strongest weapons to be used in defense of a race that has been deprived of its citizenship rights. That goal for the *Defender* made Abbott a "race leader." Roi Ottley, Abbott's biographer, captures the impact of his leadership upon his times.

This was the newspaper that moved 50,000 oppressed people between 1916 and 1918 from the sweat and toil of the boll weevil-stricken South and the paternalistic white overlords to the "freer air" of the North. And Robert S. Abbott was the man behind the call to the "promised land" that resounded throughout the Southern world. The Chicago *Defender*, circulating in some cities from work-worn hand to hand and read in secret away from resentful white eyes, was the beckoning instrument.[3]

The time was propitious. Northern industry was replacing southern plantations, and immigrants from Europe and from the American South streamed into the Midwest. Abbott openly appealed to black sharecroppers to leave the South and seek a new life in Chicago. He worked equally hard to help these black immigrants adjust to the new urban life in the North, seeking employment for them, encouraging their social and religious organizations, and keeping their needs before the black and white reading public. The newspaper became a successful business enterprise for Abbott, and its unique headlines and satirical cartoons gave black Americans throughout the United States what has been called the first popularly styled journal published by and for blacks.

Nearly a quarter of a century after he had founded the newspaper, Abbott launched his magazine, not as a supplement to the *Defender*, but as a freestanding publication owned and operated by Abbott's publishing corporation. Lucius C. Harper, longtime city editor of the *Defender*, agreed to edit the magazine.[4] His wide reading in black history and his philosophy of journalism as a vehicle for social and political protest made him especially qualified for the new assignment. At the time he had been a part of the *Defender* organization for more than a decade.

Abbott's Monthly never enjoyed the *Defender*'s popular success. Its purposes were different. Like major American magazines, it sought a more specialized audience than the newspaper's through a wider range of features: thoughtful, militant editorials intended to promote significant reactions among readers and scholarly articles contributed by black authors on a variety of subjects. Coming as it did at the time of the "Chicago Renaissance," that often-neglected phase of Americana, it saw the rise of the midland metropolis journalists and creative writers whose works have furnished a large part of twentieth-century American letters.

An editorial in the first issue of *Abbott's* claimed the new organ was needed to provide an opportunity for writers of all races. Editors solicited articles on "new, interesting and out-of-the-ordinary subjects." The journal did not intend to cater particularly to "high arts and sciences" because its staff found a measure of scientific techniques in all activities of life. *Abbott's* published book and drama reviews, true confessions, sketches of successful Negroes, some poetry and short fiction, and comments on national and world affairs. Social and political observations and recommendations appeared in editorials. Staff members wrote most of the copy, but Clarence Darrow, Thomas Fortune Fletcher, Bishop William J. Walls, the Reverend Harold Kingsley, and Horace R. Cayton contributed articles.

The prevailing interest in Africa and African culture led to Edith L. Player's "How a Voice of Africa Was Made in Beautiful Song," tracing the foundation of African tribal music and American plantation melodies in Anton Dvořák's "Symphony from the New World" and in folk songs the noted black tenor Roland Hayes made world famous. Sea chanteys black sailors sang on ocean-going vessels provided material for Lewis White's "Music and Muscle." Robert Lawrence McKiddlin discussed African political and social life in "The People of Heaven," a description of the Zulu people. Raymond Leslie Buell wrote about slavery as practiced by Liberians upon certain of their native tribes. A column titled "The Month" listed news about black people in Europe, the Caribbean, and the United States.

Abbott, one of the few black American millionaires, was a Republican, and his magazine reflected his political affiliation. By the end of its second year of publication, Abbott added a column, "This Month," to the magazine. It reported at first on outstanding black personalities around the world. As the presidential campaign of 1931 approached, however, Abbott's comments in "This Month" became more and more political. He began to write editorials. One significant comment in the column foreshadowed the editor's political change of heart. He wrote of President Calvin Coolidge:

> Mr. Coolidge is Mr. Roosevelt coming back from the outpost. It is said that his is a New England drawl. We had thought that New England had the twang and that the South lived in the drawl. But whatever it is that New England, the precious territory of the western empire, is noted for in the speech or in the affluence of ideas, Mr. Coolidge represents. His candor is delightful, but he consents with joyful dexterity.
>
> In choosing his course for 1928, he brightened American language. In 1931, he is no less original. In both instances, his conduct and his language are highly benevolent to President Hoover. Opponents of Mr. Hoover in 1928 called Mr. Coolidge to save them from the promised doom. He failed them. Opponents of Mr. Hoover in 1932 cried to Mr. Coolidge to rescue the perishing, care for the dying, but the new cry immediately met the response of the old.
>
> Instead of discouraging the Republicans, who are illustrious in the power of sufficiency no less than in an effectiveness of organized intelligence, Mr. Coolidge's decision to stand by in 1932 will be as discomforting to the hereditary foes of ordinary government as found in every contest when Republicans stood together.[5]

Abbott broke completely with the Republican party when President Hoover nominated John H. Parker of North Carolina to the United States Supreme Court. The journal joined most other black presses and the NAACP in a nation-wide campaign to influence the Senate to refuse to confirm Parker's appointment. *Abbott's Monthly* was a leader in that fight which ended in a victory for the black leadership.

Other editorials in the magazine chastised Republicans who refused to take bold stands on the racial questions of the day. Herbert Hoover showed that he and his administration controlled the machinery and direction of the Republican party, but they refused to advocate the causes most important for black Americans. According to *Abbott's* editorial comment, the Republican in the White House exacted financial tribute from black Americans for even the nominal support the party gave them. As a result of the long smoldering cleavage between Abbott and the Republican administrations of Coolidge and Hoover, the journal and its editor broke with the Republican party and threw their support to Franklin

D. Roosevelt, the Democratic candidate for president in 1933. This change in allegiance was important, for the *Defender* and *Abbott's Monthly* commanded uncommon respect among black Americans. Republican insensitivity to causes blacks considered important caused the defection as much as did the ravages of the depression. An article written by A. N. Fields, "Lily-whitism—How It Started," detailed an attitude William Howard Taft had started in 1909 that caused a chasm between blacks and the Republican party. Harding, Coolidge, and Hoover had only deepened that cleavage. Fields wrote that Booker T. Washington found it exceedingly difficult to maintain his intimate connections with the White House under President Taft. Washington had to summon aid from his most influential white friends in New York to urge the president to continue to appoint black men and women to federal positions at home and abroad. The magazine kept its audience strongly aware that Republicans had "betrayed" the Negro.

As a general purpose magazine, *Abbott's* gave appropriate attention to literary events, creative writing and the fine arts. Marc Connelly's "The Green Pastures," a lavish Broadway production that featured black singers and actors, including the principal character, Richard B. Harrison, opened during a blizzard in February 1930. The struggling economy would have seemed to weigh against a successful run for a religious play depicting black folk versions of the Bible in cynical New York City at the height of national financial disaster and rising aesthetic communism. Still, "The Green Pastures" attracted thousands of Americans to the theater, both in New York and in widely scattered parts of the country. Ruby Beckley Goodwin sought to explain this apparent paradox in *Abbott's*. She wrote, in part:

> The world is spiritually hungry. It has become cynical. People today believe in nothing. They do not believe in the Here-to-fore, or the Here-after, that is, they would like for you to believe that they do not believe. But they do—they believe in spite of their prejudices and their scoffing.
>
> There is more to "The Green Pastures" than just an illiterate Negro's conception of the Bible, nor is it a farce as probably some people who have never seen the play have been led to believe. I believe that every member of the cast feels the importance of the play and tries to the very best of their ability to interpret the part which he has to portray, whether it be a major role or a minor one.
>
> "The Green Pastures" has drawn more churchpeople into the theater than any other stage play. Noted ministers and divines from every religious denomination have come to see and study this play. The religious-minded come to grasp a firmer hold on faith; the intellectual has come to study the play from a critical, mental angle; the psychologists come to note the reactions of untutored minds to problems of infinite scope; the curious come to see something new; the so-called sophists come to scoff, but

usually they leave in silence, awed and a bit perturbed by what they have learned and seen. So you can see the play is universal in its appeal.[6]

Abbott's was not primarily a literary magazine, but it contained creative writing and it published works of Langston Hughes, J. Saunders Redding, and most of the writers who were placing their works in the other black general-purpose journals. *Abbott's* did have the distinction of publishing the first pieces of fiction written by Richard Wright, who was to become the leading black fiction writer of the 1940s and 1950s. It also published the first works presented to the public by Chester Himes, a young prisoner serving a life sentence in the Ohio State Penitentiary at Columbus at the time. He contributed five short stories to *Abbott's* before his sentence was commuted.[7] Subsequently, Himes' short fiction appeared in *Esquire, Crisis,* Coronet, New Masses, Opportunity,** and *Negro Story.**

For four years Robert S. Abbott published the journal that bore his name. When it failed to carry its financial weight among the Abbott enterprises, the pioneering publisher wrote with pride and disappointment about the purposes that motivated him to launch the project. He wanted to give the reading public a magazine that he would be proud to display in any place at any time, he wrote— one on a par with any current publication, but also so different in construction and offering that its diversity would more than compensate for its price. He was only partially successful in this venture, for price was a part of the reason the journal failed. It was excessive for black readers during the Depression. However, *Abbott's Monthly* achieved most of its publisher's aspirations. It was short-lived but significant among black journals, far more significant than most literary historians have seemed to realize.[8]

Notes

1. Robert Sengstacke Abbott (1868-1940) was born at Frederica, Saint Simon's Island, Georgia, the son of former slaves. He received his early schooling at Beach Institute in Savannah and spent a brief time at Claflin College in Orangeburg, South Carolina, before entering Hampton Institute in Virginia to study printing. After he completed his vocational course at Hampton, he went to Chicago and earned an LL.B. from Kent School of Law in Chicago. He worked for a brief time with his stepfather, who published the *Woodville* (Georgia) *Times*, before returning to Chicago. Metz T. P. Lochard, in "Phylon Profile, XII: Robert S. Abbott—'Race Leader,'" *Phylon* (Second Quarter 1947): 124, describes the founding of the *Defender*: "It was not long before he was scurrying around with a four-page sheet called the Chicago *Defender*, audaciously captioned, 'The World's Greatest Weekly.' With a quarter as starting capital, Abbott had bought some tablet paper, persuaded his landlady to let him use her kitchen, borrowed some money to pay a printer, and the Chicago *Defender* was born on May 5, 1905."

2. Lochard also reports: "Abbott labeled the movement the Great Northern Drive, the Negro's push for self-realization just as the Hindenburg Drive was the Allied push for victory in 1918. He set departure dates; he showed pictures of the best homes, schools,

and parks in Chicago next to the pictures of the worst in the South; he gave abundant space to job offers and news about the happy people who had already come." Ibid., p. 125.

3. Roi Ottley, *The Lonely Warrior: The Life and Times of Robert S. Abbott* (Chicago, 1955), p. 28.

4. Like Abbott, Lucius C. Harper was born in Georgia—in Augusta. He attended Haines Institute there, and Atlanta University, Fisk University, and Oberlin College at some time. He learned printing and began his career with *Georgia Baptist*, a religious publication published in Augusta. He worked as advance man for a minstrel troupe and developed an unusual memory for names, dates, and places. *See* Ottley, *Lonely Warrior*, p. 116.

5. "This Month," *Abbott's Monthly* (November 1931): 34.

6. "Why *Green Pastures* Became an Institution," *Abbott's Monthly* (January 1933): 6-8.

7. Himes' short fiction published in *Abbott's Monthly* gave the young prisoner an opportunity to begin a writing career while he was incarcerated. The five short stories he contributed to *Abbott's* at that time are significant pieces of black creative writing from "behind the wall." They were as follows: "His Last Day," (November 1932): 32-33, 60-65; "Prison Mass" (serialized through three months in 1933) (March, pp. 36, 61-64; April, pp. 20-21, 48-56; and May, pp. 37, 61-62); "Her Whole Existence," (July 1933): 54-57; "I Don't Want to Die," (October 1933): 21-24; and "He Knew," (December 1933): 15-18. An excellent full-length book on Himes' longer fiction is Stephen F. Milliken, *Chester Himes: A Critical Appraisal* (Columbia: University of Missouri Press, 1976).

8. In evaluating the accomplishment of *Abbott's Monthly*, Abby Arthur Johnson and Ronald Maberry Johnson, *Propaganda and Aesthetics: The Literary Politics of Afro-American Magazines in the Twentieth Century* (Amherst: University of Massachusetts Press, 1979), p. 110, write that "not until *Ebony** emerged in 1945 would a black popular magazine match the audience attracted by *Abbott's Monthly*." The same literary historians note that the first number of the magazine sold 50,000 copies, and that shortly thereafter sales soared to 100,000, breaking all records for a black popular magazine.

Information Sources

BIBLIOGRAPHY:
Dictionary of American Biography. Vol. 22, Supplement 2 1958, S.V. "Abbott, Robert S."
Johnson, Abby Arthur, and Johnson, Ronald Maberry. *Propaganda and Aesthetics: The Literary Politics of Afro-American Magazines in the Twentieth Century.* Amherst: University of Massachusetts Press, 1979.
Lochard, Metz T. P. "*Phylon* Profile, XII: Robert S. Abbott—'Race Leader.'" *Phylon,* Second Quarter 1947, pp. 124-32.
Ottley, Roi. *The Lone Warrior: The Life and Times of Robert S. Abbott.* Chicago, 1955.
INDEX SOURCES: None.
LOCATION SOURCE: Moorland-Spingarn Collection, Howard University.

Publication History

MAGAZINE TITLE AND TITLE CHANGES: *Abbott's Monthly* (October 1929-September 1933).

VOLUME AND ISSUE DATA: Vols. I-V (October 1929-September 1933).
PUBLISHER AND PLACE OF PUBLICATION: Robert S. Abbott Publishing Company, Chicago, Illinois.
EDITOR: Lucius C. Harper (1929-1933).
CIRCULATION: 37,000.

ABOUT TIME

About Time began publication as a general purpose magazine in 1973, as one of the group of publications that serve largely as local newspapers in the black community. Its chief focus is the black community in Rochester, New York. Black pride in local personalities who achieve noteworthy distinction dominates the articles and features. Departments include food and homemaking, entertainment, a poet's page, and editorials. Under "Review Column" the editor summarizes the content of each issue and comments on how the features came to be written. "Hobnobbing" highlights national news. African affairs; the unique problems blacks face in character assassinations of their local and national leaders; urban affairs, athletics, city government, and social action programs in Rochester; and the impact of political activities upon education illustrate the range of items that appear in the magazine. It is in effect a black newspaper. Its political items originally were restricted to Rochester. The magazine supported Jimmy Carter in the 1976 presidential campaign. After his election, "What Can Blacks Expect from Carter?" noted that an estimated 6.6 million black voters gave Carter 94 percent of their votes. The black agenda, the editorial continued, was well known. Blacks expected jobs, urban revitalization, national health insurance, welfare and tax reform, and an enforceable equal opportunity program. The editor warned that blacks would find solutions to these problems far more complex and elusive at close range than they appeared at a distance during the campaign.

About Time did not urge its audience to vote for Ronald Reagan in 1980. When he had been inaugurated in early 1981 and the Ninety-seventh Congress had convened, an editorial noted:

Black Americans are leery of the backward glances being advocated by many conservatives and those in the radical right.... This attitude is not one of panic. It is based on a very real historical view of black progress toward equality over the past two decades. That progress began in 1952 with the Administration of Republican President Dwight Eisenhower and picked up under Presidents John F. Kennedy and Lyndon B. Johnson with the passage of new civil rights legislation and ground-breaking black appointments.[1]

After tracing the movement toward equality under Richard M. Nixon and its reactivation under Jimmy Carter, the editorial ended by advising blacks to neither take a wait-and-see attitude toward the new White House nor panic. Instead the piece used the words of Congressman William Gray of Philadelphia's four-point formula to help meet challenges blacks face in 1981: (1) reassess coalitions with all people of good will, (2) continue to organize politically, (3) strengthen and support black institutions, and (4) renew faith. The same issue contained a long interview with Gloria Toote, one of the blacks most visible in the Republican party under Nixon and Gerald Ford.[2]

During the course of the interview, the editor of *About Time* pushed Dr. Toote to give some assurance to black readers that President Reagan would champion their causes and interests. When asked how she could build a beachhead of strength for Republicanism among blacks, given the perception that the party had not supported black interests, Dr. Toote retorted:

> I don't turn it around and I don't think my party alone can turn it around. It can only be turned around as a result of the intent of the leadership of black America to acknowledge its past failure and to encourage minority participation in both parties for the good of black America. Our leaders in this last election prevented the Republicans from being any more successful than they were.[3]

She said Ronald Reagan deserved full credit for the effort that was made on the behalf of black people by his party, and that largely as a result of his insistence, for the first time in the history of the Republican party's national platform there was language that related to black America. She insisted Reagan had placed the language there himself.

Although *About Time* is principally a local periodical of Rochester, its editorial policy is vital and national in its political scope. An editorial following the 1980 presidential election expresses the political tone of the journal.

> When the polls closed last November, fifteen incumbent black members were returned to the Congressional House of Representatives. Two former black seats were filled with new black representatives and another two brand new seats were won (one in Illinois and one in California). Black representatives in Congress increased from seventeen to nineteen members.
>
> Surely the political analysts and forecasters were looking into foggy crystal balls when they predicted voter apathy would keep black voters away from the polls. In gaining elected offices here and there, the celebration of victory was less than jubilant. We were winning the minor skirmishes but losing the major battle.[4]

The editorial chastised blacks who refused to open their doors to census takers the previous April, and, in doing so, deprived themselves of at least five additional congressmen. Those federal representatives would have brought considerably increased funds into black communities for education, employment, and housing, the editorial claimed.

About Time is not a particularly impressive publication. It serves local interests and keeps its readers aware of news and the editor's opinion about national affairs of importance. It makes little impact with its creative writing, but represents a healthy example of the community journal in contemporary society. Its "Portraits of Black Personalities" is a resource for local readers. It includes vignettes of nationally known blacks such as A. Philip Randolph, Alex Haley, Ed Bradley, Mel Goode, Andrew Young, and Edward Brooke. The December 1978 issue was a special women's edition.

Notes

1. "The Uncharted Course," *About Time* (December 1980): 4.
2. Dr. Toote, a graduate in law from Howard University and the Columbia University Graduate School of Law, served Nelson A. Rockefeller in several positions during his tenure as governor of New York. Richard Nixon appointed her Assistant Director of ACTION and later Assistant Secretary of the Department of Housing and Urban Affairs. She was the highest ranking woman in Washington in the federal government at the time. She was a member of the Reagan-Bush Trusts Teams, seconded the nomination of Ronald Reagan for president in 1976, and remained a staunch member of the Republican National Committee.
3. "Dr. Gloria E. A. Toote: A Supporting Force in the Reagan Victory," *About Time* (December 1980): 12.
4. "Election Aftermath: The Third Opportunity," *About Time* (December 1980): 12.

Information Sources

BIBLIOGRAPHY:
Wolseley, Roland E. *Black Press U. S. A.* Ames: Iowa State University Press, 1971, pp. 156-59.
INDEX SOURCES: None.
LOCATION SOURCES: Kansas State University Ethnic Studies Center; newsstands.

Publication History

MAGAZINE TITLE AND TITLE CHANGES: *About Time*.

VOLUME AND ISSUE DATA: Vols. I - (January 1973 -   ), monthly.

PUBLISHER AND PLACE OF PUBLICATION: About Time Magazine, Incorporated, Rochester, New York.

EDITOR: Carolyne S. Blount (1973-   ).

CIRCULATION: 14,000.

AFRICAN, THE: JOURNAL OF AFRICAN AFFAIRS

Africans in Harlem, Roi Ottley noted, "expend much of their energies through organizations like the African Students' Association, in attempting to arouse American Negroes to act in relieving the plight of the African blacks."[1] The *African*, published in Harlem beginning in October 1937 and continuing, with one interruption, until May 1948, was one such effort. It emanated from efforts of African leaders to establish a communications network in the United States after Benito Mussolini invaded Ethiopia in 1935.[2] Emperor Haile Selassie sent native African Malaku E. Bayen, a graduate of Howard University's medical school, and his American-born wife to the United States to stimulate sympathy among American Negroes and raise funds for war relief. Upon arrival in the United States, Dr. Bayen took up residence in Harlem after having been barred as a Negro from hotels downtown in Manhattan. He published the *Voice of Ethiopia*, a militant, pro-African newspaper that urged American blacks to save Ethiopia from the ravages of Mussolini, and he organized the Ethiopian World Federation, Incorporated.

After Bayen's death Haile Selassie dispatched his cousin Prince Araya Abebe to Harlem as his personal envoy. Agitation created by these native Africans gave rise to many organizations and periodicals that called for Americans and the rest of the democratic world to rescue Ethiopia. As their influence spread and their activities took form, black scholars and activists spoke and wrote about the aspirations of black peoples throughout the continent of Africa and the Caribbean.

The *African* was one journal of this orientation that enjoyed sustained success and attracted the attention of many Afro-American writers and public figures. The lead editorial in the magazine's premier issue made the periodical's purpose plain.

> Theories and assumptions of many varieties abound in our libraries. Millions in money and men are spent to maintain them. Anthropologists, ethnologists, psychologists, biologists, morphologists, and hosts of others are eternally looking for evidence to discount the man of Africa. Virtue is painted white and vice black so as to tie up the work of the religionists with this majestic horde in a unique schematic pattern. Where convenient, it was to prove race superiority and inferiority so as to superimpose reasons for their economic and political strangle hold on the African people. . . . It is to examine and appraise the merits or demerits of these theories and these acts of beneficence of the African "humanitarians," to relate the facts about black men in and out of Africa, to call the attention of the world to the place of Africa and Africans in the broad sweep of humanity, and to stimulate the interest of the world in recognition of 400,000,000 people, that *The African* is published.[3]

This journal of world affairs, news items of areas in which black people lived, and creative writing published book reviews read from the black perspective and presented strong activist political views. Its editorials were vital and provocative. The first one addressed some of the devastating problems of Africans caught up in the invasion of Ethiopia, and that country's dismay at the callousness with which the League of Nations treated Haile Selassie's appeals for sanctions against Mussolini's Italy. It also noted the rising unrest in Europe's African colonies, the notorious Scottsboro Case in the United States, and devised a definition of a strategic minority that could align black people in Africa and the Americas into a strong and vociferous power in world affairs. Articles appeared about the trusteeship areas of Africa that had been assigned by the League of Nations following World War I, the civil war in Spain, the proposed partitioning of Palestine, and the irrepressible conflict clearly discerned in Japan's invasion of China. "The State of Affairs" became a regular feature as a potpourri of events relating particularly to African affairs. In one feature the journal described a movement that had been launched in South African universities to combat increasing legislation intensifying racial oppression against blacks. The statement explained the group's purpose: "It intends to enroll all students regardless of their political affiliations within the newly organized South African Students Liberal League; it will issue a series of pamphlets exposing the tyrannical attacks made upon the Africans."[4]

Africans in the United States decried racial oppression in Africa, but they were equally firm in denouncing race prejudice in America. An editorial commented on the Scottsboro Case.

> For over six years the blood-boiling and hair-raising Scottsboro Case has held the attention of the world. In a way, it is unfair to America that this type of Southern justice has brought so much scorn and derision on the fair name of the land of liberty. In an interview a week ago with an African leader, the first thing which "accidentally" came up was this Alabama frame-up. Even this man who came from the hot bed of tyranny, color-barism and rank imperialist subjugation thought that the whole case was a crime against "so-called" Western Civilization.[5]

Quite aside from its emphasis on colonial Africa, the *African* committed a large portion of its columns to the independent African republic of Liberia. In "Liberia Today," "Declaration of Independence of the Republic of Liberia," and "Liberia in 100 Years of Independence," editorial and feature articles explaining the economic and social problems that abounded in that West African nation were generally commendatory. Liberia seemed, along with Ethiopia, the hopeful antithesis of colonial black Africa.

British colonialism in the Caribbean occupied a large amount of space in the *African*. Editorials, news items, and articles associated the black struggle in the

Eastern and Western Hemispheres with the work and philosophy of the late Marcus Garvey, a West Indian who had come to the United States a generation earlier and excited black Americans with his movement for black nationalism. Articles described labor unrest in the islands and stressed the color angle of that conflict.

The journal also published short stories and poetry. Claude McKay contributed poetry, and Langston Hughes' short story "Outcast" was among the fiction. The earliest issues contained sermons, one written by the black religious and political leader Adam Clayton Powell, Jr., congressman from Harlem and pastor of the world famous Abyssinian Baptist Church, reported to be the largest black church in the world. Gwendolyn Bennett, another of the Harlem Renaissance authors, contributed an essay to the *African*.

The *African* was an important black journal in the World War II era, publishing before the United States entered the war and continuing into the years of the establishment of the United Nations. Although the editorial responsibilities changed from time to time, the periodical expressed optimism that black Africa would experience wholesome nationhood and that the United Nations would serve as a salutary force in the world.

The *African* might well have represented a resurgence of the little magazine movement among blacks that blossomed in the 1940s if Claude McKay and Countee Cullen had been able to edit the journal as planned in 1938. James Weldon Johnson, a highly respected moving figure behind black literary efforts and a diplomat who was able to bring about alliances that might seem impossible, came close to bringing McKay to the *African* as editor with Cullen as his associate. In fact, an announcement of that arrangement was made in the April 1938 issue. In the next issue, however, the journal told its readers: "Due to reasons not anticipated, the world renowned poet-novelists Claude McKay and Countee Cullen, cannot now serve in the capacities of Editor and Associate-Editor respectively as announced in the last issue of the *African*."[5]

For reasons that are not clear, the *African* ceased publication from September 1938 to May 1943. Most likely, there was conflict with respect to the direction the publication should take in the war years. When it resumed publication, the editors found a new birth of zeal. In "We Rededicate," an editorial, they wrote:

Much water has flowed under the bridge and over the dam, since the last issue of *The African*. It was in many respects a regretful day, when we had to put crepe on the Editorial door, and tell the personnel to pick up its last paycheck, such as it was....*The African* comes again into being, not reborn, but reinforced, reinvigorated for the battle, the up-hill road that lay ahead. *The African* comes again into being at an historic hour. When we temporarily ceased activities the skies were pregnant with the ominous portent of war. The international clouds were sulphuric in content. Since then, they have belched their nauseating bilge over the whole earth. Since then, the artificial peace has been smashed, and we are participants in the horrific drama of all times, stupendous, nightmarish.[7]

With that issue, George S. Schuyler, an experienced journalist who had edited the *Messenger** in its last years and had distinguished himself as an essayist and columnist, joined the *African* as associate editor. J. A. Rogers, the black historian whose column on African history had appeared in the *Pittsburgh Courier* for a number of years, took a similar position. The character of the *African* changed. Schuyler began printing a column titled "Things of No Importance," and most of the contributed articles discussed the role of Africa in world peace. World affairs were addressed then in terms of the black man's relation to them rather than supplications for freedom for blacks in Africa and the West Indies. George Padmore, best known for his *Pan-Africanism or Communism* (1972), wrote several articles on black Africa and world affairs, including, "The Atlantic Charter and the Black Man's Burden." W. A. Domingo, known for his relationship to the *Crusader*,* a leftist journal published in Harlem from 1918 to 1922, wrote about the fight for freedom in the Caribbean.

The *African* ceased publication with its April-May 1948 issue. It was not able to determine a clear image for itself. It remained a champion of rights and responsibilities of black peoples on two continents, but never achieved the distinction that always seemed almost attainable. It combined political affairs with literary works, but could not successfully balance those two aspects of black American interests.

Notes

1. This observation appears in Ottley's *New World A-Coming* (New York: Arno Press and the *New York Times*, 1969), p. 42.
2. Benito Mussolini came to power in Italy in 1922 and by 1935 was seeking to resurrect the Roman Empire by overrunning Ethiopia. Haile Selassie, emperor of Ethiopia, looked to the League of Nations and to Afro-Americans to assist him in repelling the Italian armies. He was exiled from his country until Italy was finally defeated in World War II. The invasion of Ethiopia created tension among blacks in Harlem. Black weekly newspapers carried numerous stories about the war and Selassie's disappointment when he appealed to the League of Nations for assistance.
3. *African* (November 1937): 2.
4. *African* (October 1937): 3.
5. "The Scottsboro Boys: Angelo Herndon, An Example," ibid., p. 9.
6. *African* (July-August 1938): 122.
7. *African* (May 1943): 3.

Information Sources

BIBLIOGRAPHY:
"Addis Ababa Fears Its League Dues Bought a Gold Brick." *Newsweek* 6 (17 August 1935): 13.

"As Italy Marches On." *New Republic* 84 (25 September 1935): 171-72.
"England's Dilemma." *New Republic* 84 (4 September 1935): 89-90.
"Ethiopia Falls, Is the League Next?" *Scholastic* 28 (23 May 1936): 20.
Ottley, Roi. *New World A-Coming.* New York: Arno Press and the *New York Times,* 1969, p. 42.
INDEX SOURCES: None.
LOCATION SOURCES: Greenwood Press Periodicals; Schomberg Collection, New York Public Library; University Microfilm; International Microfilm.

Publication History

MAGAZINE TITLE AND TITLE CHANGES: *The African: Journal of African Affairs.*
VOLUME AND ISSUE DATA: Vols. I-IV (April 1945-April/May 1948). Ceased publication with Vol. II, no. 1 (September/October 1938); resumed with Vol. II, no. 1 (May 1943). Published monthly most years.
PUBLISHER AND PLACE OF PUBLICATION: The African Magazine Company, New York City.
EDITORS: David A. Talbot (October 1937-May/June 1938); Balfour A. Linton (July/August 1938-August 1944); R. T. Brown (October 1944-December 1945); Samuel A. Haynes (May 1946-June 1946); Associate editors (August 1946-November 1946); Akiki K. Nyabonga (January 1947-April/May 1948).
CIRCULATION: 3,500.

Charles E. Holmes

AFRO-AMERICAN JOURNAL, THE

The *Afro-American Journal* was published in Indianapolis, Indiana, from 1973 to 1977. The story of its struggle and eventual cessation is a familiar one. Originally conceived and published as a monthly magazine, the *Afro-American Journal* became a bimonthly publication by 1974, and, toward the end, combined two numbers in a single issue. Part of the magazine's difficulty derived from the fact that its staff worked on the magazine in addition to their regular work load at the Martin Center, a black community center which sponsored its publication. But its primary difficulty was financial. As its former editor and the current president of Martin Center College, Reverend Boniface Hardin, remarked, "The Journal was suspended in 1977 because its cost had become prohibitive, and we did not know how to market advertising for it."[1] The Reverend Hardin hopes to revive the journal under the control of the Martin Center College in the near future.

Though the *Afro-American Journal* was able to attract some local advertisers, circulation was only around 1,500 (some of the subscribers being university libraries), and the publishers could not depend too heavily on advertising revenue. Despite a circulation drive in 1975 which offered subscription agents a 20 percent commission, costs were clearly outrunning revenue. In 1973, the magazine sold for twenty cents a copy, by 1975 the price had jumped to a dollar, and the 1977 "two issues in one" copy of the *Journal* was priced at five dollars. Nevertheless, to the end, the publishers never altered the format or typical length of the magazine, nor apparently sought to save production costs. It was a handsome journal printed on heavy paper which normally included some illustrations, a variety of typefaces, many photographs, and often reproduced historical documents. Its contributors received no remuneration, though its editors say manuscript submissions nevertheless usually exceeded their space.

The recurring thematic emphasis of the *Afro-American Journal* seems to have been to cultivate and encourage racial pride in its black readership. Perhaps its mission was best articulated by an excerpted passage from Kofi Awoonnor's *Breast of the Earth* which the editors printed in the *Journal* in 1975. "Cultural Self-Discovery has become an essential aspect of our new quest for self and race. Pride is part of our dream of self-awareness."[2] Officially, though, the publication was described by its editors as "a commentary, historical and existential, and is desirous of representing the intellectual depth, vertical and horizontal, of Black people."[3] To achieve this "vertical and horizontal" depth the magazine divided its attention between the historical plight of blacks in America and contemporary national and international (principally African) cultural and political affairs which concerned blacks. Thus the *Journal* was a pastiche of mostly informative articles of diverse interest and range. A typical issue, for example, included a long piece on the origination of the Colored Speedway Association in 1924 and the "Gold and Glory Sweepstakes" held in Indianapolis as an alternative to the Indianapolis 500, from which blacks were barred; the second part of a two-part article on the Yoruba tribe of Nigeria; a scattering of contemporary poetry and African proverbs; a profile of the nineteenth-century emancipation lecturer and freed slave, Sojourner Truth; an analysis of the busing controversy; a description of a visit to West Africa entitled "Going Home (Spiritually)"; and, without commentary, a reprint of a handwritten indictment of slavery dated April 15, 1831 and signed simply "F.F."

The social and ethical tenor of the magazine was epitomized by the plea of the Reverend Hardin for blacks to "come on home" in his regularly featured "Editorial Viewpoint" in the July 1973 issue. "For a long time," wrote Hardin, "we didn't know where we came from and if we misbehaved as children we were told, 'You're acting like you came from Africa'—and we believed it. The Tarzan stories and the specials on T.V. about animals of Africa and Jack Parr's travels in Africa—only served to reinforce our whitewashed minds."[4] Hardin identified the source of such racial confusion as the white establishment which has passed on erroneous and misleading notions about black history and culture, "coverups, half-truths and lies, to keep Black people in their places," and equally misleading notions about social progress: "And while *the man* told us we were making progress and we were fighting the codes of Alabama and Indiana, the Knights of the Golden Circle and the Klan—some of us were bobbing our heads saying, 'Yes, we've come a long way.' Yes, we've come from Slavery 101 to Slavery 102—and Booker T. graduated with honors."[5]

Frederick Douglass and W.E.B. Du Bois, rather than Booker T. Washington, are nominated by Hardin as examples of black leaders who never forgot nor forsook their black heritage nor were beguiled by promises of progress. "It is not necessary," Hardin continued, "that you wear an Afro or African garment or hold your hand in a clenched fist to be part of our reclamation and liberation, but it is necessary that you ask the question about who you are, where you came from, and what you are going to do about it. . . . Come on home and help Black people reclaim that African Heritage, and claim of America what is rightfully ours."[6]

Neither Hardin nor others on the staff promoted any particular program, but neither did contributors shy away from pertinent political issues. In another editorial, Hardin expressed his hope that Nixon's troubles with Watergate would soon end so that public attention would once more be directed to the problems of blacks. And in still another he cautioned his readers not to allow their sympathies for the recently shot George Wallace to obscure their memory of the racial bigotry he had espoused for decades. It was political and social commitment rather than political doctrine that the *Journal* endorsed, a consciousness of oppression and struggle. In another editorial Hardin distinguished between the African and the Afro-American. "The difference between Africans and Afro-Americans is that the Africans have their minds on liberation and the Afro-Americans have been quite pleased with their oppression." The "tenacity and spirit" of Africans should provide the example for blacks at home. "If the Afro-American is to survive in this country, it is absolutely necessary that each person think, breathe, and feel liberation."[7]

That the *Journal* believed Africa provided enduring sources of inspiration and wisdom as well as self-awareness is evidenced by the frequent and purely informational pieces about Africa. For instance, one issue printed the pictures and names of the rulers of Africa without commentary, and African proverbs or folktales were often scattered throughout the magazine. There was an announcement of a symposium of South African writers held in Texas and a photo essay on the 1977 African cultural revival ("Festac") held in Nigeria.

Articles on African society shared space with a variety of pieces on American subjects of historical and contemporary interest. The *Journal* regularly reprinted a page or two from a nineteenth-century magazine (usually abolitionist publications such as the *Freeman* or William Lloyd Garrison's *Liberator**), or an original document such as a representative document of manumission dated 26 February 1814 in the hand of the slaveholder. Most of the reprinted documents were from the nearby collection of the Institute of Afro-American Studies in Indianapolis, as were many of the nineteenth-century photographs and illustrations which were typically included in the magazine. There were many historical essays, several of them rather more scholarly than journalistic, including footnotes and bibliography. Laudatory articles on prominent contemporary black historians such as John Hope Franklin and Andrew Ramsey were sometimes featured.

Typically, the historical pieces were revisionist or had revisionist implications. The character of such reinterpretations of conventional myths and mores is succinctly suggested by the following titles: "Black Imagery in the Media: Stepin Fetchit, Sweetback and Amos 'n Andy Reconsidered," "Blacks vis-à-vis Horatio Algerism: Work Does Not Make a Man Rich, but Roundshouldered," and "Of Thanks and Giving" (a critical analysis of the myth of Puritan heroism and independence, and, more particularly, an indictment of the Puritan attitude toward Indians and Negro slaves).

Analyses of current topics ranged from the specific political (such as busing and desegregation) and psychological (such as a review and criticism of William Schockley's studies of blacks and I.Q. scores), to the social (such as an analysis of blacks in relation to the so-called Youth Movement, and an informative piece on the nature and consequences of sickle-cell anemia). There were also profiles of distinguished blacks ranging from Indiana State Senator Robert Brokenburr to author Franz Fanon to jazz musician Cannonball Adderly. Finally, there were essays that possessed a purely local interest, such as "The History of the Black Man in Indiana" and "Focus on Blacks at a Suburban Indianapolis High School."

In its advertisement for manuscript submissions, the editors informed prospective contributors that the *Afro-American Journal* "offers the family person, the student and the professor a forum of expression." No doubt this policy accounted for the remarkable variety of scope and subject, as well as method and style, that characterized the publication. This is not to suggest, however, that the *Journal* suffered from diffuseness. It did achieve and maintain its own special identity. Though the treatment of subjects ranged from the scholarly to the informal to the inspirational and poetic, it did acquire a prevailing emphasis and a consistency of purpose. That emphasis and purpose were to provide its readers with a sense of historical continuity and racial identity and to treat from a variety of perspectives the sources, African and American, of a proud heritage.

Notes

1. Hardin to Dr. Walter Daniel, 19 May 1981.
2. *Afro-American Journal* (May-June 1975): 20.
3. *Afro-American Journal* (January-February 1975): 13.
4. "Editorial Viewpoint," *Afro-American Journal* (July 1973): 1.
5. Ibid.
6. Ibid.
7. "Editorial Viewpoint," *Afro-American Journal* (April 1974): 2.

Information Sources

INDEX SOURCES: None.
LOCATION SOURCES: Some college and university libraries.

Publication History

MAGAZINE TITLE AND TITLE CHANGES: *The Afro-American Journal.*
VOLUME AND ISSUE DATA: Vols. 1-2 monthly; vol. 3 bimonthly; vols. 4-5 quarterly.
PUBLISHER AND PLACE OF PUBLICATION: The Martin Center, Indianapolis, Indiana.
EDITOR: Reverend Boniface Hardin (1973-1977).
CIRCULATION: 1,500 estimate.

Thomas Quirk

ALEXANDER'S MAGAZINE

Because its variety of news was wide and its editorial policy not largely personal, *Alexander's Magazine* in many ways provides the best background history of the black experience in America of any national magazine published by blacks in the first two decades of the twentieth century. It appeared monthly from March 1905 to March 1909 in Boston. Its editor, Charles Alexander, engaged a fairly large number of persons to write articles for him, and he used reprints from other periodicals freely. His first editorial explained the magazine's purposes.

As a rule, the first news of various happenings is presented in the papers hastily. People want the news and read what is presented as news quickly and pass it along without much thought. This is about all of the attention that a large part of news items are worth. But there are constantly taking place events that bear such important relations to questions of great interest that it is essential for the student of events to have the aid of a monthly review.

Alexander's Magazine will meet an existing need if it takes up important events and questions of vital and present-day interest and gives its readers the outcome of calm, deliberate, and critical thought. The weekly paper has its place, but the race now needs strong monthly journals.

The white people who desire to learn something of the Colored citizens beyond what may be seen on the surface or gleaned from the hurried reports of daily newspapers would find in a well-edited monthly a great aid.

Such a periodical should become a powerful advocate of the welfare of the race. It should review the sayings of the weekly papers of the race and present the national conclusions that ought to be drawn from scattered views that have been hurriedly presented.

This statement introducing *Alexander's* to the reading public expresses accurately and significantly the difference between newspapers published by Negroes during the nineteenth and early twentieth centuries, and the eclectic national magazine.

The first issue contained forty-three pages and was particularly well edited and printed. It carried an article that reported on a meeting of a group of Boston Negroes who had gathered to read reports on the status of black Bostonians in the professions, business, and religion. Another item was a reprint from the *Baptist Missionary Magazine* that discussed some religious missionary work in Africa. The thirty-fifth anniversary exercises at Hampton Institute in Virginia were described, together with photographs of the principal building on campus and a note about the wisdom of a philosophy of industrial education for Negroes. The most significant feature in the premier issue was an article on socialism written by Reverdy C. Ransom, a young African Methodist Episcopal Church minister. Posing the question, "What do the Socialists plan to do with the Negro question?" Ransom pointed out that some people were saying Socialists would treat black men as well as they would treat whites while others said the opposite. Whatever the correct answer to his question, Ransom noted that 9 million people could not be ignored; that they were, and would continue to be, the "storm center for the exhibition of vigorous racial prejudice and animosities."[2] As for his own analysis of the attitude each of the prevailing political parties were taking toward the Negro at the time, Ransom wrote:

> With those who advocate the Negroes' forced elimination or self-effacement from politics, we have nothing but uncompromising dissent. The obsequious, cringing, psychophantic man, with his hat in his hand is only a thing to be despised. To be a man, one must stand erect and contend for the contention of all that belongs to a man. The Democratic Party does not seek the Negro, the Republican Party uses him, but has small use for him, in the paths that lead to honor and to power. Those who falsely picture the Negro as indolent, shiftless, lazy are one with those who seek to keep him in a condition of social, political and economic inferiority. The Negro is industrious and inspiring and is seeking to mount each round in the ladder of moral, social, industrial and political strength and progress.[3]

The publication had set its course. It would not be a Negro newspaper, yet it would take note of significant actions for the race in the Boston area; it would be an organ of race pride as it commented upon important artistic performers, educational institutions, and individuals whose emulation would be significant to the race. Further, it would comment actively on national politics which the race faced in the period beginning in 1905.

Alexander made no serious attempt to serve as a fine arts and entertainment critic. Some feature articles on these subjects, however, provide details not easily found elsewhere about the accomplishments of successful black theatrical troupes. While he could praise Negro theatrical troupes that succeeded in the entertainment world, Alexander related the changing use and nature of stage materials to the emerging improved self-image of the Negro. He disliked "coon songs" because they burlesqued the Negro, no matter whether white or black musicians wrote and performed them. Such stage materials were passing from use, he contended, because intelligent and self-respecting Negroes would no longer tolerate them. It is sometimes difficult to distinguish between the old vaudeville songs Alexander found degrading and those James Weldon Johnson, J. Rosamond Johnson, and Bob Cole popularized in the early years of the new century. But Alexander saw in the latter a turn in the right direction, as he wrote in an editorial in the April 1906 issue.

The aesthetic nature of the Negro has developed in a marked degree: more and more is he capable of appreciating the finer sentiments in song and music. The feeling stated in these coon songs occasionally find expression even now in more adroit language. These puns have now been superseded by the beautiful Negro folk songs of Cole and Johnson, such as "Under the Bamboo Tree," and "As Long as the Congo Flies to the Sea." Not long ago, the editor of the *Ladies Home Journal*, appreciating the fact that the Negro had made a revolution in music, published a series of songs by Cole and Johnson, illustrating the progress from the coon song type to the fascinating Negro lyrics of today. The pride of the Negro today would not tolerate the revival of the degrading, jingling puns of only yesterday, and we are pretty safe in saying that the coon song has seen its day.[4]

The magazine announced that Henry O. Tanner, the Negro painter, had been awarded the N. W. Harris Prize for the best entry in the painting competition at the nineteenth annual exhibition of American paintings in Chicago. His *Two Disciples at the Tomb* had been roundly praised. Alexander wrote that this distinction should make every Negro in the United States proud. Similarly, Negroes who had studied at well-known conservatories around the world and performed in operatic productions should inspire race pride.

The Atlanta race riot in the fall of 1906 left Alexander livid. Its lawlessness was inexcusable in a civilized community, especially Atlanta, where in the forty-five years since Emancipation, Negroes had accumulated over $30 million worth of property. They had surpassed every other community in the land in demonstrating their industrial, social, and ethical efficiency. The largest number of black colleges in a single American city was in Atlanta. Culture, refinement, and general intelligence among Atlanta Negroes could compare favorably with the best people in any similar community, the editor wrote. Still, shiftless, irresponsible, and ignorant mobs constantly picked quarrels with enterprising Negroes to find an excuse to carry out the dictates of "depraved and lawless ambition on the flimsiest pretense." Alexander brushed aside any evidence that Negroes had committed the outrages of which they were accused in Atlanta. The greatest injustice had been done to innocent men and women who had nothing whatsoever to do with the alleged crimes or any knowledge of the alleged criminals, he wrote. And he asked, "Would it be correct to assail President Charles W. Eliot of Harvard University because a white man robbed a bank in Cambridge or hold him responsible?"[5] He referred to the 24 September 1905 night of terror in the Brownsville section of Atlanta. Many Negroes who had heard that white mobs were approaching the area to descend upon their homes sought asylum in Clark College and Gammon Theological Seminary, local black institutions of higher education. Four black "substantial citizens" were killed in the assault upon persons taking refuge in the schools. J.W.E. Bowen, president of Gammon and one of the editors of the *Voice of the Negro*,* was beaten over the head with a rifle butt by a police officer. "Yellow journalism" had been a major cause of the riots in Atlanta, Chicago, and Washington, D.C., Alexander declared, for news stories and editorials in the daily press in all three cities had helped to create a climate of hostility toward Negroes.

The awesome disturbance had been a "terrible whirlwind" reaped upon the South for its incontinent social teachings, Alexander reasoned in his own reaction to the same position taken by a *Boston Herald* editorial, which he reprinted in the October 1906 issue of his magazine. Because the youth of Georgia had been systematically taught to hate Negroes, to rob them, to oppress them, to cheat them of their rights as citizens, and to murder them; because a large portion of the press and the political structure and pulpit sought to promote scorn and bitterness between races; the nation stood at fault and ashamed for the unnecessary harvest they had wrought. That same issue carried W.E.B. Du Bois' poem "A Litany of Atlanta," which had appeared in the *New York Independent* and bitterly lamented the Atlanta riot.

A shooting affray between black soldiers garrisoned at Fort Brown, Texas, and white civilians in the community of Brownsville sparked sharp reaction from *Alexander's*. The 13 August 1906 incident had precipitated investigation by the United States Congress for the purpose of assigning blame for the outbreak. The black soldiers were adjudged guilty of having caused the riot and were sentenced to be dishonorably discharged from the army. When President Theodore Roosevelt refused to set aside the court-martial's decision, most black newspapers and magazines protested his action and helped to make the riot and the White House's handling of the soldiers who participated in it a highly sensitive political event. According to a story which had appeared in a recent issue of the *Boston Herald* and which Alexander reprinted in his magazine's January 1907 issue, the 25th United States Infantry (Colored) Battalion had never been welcome in the Brownsville area. Unsworn testimony given to the grand jury indicated that under ordinary circumstances the disturbance in which the soldiers and local inhabitants engaged would have been considered little more than "an ordinary frontier row."

Racial explosions around the country, particularly the Brownsville incident, influenced *Alexander's* attitude toward the presidential campaign of 1908. Roosevelt supported his secretary of war, William Howard Taft, for the Republican nomination. The president's strong support among Negroes, believed to have assured his election earlier, dwindled quickly and significantly after the Brownsville affair. When the black newspapers attacked Roosevelt vigorously for his position with respect to the black soldiers, *Alexander's* published summaries of their comments. When Lyman Abbott complained about what he considered the damage of printing these comments, Alexander wrote that Abbott's editorial in the 29 December 1906 issue of his *Outlook Magazine* was "unworthy of the splendid reputation for liberality and good judgement which this journal has made in the years gone by." For *Outlook*'s information, Charles Alexander wrote, "we would say that during the past two months we have read closely 300 Negro newspapers and we find that the same diversity of opinion exists among Negro editors that characterized white editors; indeed, there is more freedom of discussion among Negroes touching their own problems than may be discovered among white people."[6]

Race riots, growing jim crowism, and the insensitivity of the federal government to black Americans' realization of full citizenship grieved Charles Alexander. But he did not believe the Niagara movement would settle any racial problems. To Alexander, W.E.B. Du Bois and his associates who called for the second session of the movement to meet at Harper's Ferry, West Virginia, in the fall of 1906, were "numbered among those persons in every community who, having accomplished little in the interest of the masses, have a feeling of self-importance."[7] Their resolutions at the gathering, he continued, "for beauty and vigor of rhetoric can hardly be equalled by any similar document issued to the public recently." But in his own estimate of the movement, Alexander wrote in his September 1906 issue that most of the speeches delivered at the convention were attempts to destroy or minimize, if possible, the influence of Booker T. Washington, "although this object is screened over by a veil like unto which hovers over the *Souls of Black Folk*."[8]

Alexander simply did not like Du Bois, probably because he considered Du Bois and his associates elitist among black Americans. The Niagara movement's members were drawn almost entirely from the ranks of college-trained professional black Americans. Lawyers, some ministers, college educators, a few government workers, and certain radical editors—including Jesse Max Barber of the *Voice of the Negro**—joined the organization. No one can fairly claim that the Du Bois group held a monopoly on promoting the causes of the race.

Alexander's never attacked the Niagara movement's expression of goals they thought American blacks and their friends should pursue for the good of the nation. Through its editor and its contributors, the journal suggested some variety in the methods black Americans should use for these purposes. One lay in its position on the emerging relationship between Negroes and the Republican party. Not a consistently active political organ, *Alexander's* could find no enthusiasm in recommending William Howard Taft for president. He had worked to redeem himself with Negro voters who believed that he could have worked more effectively than he did as secretary of war to commute the sentences of black soldiers judged guilty in the Brownsville, Texas, incident. Nothing Taft said could placate outspoken black Americans. Commenting on his speeches to black audiences in May 1906, *Alexander's* called the candidate's efforts patronizing at best. When he traced the history of the Negro race and even suggested ways it could improve itself in an address at Fisk University, Charles Alexander ridiculed the content and tone of the advice, although Taft had praised the educational opportunities offered by Booker T. Washington's philosophy. If Negroes continue to work to increase their intelligence, they may come to use the ballot effectively, Taft had said; and referring to the avalanche of complaint against attempts made in the South to circumvent Negro use of the rights of franchise gained in Reconstruction federal legislation the candidate had stated: "I cannot put myself among those pessimists who regard the settlement of the political question in the South as beyond hope." Alexander quipped that such a gradual approach to political power could hardly secure advancement for the race.

Yet, *Alexander's Magazine* did not go so far as to support a Democratic nominee for president. It criticized Taft for his reticence in stating his attitude toward the Negro and strongly favored Ohio Senator Joseph Benson Foraker for the Republican nomination. That senator had fought vigorously to exonerate the Brownsville soldiers and had openly courted the black vote. Negroes did not wish to desert the Republican party. The black press felt, though, that the Republicans had not sufficiently supported black causes in Congress; that they had not found in Roosevelt any hope to believe that erosion of the Fourteenth Amendment and the movement toward white party primaries in the South would be reversed under Taft; and that, in general, the party no longer merited black allegiance. Alexander admitted that Democratic candidate William Jennings Bryan commanded endorsement of most of the South, and he believed that Bryan would make promises that would bring Negroes into his camp if he thought such action would not offend the South. In effect, then, the black voter faced a painful dilemma: Neither Democrats nor Republicans wanted his vote. Further, Roosevelt's close ties with Booker T. Washington had seemed to signal automatic garnering of black votes no matter who ran on the Republican ticket. Bitter experience was bringing a surge of political independence among Negro voters, but Charles Alexander was not ready to advise abandoning the race's traditional pattern of political participation. His reasons were clear, as expressed in the September 1908 issue under the editorial caption, "The Negro Shall Be Loyal."

Will the Negro vote the Democratic ticket? Never! The Negro cannot afford to be a Democrat! The Negro in the South can't vote. Those few who are qualified know better than to follow men who are proud of killing them, shooting them, crowding them out of their homes, herding them together in separate cars and separate schools as so much vermin. But the

"Peerless one" endeavors to cater to the disgruntled Negro of the North. What magnificent example of political clowning, this! Does Mr. Bryan really expect to get one vote of the Northern Negro? He must forget that in the North the Negro is alive to the aspects of the situation and smart enough not to let himself be used as a dummy to elevate the Democratic party into power without therefrom deriving benefit for his race.[9]

Reluctantly, *Alexander's* endorsed Taft for president and ran small articles such as one that reported that the candidate's father, Judge Alfonso Taft, was one of the best friends the Negro had ever known and that Mr. Taft stood with Booker T. Washington who everyone knew stood for all that was beneficial to the race. The support was hardly sincere and certainly not enthusiastic. These materials might have been directed by Washington. If so, they represent a weakness rather than a strength in a system of influence upon the press.

If one has to classify it with respect to its tone and position on matters pertaining to race, *Alexander's* would have to be called hopeful. Certainly, it was not radical; and it was no advocate for accommodation. Its October 1908 issue, dedicated to the emerging "New Negro," pointed toward a renaissance within the race which later came to be recognized throughout the nation as the most dramatic and creative part of the history of the black experience in America. Charles Alexander was the first among black editors and publishers to recognize, label, and promulgate this metaphor. This seminal perception of the black American experience represents *Alexander's Magazine*'s chief contribution to American culture.

Notes

1. "The Need of a Monthly Magazine," *Alexander's Magazine* (May 1905): 41.
2. "Socialism and the Negro," *Alexander's Magazine* (May 1905): 15.
3. "After Forty Years of Freedom," *Alexander's Magazine* (April 1906): 12.
4. "The Coon Song Exists," *Alexander's Magazine* (April 1906): 12.
5. "The Atlanta Mob," *Alexander's Magazine* (October 1906): 15. *See also* "The Negro Massacre at Atlanta," *Alexander's Magazine* (November 1906): 15.
6. "The New York Outlook," *Alexander's Magazine* (January 1907): 129.
7. "The Niagara Movement," *Alexander's Magazine* (September 1907): 18-19.
8. Ibid.
9. "The Negro Vote and the Presidential Election," *Alexander's Magazine* (August 1908): 156-57.

Information Sources

BIBLIOGRAPHY:

Fox, Stephen R. *The Guardian of Boston: William Monroe Trotter*. New York, 1971.

Harlan, Louis R., and Smock, Raymond W., eds. *The Booker T. Washington Papers*, vol. 7. Urbana, Ill., 1977.

Johnson, Abby Arthur, and Johnson, Ronald M. "Away from Accommodation: Radical
    Editors and Protest Journalism, 1900-1910." *Journal of Negro History*, October
    1977, pp. 324-38.
Logan, Rayford W. *The Betrayal of the Negro: From Rutherford B. Hayes to Woodrow
    Wilson.* New York, 1965.
INDEX SOURCE: *Analytical Guide and Indexes to Alexander's Magazine, 1905-1909.*
    Westport, Conn.: Greenwood Press, 1974.
LOCATION SOURCES: Most college and university libraries; Greenwood Press Periodicals.

Publication History

MAGAZINE TITLE AND TITLE CHANGES: *Alexander's Magazine* 15 May 1905-15
    March 1909.
VOLUME AND ISSUE DATA: Vols. I-VII published monthly, dated 15th of the month.
    Vol. I contained twelve issues; Vols. II and VI had six issues, and vol. VII had
    five issues.
PUBLISHER AND PLACE OF PUBLICATION: Charles Alexander edited and pub-
    lished the magazine from his own press in Boston, Massachusetts.
EDITORS: Charles Alexander was editor throughout the life of the publication. Archibald
    Grimké was guest editor for three issues.
CIRCULATION: 5,000 estimate.

A.M.E. CHURCH REVIEW, THE

At its General Conference meeting in Baltimore in 1884, the African Methodist Episcopal Church authorized publication of a bimonthly review. The first
issue was released as a quarterly, however, in July 1884, under the title *A. M. E.
Church Review.* B. T. Tanner was appointed editor. As manager of the denomination's publishing house in Philadelphia, he had been responsible for editing the
church's newspaper, the *Christian Recorder*, for the previous sixteen years.[1] I.
Garland Penn, whose *Afro-American Press and Its Editors* (1891) is still the
classic authority on black newspapers and magazines of the nineteenth century,
wrote of the *Review*:

> It was a quarterly of never less than one hundred twenty-five pages. Its
> journalistic finish is pleasing to the eye, while its literary contributions are
> of high order. In the beginning, it was edited by Rev. B. T. Tanner, now
> Bishop Tanner; but at present its editorial head is Dr. L. J. Coppin, a writer
> of acknowledged ability. *The Review* has a circulation of 1,500, which is
> daily increasing. It goes to all points of the United States, Africa, Europe,
> Hayti, etc.[2]

The first issue contained a variety of articles, including "Thoughts About the
Past, the Present, and the Future of the African M. E. Church"; "A Scriptural

View: Or the Statement Concerning Paradise That Was Lost and Regained";
"The Greek of the Old Testament"; "The Republic of Hayti and the Revolution of
1876"; and "The Negro in Science, Art, and Literature." It also contained some
poetry and book reviews. Frances Ellen Watkins Harper contributed a poem,
"The Dying Bondsman," to the premier issue. During the next five years, most
editions carried tables of contents of other national religious journals, notably
Universalist Quarterly, Methodist Review, and the *Baptist Quarterly Review,*
together with the editor's reaction to some of the articles appearing in those
periodicals. Other comment in the *Review* supported woman's suffrage and
defended the need for a separate black church in America. Throughout the
nineteenth century, the journal published biographies of black Reconstruction
leaders.

The denomination had several objectives in establishing the *Review.* Its leaders were deeply concerned that their church cultivate and maintain an educated
ministry; hence the magazine was needed for instruction in the arts, religion, and
the scriptures for churchmen. But most significantly, those church leaders were
passionately defiant of the Christian nation—their native land—that had held so
many of them slaves for many decades. The Right Reverend Daniel A. Payne,
senior bishop of the church, wrote the lead article for the *Review,* beginning:

> About sixty-seven years ago the blasphemous spirit of American slavery
> and American caste, compelled the organization of the African M. E.
> Church. It then appeared like a star of the seventh magnitude on the
> horizon of the growing republic. Up to 1865 these two evils were among
> the sources of its popularity and prestige. Because, while these two evils
> were dominant in the M. E. Church, colored persons of intelligence and
> reflection regarded slave-holding laymen as mere hypocrites, and slave-
> holding preachers as "wolves in sheep's clothing," hence they could not sit
> with moral nor religious profit under the ministrations of the latter, nor in
> Christian fellowship with the former.[3]

Bishop Payne went on to explain that slavery and caste, as active in the North
as in the South, caused thoughtful black men and women to found an asylum in
the bosom of the A. M. E. Church. They found there freedom of thought, of
speech, and of action, and freedom for the development of a true Christian
manhood. He catalogued the accomplishments of the church after the Civil War
began and slavery was abolished; it furnished the first chaplains for the colored
regiments of the Union army, organized the first institution of learning for the
special training of freedmen, and presented the widest usefulness to the talent
and activities of that race.

Quite appropriately, the *Review* was a scholarly journal and a weapon for civil
rights, education, and religious zeal. The A. M. E. Church, an American institution, arose alongside the government of the United States. Richard Allen, one of

the founders of the denomination, completed purchasing his freedom in 1777, while the revolutionary war was being fought. He was a member of a small band of free blacks living in Philadelphia who, while the fathers of the country struggled over adopting a constitution, pulled out of St. George's Methodist Church in Philadelphia because of the indignities white members of the congregation had inflicted upon them. Their exodus led to the establishment of the African Methodist Episcopal Church, which provided Christian religion and the enlarged social, public, and intellectual services that characterized the black church before and after Emancipation. Its leaders included ex slaves and free blacks. Many were intelligent, imaginative, courageous, proud, patriotic men and women whose socioeconomic status made them militant for the rights of citizenship that they believed were theirs. Their church flourished in the years following the Civil War and reached its optimum force as a national black organization and a source of black leadership for freedmen after Emancipation.

The official magazine of the A. M. E. Church reflected that history and that sense of pride. During the first two or three decades of publication, the *Review* was a scholarly periodical featuring literature, American history, theology and biblical studies, the black church, African history, and civil and national affairs. It carried articles on politics from the black perspective. Most black leaders were Republicans at that time, due to the debt most thought they owed the party of Abraham Lincoln and to their fears that the rising Democratic party would disfranchise them and strip them of the benefits they had won with the adoption of the Fourteenth and Fifteenth amendments to the Constitution.

The editorials of the *Review* fought Jim Crow laws that were being enacted throughout the South toward the close of the nineteenth century and attacked job and housing discrimination, which Negroes who migrated North faced in almost every urban center. The *Review* was a national magazine of academic and public affairs as much as it was a church newspaper. Rayford W. Logan, the noted black American historian, wrote of the journal at the close of the nineteenth century:

A quarterly, it resembled *Harper's Magazine* in size and color, but it had smaller print on more roughly finished paper. Its circulation rose from 1,000 in 1884, to 2,800 in 1889. At that time, according to the *Review*, white church publications also had small circulations. . . . In 1900, the editor of the *A. M. E. Review* declared that its sixteen volumes constituted an encyclopedia on all subjects of direct importance to Negroes. This is an exaggeration, but the *Review*'s articles were surprisingly well written and covered not only subjects of direct importance to Negroes but broader topics such as tariff and currency. Among its principal contributors were: Douglass, Blyden, Mrs. Terrell, Bishop R. H. Cain (former member of Congress from South Carolina), Judge Ruffin, John R. Lynch, Francis Cardozo (State Treasurer of South Carolina during Reconstruction), Reverend Grimké, H. C. C. Astwood, and R. R. Wright, who later became a banker in Philadelphia and as a nonogenarian attended the San Francisco Conference on the Organization of the United Nations.[4]

The General Conference elected the editors for the *Review*. Reverdy C. Ransom, who served as editor from 1912 to 1924, brought a discernable increase to the journal's coverage of national affairs and civil rights. He had been associated with W.E.B. Du Bois in organizing the Niagara movement in 1905 and had advocated socialism as the most feasible political philosophy for Negroes. He was not narrowly partisan in the Washington-Du Bois controversy, however—he supported Booker T. Washington when Thomas Dixon, the New York pastor and anti-Negro novelist, attacked Tuskegee Institute for "miseducating" Negroes to become entrepreneurs when it should be training them as servants and tillers of the soil. On the death of Washington in 1915, Ransom wrote in an editorial:

> It has been often said that his very success was due to the triteness of his career; that he came upon the stage when philanthropy and the Republican party alike were ready to hear and try new things with the Negro. . . . By his singleness of purpose he taught us both by word and deed how to live, and by unflinching heroism amid suffering, he taught us how to die.[5]

Ransom was an ardent supporter of the NAACP and its fight against lynching. He criticized other black periodicals that, to him, were not sufficiently severe in their attack on poor relations between the races. At one time he claimed the *Review* was the only magazine published at the present "that deals comprehensively with questions that relate to the race."[6]

The *Review* lost some of its fervor during the thirties and forties. During the 1950s, it became less militant and, under the editorship of George A. Singleton, was largely an organ of communication among members of the denomination and scholars of black history. It published articles about the development of the church outside the United States and its work in the Caribbean and in almost all of black Africa. Langston Hughes wrote "Richard Allen: Founder of a Church," and other writers described the work of the Underground Railroad during slavery. The magazine paid tribute to Paul Laurence Dunbar as the first black poet to become popularly accepted by the general American public. Many articles discussed the changing nature of the Republican party. As church politics became complex and activities of candidates for bishop of the denomination became particularly bitter, much of the *Review*'s space was used for discussion of these matters.

In the sixties and seventies it has become more narrowly a denominational bulletin, reporting news within the various Episcopal districts of the church. Its vitality does not command the respect it held during the early decades of its publication.

Without question the *A.M.E. Church Review* was for many years the premier black magazine in the United States published by and for black Americans.

Notes

1. Some confusion exists as to the actual dates of the founding of the earliest denomination paper among the A. M. E. Church. The reliable historian, Daniel A. Payne, wrote in his church history:

> The year 1840 was not only remarkable for the organization of new Conferences, but also for its literary movement; for, by the statement of Rev. George Hogarth, who, at the time was the general book steward, the idea of publishing a magazine for the benefit of the Connection was considered and discussed at the Annual Conferences of this year. The General Conference, too, was held in the city of Baltimore, but not a vestige of the proceedings is handed down to us. [*History of the African Methodist Episcopal Church* (New York: Arno Press and the *New York Times*, 1969), p. 131.]

The periodical referred to in the quotation seems to have been the *Christian Advocate*.

2. Penn, pp. 126-27.

3. "Thoughts About the Past, the Present, and the Future of the African M. E. Church," *A. M. E. Church Review* (July 1884): 1. This was the first article published in the first issue of the journal.

4. *The Betrayal of the Negro from Rutherford B. Hayes to Woodrow Wilson* (New York: Collier Books, 1965), p. 321.

5. "The Passing of Booker T. Washington," Editorial, *A. M. E. Church Review* (July 1916): 3.

6. Editorial, *A. M. E. Church Review* (July 1916): 3.

Information Sources

BIBLIOGRAPHY:

Cunningham, Dorothy H. "An Analysis of the *A. M. E. Church Review*, 1884-1900." Masters thesis, Howard University, Washington, D.C., 1954.

Handy, James A. *Scraps of African Methodist Episcopal History*. Philadelphia, n.d., pp. 269-72.

Journal of Negro History, January 1938, pp. 7-12.

Logan, Rayford W. *The Betrayal of the Negro From Rutherford B. Hayes to Woodrow Wilson*. New York: Collier Books, 1965, pp. 313-24.

Payne, Daniel A. *History of the A. M. E. Church*. Nashville, Tennessee: Publishing House of the A. M. E. Sunday-School Union, 1891.

———. Recollections of Seventy Years. New York: Arno Press and the *New York Times*, 1968.

Wolseley, Roland E. *Black Press, U.S.A.* Ames: Iowa State University Press, 1971, p. 155.

INDEX SOURCES: None.

LOCATION SOURCES: Fisk University, Nashville, Tennessee; Moorland-Spingarn Collection, Howard University, Washington D. C; Tuskegee Institute, Tuskegee, Alabama.

Publication History

MAGAZINE TITLE AND TITLE CHANGES: *A. M. E. Church Review*.
VOLUME AND ISSUE DATA: Vols. I- (July 1884-), quarterly.
PUBLISHER AND PLACE OF PUBLICATION: African Methodist Episcopal Church
    Review, Atlanta, Georgia.
EDITORS: Benjamin T. Tanner (1884-1888); Levi J. Coppin (1888-1896); H. T. Kealing
    (1896-1912); Reverdy C. Ransom (1912-1924); J. G. Robinson (1924-1940);
    Howard D. Gregg (1940-1944); J. S. Brookins (1944-1950); George A. Singleton
    (1950-?); William D. Johnson (1972-).
CIRCULATION: 4,500.

AMERICAN LIFE MAGAZINE, THE: A MAGAZINE OF TIMELY FEATURES AND GOOD FICTION

Moses Jordan studied journalism at the Medill School at Northwestern University after his return from serving in World War I and founded in Chicago in 1926 a journal that was short-lived but noteworthy.[1] It was not the first black magazine published in Chicago during that city's "Negro Renaissance," which paralleled the Harlem Renaissance which is far more familiar to most Americans. *Half-Century** had begun publication in 1916 and was about to end a fairly successful tenure. *American Life* followed the line of interests that *Half-Century* had pursued. It was a general purpose periodical that carried news about Negroes around the country and made a valiant effort to attract fiction writers. The editor appealed to readers in every issue to send in creative writing for consideration for publication in the magazine. Like *Half-Century*, *American Life* was more a Chicago magazine than a national publication. It enlarged upon the function of the immensely popular weekly newspaper, *Chicago Defender*.

Inasmuch as Chicago was one of the principal points of the new black migration North during the World War I era and continuing into the 1920s, *American Life*'s features reflected the sentiment and results of that movement's impact upon Chicago. Its editorials fully supported the desire of Afro-Americans to leave the poverty and strict racial segregation of the South and to seek a better life in the urban North. It also reported on the sharp rise in the number of black churches in the city and the phenomenal development of black businesses owned and operated by men and women who had come from the South. It published articles and editorials that discussed the needs of Chicago public schools in the black belt of Chicago and the growing strength of blacks in local politics on the south side of the city.

Chicago's prominence as a musical center for blacks was clearly reflected in *American Life*. Performances by musicians and other reports of their activities appeared often in the magazine's news columns. Reviews of concerts performed by individual musicians and by church choirs were common. Most public matters were discussed under the column, "Editor's Fables" that was written by Jordan.

One particularly interesting article, "The Church Is the Mother of the Modern Drama," attacked the tendency of black clergymen to frown on the theater and entertainers. The author wrote that "the church gave birth to modern drama and was very proud of her child until the theater divorced itself from her." The Methodists, the writer claimed, had objected to the theater on the grounds that it carried the danger of corrupting the morals of children and that there was no official censorship of plays.[2]

American Life could be labeled conservative in its position on political matters. As was the case with almost all black periodicals, it took a strong stand on matters pertaining to the advancement of black Americans and their civil rights. But it was not particularly militant. Coming as closely as it did upon the end of the war, *American Life* emphasized black Americans' participation in that conflict. A regular feature that continued throughout the publication of the magazine was "Startling War Memories," a collection of reminiscences written by black veterans.

Accomplishments of individual black Americans were provided through character sketches, such as one of Benjamin Banneker, an early nineteenth-century black scientist, and through stories about the scientific discoveries of George Washington Carver, the agricultural chemist, who was teaching and conducting research at Tuskegee Institute in Alabama. His "Some Marvelous Undeveloped Resources of the South," together with "Why I Remain in the South," written by President Beverly Shaw of Haven Teachers College in Mississippi, represented the other side of the argument that blacks should migrate North.[3]

Countee Cullen and Langston Hughes, popular young poets of the period, contributed poems to *American Life*. The first and second issues contained a travelogue, "From Venice to Vienna." The magazine was also one of the first black journals to carry much advertisement for black colleges.

The demise of *American Life* indicates once more that black journals could not compete successfully with weekly newspapers for readers. Although the periodical was pertinent to its time and events, it failed for largely financial reasons and ended publication after only two years.

Notes

1. A note in the July 1926 issue of *American Life* (p. 5) remarked that the *Chicago Evening Post* had written of the first number of Jordan's magazine: "At an appropriate moment—just before the NAACP holds its annual meeting in Chicago—a young World War veteran, a student of the Medill School of Journalism, Moses Jordan, has launched a new magazine for and about Negroes. *American Life*, of which the first number appeared this month, is not another propaganda organ, but a magazine of general interest."

2. Unsigned, *American Life* (January 1927): 67.

3. George W. Carver, "Some Marvelous Undeveloped Resources of the South," *Amer-*

ican Life (April 1927): 78. J. Beverly Shaw, "Why I Remain in the South," *American Life* (June 1927): 12.

Information Sources

INDEX SOURCES: None.
LOCATION SOURCES: Fisk University Library, Nashville, Tennessee; Library of Congress.

Publication History

MAGAZINE TITLE AND TITLE CHANGES: *The American Life Magazine: A Magazine of Timely Features and Good Fiction.*
VOLUME AND ISSUE DATA: Vols I-III (June 1926-August 1928), monthly.
PUBLISHER AND PLACE OF PUBLICATION: American Life Publishing Company, Chicago, Illinois.
EDITOR: Moses Jordan (1926-1928).
CIRCULATION: 1,000 estimate.

AMISTAD: WRITINGS OF BLACK HISTORY AND CULTURE

Amistad was the first black "magabook," or "bookazine." It was begun in 1970 and continued into 1971 under the editorship of black novelist John A. Williams and Random House senior editor Charles F. Harris. *Amistad* was conceived as a semiannual publication that had the look and feel of a paperback book. Each issue normally ran to 300 pages plus in length and was published and distributed through Random House's paperback subsidiary, Vintage Books.

Apparently intended as a marketable publication that might at once be used as a primary or supplementary textbook in black studies classes on college campuses and included on the shelves of bookstores, *Amistad* represented the attempt of a major publishing house to capitalize upon a developing demand for books and articles about black history and culture. In the first issue its editors stated that they had designed the publication primarily for use in college courses in literature, history, sociology, psychology, education, political science and government, and the arts. Less practically, the president of Random House, Robert Bernstein, hoped that the bookazine might become a quarterly and that it would be a great step forward, helping black people to know and understand more about themselves and helping white people know and understand more about blacks.

The title of this publication is significant. The editors explained in the first issue that *Amistad* means friendship in Spanish. It also stands for revolt, self-determination, justice, and freedom to Afro-Americans. It was with these meanings firmly in mind that the editors designed this publication.[1]

The first issue of the magazine set the tone for subsequent issues and identified college-age students as its audience. George Davis, Oliver Jackman, and Ishmael Reed contributed short stories to the magazine. Chester Himes was also a contributor, and editor John Williams supplied an essay on Himes. There were essays on topics and figures that were already familiar or were likely to appeal to an established interest for young blacks. Thus, there were articles about James Baldwin, the slave trade, and southern writers and American letters. In sum, the editors of *Amistad* provided a publication that was at once current and, to some extent, topical but that also bore a certain resemblance to an anthology suitable for classroom use. This bookazine was multidisciplinary, stylistically accessible, and forceful. For the most part, the articles were free of footnotes, bibliography, and extensive citation.

Amistad 2, the second issue of the publication, is dedicated to Richard Wright. Not surprisingly, it contains his "Blueprint for Negro Literature." It, together with John Oliver Killens' (author of *Young Blood*) interview with himself, "Rappin With Myself," give the reader a chance to compare the two authors' aesthetics. A portion of W.E.B. Du Bois' *The World and Africa*, published in 1965, and a chapter from Toni Morrison's novel, *The Bluest Eye*, were also included. Her book was published in the same year as the magazine, 1971, and she held the copyright. Permitting contributors to hold the copyright to their work seems to have been the policy of *Amistad*, perhaps as a means to encourage scholars in black studies to submit portions of larger works in progress.

In any event, the magazine was a diverse mix of history, fiction, literary criticism, popular culture, and sometimes simple rhetoric. Such a mix guaranteed the magazine an adaptability to a variety of college courses in black studies and to stimulate student thought and discussion in a variety of ways. Thus, for instance, many of the selections might be paired in meaningful ways. Richard Wright's insistence in his "Blueprint for Negro Literature" upon the autonomy of craft and his aesthetic caution that "if the sensory vehicle of imaginative writing is made to carry too great a load of didactic material, the artistic sense is lost,"[2] contrasts sharply with John Oliver Killens' "Rappin With Myself." Here Killens confesses an admiration for Wright, but his own aesthetic perspective is much different: "How in hell could I be a writer who happens to be Black? I wasn't born pecking a typewriter. But every Black mother's child, be he ditchdigger, doctor, hustler, preacher, pimp, lawyer, or writer is born Black in a white racist society. And for a writer that is the most important thing about him, his roots." Killens rejects the "universality" of art, writes from a black perspective and for blacks, and claims "all art is propaganda." "Art is social and political. . . . Art is functional. A Black work of art helps the liberation movement or hinders it."[3] These contrasting aesthetic propositions are to some extent represented by the two fictional pieces in *Amistad* 2, "The Bluest Eye" and Paul Goods' "Commuting."

Still a third view of the artist's role is articulated by Imamu Amiri Baraka (LeRoi Jones). Baraka transcends the conventional aesthetic dilemma represented by Wright and Killens in a McLuhanesque vision in his poetic essay, "Technology and Ethos." The black artist should strive to free himself not merely of western European values and institutions but of its technology as well. "A typewriter is corny!!" he says, "machines have the morality of their inventors."[4] New technology, new forms, in constant flux, are means to a liberating spirit in art.

This is not to suggest that the conflicts and contrasts within *Amistad* 2 exist mainly between its covers. To the contrary, the prevailing emphasis of the magazine is upon a severe, sometimes strident criticism of white society, history, and culture. And the scope and method of this criticism is versatile and diverse.

The most comprehensive of the essays included in *Amistad* 2 is Du Bois' "The White Masters of the World." Du Bois begins in contemplation of the ethical and political paradoxes inherent in the white mastery of nonwhite races. The historical dialectic he saw in European and American domination has its origins in division according to race. Such racism leads to wage slavery which in turn makes possible the "gentlemen of independent means." Du Bois traces this development from its economic consequences to a Thorstein Veblen-like, ethical conclusion: It is the man of independent means who becomes a conspicuous consumer and who is responsible for the *fin de siècle* decadence of nineteenth-century Europe.

Though Du Bois is severely critical of all European colonial nations, England is held up for especial scorn. His portrait of the English lady, safe within her "lovely British home," is a devastating one.

> It will in all probability not occur to her that she has any responsibility whatsoever, and that may well be true. Equally, it may be true that her income is the result of starvation, theft, and murder; that it involves ignorance, disease, and crime on the part of thousands; that the system she enjoys is based on the suppression, exploitation, and slavery of the majority of mankind.[5]

Her contentment and happy ignorance of her own moral complicity is, according to Du Bois, the modern "paradox of Sin." This beautiful, cultured young woman "may be the foundation of which is built the poverty and degradation of the world."[6]

Narrower in their considerations than Du Bois' essay but by no means less severe in their indictments are such scholarly essays as Haywood Burns' "Racism and American Law" and Basil Davidson's "Africa Recolonized?" Both essays challenge conventional wisdom and understanding of, respectively, the American legal system and modern European and American policies toward newly constituted independent African nations. Burns maintains that white racism is woven into the very texture of our legal system, while Davidson challenges the ethical superciliousness of those who would see Africa's strife as proof that Africans are not ready for political independence. There persists, argues Davidson, an "ideological recolonization," both capitalist and communist, that tends to undermine any attempts African leaders might make to resolve their problems, problems which are historical and inherent to Africa alone. The history of colonialism and its effects was "one of contributing towards the downfall and collapse of Africa's pre-colonial and socio-economic structure, and *not* of contributing towards the organizing and raising of new structures."[7] Though Davidson admits the possibility of future upheavals in Africa, his conclusion is hopeful. An African revolution is imminent, but not necessarily a destructive one. A "saving revolution" would be a revolution "against the traditional structures of the past" and a revolution against the imposed structures of the colonial period."[8] The raising of new structures eventually will, and must, originate from African soil and African culture.

A methodological, rather than social or historical, criticism may be found in Sterling Stuckey's "Twilight of Our Past: Reflections on the Origins of Black History." Beginning with a consideration of the familiar controversy of William Styron's historical novel *Confessions of Nat Turner*, Stuckey identifies a context for exploring new approaches to the writing of American history. One such approach involves the ferreting out of evidence from unconventional sources: slave songs and spirituals, poetry and folklore. Contemptuous of the versions of black history offered by such white historians as Arthur Schlesinger and C. Vann Woodward, and their failure even to ask the pivotal questions necessary to the writing of an authoritative black history, Stuckey concludes that "only from a radical perspective can the necessary new questions and answers come to consciousness."[9] The example for future black historians should be, says Stuckey, W.E.B. Du Bois. It was Du Bois who offered the proper and still pertinent perspective on black history—its values, its methodology, and its goals.

Finally, there is in *Amistad* 2 an essay on popular culture: "The Lyrics of James Brown: Ain't it Funky Now, or Money Won't Change Your Licking Stick." In it, Mel Watkins explores the figure of James Brown and the lyrics of his songs as providing the transformation of black consciousness and values from the fifties to the seventies. Brown is, according to Watkins, a "Black troubadour," and his songs characterize "the physical, emotional and down front black life."

> His work, viewed in full spectrum, gives expression to the textural substance of black life; moreover it has reflected and sometimes anticipated the general course in which the energies of the black community would flow. From "Please, Please, Please" in the fifties, he moved to "Say It Loud—I'm Black and I'm Proud" in the sixties; and in the seventies, beyond "It's a New Day"? The answer may well be found on James Brown's next disc."[10]

A summary of the content of *Amistad* 2 serves to characterize the nature of the magazine as a whole. It was a multidisciplinary publication, a mixture of the conventionally scholarly and popular, of fiction and history, of rhetoric and analysis. Less insistent in method than in its commitment to the symbolic suggestions of its title—rebellion, equality, liberation—it responded to a need for a usable text for proliferating courses in black studies on college campuses throughout the country. It was a bold and unusual adaptation of the magazine tradition and, for a time, a very successful publishing venture.

Notes

1. The Amistad Mutiny is a significant symbol in Afro-American culture. In July 1839, Africans, led by Cinque, revolted, killed the captain and three crewmen, and seized their Spanish slave ship, *L'Amistad*, off the coast of Cuba. They sailed to Montauk, Long Island, New York, and were tried before the U.S. Supreme Court where John Quincy Adams defended them. The court ruled that they had been kidnapped, and they were freed and returned to Africa. It was the symbolic association with the Amistad Mutiny which provided a thematic, rather than a methodological or ideological, consistency of purpose and unity of organization to the selections in *Amistad*.

2. Wright, "Blueprint for Negro Literature," *Amistad* 2: *Writings on Black History and Culture* (February 1971): 18.

3. Killens, "Rappin, With Myself," *Amistad* 2 (February 1971): 103-4.

4. Barake, "Technology and Ethos," *Amistad* 2 (February 1971): 320.

5. Du Bois, "The White Masters of the World," *Amistad* 2 (February 1971): 198-99.

6. Ibid., p. 199.

7. Davidson, "Africa Recolonized?," *Amistad* 2 (February 1971): 233.

8. Ibid., pp. 256-57.

9. Stuckey, "Twilight of Our Past," *Amistad* 2 (February 1971): 289.

10. Watkins, "The Lyrics of James Brown," *Amistad* 2 (February 1971): 42.

Information Sources

INDEX SOURCES: None.
LOCATION SOURCES: Most college and university libraries.

Publication History

MAGAZINE TITLE AND TITLE CHANGES: *Amistad: Writings on Black History and Culture* (1970-1971).
VOLUME AND ISSUE DATA: *Amistad* 1 (February 1970); *Amistad* 2 (February 1971).
PUBLISHER AND PLACE OF PUBLICATION: Vintage Books, a division of Random House, New York, New York.
EDITORS: John A. Williams and Charles F. Harris (1970-1971).
CIRCULATION: 50,000 highest estimate.

Thomas Quirk

ANGLO-AFRICAN MAGAZINE, THE

Thomas Hamilton founded in New York City in 1859 the *Anglo-African Magazine*, considered the first black literary journal in America.[1] It began as a monthly periodical of thirty-two pages; and although it failed a few years later,

Hamilton's magazine has to be considered especially significant in the history of Afro-American journalism. Frederick Douglass, who began publishing his *Douglass' Monthly** that same year, after his experiences with the *North Star* and *Frederick Douglass' Paper*, wrote of Hamilton's effort:

> The new year this far brought to our public nothing more gratifying and encouraging than this new publication. The advent of a monthly magazine, devoted to Literature, Science, Statistics, etc., is no new thing under the sun and especially not new in our country. The United States abounds in such publications; but to our knowledge, nothing of the character of the magazine before us, has ever been attempted by any member or members of the colored race in the United States.[2]

Hamilton, who wrote in the first issue of *Anglo-African* that he had cherished since childhood a dream of publishing a magazine, had worked as a boy in Manhattan's newspaper district. He felt he had gained there significant knowledge about the profession, especially its technical aspects. The high-quality appearance of his magazine attests to that skill. His primary reason for going into journalism was the same motivation that took most blacks into it. Slavery, especially in the antebellum years, was odious to any black American. Abolition of slavery was the chief aim of the race, and journalism was one way to make their feelings about the hated institution known. Hamilton expressed that purpose in an editorial.

> Negroes, in order to assert and maintain their rank among men must speak for themselves. No outside tongue, however gifted with eloquence, can tell their story; no outside organization, however benevolently intended, however cunningly contrived, can develop the energies and aspirations which make up their mission.[3]

The *Anglo-African* was intended to be a weapon for Negroes in the time of the irrepressible conflict leading up to the outbreak of war, but it also served as a newspaper for and about blacks. It would "chronicle the population and movements of the colored people" with respect to their religious organizations, as well as their moral and economic standing. It made statements about their educational condition and their legal status in the several states, their claims for citizenship in various parts of the country, and it provided biographies of noteworthy black men throughout the world. Those purposes have been common to all general-purpose black journals.[4]

The *Anglo-African* is remembered for its literary content as well as for its chronicle of the life of black Americans on the eve of the Civil War. Hamilton was able to attract the best Negro minds in the nation as contributors to his journal. They figured largely in the antislavery movement: Alexander Crummell, Edward W. Blyden, Martin R. Delany, J.W.C. Pennington, William Wells

Brown, John Mercer Langston, George B. Vashon, Frances Ellen Watkins Harper, Daniel A. Payne, and James McCune Smith represented the professions and public figures.

Titles of some articles appearing in the journal included: "A Statistical View of the Colored Population from 1790 to 1850," "American Caste and Common Schools," "On the 14th Query of Thomas Jefferson's Notes on Virginia," "Thoughts on Hayti," "A Chapter in the History of the American Slave Trade," and "The Effects of Emancipation in Jamaica." *Anglo-African* has been called the black man's *Atlantic Monthly*.

Although Hamilton did not list literary works as one of the emphases of the magazine, creative writing became a significant part of its offerings. The use of imaginative writing as a part of the fight for civil rights—the strategies so common to the Harlem Renaissance and the black arts movement many years later—was first expressed in *Anglo-African* by Frances Harper, an abolitionist and creative writer. Her "Two Offers" was the first piece of short fiction contributed to a black journal in the United States.[5] Moreover, she requested blacks to use their talents in creative writing to fight for citizenship rights on the theory that issues might not be so commanding as matters of the human heart, which could engage the sympathies and the attention of all people. William Wells Brown, the first Negro to write and publish a novel, and Martin R. Delany, author of the novel *Blake, or the Huts of America*, both published works in the magazine.

When the journal was forced to cease publication in 1862, Hamilton's relatives converted it into a weekly magazine under the title *Weekly Anglo-African* which continued until 1865.

Notes

1. Mary Fair Burks, "The First Black Literary Magazine in American Letters," *College Language Association Journal* (March 1976): 318-21.
2. "Editor's Apology," *Anglo-African Magazine* (January 1860): 1.
3. These purposes are quoted in I. Garland Penn, *The Afro-American Press and Its Editors* (Springfield, Mass., 1891), p. 119.
4. Burks, "First Black Literary Magazine," p. 319.
5. "Our Greatest Want," *Anglo-African Magazine* (November 1859): 2.

Information Sources

BIBLIOGRAPHY:
Burks, Mary Fair. "The First Black Literary Magazine in American Letters." *College Language Association Journal*, March 1976, pp. 318-21.
Johnson, Charles S. "Rise of the Negro Magazine." *Journal of Negro History*, January 1928, pp. 11-12.
Penn, I. Garland. *The Afro-American Press*. Springfield, Mass., 1891, pp. 118-20.
INDEX SOURCES: None.

LOCATION SOURCES: Library of Congress; Moorland-Spingarn Collection, Howard University, Washington, D.C.

Publication History

MAGAZINE TITLE AND TITLE CHANGES: *The Anglo-African Magazine*.
VOLUME AND ISSUE DATA: I-III (January 1859-April 1861), monthly.
PUBLISHER AND PLACE OF PUBLICATION: The Anglo-African Magazine, New York, New York.
EDITOR: Thomas Hamilton (1859-1861).
CIRCULATION: 500 estimate.

——— B ———

BLACK ACADEMY REVIEW: QUARTERLY OF
THE BLACK WORLD

An interdisciplinary quarterly devoted to the defense and edification of black civilization in all its dimensions and variations, *Black Academy Review* was one of many scholarly journals launched in the 1970s. Based at the State University of New York at Buffalo, the *Review* was the official magazine of the Black Academy Press, Incorporated, organized in March 1970 at Buffalo. Its articles were directed toward a general academic audience. The editorial statement in the first issue announced that the journal would publish essays on major matters confronting the "black pluriverse" as well as literary and semitechnical discussions on black colonization in Africa, the West Indies, the Americas, and elsewhere. It did not claim to be a protest quarterly—it intended to represent the black diaspora after the fashion of *Black World*.*

S. Okechukwu Mezu, president of the press and editor of the magazine, is a Nigerian who holds degrees in French, German, and law from American universities. He considered his academy a direct descendant of organizations like the American Negro Academy set up by Alexander Crummell in 1897 as a vehicle for black American intellectuals to defend other blacks and to promote research on black problems.[1] Similarly, recalling W.E.B. Du Bois' manifesto issued in 1905 at the Niagara Conference that, together with other organizations and efforts, led to the establishment of the NAACP, Mezu noted the parallel between his enterprise and Du Bois'.

> Here today in Buffalo, on the same Niagara Frontier, is being constituted Black Academy Press, Inc. as the black intellectual seeks to reclaim his rights in a multiracial society and affirm his responsibility to his people in our complex pluriverse. The organization is Black to emphasize its primary but not exclusive orientation and control; Academy, to underscore the honesty, excellence and high standard the organization wishes to maintain;

Press to show that it intends to be a full fledged business concern in the most extensive use of the word. It plans to cater firstly to the University community, secondly to the high school system and last but not least to the general public.[2]

The academy's publishing house sought to take advantage of the boom in black studies programs and the proliferation of books in that area and planned to divert black authors from going to publishing establishments outside the United States in order to have their works placed before the reading public. Writers and scholars would find in the press an opportunity to own shares in the corporation and a voice in its management. The *Review* would publish special issues and bibliographical supplements detailing current scholarship in the areas of intercultural relations and world politics among black peoples.

For the first issue the editor wrote the lead article, "Poetry and Revolution in Modern Africa." Roger Landrum of Teachers, Incorporated, wrote "Chinua Achebe and the Aristotelian Concept of Tragedy" for the same issue. Other articles included Dudley Randall's "Poets of the Broadside Press," Arnold Gibbons' "Minority Programming on American Commercial Television," and Edward A. Jones' "White Experts, Black Experts, and Black Studies." Subsequent issues contained essays and reports on special programs for the disadvantaged, such as academic skills centers in colleges and compensatory education projects in public schools. The *Review* paid homage to W.E.B. Du Bois, Frantz Fanon, and Ralph Ellison. Pan-African and Caribbean subjects had a special emphasis in the publication. Caribbean linguistics and literature, literary criticism of black writing in the United States, and Negro theater in Brazil provided some of the most significant pieces in the journal. Special issues were devoted to modern black literature, educational controversy concerning the government takeover of Nigerian schools, and culture and religions.

Native Africans on the staff, together with Americans who had taught English in Nigeria with the Peace Corps, brought to the *Review* firsthand knowledge of the interesting relationship between American and African black writing. However, the journal showed, perhaps too clearly, the strains of the civil war in Nigeria in the early 1970s. As it became narrowly focused on Nigerian affairs, the magazine lost its appeal to its larger original American audience. Like most of its contemporaries, it ceased publication for lack of sufficient financial resources.

Notes

1. Alexander Crummell (1819-1898), minister and scholar, spent much of his career advocating and defining the aims and ideals of the Liberian settlement. Near the end of his life, he founded the American Negro Academy. Among its prominent members and early officers were W.E.B. Du Bois, John W. Cromwell, and the Reverend Francis J. Grimke. The academy was organized to promote literature, science, art, and higher education. It published a series of occasional papers on those subjects. For Crummell, *see* Kathleen O.

Wahle, "Alexander Crummell: Black Evangelist and Pan-Negro Nationalist," *Phylon* (Winter 1968): 338-95.
    2. "The Philosophy of Black Academy Press, Inc.," *Black Academy Review* (Spring/Winter 1970): 3.

Information Sources

BIBLIOGRAPHY:
Katz, Bill. *Magazines for Libraries.* 2d ed. New York, 1972, p. 106.
INDEX SOURCE: *Index to Periodical Articles about and by Negroes.*
LOCATION SOURCES: College and university libraries; University Microfilms.

Publication History

MAGAZINE TITLE AND TITLE CHANGES: *Black Academy Review: Quarterly of the Black World.*
VOLUME AND ISSUE DATA: Vols I-V (Spring/Winter 1970-Spring 1974), quarterly.
PUBLISHER AND PLACE OF PUBLICATION: Black Academy Press, Incorporated, Buffalo, New York.
EDITOR: S. Okechukwu Mezu (1970-1974).
CIRCULATION: 5,000.

Mark A. Reger

BLACK AMERICAN LITERATURE FORUM

In 1967 Indiana State University at Terre Haute launched the *Black American Literature Forum* (originally called the *Negro American Literature Forum*) in the midst of national unrest on college and university campuses, calling for courses that explored the black American experience. The *Forum*'s first editor wrote that the journal's editorial policy was to run the gamut of Negro American literature at all levels of education, from kindergarten to the university. In its earliest issues, the magazine focused its content on teaching black writing and introducing students to black authors whose names and works had generally been excluded from textbooks on American literature.[1]

Beginning as a modest publication, the *Forum* dedicated a large portion of its first issue to the memory and works of Langston Hughes, who died in the same year the magazine began publication. Arna Bontemps, a celebrated black writer, and Donald C. Dickenson, a librarian at the University of Missouri, set the course for the small but well-edited journal with their reminiscences of Hughes. Other early articles discussed the Negro in modern literature and films and the integration of minority literature into university and high school curricula. Within the first few years of publication Arthur Davis, Darwin Turner, and Charlene Rollins—among other distinguished black scholars of Afro-American culture—wrote for the magazine. Their contributions discussed Carl Sandburg and the Negro, Charles Chesnutt's short fiction as tragic racial parables, the development of Negro American drama, planning a program in Negro American Studies, growing up in the Harlem Renaissance, and comprehensive bibliographies of black writing.

Within the first four years of publication, the *Forum* presented a balance between teaching methods and literary analysis of works written by twentieth-century black authors. Some of those articles included: "Against Invisibility: The English for Probing Black and White Youth," "Teaching of Protest and Propaganda Literature," "Alain Locke and the 'New Negro' Movement," "Promoting Racial Understanding Through Books," "Traditions of Negro Literature in the United States," "The Politics of Passing: The Fiction of James Weldon Johnson," and "On Teaching Works By and About Black Americans: A Review of Articles."

Various issues of the journal provide an unusual mixture of discussions of Afro-American writing, covering Charles Chesnutt, Booker T. Washington, W.E.B. Du Bois, Zora Neale Hurston, Ralph Ellison, Richard Wright, Jean Toomer, Ed Bullins, Melvin B. Tolson, Le Roi Jones, Gwendolyn Brooks, Lorraine Hansberry, Al Young, Adrienne Kennedy, Ishmael Reed, and Chester Himes. One of the excellent bibliographies is "The Harlem Renaissance and After: A Checklist of Black Literature of the Twenties and Thirties." The winter issue has usually contained a valuable bibliography. The articles are always well documented, brief, cogent, scholarly, and well chosen for valuable insight and commentary about the black American experience.

While *Black American Literature Forum* has remained essentially a literary journal, it has not failed from time to time to take serious note of the larger problems of blacks living in the United States. One illustration of the manner in which this larger racial context has been related to black contemporary writing lies in the following comment:

Most whites but few Blacks prefer thinking that social, political and economic conditions for America's thirty million Blacks have improved considerably in the last decade. These same people point to the schools for evidence of this wild claim. They point to the increased numbers of Blacks in colleges or to the fact that a Black is now president of a large Midwest university.

Nonsense. These are the exception, otherwise they would not be newsworthy, not the rule. It is one thing to look at the figures for Blacks *entering* college—which continue appallingly low—and quite another matter to look at the figures for Blacks who graduate. This infectious American habit of accenting miniscule gains while overlooking or distorting harmful realities led one American President to deny that this country owned U-2 planes even as one was shot down by the Russians. And in Chicago, it permits the mayor to publicly claim that there are no slums in his city.

This issue of *NALF* slices through some of the comfortable lies about the state of America's educational institutions and her Black citizens. This issue has a rondo form, familiar in music, but criminally discoverable too in the Black American experience. The issue opens with students rapping about the broken promises they've experienced in colleges; it closes with a vignette which rips off the rationalizations routinely offered for mistreatment of and discrimination against Black Americans. In that story, the little girl is called a "Nigger" and that, when the rhetoric and stratagems are stripped away, is precisely what Blacks continue to be treated as in educational institutions whether they be students, teachers, or administrators. In that story, the little girl is called a "Nigger" and that, when the rhetoric and stratagems are stripped away, is precisely what Blacks continue to be treated as in educational institutions whether they be students, teachers, or administrators. In that story, the little girl is called a "Nigger" and that, when the rhetoric and stratagems are stripped away, is precisely what Blacks continue to be treated as in educational institutions whether they be students, teachers, or administrators.

Each contributor to this issue is Black. Half of them are students under thirty; others are professors, several are administrators. The range of view is wide, reminding the reader that there is *no* single Black point-of-view. True despite the fact that *all* Blacks struggle to survive and to thrive in the grip of the terrible, inescapable institutional and personal racism designed to defeat them, which is America.[2]

Notes

1. "Editorial," *Negro American Literature Forum* (Winter 1967): 11.
2. Ernece B. Kelly, "Guest Editor's Note," *Negro American Literature Forum* (Fall 1970): 79.

Information Sources

INDEX SOURCES: *Abstracts of English Studies*; *Current Index to Journals in Education*; *Index to Periodical Articles about and by Negroes*; *Modern Language Association International Bibliography*.
LOCATION SOURCES: Most college and university libraries; University Microfilms.

Publication History

MAGAZINE TITLE AND TITLE CHANGES: *Negro American Literature Forum* (Fall 1967-Fall 1976); *Black American Literature Forum* (Winter 1976 to present).
VOLUME AND ISSUE DATA: Vols. I-XIV, quarterly.
PUBLISHER AND PLACE OF PUBLICATION: Indiana State University, Terre Haute, Indiana.
EDITORS: John F. Bayliss (Fall 1967-Spring 1977); Hannah Hedrick (Fall 1976); Joe Weixelman (Spring 1977-).
CIRCULATION: 5,000.

BLACK BUSINESS DIGEST

In the first issue of *Black Business Digest*, executive editor Albert D. Hendricks wrote about the philosophy of his journal, which began publication in July 1970 in Philadelphia. His editorial began, "*Black Business Digest* was created for the express purpose of promulgating the black business story."[1] He predicated one of his motivations upon a passage from the writings of philosopher Peter Drucker, which he quoted in the same editorial.

> We know much more about communications than we have been able to apply. We know, for example, that the communicator does not communicate— he only utters. Whether or not he gets through depends less on his eloquence and logic and more on the frame of reference available to the perceiver by virtue of his experience. The communicator's success depends largely upon how well he understands the perceiver.[2]

To Hendricks, this statement meant that the black businessman was compelled to fully understand the details and elements of the exploding new markets. Hendricks' journal would interpret these dynamics and relay them to the black businessman. Each month he would present stimulating articles written by well-known experts active in promoting black business programs; statistics on economic trends; news of government programs geared to assist small business; demographic data to help big business expand; and reviews of current books on economics, modern management techniques, labor unions, and business education opportunities. He believed there was a willing audience in the nation, eager to become an effective element in black enterprise.

The *Digest*, then, would address the more than 500,000 black professionals, managers, and entrepreneurs who, in 1970, could generate a minimum cash flow of $5 billion for purchase of goods, equipment, and services in urban America. While the journal was interested primarily in alerting blacks to their new opportunities in business, it was interested in both black and white "perceivers."

To achieve these purposes, the *Digest* adopted a format that included national black business directories; articles about American industry and its involvement in increasing minority job opportunities; the revitalization of the inner cities; activities of the Office of Equal Opportunity and Small Business Administration; economics in Africa; a Youth Corner; and discussions of new black businesses.

The March 1971 issue carried a special section on "Black Capitalism—Point of Conflict." The centerpiece for the symposium on this subject was "An Economic Agenda for Black Americans," an address Andrew F. Brimmer, a black member of the Board of Governors of the Federal Reserve Bank, had delivered recently at Atlanta University. The chief rebuttal to Brimmer's thesis was prepared by Dunbar McLaurin, president of Ghettonomics, a Harlem-based firm of black economic consultants. McLaurin attacked "brimmerism" as a fatalistic and self-defeating approach to economics for Afro-Americans that was irrelevant to their needs. He called it "tokenism in banking and finance" which brought blacks to the brink of economic opportunity without taking them into the mainstream.

Topics of other provocative features and articles appearing in *Black Business Digest* during its three-year publication life included Jesse Jackson's PUSH project; black members of directorates of major national corporations; Leon Sullivan's Black Expo '71, sponsored by the Philadelphia chapter of the National Negro Business League; growing black business ownership resulting from Executive Order 11625 issued by Richard Nixon on 13 October 1971; and a special report on black women executives. The journal always published strong editorials that explained the status of the black economy and made evaluations of new directions that seemed feasible.

Black Business Digest could not compete with *Black Enterprise*,* also a magazine that arose in the 1970s and gained quick acceptance by the advertising world. Because it could not sustain itself to continue publication, *Black Business Digest* was short-lived. It does represent, however, some of the thrust of business journalism among Afro-Americans during the unusually fertile 1970s.

Notes

1. "As Black Business Digest Sees It," *Black Business Digest* (July 1970): 4-5.
2. Ibid.

Information Sources

INDEX SOURCES: None.
LOCATION SOURCES: Library of Congress; Harlan Hatcher Graduate Library, University of Michigan; many college and university libraries.

Publication History

MAGAZINE TITLE AND TITLE CHANGES: *Black Business Digest*.
VOLUME AND ISSUE DATA: Vols. I-III (July 1970-October 1973).
PUBLISHER AND PLACE OF PUBLICATION: Compeers, Inc., Philadelphia, Pennsylvania.
EDITORS: Albert D. Hendricks, executive editor; Vincent A. Capozzi, managing editor (1970-1973).
CIRCULATION: 3,000.

BLACK CAREERS

The fruits of the civil rights movement of the 1960s led directly to a new and broadened scope of educational and employment opportunities for black youth in the United States. That trend opened new areas for periodicals directed toward blacks. *Black Careers*, which began its present publication with a free introductory issue for May/June 1971, is a successful prototype of that phenomenon.[1]

Black Careers is a reference publication and instructional aid that offers readers significant information about career opportunities and advancement. It is a valuable tool for teachers and counselors who deal with problems of motivating contemporary students toward educational opportunity on a day-to-day basis.

Black Careers primarily provides the minority student in college with a vivid presentation of the achievements of minority persons in business and industry. It also provides nonminority Americans with a clear picture of the aspirations, the problems, and the gains of minority Americans.

"Viewing the Service Academies," an editorial in the first issue, identifies the subject of that special issue. Traditionally, black Americans have seldom been welcomed into the national service academies. The armed services were not integrated until midcentury, and even then peacetime commissions for graduates of the several officer-training institutions were rare among blacks. In the early 1970s, however, new opportunities created by the movement to equalize the chances of all persons to make career choices were presented by the service academies as well as American industry. The editorial in *Black Careers* pointed out that the academies are, first and foremost, colleges that are extremely efficient seats of higher education. Inasmuch as most blacks could not afford the tuition required for a private school education comparable to that offered by the service institutions, high school seniors were advised to take advantage of the change in attitudes toward blacks in the services.

Each year one special issue of *Black Careers* is entitled "A Guide to Black Colleges and Universities." It is an up-to-date and especially useful list giving the names and locations of schools, degrees offered, and enrollments and number of graduates over a six-year period. This last feature indicates one aspect of racial pride the magazine emphasizes. The black college is a uniquely black institution which this journal considers worthy of enrolling the best minds among black youth.

More than simply listing new areas in which young graduates might find employment, the articles in *Black Careers* explore the realities of employment in the black American experience. Black history issues highlight achievements among blacks which are intended to raise the aspirations of youth. Other issues focus on nonconventional career opportunities for black youth in science, industry, and business. Articles in these issues often make clear the fact that opportunities to prepare for such careers are available in black schools as well as the better-known, traditionally white institutions. "Management Speaks" is an uncommonly effective feature that presents questions placed to 100 business editors about career positions for blacks. One special report is a conversation with Samuel D. Proctor, a graduate professor of education at Rutgers University School of Education, and senior minister at the famous Abyssinian Baptist Church in Harlem. Inasmuch as Proctor has served as president of two traditionally black colleges and has held a variety of significant positions in education and government, his comments about the tensions black students often feel in studying at traditionally white universities are of special value and particular relevance. His honest and informative response to the questions many students raise about the relative merits of enrolling in a white college instead of one that is historically black is an important dimension in counseling the college-bound black student in the seventies. Articles such as these are examples of *Black Careers'* successful efforts to approach special questions of career choice and educational opportunity for blacks.

Note

1. *Black Careers* was formerly *Project Magazine*. Volume numbers are carried from the older periodical. The two journals are sufficiently different for a profile to be fashioned specifically for *Black Careers*.

Information Sources

INDEX SOURCES: None.
LOCATION SOURCES: Black college libraries; Moreland-Spingarn collection, Howard
    University, Washington, D.C.; Library of Congress.

Publication History

MAGAZINE TITLE AND TITLE CHANGES: *Black Careers* (May/June 1971 to present).
VOLUME AND ISSUE DATA: Vol. VII, no. 3 began the new publication in 1971.
    (*Project Magazine* began publication with vol. I in Fall 1969). Bimonthly.
PUBLISHER AND PLACE OF PUBLICATION: Black Careers, Inc., Philadelphia,
    Pennsylvania.
EDITOR: Emory W. Washington, editor-in-chief (1971-   ).
CIRCULATION: 175,429.

Mark A. Reger

BLACK CHURCH, THE

The Black Ecumenical Commission of Massachusetts introduced the *Black Church* to the public in May 1972. Commission associates in the Massachusetts Bay Area considered their journal a breakthrough in religious publishing, although theirs was by no means the first black church periodical. Leaders were respectfully conscious that in beginning their magazine they were following a long and honored tradition in black religious circles. In the nineteenth century the church published potent organs dealing with religious and civic affairs and powerful appeals for education and political agitation. *Christian Recorder*, *A.M.E. Church Review*,* *Sunbeam*, *Baptist Reflector*, *African Biblical Review*, and *Star of Zion* are only a few of the papers and magazines that represent this heritage. Some denominational papers continued well into the latter half of the twentieth century, but most church news by then was disseminated by way of the church page in weekly and daily newspapers. The promoters of *Black Church* felt they had no ecumenical medium in which to discuss the problems and aspirations of black churches and their congregations—their past and their future. Moreover, the black nationalist movement of the 1960s had transformed the function of the black church in American society. It returned to the social activism role it had played in the nineteenth century as it became an essential cultural factor in American life, far more complex than a meetinghouse for Christian worship. This new need for an ethnic medium of religious expression and the work of the church gave rise to the establishment of the *Black Church*. It was an attempt to tie literary expression to the new consciousness of black Christians as part of the nationalism movement. Its founders created what they called "the first ecumenical Black caucuses to be established on a regional basis since the founding of the National Committee on Black Churches in 1967."[1] The Ecumenical Commission made some funds available to pay for the first issue of the quarterly. The journal was expected to become self-supporting by the time the second issue would be published.

In his preface to the first number, editor Jefferson P. Rogers wrote that the *Black Church* was designed primarily to present in-depth interpretations of the historic role of black Christianity in American culture and the entire American church. That purpose would be served by publishing penetrating, factual analyses of the church's past, and articulation of its present efforts to guide American society in the direction of wholesomeness and radical sanity. Realizing that blacks have the responsibility of telling the story of their church's centrality "in the terrible march of Blacks to 'the Promised Land' of inner freedom,"[2] the editorial staff chose for the first four issues of *Black Church* principal articles drawn from addresses that had been delivered at important religious conferences. They covered a variety of subjects, including: "The Crisis in the American Church," "The Black Man's Environment and His Minority Status—A Challenge to the Black Church," "The Black Church Now," "Black Worship: Black Church," "Another View of the Minority Student and the Law School," and "The A.M.E. Church, A Study in Black Nationalism." Benjamin E. Mays, a distinguished black minister and educator, wrote in the black man's environment article that his minority status required every black man to make a significant connection with his church in every area in which blacks lived. Alain Rogers wrote in the A.M.E. Church article that contemporary development of black consciousness could best be studied through a careful analysis of the history of that denomination. For, unlike the NAACP, the "Tuskegee Machine," or Marcus Garvey's Universal Negro Improvement Association, the A.M.E. Church had come closer to forming a black nation within the United States than had any other organization in history.[3]

The magazine struggled for a viable focus during the two years of its publication. Rogers resigned the editorship to accept a pastorate in New York State, and Gayraud Wilmore replaced him. In his first "Word from the Editor" he wrote that the journal's staff was gaining experience and ability and could continue to improve the literary quality, style, and layout of the *Black Church*. He was concerned, however, with more important problems. One was the identity of the magazine. To serve as a medium for current news and religious interest for lay people and a communications and educational resource for pastors seemed to him a "rather large and fuzzy order." He understood that *Black Church* considered itself "a message beamed primarily to the Black family, to help it realize a Black Christian consciousness of the distinctiveness and relevance of Black religion for the liberation of the oppressed—particularly the Black poor."[4] He thought that the magazine wanted to relate black religion and theology to every aspect of black life and culture. But he also saw other more institutional reasons for the journal's existence; reasons related to the purpose and program of the Black Ecumenical Commission and the National Conference of Black Churchmen, and to the mobilization and empowerment of black people in areas of social, political, and economic strength; locally, regionally, and perhaps internationally. If that was the identity of *Black Church*, Wilmore asked how he could confirm and strengthen this image in the issues that would come before his staff. The more urgent problem arose from what he called "the apathy and lack of cooperation on the part of churches that have pledged themselves to support *Black Church* with subscriptions and promotion in the congregations and the communities."[5]

Lack of that support caused *Black Church* to cease publication, largely because it could not project a focus that would generate sufficient interest among black churchmen to sponsor a religious magazine of this nature. In a larger sense, radical black ministers probably found themselves out of synchronization with their memberships as the clergy forged a new black theology that seemed *avant garde* to many congregations unwilling to use the church as an instrument of social change. *Black Church*, despite its short life, was a medium of the black church during the sixties and seventies and reflected the uses of that institution as an agent for change.

Notes

1. "Editor's Preface," *Black Church* (May 1972): ii.
2. Ibid.
3. *Black Church* (Spring 1973): 4.
4. Ibid.
5. Ibid.

Information Sources

BIBLIOGRAPHY:
"Editor's Preface." *Black Church*, May 1972, pp. v-vi.
Wilmore, Gayraud S. *Black Religion and Black Radicalism*. New York, 1972.
INDEX SOURCES: None.
LOCATION SOURCES: Atlanta University Library, Atlanta, Georgia; Fisk University Library, Nashville, Tennessee; Moorland-Spingarn Collection, Howard University, Washington, D.C.

Publication History

MAGAZINE TITLE AND TITLE CHANGES: *The Black Church* (May 1972-Spring 1974).
VOLUME AND ISSUE DATA: Vols. I-IV (May 1972-Spring 1974), quarterly.
PUBLISHER AND PLACE OF PUBLICATION: Black Ecumenical Commission of Massachusetts, Boston, Massachusetts.
EDITORS: Jefferson P. Rogers (May 1972-March 1973); Gayraud Wilmore (March 1973-May 1974).
CIRCULATION: 1,000.

BLACK COLLEGIAN, THE: THE NATIONAL MAGAZINE OF BLACK COLLEGE STUDENTS

A general-purpose magazine addressed to black college student audiences, *Black Collegian* contains feature articles, and reviews of books, films, and plays. It carries little editorial comment. Its format follows the pattern of literary and special-interest periodicals more than that of the news media. Its special issue on black women is one of its most impressive editions. It includes such articles as "Role of Black and White Women," "From the Classroom to Their Corporations: How Two Black Women Made It," "Career Opportunities for Black Women in the 1980s," and "What It Means to Be a Black Woman." Articles are written by staff members and invited authors. Although that issue was devoted to black women, its focus reflects the consistent concerns of the magazine. Founded in 1968, this magazine, like others designed for black youth in the sixties and seventies, provides useful data relating to career choices. *Black Collegian*'s *raison d'être* arises from the new emphasis on expanded job opportunities for black youth which is an outgrowth of federal legislation fostered by the civil rights movement of the 1960s. One goal of black organizations at that time was realized: National corporations turned for the first time to black colleges and universities to fulfill their obligations and commitments to equal employment opportunities for American blacks.

Black Collegian publishes job issues each year. In 1980, more than 200 businesses and professional firms sponsored the special edition that appealed to black youth graduating from colleges and universities. Their direct relationship to the magazine appeals to young people seeking to enter the world of work and, at the same time, the supporting enterprises find in this magazine an effective advertising medium addressed to black America.

Aside from its primary orientation to career counseling and articles relating to interpersonal relations in national industrial organizations, *Black Collegian* contains a significant literary component. Hoyt W. Fuller, one of the most highly respected black literary and editorial figures of the day, who has edited *Negro Digest,* *Black World,* and *First World,* occasionally writes book reviews for the *Collegian*. His name lends high visibility to the concern for literary matters. One most unusual item in a recent issue is an imaginary conversation between Carole Gregory and Zora Neale Hurston, the significant black woman author of the Harlem Renaissance era whose works have been revitalized by the contemporary novelist, Alice Walker.[1] Sonia Sanchez and Toni Cade Bambara, popular black women writers, are among others who have contributed essays to the magazine.

In recent years, the *Collegian* has refined the scope and quality of its subject matter. A section on religion has explored "Sound of Blackness" with discussions of the black church's music and preachers. "Dynamics in the Religious Antebellum Community" presented an in-depth historical portrait of the impact of the church as a social force in slavery times among free and slave blacks. Other historical subjects include a pictorial essay on the civil rights movement and "Economic Programs of Marcus Garvey," which related that black leader of the 1920s to contemporary Afro-American aspirations. Black history in Africa and the United States is featured with "Survey of African Independence," "Conflict and Famine in East Africa," "Liberia: A Dream Deferred," "South African Divestment Campaign," "Meaning of Malcolm X," "The Sally Hemmings Controversy," and "Black American Landmarks." Current social problems of youth are addressed in essays on suicide among young blacks, sickle-cell anemia, and educational challenges for the twenty-first century. Sections on fashion, art, and sports are regular parts of the magazine. Interviews with familiar blacks in a variety of fields of work appear, featuring a wide range of personalities including James Baldwin, Smokey Robinson, Sugar Ray Leonard, Andrew Young, and Natalie Cole.

This journal addressed to the interests and needs of the black college student has kept its focus on career advisement through its special issues on engineering, energy, money and banking, communication, and health. *Black Collegian* offers readers significant advice and information on procedures for applying to graduate and professional schools. It is an important and successful venture in journalism for the black American college student.

Note

1. See *Black Collegian* (April/May 1980): 146-50 for this feature.

Information Sources

INDEX SOURCES: *Index of Periodical Articles by and about Negroes: American Humanities Index.*
LOCATION SOURCES: Most black college libraries; University Microfilm International.

Publication History

MAGAZINE TITLE AND TITLE CHANGES: *The Black Collegian: The National Magazine of Black College Students.*
VOLUME AND ISSUE DATA: Vols. I-XII, 1968-present. Bimonthly during the school year.
PUBLISHER AND PLACE OF PUBLICATION: Black Collegian Services, Inc., New Orleans, Louisiana; Preston J. Edwards, publisher.
EDITORS: N. R. Davidson (1970-present); Preston J. Edwards (1970-78); Kalamajyal Salaam (1978-present).
CIRCULATION: 200,000.

BLACK CREATION: A REVIEW OF BLACK ARTS AND LETTERS

A statement inside the front cover of early issues of *Black Creation* claimed that this journal, while perhaps not the best, was one of the few magazines that was truly in tune with the heartbeat of black America. In actuality, *Black Creation* was probably the finest—and most diverse—black arts magazine in America in the 1970s.

Founded in 1970 in New York City and published quarterly by the Institute of Afro-American Affairs of New York University, *Black Creation* was concerned about both quality and the need for diversity of art forms and viewpoints. Thus, a representative early table of contents included "Novel Excerpt," "Film," "Art," "Photo Essay," "Fiction," "Theater," and "Book Review"; all of these categories were generously interspersed with individual poems. In later issues of *Black Creation*, the categories "Music" and "Dance" were added, and even later there appeared a section devoted to "Mini-Views" of movies and records. Soon after this a section devoted to outside comment was incorporated; and then, when *Black Creation* became an annual in 1974-75, a whole new area called "Kaleidoscope" was included.

As is customary at the birth of so many magazines, many of the editors of *Black Creation* were also creative writers who subsequently had their materials published in the magazine's pages. Elouise Loftin, for example, was both associate editor (for poetry) and the author of several poems which appeared in *Black Creation* from time to time (one of her more famous being "Sunni," about a woman whose total wisdom about her life and the life of her people is explained by the fact that "Her mother's womb had a window/so she knew exactly what she/was coming into). Jose Angel Figueroa also was an associate editor whose poetry appeared occasionally, and other editors provided the magazine with both journalistic and creative prose.

Because *Black Creation* was both a politically/socially/artistically sensitive and a secure magazine, it showed a good deal of innovation and growth in its structure and materials. Perhaps most impressive was its development of "Regional Editors" very early in its existence; an innovation that had a very interesting and perceptive rationale. As editor in chief Fred Beauford noted in the Winter 1973 issue:

> We now have editors across the country and abroad reporting on the arts from their communities. This is exciting because one of the biggest problems facing Black journalism is to cover fairly all segments of the community. And for lack of funds (or imagination) many so-called national publications never really leave their backyards. . . . Add to that the fact that too often magazines centered in New York or Chicago project only artists and ideas from these two centers and proclaim that these are the only ideas and artists that represent Black arts. . . .
>
> So, starting with this issue, we have tried to do something about this. Now we have people in San Francisco, Boston, Houston, New Orleans, Paris and London. We would also like to get into contact with people in the Mid-West, Mid-South, Africa and the Islands. If you know of anyone who is interested in reporting on the cultured happenings in their communities, tell them to drop us a line.[1]

Related to this was *Black Creation*'s introduction, also in Winter 1973, of a full "Comment" page, given over to a thorough discussion of some point by someone not on *Black Creation*'s staff. Walter D. Myers, senior editor at Bobbs-Merrill, was the first "commentator." *Black Creation* was clearly in the forefront, democratically reaching out to the community it both served and drew upon.

Another major aspect of this kind of outreach and community support was *Black Creation*'s initiation of a literary contest in the areas of fiction, essay, and poetry. After acquiring some very select judges to review the materials submitted (John A. Williams—fiction; Nikki Giovanni—poetry; and E. R. Braithwaite—essay), *Black Creation* ran an extensive contest in which "the quality of the submissions was rich" (Williams) and "all the poems. . .were quite exciting, quite full of ideas and energy" (Giovanni).

With the success of the literary contest, *Black Creation* developed a photography contest, once more reaching to the community while simultaneously emphasizing a black art form which generally had been overlooked and which *Black Creation* set out in earlier issues to stimulate and nurture (for example, in its extensive, five-page dialogue on "The Black Photographer").

Black Creation also pioneered the area of black films and black filmmakers, partially as a result of the expertise and verbal vitality of associate editor James Murray, partially because of the huge "explosion" of black films in the early seventies, and partially because so many of those rapidly produced films were considered exploitative of the black community (both in luring black viewers to the ticket windows and in purveying perverted images of blacks). *Black Creation* responded by devoting a full nineteen pages to "The Expanding World of Black Film" in its Winter 1973 issue. As the editors noted in their preface to this special series of articles,

> The future—both immediate and long-range—of visual communications, particularly film, looms as one of the most important influences on the destiny of Black life in America and the entire Third World. Film as art and as conveyor of realistic images has been overwhelmed by commercial and economic influences, and the greatest losers to date have been Blacks, whose image during the entire history of this relatively new medium has been consistently demeaned and exploited from one extreme to the other without significant challenge.[2]

It was up to *Black Creation* to offer this "challenge," the editors thought, and as a result, this "special study" became one of the major achievements of the magazine's six-year history.

Another unique area of exploration and analysis was the world of community and/or developing black theater. Thus the Summer 1972 issue made a fairly extensive study of the various black community theaters in the New York City area; and the next issue journeyed South to analyze "the Free Southern Theater," an outgrowth of the Student Nonviolent Coordinating Committee (SNCC) and the civil rights movement in New Orleans, and "the first radical Black theater the South, or the country, has ever known" (that is, a theater whose articulated philosophy was that "art is the highest form of politics"). So strong and continuous was *Black Creation*'s interest in political/community theater that in addition to a fairly extensive interview with Ed Bullins, associate director of Harlem's New Lafayette Theater, (Winter 1973) and an in-depth look at Barbara Ann Teer's National Black Theater in Harlem (Summer 1972) the magazine later ran an article on "South Africa's Theater of Commitment," noting the similarity between the various theaters, their approaches, and, especially, their artistic/political/social goals.

Still another highlight of *Black Creation*'s early issues was its development of a "Mini-Views" section that reviewed movies and records, and the utilization of that format by associate editor/film reviewer James P. Murray. Partially because of the limited space within which he had to work and partially because of his own flair for words, Murray soon became the magazine's most energetic and intensely vital writer. Some fairly representative samples of his style include his review of the movie *Slaughter* as "this summer's latest example of exploitation overkill," a "silly film" in which "neanderthal dialogue makes it [the formula violence and action] all inadvertent burlesque."

Despite all its unique emphases and successes, by 1974 the economic foundation of *Black Creation* had become so weak "due to financial exigencies that face all publications today" that it ceased quarterly publication for annual. With this shift in format came many other major shifts. "Kaleidoscope" appeared, a new section with three narrow columns per page that looked and functioned like a newspaper for the arts. "Money, Money, Who's Got the Money?" was the title of one small part of Kaleidoscope, and that part contained several small articles regarding funding sources, including complete addresses and what sort of specifications they generally had for awarding grants. Other articles throughout Kaleidoscope looked almost like advertisements or announcements for new magazines, new art centers, new schools of writing, and so forth. "*Onyx*: Magazine for Men" was the "birth announcement" heralding "the soon-to-be-published *Onyx*, a magazine geared to Black men." "Freelance Writers Take Note," another headline urged, and then provided the information necessary to pay sixteen dollars a year in order to receive *Freelancer's Newsletter*. Likewise, "New Third World Greeting Card Publishing Company" was a short "spot" which announced that "*The House of Gemini*, with a collection geared to Black and Spanish consumers, opened in early 1973, obtaining its first contract with F. W. Woolworth Company."

Furthermore, there was even a kind of artists' society column entitled "Visuals 1974" where one learned that "the *Jacob Lawrence* retrospective which opened on May 6, 1974, at the Whitney Museum of American Art in New York was the most important art exhibit held during the year 1974"; that "earlier, in April, in conjunction with a one-man show by the late artist *Palmer Hayden*, the Studio Museum in Harlem sponsored an 'Informal Evening of Conversation' focusing on the art of the Harlem Renaissance"; and that participants in that "Conversation" included "*Mrs. Countee Cullen*, wife of the late Harlem poet, *Jean Hutson*, curator of the Schomburg Collection of Afro-American literature, and artists *Joseph Delaney, Ernie Critchlow, Norman Lewis, Ellis Wilson, Bob Blackburn, Hale Woodruff*, and *Art Coppedge*." It is interesting to note that the names of people and companies were generally italicized, in true social page fashion.

In addition to the new personnel and the drastically new and different Kaleidoscope, there were two other changes of major note. The first was a strong move toward African and other international materials and perspectives. Thus there was a two-page article on "South Africa's Theatre of Commitment," immediately followed by a four-page study of "Contemporary Egyptian Art," and a three-page analysis of the "Birth of Puerto Rican Literature." The second major change was in the size of the magazine (ninety-six pages instead of the usual sixty or so), which left room for a very large book review section, with some fairly substantial assessments of works by Angela Davis, Toni Morrison, Dudley Randall, and others.

In the final analysis, despite its shift to annual publication (with whatever economic savings that may have entailed), *Black Creation* died after that one issue, a victim of American inflation and the Nixonian end to the active civil rights and black expression movements.

Notes

1. *Black Creation* (Winter 1973): 2.
2. Ibid., p. 6.

Information Sources

INDEX SOURCES: None.
LOCATION SOURCES: Scattered copies can be found in the Atlanta, Georgia, public library and in most black college and university libraries; Library of Congress.

Publication History

MAGAZINE TITLE AND TITLE CHANGES: *Black Creation: A Review of Black Arts and Letters* (Fall 1970-Fall 1974-75).
VOLUME AND ISSUE DATA: Vols. I-IV, quarterly; final issue, annual 1974-75.
PUBLISHER AND PLACE OF PUBLICATION: Institute of Afro-American Affairs, New York, New York.
EDITOR: Fred Beauford (1970-1975).
CIRCULATION: 2,500 estimate.

Noel Heermance

BLACK ENTERPRISE

Although *Black Enterprise* began publication in August 1970, it represents an entirely different genre of black journalism from the literary and general-purpose periodicals of the seventies. Its financial base is secure because it is grounded in the alignment of members of the American corporate structure and geared to American business as the center of the nation's life. *Black Enterprise* focuses on the practical side of the economics of black Americans as a part of the financial fiber of the nation. The concept of *Black Enterprise* enlarges upon the basic premises of Booker T. Washington's National Negro Business League network, strengthened by the political and social realities black and white Americans have come to accept in the latter half of the twentieth century. Thus, the journal is not narrowly black, although it emphasizes the Afro-American and African consciousness of economics. At the same time, it effectively joins that consciousness to the financial power structure of the Western world. Its areas of interest are business, jobs, and career potential. The magazine itself is viewed as a source for practical answers and information on business trends as well as career and business opportunities.

Black Enterprise emerged from the careful thinking and planning of an advisory board from the business and governmental sectors of American society. Its promoters realized that the traditional method of publicizing the few blacks who had made a breakthrough into some aspect of American life heretofore unavailable to blacks was limited. The answer to black economic needs was not, as they saw it, the monthly projection of the few who had made it. Rather, it was fostering conditions that would encourage black economic development as a basic element of the general economy and of the aspirations of most blacks. Many individuals and organizations participated in the formation of this particular thrust for a magazine: Whitney Young, Jr., then director of the National Urban League; Capital Formation, the National Association of Marketing Developers; the National Business League; the Congress of Racial Equality; the Organization of Industrial Centers; the Office of Minority Business Enterprise; and the Black Advisory Council of the Small Business Administration. That amalgam itself reflected a racial force that could not have been possible during the days that followers of Booker T. Washington fought with W.E.B. Du Bois' disciples over the relative merits of business and culture. By the era of the seventies, the cleavage between the two had become moot.

From its first issue, *Black Enterprise* had already gained the support of a good number of American corporations which advertised in the new magazine to demonstrate their belief in the relevance of a publication concerned with the encouragement of black economic development. Earl G. Graves, publisher and editor of the journal, noted, though, that the value of *Black Enterprise* must be proven in its relevance to the times and to the black community.

Theoretically, *Black Enterprise* asked the age-old question of whether the national economic system works for blacks. The scope of the question was new, however. An early editorial set forth the magazine's basic purposes.

> The economic problems of our cities, where a majority of black people live, will not yield simply because we decry conditions there. Nor will stubborn rural poverty disappear because we bemoan that fact. What has become increasingly clear is that black people need economic power if conditions are to be changed.
>
> The routes by which blacks enter the world of business and gain economic power are many and varied. We shall examine many of them on many of these pages. We shall write about the lives of men like Albert Corley who started with $1,000 and a dream. We shall write about those who failed, for there is profit in that story, too.
>
> We shall cover the careers of those who are "Making It" in the corporate world and the problems of the shopkeeper who wants to improve his business. We shall include the thoughts of theorists and practitioners alike. In short, *Black Enterprise* is your magazine, providing information and a wealth of shared experience for those who venture into the precarious world of business.[1]

In order to provide "a unique service to both black and white Americans" within the context that the health of the nation depends upon the extent to which "our ethnic minorities will participate in and profit from its economic system,"

Black Enterprise organized itself into departments: "Publisher's Page," "In the News," "Washington Page," "Making It," "Travel," "Personal Finance," "On the Move," "Career Marketplace," "Classified Advertisements," "Economic Perspectives," and "Facts and Figures." It employed a full staff to manage the conventional responsibilities of a commercial magazine with photographs and illustrations. Its annual careers issues perform a significant service for American youth planning to study for a career, as well as for those who are leaving colleges and universities for a life vocation.

While *Black Enterprise* is a magazine of business orientation, it does not neglect the political and social implications of black economics. It conducts an annual survey to give readers an opportunity to express their views on economic issues in the United States. Its "Publisher's Page" contains trenchant editorial comment. Publisher Graves wrote "Our Time to Take Charge," about some reactions to actor Ben Vereen's controversial blackface performance at President Reagan's inaugural gala in January 1981. He noted that he had received a number of letters and telephone calls from readers who were incensed by the performance, reflecting their sensitivity about the political status of blacks in a period "when the national mood is being manipulated into a search for scape-goats and simplistic solutions to our nation's problems."[2] He wrote that the infusion of black talent into the federal bureaucracy was one clear accomplishment of the Carter administration. It changed the face of the federal government and provided channels of access that blacks had not previously known. The phenomenon affected blacks curiously, for while everyone understands the changes in personnel in federal agencies that accompany the beginning of a new administration, blacks were not welcome in the Reagan order, and those who had gained government experience were not received enthusiastically by business, as whites with government experience often are. The editorial concluded, "The experience of the blacks who worked in the Carter administration is a reminder that, whatever our current status, none of us is immune to the winds of retrenchment and reaction. None of us can afford to sit back and wait to see what is going to happen."[3]

Political developments in the United States are critically important to all Americans—particularly to blacks, the publisher observed. The Vereen incident and the loss of black influence in the Reagan victory at the polls in 1980 prompted *Black Enterprise* to place strong emphasis on its presentation to its readers of a new generation of black leadership that is emerging in the country. It is the magazine's and the race's challenge to harness that talent into a strong political and economic force that will serve the needs of black communities all over the country, the publisher stated. This focus is central to the purposes for which *Black Enterprise* was established.

Population shifts among blacks created new patterns around the country that were also matters of interest and concern. Changes in congressional representation in the 1982 reapportionments could affect economic clout. In its continuing forward look at black potential for economic power, the journal recognizes that a strong and independent Africa is necessary for black progress in the United States. W.E.B. Du Bois had made that observation many years earlier. Senior editor Emile Milne's feature article "Pursuing the African Dollar" was written to show the opportunities for cooperation between Africans and Afro-Americans in the economic sphere. Milne wrote that "the African need for expertise, technology, and consumer goods can help build an economic base which should ensure that progress will continue on both sides of the Atlantic."[4]

New vistas in careers provide the aura for the annual careers issues of *Black Enterprise*. The lead story in a recent issue, "Wanted: Engineers and Scientists," noted the need for blacks to shift their thinking about education. The article pointed out that the growing complexities of the world would require new machinery and vocabulary for persons who would succeed. Growth in the need for teachers and social workers, while always necessary, would be slow. The problem for blacks, however, the author explained, lay in inadequate schools, lack of parental know-how, and the absence of role models—barriers that limit a black youth's abilities to move into the advancing world of science and business. *Black Enterprise* places unusual value on its classified sections as career guides for black persons entering the significant economic mainstream of the nation.

With a combination of black pride, news about blacks who have made it, analysis of the economic system upon which the United States turns, articles about the economy of the black world, and provocative editorials on the political implications of black economics in the nation, *Black Enterprise* represents the final accomplishment of several early attempts to bring awareness and activism to blacks that might involve them in the ongoing dynamics of American economics. The attractive and well-balanced magazine represents a significant new dimension in black journalism that transcends a special-subject magazine, for the subjects it presents affect all black Americans.

Publisher Earl G. Graves has taken deep interest in the annual careers issues he has published and has commented regularly on directions for education for black Americans. He was quick to point out that when integration became a reality in the 1960s and corporations opened their doors to blacks for the first time the demands for appropriate education to take advantage of the new opportunities changed drastically. He was aware that few blacks held degrees in business and accounting, for example, simply because they never expected to be able to make a reasonable living with those skills. His estimate of the status of blacks in the business world and *Black Enterprise*'s relationship to its promotion is seen in an excerpt from one of Graves' editorials.

These new opportunities and the willingness of some corporations to seek black talent is why we started our new Career Marketplace section in the December 1980 issue. Our new Classified section provides access to potential corporate clients for those readers who want to advertise their goods, services, or talents.

But there are also strong pockets of resistance to black progress, even in new sophisticated fields that need our talents. America's economic problems have profoundly affected us. If we are ever to break out of the last-hired, first-fired category, we must move into areas of growth that promise security and advancement.

In the next two decades the competition for jobs, even among the highly educated, will be intense. We are not afraid of competition. All we have ever asked for was a chance to compete equally. Those who wish to turn back the clock should understand that we will continue to struggle. We have contributed too much to this country to be stopped by old ideas in new bottles. We *will* have our share of America's bounty. We have earned it.[5]

Notes

1. "A Word from the Publisher," *Black Enterprise* (August 1970): ii.
2. *Black Enterprise* (April 1981): 7.
3. Ibid.
4. Milne, "Pursuing the African Dollar," *Black Enterprise* (April 1981): 29.
5. "New Career Vistas," *Black Enterprise* (February 1981): 7.

Information Sources

BIBLIOGRAPHY:
"Advertising with Special Care." *Black Enterprise*, June 1980, p. 71.
Brimmer, Arthur F. "Business Services: A Growth Industry." *Black Enterprise*, January 1981, p. 57.
————. "Economic Integration and the Progress of the Negro Community." *Ebony*, August 1970, pp. 118-21.
Clemons, John G. "Making of *Black Enterprise.*" *Black Enterprise*, August 1980, pp. 106-8.
Graves, Earl G. "The Meanings of Black Enterprise." *Black Enterprise*, May 1975, p. 6.
"Use Different Advertising Tack for Blacks." *Advertising Age*, 14 February 1977, p. 66.
"What Do You Think?" *Black Enterprise*, February 1980, p. 7.
INDEX SOURCES: *Business Periodicals Index; Index to Periodical Articles By and About Negroes; Public Affairs Information Service; Reader's Guide to Periodical Literature; Work-Related Abstracts.*
LOCATION SOURCES: University Microfilms.

Publication History

MAGAZINE TITLE AND TITLE CHANGES: *Black Enterprise* (August 1970 to present).
VOLUME AND ISSUE DATA: Vols. I-XI (August 1970 to present), monthly.
PUBLISHER AND PLACE OF PUBLICATION: Earl G. Graves Publishing Company, New York, New York.

EDITORS: Earl G. Graves, publisher and editor; Pat Patterson, editor at large.
(1970-   ).
CIRCULATION: 230,000.

BLACK MAN, THE: A MONTHLY MAGAZINE OF NEGRO THOUGHT AND OPINION

James Weldon Johnson wrote in *Black Manhattan* that Marcus Garvey was a "tragic figure," not unlike "that former and greater dreamer in empires, exiled to another island." Johnson wrote of the man shortly after Garvey, the charismatic and enigmatic black leader, had been imprisoned in the United States for mail fraud and exiled to his native Jamaica. The heart of the tragedy, Johnson continued, was that to this man came an opportunity such as comes to few men and "he clutched greedily at the glitter and let the substance slip through his fingers." Johnson, who knew Garvey at close range, also knew the West Indian native's strong impact upon Harlem through his Universal Negro Improvement Association, which engaged the attention of the nation in the World War I era. His influence on black popular journalism drew judicious praise from even his strongest critics. His *Negro World* newspaper, the official organ of his association published in New York City, was, as Claude McKay wrote, "the best edited colored weekly in New York." Within the space of a few months it became a leading black weekly journal that was most effective in promulgating the Garvey movement. The front page always carried a lengthy editorial addressed to "Fellowmen of the Negro Race" and signed "Your Obedient Servant, Marcus Garvey, President General." Garvey turned over editing that paper to the able William H. Ferris, who enlisted the aid of Hubert H. Harrison, Eric Walrond, Hudson C. Pryce, and other talented black writers. *Negro World* was the antecedent of Garvey's magazine *Black Man*, which he published in Jamaica for two years beginning in December 1933 before moving it to London in 1935 and continuing until the summer of 1939.[1] The twenty-four issues were published over a period of five and a half years, ceasing only when Garvey suffered a paralyzing stroke. Although *Black Man* was never published in the United States, Garvey's involvement with Americans and the journal's strong emphasis on the black experience in the United States make the periodical vital to any study of black magazines.

Black Man reflects its times and promotes Garvey's association. The first issue contained the usual statement of introduction to the public, "The *Black Man* Makes Its Bow." Garvey writes:

The "Blackman," [*sic*] as a new Monthly Magazine, makes its bow to the Negro peoples of the world. Its advent was long expected, but delayed because of stress of financial circumstances. Those who have looked for it may expect to have the regular issues sent to them by keeping in close contact with our activities, as it is our desire to inaugurate, through its columns, an intensified world campaign to again arouse the Negro to the seriousness of his responsibility, so that he may look forward hopefully to a better day nationally and internationally.

The first issue also contained an opinion column written by Garvey, titled "The World As It Is," in which he praised Adolf Hitler for his German nationalism while criticizing his persecution of Jews. He gave a simplistic version of the complex world monetary problem but showed sagacity in advising President Roosevelt to engage a "brain trust" to meet the combined genius of Europe in the national finance challenge. Lynching in the United States was especially reprehensible to him. People outside America could not understand how a country "dotted with universities and colleges and having so many cultural institutions can perpetuate such a horrible thing like lynching without taking definite steps to protest the reputation of the nation." Garvey, who was strongly opposed to communism, criticized the party for establishing the *Negro Worker* in Germany. To him, Negroes on the editorial staff of that newspaper were doing their race a great deal of harm by trying to influence black Americans to assume the responsibility of propagating communism. Negroes' economic troubles were so great and their preparation to take care of themselves so scant that Garvey felt it was almost criminal to lead blacks to estrangement between themselves and their employers. "We would prefer the Communists carrying out their purposes by themselves, and then in their success, admitting the Negro to the right of partaking in the benefits of the new system they seek to establish, rather than placing the onus on the Negroes at this early stage, making them a target of an organized political opposition."

Garvey used his editorial to continue tirades he began against certain black Americans during his years of popularity in the United States. George S. Schuyler—journalist, novelist, essayist, and later editor of the *Messenger** and the *Pittsburgh Courier*—was a frequent target of his criticism. In one particularly scurrilous attack, he wrote:

When we were in America, we helped George S. Schuyler to become known, and that we furnished him with his subjects for his attempted journalism. For several years he could find no other topic to write on of importance, but to discuss us, and in his then rudeness, he said contemptible and rude things that caused us to have thought very little of him as a journalist. When he switched from us, he turned to other public men and movements, and attempted to criticize them in the same way. That was his start in journalism. By abusing other people he became known, but up to now he is still the pretending journalist and ignorant Schuyler. He knows nothing of what is going on, except what he culls from other journalists of intellectual worth.[2]

In other comments, Garvey referred to Schuyler as "a dangerous Negro to the American people" and "a defeatist of the worst kind" who had never attempted anything constructive in the interest of the American black, but had "attacked and mercilessly libelled nearly every honest Negro and Negro movement, seeking to do good for the race in America."

When W.E.B. Du Bois' serious struggles with the NAACP began to bring criticism of that long-respected black leader that led to his leaving his position as editor of the *Crisis*,* which he had helped to found nearly twenty-five years earlier, Garvey was delighted. He wrote that the "flood gate of criticism" had been opened against Du Bois because he had written disparagingly of his colleagues, notably Walter White, secretary of Garvey's association, and had expressed himself compromisingly on the segregation issue. "Whilst Du Bois has been glorified by a lot of people who do not think seriously and deeply, we never held any high opinion of him as a leader, and up to now we have not changed in our way of thinking," Garvey wrote in a lead editorial in his magazine. He went on to write that Du Bois might have been an exceptional character in the early life of American Negro education, but that the education of which he boasted was merely a kind of imitation of "that white culture he seems to like so much." Du Bois never was a leader; only an opportunist. He had no qualities of a leader, for he was too selfish to care for "anything else but Du Bois."[3]

Garvey disagreed strongly with black leaders who wanted segregation abolished for the sole purpose of being "socially near to the white man." He believed man should be able to select his own company on a social level. His interpretation of the history of segregation in America was unusual, as is shown from a passage from one of his editorials.

It was segregation of the Old Colonists of America that created the American nation. If they hadn't segregated themselves from the old countries there would be no American Republic today, and those who are descendants of the Colonists would not be able to be carrying out in America today, social and political segregation. So if the thing is well considered, it will be seen and realized that some kind of segregation is good, for the right kind generally leads to the accumulation of strength and the demonstration of unusual worth. If the Negro can be segregated to make him a powerful national unit, then we say, let him be segregated. If he is going to seek the abolition of segregation just for the purpose of social privileges that he will never fully enjoy, then we say he has the wrong idea. This is the idea of fools like Schuyler. Schuyler likes good company because it is white, and so he fights segregation. He cannot create company for himself, he cannot so create as to allow other people to seek association with him and his race, in the same way he and his followers seek association with others.

Garvey wrote that Du Bois could take the NAACP no further than he had gone with it. He had to resign because he could not continue abusing the white man "when the American Negro is at the white man's Soup Kitchen." He reminded his readers that when the Universal Negro Improvement Association suggested and advocated a program of economic independence for blacks, Du Bois was one of the principal men to fight against it. His opposition to Garvey's movement, the editorial claimed, had sabotaged the "one thing that would have saved the American Negro."

He was equally strong in renouncing Father Divine, who was outraging his race by calling himself "God." And he disliked Paul Robeson's roles in *Emperor Jones* and *Sanders of the River* on the grounds that his portrayal of the Negro in these works would make one think blacks were unworthy of a place of any significance in world civilization.

Monroe Trotter, editor of the *Boston Guardian* newspaper, was admired by Garvey. Trotter, a supporter of Du Bois in his philosophical argument with Booker T. Washington at the turn of the century and a consistent civil rights militant, deserved better assistance in his fight for equality among the races than blacks gave him, Garvey wrote in an editorial upon the occasion of Trotter's death.

> The American Negro could have well afforded to lose a thousand of their present-day pseudo-leaders without regret, rather than losing William Monroe Trotter. We knew Mr. Trotter well. We admired him very much and watched his career with deep interest. He was not one who assumed leadership for the purpose of enriching himself, and his very death has proved that. Unfortunately, there is no fraternity among the better class Negroes that would lead them to hold up the hand and support one who is of use to the race, hence, probably, it was impossible for Trotter to gain help when his difficulties pressed upon him.[4]

Black Man was primarily the communications organ of Garvey's association. It carried news of conventions and activities in that organization, but its editorials expressed opinions about Benito Mussolini's invasion of Ethiopia and Haile Selassie's attempts to convince the League of Nations to support the integrity of his nation. Garvey differed with Haile Selassie and carried on a long argument with him about the role his nation should play in black nationalism but was unrestrained in his criticism of fascism and communism which were gaining power in Europe in the years preceding World War II.

Most black American intellectuals rejected Garvey's leadership at the height of his association's movement. Few failed to realize the strength of his personality and the feasibility of some of his ideas, however. After Garvey was released from prison and deported to Jamaica, scholar Charles S. Johnson, editor of *Opportunity*,* wrote:

No one dismisses his name now four years after his conviction, as that of a mere criminal and exploiter of ignorant Negroes. It would be worth the inquiry to learn why this lone black figure, bumptious and flamboyant as he is, can call forth in such concert the interests of those governments with black subjects, in protecting them from his doctrines. There are faint flashes of irony in the solicitude. Most important in the philosophy which he preached were these: The black peoples of the world are entitled to a country and government of their own where they can develop their own culture, industry, and commerce, and elevate themselves to an equal status with the white races of the world.

Black Man illustrates the unique quality in Garvey that Johnson suggests in his comment. Eric Walrond, a recognized writer of the Harlem Renaissance era and a West Indian, joined Garvey in London and wrote a series of articles for the magazine. Little is known about the reasons for the late relationship that developed between the two men, but the Walrond features add interest to the journal.

Garvey's prolonged illness before his death, the magazine's dire financial straits, and the beginning of World War II led to the *Black Man*'s end.

Notes

1. After Garvey returned to Jamaica from the United States, he initiated publication of a daily newspaper called the *Blackman* from 30 March 1929 to 7 February 1931. The monthly magazine the *Black Man* is the successor to that daily newspaper. In effect, the new journal combined the New York based *Negro World* and the *Blackman* as a single official organ of the Universal Negro Improvement Association.

2. Schuyler is generally considered conservative among black writers. His magazine articles and fiction satirized all race-oriented organizations as "hustlers." He criticized the one dimensional emphasis on race practiced by the NAACP and the National Urban League at the same time he attacked the Ku Klux Klan for the same purpose. Although most black intellectuals disapproved of Garvey's flamboyant leadership and grandiose economic plans, Schuyler was particularly cruel in his "Shafts and Darts" column in the *Messenger*. He suggested criminal intent in Garvey's ill-fated Black Star Line shipping disasters.

3. Garvey wrote in his "First Message to the Negroes of the World from Atlanta Prison" dated 10 February 1925, "Du Bois and that vicious Negro-hating organization known as the Association for the Advancement of Colored People are the greatest enemies the black people have in the world."

4. Trotter is best known as an early exponent of revolt against Booker T. Washington and the "accommodationist" social philosophy Washington advocated for Negroes at the turn of the century and in the early years of the twentieth century. The *Boston Guardian*, Trotter's newspaper, served as a counterbalance to the *New York Age*, a paper Washington was accused of influencing unduly. Extreme financial reversals that pointed toward Trotter's losing control over the *Guardian* led him to commit suicide in 1934. Garvey and Trotter seem to have had some affinity in their racial attitudes and to have had contacts with each other that have not been fully explored. *See* Stephen R. Fox, *The Guardian of Boston* (New York, 1971), chap. 8, pp. 236-56.

Information Sources

BIBLIOGRAPHY:
Anderson, Jervis. *A. Phillip Randolph: A Biographical Portrait*. New York, 1972.
Cronon, Edward David. *Black Moses*. Madison, Wis., 1955.
————, ed. *Marcus Garvey: Great Lives Observed*. Englewood Cliffs, N.J., 1973.
Davis, Arthur P. "George S. Schuyler." *From the Dark Tower: Afro-American Writers 1900 to 1960*. Washington, D.C., 1974, pp. 104-8.
Fox, Stephen R. *The Guardian of Boston*. New York, 1971.
Johnson, Charles S. "Garvey and the 'Garvey Movement.' " *Opportunity*, January 1928, pp. 4-5.
Johnson, James Weldon. *Black Manhattan*. New York, 1930.
Kornweibel, Theodore, Jr. *No Crystal Stair: Black Life and the Messenger, 1917-1928*. Westport, Conn., 1975.
Schuyler, George S. "The Separate State Hokum." *Crisis*, May 1935, pp. 113-16.
Young, James O. *Black Writers of the Thirties*. Baton Rouge, La., 1973.
INDEX SOURCES: None.
LOCATION SOURCE: The complete file of *Black Man* is available in reprint through Kraus-Thompson Organization Limited, Millwood, New York.

Publication History

MAGAZINE TITLE AND TITLE CHANGES: *The Black Man: A Monthly Magazine of Negro Thought and Opinion* (December 1933-June 1939).
VOLUME AND ISSUE DATA: Vols. I-IV, irregular; dated on monthly basis. After the appearance of the first issue, five issues were published in 1934 and 1935; four in 1936 and 1937; three in 1938; and two in 1939.
PUBLISHER AND PLACE OF PUBLICATION: Blackman Publishing Company, Kingston, Jamaica, B.W.I. (December 1933-May/June 1934); Blackman Publishing Company, London, England (November 1934-June 1939).
EDITOR: Marcus Garvey (1933-1939).
CIRCULATION: 2,500 highest estimate.

BLACK ODYSSEY: A MAGAZINE ON TRAVEL AND LEISURE

Before passage of the Civil Rights Acts of 1964 and 1965, black Americans experienced painful incidents when traveling in the United States. Bus and train transportation were color segregated. Persons who traveled by private conveyance were similarly prevented from purchasing accommodation in public hotels and entering public eating facilities. In the South and in many nonsouthern states, black travelers were hard pressed to find board and lodging because of routine discrimination. Accordingly, several publications and guides were published that directed blacks to Negro places of accommodation and to those scattered firms that occasionally were open to them. In the 1940s, *New Negro Traveler and Conventioneer** was the most popular among those periodicals.

Black Odyssey, founded in January 1979, is different. It concentrates upon places around the world that may particularly interest the black American vacationer. The publisher, Ella Ferguson, entered the highly competitive magazine marketplace for one principal reason: "The main factor was that no one else was attempting, on a nationwide and fulltime basis, to monitor the spending by black America of more than $7 billion annually on travel and another $3 billion on leisure time activities."

The magazine regularly includes articles about places to visit including available activities and facts about the culture and economy. Editorials, letters from readers, general travel ideas, and a presentation focusing on a given location each month make up the body of the periodical. Good photography of the type used by travel agencies and commercial carriers makes the magazine physically attractive.

Inasmuch as the feature articles provide historical and current facts about featured locations and discuss how citizens there react to Afro-Americans, the magazine serves a broader purpose than a mere travel brochure. It has cooperated creatively with tourist bureaus of several African countries to attract black Americans to those areas. Observations on relationships between these countries and the United States government often appear in the articles.

Information Sources

BIBLIOGRAPHY:
Ferguson, Ella. "Well, We've Done It." *Black Odyssey*, February, 1979, p. 1.
Miles, Frank W. "Negro Magazines Come of Age." *Magazine World*, 1 July 1946, p. 12.
INDEX SOURCES: None.
LOCATION SOURCES: None.

Publication History

MAGAZINE TITLE AND TITLE CHANGES: *Black Odyssey: A Magazine on Travel and Leisure.*
VOLUME AND ISSUE DATA: Vol. I- (January 1979 to present), monthly.
PUBLISHER AND PLACE OF PUBLICATION: J.F.F. Communications, Inc., Jamaica, New York.
EDITOR: Ella Ferguson, editor and publisher (1979-).
CIRCULATION: Information unavailable.

Mark A. Reger

BLACK OPALS

During the period of the Harlem Renaissance, black creative writers in Philadelphia published a journal that brought their talents to the attention of the growing reading public. The first issue of *Black Opals* appeared in the spring of

1927. The periodical was part of the continuing discourse about the proper direction for black writing. Arthur Huff Fauset, uncle to Jessie Redmond Fauset, was the leader of the Philadelphia group. He had published *Freedom!* in 1926, a children's book that assembled black heroes around a Negro Round Table and which was widely used in Philadelphia public schools. Fauset's short story *Symphonique* won a prize for fiction in *Opportunity** magazine's second literary contest and was included in Edward J. O'Brien's popular *Best Short Stories of 1926*. "Brentano's Book Review" praised the Fauset story among other works in O'Brien's annual selection.

> By far the most signal achievement in this collection is *Symphonique*. It is a Negro story by a Negro author, a study of primitive reactions to the stirrings of religion and of love. Cudo is a natural-born pagan, and his desires are simple and primary. His greatest desire is for Amber Lee. . . And the story—no, technically, it isn't a story, it is rather a verbal symphony— tells of his desire, his temptation, and his final conquest of self. And it tells it in a passionate cadenced prose that beats and throbs like the primitive beat of heathen drums in an African jungle, sweeping the reader along in a breathless, aching sympathy, a tense sharing in exotic, primeval emotions such as hark back to just one other book in my own range of memories: Haldane McFall's *House of the Sorcerer*. Arthur Huff Fauset is a name to be carefully registered on the tablets of memory, for he is bound to do some surprising work in the near future.[1]

The encomium appeared in black magazines and newspapers and gave some status to the growing strength of black writing during the period. Fauset did not become a well-known black writer, but he did encourage literary efforts among his fellow Philadelphians. With a group of them, he published *Black Opals* as an outlet for students of the local high schools as well as Philadelphia Norman School, Temple University, and the University of Pennsylvania. The names of his associates in the effort were never familiar, but Langston Hughes and Alain Locke lent their influence to the enterprise. Locke wrote "Hail Philadelphia!" for the first issue in an attempt to assuage the cleavage between conservative and radical voices among the black writers and scholars. Fauset was basically conservative but seemed willing to present works of either side in the journal.

Countee Cullen, new literary editor of *Opportunity* magazine at the time, noted that the Philadelphia writers planned to make *Black Opals* a quarterly. He praised "some highly commendable material" in the first issue, especially two poems written by Nellie R. Bright and Mae V. Cowdery. Cullen wrote that *Black Opals* "is a venture we should like to see sweeping the country."[2] Gwendolyn Bennett, an art teacher at Howard University and a poet in her own right whose "Ebony Flute" column in *Opportunity* was a rich source of comment about black writers and their works, was guest editor. W.E.B. Du Bois, editor of

*Crisis** and ostensibly the "old head" among the black artist-scholars of the time, wrote that he was happier with *Black Opals* than he had been with earlier efforts of black writers to publish a literary "little" magazine.

Black Opals ceased publication after the June 1928 issue which was edited by an editorial board. It was not properly a magazine. Its sponsors simply published a series of three journals that contained writing produced by a small, black literary circle in Philadelphia similar to groups that grew up in several cities in the United States during the period. Their presence and the quality of their work make the point that Harlem was not the sole locale of the black arts movement in the post-World War I period.

Notes

1. Quoted in "The Ebony Flute," *Opportunity* (March 1927): 90.
2. "The Dark Tower," *Opportunity* (June 1927): 180.

Information Sources

BIBLIOGRAPHY:
Bennett, Gwendolyn. "Ebony Flute." *Opportunity*, February 1928, p. 56.
Cullen, Countee. "The Dark Tower." *Opportunity*, June 1927, p. 180.
Johnson, Abby Arthur, and Johnson, Ronald Maberry. *Propaganda and Aesthetics: The Literary Politics of Afro-American Magazines in the Twentieth Century.* Amherst, Mass., 1979, pp. 93-4.
INDEX SOURCES: None.
LOCATION SOURCES: Moorland-Spingarn Library, Howard University, Washington, D.C.; Library of Congress.

Publication History

MAGAZINE TITLE AND TITLE CHANGES: *Black Opals* (Spring 1927-June 1928).
VOLUME AND ISSUE DATA: Vols. I-III (Spring 1927-June 1928), biannual.
PUBLISHER AND PLACE OF PUBLICATION: Arthur Huff Fauset, Philadelphia, Pennsylvania.
EDITORS: Arthur Huff Fauset, Vol. I (Spring 1927); Gwendolyn Bennett, guest editor, Vol. II (Christmas 1927); Editorial Board, Vol. III (June 1928).
CIRCULATION: 500 estimate.

BLACK PERSPECTIVE IN MUSIC, THE

Eileen Southern, foremost contemporary authority in the United States on the history of black music, established the *Black Perspective in Music* in the spring of 1973.[1] Its purpose is to promote the opportunity for free expression of ideas and opinions by persons interested in black American and African performing arts, particularly from the creative point of view. Regular features include articles by musicologists, artists, ethnologists, historians, composers, and performing artists; interviews with well-known personalities in the performing arts; announcements of special events in music; and periodical surveys of bibliographical material. From the beginning, the periodical's strength has lain in its articles and bibliographies. Both have covered a wide range of subjects and personalities which provides a significant resource for black music. That scope includes popular and academic perspectives.

The range of articles contained in a single issue, Spring 1975, may be seen from a listing of its contents. Richard Turner's "John Coltrane: A Biographical Sketch," details incidents in the life and accomplishments of this highly artistic popular musician's career from the fifties until his untimely death in 1967. Samuel A. Floyd, Jr., recalls the activities and experiences of black navy musicians who were stationed at Great Lakes Naval Training Center during 1942-45, in the World War II period. Atlanta, Georgia's, importance as an educational, cultural, and social center for the black populace of the South is viewed through the biography of Henry Hugh Procter, who became a leading force for black music while he pastored the First Congregational Church in Atlanta. Altona Trent Johns' article discussed Procter's role as a black musical impresario presenting music festivals between 1910 and 1920, before leaving Atlanta for a pastorate in Brooklyn, New York. "Racial Bigotry and Stereotype in Books Recommended for Use by Children" reports on a conference the New York State Education Department and the New York State Teachers Association conducted in May 1972 to explore what the writer Ruth Zinar considered glaring instances of stereotyping, tokenism, and misrepresentation of minority groups in children's books.

Leonard Goines' "Africanism Among the Bush Negroes of Surinam" discusses life among the only African tribal society living in the Western Hemisphere, and Addison W. Reed contributes a chapter of his doctoral dissertation, "The Life and Works of Scott Joplin." Other features in the issue are conversations with Andrew Cyrille, a black drummer, and Hale Smith, an Afro-American composer; a historical perspective, "Black Musicians and Early Ethiopian Minstrelsy"; "New Books," "New Music," and "Doctoral Dissertations"; and book and record reviews. These contents are typical of the *Black Perspective in Music*.

Special issues have included one devoted to the accomplishments of William Grant Still which was introduced by an editorial that reads, in part:

> For this special issue in honor of William Grant Still we have borrowed an idea from a delightful tradition of musicology where the friends, colleagues, and students of a great scholar contribute articles to a publication planned as a birthday present. We are improvising on the theme, however—in keeping with the black tradition. Normally the articles in a *festchrift* all are written by musicologists on diverse subjects related either to the scholarly interests of the man being honored or to their own special interests. In *this*

birthday offering, it is the writers who are diverse, and their contributions reflect their talents and skills as well as their desires. Thus, there are essays from the musicologists and music educators, reminiscences from the practicing musicians, and compositions from the composers. All of the contributions are given with love and appreciation to Dr. Still for his great achievement in music.[2]

"Singing in the Streets of Raleigh, 1963: Some Recollections" relates music to the civil rights movement of the 1960s and provides unique insight into the social and political uses an ethnic group makes of art forms its forebears have created at another time. The author called the period "a *singing* movement in which singing was integral to the many activities in an even more pervasive and basic manner than the demonstrations and rallies and sit-ins and jail-ins, because singing was a vital component of each aspect of these freedom movements." The article leans heavily toward the musicological and ethnomusical aspects of the freedom movement songs, but their force is unmistakable, as a portion of a story related in the piece shows:

I remember one evening I was in the State Capitol working when I heard a heavy-beated pulsating song sung by a large group of men and women. I was alone in the building, yet the music was coming from all around me, it seemed, and was drawing closer.... Then, through a window, I saw them, hundreds of them, almost all of the Negro young people. They carried torches. Their cadence was the beat of threatening men and women, of natives in the streets.[3]

Those singers were primarily students from Shaw University, Saint Augustine's College, and J. W. Ligon High School—black Raleigh institutions—but the dramatic event was replicated in many American towns and cities. Recollections such as these represent the broad visage of *Black Perspective*'s content.

Other articles are technical, such as "Afro-American Sacred Songs in the Nineteenth Century," "Fugitive Notes on Notation and Terminology in African Music," "Musical Sources for the History of Jazz," "Black Spirituals: An Analysis of Textual Forms and Structures," and "An Analysis and Comparison of Piano Sonatas by George Walker and Howard Swanson." The Bicentennial number was especially ambitious and appropriately comprehensive. Its contents were introduced by an editorial that described the scope of the features and emphasized the sources of scholarship for Afro-American music in performance, history, and social use.

This special Bicentennial Number of *The Black Perspective in Music* offers an overview of the musical activities of black Americans through the eyes of the nineteenth century. Press releases, advertisements, articles in periodicals and newspapers, programs, photographs, cartoons, music—all these kinds of primary sources reveal more information about the musicians and their music, about the times during which they flourished, no matter how flawed or how biased were some of the writers, than it is possible to obtain from secondary sources. The material presented here is representative of the diverse musical activities engaged in by blacks during the nineteenth century, from the folk music of the masses which obviously originated in an earlier era, to the ragtime that emerged just as the century was drawing to a close. It is our hope that readers will enjoy this excursion into the past.[4]

"Black Entertainers on Radio, 1920-1930" provides unusually valuable information on black musicians who participated in the mass entertainment industry early in the twentieth century. "Black Music Concerts in Carnegie Hall, 1912-1915" reports and evaluates black performers who reached the premier concert hall in the United States before World War I and the Afro-American cultural organizations in New York City that helped to give rise to the musical portion of the Harlem Renaissance. "Social Dance Music of Black Composers in the Nineteenth Century and the Emergence of Classical Ragtime" discusses and illustrates the essential differences between quadrilles, cotillions, waltzes, marches, mazurkas, and other European-American dance pieces, and the distinctive American classic, ragtime.

The *Black Perspective in Music* is an unusual source for contemporary scholarship in Afro-American culture. Its features balance technical articles intended for students of the arts with general information. Valuable for musicologists, performers, and the general public, this journal is outstanding among black periodicals.

Notes

1. Eileen Southern wrote *The Music of Black Americans: A History*. This source was preceded by *Music and Some Highly Musical People* by James M. Trotter and *Negro Musicians and Their Music* by Maude Cuney-Hare. Southern is also the editor of *Readings in Black American Music* and the author of the *Buxheim Organ Book* as well as various articles in significant journals on Renaissance and black American music. She has been cited for her scholarship by the University of Chicago, the Voice of America, the National Association of Negro Musicians, New York University, and Harvard University. She heads the Afro-American Studies department at Harvard University.

2. "Editorial," *Black Perspective in Music* (May 1975): 131.

3. Clyde Appleton, "Singing in the Streets of Raleigh," *Black Perspective in Music* (Fall 1975): 243-52.

4. "Editorial," *Black Perspective in Music* (July 1976): 131.

Information Sources

INDEX SOURCES: *Music Articles Guide; Music Index; RILM Abstracts of Music Literature; Jazz Index.*

LOCATION SOURCES: Most college and university libraries; University Microfilms; International Microform.

Publication History

MAGAZINE TITLE AND TITLE CHANGES: *The Black Perspective in Music* (Spring 1973 to present).
VOLUME AND ISSUE DATA: Vols. I-III (Spring 1973 to present), semiannual.
PUBLISHER AND PLACE OF PUBLICATION: Foundation for Research in Afro-American Creative Arts, Inc., Cambria Heights, New York.
EDITOR: Eileen J. Southern (1973-).
CIRCULATION: 1,000.

Addison W. Reed

BLACK POLITICIAN, THE: A QUARTERLY JOURNAL OF CURRENT POLITICAL THOUGHT

The *Black Politician* was novel in its field. Founded in 1969 as a quarterly by the Center on Urban and Minority Affairs of Berkeley, California, it was edited by Mervyn Dymally, at the time a state senator from Los Angeles. The *Black Politician* was established to fill "a need in the classroom and among the public for a single authoritative reference source on the political tendings in the black community."[1] It was not revolutionary. Instead, as stated in its first editorial, it was bipartisan and sought to cover "the full spectrum of current political thought" among Afro-Americans. In devoting itself exclusively to political issues, the *Black Politician* was unusual among black journals.[2]

Its format contained eight to ten full-length articles, primarily dealing with some aspect of the relationship of blacks to contemporary political concerns. The scope of coverage extended to such matters as "The Role of the Black University," "Soledad Report: One Year Later," and "Justice and the Urban Indian." Most issues also contained articles that discussed problems of Mexican-Americans. Special emphasis was given to blacks in Congress and the relationship of the Black Caucus there to President Richard Nixon. Issues like revenue sharing were presented in the form of a debate. In one of these features, Richard Hatcher, the black mayor of Gary, Indiana, took the negative side of the debate on whether cities should receive revenue sharing, and Nelson Rockefeller, governor of New York at the time, took the affirmative.

Some well-known blacks wrote for the journal. Edward W. Brooke, the senator from Massachusetts, contributed "A Perspective on Africa." Andrew F. Brimmer, a member of the board of the Federal Reserve Bank, wrote "Economic Agenda for Black Americans." Imamu Amiri Baraka (LeRoi Jones) contributed an article on "Strategies and Tactics of an Afro-American Poetry." Other examples of typical essays are "Focus on Georgia Politics," "Black Visibility in the

Political Arena," "Third Party Politics," "Chicanos in Politics," "Mississippi Freedom Democratic Party," and "Black Members in White Legislatures."

By the end of its second year of publication, Dymally wrote of the journal that it had striven to meet the demand for a medium of political thought focusing on black and other minority politicians and their constituencies. He felt the publication had carried out reasonably well the confidence that had been placed in it by subscribers and by the Urban Affairs Institute of Los Angeles which had made a grant that had provided cost of publishing the journal for two years.

The *Black Politician*'s articles were informative and unusual. They expounded no particular political philosophy other than the new and growing trend of blacks and other minorities to participate significantly in city, state, and national legislative bodies. Its articles on education and the arts were related to politics. The *Black Politician*'s editorial comment, "What the Press Is Saying," reported on news of appropriate political issues and personalities around the nation. Some book reviews and letters to the editor were included in the journal. The journal's contents provide a significant perspective on that era in American history when the civil rights movement made it possible for minority persons to become actively involved in public affairs as elected officials. It was, indeed, a fresh approach to black participation in politics, compared with earlier periods when those activities were centered around a few especially placed representatives of the major parties in urban areas.

Notes

1. Roland E. Wolseley, *Black Press U.S.A.* (Ames, Iowa: Iowa State University Press, 1971), p. 141.
2. Editorial, *Black Politician* (July 1969): 3.

Information Sources

BIBLIOGRAPHY:
Katz, Bill, and Gargal, Berry. *Magazines for Libraries*. 2d ed. New York, 1972, p. 107.
Wolseley, Roland E. *Black Press U.S.A.* Ames, Iowa: Iowa State University Press, p. 141.
INDEX SOURCES: *Historical Abstracts*; *America: History and Life*.
LOCATION SOURCES: Many college and university libraries.

Publication History

MAGAZINE TITLE AND TITLE CHANGES: *The Black Politician: A Quarterly Journal of Current Political Thought*.
VOLUME AND ISSUE DATA: Vols. I-III (July 1969-July 1971), quarterly.
PUBLISHER AND PLACE OF PUBLICATION: The Urban Affairs Institute, Los Angeles, California.
EDITOR: Marvyn M. Dymally (July 1969-July 1971).
CIRCULATION: 2,500.

BLACK POLITICS: A JOURNAL OF LIBERATION

One example of the several extreme, black revolutionary periodicals that sprang up during the 1960s is *Black Politics: A Journal of Liberation*, which published six issues during 1968 from Berkeley, California. Its editors included a "Statement of Purpose" in the first number which read, in part:

> *Black Politics* is an independent journal whose purpose is to provide a forum for vanguard theories and ideas that deal with currently crucial issues.
>
> We support the liberation struggles of the oppressed masses of the world.
>
> We oppose the war in Vietnam and uphold the right of the people to determine their own destiny.
>
> We are a part of the Black Liberation Movement and believe that freedom, justice, and equality must be attained by those means that the oppressed think necessary.[1]

The statement continued that editorials would represent the official position of the journal, but that articles would be presented on the basis of their relevancy to the struggle and did not necessarily represent the opinions of the editorial board.

The first editorial was about Malcolm X, the black religious and political leader whose assassination in 1965 ended the career of a prophet of black liberation whose influence had extended beyond the borders of the United States into the Middle East, Africa, and Latin America. *Black Politics'* editorial called Malcolm X "one of the most slandered public figures of our time; yet he was an honest leader of his people who was willing to work with any group" that was determined to fight against injustice done to blacks.[2] The piece went on to point out that it was the duty of every Afro-American to protect his people against mass murderers, bombers, lynchers, flayers, and exploiters. It glorified Malcolm X as the "Moses of all oppressed people in the United States who looked forward to alliance of black and white revolutionaries."

The same issue contained an article written by Charles Williams, "The Murder of Malcolm X, the Kennedy Assassination, and the CIA," which detailed Malcolm X's separation from Elijah Muhammad and his new insight into racism, capitalism, and war. From that time, Williams claimed, Malcolm X was a marked man, by those who feared he might convince African members of the United Nations to raise the question of persecution of Negroes in the United States. Malcolm X was under constant surveillance by the U.S. Justice Department, according to Williams, and reports persisted that attempts had been made to poison him in Cairo at a conference in 1964. A waiter who had allegedly tried to carry out the Justice Department's scheme disappeared from the banquet hall after he was detected. The article expressed the belief that Malcolm X was marked for extinction by the United States government for his outspoken opposition to the Vietnam War. The author concluded that Malcolm's death was, indeed, a cruel blow to militants who saw in him the promise of a better world.[3]

"In Memory of El-Hazz El-Shabazz," an unsigned article, was written to refute white journalists' claims that Malcolm X was a "folk hero for black militants." The author declared Malcolm X was a national hero and a world hero to all black peoples who, like Marcus Garvey, understood black power as the center of black communities.[4] The first issue, together with all subsequent ones, contained a list of suggested reading on black revolutionists and black power.[5]

The second issue of *Black Politics* described the details of a national disgrace at Orangeburg, South Carolina, in which students at the black South Carolina State College in that town conducted a sit-in at a bowling alley on the edge of the campus which refused to accept black patrons. More than 600 students from South Carolina State and Claflin colleges marched upon the Orangeburg police station demanding the release of twenty of their fellow students who had been arrested for sitting in at the bowling alley. Those arrested were released, but as the marchers started to return to campus they were attacked by the police. Some students were killed and many were seriously injured.[6]

Largely as a result of these reactions on the part of local authorities to black college students' attempts to peacefully integrate public accommodations in the South, *Black Politics'* editorials and articles took up Stokeley Carmichael's plea to get guns for the coming race war. The journal published a feature "How to Acquire the Rifle" (as a weapon for defense). It also published several articles on the economic aspects of the African slave trade in the Americas. Other items explained Marxism and labor unrest in the Caribbean and organized antiblack sentiments in the American military forces.

Black Politics was short-lived but highly articulate. It was not an "underground" sheet, although its circulation was small. It was well edited, though mimeographed, and is a fair example of the stance of black revolutionary politics. The final issue was dedicated to Huey P. Newton, minister of defense of the Black Panther Party which was at the time beleaguered by the Justice Department.

Notes

1. *Black Politics* (January 1968): 2.
2. Malcolm X fused religion with politics by serving as leader of a faction of the Black Muslims and of black nationalists. His relationship to American politics and religion from the black perspective has been described in many ways. One writer has stated, "The Black revolution he [Malcolm X] envisioned was primarily secular, but his incisive analysis of the role of Christianity as an exploitative religion and his understanding of the spiritual quality of an ultimate commitment—the power of faith which had shaken the

foundations of his own life and impelled him to give himself to the liberation struggle—gives him unquestionable standing as a religious leader, if one understands the meaning of religion in the Black experience." [Gayraud S. Wilmore, *Black Religion and Black Radicalism* (New York, 1972), p. 225.]

3. "The Murder of Malcolm X, the Kennedy Assassination, and the CIA," *Black Politics* (January 1968): 6.

4. "In Memory of El-Hazz El-Shabazz," *Black Politics* (January 1968): 12-14.

5. The term "black power" arose from the shock black Americans felt as a result of the shooting of James Meredith, the first black person to be admitted to the University of Mississippi in modern times, as he marched ten miles into Mississippi on a walk from Memphis to Jackson to demonstrate the need for integration. Stokeley Carmichael of the Student Nonviolent Coordinating Committee (SNCC) and Floyd McKissick of CORE joined with Martin Luther King, Jr., to continue the march Meredith had started. Along the way, McKissick, the leader of CORE, told an audience at Greenwood, Mississippi, "What we need is black power." The term was picked up and chanted over the nation. It reflected the mood of black Americans in 1966, replacing powerlessness. *See* Arvarh E. Strickland and Jerome R. Reich, *The Black American Experience: From Reconstruction to the Present* (New York: Harcourt Brace, 1974), pp. 267-47 for a cogent explanation of the genesis of the term.

6. "Real Truth About the Massacre at Orangeburg," *Black Politics* (March 1968): 8-10.

Information Sources

BIBLIOGRAPHY:
Carlisle, Rodney. *The Roots of Black Nationalism*. Port Washington, New York: Kennikat Press, 1975, pp. 152-60.
Carmichael, Stokeley, and Hamilton, Charles V. *Black Power: The Politics of Liberation in America*. New York: Vintage, 1967, pp. 276 ff.
Meier, August, and Rudwick, Elliott. "How CORE Began." *Social Science Quarterly*, March 1969, pp. 789-99.
Myrdal, Gunnar. "The Racial Crisis in Perspective." In *The Black American and the Press*, edited by Jack Lyle. Los Angeles: Ward Ritchie Press, 1968, pp. 5-14.
Strickland, Arvarh E., and Reich, Jerome R. *The Black American Experience: From Reconstruction to the Present*. New York: Harcourt Brace, 1974, pp. 246-47.
INDEX SOURCES: None.
LOCATION SOURCES: Library of Congress; Moorland-Spingarn Collection, Howard University; New York Public Library, New York, New York; University of California at Los Angeles Research Library.

Publication History

MAGAZINE TITLE AND TITLE CHANGES: *Black Politics: A Journal of Liberation*.
VOLUME AND ISSUE DATA: Vol. I, Nos. 1-8 (January-Summer 1968), monthly through March 1968, quarterly for Summer 1968.
PUBLISHER AND PLACE OF PUBLICATION: Black Politics, Berkeley, Calif.
EDITORS: Board members: Richard Assegai, Tom Sanders, Ed Turner (1968).
CIRCULATION: 500 estimate.

BLACK REVIEW

A magazine in paperback book format, *Black Review* contains graphics, poetry, prose fiction, and critical essays, some of which had appeared elsewhere. Its two issues were published in 1971 and 1972. All of the works represent the cultural nationalism among black Americans that arose out of the 1950s and 1960s and the new literary expression of that era, although some essays use a historical context for their examination of contemporary works. During the period covered by *Black Review*, the quest toward the integration of blacks into the white American culture gave way to a new examination and exploration of Afro-American heritage and its roots. Creative artists worked with social and political activists to establish a racial aesthetic and to revitalize deteriorating black urban communities. Black drama and poetry became essentially a "people's art" that brought rank and file men, women, and children into the vitality of the works of their creative artists. This new social and political context was the backdrop for the first issue of *Black Review*. Editor Mel Watkins wrote in the introduction:

> Its aim is to provide a platform from which various aspects of black culture may be examined and discussed and a showcase in which the works of black writers and poets, particularly the young, may be displayed. It is intended to encompass the wide spectrum of opinion and viewpoint that exists in the black community and allow discourse between dissident factions. But its primary function is to further the black man's independent analysis and defining of black American culture, in the hope that it be better understood and more richly developed. Non-black writers will appear when it is felt that their examination of some aspect of their culture illuminates the interrelated aspects of black life. Toward these ends, the selections for the initial issue of *Black Review* have been chosen.[1]

Novelists Barry Beckham, Cecil Brown, George Davis, Shane Stevens, and Edgar White contributed fiction to the first issue. Ed Bullins, resident playwright of the New Lafayette Theatre in Harlem and editor at that time of *Black Theatre*,* provided a short prose piece. David Henderson, Carole Clemons, and Alicia L. Johnson are poets whose works appeared in the first issue along with Edgar White's one act play, "Seigismundo's Tricycle: A Dialogue of Self and Soul." Julius Lester, Reginald Major, and Nikki Giovanni wrote essays about the revolutionary possibilities in contemporary American society.

George Kent's "Richard Wright: Blackness and the Adventure of Western Culture" is an important critical essay. It relates Wright's fiction to the pre-1950 aspirations of black Americans. Their goals then were attached to issues the liberal establishment could help to foster: New Deal legislation, Supreme Court edicts, NAACP persistence, and freedom marches. These were the machinations of a race bent on achieving social integration. When, in the 1960s, American cities burned as a result and illustration of widespread social unrest, the nation realized the true meaning of Richard Wright's portrayal of frustrated black youth. Critics realized reluctantly that *Black Boy* is a great social document. For in it, Wright captures the stirrings of the black masses, not unlike W.E.B. Du Bois' representation in the *Souls of Black Folk*, written before Wright was born. Both wrote about the double consciousness that living black in America imposed. After his telling analysis of major Wright fiction as an expression of the black national consciousness, Kent concludes:

> Wright's vision of black men and women rendered in the four books that I have discussed stormed its way into the fabric of American culture with such fury that its threads form a reference point in the thinking and imagination of those who have yet to read him. Quickly downgraded as more art-conscious black writers made the scene, he seems now all too prophetic, and all too relevant, majestically waiting that close critical engagement which forms the greatest respect that can be paid to a great man and writer.[2]

This approach to the racial aesthetic that had asserted itself by the beginning of the 1970s is a composite social, psychological, and artistic truth. It is the author interpreting his race.

Cecil Brown's essay, "James Brown, Hoodoo and Black Culture," scores black ethos in the new key of the art-heritage movement. It traces the belated recognition jazz vocalist James Brown has received from American blacks. Intellectuals ignored him for going on the air with his "cool it" messages during the urban riots. "What is becoming apparent is that Brown and artists like him are themselves examples of the positive aspects of black life," the essay continues.[3] These musicians and their music symbolize the honest use and development of black folklore that they have projected in place of racial conflict.

In this particular case, the art form—popular music—may be traced to black "hoodoo" culture. "Funky," "heavy," "it's a groove," "deep," "bad," "down," "in there," "out there," "out of sight," and "gone" are linguistic aspects of African culture, the author explains. In the language and religion of historical blackness, the voodoo culture produces poems, novels, and lyrics that are *about* things. Brown makes the point that when James Brown sings about being black and proud, the statement and the art are black and proud. This analysis defines and exemplifies the black aesthetic. It separates the folk art from the literary; it gives sense to the "I'm black and proud" shout emanating from popular musicians.

For the second issue of *Black Review*, "A View of the Artist," the brief introduction sets forth a racial ethos compatible with what the most penetrating essays had expressed in the earlier publication.

Blacks were united by their distinct culture, and every culture is dependent upon the development of its images. It is the attempt to disguise the dynamics and images of the black culture that is partially responsible for the dilemma now confronting white America. It is unnecessary and misleading for whites to give black people the impression that they are establishing the black image, and it is unfortunate for those whites who have never questioned the lie that they live and propagate. The corrupt protagonists controlling what is the American image in the art world are responsible for the lack of awareness of the black image, the black artist and the black aesthetic. I am not trying to establish a black image for black people and certainly not for white people. That image has already been established. I am simply the reflection of that image, and it is my hope that I can mirror the dynamo of our antecedent heritage despite the temerarious and presumptuous canons of the establishment art world.[4]

The tone here is a bit more belligerent than that of the introduction to the first issue. But this volume also contains essays, prose fiction, and graphics. Its principal value lies in Larry Neal's "Eatonville's Zora Neale Hurston: A Profile," which celebrates that author's use of folklore in the Harlem Renaissance period. The essay is biographical and critical. It emphasizes Hurston's success in employing the literary possibilities of black folk culture in her writing. She made a worthy contribution to Afro-American literature by establishing some "new categories of perception; new ways of seeing a culture that had been caricatured by the white minstrel tradition, made hokey by the dialect poets and finally made a 'primitive' aphrodisiac by the new sexualism of the twenties."[5]

As a magazine-book, *Black Review* is a distinct kind of journal: a collection of Afro-American literature valuable not so much as a showcase for young writers, but as the publisher of at least two significant pieces of literary criticism on the development of a distinct aesthetic in black American fiction.

Notes

1. *Black Review* (1971): 6.
2. Ibid., p. 34.
3. Ibid., p. 180.
4. Ellsworth Ausby, "A View of the Artist," *Black Review* (1972): 8.
5. Ibid., p. 15.

Information Sources

BIBLIOGRAPHY:
Katz, William. *Magazines for Libraries*, Vol. 1. New York, 1974, p. 108.
INDEX SOURCES: None.
LOCATION SOURCES: Academic libraries.

Publication History

MAGAZINE TITLE AND TITLE CHANGES: *Black Review*.
VOLUME AND ISSUE DATA: Nos. I-II (1971-1972), annual for two years.
PUBLISHER AND PLACE OF PUBLICATION: William Morrow and Company, New York, New York.
EDITORS: Mel Watkins (1971). No editor listed for 1972.
CIRCULATION: Not available.

BLACK SCHOLAR, THE: JOURNAL OF BLACK STUDIES AND RESEARCH

The Black World Foundation was founded in 1969 with Nathan Hare, a black sociologist, as president. The organization's journal, the *Black Scholar*, appeared first in November of that year. Robert Chrisman, vice-president of the foundation, became editor. His statement in the first issue expressed the periodical's purposes.

We recognize that we must re-define our lives. We must shape a culture, a politics, an economics, a sense of our past and future history. We must recognize what we have been and what we shall be, retaining that which has been good and discarding that which has been worthless. *The Black Scholar* shall be a journal for that definition. In its first pages, Black ideologies will be examined, debated, disputed and evaluated by the Black intellectual community.[1]

The foundation itself was a nonprofit organization with the goal of creating, publishing, and distributing black educational materials. In a time of unusual social struggle and strong determination for black self-realization, the foundation recognized that black liberation depended upon research and dissemination of information that would provide a dialogue for a revolutionary black ideology. Through its Center for Research, Planning, and Statistics the Black World Foundation published its journal monthly, ten issues each year plus "basic black books by old and new writers, including booklets, pamphlets, textbooks, poetry, art reproductions, photographic essays, etc." It proposed to conduct symposia and seminars on every phase of black America, to establish dialogue with various liberation groups and factions in the United States, and to maintain liaison with African cultural groups for the purpose of developing a new cultural resistance that would cover all areas of educational curricula. The foundation declared a black cultural revolution was essential for the nation. Its journal would be a periodical of black studies and research promoting the revolution.

An impressive array of professional persons, educators, and writers made up the original list of contributing and advisory editors for the journal. Included were Andrew Billingsley, then assistant chancellor for academic affairs at the University of California at Berkeley; Prince Cobb, psychiatrist at the University of California Medical Center; Charles V. Hamilton, professor of political science at Columbia University; and Don L. Lee, black poet-in-residence at that time at Northeastern Illinois University. The number has grown steadily.

The lead article for the first issue described the Pan-African Cultural Festival recently held in Algiers. Nathan Hare reported on it and carefully outlined the kinds of struggle blacks were experiencing from San Francisco to Dakar to the District of Columbia. Hundreds of delegates came to the festival from thirty-one independent African countries, as well as representatives from six movements for African liberation from Palestine, Angola, Mozambique, and the Congo. They joined the Black Panthers and others from the American continents. There, exiled Eldridge Cleaver chose to reveal his whereabouts and expatriate Stokeley Carmichael came with his South African-exiled wife, Miriam Mekega. LeRoi Jones could not come because his passport had been held up. But the young poet Don L. Lee, Hoyt Fuller of *Negro Digest*,* and other Americans who shared the new revolutionary trend attended. For the issue of *Black Scholar* that reported on the festival, Eldridge Cleaver wrote "Education and Revolution." Carmichael contributed "Pan-Africanism—Land and Power," and John O. Killens wrote "The Artist in the Black University." Roosevelt Johnson's "Black Administrators and Higher Education" also appeared.

Other issues the first year honored W.E.B. Du Bois as the patron saint of black radicals who, during his lifetime, had never ceased to fight for full "manhood rights" for blacks. An editorial complained bitterly that Shirley Graham Du Bois, his widow, had been denied entry into the United States to speak at a Fisk University ceremony honoring her husband's having received his baccalaureate degree there. The United States government ruled against her on the basis of Section 212-2-218 of the Immigration and Nationality Act. Because of her association with Du Bois and her active opposition to racism, neocolonialism, and apartheid, the attorney general ruled that she was a subversive. His refusal to grant her entry was called the latest in a long series of sustained harassments by the government of Du Bois and his family. The editorial recalled that in 1950 the eighty-two-year-old scholar had been arrested, charged as an "unregistered foreign agent," and brought to trial in chains. Although he was acquitted, he was "race-baited and red-baited" by Richard Nixon and J. Edgar Hoover, who led the campaign to eliminate W.E.B. Du Bois campus clubs from American colleges and universities, according to the editor.

Less than a year after its first appearance, Hare could write that the journal had grown without benefit of any "angels," foundation grants, or any source of income except subscriptions and purchases. He was proud that *Black Scholar* had been able to bring its readers some of the best thinking of the time written by

Pelson, who wanted to expose the "neo-colonial exploitation of black cities," which would be the most distressing problem of the seventies. The greatest accomplishment of *Black Scholar*, Hare wrote, lay in its ability to bridge the gap between the academy and the street.

The scholarly and carefully structured magazine would, indeed, bring the scholar and the community together to study at close range the significance of the black experience in America. A large part of its purposes would be accomplished through black studies programs in the schools. In "A Force to Burn Down a Decadent World" Hare lamented the disarray into which many black studies programs had fallen.[2] Few were worth the name they bore, despite the hard work many dedicated black people had given to the effort. They were stymied by cunning opposition from "oppressors and their collaborators." In content, some programs were restricted to recounting historical travails and ferreting out black contributions to a diabolical civilization. Typical programs allowed Afro-Americans to "re-discover our identity and increase our self-respect, but otherwise our intellectual life remains in the throes of bourgeois abstractions. . . and our education is separated from our daily lives."

Black studies, as conceived by the cultural revolutionists, was never meant to be a means of merely learning about the past. The plan was, instead, a pedagogical innovation designed to avoid the study of blackness alone. It was to be a new approach to scholarship and teaching which would prepare black students to function in hard times ahead while learning how to clear the way for the ultimate humanization of the decadent American society. To that extent, black studies would always be revolutionary if they would be useful. Such a curriculum would necessarily include analyses of race and class and studies of oppressors as well as victims. Moreover, it must include the study of the march toward freedom of peoples in other areas of the world—their failures and successes, their goals and strategies, and their tactics. Without these focuses, Hare wrote, no black studies program could serve a significant purpose. His attempt to establish this kind of dynamic curriculum at San Francisco State University brought about a bitter struggle between black faculty and students on the one hand and the administration on the other. In recalling that dramatic fight, the publisher wrote:

> San Francisco State College, where the cry for Black Studies (as such) was born, is a model of this confusion today and, no doubt, a prototype of what lies ahead for black studies everywhere. A long and costly strike there two years ago was pitched on a principle of "non-negotiability" (by which was meant no compromise), a bold new concept in hypocrisy of American arbitration and rebellion. But, as we enter the present year, the Negroes at San Francisco State are still seeking to negotiate with S.I. Hayakawa and his ilk, despite the fact that he has even fired or caused to resign more than half a dozen blacks who were not revolutionary enough to support the strike.[3]

Black Scholar's greatest value lies not so much in its promotion of black studies curricula as in the research it publishes on a broad scope of subjects from the revolutionary perspective. Richard Hatcher, black mayor of Gary, Indiana, and Shirley Chisholm, black congresswoman from Brooklyn, wrote on the basic racism of the daily American press. Both noted that few newspapers attempt to employ or to represent in their news coverage a reasonable proportion of the black population living in their home areas. Chisholm reported the press was racist and sexist as she related the story of her invitation to attend the all-white, all-male Gridiron Club as a token guest. Frances B. Ward wrote "The Black Press in Crisis," lamenting the diminution of the once-powerful *Pittsburgh Courier* and *Baltimore Afro-American* newspapers which had not been able to regain their lost status in black America despite the current civil rights movement and better economic conditions for Negroes.

The economy, housing, black psychology, public education, black social classes, Pan-Africanism, women's problems, the child, and the American government's relations with nonwhite peoples were discussed in issues of the journal. Special Bicentennial and creative writing numbers appeared in the mid seventies. Maya Angelou, Gwendolyn Brooks, Imamu Amiri Baraka, Sonia Sanchez, and Alice Walker contributed poetry. Gayle Jones, Clarence Major, John Stewart, Woodie King Jr., and Cecil Brown published their short fiction. Ed Bullins' play "Malcolm '71: Or Publishing Blackness" is another important work that appeared in the journal.

Black Scholar is an independent magazine that supports itself through subscriptions and some advertisement. It is an attractive journal that captures the most articulate expressions of the revolutionary spirit of the times. It gained ready acceptance among the intelligentsia of revolutionary black and white Americans in a period that was particularly sensitive to a swiftly changing nation, and it has maintained its visibility. It reached its zenith of influence in the mid seventies, but the scholarly research that its sponsoring foundation carried on has seldom been paralleled in other periods of the history of black scholarship, with the possible exception of Du Bois' early work in sociology at the turn of the century in the *Atlanta University Studies*.

In recent issues, the "Black Book Round-up" has proved a unique feature. The "Poets' Corner" was added in 1979 as a regular item. Complete numbers have been devoted to Latin America/Caribbean; Africa: The New Societies, Black Politics: 1980; Black Anthropology; The Black Struggle: Miami and the Caribbean; and Black Education: 25 Years After Brown.

Notes

1. *Black Scholar* (November 1969): inside front cover.
2. *Black Scholar* (April/May 1971): 23-30.
3. Ibid.

Information Sources

BIBLIOGRAPHY:
Cummings, Robert. "African and Afro-American Studies Centers." *Journal of Black Studies*, March 1979, pp. 291-310.
Hare, Nathan. "Combating Black Apathy." *Black Scholar*, November 1973, pp. 38-42.
"On Black Media." *Black Scholar*, September 1973, inside cover.
Wolseley, Roland E. *The Black Press, U.S.A.* Ames: Iowa State University Press, 1971.
INDEX SOURCES: Microfiche University Microfilm International; *Social Science Index; Index to Periodical Articles by and about Blacks.*
LOCATION SOURCES: Most college libraries.

Publication History

MAGAZINE TITLE AND TITLE CHANGES: *The Black Scholar: Journal of Black Studies and Research* (November 1969 to present).
VOLUME AND ISSUE DATA: Vol. I- (1969 to present), published six times a year.
PUBLISHER AND PLACE OF PUBLICATION: Black World Foundation, Sausalito, California.
EDITORS: Robert Chrisman (November 1969-November 1974); Robert L. Allen (December 1974 to present).
CIRCULATION: 18,000.

BLACK SPORTS

A magazine devoted entirely to news and issues about black athletes did not appear in the United States until *Black Sports* was launched in 1970. Sports has long been popular in the nation, and the preponderance of blacks in collegiate and professional baseball, basketball, and football has long been a source of news items and feature articles. All black communications media have included sports, and some weekly newspapers have included it in their entertainment sections. The all-Negro baseball teams that enjoyed success as spectator attractions in the first decades of the twentieth century received little notice in the white newspapers and magazines. Jackie Robinson, who starred in football, track, and baseball at UCLA, was playing on the Kansas City Monarch Negro baseball team when Branch Rickey signed him to his farm team in Montreal in 1945. Two years later, Rickey announced that Robinson would be added to the roster of the parent club. His accomplishment made Robinson a source of uncommon pride for black Americans. He was the forerunner in white organized baseball. His extraordinary athletic talent and his personal struggle to gain acceptance as a professional black athlete in his native land in the mid twentieth century was an impetus for black sports news, even as Joe Louis had been for boxing beginning a decade earlier. Black football players—first the few at northern white universities, and later unusually talented students at black colleges—found their way into professional football as it competed with baseball to become a companion American pastime. Basketball followed.

This scenario led, in large measure, to the spate of black tabloids and magazines. It led specifically to *Black Sports*, a popular and financially successful periodical that added a significant dimension to black journalism in the United States.

Started in 1970, the era that spawned dozens of black periodicals of many types, *Black Sports* has served several purposes. As expected, its format is arranged to inform its audience about black athletes. Most of the feature articles are written by the editorial staff. They present sports personalities, the state of the art in the several sports in which blacks participate, and news stories centering around athletics in the United States. The articles usually focus upon a black perspective, with details that do not appear in stories about the same incidents in the daily white press or in the better-known sports magazines. To that extent, *Black Sports* is a newspaper about black athletes and their activities.

Departments in each issue include "Man on the Sideline," a letter-to-the-editor feature; "Locker Room Chatter," "Tips on Sports," "Locks on Jazz," and "College Athlete of the Month." "Historically Speaking" is an invaluable collection of black sports history about college teams, individual portraits of athletes, and black professional teams. The features are well illustrated with excellent photographs.

Much of the vitality of the magazine lies in its "Publisher's Statement." Some have concentrated on the dearth of blacks in sports management and a variety of other provocative subjects. A recent column expressed the growing responsibility of sports media beyond the newspaper function. "Ours is not just to report the 'game' to our enthusiastic audience but rather to begin to change our perspective as the reverberating implications and social needs dictate," publisher Allan P. Barron wrote. The publicized problem of drugs in professional sports concerns *Black Sports*, whose staff considers athletics no longer a "toy department item in the scope of human affairs." Barron believes his periodical must "present athletics in a contemporary environment in such a way that sports can stimulate positive social and cultural interchange and development."[1]

In this function, particularly, *Black Sports* serves and transcends the concerns of a newspaper for, about, and by blacks. It takes a novel and intelligent view of sports as a vital source in the American society for which it is a spectacle, a business enterprise, and a profession.

Note

1. *Black Sports* (February 1978): 4.

Information Sources

BIBLIOGRAPHY:
Barron, Allan P. "Publisher's Statement." *Black Sports*, February 1978, p. 5.

Katz, William, ed. *Magazines for Libraries*. New York, 1972, p. 17.
INDEX SOURCE: *Index to Periodical Articles about and by Negroes*.
LOCATION SOURCES: Many college and university libraries; public libraries; University Microfilm.

Publication History

MAGAZINE TITLE AND TITLE CHANGES: *Black Sports* (February 1970 to present).
VOLUME AND ISSUE DATA: Vols. I- (February 1970-), monthly.
PUBLISHER AND PLACE OF PUBLICATION: Allan P. Barron, Black Sports, Incorporated, New York, New York.
EDITOR: Rudy Langlais (1970 to present).
CIRCULATION: 10,000.

BLACK THEATRE

Black playwright Ed Bullins began publishing *Black Theatre* in 1968 in Harlem. His purpose was to survey the activity in black experimental community workshop theaters that sprang up throughout the country in that decade. *Black Theatre* presented new revolutionary plays and articles supporting and advocating a black national theater.[1] Playwrights engaged in the movement sought a new identity that had not been known before. They needed new forms and techniques in the drama to serve their new purposes. This was a pioneer venture in that it sought to define a new culture for a part of American drama by discussing and demonstrating the product. *Black Theatre* joined *Black Dialogue*, *Soul Book*, and the *Journal of Black Poetry** as the foremost black revolutionary journals of black literature written for and by blacks.

The home of the new drama and the journal was the New Lafayette Theatre in Harlem. The name of that institution had grown to be racial legend in the United States. It was the most successful black theater activity in Harlem in the 1920s. Moreover, it was the center of the Harlem Work Projects Administration (WPA) Theatre Project that flourished in the 1930s. That period saw the rise of federally supported community theater in Harlem and the bitter arguments that raged over whether whites or blacks should control its management and choice of offerings. Blacks were staunch in their demands that the government funds be used to continue and enlarge upon the works of Rose McClendon and other black actors who had labored to bring theater to Harlem. At the same time, they strove to make the WPA's purpose of giving some monetary assistance to actors and artists a reality for blacks in New York City.[2]

Toward the end of the 1960s, black drama had become a recognized part of the black revolutionary movement in politics and the arts. *Negro Digest** and *Black World**—both John H. Johnson publications—had been significant media for the definition and expression of the special uses of black militancy in the theater. It was a movement that sharpened the unique application of Afro-American creative arts from their beginning to the present in the national culture. The black nation-within-a-nation found a vehicle for self-expression in creative writing and acting. But the wider power of drama became a tool for political manifestation. The medium was particularly felicitous. For playwright and audience could establish and articulate a dialogue that was not possible in fiction or poetry or the essay. Black awareness and motivation to political action were expected from the new drama. LeRoi Jones (later Imamu Amiri Baraka) and Ed Bullins in particular described their plays as black revolutionary drama. Their artistic and political thrust was anti-integrationist and antibourgeoisie. They established and practiced a non-Western aesthetic which defied conventional dramatic criticism by white critics who had always reviewed American theatrical productions, and who, in judging the playwrights, became a vehicle for a new meaning for racial aspirations. Most black playwrights working in the revolutionary trend contributed articles to the new journal, including Ben Caldwell, LeRoi Jones, Woodie King, and John O'Neal. Their essays covered a variety of subjects. Reviews of plays stated by black community drama groups were an integral part of each issue. To that extent, it served as a newspaper about new performances. Some poems were published in each issue, including one written by LeRoi Jones and one by Dionne Warwick.

The first issue carried reports on black theater in San Francisco, Philadelphia, New Orleans, and other smaller towns in the South. It described activities at the Free Southern Theatre Workshop which had been held early in 1968 in New Orleans. Bullins contributed an article he had been commissioned to write for the *New York Times* "on anything you'd like" which he had refused to submit because the *Times* had rejected a piece the paper had previously commissioned LeRoi Jones to write on revolutionary theater. A Mr. Peck at the *Times* had found the essay "interesting" but "not for them."[3] Joe Conclaves, later editor of the *Journal of Black Poetry*,* contributed "The Actress," a poem dedicated to the recently deceased black stage and motion picture personality Dorothy Dandridge. "Two on Cruse: A View of the Black Intellectual" was prepared as a symposium piece on the black theater in Harold Cruse's book, *Crisis of the Black Intellectual*. Larry Neal and Askia Muhammed Toure participated in the symposium. Other items in the first issue included an interview with LeRoi Jones about his drama and Spirit House, his project as a school for black consciousness and play production. Two recently produced black plays were reviewed—Erroll John's *Man on a Rainbow Shawl* and Louis Spain's adaptation of Richard Wright's short story, *Daddy Goodness*.

In addition to publishing black plays and ritual drama, *Black Theatre* kept its readers aware of important development in theatrical activities among blacks in a variety of forms. The second issue carried a formal report of a creative workshop held at the Third Annual Black Power Conference in Philadelphia 29-31 August 1968. Other essays discussed the Yard Theatre movement in Jamaica and interviews with black writers who were part of the new theater.

Black Theatre contains valuable collections of black plays written during the late 1960s and early 1970s. Its essays show clearly the relationship between creative writing and political activity. Together with the several proceedings of black nationalist and Third World conferences on a new aesthetics as well as a new political alignment of black peoples in the world, the journal is a significant document of the Western Hemisphere and its dynamics in art and politics in the early decades of the second half of the twentieth century.

Notes

1. *See* "Evolution of a People's Theatre," in *Black Drama Anthology*, ed. Woodie King and Ron Milner (New York, 1972), pp. vii-x, for a succinct discussion of the periods of development of black drama in the United States in the twentieth century.

2. For some understanding of the nature of the controversy that the Harlem Theatre Project of the WPA brought to Harlem, *see* "Federal Aid for Negro Theatre in Harlem Assured," *New York Age*, 30 November 1935, pp. 4, 8; William E. Clark, "WPA Theatre Project in Harlem with Eight Executives Draws Howl from Negro Actors," ibid., 14 December 1935, p. 4; and "Resentment Grows at Proposed Negro Theatre Project," ibid., 11 December 1935, p. 4.

3. "Black Theatre News," *Black Theatre* (Fall 1968): 4-6.

Information Sources

BIBLIOGRAPHY:
Brown, Lloyd D. "The Cultural Revolution in Black Theatre." *Negro American Literature Forum*, Spring 1974, pp. 159-64.
Bullins, Ed, ed. *The New Lafayette Theatre Presents: Plays With Aesthetic Comments by Six Black Playwrights*. Garden City, New York, 1974: pp. 2-5.
Orman, Roscoe. "The New Lafayette Theatre." *Black Theatre*, June 1970, pp. 12-13.
Perkins, Eugene. "The Black Arts Movement." In *The Black Seventies*, edited by Floyd B. Barkham. Boston: Peter Sargent Publishers, 1970, pp. 85-96.
Steele, Shelby. "Notes on Ritual in the New Black Theatre." *Black World*, June 1973, pp. 4-13, 78-84.
Taylor, Willene Palliam. "The Reversal of the Tainted Blood Theme in the Works of Writers of the Black Revolutionary Theatre." *Black American Literature Forum*, Fall 1976, pp. 88-91.
INDEX SOURCE: *Index to Periodical Articles by and about Negroes.*
LOCATION SOURCES: Library of Congress; University of Illinois; Vanderbilt University; many black college and university libraries.

Publication History

MAGAZINE TITLE AND TITLE CHANGES: *Black Theatre* (formerly irregularly published as *Black Theatre News*).
VOLUME AND ISSUE DATA: Nos.1-6 (Fall 1968-Spring 1972).
PUBLISHER AND PLACE OF PUBLICATION: New Lafayette Theatre, New York, New York.
EDITOR: Ed Bullins (1968-1972).
CIRCULATION: 3,500.

BLACK WORLD

Negro Digest* enjoyed popular success as a part of the Johnson Publishing Company for nearly twenty years. With the May 1970 issue, the digest became *Black World.*

Beginning with the May 1970 issue, *Negro Digest* will have a new name. The magazine will continue its focus on Black ideas, fiction, poetry and the arts, and it will redouble its efforts to bring clarity and insight into the problems and prospects of the children of Africa wherever they happen to be.[1]

Managing editor Hoyt W. Fuller retained his position with the new magazine. He had moved the *Digest* from a collection of reprinted articles and some special features into essentially a literary journal that reflected the controversies surrounding the rise of the second black literary renaissance that many persons consider the thrust of the 1960s and part of the 1970s. The black aesthetic became the byword in Afro-American cultural circles. A generation earlier, authors and politicians in the 1920s had used the "New Negro" metaphor to give vitality to black writing as an ally to political and social purposes. The proper subject for black authors was the question of the twenties. W.E.B. Du Bois conducted a survey in the *Crisis** to get black and white authors to comment on the subject. In the 1930s, Richard Wright published his "Blueprint for Negro Writers" in the ill-fated *New Challenge* magazine.[2] Fuller polled writers in the middle and late 1960s and found the subject still lively and the consensus still evasive. Some believed black writing should serve as a weapon of revolution. Others disagreed. All realized that black creative writing had attracted the attention of the Western world. "Negro" had become a term of derision in the literature, sociology, and politics of the new black nationalism. The *Messenger** and the *Liberator** had debated the use of the term in the twenties and *Colored American** and *Alexander's Magazine** published articles on the subject at the turn of the century.

The emphasis was different in the sixties. "Black" was solidly in vogue, and the word referred to an ethnic group, no matter the name of the land in which its black people lived. *Black World*, then, was the appropriate title for a journal that would meld black politics with black art, even as the "radical" periodicals had done decades earlier. Fuller did not lead the movement. He followed it. And with the new magazine, he came to be one of its chief exponents.

In his "Notes" for the first issue of *Black World*, Fuller wrote that authors of the eight articles, the short stories, and the poems in the premier number made it abundantly clear that black peoples on both continents—Africa and the Americas—had grave and similar problems and a common source in the experience of colonization and enslavement. He expressed the hope that black people everywhere had reached a maturity that would cause them to understand that the empowerment of black people of Harlem is not possible until black men are in full control of that experience. *Black World*, he wrote, would routinely publish articles that would probe and report on the condition of peoples and their struggles. Hence, the title. Still, the journal would continue the tradition of *Negro Digest* by publishing thoughtful essays, fiction, and poetry written by "known and unknown" authors. His description referred to what was to become a revolutionary periodical.

Black historian Charles V. Hamilton set the tone for the renamed magazine's content with the lead article, "Brown Americans and the Modern Political Struggle," which related the then current black national aspiration to those of the late nineteenth century and the early decades of the twentieth century. Other articles warned against "racist researchers" who would exploit and misinterpret the new social tensions and identified the black revolution as a common phenomenon in Africa and the United States. The Afro-American world view was established. Black consciousness would be fostered and it would relate to national politics and to the creative arts. In its black literature emphasis, *Black World* would keep before its readers the ever-broadening scope of literary form as a reaction to living black throughout the world. That focus led naturally to the Pan-African movements and the many national and international organizations in which Fuller held membership and association. Most importantly, *Black World* had the popularity and the financial stability of the Johnson Publishing Company behind it. It would thrive where many other periodicals with similar orientation failed.

Black theater, particularly, enjoyed the special attention of the journal. The Annual Theatre Issue of April 1973—the first of a yearly series—contained Carlton W. Molette's significant article "Afro-American Ritual Drama," an interview with playwright Lonne Elder, and "Reports on Black Theatre, U.S.A.," which reported on activities in drama in New York City, Cleveland, Chicago, Washington, D.C., Atlanta, Seattle, and New Orleans. The issue is a valuable document on black theater at the beginning of the 1970s. *Black World* could chronicle and interpret black arts better than the special subject journals, and it could reach a far larger audience than they could expect to attract.

Fuller brought into *Black World* a fortuitous fusion of academic scholars, performing artists, creative writers, and persons who knew most dimensions of the black experience. It reported on blacks who broke into the mainstream of American society and interpreted rising nationalism among blacks outside the United States. It kept alive and visible the heightened black consciousness that had blossomed during the social civil rights movement at a time in the mid-seventies that saw some waning of that emphasis. The breakdown of racial segregation *de jure* took some momentum out of the popularity of the revolutionary spirit among black Americans. Nathan Hare, recent editor of the *Black Scholar** and a dynamic leader in establishing black studies programs at San Francisco State College, explained the attenuation in "What Happened to the

Black Movement," an article printed in *Black World* during the last year of its publication. Hare wrote, "We became preoccupied with the past, bogging ourselves down in bygone glories," as he referred to the spate of African hairdos, names, and clothing prevalent during the height of the black consciousness days. He complained that blacks had lost the revolutionary initiative that prevailed then, but he did not despair. For he believed disillusionment with the tensions of black American life would again kindle the revolutionary spirit.[3]

Fuller would agree with Hare's assessment of the preoccupation with faddish, external symbols of Africanism during the 1960s. For in *Black World* he kept the revolutionary spark aglow. He usually wrote the column "Perspectives" that was a commentary on black social, political, and literary affairs.[4] Throughout his editorship of the journal, Fuller amassed an anthology of black creative writing and literary criticism that surpasses in quality and quantity that of any academic-subject journal. The creative writing was not always good. The weakness in much of it supported some authors' claim that a black aesthetic was little more than racist propaganda, an anomaly in a multiethnic society.

Some of these reactions against radical black writing had surfaced during the life of *Negro Digest*. As an aggressive and incisive editor who selected and solicited articles that explored the depths of the essential controversies of his time, Fuller's influence on American magazine journalism was profound. He drew effectively upon the growing area of scholarly criticism for Afro-American writing. Although he was a clear advocate of the black aesthetic school of scholarship and wrote often on the subject, he invited and published comment from scholars and critics who opposed his point of view. Through his "Perspectives" column he provided a wealth of news about authors and their works, cultural events, and political affairs and personalities. The journal's book reviews were brief essays that reflected seasoned scholarship unique among literary magazines. *Black World* brought into sharp focus the agonizing problem of white critics attempting to evaluate black writing. Within the concept of the black aesthetic there was the strong position that the purist view of literature left unanswered some essential questions about the motivation to create and the elements and the quality of the creative artist's product. Through its multitude of well-qualified critics, *Black World* allowed for pursuit of the several dimensions of the role of the black critic in analyzing the black artist's writing.

In the same statement in which he announced the change of title from *Negro Digest* to *Black World*, Fuller wrote that he had been urged to bring the title into the trends of the times so that it would reflect the actual character of the publication. Still, the second run of *Negro Digest/Black World* did not enjoy the commercial success of the first. Only about half of the 1963 and 1967 pressruns were sold. Although the new journal carried a large and varied number of articles that would seem to appeal to a wider audience than the original organ, its focus was too narrow for the popular success necessary to keep it in publication.

Notes

1. *Negro Digest* (April 1970): 6.
2. *See* Walter C. Daniel, *"Challenge Magazine*: An Experiment That Failed," *College Language Association Journal* (June 1976): 494-503.
3. "What Happened to the Black Movement?" *Black World* (January 1976): 28.
4. *See* Abby Arthur Johnson and Ronald Maberry Johnson, *Propaganda and Aesthetics: The Literary Politics of Afro-American Magazines in the Twentieth Century* (Amherst, Mass., 1979), chapter 6, for a detailed discussion of Fuller's conversion to revolutionist.

Information Sources

BIBLIOGRAPHY:
Fuller, Hoyt W. "All in a Name," *Negro Digest*, February 1970, p. 97.
————. "Negro Writer in the United States." *Ebony*, November 1964, pp. 126-28.
Hare, Nathan. "Division and Confusion: What Happened to the Black Movement?" *Black World*, January 1976, pp. 20-32.
Joyce, Donald Franklin. "Magazines of Afro-American Thought on the Market: Can They Survive?" *American Libraries*, December 1976, pp. 673-78.
Miles, Frank W. "Negro Magazines Come of Age." *Magazine World*, 1 June 1946, p. 18.
Reichley, A. James. "How John Johnson Made It." *Fortune*, January 1968, pp. 152-53, 178-80.
INDEX SOURCE: *Index to Periodical Articles by and about Negroes.*
LOCATION SOURCES: Most college and university libraries.

Publication History

MAGAZINE TITLE AND TITLE CHANGES: *Black World* (May 1970-February 1976).
VOLUME AND ISSUE DATA: Vols. XIX-XXV, no. 6, monthly. (*Black World* assumed volume numbers of *Negro Digest*.)
PUBLISHER AND PLACE OF PUBLICATION: Johnson Publishing Company, Chicago, Illinois.
EDITORS: John H. Johnson, editor and publisher; Hoyt W. Fuller, managing editor. (1970-1976).
CIRCULATION: 55,000.

BRONZEMAN, THE

The *Bronzeman* began publication in Chicago a few months before the stock market crash of 1929 and continued well into the depression. As a popular periodical, it achieved no literary distinction and contained little significant political editorial opinion. It was circulated nationally, although most of its news features centered around local activities. Accordingly, it became, along with *Abbott's Monthly*,* a significant source of information about the social, religious, and cultural life of black Chicago. Its editor, Carswell W. Crews, was active in the African Methodist Episcopal Church; consequently, the journal contains editorials and news accounts of that denomination's activities and of Wilberforce University, the church's leading college. At one time Crews ran unsuccessfully for editor of the *A.M.E. Church Review*,* generally considered the oldest black journal in the nation. The *Bronzeman* could not survive the depression, but it stands as an often overlooked black publication during the second phase of the "Chicago Renaissance."[1] The cultural climate of Chicago during the life of the *Bronzeman* contributed to the milieu that gave rise to the works of Gwendolyn Brooks, Margaret Walker, and Richard Wright, principal luminaries of the black Chicago school of writers. The *Bronzeman* did not publish any of these writers, whose fame was to come later. Its best-known contributors were Charlene Rollins, the outstanding children's librarian who managed the book review section, and Marita Bonner, whose short fiction also appeared regularly in the *Crisis*.* Editor Crews invited contributors to submit short stories of adventure, mystery, and love and true stories that conveyed "helpful messages and confessions," as well as articles dealing with Negro life in all phases. The *Bronzeman* offered to pay for any contributions it published. Its fiction was always illustrated.

The format included a collection of paid advertisements for private and public black colleges headed "Educational Service for Parents." "Bouquets and Bomb-shells" contained letters to the editor. Crews usually wrote editorials under a regular column, "Take It or Leave It," and Chicago ministers wrote columns on religion.

Popular-appeal features included contests for the best essays on such subjects as "Who Is the Most Unusual Man (or Woman) in Your Town?" and a gallery of photographs of black women from around the country under the caption "Bronze Beauties." "When Opportunity Knocked" reported success stories about black girls who found employment in business firms, such as the telephone company and department stores. The small number of poems used were usually religious, romantic, or concerned with racial pride. "Junior Bronzeman" was a monthly page of letters, lists of famous black Americans whose birthdays fell within that month, and lists of children's books.

Upon the occasion of the seventy-fifth anniversary of the founding of Wilberforce University and the fiftieth of Tuskegee Institute, Crews wrote in an editorial, "One can hardly over-emphasize the magnitude of the work nor the service performed by the two institutions, each seeking in its own way to reach the same end—making the Negro an indispensable factor in American life."[2] He observed that Wilberforce had survived the bitter debate between proponents of higher education versus industrial education for blacks and noted that during that philosophical conflict Tuskegee had millions of dollars lavished upon it, while Wilberforce had to struggle along on such scant support as the A.M.E. Church had been able to give along with small gifts from a few whites.

National interests were cast into a local perspective, such as the strong antiwar sentiment expressed in Crews' reaction to a Memorial Day service held in a

Chicago church some twenty years after the end of World War I. The editor related the ill effects of the war to the depression, writing about the thousands of wrecked lives, the black boys who sacrificed themselves for a democracy that never came to their land for their people, and the farce "whereby men too old to fight may decree that the youth of any nation give up all to satisfy a caprice." Upon this background of the devastations of war, Crews placed the picture of soldiers still facing hunger and deprivation because their government would not find jobs for them.

Editorials in the *Bronzeman* offered no profound remedies for the bleak aftermath of the war most black Americans experienced. The editor was basically conservative in his political outlook, although he failed to support specific candidates for office. Following the deaths of three blacks in Chicago in a fracas with the police, Crews wrote that once more attention had been focused on what was termed "the growing Red inclination of Negroes." To him, the political implications of black resistance to their economic lot was far from ideational. They were not Reds—"not yet." They were hungry. For the most part, they knew nothing about communism, "but a hungry man is ready material for Red propaganda."[3] Communism involves, along with other things, assault on capitalism, he explained. To date, no Negroes had risen to that type of action. No one had committed acts of violence against government property or capitalistic property. So far, there was only harangue, people listening to arguments, and gatherings to return dispossessed tenants' furniture to the apartments from which they had been evicted. Crews contended the effective solution to unrest among American blacks was simple: Give them work. Then no idle crowds would be available for white Reds to agitate and inspire to mischief. Crews believed the responsibility to bring about national economic recovery lay with the national government— particularly with the White House. He strongly denounced President Herbert Hoover's attitude toward the Veterans' Bonus March on Washington.

> These men are no beggars; they ask their Government for the bonus only because it is too stupid to provide them with work. Give them jobs and the bonus can go hang! Of course, the Government says it has no money to pay bonuses. It would be very interesting should war break out tomorrow to see how soon millions would be forthcoming to hustle these same men into uniforms, equip them with submarines, aircrafts, and other deathdealing devices and send them into the jaws of death.[4]

When Franklin D. Roosevelt won the Democratic nomination for president in 1932, Crews praised the choice. He wrote that it would take a man of magnetism on the Republican side to even make an interesting race. He saw no one on the horizon. In a kind of fantasy, he suggested that a race between Theodore Roosevelt and Franklin Roosevelt would be interesting. He was hardly serious, but the statement does reflect on the days in which blacks held the elder Roosevelt in high esteem and would have voted for him simply because he was a Republican. By the 1930s, that attitude had passed.

The *Bronzeman* was a black popular magazine intended to entertain and to provide examples of success among American blacks. Its features appealed to a family audience and seldom were controversial. Its "Letter from Hollywood," a monthly report on the motion picture industry, provides valuable data on black entertainers. Moreover, the magazine contains significant stories about popular, classical, and sacred music among blacks in Chicago. It published one or two important articles on the rise of black gospel music, a depression phenomenon that arose in Chicago churches.

Despite persistent financial problems common to any journalist, Crews remained optimistic throughout the life of the *Bronzeman*. His own assessment of the magazine appears in an excerpt from one editorial.

With this number, *Bronzeman* enters its third year of journalistic life. That's setting a pace. There are two magazines published or rather edited by Negroes which outrank *Bronzeman* as to age, but these are mouthpieces of organizations. *Bronzeman* leads the field and has enjoyed a longer life without interruption of issues of any magazine of its kind.[5]

That claim is true. His reference to the other two magazines at the time were the *Crisis*, the official journal of the NAACP, and *Opportunity*,* the publication of the National Urban League. They both outlived the *Bronzeman* but they also suffered the ravages of the depression years. The *Bronzeman* is the only popular magazine begun in the depression that lived as long as it did.

Notes

1. Bernard Duffey, *The Chicago Renaissance in American Letters: A Critical History* (Lansing, Mich., 1956), and Dale Kramer, *Chicago Renaissance: The Literary Life of the Midwest, 1900-1930*, (New York, 1966) discuss Chicago milieux that would cover the period of the publication of the *Bronzeman*, but make no mention of black writing.
2. *Bronzeman* (August 1931): 6.
3. "Give Them Work," *Bronzeman* (June 1932): 2.
4. Ibid.
5. *Bronzeman* (March 1931): 2.

Information Sources

BIBLIOGRAPHY:
Detweiler, Frederick G. *The Negro Press in the United States*. Chicago, 1922.
Johnson, Abby Arthur, and Johnson, Ronald Maberry. *Propaganda and Aesthetics: The Literary Politics of Afro-American Magazines in the Twentieth Century*. Amherst: University of Massachusetts Press, 1979.
Kornweibel, Theodore, Jr. *No Crystal Stair: Black Life and The Messenger, 1917-1938*. Westport, Conn., 1975.

INDEX SOURCES: None.
LOCATION SOURCES: Schomberg Collection, New York Public Library; Spingarn-Moorland Collection, Howard University, Washington, D.C.; University of New Mexico, Albuquerque.

Publication History

MAGAZINE TITLE AND TITLE CHANGES: *The Bronzeman* (March 1929-October 1933).
VOLUME AND ISSUE DATA: Vols. I-V (March 1929-October 1933), monthly.
PUBLISHER AND PLACE OF PUBLICATION: Fireside Publishing Company, Chicago, Illinois.
EDITOR: Carswell W. Crews (1929-1933).
CIRCULATION: 1,500 estimate.

BROWN AMERICAN, THE

Inasmuch as the *Brown American* was published, beginning in April 1936, under the auspices of the Institute of Race Relations, its emphasis on social affairs becomes clear and justifiable.[1] Yet, editor Joseph Y. Baker seemed to write with his own sense of freedom as he complained about the resurgence of lynching in the United States and the lack of attention shown it by President Roosevelt and equally condemned the Republican party which, during the long years of its reign, had taken no steps to eliminate the practice either. The record would show, he wrote, that what prevented the Congress of the United States from "unsheathing its sword" against lynching was the united efforts of that same willful group which then stood in the way of the passing of an antilynching bill. *Brown American* started as a conservative black magazine in an era in which radical political thought abounded in the nation. Yet, this conservative point of view should not in any way be construed as failure to condemn social abuses at the official level, especially with respect to race relations.[2]

In his "Editor's Page" for the November 1936 issue, Baker referred significantly to the age-old Booker T. Washington-W.E.B. Du Bois dichotomy over the direction of black leadership. While he honored both positions, he synthesized their philosophies concretely when he stated, "Brain and labor must be not only reconciled but coordinated in an ever-moving harmonious power. . . stripped of their trappings, both these theories move toward one goal—a unified America." He then went on to point out that it is particularly significant to look at these two great black leaders at a time when the power of the government was being used to array the two forces against each other, rather than to mold and weld them into a new power. He observed that it was exceedingly pathetic to attempt to imagine what the great Washington would think of the matter of legislating people into idleness and want and "removing forever from the shoulders of labor the dignity with which he longed to clothe it." Obviously, he referred to the New Deal legislation and Roosevelt's approaches to national recovery from the depression.

Baker's own political position became clear as the presidential election of 1936 began. He had promised that his magazine would not take sides in such discussions, but he wrote in his personal column:

> Few people are wild enough to hold that we have a perfect Nation; fewer would approach believing that we have exhausted our rise. There are still problems which must be solved. Capital and Labor must close the void between themselves—but nothing, not even a New Deal, can suffice for the normal growth of human-kind; and surely nothing can be accomplished using the very power of democracy to incite to riot and mutual destruction [of] those forces which have in their loins a Greater America.[3]

With the election over and the inauguration of Roosevelt for his second term imminent, Baker called upon the chief executive to serve the large number of citizens who had voted for him "without discrimination, without fear, and with true statesmanship." True, his plurality in the voting had been extremely impressive and he may very well have interpreted his reelection as a mandate to keep to his guns, yet Roosevelt was president of the people of the United States. Baker could not agree that substitution of vagrancy for labor, as he called the public relief projects, would bear fruit. And he pledged himself to oppose with all his strength anything that "gnaws at the basics of the Nation, for Negroes have too large a stake in it to see it scrapped now."[4]

Baker reminded his audience of his avowed friendliness to American business. He did not believe that government should dominate business to the point of making it crawl and lose its dignity, but he finally realized that American business had done little or nothing to gather unto itself the support of 12 million black Americans, many of whom registered and voted. He argued that Negroes needed jobs *and* representative positions that might be interpreted as tokens of goodwill. Along with doing the dirty work, he wrote, Negroes could support business in its struggle against the growing strength of organized labor. He advised that Negroes should ask for some opportunity to take a hand in the creation and running of things, and that American business would be doing itself a favor if it took a step in their direction. The crux of his argument was contained in his clarion call to the nation: "Let's face the music and build a higher wall against Communism, which is clamoring at our gates."[5]

Baker identified two deplorable problems which to him were vexing the nation and bearing directly upon the interests of the average black citizen. One was the ruthless attack upon the Supreme Court of the United States. The other was the "increasing condonement of lawlessness" he saw in the sit-down strikes. While he agreed that the recent Scottsboro Case, the Texas primary case, and decisions on Jim Crow laws on southern railroads could not endear the Supreme Court to

Negroes, he felt the race should cast its lot against "the looting of halls of justice and the condonement of lawlessness." For although the Negro's plight may be sad, there are ills he never dreamed of in the philosophy of those who would render the Constitution mere scraps of paper. As much as blacks may resent the runabout business traditionally has given them, Baker wrote, the silence in the White House on the sit-down issue represented a calloused indifference that could benefit no one. The choice was clear: The Negro would ally himself with business in order to assist in saving the nation.[6]

As the nation saw its interests rather naturally merge with the Allies who were already fighting World War II in western Europe, Joseph Baker became particularly concerned about the position that Negroes should take with respect to the impending crisis. "We American Negroes are particularly proud of a tradition of which we often boast." That tradition, he continued "has set Negroes aside in times of conflict and danger to this nation as a people who may be trusted, even with the most sacred possessions of the land."[7]

Although he deplored the manner in which the conventional black military units had been mistreated by officialdom in the nation, Baker was confident in his declaration that there was no "Fifth Column" within the Negro race in this nation and that there would be none. But he did remind all America that if "the egg now being laid by those who would divide us ever hatches, the heat that will bring it about will be generated by our own sluggishness."[8] To him, conventional loyalty needed to be buttressed by democratic treatment in the nation in order for Negroes to contribute their not inconsiderable resources to a nation as it prepared to go to war.

When Wendell L. Willkie sought the Republican nomination for president in 1940, Baker addressed an open memorandum to him in which he mentioned that for more than five years *Brown American* had been talking about the need for a strong American businessman to come to the fore and take up the burden of his group and the gauntlet thrown down by the New Deal. Although the Negro race did not support Willkie, they were pleased that he had come forward, seeming to represent a strong adversary for the Democratic party. A fast-maturing race, faced with the end of a devastating depression and disillusioned with upward social and economic movement, would not in any way simply support the conventional labels of the two main parties. It would take more than such jargonistic expressions as "great progress" for the race to support any candidate. Again, despite his rejection of the basic economic philosophy of the New Deal, editor Baker made it clear that he would never recommend a blind political course for the Negro race.

Once the election was over, it became evident that Baker's real political philosophy had ripened during his editorship of the magazine.

Now, our position is not political. We support the Republican Party, as a unit, in the nation because it is our conviction that it represents the link, long lost, between a prosperous, business-like country and one which muddles through. But employment in private industry is no proud possession of anybody. It is a result of an economic theory; it is good practice in the art of conservation and the refusal to waste, willfully and wildly, the nation's resources.[9]

This he considered his pledge of allegiance as the loyal opposition within the nation.

Despite its clear, and real, commitment to an interpretation of national and international events and, to a certain degree, to political advocacy, *Brown American* made an equal appeal to interests of the readers other than the purely political. Its pages included articles on fashion, sport, entertainment, and travel. The *Brown American* had a special interest in black youth and frequently featured profiles of dedicated workers interested in opportunities for work and play for young Negroes in its regular column, "I Work With Youth." It also often reviewed books and plays. Thus, for instance, it lauded the work of Zora Neale Hurston, though its editors seem to have taken greater interest in her as an anthropologist and folklorist than as a novelist; and, despite its decided devotion to preserving democratic institutions, it had nothing but high praise for Richard Wright's *Native Son*. More than once it featured articles on the "Brown Bomber," Joe Louis, and it provided a profile of female sprinter Jean Lane. But the predominant sports interests of the magazine were football and, interestingly, tennis.

As was typical of the eclectic black magazine, *Brown American* cultivated racial pride through profiles of notable black Americans, which appeared as features of such regularly offered columns as "Interesting People," "By Candlelight," "Race," and "America's Men of Goodwill," the last of which paired prose sketches and photographs of notable black and white Americans. Among these profiles were those of composer James A. Bland, author of over 700 ballads including "Carry Me Back to Old Virginny"; Hollywood hat designer Mildred Blount, who designed the hats worn by Vivien Leigh in *Gone With the Wind*; and the "concert Cinderella," soprano Dorothy Maynor.

These profiles complemented the social and political emphasis of the magazine and ran side by side with such feature articles as a three-part study of "The Negro and Democracy," which included as contributors Dr. Frederick D. Patterson, president of Tuskegee Institute, and Dr. Kelly Miller, professor emeritus at Howard University, both of whom shared Baker's moderate political philosophy. Other political articles included two-part studies on "Relief" and "The Negro and the Railroads," and a study that concluded with a cautious and moderate endorsement of socialized medicine.

But try as it might to emulate the *Nation*, the *Brown American* remained a Philadelphian magazine and was bound to present features of prevailingly local interest. Thus, there were articles on Philadelphia black society, vacation spots in Pennsylvania, and working conditions and employment opportunities on the Pennsylvania Railroad. Many of the featured articles were local success stories, such as those of Philadelphia-born singer Vivian Chisolm; Beatrice Bradley Clare, "the first Negro Art Instructor in Philadelphia"; Dr. Boyer, a local physician and tennis afficianado; and George Dickerson, "Dean of Negro Lawyers in Philadelphia."

During the war, which itself had altered the nature of the magazine's appeal in subject matter and the makeup of its readership, *Brown American* shifted its emphasis from entertainment, prosperity, and leisure to leisure and patriotic sacrifice. And with so many men now in Europe or Asia, it increasingly directed its appeal to a feminine audience. It ran an article on women in industry and included more frequent and lengthier sections on homemaking and fashion.

In the final issue of *Brown American*—Summer/Fall 1945—Baker once more called attention to the purposes for which the publication had been launched.

The danger in this Nation now that the hump of the war is over and only the cleaning of the debris remains is a pending revival of the preaching of ways of life foreign to American blue-prints. Whether Russia was, or still is an ally is not pertinent to a discussion as to our reaction to any form of proletarianism. Communism is poison to Negroes and every other minority, whether here, or in Palestine or Rome. And Negroes will do well to fight it.[10]

It was this sort of moderate and clear-eyed consideration of the forces at work at home and abroad, as they related to the future and progress of the Negro, that distinguished *Brown American* from the very beginning. Though nothing in this last issue betrays an awareness that this number, in fact, would end the nine-year life of the magazine, Baker's editorial strikes a note of finality, at once conclusive and hopeful.

But there is a responsibility which cannot be shirked. The best minds in this Nation—and they are by very far the industrial and not the political minds—must make barren the soil upon which the seed of the philosophy of "rolling blood" might fall. They must shape their own destinies and plans, as well as force whatever recalcitrant politicians there may be, into line—; for upon it pivots the future of men and women of all color.[11]

Most of the commentary on the United States in *Brown American* was written by Baker. He was a conservative Republican, one of a vanishing breed among blacks in the Franklin D. Roosevelt era. The journal recorded that perspective of social conditions, politics, religion, and education during that period. Its features on entertainment were almost totally limited to discussions of the black drama. This emphasis makes the *Brown American* a good research tool.

Notes

1. The Institute of Race Relations had been organized and, for three summers before 1936, had met at Swarthmore College in Pennsylvania under the auspices of the American Friends Service Committee. The directors of the institute for 1936 were Dr. Ralph Bunche, then professor of political science at Howard University in Washington, D.C.; and Dr. George E. Simpson, professor of sociology at Temple University in Philadelphia.

2. *Brown American* was superseded by the *Negro Statesman*, the official publication of the National Council of Negro Republicans, issued from Philadelphia, November 1945 to July 1948. *Brown American*'s Republican orientation originally was compatible with the tradition of black Republicanism prevalent among northern urban blacks well into the Roosevelt administration.

3. "Editor's Page," *Brown American* (November 1936): 2.
4. Ibid.
5. "Rededication," *Brown American* (January 1937): 2.
6. Ibid.
7. "This Matter of Law and Order," *Brown American* (May 1937): 2.
8. "Come and Be Counted," *Brown American* (August 1939): 2.
9. "A Memo to Mr. Willkie," *Brown American* (August 1940): 2.
10. "Come Now Let's Face It," *Brown American* (Summer/Fall 1945): 2.
11. Ibid.

Information Sources

BIBLIOGRAPHY:
Buni, Andrew. *Robert L. Vann of the Pittsburgh Courier: Politics and Black Journalism.* Pittsburgh: University of Pittsburgh Press, 1974, pp 208-9.
Strickland, Arvahr E., and Reich, Jerome R. *The Black American Experience: From Reconstruction to the Present.* New York, 1974, pp. 78-87, 142-46.
INDEX SOURCE: *Index to Selected Periodicals Decennial Cumulation 1950-1959.*
LOCATION SOURCES: Library of Congress; some black colleges and universities; Moorland-Spingarn Collection, Howard University, Washington, D.C.; Negro Universities Press Reprint.

Publication History

MAGAZINE TITLE AND TITLE CHANGES: *Brown American* (April 1936-Summer 1945).
VOLUME AND ISSUE DATA: Vols. I-X (April 1936-Summer 1945). Monthly, April 1936-June 1941; "Two Editions in One Cover," January 1942; quarterly, Spring 1942-Summer 1945.
PUBLISHER AND PLACE OF PUBLICATION: National Association of Negroes in American Industry, Philadelphia, Pennsylvania.
EDITOR: Joseph Y. Baker (1936-1945).
CIRCULATION: 5,000.

Thomas Quirk

BROWNIES' BOOK, THE

BROWNIES' BOOK, THE

W.E.B. Du Bois, editor of the *Crisis*,* together with his business manager, Augustus Dill, and literary editor, Jessie Fauset, organized a company in 1920 to publish the *Brownies' Book*, a children's magazine intended to promote universal brotherhood and to reduce the stigma Afro-American children felt because they were black. Du Bois planned to use the publication to make black children familiar with their history and the accomplishments of members of their race, and to teach them "delicately a code of honor and action in their relations with white children." *Brownies'* was popular but short-lived. When it discontinued publication, Du Bois wrote a "Valedictory" in which he recounted the need for literature adapted to children who live in a world of varied races. He had been satisfied with the magazine's success and the enthusiastic reception subscribers had given it. He and his associates had published the journal at their own expense, but the economic depression following the war forced their decision to cease publication. The project was an aesthetic and literary innovation. Moreover, it provided Du Bois one way to pursue his long-standing concern that there was "no place for black children in the world." With this pioneer accomplishment in children's literature, he sought to erase the image of black children that was found in most popular American magazines. He expressed in childlike terms his analyses of current society and advice to black children caught up in the confusing need to develop a viable self-image in a basically hostile environment in which their textbooks, daily newspapers, and national magazines gave them little reason to feel good about themselves and their progenitors.[1] Du Bois fretted over the generation of white children growing up and developing without a notion that there were children of other colors and cultures. For them and for nonwhites around the world, the magazine rendered a valuable service.

Du Bois' editorial persona, "The Crow," gave him a continuous voice for his juvenile audience. He introduced himself in the magazine with the following explanation of his role:

> The crow is black and O so beautiful with dark blues and purples, with little hints of gold in his mighty wings. He flies far above the Earth, looking downward with sharp eyes. What a lot of things he must see and hear and if he could only talk—and lo, *The Brownies' Book* has made him talk to you.[2]

Du Bois respected young people and expected them to be interested in other people in the world and to respect them. He believed, too, that his youthful audiences could understand much of the world about them if someone told them about it in appropriate language. In "As the Crow Flies" he discussed national and international problems. He lamented the absurd loss of life and money the recent war cost, and he ridiculed President Woodrow Wilson for declaring war on Germany and its allies in order to make the world safe for democracy while at the same time he failed to fight for democracy for black Americans at home. Without making a frontal attack on the failure of the European experiment in idealism after the armistice, he discussed the protectorate policy that gave some measure of self-government.

His chief concern was for the absence of democracy among "darker races" of the world, although he favored the Irish in their "troubles" and the South American peasants who stirred to gain some measure of self-determination. The Bolshevik revolution would succeed as a popular uprising, he predicted, and he called the 1920 presidential election in the United States an enigma in democracy, with Socialist candidate Eugene Debs receiving votes while incarcerated in the Atlanta federal penitentiary. California's recently passed law making it illegal for Japanese inhabitants to buy land was incongruous with the American Dream, he wrote; and he held little faith in the League of Nations' ability to promote a truly egalitarian world.

Du Bois' role as "The Crow" allowed him to fly throughout the world and select folktales and legends from Europe, Africa, the Caribbean, and Latin America to help him illustrate the bonds common among "colored peoples" and to expose his young readers to cultures other than their own. Contemporary black creative writers published their works in the journal. Jessie Fauset's fiction appeared in practically every issue. Georgia Douglass Johnson, Joseph Cotter, and Leslie Pinkney Hill contributed poetry. The youthful Langston Hughes published one of his earliest pieces of prose fiction, "Mexican Games," several poems, and a short play. Willis Richardson published several of his plays for children. Black painters designed covers for each issue. "We are going to reserve a very small bit of this magazine for grownups," Du Bois explained when he initiated a column that printed letters from adults. In "The Jury" he published correspondence between young readers and himself, and in "The Judge" he gave advice to readers. He taught Negro history through a series of biographies of black heroic figures. Advertisements were limited to promotion of books, schools, and courses in self-improvement.

Notes

1. The most popular children's magazine, *St. Nicholas*, must have been among the forces that motivated Du Bois to establish *Brownies' Book*. In its July 1920 issue, this magazine pictured school boys marching in the May Day Americanization parade. A small group of children is seen sitting on guns aboard the *Pennsylvania*, flagship of the American fleet, feeling "proud to be nieces and nephews of Uncle Sam." Not one of them is black. An early issue of *Brownies' Book* showed Afro-American Sunday school children marching to protest the lynchings and brutalities taking place in the South. *See* Elinor Desverney Sinnette, "The *Brownies' Book*: A Pioneer Publication for Children," *Freedomways* (Winter 1965): 133-42.

2. "The Crow," *Brownies' Book* (January 1920): 10.

Information Sources

BIBLIOGRAPHY:
Diggs, Irene. "Du Bois and Children." *Phylon*, December 1976, pp. 370-99.
Emanuel, James A. *Langston Hughes*. New York, 1967.
Green, Dan S. "W.E.B. Du Bois: His Journalistic Career." *Negro History Bulletin*, March/April 1977, pp. 672-77.
Sinnette, Eleanor Desverney. *"The Brownie Book." Negro History Bulletin* 18 (December 1968): 8-10.
INDEX SOURCES: None.
LOCATION SOURCES: Fisk University Library; University of Nashville Library; Yale University Library; Moorland-Spingarn Collection, Howard University Library; Library of Congress.

Publication History

MAGAZINE TITLE AND TITLE CHANGES: *The Brownies' Book*.
VOLUME AND ISSUE DATA: Vols. I-II (January 1920-December 1921).
PUBLISHER AND PLACE OF PUBLICATION: Du Bois and Dill, Publishers, New York, New York.
EDITOR: W.E.B. Du Bois (1920-1921).
CIRCULATION: 1,000 highest estimate.

BUFFALO

A special-purpose magazine founded in February 1980 for the black American military professional, *Buffalo* takes its name from the historical involvement of black soldiers in the conquest of the American West. After the Civil War, the Department of the Army added to its regular forces four cavalry regiments, one of which was the Tenth United States Cavalry, a black regiment. Freedmen also served in the Ninth Cavalry and in the newly created Twenty-fourth and Twenty-fifth Infantry divisions. These organizations established a black tradition in American military history. From the late 1860s until the last Indian fight in the West in 1918, against a band of Yaqui, the Tenth Cavalry became known primarily as an Indian-fighting regiment. Headquartered at Fort Riley, Kansas, it was significant in protecting the development of the railroad into the West. The buffalo became the regimental coat of arms. The Indians were the first to use the term "Buffalo Soldiers" to refer to the black soldiers who secured the Union in that part of the country. The name and the symbol have been associated with black soldiers ever since. The Twenty-fourth and Twenty-fifth Infantry divisions have seen action in war and in peace throughout the first half of this century and have been engaged in some of the most thorny race relations known between civilians and soldiers in United States history.[1]

The magazine makes clear its independence of any organized national military establishment. "*Buffalo* is not a publication of the United States Department of Defense, nor are its views and statements representative of that department, or its military departments."[2] Instead, it commemorates black military history with features about personalities, tactics, and events that reflect the role of black Americans in the military posture of the nation. One issue contains a memorial tribute to the recently departed general, Daniel "Chappie" James, celebrated commander in chief of North American Air Defense Command (NORAD) at the time of his death. His long and brilliant career is remembered in connection with United States policy toward blacks in the military. Few Afro-Americans had attended the service academies at the outbreak of World War II. General James was a product of the racially segregated Army Air Corps and its separate training program at Tuskegee Army Air Field. President Harry Truman integrated the armed forces after the close of World War II.

The saga of the "Buffalo Soldiers" is told in glowing detail as a part of the romance of the American westward movement and the little-known role blacks played in that expansion. "Brown Eyes with Earth-Shine," in the same issue, reports on the three black members of one of NASA's astronaut teams. The orientation toward black history in the magazine also extends to features about black cowboys in the frontier West and well-documented articles about early black civilizations in the Americas before the voyages of Columbus.

Carl Rowan, a noteworthy American journalist and diplomat, is director of editorial services for the journal. Occasionally he writes a column of personal reminiscences, like "Memories of a Marvelous Teacher," a tribute to Bessie Taylor Gwynn, who taught him literature, history, and "several other subjects" when he was a student in a little "Jim Crow high school in McMinnville, Tennessee, four decades ago."

William Raspberry, a syndicated black newspaper columnist like Rowan, writes editorials from time to time. He is especially interested in the problems of inner-city black schools and wrote in one editorial asking for understanding, even among blacks, for problems the school-age young person faces in current society. His advice in this respect includes a point of emphasis.

We look at our children and see potential, and we see to it that that potential is developed—not by railing against racism but by giving our children the resources to combat it. Of course they will be confronted with racism, we'll tell them, but that doesn't mean that they should give up, only that they must try twice as hard, be twice as good.[3]

Raspberry's counsel comports well with the vitality of the magazine. For while it is published for the military black professional, it falls into the category of most black journals. It celebrates the accomplishments of black persons—primarily those associated with the military—and keeps readers abreast of news about personalities and events that fall within its focus.

Notes

1. One of the most controversial events in American history involving the Twenty-fifth Infantry division in civilian conflict can be found in Ann J. Lane, *The Brownsville Affair: National Crisis and Black Reaction* (Port Washington, N.Y., 1971).
2. *Buffalo* (March 1981): frontispiece.
3. *Buffalo* (March 1981): 2.

Information Sources

BIBLIOGRAPHY:
Carroll, John M., ed. *The Black Military Experience in the American West.* New York, 1971, pp. 173-79.
Katz, William Loren. *The Black West: A Documentary and Pictorial History.* New York, 1971, pp. 199-243.
Strickland, Arvarh E., and Reich, Jerome R. *The Black American Experience: Reconstruction to the Present.* New York, 1974, pp. 105-6.
INDEX SOURCES: None.
LOCATION SOURCES: Many college and university libraries.

Publication History

MAGAZINE TITLE AND TITLE CHANGES: *Buffalo* (February 1980-).
VOLUME AND ISSUE DATA: Vol. I- (February 1980-), monthly.
PUBLISHER AND PLACE OF PUBLICATION: Buffalo Publishing Company, Fayettesville, North Carolina.
EDITOR: Ariel P. Wiley (1980-).
CIRCULATION: 1,500.

C

CALLALOO: A BLACK SOUTH JOURNAL OF ARTS AND LETTERS

When *Callaloo* first appeared in 1977, issued by the Department of English at the University of Kentucky, one of its coeditors wrote that it was coming into being at the time of the demise of *Black World** and many of the community-based literary magazines that sprang up in the late 1960s and early 1970s. A year later, Editor in Chief Charles H. Rowell reported on the life of *Callaloo* during that first year and the purpose it planned to continue to serve.

> But after the publication of *Callaloo* No. 1, we encountered the inevitable problem: inadequate money to finance the publication of the second and third issues planned for 1977. Neither sales from the first issue nor contributions from the community produced sufficient income for additional issues. Yet during this one year period, we have been able to acquire a substantial sum of money from individual contributors and from two large financial supporters to continue this non-profit community project.
>
> As the first issue indicated, *Callaloo* is an independent organ of the Black South community. Although we have accepted generous financial support for the journal from the University of Kentucky and the Coordinating Council of Literary Magazines, *Callaloo* will remain independent, free of editorial control. We have preserved this freedom in order to remain true to the original purpose of the journal.
>
> The central purpose of *Callaloo* is to present, without outside control, the creative writing, critical thought, and visual arts of the Black South, a community whose creativity has been grossly neglected. Historians of Black America have carefully documented the economic, political, and social conditions which led to the exodus from the South. They have also recorded the various results of that second diaspora. What has been ignored

is the Southern experience which served as the origin of Afro-American culture. It was in the South thàt the majority of African slaves, while retaining and adapting remnants of African culture, created a new Black culture. It was only then that the new culture was transported North and West. In our efforts to publish creative and critical works by Black Southerners, we hope to remain faithful to that reality and history.[1]

Yet, *Callaloo* was not a regional journal. It published works of black writers and visual artists from regions of the United States other than the South and from other countries. Its editors felt that black southerners faced special publishing problems which could stifle their imaginations without outlets such as *Callaloo*.

The dearth of media for artistic expression the editors described brought a wide variety of poems, short stories, and interviews to the journal. Inasmuch as the other black little magazines had reached their nadir, any new publication attracted the attention of creative writers and students of the history and criticism of black American writing. Accordingly, *Callaloo* soon enjoyed popularity as a new independent organ of the black southern community.

One of its most important issues was devoted entirely to the works of Ernest J. Gaines, a highly productive, contemporary American black writer.[2] The special Gaines issue contains Isaac J. Black's poem, "When I Read Gaines"; Michael S. Harper's poem "Peace on Earth," inspired by a line from one of Gaines' poems; an excerpt from a novel that Gaines was writing at the time with the working title, "The Revenge of Old Men"; an interview Gaines gave at Louisiana's Southern University about his popular *Autobiography of Miss Jane Pittman*; another interview with Gaines conducted by editor Charles H. Rowell, entitled "This Louisiana Thing That Drives Me"; "Home," a photo essay by Gaines that presents photographs of places in rural Louisiana that influenced the author and his work. Alvin Aubert, founder and editor of *Obsidian*, another black literary journal, wrote "Ernest J. Gaines' Truly Tragic Mulatto." John Wideman, himself a novelist and critic, wrote *"Of Love and Dust*: A Reconsideration" which considered that novel's plot to lie at the center of the Afro-American tradition. Other critical articles on Gaines' work included *"Jane Pittman* and the Oral Tradition," "Scene and Life Cycle in Ernest Gaines' *Bloodline*," and "Bayonne or the Yoknapatawpha of Ernest Gaines," originally published in French in *Recherches Anglaises et Américaines*. Michel Fabre, the celebrated critic who wrote about the works of black American writers, was author of that essay. "Ernest J. Gaines: A Checklist, 1964-1978" is an invaluable listing of bibliographies, interviews, and biographical and critical essays about the prolific American writer. The Ernest J. Gaines special issue is clearly the most valuable number of *Callaloo*.

The journal has continued to explore writing by and about southern blacks and has added some studies in folklore that present well the literature and photography of the region.

Notes

1. "Editor's Notes," *Callaloo* 3 (February 1978): 4.
2. Ernest J. Gaines was born in Oscar, Louisiana, 15 January 1933. He attended San Francisco State College and Stanford University in the late 1950s. In addition to numerous short stories and novellas which have appeared in magazines, he has published several novels that have gained wide recognition, including *Catherine Carmier* (1964); *Of Love and Dust* (1967); *Bloodline* (1968); *Long Day in November* (1971); and *Autobiography of Miss Jane Pittman* (1971).

Information Sources

BIBLIOGRAPHY:
Davis, Arthur P., and Redding, Saunders. *Cavalcade: Negro American Writing From 1760 to the Present.* Boston: Houghton Mifflin Company, 1971, p. 704.
Shockley, Ann Allen, and Chandler, Sue P. *Living Black American Authors: A Biographical Directory.* New York: R. R. Bowker Company, 1973, p. 53.
INDEX SOURCES: *American Literature*; *Obsidian*.
LOCATION SOURCES: Major university libraries.

Publication History

MAGAZINE TITLE AND TITLE CHANGES: *Callaloo: A Black South Journal of Arts and Letters.* (January 1977-).
VOLUME AND ISSUE DATA: Vols. I-IV (January 1977 to present), triannual: February, May, October.
PUBLISHER AND PLACE OF PUBLICATION: Callaloo/Charles H. Rowell. Department of English, University of Kentucky, Lexington, Kentucky.
EDITOR: Charles H. Rowell (1977-).
CIRCULATION: 500.

CHALLENGE/NEW CHALLENGE

Dorothy West intended her new magazine, *Challenge*, to recapture in the mid 1930s the vitality that had characterized Afro-American writing during the Harlem Renaissance but had declined perceptibly during the depression. The ambitious editor hoped to arouse anew the best-known voices that had dominated the post-World War I years and to foster the development of new young black voices she believed were studying and writing in black colleges. She hoped to establish a "new movement" in Afro-American writing. Name writers responded to her call, and some post-Renaissance works appeared in *Challenge*. But West never found the wealth of high quality writing she expected from college students, and the old names could hardly mount a new renaissance. Significantly, the race, the nation, and large parts of the world were leaning toward a proletarian artistic view West never understood. Under pressure from critics who ridiculed her "pale pink" tone in *Challenge*, in 1937 West added Richard Wright as associate editor and changed the journal's name to *New Challenge*. The experiment failed miserably and publication was discontinued after one issue. Yet, the "little magazine" is a part of the history of literary journalism in the United States, for West was able to attract some of the most prominent black writers to her project, and *New Challenge* did publish Richard Wright's often-discussed "Blueprint for Negro Writing."

James Weldon Johnson, then creative writing professor at Fisk University, wrote the foreword to the first issue of *Challenge*. In it he praised black writers for the force he believed they could bring to the struggle to break down and wear away the stereotyped ideas about the Negro, creating enlightened opinion about the race. He wrote that sincere artists could advance this aspiration without resorting to propaganda and cheap applause. "It seems to me that the greatest lack of our younger writers is not talent or ability, but persistent and intelligent industry."[1] West and Johnson believed the passing of the Harlem Renaissance did not necessarily signal the decline of talent among Negro writers, but that a new magazine would provide a renewal of their talent and encourage their output.

For several issues of the journal, their faith seemed justified. Pauli Marray, Countee Cullen, Harry T. Burleigh, Arna Bontemps, Helene Johnson, and Langston Hughes contributed to the March 1934 number. The beginning was auspicious, particularly with respect to the response received from some of the most prominent black writers, but the second issue did not appear until September 1934. West explained that the magazine had become a quarterly with that issue, rather than the monthly she had planned. She said that the writing she received for publication was disappointingly poor. Admitting embarrassment, she had to fall back on the "tried and true voices." Arna Bontemps wrote that he was not surprised that the outpouring from the younger writers was not coming forth. "We're not washed up by a jugful," he continued. "It is a pretty pose, this attitude about 'old before our time.' I will not have it." He said he believed the "promised land" for Afro-American literature lay ahead.[2] In the same vein, Carl Van Vechten criticized the claim that the "Renaissance" that had been launched so bravely had not continued its voyage "on the seas of art as triumphantly as might have been wished." To him, the Negro of 1934 was "on a much more solid base as an artist and as a social individual" than he was in the mid twenties. James Weldon Johnson's *Along This Way*, Langston Hughes' *The Ways of White Folks*, and Zora Neale Hurston's *Jonah's Gourd Vine* proved his conclusion, he wrote.

Apparently, although enough satisfactory writing for a new journal did appear, a different problem arose. West wrote about it in the January 1936 issue.

> Somebody asked us why *Challenge* was for the most part so pale pink. We said because the few red articles we did receive were not literature. We care a lot about style. And we think a message is doubly effective when

effectively written without bombast or bad spelling.... We would like to print more articles and stories of protest. We have daily contact with the underprivileged. We know their suffering and soul weariness. They have only the meager bread and meat of the dole, and that will not fail their failing spirits. Yet the bourgeois youth on the southern campus, who should be conscious of these things, is joining a fraternity instead of the brotherhood of serious minds. Leadership of the literate is infinitely preferable to the blind leadership of the blind.[3]

This was a strong statement for West and an indication of her readiness to move from the "integrationist" stance of the older black journals toward an activist dimension to black writing. Two issues later, West wrote that she wanted to publish a "progressive magazine"; that she had no intention of dictating to writers the style, choice of subject, or content of works they should submit for consideration for *Challenge*. Her ambivalent response to the prodding she was getting from forces she did not understand well or accept shows in her complaint that she "would defeat the purpose of the magazine, mainly to foster developing talents, if we rejected those early gropings toward style, social consciousness and adulthood." She had been disappointed with the poor quality of writing received from college students but chose to believe the letters she had sent to English-department heads had never reached the students. Her interest had turned, she wrote, to a young Chicago group of writers that was holding regular meetings to read and discuss their writing. When she learned that these writers had attacked the lack of vitality in *Challenge* she offered them a special section in a forthcoming issue that might show how the magazine had failed.

That special edition appeared in the fall of 1937 under the title *New Challenge*, with Marian Minus as one of its editors and Richard Wright as associate editor. Editorial comment held that the "new" magazine wished to transcend its "pale pink" hue while not attempting to "restage the 'revolt' and 'renaissance' which grew unsteadily upon false foundations 10 years ago." For a literary movement among Negroes should first of all be built upon the writer's placing his material in the proper perspective with regard to the life of the Negro masses. This focused editorial policy, compatible with the Chicago school that had grown up around the John Reed clubs, led West to write: "We want to indicate, through examples in our pages, the great fertility of folk material as a source of creative material." She wanted *New Challenge* to provide a medium of literary expression for all writers "who realized the present need for the realistic depiction of life through the short focus of social consciousness." She went so far as to write that "Negro writers themselves and the audience which they reach must be reminded, and in many instances taught, that writing should not be *in vacuo*, but placed within a definite social context." The special issue that was fashioned to represent these new editorial directions contained short stories written by Norman MacLeod, Benjamin Appel, Vlademar Hill, George B. Linn, and Clarence Hill.

Poetry was contributed by Frank Marshall Davis and Margaret Walker. Allyn Keith's article, "A Note on Negro Nationalism," and Eugene Holmes' essay, "Problems Facing the Negro Writer Today," implemented parts of the new purpose.

Richard Wright's "Blueprint for Negro Writing," which was included in that issue, represents the most significant article that appeared during the three years of the magazine's publication. Some of Wright's revolutionary poetry had by this time already been published in *Left Front, The Anvil, New Masses, Midland Left, International Literature*, and *Partisan Review*. He had already published some short fiction. He wrote in an issue of *Daily Worker* to elaborate upon the purposes of *New Challenge*, noting that thousands of Negro workers, students, and intellectuals whose lives had been touched by recent social and economic changes constituted the new audience young writers were aiming to mold and direct, and that they would contradict the Harlem school of expression, exploited by publishing for the jaded appetites of New York bohemians. He wrote that in Washington, Memphis, and Detroit organizations were emerging to organize young writers on a plan similar to the purpose and structure of John Reed clubs which had influenced many young white writers within the recent past. Writers in the new clubs would be black, but Wright predicted whites would join them in producing literature that would deal with minority themes and conditions of life.[4]

West tried to modify her precarious magazine into a proletarian organ. She believed she was following the wave of the future in Afro-American writing. With Richard Wright, the brightest name on the horizon of developing black writers, as her associate editor, her venture seemed secure. But it failed and so did her commitment to providing rising young black writers a journal in which they could publish their poetry and fiction. She learned, too, that mere theories of aesthetics could not sustain a black literary magazine. *New Challenge* did, however, foreshadow the fusion between art and politics that would find stronger expression in *Black World** and similar journals a generation later.

Notes

1. *Challenge* (March 1934): frontispiece.
2. "Dear Reader," Ibid., p. 39.
3. *Challenge* (January 1936): 38.
4. "Blueprint for Negro Writing," *New Challenge* (Fall 1937): 53-64.

Information Sources

BIBLIOGRAPHY:

Cruse, Harold. *The Crisis of the Negro Intellectual*. New York, 1968.

Daniel, Walter C. "*Challenge Magazine*: An Experiment That Failed." *College Language Association Journal*, June 1976, pp. 494-503.

Johnson, Abby Arthur, and Johnson, Ronald Maberry. *Propaganda and Aesthetics: The Literary Politics of Afro-American Magazines in the Twentieth Century*. Amherst: University of Massachusetts Press, 1979.

INDEX SOURCES: None.
LOCATION SOURCE: Negro Universities Press.

Publication History

MAGAZINE TITLE AND TITLE CHANGES: *Challenge* (March 1934-? 1937); *New Challenge* (Fall 1937).
VOLUME AND ISSUE DATA: Vols. I-II; monthly, irregular.
PUBLISHER AND PLACE OF PUBLICATION: Dorothy West, Boston, Mass.
EDITORS: *Challenge*: Dorothy West (1934-1937); *New Challenge*: Dorothy West and Marian Minus; Richard Wright, associate editor. (Fall 1937.)
CIRCULATION: 500 highest estimate.

CHAMPION MAGAZINE: A MONTHLY SURVEY OF NEGRO ACHIEVEMENT

Fenton Johnson, editor and founder of *Champion Magazine*, was in his late twenties when he began publishing the journal. He had been educated in the public schools of his native Chicago and at the University of Chicago and Northwestern University. He had received some recognition for his poetry, much of which he had published himself and some of which had appeared in little magazines. After having taught school in the South for a few years, Johnson returned to Chicago to make his living with his literary and publishing endeavors. *Champion Magazine*, which first appeared in September 1916, was the most ambitious of his several projects and deserves more attention than it has received from students of Afro-American letters.[1]

In the premier number of *Champion*, Johnson wrote that his journal had been born "of the desire to serve a struggling race impartially" and "to come out of the wilderness with the aim to make racial life during the twentieth century a life worth living." He wrote that America could not accomplish her purpose so long as her people were unassimilated. Yet he believed that the Negro, due to a prejudice born of politics and the spirit of slavery, had remained alien in his native land. And he would remain so as long as his problems were placed in the hands of the propagandists. The great mission, then, of his magazine would be reconciliation of the races. He would seek to promote a better feeling between white and black Americans and to lift up the spirit of the Negro so he might be able to realize that he was a force in world achievement. *Champion*, Johnson promised, "will do all in its power to impress upon the world that it is not a disgrace to be a Negro, but a privilege."[2] In "A Confidential Talk" in the same issue, Johnson wrote that he wanted *Champion* to be a magazine for the masses "for the masses, after all, have the greatest intelligence."[3]

The reconciliation of the races that Johnson sought and the reference to propagandists may well have been his way of referring to the crossroad black Americans had reached with the recent death of Booker T. Washington, principal of Tuskegee Institute in Alabama and acknowledged leader of one faction of Negroes. He was considered an "accommodationist" by "radicals" who agitated for full citizenship at the turn of the century and the period of fast-vanishing civil rights that had been won by the Fourteenth and Fifteenth amendments to the Constitution. The nation was, indeed, watching closely to see who would succeed Washington at Tuskegee and by extension take on his leadership position philosophically and economically.

Appropriately, then, from the black perspective the inauguration of Robert Russa Moton as Washington's successor at Tuskegee was a major news event, and *Champion* covered the ceremonies. Its reporter was copious in his praise of Washington and the monument to him that was the institute. "The beauty and magnitude of the place cannot be imagined. Tuskegee, like the Niagara Falls, the Grand Canyons of Colorado and the Desert of Sahara must be seen; it cannot be told."[4] Moton, the story continued, put stress on the "Tuskegee Spirit" in his inaugural address. Part of it set forth the direction the new principal would take.

If we are to be true to the great and sacred trust, if we are to carry out the aims and purposes of Booker T. Washington, the founder of this institution, we must each cherish and maintain the spirit which has always permeated the life and work of this school—the spirit of self-forgetfulness—the spirit of service and sacrifice—the Tuskegee spirit— the spirit of cooperation and consecration. It is only in this spirit that Tuskegee Normal and Industrial Institute can continue to render service to the Negro, to this state, and to this nation.[5]

In his editorial on Moton at Tuskegee, Johnson wrote that the eyes and ears of the world were turned upon the new principal. "What will he do now that he has control of the Booker T. Washington machine?" he asked. And he answered his own question by stating that he believed Moton would be true to the trust placed in him. True, he was not "the genius Washington was," but he possessed the insight of one who could profit from the mistakes of others. The editor's principal message in the Moton matter seemed to be that the industrial South could not triumph in an atmosphere of racial conflict. "The world at large desires to see Mr. Moton practice the doctrine that made Booker T. Washington great: 'I will let no man drag me down by making me hate him,'" the editorial concluded.[6]

Racial harmony in the South was an essential part of Johnson's social and economic philosophy. Writing on the Negro exodus north, he pointed out that race problems followed Negroes to the urban North. They were forced to compete with white unskilled labor in either part of the nation. The war was responsible for this social innovation. And yet the world moved on and irresponsible elements of the South continued lynching and all the other evils of propaganda. He welcomed the exodus of Negroes so long as they could become a part of a trained labor force. Otherwise, he saw little opportunity to avoid a critical racial confrontation over menial jobs that paid little to black or white workers.

In other editorials, Johnson advocated respect for Negroes, abolition of lynching, and encouraged the racial movements established by the NAACP and the National Urban League. He particularly praised the work and the philosophy of the National Negro Business League that had been founded in the North by Washington.

Champion devoted a full page of each issue to Negro theatrical and sports news and personalities. It also contained "Paste Pot and Shears," a feature that reprinted portions of editorials from numbers of daily newspapers. Himself a poet who had produced no small amount of published works, Johnson published creative writing in his journal, including some of his own. He was able to get important black public figures to contribute articles for his periodical, including Benjamin Brawley and Joseph S. Cotter, early black creative writers, and such well-known scholars as Richard Greener and William Pickens. Marcus Garvey, later known for his Negro improvement association, wrote two articles for *Champion* before his name became a household word in Harlem.

Upon the occasion of the anniversary of the hundredth anniversary of the birth of Frederick Douglass, Johnson wrote a tribute that expressed his own view of American Negro leadership.

Douglass's greatness lay in the force that he gave to his convictions and his keen insight into the future needs of his people. Other men of color fought for abolition of slavery; other men of African descent were political leaders during the era of Reconstruction; but none moulded so successfully his ideals into the American conception of racial justice as this former Maryland slave. Turner and Vesey were martyrs, but their martyrdom did little to shake the Gibraltar of slavery; Redmond and Ward were brilliant agitators, but their agitation compared to the work of Douglass was as the dashing of waves against rocks. To him of all men, save Charles Sumner and Thaddeus Stevens, is due the credit of the Fifteenth Amendment, which gave the emancipated black the political right to defend his liberty. . . . He was the first among us to conceive the idea of equal rights for all races; he anticipated Booker T. Washington on the subject of industrial education by at least thirty years; he stemmed a Negro exodus that would have been as far-reaching as the exodus of today by his conservative estimate of the best element in the South. . . . We cannot call him a radical. He was eloquent.[7]

Unfortunately, *Champion Magazine* survived for less than a calendar year. It was one of the best edited of the many black journals that found too little financial support to continue publication. Johnson's sound education and his writing skill made the magazine unusual among its contemporaries, but the time was not propitious for a self-sustaining black magazine in the United States.

Notes

1. Fenton Johnson (1888-1958) is best known for his poetry, although he is considered a minor Afro-American poet. James Weldon Johnson included Fenton Johnson's poetry in his first anthology of Negro poets because he was "one of the first Negro revolutionary poets"—one of that group who used dialect and, at the same time, threw over the traditions of American poetry to work in the "new" medium. At the age of nineteen he had already had several of his plays performed in Chicago's Pekin Theatre. The *Crisis** published several of his short stories. After the failure of *Champion Magazine*, Johnson published and edited the *Favorite Magazine* briefly.
2. "The Editor's Blue Pencil," *Champion Magazine* (September 1916): 3.
3. *Champion Magazine* (September 1916): 2.
4. John W. Felton, "The Inauguration of Major Robert R. Moton," *Champion Magazine* (September 1916): 5.
5. Ibid.
6. "Robert Russa Moton," *Champion Magazine* (September 1916): 6.
7. "The Editor's Blue Pencil: Frederick Douglass—One Hundred Years Ago," *Champion Magazine* (February 1917): 3.

Information Sources

BIBLIOGRAPHY:
Huggins, Nathan Irvin. *Voices from the Harlem Renaissance*. New York, 1976, p. 324.
Peplow, Michael W., and Davis, Arthur P. *The New Negro Renaissance: An Anthology*. New York, 1975, p. 526.
Wagner, Jean. *Black Poets of the United States from Paul Laurence Dunbar to Langston Hughes*. Urbana: University of Illinois Press, 1973, pp. 179-83.
INDEX SOURCES: None.
LOCATION SOURCES: Fisk University; Schomberg Collection, New York Public Library.

Publication History

MAGAZINE TITLE AND TITLE CHANGES: *Champion Magazine: A Monthly Survey of Negro Achievement*.
VOLUME AND ISSUE DATA: Vol. I, Nos. 1-8 (September 1916-April 1917), monthly.
PUBLISHER AND PLACE OF PUBLICATION: Champion Magazine Publishing Company, Chicago, Illinois.
EDITOR: Fenton Johnson (1916-1917).
CIRCULATION: 1,000 estimate.

Charles E. Holmes

COLLEGE LANGUAGE ASSOCIATION JOURNAL

Therman B. O'Daniel, the first editor of the *College Language Association* (*CLA*) *Journal*, wrote in the November 1957 inaugural number that the journal "was founded in order to provide another medium of scholarly expression for members of the College Language Association, and to provide the same expression outlet for other persons with similar scholarly interests, who, though not members of the Association, might wish, from time to time, to make acceptable contributions to its official publication."[1] O'Daniel emphasized the journal's openness. It would not be limited or restricted by period, genre, or topic. Acceptable creative materials were solicited. In a general sense the *CLA Journal* adopted the following format: six to eight articles on widely mixed literary topics; book reviews limited to 500 words; a section entitled "CLA News," which included information about member institutions and individual members of the association; and a list of the CLA officers and committee members. The *CLA Journal* also lists its membership annually, along with an index to each volume. This format has remained consistent throughout the twenty-four year history of the journal. One item of particular interest in the first issue is an announcement of the annual original short story and poetry contest for college students and teachers.

Perhaps the most revealing statements concerning the birth of the *CLA Journal* come in the last paragraph of Professor O'Daniel's position paper. "The journal represents the third stage in the evolution of an official CLA publication. It began with a mimeographed newsletter, evolved into a printed bulletin, and now is a full-fledged periodical." In order to succeed, Professor O'Daniel noted three criteria: "A trial run in order to work the 'kinks' out of its joints; a philanthropic angle to free it from worry about that mundane commodity called money; and the courage to face both the pleasant possibility of enjoying a long *run*, and the embarrassing possibility of being an overnight *flop*." The "kinks" were worked out since there were very few. The format required advanced planning, at which Professor O'Daniel was most adept, and it was his leadership that established the excellence of the journal. Obviously, the journal has enjoyed a long run, and it is financially solvent as it was in the beginning. This is a remarkable feat, since most of the revenues involved in the publication of the *CLA Journal* are generated from CLA membership, limited to less than 250 persons.

The first issue was indeed crucial since there was some risk involved with the venture. Besides the essay by Professor O'Daniel entitled "The *CLA Journal*," seven other articles appeared. Two book reviews, the CLA news section, the CLA standing committees, and the list of officers of the College Language Association completed the contents. The list of contributors is revealing. Blyden Jackson, Herman H. Long, and James W. Byrd were all recognized as leading scholars, and each added authenticity to the fledgling journal. Professor Byrd's contribution was especially significant. Entitled "Stereotypes of White Characters in Early Negro Novels," the article covered new ground and was especially appealing to white scholars since Professor Byrd chose to emphasize the other side of stereotyping by race. It is now apparent that one major criterion for publication in the *CLA Journal* is objective scholarship. Great pains were taken to avoid theses ridden and racist articles. Although never explicitly stated, a check of subsequent issues through 1980 substantiates this view. Very few Afro-American periodicals can make the same claim.

The published minutes of the 1960 CLA business meeting indicate the growth of the journal and its widening prestige.[2] The 1961 budget called for one additional issue with a fourth to follow if it were deemed financially possible. In celebration of its tenth anniversary, the *CLA Journal* became a quarterly publication with its September 1966 issue. The new number was issued in June.

The editorial stance of the journal has remained consistent, a reflection of the original stated mission of the *CLA* editorial board and the firm tenure of editor O'Daniel. Rather than adopting any overt political or philosophical stance, the journal carefully adheres to academic standards for scholarly publications. If anything, the *CLA Journal* has grown increasingly more scholarly, covering the widest possible range of topics in world and American literature. The only noticeable trend, which is slight indeed, has been an emphasis on Afro-American literature beginning in the mid 1960s, peaking in the mid 1970s, and gradually lessening at the present time. This trend can be accounted for by the interest in such studies. During this period of concern for and about Afro-American literature, the *CLA Journal* emerged as the leading scholarly periodical controlled and sponsored in the main by Afro-American academicians. Moreover, many of the articles on Afro-American literature published by the journal served to resurrect interest in certain neglected writers, including Rudolph Fisher, Zora Neale Hurston, Willard Motley, and Charles W. Chesnutt.[3]

The single most significant addition to the original format of the *CLA Journal* has been the inclusion of an annual bibliography of Afro-American, African, and Caribbean literature. This bibliography, limited to sources published in English, was begun in 1976. The first one was compiled by Vattel Rose, Jennifer Jordan, Virginia Barrett, Dorothy Evans, Enid Bogle, Lorraine Henry, and Leota Lawrence. Although not comprehensive, the bibliography is unique and a welcome addition to the journal.

Ten categories are used in the bibliography, including: (1) Anthologies and Collections, (2) Autobiography and Biography, (3) Bibliographies, Indexes, and Checklists, (4) Drama, (5) Faction, (6) Fiction, (7) Folklore, (8) General Literary Criticism and History, (9) Poetry, and (10) Miscellaneous. Another helpful aspect of the bibliography is the annotation of material that is not self-explanatory.

The *CLA Journal* enjoys a continued growth and remains the flagship of scholarly Afro-American journals. Its editorial policy has continued the same under the leadership of editor Edward A. Jones of Morehouse College, beginning in 1978. Its circulation remains one of the indicators of its influence.

Notes

1. *College Language Association Journal* 1 (November 1957): 1.
2. "Second Business Session," *CLA Journal* 4 (September 1960): 75.
3. See *CLA Journal* 9 (September 1965) for the beginning of this development.

Information Sources

INDEX SOURCES: *Humanities Index*; *PMLA Bibliography*.
LOCATION SOURCES: Most college and university libraries.

Publication History

MAGAZINE TITLE AND TITLE CHANGES: *College Language Association Journal*
(November 1957 to present).
VOLUME AND ISSUE DATA: Vols. I- (November 1957 to present), quarterly.
PUBLISHER AND PLACE OF PUBLICATION: Morehouse College, Atlanta, Georgia.
EDITORS: Therman B. O'Daniel (November 1957-March 1978); Edward A. Jones (June
1978-).
CIRCULATION: 5,000.

Brian Joseph Benson

COLORED AMERICAN

Although some black journals were launched during the nineteenth century,
Colored American, first issued in May 1900 from Boston, is usually considered
the first black "general purpose" magazine. It followed the appearance of *Mun-
sey's, McClure's,* and *Cosmopolitan,* which presented inexpensive alternatives
to the so-called quality periodicals—*Atlantic Monthly, Harper's Magazine, Century,* and *Scribner's.* More and more Americans were becoming literate, and the
new journals were priced within reach of the mass of citizens. The movement
toward inexpensive alternative magazines fired the imagination and the ambition
of Walter W. Wallace, a young black man who had migrated from Virginia to
Boston. Three black friends—H. A. Fortune, Jessie Watkins, and Peter B.
Gibson—joined Wallace in a partnership that led them to establish the publishing
firm that issued *Colored American.* Their journal would take a new path for
black journalism. It would combine the passion of Frederick Douglass type
pre-Emancipation militancy, creative writing, news about blacks and their institutions, and the strength of commercial advertisement to bring to the nation an
opportunity to know about the activities and opinions of the twentieth-century
Afro-American.

Colored American provides a significant chronicle of the black perspective on
the national posture during most of the first decade of the new century. Its first
issue promised a publication of merit for every Negro family that would be "a
credit to the present and future generations." It would be devoted to the "higher
culture of religion, literature, science, music and art of the Negro universally,"
and would act as a stimulus to old and young; "the old to higher achievements,
the young to emulate their example." The editorial and publishers' announcement stated that "American citizens of color have long realized that for them

there exists no monthly magazine, distinctly devoted to their interest and to the development of Afro-American art and literature." Some American magazines had been liberal in their kindly treatment of certain Negro individuals and subjects, but as a rule they failed to sufficiently recognize Negro efforts, hopes, and aspirations. *Colored American* would meet this need and offer the race a medium through which it could demonstrate its ability and tastes in fiction, poetry, and art, as well as historical, social, and economic literature. Above all, the magazine would aspire to develop and intensify the bonds of that racial brotherhood "which alone can enable the people to assert their racial rights as men and demand their privileges as citizens." No philanthropic, political, sectarian, or denominational "clique" would in any way influence, direct, or control the management of the magazine. No editor in chief was listed regularly on the masthead during its first years, although Pauline Hopkins is often considered to have served that purpose.[1]

Colored American's most compelling purpose grew from the nation's new social direction as the South attempted to "crush the manhood and self-concept out of the Negro"; to "smile upon the servile, fawning, cowardly and sycophantic Negro and frown upon the brave, manly, and aggressive Negro." The journal's editorials held that the South was bent upon a policy of extermination or subjugation of the black American. Illustrations pointed to the 1,500 blacks lynched between 1890 and 1900, and the failure of the Supreme Court to support the spirit of the Fourteenth and Fifteenth amendments to the Constitution. A remedy for this intolerable national direction lay in the steady growth in number and strength of Afro-American newspapers and magazines. To *Colored American*'s editors, the parallel growth in moral, intellectual, and material development of 10 million black Americans made it absolutely necessary for them to create their own channels of news and opinion. American schools and colleges were "ceaselessly sending out men and women prepared for the work of intelligently handling the ethical, economic, civic, literary, scientific, and religious questions demanded by the enlarged and enlarging intelligence of the masses." Already a literary cult existed within the race. Some representatives, such as Booker T. Washington, Paul Laurence Dunbar, W.E.B. Du Bois, and Charles W. Chesnutt, enjoyed national and international reputations. Moreover, they compared favorably in moral force and literary ability with the best white writers the South had produced since the war. Accordingly, there was every justification and necessity for a journal like *Colored American*.[2]

Throughout its life, the journal carried out its stated purposes. Most popular black American scholars and public figures contributed articles. Editorials, news items, and opinion essays covered a wide range of subjects: education, national politics, jim crow practices, socialism, black journalism, religion, business, labor, and entertainment. All these subjects reflected a black viewpoint.

Despite emphasis current scholarship has placed on *Colored American* as part of Booker T. Washington's public relations empire, through which he allegedly promoted industrial education at the expense of higher education and directed "assimilationist" politics for black Americans, the magazine reflects a broad range of Afro-American thinking. George Washington Forbes, coeditor of the *Boston Guardian*, Monroe Trotter's vigorously anti-Washington weekly newspaper, attacked Washington's approach to black social and political advancement in an early issue. During most of its first four years, *Colored American* tended to praise black leaders. It supported economic development and patronized black businesses. It was, itself, a black enterprise doing business as the Colored Co-Operative Publishing Company, which issued the journal and published some books, including Pauline Hopkins' *Contending Forces*. But the company failed, and its founders sold it for debt to Colonel William H. Dupress, a black Bostonian of means. According to an unsigned article in the *Crisis*, Hopkins was not "conciliatory" enough to survive the change in ownership. She had been too militant an editor.

Booker T. Washington was said to have obtained a controlling interest in *Colored American* at this time. Its editorial offices were moved from Boston to New York in 1904, and Fred R. Moore, a Washington colleague who had become editor and publisher of the *New York Age* newspaper, was made editor and publisher of *Colored American*.[3] The next year, Moore wrote that the financial status of the journal had become precarious in Boston largely because of mismanagement by the original owners. To those persons who criticized the move from Boston and the change of ownership, Moore replied that "this particular class gave small support when the property was in Boston and its success is certainly not dependent upon them now." He said that a more broadminded clientele had come to the journal in New York, and he predicted that the magazine would continue publication notwithstanding the withdrawal of support of certain persons. Moore's editorial on the subject suggested that some Bostonians opposed Washington's association with *Colored American*. He declared that he and the journal would support Washington's policies "because we believe in them, and we shall endeavor to make friends for the race wherever possible." He would continue to publish "doings of the race" in business and education and to criticize "in a dignified way those policies that do not seem in the best interest of the race."[4] Moore also categorically denied Du Bois' claim that Washington had paid $3,000 to certain black publications to advocate his policies in five urban areas. Moore challenged Du Bois to prove his allegations.

Clearly, Washington used black periodicals to publicize Tuskegee Institute, the school he founded and headed, and no doubt he held financial interests in the *New York Age* and *Colored American* at some time. He was a popular contributor to the *New York Times* and to most leading national magazines of the day. Without attempting to argue whether Washington "managed" the news about himself, it is interesting to note that seven articles signed by him appeared in *Colored American*. In these essays, Washington appealed for a permanent and satisfactory resolution of the "Negro question" that would command the respect and confidence of all Americans. He asked for "absolute, unchangeable justice for all parties" in "The Calm Before the Storm," a portion of an address he had delivered before the General Conference of the African Methodist Episcopal Church that met in Norfolk, Virginia, in 1900. In other essays, he defended his faith in industrial education and said the race needed a professional class "educated to perform services the nation needs." But he maintained that the habits of thrift, love of work, ownership of property, and understanding of the economy lay naturally in the foundation gained through an industrial education. He praised black men who had been able to provide well-appointed homes for their families. In a forum on the race question, Washington took issue with white and black Americans who asserted "with a great deal of earnestness" that there was no difference between white and black men in the country. He declared there was a difference, not inherent or racial, but one which grew from the unequal opportunity of the past. He criticized education for blacks patterned after New England schools. The youth of New England had a hundred years of a strong economy, family landownership, and community culture to draw upon, he observed, but the Negro had little or none of these assets. Accordingly, his education should be fashioned along lines that would teach him to earn a living and to live "intelligently and economically." Washington admitted his position would seem to suggest that he was putting stress on what people called the "lower things life"—the material, and that he seemed to overlook the higher side—the ethical and the religious. He argued that that was not the case. He was advocating the *means* to the higher.

Perhaps the model for the education format Washington preferred for the race lies in his discussion of the Negro town of Wilberforce, Ohio. A black institution was established there in 1856 when antislavery agitation was at its height in that state. There Professor William S. Scarborough, a national authority on the classics and author of a widely used Greek-language textbook, and Professor Joshua H. Jones, a businessman and president of the college, lived and worked. They reflected higher education at its best. The college also had a normal and industrial department established in 1887 by the Ohio legislature. Wilberforce University, the only college operated for and by Negroes north of the Mason-Dixon line, lay next to Springfield, Ohio, the scene of bitter race riots in 1905, and just west of Dayton, Ohio, the home of Paul Laurence Dunbar, the celebrated black poet. To Washington, Wilberforce represented the proper combination of higher and industrial education. His essay on that college and its community expressed a model for black education which clarified, to a large extent, Washington's thinking on the subject at that time. Education for Afro-Americans was a burning public issue. *Colored American* carried more articles on education than any other single matter. Washington was, at the turn of the century, the acknowledged spokesman for black America. What he said and wrote was read widely. For this reason, *Colored American* became an important medium of expression of theories and practices of black education.

The rise of racial segregation in public accommodations engaged editorials, news items, and opinion articles in *Colored American*. An article reported on Virginia's law requiring racially separate accommodations, which the legislature adopted without a dissenting vote. Four years earlier, the same body had rejected a similar proposal, but now Negroes had become obnoxious to white people and had to be "put to themselves." *Colored American* editorials bristled with indignation, for painful evidence that Reconstruction had not brought the promised equality under the law was evident throughout so much of the nation. "Despite all our efforts along the line of civilization, we are unfit for human treatment," a writer complained. Valor in war and decorous conduct in peace did not merit such treatment. "The records of the past and the demonstrations of the future teach us to believe that in any government the tendency of whose laws is to create classes among its citizens is doomed to failure," the journal predicted. The Virginia law affected the freedom of movement of blacks in Washington, D. C. Commissioners of the District of Columbia denied jurisdiction when a black minister in Washington complained about segregation. Black rail passengers who traveled south from Washington were required to move to "colored" cars as soon as the train reached its first stop in Virginia. Despite protestations in the press and court action, segregation on public conveyances and in public buildings continued.

In 1905 a group of citizens in Nashville, Tennessee, fought back against separate streetcar seating. *Colored American* editorials praised the group's efforts. Boycotts of streetcars in Houston and San Antonio, Texas, brought compliments from the journal. The beginnings of jim crowism in Kansas public schools particularly troubled the editors of the magazine who noted that as early as 1904 Kansas had led the nation in establishing a progressive society. Editorials questioned whether the South should develop a double set of schools, one for whites and one for blacks. Not only was such a practice "a prejudice, a vanity, a sin if not a crime," it also presented a double burden to that part of the country that could least afford the economic luxury of racially separate public schools.

Colored American's columns complained bitterly that America had stood by and allowed Negroes to be jim crowed in politics, religion, education, business, common carriers, theaters, and hotels without a ripple of dissent from those that could have reversed the trend, such as Congress or the Supreme Court. The editors saw that the William Jennings Bryan wing of the Democratic party intended to attack the Fourteenth and Fifteenth amendments on a national basis as the unstated plank in their campaign for the presidency. Jim crow was not restricted to the South. President Charles W. Eliot of Harvard University had promised that if black students came to that institution in appreciable numbers he would establish "distinct departments for whites."

Editorials in the journal expressed disappointment with the Republican party's attitude toward the Negro and distrust and disdain for the directions the Democrats were taking. Charles Winslow Hall wrote that the black voter must make, in the election of 1900, "the most important decision of his whole political experience, and one that, however solved, must be of necessity the better choice of two evils." He noted that the Republicans had in 1860 overthrown that "unholy alliance between the slave power of the South and the greedy commercialism and political selfseeking of its Northern allies"; and that the Civil War had, through military intervention, conferred universal suffrage upon the freedmen and had, for a season, protected them and loyal whites of the South against their enemies. But that same party had later surrendered its noble purposes. To the writer, the Republican party had declared the Negro innately inferior to the white man and unqualified for elected office or diplomatic appointment.

Repudiation of Republicans did not mean support of Democrats by *Colored American*, however. Articles and editorials claimed the Democratic party included leaders whose attitude toward the black race was antagonistic. Some were said to be utterly cruel. There was hope for that party, though, for indications showed that its younger members favored opportunities for colonials, improved conditions in labor and business, and an honest and impartial currency system. The new Democrats deserved the vote of any American, notwithstanding the Negro's traditional loyalty to Republicans. Perhaps the two parties did not present all the alternatives for the black voter. *Colored American*'s editorials did not advocate support for the rising Socialist party but explained the tenets of that political group to its audience.

One extraordinary resource for studying Afro-American culture in entertainment and the arts lies in several reviews, news items, and articles that the journal featured. They focused upon accomplishments of black Americans performing on the stages of the theaters and concert halls of the nation, as well as those performing in artists' studios. Race pride was a hallmark of the publication. Robert Cole, one of the most successful of all black vaudeville performers, wrote "The Negro and the State" to detail proof that blacks had been an integral part of the major dramas of the Western world. Tracing the way in which certain ancient Greek playwrights, Shakespeare, and the French had written blacks into their significant stage works, Cole noted that black Americans had learned to work effectively in the sphere of comedy. He anticipated an Afro-American drama in which black writers would write effectively of their lives in the United States.

During the nine years of its publication, *Colored American* reflected an Afro-American perspective of life in the United States which was vital and varied. Despite influences Booker T. Washington may have exercised on the journal, it remains one of the most important publications that was produced for blacks by blacks in the nation during the first decade of the twentieth century.

Notes

1. Considerable confusion exists concerning the editorship of the magazine during its early years of publication. William Braithwaite in his "Negro America's First Magazine" (*Negro Digest* [December 1947]: 21-25), specifically states that Pauline Hopkins was

editor throughout the time *Colored American* was issued from Boston. Her name appeared as literary editor on the masthead beginning with volume 6, November 1903, and continuing until the magazine was sold to a new interest and moved to New York. Earliest numbers contained her fiction and biographies of black persons in her regular column, "Famous Men of the Negro Race." At times she wrote under *noms de plume*, one of which was Sarah A. Allen.

2. William Braithwaite contributed poetry, as did James D. Carruthers, both popular black American poets in the early years of the twentieth century. Lester A. Walton who became well known for his theater reviews and articles on entertainment for the *New York Age* wrote "The Future of the Negro on the Stage."

3. The July 1904 issue contained the notice that the magazine would hereafter be issued from a new address: Colored Co-Operative Publishing Company, 181 Pearl Street, New York. Fred R. Moore, listed as publisher and general manager, expressed appreciation for the cordial support the public had given the magazine during its stay in Boston and hope for "a larger measure of support now that it is located in the great metropolis." The May/June 1904 issue carried a lengthy article, "Biographies of the Officers of the New Management of Our Magazine."

4. When the magazine passed into the hands of Moore and the Washington enterprises, the emphasis of its articles changed from literary and cultural subjects to politics and business. Reports on the activities of Washington's National Negro Business League often appeared. T. Thomas Fortune, also later associated with the *New York Age* and one of the principal figures in black newspaper journalism, wrote frequently on a variety of subjects for the journal. He reported on the 1904 Democratic national convention which met in Saint Louis, denouncing Democrats William Jennings Bryan and Alton Brooks Parker and endorsing Republican candidate Theodore Roosevelt.

Information Sources

BIBLIOGRAPHY:
"Biographies of the New Officers of Our Magazine." *Colored American*, May/June 1904, pp. 443-49.
Bond, Horace M. "Negro Leadership Since Washington. "*South Atlantic Quarterly*, April 1925, pp. 115-30.
Braithwaite, William S. "Negro America's First Magazine," *Negro Digest*, December 1947, 21-26.
"Colored Magazines in America," *Crisis*, November 1912, pp. 33-36.
Harlan, Louis R. "The Secret Life of Booker T. Washington." *Journal of Southern History*, August 1971, pp. 393-416.
Johnson, Abby, and Johnson, Ronald M. "Away from Accommodation: Radical Editors and Protest Journalism, 1900-1910." *Journal of Negro History*, October 1977, pp. 325-38.
Meier, August. "Booker T. Washington and the Negro Press: With Special Reference to *Colored American Magazine*." *Journal of Negro History*, January 1953, pp. 68-90.
Shockley, Ann Allen. "Pauline Elizabeth Hopkins: A Biographical Excursion into Obscurity." *Phylon*, Spring 1972, pp. 22-26.
Thornbrough, Emma L. "More Light on Booker T. Washington and the New York *Age*," *Journal of Negro History*, January 1958, pp. 34-49.

INDEX SOURCES: None.
LOCATION SOURCES: Greenwood Press Periodicals; Moreland-Spingarn Collection,
Howard University, Washington, D.C.; Cleveland Public Library.

Publication History

MAGAZINE TITLE AND TITLE CHANGES: *Colored American* (May 1900-October
1909).
VOLUME AND ISSUE DATA: Vols. I-XVII, monthly.
PUBLISHER AND PLACE OF PUBLICATION: Colored Co-Operative Publishing Company, Boston, Massachusetts (May 1900-May 1904); Colored Co-Operative Publishing Company, Fred R. Moore, Publisher (June 1904-October 1909).
EDITORS: Walter W. Wallace (May 1900-October 1903); Pauline Hopkins (November
1903-September 1904); Fred R. Moore (June 1904-October 1909).
CIRCULATION: 15,000 highest.

Brian Joseph Benson

COLOR LINE

Three young working black Americans launched *Color Line* in 1946 in order
to place before as large a segment of Americans as possible the daily facts of
Negro social progress and interracial cooperation. They believed a publication
with this focus could accelerate acceptance of black Americans as able and
integral parts of the national economic and cultural society. The slight periodical
would disseminate data on a nonpartisan, nonsectarian, independent basis. Its
one criterion for inclusion of an item in the magazine was simple: Has the
organization or individual contributed something to Negro progress or American
unity?

With this purpose, *Color Line* called itself a monthly review of democracy in
action for busy Americans. It proposed to present, in easy-to-read, capsule form,
authentic and "informative facts, figures and fashions" about the Negro American. It would serve primarily as a newsletter. The editors and publishers assumed
that their periodical would prove useful to persons who believed sociologists,
politicians, and educators who said they wanted to unify the nation. They placed
significant credence in a national sense of fair play to show that truth is the
enemy of intolerance and facts are "the scourge of prejudice." *Color Line* did not
seek to lead or to teach. Its editors never projected their own views on any
subject; they sought, rather, to present the past and continuing history of the
Negro's participation in American life. They reported on both the struggles and
the achievements of black and white Americans who felt the nation would not
reach its destiny until the Constitution was applied literally to every citizen.

The special function of the magazine was to highlight events, overlooked or
underplayed by the daily press, which deserved a place in any interpretation of

daily race relations. Entries were necessarily brief. "We cannot be either complete or exhaustive but if our kaleidoscope moves some readers to further study the Negro's contribution to America and others to a better realization of the Negro's worth as a fellow citizen, then we will have made a definite contribution to America," an early editorial stated.[1] Labor and the Negro; friends and interracial cooperation; religion and the Negro; the Negro in sports; history, women, and equal justice; Negroes in the theater and in politics; and issues of the day represented news categories the editors used to carry out their purpose. These brief statements formed a news service that could not have been rendered so comprehensively and succinctly by a larger newspaper or magazine. There was no advertisement in the publication; it was sustained totally by subscriptions and gifts.

The second issue of *Color Line* carried a "Thank You" editorial expressing appreciation for the warm reception the reading public had given the magazine. A companion editorial reminded its audience that while the recently ended war had seemed to lessen some of the problems of racial tension within the nation, tales from the battlefields of the American race war tended to blot out the slow and unspeculated story of increasing national unity.

News items during 1946 show the extraordinary rigidity of the nation's racial climate at that time. Negroes were elected to state legislatures in Colorado, Illinois, Indiana, Kansas, Massachusetts, Michigan, Missouri, New Jersey, New York, Ohio, Pennsylvania, Vermont, and West Virginia. Benjamin Davis, Jr., the Communist party candidate for attorney general in New York, received the largest vote ever polled by his party for state office. In a city election in Norfolk, Virginia, the largest Communist vote came from the Negro district. And in Dade County, Florida, a Negro who ran for the school board on the Republican ticket lost by only a small margin. William L. Dawson of Chicago and Adam Clayton Powell of New York City, both Democrats and the only black members of Congress, retained their seats despite Republican election sweeps in many states. Ralph J. Bunche, a Negro State Department official and Harvard Ph.D., became director of the Trusteeship division of the United Nations. Charles S. Johnson, a sociologist and former editor of *Opportunity*,* was elected the first black president of Fisk University. The University of Minnesota appointed Forrest O. Wiggins to an instructorship in philosophy.

In approaches to civil rights through the courts, the Arkansas Supreme Court reversed the conviction of Negro publishers of the *Arkansas State Press* who had been fined $100 and sentenced to ten days in jail for printing a news story with the headline "Strikers Sentenced to Pen by Hand-Picked Jury." Florida's supreme court upheld a lower court decision declaring unlawful the segregation of blacks and whites by restrictive residence zoning, and the United States Supreme Court ordered a lower court in Alabama to hear a case challenging the board of registrars in Macon County for excluding Negroes who sought to register to vote. A suit to enforce equal school facilities for black and white students had been scheduled for hearing in Virginia, and the Veterans Administration had agreed to use Negro dentists in its rehabilitation programs for ex-servicemen.

Cultural and entertainment news included the Carnegie Hall premiere of "Concerto for the Jazz Band" which Dmitri Shostakovich wrote for Lucky Millinder's orchestra. Langston Hughes wrote the lyrics for playwright Elmer Rice's *Street Scene*. Negro baritone Harry T. Burleigh retired after having served fifty-two years as soloist in Saint George's Episcopal Church in New York City. Broadway plays and musicals that employed black performers included *Annie, Get Your Gun*; *Another Part of the Forest*; *Call Me Mister*; *Cyrano de Bergerac*; *Showboat*; and *The Ice Man Cometh*.

Fred Rosenberg, who joined the publication as its associate editor in March 1947, wrote "Let's Get Acquainted":

> If *Color Line* is to be a mirror and forum for the recording of increasing national unity and justice, you must do the reporting. We will do the recording....Therefore, please let us know what is going on in your community on the *Color Line* scene. Has your club, school, or group taken any recent stand on discrimination? Is your church, club or lodge holding a lecture on inter-racial understanding? Know a good story, poem or fact that others should hear? This column is to be the record of *your* contribution to America. We also want to create *Color Line* clubs all over the country. Let us know if you are interested and we will help you get started because we realize only too much that the trend of race relations depends much more upon what *you* do about it than about what *we* write about it.[2]

A few months later, Rosenberg thanked readers for their enthusiastic response and indicated that limited space and growing financial problems did not permit the magazine to carry out its original plan for using most items club members sent to the editor.

"Trends in Interracial Cooperation" in the next two issues furthered the focus of the publication. *Tower Time*, student newspaper at the University of Missouri, was suspended when its editor refused to destroy an article calling for admission of Negroes to the university. When printers refused to print the newspaper, the article was mimeographed and distributed widely. The New York Society for Ethical Culture joined the drive against segregation by showing, through maps, pictures, and graphs, that jim crow cost the nation a significant price in lives, morale, and dollars. A touring biracial group of lecturers sent south by the Fellowship of Reconciliation to publicize and demonstrate the Supreme Court's decision outlawing segregation in interstate bus travel had to seek protection from a mob that confronted them in Chapel Hill, North Carolina. A white student pledged Alpha Kappa Alpha, a black sorority, at the University of Southern California. The mayor of Savannah, Georgia, appointed a Negro advisory committee to keep the city administration in close touch with race relations in the community.

Its "birthday issue" in August 1947 was also the last one for *Color Line*. The last editorial did not suggest that the publication would go out of existence; instead, it ended on a rather strong note of hope:

We thank the many persons who helped *Color Line* get its start. We thank the columnists and reviewers whose printed plaudits directed many letters to our office asking for *Color Line*. To them, proven friends, we turn again for continued help in getting our little publication into places where it can do the most good for America—into the hands of millions of Americans who are still unconvinced that the Negro American is ready, willing and able to take his rightful place beside his white brother in the factory, office and farm, behind the throttle of locomotives and on the construction gangs pushing steel girders into the sky, behind a sales counter and in the ticket booth—yes, even on the bench of the Supreme Court of the United States. For it is only in that way will America's voice truly sound like thunder when it utters the sacred word "democracy," in the council of the nations of the earth.[3]

Color Line was a small but fairly significant news magazine that did not seek to feature scholarly essays or creative writing. It did not take editorial positions on politics, economics, or social issues of the time. It was what it had pledged its audience to be: a national news organ that would focus on interracial cooperation and Negro advancement within the nation at mid century. Its greatest worth lies in its use as a document reflecting the status of race relations in the years immediately following World War II without editorial opinion.

Notes

1. *Color Line* (August 1946): 8.
2. *Color Line* (March 1947): 18.
3. "Our Birthday," *Color Line* (August 1947): 4.

Information Sources

INDEX SOURCES: None.
LOCATION SOURCE: Greenwood Press Periodicals.

Publication History

MAGAZINE TITLE AND TITLE CHANGES: *Color Line* (July/August 1946-August 1947).
VOLUME AND ISSUE DATA: Vol. I-vol. II, no. 6 (July/August 1946-April 1947), monthly; Vol. II, no. 7 (July/August 1947), bimonthly.
PUBLISHER AND PLACE OF PUBLICATION: Carver Features, Mount Vernon, New York.
EDITORS: Paul R. Simms, editorial director; Gerald L. Brooks, managing editor; Fred Rosenberg, associate editor. (1946-1947.)
CIRCULATION: 400.

COMPETITOR, THE: THE NATIONAL MAGAZINE

Robert L. Vann, a young North Carolina-born lawyer, began his law practice in 1910 shortly after his graduation from the University of Pittsburgh. That same year he founded the *Pittsburgh Courier*. Within the next decade that newspaper became one of the best-known and most widely read black periodicals in the nation. In January 1920 Vann issued the *Competitor: The National Magazine*, edited as his special, personal venture. Such a publication was needed, he wrote, to serve a pressing need for a journal of national scope, constructive policy, and "replete with matters calculated to inspire the race to its best efforts in everything."[1] Vann sensed the dynamics of the "New Negro" emphasis of the post-World War I era. He wanted his magazine to "give rise to fostering a vision for the new understanding within the race toward a good and proper direction for a people who were forsaking the older things for something new and who were learning they could produce within their own ranks clean and wholesome literature."[2] They were, he wrote, thinking less of color and more of the nation and its opportunities. Black Americans had shown in the Great War sacrifice and loyalty equal to that of any other group of citizens. Now they would not hesitate to insist upon rights other citizens enjoyed. Conscious of the American inclination to brand personalities and publications as "radical" or "conservative," and intimately familiar with the potential divisiveness in the several current movements for racial advancement, Vann carefully formed a policy for the magazine he published for eighteen months during this protean period of American history.

The Competitor is not published in opposition to any organization or in opposition to any man or set of men. It has no selfish purposes to espouse. Rather, it is dedicated to the consummation of a profitable and dignified relation between all Americans. *The Competitor* will not bear aloft the burning torch of the Bolshevist, Anarchist or blind radicals, nor will it tolerate a cringing coward who declines to defend his honor or his home against any invading foe. *The Competitor* believes there is need of a new National Conscience; there must be a new system substituted for the old; there must be a conference between the various races and groups with a sincere desire to instruct all Americans in progressive American ideals.[3]

Part of that national consciousness lay in commitment to reconstructing the social order, the military posture, and national politics. Fourteen months had passed since the formal close of the war, the editor complained, and the United States languished in a "needless series of mental paroxysms" brought on by debate over the League of Nations, bolshevism, labor crises, race riots, Prohibition, and the spiraling cost of living. Germany had set out to rebuild as soon as the fighting had stopped. Great Britain, France, and Italy had achieved notable measures of reconstruction despite their own special problems. But the United States still clung to its tradition with embarrassing tenacity, Vann wrote. Thus, the nation failed to move ahead in its domestic and international affairs. It could not rid itself of race prejudice or stop lynching and riots. And it could not decide what to do about Japan. Debate over whether the United States should join the League of Nations seemed appropriate, for the country had entered the war for more noble purposes than securing and justifying spoils for the victors. But the lengthy acrimony between Congress and President Woodrow Wilson had laid waste the nation's energies and obfuscated its priorities. To the average American the war was over. People wanted to bind their wounds and return to their normal activities as rapidly as possible, Vann wrote.

Woodrow Wilson had led the nation into war to make the world safe for democracy. That rubric became the metaphor for the *Competitor*'s presentation of its position on the eternal "Negro Question." People had learned to think of democracy in terms of themselves—the masses—and their interests in counterdistinction to the classes. Radical economic theories and practices, though, would not suffice for the nation's needs at the time. The editor totally rejected Americans who believed that equality meant the wealthy should be reduced to poverty and exchange places with the pauper. Democracy, to him, was a product of the people. It could evolve naturally, provided citizens made its operation possible, easy, and permanent.

Considerably before the publication of Alain Locke's *The New Negro: An Interpretation* in 1925, Robert Vann articulated his meaning of the key term. "The New Negro," he claimed, was a misnomer; for Negroes had always wanted the materials and opportunities now demanded in the postwar period. Their progenitors simply did not know how to frame demands for their aspirations. Nor did they realize they could achieve them. They believed their hopes lay only in quiet patience and supplication. But their progeny operated differently. The new generation demanded outright that which they felt they deserved. And the *Competitor* became the medium of expression for the vitality of this black national posture. It comported well with the editor's call for social reconstruction in the United States.

Even with the new approaches to full citizenship, Negroes could not depend solely upon social service agencies and their methods to attain their goals. Nor could any known style of popular leadership serve the purpose. Vann claimed the race had not provided itself with effective individual leaders in the past and did not seem inclined to do so in the future. Frederick Douglass had led without receiving the common necessities of life; Booker T. Washington's services were financed by Andrew Carnegie and other white philanthropists; W.E.B. Du Bois would have been sorely handicapped without the support of the NAACP; Robert R. Moton had followed the course financed by white friends who made Tuskegee's founding and maintenance possible. Monroe Trotter tried in vain to rise to leadership with Negro support and personal sacrifice. Moreover, every man who had attracted public attention had been plagued unmercifully by "those stage acrobats who never fail to nominate themselves as the one and only fit leader of the race," Vann wrote. Any person who rose to the level of comparative comfort "where he can afford to devote his time and some of his saving to the cause" immediately became the victim of a campaign of destruction. Primarily for these reasons, Vann preferred collective leadership to individual leaders. To him, no single personality, no matter the level of his sacrifices, could achieve the desired goal of a race devoid of a leisure class of men of wealth.

In editorials and contributed articles, the *Competitor* soundly rejected bolshevism as a panacea for Negroes' problems. Kelly Miller, dean of Howard University, wrote that in the process of radical adjustment taking place in the world in the relationships of rich to poor and laborer to overlord, the strong men and the weak, the white and the nonwhite—all must be adjusted in harmony with the progressive spirit of the times. To Miller, the war had upset everything and settled nothing. Radical politicians and economists would not accomplish desired goals, however. "Riotous Reds" in Russia, Socialists in Italy, and Laborites in England, he wrote, could only bring distress to their nations. Those strains of radicalism in the United States that prompted labor unions to defy the federal government to win concessions from it and the courts portended disaster.

Indeed, the times were out of joint, and Woodrow Wilson was ill equipped to set them right at home or abroad. Miller quipped that the president had proclaimed himself "Chief Magistrate of Mankind," but his charity had never reached home. He believed in democracy for humanity but not for Mississippi. His "marvelous assumption of superior insight" led Wilson to propound preachments and compound idealistic theories that could hardly serve the nation he headed. The *Competitor* attacked President Wilson repeatedly for his failure and particularly for his racial attitude which excluded Negroes from any significant role in the government. His personal arrogance and bigotry had gained for him the distinct disfavor of the magazine.

The *Competitor* lashed out at race riots and lynchings prevalent during the "Red Summer" of 1919 and continuing into 1920. Walter S. Singleton wrote an analysis of the race riot in Washington, D.C., and joined the majority of the black press in blaming daily newspapers in Washington for inciting the disturbance.[4] Singleton reasoned that riots emanated from race prejudice based on belief in the inherent inferiority of Negroes; that contact with a Negro on equal terms embarrassed and degraded a white man; and that black Americans who sought to realize the promise in the Declaration of Independence and the Constitution of the United States became public enemies in the Washington social environment. They were marked to be reduced to the lowest terms or exterminated.

Singleton thought the existing condition could be explained rather clearly. Slavery had been abolished in the District of Columbia in 1862, but the native white population had remained essentially proslavery in practice and sympathy. With the declaration of war against Germany, large numbers of southern war workers came to Washington. Their distaste for riding streetcars with Negroes led to open violence. Further, the major of police in Washington devoted so much of his time and resources to enforcing Prohibition in the "bone dry" area that protection of life and property and personal security became secondary considerations for the police. These conditions contributed to racial tensions in a crowded wartime capital where Negroes already fretted over their steadily deteriorating social and economic status.

Although lynching became the subject of editorials throughout the life of the *Competitor*, Vann agreed with Tuskegee Institute's Robert R. Moton that within ten years the hated practice would pass. This expression of bright hope in no way represented "gradualism" however, for the organ consistently called for strong federal legislation to stamp out lynching. Vann laid primary responsibility for legal prohibition of lynching upon the White House. He did not hesitate to claim that Wilson's own personal attitude toward Negroes had contributed to the national malaise that permitted and encouraged the practice. Understandably, Vann was elated with Warren G. Harding's speech at Warren, Ohio, 22 July 1919, in which the Republican candidate for president said, "I believe the Federal government should stamp out lynching and remove the stain from the fair name of America."

Presidential nominating conventions and the election campaigns of 1920 engaged an uncommon emphasis in the *Competitor*'s editorials. By the time the parties had chosen their nominees and adopted their platforms, the magazine noted that one would have to look to the past records of both parties in order to find the issues of importance. Each addressed the League of Nations, lynching, immigration, relations with Mexico, and labor. Each sought to present a safe policy on these matters and to minimize their past failures. The *Competitor* favored Warren G. Harding and the Republican party. Their views were saner and safer than the opposition's.

After election day, the *Competitor* claimed that, in electing Harding, the people had spoken through their ballots and had "reaffirmed the solid strength of the Republic." Negroes had provided the balance of decision in Illinois, Indiana, Iowa, Michigan, Ohio, and Maryland. Their traditional loyalties to the Republican party had assured the election. "What does the election of the Republicans mean to 14,000,000 black citizens of the United States?" the magazine asked. It assured its readers that the new government could be trusted to honor its debt to Negroes and to respond to well-known expectations. It would enact legislation prohibiting lynching; ensure that Negroes would not lose their jobs to foreigners; reestablish patronage positions Woodrow Wilson had taken away; and restore the right of equal accommodation on common carriers. These expectations were not wild dreams. "They are simple rights which all other American citizens enjoy without molestation and embarrassment," Vann wrote.

The *Competitor*'s vitality lay in its editorials and contributed articles. They reflected a view of the American experience on a national basis at a seminal period in black social, political, and economic life. The magazine's general format included feature articles, creative writing, entertainment, and news items presented for black consumption. Its masthead contained names of contributing editors, including Henry Allen Boyd, Archibald Grimké, James Weldon Johnson, Robert R. Moton, Mary B. Tolbert, Robert H. Terrell, R. R. Wright, Jr., Emmett J. Scott, Eugene Kinkle Jones, Walter S. Buchanan, Alice Dunbar-Nelson, and William S. Scarborough. Julia Bumbry-Jones conducted a woman's department especially concerned "about things pertaining to women and a medium of exchange for professional minds on questions of current interest and importance."

The journal provides an important resource for the study of black arts and entertainment of the period. Angelina W. Grimké, a black playwright, wrote an analysis of her play *Rachel*. Bert Williams, the foremost black vaudeville personality, discussed commercial stage entertainment. Lester A. Walton, who enjoyed some distinction as a drama critic in the *New York Age* and *The Messenger*,* wrote articles on the drama. Every issue contained at least one article about Negroes in sports, including discussion of working conditions and racial discrimination in organized athletics and news about black intercollegiate sports. Throughout its publication life, the *Competitor* included some short fiction and poetry in most issues, although none of the writers achieved any notable reputation during the renaissance of black letters, with the exceptions of Angelina Grimké and Alice Dunbar-Nelson.

Several conditions contributed to the demise of the *Competitor*. Its format and scope represented an ambition Vann could not sustain. Its glossy stock, numerous photographs, and issues averaging 120 pages cost more than the editor could afford. The magazine sold for twenty cents a copy, considerably more than the price of most black newspapers. Vann could not secure the advertising he needed. The *Competitor* enjoyed no organizational support as did the *Crisis*,* the official organ of the NAACP. Neither did it have the exotic appeal of the *Messenger*,* a radical publication popular in Harlem. The *Competitor* resembled white eclectic magazines before black readers had developed strong support for a publication of this type. Given the precarious financial circumstances his newspaper faced at the time, Vann could ill afford to launch a magazine. During its brief life, the *Competitor* provided a valuable voice for black Americans. Its strength lay particularly in its promulgating the concept of the "New Negro" outside Harlem into the western fringes of the East.

Notes

1. "Why This Magazine?" *Competitor* (January 1920): 2.
2. Ibid.
3. Ibid., pp. 14-16.
4. "Washington Before and After the Riots," *Competitor* (January 1920): 14-16.

Information Sources

BIBLIOGRAPHY:
Buni, Andrew. *Robert L. Vann of the Pittsburgh Courier: Politics and Black Journalism.* Pittsburgh: University of Pittsburgh Press, 1974.
Dahlinger, Charles W. "The Rising Tide of Color." *Western Pennsylvania Historical Magazine* 4 (April 1921): 72-73.
Joyce, Donald Franklin, "Magazines of Afro-American Thought." *American Libraries,* December 1976, pp. 678-82.
INDEX SOURCE: Grant, Mildred Bricker. *Indexes to "The Competitor".* Westport, Conn.: Greenwood Press, 1978.
LOCATION SOURCES: Library of Congress; Moreland-Spingarn Collection, Howard University Library; Greenwood Press Periodicals.

Publication History

MAGAZINE TITLE AND TITLE CHANGES: *The Competitor: The National Magazine* (January 1920-June 1921).
VOLUME AND ISSUE DATA: Vol. I, no. 1-Vol. III, no. 4, monthly.
PUBLISHER AND PLACE OF PUBLICATION: Continental Publishing Company, Penn Building, Pittsburgh, Pennsylvania.
EDITOR: Robert L. Vann (1920-1921).
CIRCULATION: 65,000.

CRISIS, THE: A RECORD OF THE DARKER RACES

Mary White Ovington, one of the founders of the National Association for the Advancement of Colored People, recalled once how the *Crisis* magazine got its name.

I remember the afternoon that *The Crisis* received its name. We were sitting around the conventional table that seems a necessary adjunct to every board, and were having an informal talk regarding the new magazine. We touched the subject of poetry.
"There is a poem of Lowell's," I said, "that means more to me today than any other poem in the world—'The Present Crisis.' "[1]

William Edward Burghardt (W.E.B.) Du Bois, director of research and publication for the fledgling NAACP he had helped to create, thus began, in November 1910, his long editorship of the *Crisis.* Officially it was the organ of the association. The board of directors pledged fifty dollars a month to support the publication. Its editorial board included NAACP members Oswald Garrison Villard, J. Max Barber, Charles Edward Russell, Kelly Miller, and William S. Braithwaite.

Mary D. Maclean, another member of the organization and a staff writer for the *New York Times*, agreed to assist with editorial duties. Robert N. Woods, a printer who headed the Negro Tammany political organization in New York, assumed responsibility for the technical direction. He also arranged credit for the printing and the cost of the paper.

The first issue contained sixteen five-by-eight-inch pages and a cover bearing one woodcut print of a Negro child. Four pages reported race news under the title "Along the Color Line." The first editorial explained the object and policies of the new periodical. It would set forth facts and arguments to show the dangers of race prejudice; serve as a newspaper to record important events and movements bearing on interracial relations; review books and press comments; and publish a few appropriate articles. The new organ could not pay contributors. It would appeal to readers through innovations in practices used by the black press, including photographs as a part of news about black Americans. This feature interested Du Bois particularly because the white press used black Americans' photographs only when they had committed crimes, and the black press used them only if the personalities paid for the privilege.

By the close of its first year of publication, the *Crisis* counted a monthly paid circulation of 9,000. It had achieved early success, although some readers complained that the tone was "bitter" and the news "depressing." Du Bois replied testily that the *Crisis* did not "try to be funny." It was a newspaper that would tell the truth about racial antagonism in the world. By encouraging and castigating his readers, the editor sought to keep the magazine healthy. He wrote that he remembered all too well the "graveyards of ambitious and worthy ventures" in which *The Colored American** and *The Voice of the Negro**—once-promising black monthlies—lay. He realized Negroes had not become sophisticated enough to fully support a magazine after the fashion of national white monthly organs. But he believed he could sell 50,000 copies of the *Crisis* without difficulty. He could distribute issues through agents largely because the NAACP had captured the imagination of Negroes throughout the nation. Its members normally subscribed to the magazine at the same time they joined the association. Du Bois did not wish the *Crisis* to become a mere house organ and reporting vehicle for the NAACP. He envisioned a broad-based national magazine that could make the best use of its relationship to the parent organization.

Du Bois enjoyed freedom and security in his position that no other Negro editor had known previously. This preferred and unique position provided him an effective rostrum, but he took the responsibility seriously to tailor his editorial comments and choice of articles to the magazine's expressed policies and purposes. And he sought to ensure the national role he had sought and gained for himself, the NAACP, and the *Crisis*. At long last, he had acquired a medium to espouse the "radical" position of black leadership that he had nurtured through his philosophical conflict with Booker T. Washington. Through the *Crisis* Du

Bois found a secure and effective route to supplant Washington as the leading black American spokesman.

Lynching was, to Du Bois, *the* national disgrace, and he undertook to make certain every reader of the magazine understood the impact of that hated practice. He held little faith in current methods of stamping out the ever-increasing menace. Accordingly, he placed the *Crisis* solidly alongside the NAACP's efforts to keep lynching before the American public, to report on it in detail as black men and women died at the hands of mobs which took the law into their own hands during the World War I era, and to keep alive the argument for a federal antilynching law. His position on other major national issues reflected a black perspective. Woman suffrage received his endorsement only because it was a human question. "Whatever concerns mankind, concerns us," he wrote; and he argued that any agitation, discussion or reopening of the problem of voting must inevitably lead to a discussion of the right of black folk to vote. Votes for women would mean votes for some 3 million black women. Therefore, the movement was good.

For all his orientation toward egalitarianism, Du Bois held no particular interest in the organized labor movement, except when the unions discriminated against black workers. One of his most strongly worded editorials on the subject reads, in part:

> We know, and all men know, that under ordinary circumstances, no black artisan can today work as printer, baker, blacksmith, carpenter, hatter, butcher, tailor, street or railway employee, boilermaker, bookbinder, electrical worker, glass blower, machinist, plumber, telegrapher, electrotyper, textile worker, upholsterer, stone cutter, carriage maker, plasterer, mason, painter—or any other decent trade, unless he works as a "scab," or unless in some locality he has secured such a foothold that the white union men are not able to easily oust him. That policy was not always avowed but it was perfectly well understood. Some unions, like the printers and the carpenters, admit a lone colored man here and there so as to more easily turn down the rest. Others, like the masons, admit Negroes in the South where they must, and bar them in the North where they can.[2]

The *Crisis* editorials often discussed education for black Americans. Du Bois understood well that a nation trying to provide education for 10 million people largely by private philanthropy faced particular problems. Private financing was inadequate and undesirable as a means of paying for education for black youth. Donors could and did dictate the curriculum and social posture of schools they supported. The system encouraged sycophancy and mitigated against a desirable scope of choices of educational emphases. Du Bois praised Fisk, Atlanta, Virginia Union, and Shaw universities, in particular, as worthy institutions of higher education. He advocated substantial financial resources for these schools and believed black colleges should be headed by black administrators. To him, Atlanta needed public elementary schools more than it needed more private schools; for these "academies" already offered sufficient training in industries, agriculture, and some professional work. Du Bois proposed a plan which would ensure that private monies would be channeled to the most viable black schools and would, at the same time, thwart unscrupulous persons who exploited potential contributors. That plan would require the NAACP to offer an impartial, thoroughly reliable bureau on board lines with maps and figures at command which could furnish unbiased facts. The proposal seemed consistent with the association's purposes in establishing its research and publicity arm for which it published the *Crisis*. Du Bois failed, however, to anticipate the publicly supported elementary, secondary, and postsecondary schools that would spring up in all states of the South and exist alongside the private "academies" and black colleges.

Each spring the *Crisis* published photographs of selected black Americans who received degrees from American colleges and universities—white and black. The magazine became a principal source of information concerning black education.

The presidential election of 1912 found Du Bois expressing in the *Crisis* a departure from the traditional pattern of black politics. He wrote that he could sympathize with "faithful old black voters who will always vote the Republican ticket." He could even "respect their fidelity but not their brains"; for the Grand Old Party had betrayed the Negro with reckless insensitivity. The Democrats had always been "the avowed enemy of the Negro." Yet Du Bois hoped Woodrow Wilson, the Democratic nominee for president, would "view intelligently his responsibility to black Americans." He based that hope on little more than a kind of elitism that had little to do with anything the candidate had done or said to inspire confidence among black voters. He had been president of Princeton University, and Du Bois seemed to think that qualification was sufficient to recommend Wilson to his readers. Du Bois was wrong. Within a short time after his move into the White House, Woodrow Wilson and his staff began to set back the progress Negroes had made in politics and political appointments. In two open letters to the president published in the *Crisis*, Du Bois appealed to Wilson's sense of fairness and intelligence to reverse the trend he seemed to be establishing in race relations. Du Bois realized he had taken a calculated risk in supporting Wilson and had lost. His own sense of fairness caused him to express his serious disappointment with the new administration to his black readers.

When the United States entered World War I, many black editors and publishers took the national emergency as an opportunity to call loudly for the first-class citizenship Du Bois and others had advocated since the turn of the century. They were stunned when Du Bois published in the *Crisis* his famous "Close Ranks" editorial, asking black men and women to lay aside their forward push for equality until the present emergency was over. They must have thought he sounded like the Booker T. Washington he had so soundly criticized for his Cotton States Exposition speech, often called "The Atlanta Compromise" by Du Bois. His detractors made public an arrangement Du Bois had attempted to complete with the War Department that would have given him a military appointment as an army officer in the segregated black officers' training center established at Fort Des Moines, Iowa. It was said that the editor had compromised his position on social justice in order to ingratiate himself with the War Department. He had already asked the NAACP Board of Directors for special permission to continue as editor of the *Crisis* at his regular salary while he held the temporary commission in the army. The appointment did not materialize, and relations between President Wilson and Negroes deteriorated further as the war progressed and after it ended. Du Bois was chosen to write reports from Europe on the activities of black American soldiers in the war, and to publish these reports in the *Crisis*.

As the Republicans prepared for their nominating convention for the 1916 election, Du Bois wrote: "Very quietly and on tiptoe the Republican party has completed its disfranchisement of the Negro voters in the South." He could not endorse Wilson for reelection with any enthusiasm, but he did not feel confident with Charles Evans Hughes, the Republican nominee. Of him Du Bois wrote: "He is practically the only candidate for whom Negroes can vote," as final advice to his readers in that campaign.

After the war Du Bois turned his attention and the magazine's toward wider notice of emerging organizations of black persons in other parts of the world besides the United States. This activity engaged his energies throughout the remainder of his life. The subtitle of the *Crisis*: *A Record of the Darker Races* became an emphasis of the magazine at that time.

Du Bois' extraordinary interest in the creative arts will recommend him and the *Crisis* to posterity long after his civil rights and educational confrontations have paled. For no matter how many other persons may deserve praise and credit for the rise of the fine arts—their performance, creation, and promotion—among Negroes during the Harlem Renaissance, Du Bois leads all others. He wrote poetry, fiction, and some drama. Most of his prose contains unmistakable poetic essence. His active work as a patron of black creative and performing artists is far too comprehensive to attempt to chronicle in a discussion of the *Crisis*, but the magazine served him well in these purposes. And it provided a publication source for black writers that would hardly have been available to them otherwise. His appointment of Jessie R. Fauset, a young Cornell University graduate and promising writer of fiction who later became well known as a black American novelist, to the *Crisis* as its literary editor represents a significant event in the history of American letters. Elliott M. Rudwick provides a summary of the *Crisis*'s part in those activities.

The artistic renaissance was probably the crowning glory of the Negro society which The *Crisis* sought to develop. Although Du Bois still said that

Negroes wanted to be "full-fledged" Americans, he portrayed the white American culture as effete and materialistic. He contended that isolation motivated Negroes to accept "new stirrings" within themselves as an artistic and creative nature. While he admitted that Negro art "often lacks careful finish," he admired its honesty and he hoped that it would be supported within the race. He regarded the *Crisis* as the Negroes' chief talent scout, and during the 1920's he helped to sponsor contests and to secure prizes for literary works. On *Crisis* covers, he proudly introduced Negro painters Richard Brown and Wilbur Scott, and he "helped to discover" Jessie Fauset, the novelist and Langston Hughes, the poet. In 1922, he proposed an annual "Institute of Negro Literature and Art." Angered that Roland Hayes received no offers to record serious music, he announced the formation of a Negro phonograph company dedicated to supporting Negro musical artists. There is no evidence that either of these enterprises came to fruition. He also plugged "Negro drama" and especially Ethiopian Art Players. The renaissance was essentially directed by mulattoes, and Du Bois found it difficult to convince them to appreciate blackness as a standard of beauty. He was deluged with protests when he commissioned paintings of darker Negroes for *Crisis* covers.[3]

Ironically, Du Bois was forced to resign from editorship of the *Crisis* on the basis of a protracted feud with the NAACP over the association's official position on segregation. His own experience with the nation's political parties, labor unions, industries, and institutions of education led him to believe racial integration was not feasible in the United States. Almost from the beginning of the publication of the *Crisis* Du Bois had sought a high degree of freedom as its editor, and his insistence had made some officers of the association uncomfortable. The cleavage broadened during the thirties. Du Bois refused to accept and abide by an action of the board which sought to forbid all criticism of the officers and policies of the NAACP in the magazine. Interracial cooperation in national institutions faced tension throughout the nation. Private colleges were passing from white administrators to black presidents. Racially mixed religious denominations found strong agitation for black officers in their governance structures. No wonder, then, the NAACP could hardly continue in the manner in which it had been organized. The association could not meet the demands of its change gracefully. But Du Bois understood the essence of the problem.

I had planned to continue constructive criticism of the National Association for the Advancement of Colored People in *The Crisis* because I firmly believe that the National Association for the Advancement of Colored People faces the most grueling tests which come to an old organization. Founded in a day when a negative program of protest was imperative and effective, it succeeded so well that the program seemed perfect and unlimited. Suddenly, by World War and chaos, we are called to formulate a positive program of construction and inspiration. We have been thus far unable to comply.

Today this organization, which has been great and effective for nearly a quarter of a century, finds itself in a time of crisis and change, without a program, without effective organization, without executive officers who have either the ability or disposition to guide the National Association for Advancement of Colored People in the right direction.[4]

On 26 June 1934, W.E.B. Du Bois officially resigned from the editorship of the magazine he had built into the single most identifiable vehicle for American black expression of the national experience.

Roy Wilkins, former managing editor of the *Kansas City Call* who had come to the NAACP in 1931 to serve under Walter F. White as assistant executive secretary, succeeded Du Bois as editor of the *Crisis*. His hands-on experience with the association left no room for doubt as to the direction the magazine would take under his leadership. He wrote editorials and some feature articles, like his predecessor. He was a forceful editor, but his style differed from that of Du Bois. During the fifteen years of his association with the *Crisis*, Wilkins maintained a close relationship between the periodical and the association. He worked as strenuously as Du Bois to secure an antilynching bill. He attacked wage discrimination among the races on federal projects in the South, Italy's invasion of Ethiopia, the social, political, and economic ramifications of World War II, and the postwar recovery. As soon as the members of the Seventy-fourth Congress took office in 1935, the NAACP and the *Crisis* dramatized the need for legislation to outlaw lynching. Promptly upon convening Congress on 3 January, Senators Edward P. Costigan of Colorado and Robert F. Wagner of New York agreed to reintroduce their antilynching bill in the Senate and Congressman Thomas F. Ford of California agreed to present companion legislation in the House. Walter F. White explained the urgent need for the bill in the *Crisis*.

Developments since Congress adjourned have given proof... that there can be no end to lynching unless there is federal legislation. The perverted and fiendish mutilation of Claude Neal at Mariana, Florida, late in October, revealed as few other lynchings in the history of the United States that there are states in America where it is useless to expect any effective action against lynching by local authorities. At the date of this writing, the lynching record for 1934 lends striking affirmation to the contentions of the supporters of the Costigan-Wagner bill. Of 17 lynchings, two occurred early in January. Then there was a complete cessation of lynching until it was evident, in June, that Congress would adjourn without voting on the bill. 15 lynchings, among them the one widely advertised in advance in Mariana, occurred between June and the end of November.[5]

Some Americans claimed the proposed bill would promote rape and attacked congressmen who sponsored and supported the legislation. Arthur W. Mitchell, the first Negro Democrat to sit in Congress, reportedly said in an interview that he was not in Congress to represent the Negro race or to look after "race matters." "It is difficult to imagine how hard the Negro's plight would be in this country if all congressmen took the position that they have nothing to do with Negro affairs," Wilkins wrote in response to Mitchell's remark.

With the Japanese naval and aircraft attack on Pearl Harbor and President Franklin D. Roosevelt's almost immediate declaration of war, Wilkins, like Du Bois a generation earlier, called on Negroes to support the war effort wholeheartedly. He regularly admonished Negroes to maintain their faith in America throughout the war years. At the same time he joined other black editors in highlighting stories of injustice against Negroes in the armed forces. Their efforts led President Harry S. Truman to desegregate all the military services. In his final editorial in the Crisis, Wilkins pointed the direction black activities would have to take in the coming decades in order to keep alive the forward movement toward full citizenship.

From now on Negro voters are going to keep a sharp eye on their Congressmen. They are not going to take the side-tracking of the civil rights program lying down. They want civil rights programs to become the first order of business in the second session of the 81st Congress when it meets in January. Negroes are restless, tired of empty promises and broken pledges. And they know that the most effective place to register their disapproval of Congressional inaction is at the ballot box.[6]

In the 1950s the Crisis faced unusual financial straits. Its advertising revenue had always been small, inasmuch as most of it was college advertisement. Big advertisers avoided the magazine because it was considered a house organ, and it did not enjoy Audit Bureau of Circulation rights. Too, it was still a controversial civil rights journal in the perception of most Americans. With several promotion efforts among NAACP members, the periodical began to make a small profit in the mid 1950s. Its circulation returned to about 100,000 copies a month.

School desegregation, political assassination of the Kennedys and black civil rights leaders, general social unrest in the United States, and the rise of nationalism in colonial Africa and Asia caused the Crisis to focus upon a broader scope of problems than it had known in its earlier years. Lynching had become rare—that is, in the conventional sense of the practice—and the art of communication had become refined to the extent that a news-opinion magazine such as Du Bois had founded earlier in the century was no longer a necessity. During this period of national and world turbulence the Crisis served primarily as the organ of the NAACP. It published statistical reports and analyses of inner-city riots, campus unrest, and the Vietnam War alongside other national journals. It celebrated the election of black mayors in Cleveland and Springfield, Ohio; Gary, Indiana; Chapel Hill, North Carolina; and Fayette, Mississippi, and the election of Edward Brooke, the first black United States senator since Reconstruction. It appeared for a time that some of the sense of crisis Du Bois and his associates had felt so keenly when they established the periodical had begun to take a different direction, if not to dissolve.

During this formidable period of national history, the NAACP came under severe attack by elements within the race who gave a new meaning to the "radicalism" Du Bois had espoused in the first half of the century. The Southern Christian Leadership Council (SCLC), Student Nonviolent Coordinating Committee (SNCC), Congress of Racial Equality (CORE), and other race advancement movements weakened the stature of the NAACP and the *Crisis*. Other black publications arose to provide media of expression along many lines for a variety of black opinions. The white press and television joined in the communication of black activism and concerns.

The *Crisis* had published through most of the twentieth century a seminal medium for expressing the black American experience. It had not veered essentially from the course its founders had set, although times and changing circumstances affected the direction. At the close of the decade of the sixties, editor James W. Ivy wrote a fitting tribute to the accomplishments of the magazine and to its future purposes. He declared that the *Crisis* deserved to go on for another sixty years, for increasing exposure of the American Negro to mass media had not eliminated the need for hard-hitting, informative journals. They were needed, he continued, to perform the same function carried on by Jewish and Catholic periodicals. *Crisis* does not enjoy the prestige it earned under Du Bois and Wilkins. But it has adjusted its contents and format to the 1970s and the 1980s.

Notes

1. "How the NAACP Was Born," *Crisis* (August 1914): 187.
2. "Organized Labor," *Crisis* (July 1912): 131.
3. "W.E.B. Du Bois in the Role of *Crisis* Editor," *Journal of Negro History* (July 1958): 216.
4. "Editing the *Crisis*," *Crisis* (March 1951): 48.
5. "The Anti-Lynching Bill," *Crisis* (February 1935): 22.
6. *Crisis* (March 1951): 154.

Information Sources

BIBLIOGRAPHY:
Bond, Horace M. "Negro Leadership Since Washington." *South Atlantic Quarterly*, April 1925, pp. 115-30.
"*The Crisis*, Voice of the NAACP," *Crisis*, August/September 1978, p. 221.
Du Bois, W.E.B. "The Colored Magazine in America." *Crisis*, November 1912, p. 35.
———. "Editing the *Crisis*." *Crisis*, March 1951, pp. 147-51, 213.

Green, Dan S. "W.E.B. Du Bois: His Journalistic Career." *Negro History Bulletin*, March/April 1977, pp. 672-77.

Harlan, Louis R. "The Secret Life of Booker T. Washington." *Journal of Southern History*, August 1971, pp. 393-416.

Hughes, Langston. *Fight for Freedom: The Story of the NAACP*. New York: Berkeley Publishing Company, 1962, pp. 14-23.

Johnson, Abby Arthur, and Johnson, Ronald M. "Away from Accommodation: Radical Editors and Protest Journalism, 1900-1910." *Journal of Negro History*, October 1977, pp. 325-38.

Kellogg, Charles Flint. *A History of the NAACP: Volume 1, 1909-1920*. Baltimore: Johns Hopkins University Press, 1967, pp. 89-115.

Moon, Henry Lee. "History of *The Crisis*." *Crisis*, November 1970, p. 5.

Wilkins, Roy. "The Crisis, 1934-49." *Crisis*, March 1951, pp. 154-56.

———. "The Decade, 1960-1970." *Crisis*, February 1973, pp. 46-49.

INDEX SOURCES: *Historical Abstracts*; *History and Life*; *Index to Periodical Articles by and about Negroes*; *Current Index to Journals in Education*; *American Humanities Index*; *Index to Selected Periodicals: Decennial Cumulation 1950-1959*; *Analytical Guide and Indexes to "The Crisis: A Record of the Darker Races," 1910-1960: Index and Literary Index*.

LOCATION SOURCES: Most college and university libraries; many public libraries; Greenwood Press Periodicals.

Publication History

MAGAZINE TITLE AND TITLE CHANGES: *The Crisis: A Record of the Darker Races* (January 1910-).

VOLUME AND ISSUE DATA: Vols. I- . Monthly; sometimes bimonthly.

PUBLISHER AND PLACE OF PUBLICATION: National Association for the Advancement of Colored People, New York, New York.

EDITORS: W.E.B. Du Bois (1910-1934); Roy Wilkins (1934-1949); James W. Ivy (1950-1966); Henry Lee Moon (1966-1974); Warren Marr II (1974-).

CIRCULATION: 116,000 highest.

CRUSADER, THE

The *Crusader* began publication in Harlem, September 1918, by means of a donation from the West Indian importer J. Anthony Crawford, whose patronage enabled Cyril V. Briggs to move from the editorial staff of the *Amsterdam News*. With the financial support of Crawford and the experience Briggs had gained on one of the most successful black weekly newspapers of the time, the *Crusader* enjoyed a promise seldom available to black periodicals. Crawford actually intended to create a periodical to support his secret African Blood Brotherhood organization which promoted freedom for black Africa and formation of a separate black state.[1] The post-World War I period was the era of black radical journalism which grew out of a sense of corporate cynicism black Americans felt after their return from Europe. They had saved that continent for democracy, which they could not find at home. The new spirit of defiance was different from any motivating force blacks had experienced previously in the United States. James Weldon Johnson, the eminent black writer and cultural historian, describes the summer of 1919 as the "Red Summer" because of the violent racial conflicts in the major cities of the nation. The new radicalism was one response to the frustration blacks felt at the close of the war. Johnson wrote, "It was something different from the formal radicalism of pre-war days; it was radicalism motivated by a fierce race consciousness."[2]

That milieu fostered a new trend in black newspapers and magazines. Those already in existence for the most part took on fresh vigor, reflecting the spirit of the times. But the new ones—particularly the *Messenger*,* the *Challenge*, the *Voice*, the *Crusader*, the *Emancipator*, and the *Negro World*—added a new dimension to black journalism. They represented an essential radicalism with respect to the proper national ecology that would give rise to self-realization for Negroes, and their editors possessed a remarkable command of forceful and trenchant language.

Harlem had become the center of the world for black peoples. Briggs and Crawford were West Indians, as was Marcus Garvey. A. Philip Randolph and Chandler Owen, editors of the *Messenger*, were American southerners who had migrated north. In addition to the southerners, large numbers of other black people had come from Jamaica, Trinidad, Barbados, Martinique, Saint Vincent, Saint Lucia, Dominica, British Guiana, Saint Kitts, Antigua, the Virgin Islands, Bermuda, and the Bahamas. The majority spoke English, but some spoke French, Spanish, or Dutch. Black immigrants to Harlem differed from one another in place of origin. But they shared the common onus of color, and that characteristic created an *esprit de corps*. Those immigrants provided the backdrop for the *Crusader*.

Briggs wrote in his first editorial that his aims were as high as the heavens. He wanted his magazine to please, delight, and inspire pride in race. He felt he could fight the battles of black Americans in the pages of his journal. He supported issues, proposals, and personalities that were not necessarily favored by the conventional black press. Like the growing chorus of emerging black public figures at the time, *Crusader* editors and contributors rejected both the Republican and the Democratic parties and helped turn some other black periodicals from their traditional allegiance to the Republican party. They did not embrace socialism, as did Randolph and Owen of the *Messenger*, but with Briggs and his activist associates they made Harlem an integral political community. Few well-known black scholars or commentators contributed articles to the *Crusader*. It primarily reflected Briggs' political ideas. Its public purpose was to fight for the elimination of racial discrimination and oppression of blacks. Occasionally it carried advertisements for membership in the African Blood Brotherhood.

Like the other radical editors, Briggs and his associates sponsored mass meetings in Harlem churches to inform blacks of the strength and activities of the Ku

Klux Klan and its revival after the war. Briggs wrote that capitalism and the Klan worked hand-in-hand to exploit and oppress blacks. He saw little difference between motivations for lynching and those for abusing black workers. He incurred the suspicion of Attorney General A. Mitchell Palmer, who considered the editorials of most of the radical black periodicals at the time a part of a "Red Plot" to overthrow the government of the United States.[3] Briggs praised black Americans who defended themselves in race riots in Washington, D.C., and Chicago in the summer of 1919, claiming they should take justifiable pride in the prowess and resourcefulness they had displayed in fighting back against attackers.

Briggs rejected Marcus Garvey and his Universal Negro Improvement Association largely because he considered its base "egocentric politics." In his violent confrontation with Garvey, Briggs assisted the United States government in charging the "Black Moses" with using the mails to defraud investors in some of the association's shipping interests.

Occasionally Briggs wrote articles about the theater for the *Crusader*. He had a deep interest in the Lafayette Theatre, a group of black actors and playwrights who made the theater popular in Harlem. Comedian Bert Williams wrote personal reminiscenses for the magazine, and Lester Walton, who enjoyed a good reputation as drama critic for the *Messenger* and other periodicals, contributed some features. Aside from Claude McKay, who published a few poems in the *Crusader*, other contributors were commonplace. Each issue did contain some literature, however.

Alongside the *Messenger*, the *Crusader* is not so often mentioned for its role in the Harlem of the twenties. It was, nevertheless, a strong and vital force in establishing the "New Negro" concept of the period.

Notes

1. *See* Theodore Kornweibel, Jr., *No Crystal Stair: Black Life and The Messenger, 1917-1928* (Westport, Conn.: Greenwood Press, 1975), p. 46 for discussion of these periodicals.

2. *Black Manhattan* (New York, 1930), pp. 246-47.

3. Kornweibel, *No Crystal Stair*, pp. 81-99 provides significant discussion of the part the Justice Department and the Lusk committee in New York played in the confrontation with the black press.

Information Sources

BIBLIOGRAPHY:

Boone, Dorothy Delores. "A Historical Review and a Bibliography of Selected Negro Magazines, 1910-1969." Ph.D. dissertation, University of Michigan, 1970.

Cronon, E. David. *Black Moses: The Story of Marcus Garvey and the Universal Negro Improvement Association*. Madison, Wis., 1955.

Cruse, Harold. *The Crisis of the Negro Intellectual: From Its Origins to the Present*. New York, 1967.

Record, Wilson. *The Negro and the Communist Party*. New York, 1971.

INDEX SOURCES: None.
LOCATION SOURCES: Schomberg Collection, New York Public Library; Moorland-Spingarn Collection, Howard University, Washington, D.C.

Publication History

MAGAZINE TITLE AND TITLE CHANGES: *The Crusader* (September 1918-April 1921).
VOLUME AND ISSUE DATA: Vols. I-IV (September 1918-April 1921), monthly.
PUBLISHER AND PLACE OF PUBLICATION: Cyril V. Briggs, editor and publisher, New York, New York.
EDITOR: Cyril V. Briggs (1918-1921).
CIRCULATION: 8,000 highest.

D

DOUGLASS' MONTHLY

Frederick Douglass had already become the most celebrated black abolitionist in the United States before he entered upon a career in journalism. His *Narrative*, which described and documented his own experiences as a slave, together with his unique popularity as a lecturer with white abolitionists in the United States and Great Britain, gave him his visibility. But Douglass was seldom content with anything less than abolitionist activities that seemed destined to bring to a conclusion the hated institution of slavery which he knew firsthand. He argued with the major white organizations that worked for emancipation of the black American slaves, holding that they often sidestepped the principle of freedom for black southerners to engage in what he considered peripheral issues. "It is enough to make a man's blood run cold now-o-days to read the so-called antislavery papers of our country," he once wrote in a statement that explains his principal reason for entering the publishing business. He wrote often for black and white papers that dedicated themselves to abolishing slavery.[1] Douglass wanted to attack slavery "in all its forms and aspects; advocate Universal emancipation; exact the standard of public morality; promote the moral and intellectual improvement of the colored people; and to hasten the day of freedom to all three million enslaved fellow-countrymen." That purpose was expressed in the first issue of the *North Star*. Later titled *Frederick Douglass' Paper*, both were antecedent to *Douglass' Monthly*, published continuously from January 1859 through August 1863.[2] In his *Monthly*, Douglass wrote in his uncommonly passionate style of his disdain for slavery and his impatience with any attitudes or activities that seemed to him to delay emancipation. The journal provides an unusual compendium of his observations on the contending forces that engaged the energies and thoughts of Americans during the days preceding the Civil War and the anxious considerations of Reconstruction and enfranchisement of the freedmen.[3]

Douglass' lead editorial in the first issue of *Douglass' Monthly* took to task what he called "the heartlessness displayed in dealing with the sin and crime which is eating out the very heart of all that is precious and worth struggling for" in the fight against slavery. While "humanity, justice, and freedom" were "thawing the icy heart of Russia into life, and causing, even there, the iron hand of despotism to relax its terrible grasp upon the enslaved peasantry," the United States was buried in stone-dead indifference to the only true and vital issue that freedom has any right to make with slavery, Douglass complained. The many issues that were beclouding the nation's clear view of its moral responsibility—that slavery should not commit any further aggression upon the North; that slavery should or should not be permitted in Cuba or in Kansas; whether the Dred Scott decision was binding upon Congress—all these matters were engaging debates in the antislavery journals. And they had caused the North to lose sight of the one true issue of abolitionist commitment. "The whip-scarred millions now toiling in bondage have claims upon us more powerful and telling, more authoritative and imperative, backed up by all the ties of nature, and nature's God, than any of the appeals made to us in behalf of 'free white labor'."[4]

Douglass could not find the emotion to weep for the lot of that labor for it was free and could take care of itself. It had the ballot box and the sword for its resources and needed no special protection from the abolitionist press. Black labor, though, remained in chains, "under the merciless lash, sold on the auction block, crushed in spirit, and bleeding at heart." An insolent and bloodthirsty aristrocracy joined with the "cold, clammy, and blood-stained walls of the American Church, in which a hypocritical clergy mock God with sepulchral incantations from Sabbath to Sabbath, calling it divine worship." The clergy and the lukewarm abolitionists formed an unholy alliance, to Douglass' way of thinking—a placebo which postponed the forces that should be working for the speedy end of the hated institution of slavery. "Abolitionists, return to your principles," he shouted at his associates, and he challenged them to come back and do their first work over and make the slave first and last their considerations. He reminded them that William H. Seward had spoken well when he said slavery would end if the nation *willed* it to end.

Douglass' Monthly reported on a resolution the Church Anti-Slavery Society had submitted to the general association of Connecticut placing the Christian church and its ministry once more strongly in the fight against slavery. One part of the resolution read:

that the responsibility of a longer continuance of slavery in the United States rests mainly with Christian churches and ministers, and that the Church Anti-Slavery Society, which seems to have arisen from this deep conviction, should have the earnest cooperation of the friends of freedom and Christianity in its honest attempt to array the churches against slavery, and to procure from them an expression of Christian abhorrence of slaveholding.[5]

Douglass felt strongly that abolition was a moral issue as well as a civil concern and that the Christian church should be in the forefront of the antislavery fight.

He was bitterly disappointed, then, when he learned that the general association of Connecticut Congregational ministers had indefinitely postponed the antislavery resolution that had been presented to it by unanimous vote of the Church Anti-Slavery Society.

The presidential election of 1860 brought forth from the *Monthly* cogent analyses of the national political parties, particularly with respect to their positions on slavery. Its editorials agreed that the most vital element in the Republican party was antislavery sentiment in the North. Its ancestry—growing out of the old Liberty party, the Abolition party, and the Free Soilers—made clear that, by the summer of 1860, the Republican party stood for equality, advancement, suffrage, citizenship, and emancipation. Opposition to slavery was supported for several reasons. "One man is opposed to slavery because it is an expensive and a non-remunerative system of labor, impoverishing the States and the communities, where it is established." Others believed it created an aristocratic class in slave states that despised labor and looked with contempt upon those who worked for a living. A third reason was that those whose interests were mainly involved in the slave system had endeavored to make the principles and practices of slavery dominant throughout the country. They had striven to make themselves masters of the United States even as they were masters of their slaves, an editorial claimed. Most importantly, Republicans had been clear in expressing their belief in an egalitarianism that agreed that the Negro was a man. Senator Charles Sumner had held the Negro up before the Senate as one who had been "wronged and imbruted as a human being whose degradation insulted the whole of humanity." The Republican party could teach the people for once in a political campaign the sacredness of human rights, the brotherhood of man, and expose to all the foul and terrible abomination of southern slavery. In so doing, the party would strengthen the abolition element of the country and show that no feigned loyalty to the South should make or honor any pledges to carry out the cruel Fugitive Slave Laws. To the *Monthly*, the Republican party's task and goal were clear. It needed simply to stand for the same rights for white men and for black men and not engage in the "miserable twaddle" of some difference between the two.

The Democratic party, after twenty years of discouraging all antislavery tendencies in the country and exalting the strength of slave power, was hopelessly divided and broken up in its political organization. It had been regarded in the North and in the South as the natural ally of slavery. The vital elements of the party, according to the *Monthly*, had been "hatred of negroes and love of spoils." It enjoyed a semblance of stability when the Whig party crumbled under the sturdy blows of the abolitionists in 1852 but was no longer a viable force in the upcoming presidential campaign. Crafty and greedy candidates had decimated the historical strength of Democrats. The *Monthly* could make clear its endorsement of the Republican party and Abraham Lincoln, its nominee, with a ringing declaration.

We wish only to send up a jubilee shout over the fact that the wisdom of the crafty has been confounded, that the counsels of the wicked have been brought to naught, and the Democratic Party, the bitter and malignant persecutor of our sable race, has fallen mortally wounded in the house of its friends in Baltimore. The condition of the scattered factions who still cling to the name of the Party, makes it almost certain that Abraham Lincoln and Hannibal Hamlin will be president and vice president of the United States in 1861.[6]

Abolition of slavery was the efficient cause for the publication of *Douglass' Monthly*, but the editor and his journal did not separate freeing the slaves from their equally strong insistence upon full citizenship rights for all black Americans. Some white and black voices in the nation advocated migration of Negroes to some other country even if emancipation came. Colonization projects in Africa became popular during the life of the *Monthly*, and other persons promoted separatist societies in Haiti. Douglass fought tenaciously for assimilation of blacks into the mainstream of American social, economic, and political life. On the eve of the issuance of President Lincoln's Emancipation Proclamation, Douglass wrote in his journal:

During a period of more than 30 years, there has been shown at different times a disposition, more or less strong, on the part of the free colored people of the United States, to migrate and blend their destinies with those of people of the free and independent Republic of Hayti. We have often regretted this disposition, believing that the place for the free colored people is the land where their brothers and sisters are held in slavery, and where circumstances might some day enable them to contribute an important part to their liberation. We have also used our pen and our voice against all emigration, because we have seen that the habit of looking away from America for a home, induces neglect to improve such advantages as are afforded by our conditions here, and raised hopes in our oppressors that they should yet be rid of us when they would the more securely hold these of our color in merciless bondage....Now, sir, it seems to me that the slavery party will gain little by driving us out of the country, unless it drives us off this continent and the adjacent islands. It seems to me that it would be, after all, little advantage to slavery to have the intelligence and energy of the free colored people all concentrated in the Gulf of Mexico. Sir, I am not for going anywhere; I am for staying precisely where I am, in the land of my birth. But, sir, if I must go from this country; if it is impossible to stay here, I am then for doing the next best and that is to go wherever I can hope to be of most service to the colored people of the United States of America.[7]

As southern states began to withdraw from the Union, Douglass decried the "perilous and dilapidated confusion of the Federal Union." But he used his editorials to ridicule the attitude of the North which he wrote would "crimson the cheeks of their children with shame." History would record, he wrote, that in the conflict to that date, the South had acted with manly spirit, even in support of its "villainous and wicked cause" while the North had acted the "part of miserable cowards, insensible alike to the requirements of self-respect and duty." They were frightened, he claimed. They had been singing and shouting *free speech*! for the last ten years, and yet "one rebellious frown of South Carolina had muzzled the mouths of all our large cities, and filled the air with whines for compromise." Douglass complained that statesmen in and out of Congress had neither an understanding of the problem the nation faced nor its remedy. To him the panacea was simple, for slavery was the root cause of the conflict, notwithstanding the bevy of discussions that had emerged to disguise the fact, and the abolition of slavery would cure the ill. Any union which could be possibly patched up while slavery continued to exist, he wrote, must either completely demoralize the whole nation, or remain a heartless form disguised under the smiles of friendship; a vital, active, and ever-increasing hate that would be sure to explode into violence.

Douglass was equally adamant about the futility of trying to seek a plan for reconstruction of the Union as Abraham Lincoln entered the White House. To him, the cotton states had set up their separate and independent government and nothing could save the Union from the degradation it faced. Any peace conference implied rejection of the Constitution on which the nation had been founded. Any alteration of that document could mean making the Constitution express the image of slavery itself and the North the worshippers of the new aberration. To consider such a plan was abhorrent to Douglass. Moreover, it would call for cementing another union with the slaves' blood. He was opposed and feared that the North would not hold its resolve to save the Union by whatever strong methods the necessity required. No compact or compromise or argument or covenant into which the North and South might enter that would result in strengthening and perpetuating slavery was acceptable.

The abolition of slavery in the District of Columbia encouraged Douglass, but the eventual issuance in 1863 of the Emancipation Proclamation was cause for jubilation. The thought of a country unified in sentiments, objects, and ideas had seldom occurred to most politicians, the editor wrote, but he believed the far too tardy action of the president would save the Union. He also believed that Europe would find a new respect for the United States in that action. When rumors abounded that officers and men on the field fighting for the Union army laid down their arms and threw up their commissions when they heard about the Emancipation Proclamation, Douglass wrote that any such action would be the greatest argument in favor of the president's edict. It would prove that such dissenters had been more concerned with preserving slavery than with defending the Union.

"Let the army be cleansed from all pro-slavery vermin, and its health and strength will be greatly improved," Douglass exclaimed.

Clearly, *Douglass' Monthly* was an abolitionist journal. It did not end its vital arguments and presentations, though, with the Emancipation Proclamation. For as soon as that official action had been taken by the president, the larger and equally vexing problem of what to do with the Negro prevailed throughout the nation. In an address in the Church of the Puritans in New York City, Douglass spoke on "The Present and Future of the Colored Race in America." He published the address the next month in his journal, in which he wrote:

> What shall be done with the Negro? Meet us not only in the street, in the Church, in the Senate, and in our State Legislatures; but in our diplomatic correspondence with foreign nations, and even on the field of battle, where our brave sons and brothers, are striking for Liberty and country, or for honored graves.
>
> This question met us during the war; and will certainly meet us after the war, unless we shall have the wisdom, the courage, and the nobleness of soul to settle the status of the Negro, on the solid and immovable bases of Eternal justice.
>
> I stand here tonight therefore, to advocate what I conceive to be a solid basis, one that shall fix our peace upon a rock. Putting aside all the hay, wood, and stubble of expediency, I shall advocate for the Negro, his most full and complete adoption into the great national family of America. I shall demand for him the most perfect civil and political equality, and that he shall enjoy all the rights, privileges and immunities enjoyed by all members of the body politic. I weigh my words and I mean all I say, when I contend as I do contend, that this is the only solid, and final solution of the problem before us.[8]

During 1863, financial problems caused Douglass to cease publishing his journal. In so doing, he concluded a journalistic career that covered some fifteen years of writing for abolitionist publications, or editing and publishing his own. *Douglass' Monthly*, in particular, represents its editor's most vital expressions of the essence of full American democracy for black and white citizens of the nation. The journal includes Douglass' rejoinders to most of the arguments for slavery and against emancipation and full citizenship for American slaves. It is also a newspaper about the practice of slavery and efforts to avert its atrocities. It was an abolitionist periodical but it also reported on the Haitian revolution and other news outside the United States. Its coverage of the October 1859 trial of John Brown for insurrection is the most complete that can be found in any single periodical, including a reporter's transcript of the proceedings at the trial; editorials about the incident itself; the full text of Henry Ward Beecher's sermon on the trial delivered at his Brooklyn, New York, church; and a wide collection of comments from other magazines and newspapers.

Notes

1. Patsy Brewington Perry's "Before the *North Star*: Frederick Douglass' Early Journalistic Career," *Phylon** (March 1974): 96-107, details Douglass' interest in producing
his own newspaper as early as August 1841, after he had made "a moving impromptu
speech at a meeting of abolitionists convened in Nantucket" while he was working as a
lecturer for the American Anti-Slavery Society. From that time until he launched his
weekly, the *North Star*, in December 1847, Douglass wrote regularly for the *Standard*,
the *National Watchman*, the *Mystery*, and the *Ram's Horn*, leading abolitionist journals.

2. Some historians note that, perhaps, at some time during 1860 Douglass was unable to
publish the *Monthly* owing to his having been forced to reside abroad a portion of that year
to avoid being returned to slavery at the request of his former owner.

3. This format was decidedly different from that of *Frederick Douglass' Paper*, which,
in addition to the abolitionist articles and news about slavery, had an unusually well-
balanced selection of book reviews, original poetry and fiction, and slave narratives.

4. "The True Issue," *Douglass' Monthly* (January 1859): 1.

5. Ibid.

6. "The Republican Party," *Douglass' Monthly* (August 1860): 308.

7. "Proclamation Proclaimed," *Douglass' Monthly* (October 1862): 1.

8. "What Shall Be Done with the Freed Slaves?" *Douglass' Monthly* (November
1862): 1.

Information Sources

BIBLIOGRAPHY:
Bontemps, Arna. *Free at Last: The Life of Frederick Douglass*. New York, 1971.
Dann, Martin E. *The Black Press: 1827-1890*. New York, 1971, pp.14-26.
Penn, I. Garland. *The Afro-American Press*. Springfield, Mass., 1891, pp.66-70.
Perry, Patsy Brewington. "Before *The North Star*: Frederick Douglass' Early Journalistic
    Career." *Phylon*, March 1974, pp.96-107.
———. "The Literary Content of *Frederick Douglass' Paper* Through 1860." *College
    Language Association Journal*, December 1973, pp.214-29.
INDEX SOURCES: None
LOCATION SOURCES: Greenwood Press Periodicals; Negro University Press Reprints;
    Schomberg Collection, New York Public Library, New York, New York.

Publication History

MAGAZINE TITLE AND TITLE CHANGES: *Douglass' Monthly* (January
    1859-August 1863).
VOLUME AND ISSUE DATA: Vols. I-VII , monthly. It appears that the first seven
    issues of Vol. I were published as part of *Frederick Douglass' Paper*, an anteced-
    ent to *Douglass' Monthly*.
PUBLISHER AND PLACE OF PUBLICATION: Frederick Douglass, Rochester, New
    York.
EDITOR: Frederick Douglass (1859-1863).
CIRCULATION: 3,000 estimate.

E

EBONY

John H. Johnson, who had experienced unprecedented success for black journalists with his *Negro Digest*,* published the first issue of *Ebony* in Chicago in November 1945. The World War II milieu gave rise to the publishing company Johnson had founded. As had been the case during World War I, the black press was harassed by governmental forces in the 1940s. Their editorials were offensive as they attacked treatment of black troops in training camps in the South, job discrimination in war-related industries, and the expectations of blacks as an outgrowth of this nation's going forth once more to assist European nations to achieve democracy.[1] When World II was over, the giants of the black weekly newspaper press declined in influence. Television was the new medium of communication. And the white press, long known for ignoring news about blacks, found itself forced to give attention to the social revolution of the 50s and 60s. Black magazines replaced black national newspapers in large measure. Moreover, they have continued to enlarge upon the purposes of the black press as enunciated since the founding of *Freedom's Journal** in 1827.[2]

No single periodical has served this purpose so effectively as *Ebony*; though it was not the first of Johnson's publications. *Negro Digest* went on the newsstands in November of 1942. Within a year, it had reached a monthly circulation of some 50,000. *Ebony*, considered by most an Afro-American version of *Life* magazine, appeared three years later. Its chief objective was not unusual. Like periodicals that had preceded it, *Ebony* sought to report success black people were experiencing in various aspects of American life. Unlike some other journals, it emphasized the bright side of black life. In imitating *Life*, Johnson established a practice of launching magazines with formulas and formats that had been used successfully by publishers for primarily white readers.[3]

Ebony's first issue contained a brief statement of editorial policy, "Backstage," that committed the magazine to reporting on everyday achievements of blacks from Harlem to Hollywood. "When we talk about race as the Number 1 problem in America, we talk turkey," Johnson promised. The several departments in the inaugural number were Race, Youth, Personalities, Culture, Entertainment, and Humor. News and opinion items under those headings included notes on "Catholics and Color," "The Truth About Brazil," "60 Thousand Jobs or Else," "Children's Crusade," "Bye-Bye to Boogie," "Richard R. Wright's Citizens and Southern Bank in Philadelphia," "African Art for Americans," "Book Boom for Negro Authors," and "Film Parade." The photo-editorial that remained a feature of *Ebony* for many years discussed postwar unemployment problems for blacks. E. Simms Campbell, a distinguished black cartoonist who had won his reputation with *Esquire* magazine, contributed "Campbell's Comic."

The second issue was a bit late because Johnson was unprepared for the tremendous response *Ebony* received from the public. Six months later, the publisher announced that *Ebony* would accept advertising. He wrote letters to chief executives of large corporations on the theory that his new magazine could only approach major advertising revenue circles as foreign territory. He argued that if the president of the smallest country in the world came to the United States, he would be received by the president as a matter of protocol. His first account was secured with Zenith Corporation. It represented a seminal breakthrough for black journalism. Thus, with photojournalism for blacks, unprecedented advertising accounts, and an impressive array of talent on his staff, Johnson brought an entirely new vigor to the conventional subjects black periodicals had always projected. In addition to those already mentioned, he added "Date with a Dish," "Eligible Bachelors," "Fashion Fair," "Washington Notebook," "*Ebony* Bookshelf," and "Speaking of People."

Ebony began publication as an imitation of *Life* magazine, and in doing so, it established an unstated assumption that the United States was, indeed, a two-society nation. There was a white life and there was a black life. The two seldom met in self-image. *Ebony* extracted a journalism model and economic clout from one and used these to propel the accomplishments and aspirations of the other without the encumbrances of philanthropy that had obligated almost ever previous black institution. In the highest tradition of an American cultural artifact, *Ebony* served an ongoing utilitarian purpose with each issue. Moreover, it chronicled a storehouse of pertinent information about blacks in contemporary and past times. Through its popular appeal, it informed white and black Americans about the values each sought and cherished. And in so doing, it advanced the achievement of Johnson's goal of interracial understanding.

Unlike *Negro Digest*, *Ebony* published editorials in the early years. They were Johnson's medium for "talking turkey." After the war, he decried the shortage of black skilled labor. And he attributed that dearth to the mis-education of blacks. Black colleges, he wrote, had leaned over backwards to emphasize academic studies at the expense of the vocations, and in making that choice, they had deprived their students of a way of making a living in the fast-developing industrial postwar economy. Another cause for the scarcity lay in the widespread discrimination labor unions practiced against black artisans.

Ebony was active politically. Johnson supported Harry Truman for reelection in 1948 because he was electable and Henry Wallace was not. He encouraged blacks to think politically in terms of economics rather than race. His strongest editorials praised the collapse of white Democratic primaries in the early 1950s, because of the impetus that movement would give to black voter registration. He endorsed Adlai Stevenson for president in 1953 because he believed Stevenson had demonstrated unmistakably his feeling and friendship for Negroes. John Sparkman, Stevenson's running mate from Alabama and an acknowledged racist, was no more objectionable to Johnson than John Nance Garner or Harry Truman, who had been Franklin D. Roosevelt's vice presidential candidates. Johnson entreated his readers to stand muster at the polls and pass the most important intelligence test of the time by voting for Stevenson. He could not support Dwight D. Eisenhower. The general's 42 years of military service hardly qualified him for the presidency. Further, he had testified before the Senate Armed Services Committee that the army was justified in its jim crow practices. After Eisenhower was elected president and his administration integrated schools on military bases and Veterans Administration hospitals, *Ebony* praised the president for his role in carefully planning and carrying out the desegregation proposals.

After the first ten years of its publication Johnson wrote of *Ebony*:

Ebony was started ten years ago to mirror the brighter side of Negro life. On the whole, the Negro has had a good life in America during that period, and reporting on his activities has been for us both a privilege and a pleasure. Because it has filled a long felt need of the Negro for recognition and respect, *Ebony* has succeeded beyond our fondest hopes.

The chief criteria we use in determining the suitability of any story which will appear on the pages of *Ebony* is success and achievement in any field. In so doing, we have featured lawyers and farmers, school teachers and chorus girls, ministers and bellboys, scientists, and bootblacks.

We believe that *Ebony* has helped the Negro gain a new respect and dignity by showing him as a fellow human being, with the same qualities and capacities as other members of his species.

We believe that *Ebony* has increased the Negro's pride in himself and his heritage by presenting his historical contributions to the development of our American culture.

We believe *Ebony* has promoted interracial understanding by emphasizing the positive and minimizing the negative aspects of race relations.

Finally, and certainly by no means least of all, we believe *Ebony* has given hope and inspiration to our young people. By portraying through words and pictures the success stories of great Negro Americans, we have proved for our youth that their dreams, too, can come true, and that any goal in life can be achieved if we put into it enough study, work and faith.

We shall in the future continue to report honestly and accurately, the noble determination of the Negro people to gain full equality.[4]

Ebony was one of the most reliable sources of news of the civil rights movement of the late fifties and the sixties. Johnson's editorials condemned what he considered the stereotyped "Uncle Tom" figures among black faculty and administrators and praised the rise of student activism. He recognized and understood the dilemma Alabama State, South Carolina State, Alcorn A. and M., Southern, Florida A. and M., and North Carolina A. and T. colleges and universities faced as southern black institutions grappled with the embryonic social revolution on their campuses. The magazine stood solidly behind persons in those schools who were determined to eliminate segregation in higher education. *Ebony* held that blacks could remain proud of their heritage and of the black colleges they had founded and sustained. At the same time, though, the journal placed upon those institutions a major responsibility to provide leadership in fighting for black citizenship advancement.

During those turbulent years, Martin Luther King, Jr., published an article describing his visit to India, and he ran a regular "Advice for Living By" question-and-answer column in the magazine. *Ebony* also provided news and analyses of the dramatic rise of nationalism among black African colonials, including biographical sketches of black diplomatic and government officials in the new nations and representatives from those countries in embassies in the United States and in the United Nations organization.

Ebony supported John F. Kennedy for president in 1960 and held high hopes for his new idealism for the nation. Simeon Booker wrote, upon the occasion of his inauguration, that the president and his vice president would try to pass liberal social and economic legislation; they would face an uphill Capitol Hill battle in doing so, but would have the encouragement of Negroes in their fight.[5]

Reaching an estimated 6 million readers by the time of its thirty-fifth anniversary in 1980, *Ebony* had recorded, illustrated, and commented upon the dynamic second half of the twentieth century. Johnson has been honored and written about more than any living black journalist during that period. *Ebony* has become and continues to be the accepted symbol of a black medium for black people. It has covered the civil rights movement, the *de jure* desegregation of America, the black arts, the Vietnam War, and the affirmative action dilemma of the late seventies and early eighties. One of its special issues, "Blacks and the Money Crunch," was prefaced by Johnson's timely, succinct statement of *Ebony's* history and its relationship to current problems. The bicentennial issue, "200 Years of Black Trials and Triumphs" is a course outline in American life and history.

Ebony is a veritable library of the second half of the twentieth century from the black perspective. Its emphasis remains centered on black history, entertainment, business, health, personalities, occupations, and sports. Departments have not changed radically over the years. Practically every significant American—black and white—has been interviewed by or contributed to *Ebony*. Johnson often speaks with justifiable pride of the large number of graduates of black colleges his enterprise has employed now for more than a generation.

Notes

1. For further understanding of the historical problem the black press has experienced with the official American public, *see* John H. Burma, "The Future of the Negro Press," *Negro Digest* (December 1947): 67-70; F. G. Detweiler, "The Negro Press Today," *American Journal of Sociology* (November 1939): 391-400; and Jack Lyle, ed., *The Black Americans and the Press* (Los Angeles, Calif. World Ritchie Press, 1968).

2. *See* Henk La Brie II, "Black Newspapers: The Roots Are 150 Years Deep," *Journalism History* (Winter 1977-78): 111-13.

3. Roland E. Wolseley, *The Black Press, U.S.A.* (Ames, Iowa, 1971), pp.64-65, notes that *Negro Digest* suggests *Reader's Digest*; *Ebony* is like *Life*; *Jet* like the defunct *Quick*. The Johnson publications have outlived all of those they are said to have imitated except *Reader's Digest*.

4. "A Message From The Publisher," *Ebony* (November 1952): 97.

5. "What Negroes Can Expect From Kennedy," *Ebony* (January 1961): 36.

Information Sources

BIBLIOGRAPHY:
Cartwright, Margarite. "Magazines in Sepia." *Negro History Bulletin*, January 1954, pp. 74, 94.
"Color Success Black." *Time*, 2 August 1968, p. 32.
"*Ebony* Circulation Nears 200,000 Mark." *Advertising Age*, 18 March 1946, p. 31.
"*Ebony* Making a New Market Pay Off." *Business Week* 1177 (22 March 1952): 38.
"*Ebony* Publishes Largest Issue: Has 450,000 Circulation." *Advertising Age*, 17 September 1951, p. 81.
Johnson, John H. "The Publisher's Statement." *Ebony*, August 1980, p. 31.
————"First Ten Years." *Ebony*, November 1953, p. 9.
————"The *Ebony* Family." *Ebony*, November 1980, pp. 32-42.
Joyce, Donald Franklin. "Magazines of Afro-American Thought." *American Libraries*, December 1976, pp. 678-83.
Miles, Frank W. "Negro Magazines Come of Age." *Magazine World*, 1 June 1946, pp. 18, 21.
Reichley, A. James. "How Johnson Made It." *Fortune*, January 1968, pp. 152-53, 178-80.
Rinder, Irwin D. "A Sociological Look Into the Negro Pictorial." *Phylon*, Spring 1959, pp. 181-87.
Robinson, Louis. "The Black Press: Voice of Freedom," *Ebony*, August 1975, pp. 82-88.
"The Story of *Ebony*." *Ebony*, November 1953, pp.122-24.
Wolseley, Roland. *The Black Press, U.S.A.* Ames: Iowa State University Press, 1971, pp. 61-63.

INDEX SOURCE: *Reader's Guide to Periodical Literature*.
LOCATION SOURCES: University Microfilms; most public and academic libraries.

Publication History

MAGAZINE TITLE AND TITLE CHANGES: *Ebony*, November 1945 to present.
VOLUME AND ISSUE DATA: Vols. I-XXXVI, monthly.
PUBLISHER AND PLACE OF PUBLICATION: John H. Johnson, Editor and Publisher, Johnson Publishing Company, Chicago, Illinois.
EDITORS: John H. Johnson (1945-); Herbert Nipson, executive editor; Lerone Bennett, Jr., senior editor.
CIRCULATION: 1,225,000.

EBONY JR.

The Johnson Publishing Company, the most successful magazine enterprise among Afro-Americans, began publishing *Ebony Jr.*, a children's periodical, in January 1973, almost thirty years after it had launched the exceptionally popular *Ebony*.* It was the first effort at publishing a general-purpose magazine for children since W.E.B. Du Bois' short-lived *Brownies' Book*.* Du Bois set up a company to produce and market that journal, although Augustus Dill and Jessie Fauset—both associates of his at the *Crisis** staff—became his partners in the new endeavor.

Ebony Jr. is fashioned for children in grades kindergarten through six. Its special address is to black children. It contains stories, articles, word and mathematical games, songs, contests, and a calendar of events in the lives of black Americans. The contents are edited especially to assist elementary school children to strengthen their reading skills and to appreciate their Afro-American heritage. "A Guide for Use of *Ebony Jr.*" describes ways teachers may use the features in each issue for reading comprehension, vocabulary building, word attack, and "bridging" between black and standard English. "Ebony Jr. News" carries short letters from children and news items about children's activities. The magazine also conducts a writing feature for young poets.

Like adult general-purpose periodicals, *Ebony Jr.* concentrates on black personalities, including popular entertainers. One novel article in a recent issue, "Talking with W.E.B. Du Bois," is an imaginary interview with the noted black scholar. Its content is biographical and contains two color illustrations from the *Brownies' Book*.

With the extraordinary financial security of the popular Johnson Publishing Company as its support, *Ebony Jr.* enjoys the opportunity to provide a well-edited journal for black children that no other known source could provide.

Information Sources

BIBLIOGRAPHY:
Hall, Carla. "John Johnson—Still Climbing on a Jet Stream." *Chicago Sun-Times,* 19
October 1980, section 2, p. 10.
Katz, Bill, and Richards, Berry G. *Magazines for Libraries.* 3 ed. New York, 1978, pp.
241-2.
Van Order, Phyllis, ed. *Elementary School Library Collection: A Guide to Books and Other
Media.* 11th ed., phases 1, 2, 3. Newark, N.J.: Bro-Dart Foundation, p. 42.
INDEX SOURCE: *Subject Index to Children's Literature.*
LOCATION SOURCES: College and university libraries; public libraries.

Publication History

MAGAZINE TITLE AND TITLE CHANGES: *Ebony Jr.*
VOLUME AND ISSUE DATA: Vols. I-VIII (January 1973 to present), monthly, bi-
monthly June/July and August/September.
PUBLISHER AND PLACE OF PUBLICATION: Johnson Publishing Company, Chica-
go, Illinois.
EDITOR: Constance Johnson (1973-).
CIRCULATION: 400,000.

EDUCATION: A JOURNAL OF REPUTATION

Education: A Journal of Reputation was launched by three black New Yorkers—
Harry T. Stewart, Johnnie Kelly, and H. S. McFarland—following the Harlem
riot of 19 March 1935. The men pooled their resources to publish a magazine
they believed would contribute to better racial understanding among white shop-
keepers and black residents in Harlem. Allegedly, the disturbance arose because
a black boy accused of stealing a small knife from a 125th Street store was said to
have been beaten to death. The riot caused property damage estimated at $200
million and cost at least three lives. Interracial committees sought to identify the
causes of the violence. Most investigators agreed that resentment of racial discrimination and poverty among blacks in the midst of plenty contributed to a
general unrest in the area. Shortly before the riot, white Harlem businessmen
forced through a boycott to hire Negroes had secured an injunction on the basis
of the Sherman Anti-Trust Act. As a result of their court action, many merchants
fired their newly hired blacks. Frustration over a series of events led Mayor
Fiorello La Guardia to appoint a commission on race to attempt to quell strife and
the growing discomforts of the national depression. Stewart, Kelly, and McFarland
believed they could contribute best to efforts to bring racial peace in Harlem by
issuing a monthly magazine and distributing it locally. McFarland served as

editor. In *Education*, he sought to educate Harlemites to their potential for solving their own problems, to advertise the virtues rather than the vices of the community, and to work to broaden considerably the scope of employment for blacks. He wanted to find intelligent solutions to housing conditions and to increase black representation in state and national legislatures.

McFarland called for articles that he could publish in the magazine on the mayor's committee and the Scottsboro Case. At a time when many persons were questioning whether the American system of government could survive the depression and the attendant racial disturbances, the little magazine, through an editorial titled "Why I Believe the United States Will Remain a Constitutional Democracy for Several Generations to Come," expressed the editor-publishers' political posture. They believed that in an atmosphere of growing agitation for advancement for socialism and/or communism as a remedy for the nation's ills, black people should work within the system to solve their problems. McFarland used an item from *Pravda*, "A Picture of Harlem," that called the community the most discussed and least understood Negro area in the world, as a basis for one of his early editorials.

Without disagreeing with that part of the story that pointed out the problems blacks faced in Harlem, McFarland wrote that the American proletariat, black and white, were not dreamers. They were practical, peace-loving, and law-abiding people firmly resolved to adhere to the time-honored system of orderly, democratic government. The editor criticized *Pravda* for using social and economic distress in the United States as an indication that the black population would turn to communism. Russian writers, he said, who looked at Harlem through flaming red glasses might well remember that the Negro is decidedly American, and as such is thoroughly capable of solving his own problems. He did not agree with the Russian reporters that Father Divine's Peace Missions were an indication that American blacks felt they should turn from Christianity to a "Moses" who would lead them out of economic bondage.

Education published some creative writing, but it focused primarily upon living conditions in Harlem. Some articles included "A Brief History of Negro Representation in the Democratic Party in the City of New York," "West Indian Women at Home and Abroad," "Problems of the Negro Lawyer," "Lack of Dependability Mars our Progress," and "The School System of Harlem." The editor praised Mayor La Guardia for his promise to insure additional and improved parks, hospitals, and low-cost housing in Harlem. He moved slightly to the left of his original political positions when, in the last two issues of the magazine, he advocated Angelo Herndon, the well-known black Communist, in his campaign to become representative of the twenty-first state district to the New York General Assembly.

Education is an extremely slight publication that has little value other than as a chronicle of some details on Harlem during the mid thirties. Its articles on tensions between landlords and tenants and the long, often acrimonious negotiations between them, present a comprehensive perspective on this festering socio-economic issue. When the magazine added news on a national or international level, it lost its validity. Its focus had been traditionally narrow, poignant, and effective. It could not compete with other black periodicals better qualified to engage in the broad dimensions of journalism. It also lost ground when it moved left editorially. It served its original purposes well during its brief life. The only distinctive features in *Education* are Arthur Schomberg's article "Great Negro Tragedians" and several personal interviews with black entertainers including Josephine Baker and Mercedes Gilbert.

Information Sources

BIBLIOGRAPHY:

Bergnab, Peter M., and Bergman, Mort M. *The Chronological History of the Negro in America*. New York, 1969.

Osofsky, Gilbert. *Harlem: The Making of a Ghetto*. New York, 1971.

Sitkoff, Howard. *A New Deal for Blacks: The Emergence of Civil Rights As a National Issue. Volume I: The Depression Decade*. New York, 1978.

Weiss, Richard. "Ethnicity and Reform: Minorities and the Ambiance of The Depression Years." *Journal of American History*, December 1979, pp. 655-85.

INDEX SOURCES: None

LOCATION SOURCES: Library of Congress; Schomberg Collection, New York Public Library; Greenwood Press Periodicals.

Publication History

MAGAZINE TITLE AND TITLE CHANGES: *Education: A Journal of Reputation.*

VOLUME AND ISSUE DATA: Vols. I-II (April 1935-September 1936).

PUBLISHER AND PLACE OF PUBLICATION: Negro Needs Society, Corona, New York.

EDITOR: H. S. McFarland (1935-1936).

CIRCULATION: 1,000.

ENCORE AMERICAN AND WORLDWIDE NEWS

Encore American and Worldwide News is designed to be a news monthly for blacks. Its editor points out that hers is not a magazine of so-called black news, but of all the news of the world reported from a black perspective. As founder and editor in chief of *Encore*, Ida Lewis was the first black woman publisher of a national magazine. Previously, she had been involved in the launching of *Essence** magazine, which she served as editor from its founding in 1970 until 1971 at which time she was ousted during an intramural fight. Her own uncommon professional experience as a journalist which includes service as a correspondent in Africa and Europe made it possible for her to draw around herself a cadre of persons to work for her new enterprise, *Encore*. She started with $40,000 raised through loans, and volunteer manuscripts from friends. She brought out the first issue in May 1972 and immediately placed upon the journal a stamp of individuality. It carried in its inaugural number a debate between black poet Nikki Giovanni and Soviet poet Yevgeny Yevtushenko over the racial overtones in the term "black power"; an interview with a Chinese physician on women's liberation in the Cultural Revolution; and the beginning of a regular feature, "America: Neither Black Nor White" which included essays written by black, Puerto Rican, Chicano, and American Indian spokespersons. The first issue was tentative. Four months after its appearance, Lewis went into regular production of a monthly journal that was compelled to compete with the unusual financial backing *Essence* had received in its introduction to the public two years earlier.[1]

The September 1972 issue of *Encore* reflected Lewis' worldwide connections and the unique perspective she would bring to the magazine's audience. She reported on the problem of unrest among British West Indian troops stationed in Northern Ireland to keep peace between warring Catholics and Protestants. She also included news items from China, Haiti, and the French Antilles. One of her associate editors remarked at the time that *Encore* had broad international perspectives that ranged beyond Harlem. Domestic issues were covered in a format divided into departments: law, medicine, fashion, architecture, travel, cinema, books, and art. *Encore* was consciously directed toward the educated, affluent black audience. The 75,000 copies prepared for the first two-monthly schedule were sold out. Some advertisers soon came, giving security to a journal that had been started with credit, a bank loan, and a commitment to low overhead. Lewis considered the proliferation of black periodicals in the seventies healthy rather than discouraging, and fashioned a new dimension for black journalism which found a way to carry out the meaning Lewis gave to the title she chose for the journal. She once wrote that *Encore* denoted further interpretation and a hearing again of the news in terms of the needs of black people. Other editors and publishers had felt the need but had not been nearly so successful in devising a viable medium for that purpose.

Encore is a general-purpose magazine that reports on national and international affairs and emphasizes personalities and events among black Americans—historic and current. Editorial comment is contained in "In Focus," a brief summary of contemporary matters. The format of the journal includes several sections. "Newscheck" is a collection of brief paragraphs of news items around the world as they relate to black people. "Remembrance of Things Past" is a valuable source of information on personalities in Afro-American history. "Within the Nation" contains in-depth stories on current affairs—pornography, Marines in the Ku Klux Klan, overpopulation of prisons, and national problems of social and political importance. The "International" news column usually concentrates upon race relations in the Caribbean, Europe, and Africa. "People in the News" is a series of short items about well-known blacks and their accomplishments.

In addition to these regular departments, *Encore* provides a wide range of entertainment news. There are features on blacks in theater, music, art, and motion pictures. Other articles address problems in religion and news about religious organizations. The book reviews are general in nature, although they relate to blacks. Although Nikki Giovanni has served as editorial consultant for the magazine, it publishes little creative writing. Since January 1975, the journal has appeared biweekly.

Articles and editorials were vociferous in the 1980 presidential campaign. "Can Blacks and Communists Unite?" was written following the violent confrontation between communists and Ku Klux Klan members in Greensboro, North Carolina, in November 1979. Editors expressed the fear that communists might have inroads among blacks in the South at a time when traditional black-rights organizations were suffering dwindling funds and loss of members.

An editorial in April 1980 took a strong position: that Islam is not anti-American. It made the provocative point that inasmuch as Islam claims 576 million of the world's people, forty-two different nations, and the world's major oil producers, the United States cannot succeed with a foreign policy that perceives Muslims as ignorant. Hostility toward Islamic nations, the editorial continued, is nonproductive for the United States government as a continuing policy.

In "Carter or Kennedy—What's the Difference?" *Encore* pointed out that there was a distinction between the two candidates for the Democratic presidential nomination. Those differences lay in their attitudes toward employment and inflation, the federal budget, energy, health care, urban affairs and revitalization, civil rights and affirmative action, rights and privileges of women, criminal justice and law enforcement, and foreign policy. The position paper pointed out that despite pressure on Kennedy to move to the right, unlike Carter, the Massachusetts senator has for the most part remained a liberal of the old school. *Encore* supported Kennedy for the nomination because of his voting record which had earned him the support of American blacks.

Leadership among blacks and whites is a most important part of the editorial position of *Encore*. The journal has attacked again and again what it considers the "bankruptcy of black leadership." It is a liberal journal in its politics, but it requires old-fashioned integrity and clean aggressiveness of political leaders. The nature of its contents makes *Encore* a news and opinion periodical that enjoys unusually strong circulation. It is one of the few biweekly organs geared to black audiences.

Note

1. *Essence* represents a radical departure from the publishing opportunities previously available to black journalists. It was supported from the beginning as a joint venture between the Chase Manhattan Bank, the Morgan Guaranty Trust Company, and the First National City Bank of New York. With the artistic reputation of Gordon Parks, a popular black artist and professional photographer, four young black college-trained people repre-

senting a combination of professions initiated *Essence* without the restraints black publishers had almost always faced previously. Ida Lewis was part of the venture.

Information Sources

BIBLIOGRAPHY:
"Black Perspective." *Time*, 30 October 1972, p. 85.
Shockley, Ann, and Chandler, Sue P. *Living Black American Authors: A Biographical Directory*. New York, 1973, p. 97.
INDEX SOURCE: *Index to Periodical Articles by and about Negroes.*
LOCATION SOURCES: Many college and university libraries; University Microfilms International.

Publication History

MAGAZINE TITLE AND TITLE CHANGES: *Encore* (Spring 1972), quarterly.
Encore American and Worldwide News (6 January 1975), biweekly.
VOLUME AND ISSUE DATA: Vol. I (Spring 1972), continued monthly from September 1972. Volume numbers have been consecutive since.
PUBLISHER AND PLACE OF PUBLICATION: Ida Lewis, Publisher, Tanner Publications, Inc., New York, New York.
EDITOR: Ida Lewis (1972-).
CIRCULATION: 150,000.

ESSENCE: THE MAGAZINE FOR TODAY'S BLACK WOMAN

Essence ushered in an entirely new dimension to black magazine journalism. Previously, black social progress organizations had represented the most financially stable black magazines—that is, until John H. Johnson established his pace-setting publishing company with *Negro Digest** in 1942. Few privately owned magazines had prospered, even those initiated by Robert S. Abbott and Robert L. Vann, both of whom had established unusually successful national weekly newspapers. Denominational periodicals and academic, professional subject-matter journals survived primarily from membership subscriptions and patronage from black college libraries. Little literary journals and scholarly periodicals published by black colleges depended on more precarious backing than any other black media. The new emphasis on broadened employment opportunities for blacks in areas they had participated in only nominally at an earlier time gave rise to *Essence*. Jonathan Blount, an advertisement salesman for New Jersey Bell, first proposed a black woman's magazine two years before *Essence* appeared in May 1970. He and Clarence Smith, a salesman for Prudential Insurance, were among fifty young blacks invited by the Wall Street brokerage firm of Sherson, Hamill, and Cox to discuss ideas for black business ventures. There they met Cyril Hill, a printing expert, and Ed Lewis, a financial planner. The four men formed a partnership and sold their proposal for a black women's magazine to influential financiers on Wall Street. They engaged the noted photographer and author Gordon Parks as their editorial director and planned their first issue. Parks brought along his son, Gordon Parks, Jr., and another free-lance writer, Gilbert Moore. The partnership employed Ida Lewis, an experienced and talented journalist with national and international reporting experience, as the first editor.[1]

Such a collection of talent had never before amassed its resources to produce a black journal. The staff agreed upon a militant tone for the new magazine that would not be incompatible with the new black nationalism. But they also made clear that they wanted a periodical "more woman and less black" than their contemporary competitors. It would particularize for women the market and audience *Ebony** had cultivated for blacks in general. The editor of the *Journal of Black Poetry** a little literary journal, complained bitterly that *Essence* was not worthy of pointing out a direction for black culture because its staff and contributors were racially mixed and its promoters were white. *Essence* replied by including in its original format black creative arts. It was "black is beautiful" in a new key. The management confidently made a first press run of 175,000 copies. The journal was clearly geared to the interests of young black women. First-rate advertising accounts came almost immediately.

The first issue contained Parks' photographs of Rosa Parks, Shirley Chisholm, Barbara Ann Teer, and "Muslim" Woman as the "Mother of Black Nations." "Our World" included features written by highly respected black men and women: Louise Meriwether's "Black Man, Do You Love?", Gilbert Moore's "Five Shades of Militancy," Alvin Poussaint's "The Psychiatric Dimension: Black Woman's Double Subjugation," and Alice Childress' "Mothers' Day, 1970." Another feature, "Folks Are Rapping On," reported on news about the activities of black entertainers. "On the Wire" recorded observations about blacks on the public national and international scenes. The Culture section contained poems, essays, and a short story. Other departments were titled "Fashion," "Beauty Notes," and "Home and Family." The publisher's statement spoke directly to the black woman's intelligence as well as her physical beauty.

> With the swelling wave of black consciousness around the world, you, the Black woman, are at long last coming into your own....*Essence* will publish the most significant developments in public affairs, education, entertainment, and the arts as they relate to our Black community, as well as fiction, poetry, and features on Black heritage, travel and careers.... *Essence* will serve as a forum for Black discussion and a showcase for Black talent.[2]

A free-lance writer who admitted he had never read *Ebony* or *Essence* or known anyone who read either of them, wrote a comparison of the two black journals. "*Ebony* is the oldtimer," he wrote, the one that tried to keep up with the times, giving space to younger black celebrities, new black fads and styles, "the angrier black rhetoric," as well as giving some attention to Thurgood Marshall and Martin Luther King, Jr. *Essence*, to him, was different. It was aimed specifically at young black women. "It's sassy, a NOW magazine," that was laid out better than *Ebony* and relied more on prose, less on pictures. The writer concluded that *Essence* was a "black *Cosmopolitan*."[3]

For its tenth anniversary issue, a member of *Essence*'s staff who had been with the magazine since its inception described the periodical in quite different terms from the writer quoted above.

> Looking back on those first issues, I wonder what made the publishers actually try to deal with us at all. We didn't know what we wanted but screamed when *Essence* didn't give it to us. We didn't know where we were headed but demanded that *Essence* guide us there. The magazine was as schizophrenic as the times, and no matter what was printed, a vocal segment of our community was offended. It's a good thing Black women had no other magazine to turn to—otherwise *Essence* might have been in a no-win situation. Of course, there was *Ebony*, but it didn't feature red, black and green patent leather shoes the way *Essence* did. *Jet* [*] didn't tell you how to fashion your hair into a Gibson Girl Afro like *Essence* did. *Negro Digest* didn't print stories like "Sensuous Black Man, Do You Love Me?". . . *Essence* was the first publication to look at us realistically, just as we were, and not turn and run the other way.[4]

That statement might well define the reasons for the magazine's success. But there was more. In an early editorial, "Perspective: Black Is the Pursuit of Excellence," the editor wrote that the journal would "build on the positive elements of our heritage. We do not pretend to be leaders of a revolutionary movement." In that retort to the black-arts spokesmen who attacked the magazine for its own purposes, the editor continued, "We do not intend to go through the 'Mirror-mirror-on-the-wall-who-is-the-blackest-of-them-all?' syndrome." She reiterated that *Essence* was a black woman's magazine. "We are convinced that we can best serve the Black woman by encouraging her to fulfill herself."

The staff made good on their promise. The journal enjoyed success from its first issue. The format successfully combined creative arts with public affairs, women's special interests, and major advertising copy. It published works about, of, and interviews with popular black American writers including James Baldwin, John Killens, Larry Neal, Nikki Giovanni, Charles Gardone, Alice Walker, Ishmael Reed, Maya Angelou and Dudley Randall. Articles on public affairs were contributed by John Henrik Clarke, Jesse Jackson, and Angela Davis. Lindsay Patterson and Raoul Abdul wrote on theater and entertainment. One particularly impressive feature in the first Christmas issue was Albert Cleage's "Jesus Was a Black Messiah."

By the beginning of the 1980s, *Essence* had moved into a mode that emphasized departments providing information on women's interests, travel, the world of work, some labor news, and a small amount of creative writing. The new trend in this respect is illustrated by an announcement: "We'd like to thank all writers who have sent their poetry to *Essence*, however, we no longer accept unsolicited submissions." Another indication of the shift in emphasis in focus on the black woman appears in a recent editorial under the feature title "Common Ground," which places the expectation level of the black woman into realistic perspective.

> Everyone, including me, would like to believe that we Black women are leapfrogging into the land of plenty. We buy the myth that right timing, MBAs and affirmative action are springing us into the inner sanctum of the boardroom. This seductive portrait has us as attached, navy-suited dynamos cutting our executive suite teeth with high-rolling, hip-switching savvy. We are somehow Lola Falana, Patricia Roberts Harris, and Mary McLeod Bethune rolled into one, upscale, uppity, and ubiquitous Black businesswoman—MS. Biz.[5]

The image is a myth, the editor continued. One that black women must learn to handle. For the cold, unrelenting reality is that few black women reach a higher rung in life than their mothers reached, and the odds are just about as overwhelming. "In general we are outnumbered in high-paying positions by white women, Black men and white men—and not in that order," the comment pointed out. The piece made it clear that black women and men need numbers, push and help from one another. They do not need myths.

Essence continues to work successfully at the purposes its promoters and editors set for it at the beginning of the seventies. Its advertising accounts are impressive. They filled thirteen pages in the first issue and have multiplied to many times that number in current issues.

Notes

1. At one time some members of the staff claimed that *Playboy* magazine was taking over the controlling interest in *Essence* and setting editorial policy. The charge was denied; a new editor in chief was appointed, and the tone of the magazine was changed somewhat. It moved into the trend of general-purpose periodicals of the time, balancing strong women's interests with creative writing and national affairs.

2. *Essence* (May 1970): 8.

3. M. J. Sobran, Jr., "Having It Both Ways," *National Review* (8 November 1974): 1303.

4. "Editorial," *Essence* (May 1980): 14.

5. Ibid., p. 26.

Information Sources

BIBLIOGRAPHY:
Alexander, Daryl Royster. "Common Ground." *Essence*, March 1981, p. 79.
Allen, Bonnie. "The Making of *Essence*." *Essence*, May 1980, pp. 83-95, 166-67.
"Black Market." *Newsweek*, 17 July 1972, p. 71.
"Black Venture." *Time*, 4 May 1980, pp. 79-80.
"Meaningful Images." *Newsweek*, 11 May 1974, p. 74.
Sobran, M. J., Jr. "Having It Both Ways." *National Review*, 8 November 1974, pp. 1302-3.
"Some Notes." *Journal of Black Poetry*, Summer 1972, p. 3.
INDEX SOURCES: *Index to Periodical Articles by and about Negroes*; *Arts and Humanities Citation Index*; *Reader's Guide to Periodical Literature*.
LOCATION SOURCES: Most college and university libraries; urban public libraries; University Microfilms.

Publication History

MAGAZINE TITLE AND TITLE CHANGES: *Essence: The Magazine for Today's Black Woman*.
VOLUME AND ISSUE DATA: Vol. I- (May 1970 to present), monthly.
PUBLISHER AND PLACE OF PUBLICATION: Edward Lewis, Publisher and Chief Executive, Essence Communication, Boulder, Colorado.
EDITORS: Ida Lewis (May 1970-June 1971); Marcia Gillespie (July 1971-May 1980); Daryl Royster Alexander (June 1980-).
CIRCULATION: 600,000.

F

FIRE!!: DEVOTED TO YOUNGER NEGRO ARTISTS

The first and only issue of *Fire!!* appeared in November 1926 with the subtitle, "A Quarterly Devoted to Younger Negro Artists." As the first black "little magazine," it arose in response to the popular black creative artists' desire for a periodical entirely concerned with the arts. They said they intended to rebel against Alain Locke, W.E.B. Du Bois, Benjamin Brawley, and the other "old heads" whose ethnoaesthetic seemed tied too closely to a "decadent bourgeoisie" element in the black political world. Writers among the group had gained public visibility through *Crisis** and *Opportunity*,* organs of the black political and social organizations the NAACP and the National Urban League, respectively. Du Bois at *Crisis* and Charles S. Johnson at *Opportunity* actively promoted black creative art through creative writing contests. Walter White, executive secretary of the NAACP, used his considerable influence with New York businessmen to secure publishing opportunities for Countee Cullen and Claude McKay in particular. Cullen and Gwendolyn Bennett wrote literary columns for *Opportunity*. But *Fire!!*'s promoters wanted a magazine like *Poetry*, *Palms*, and *Carolina Quarterly*, white literary organs intended solely for writers and illustrators. The young writers argued with Alain Locke's subject matter and aesthetic assumption in his *New Negro: An Interpretation* (1925) which they said was published with the imprints of the NAACP and the National Urban League and issued by a white publishing house. To them, the fiery passion of the new breed of writers needed its own medium, one paid for and completely controlled by them. So Langston Hughes, Wallace Thurman, Gwendolyn Bennett, Richard Bruce, Zora Neale Hurston, Aaron Douglas, and John Davis edited the "Premier Issue" of *Fire!!* with some financial assistance from nine patrons. Each member of the editorial board pledged fifty dollars to cover the initial cost of printing and distribution. They hoped patrons would underwrite the expenses of subsequent issues.[1]

Countee Cullen, one of the brightest of the young writers and a literary columnist for *Opportunity*, wrote of *Fire!!*:

With its startlingly vivid Douglas cover done in red and black, *Fire!!*, on the whole, represents a brave and beautiful attempt to meet our need for an all-literary and artistic medium of expression. Its contents are, in places, exemplary of the tyro, but in the aggregate there is enough writing and art in the issue to establish for it a definite *raison d'être*. There seemed to have been a wish to shock in this first issue, and, though shock-proof ourselves, we imagine that the wish will be well realized among the readers of *Fire!!*. . . . The laurels of the issue, we think, ought to be divided between Aaron Douglas for his three caricatures and Zora Neale Hurston for her play "Color Struck." Both these contributions are noteworthy for their method of treating racial subjects in a successfully detached manner. This sort of success, more than any other, argues good for the development of Negro artists.[2]

Du Bois did not comment extensively on the new journal. His response was not what the young writers might have expected. In *Crisis*, he acknowledged receipt of the magazine, praised Douglas' striking illustrations, and studiously avoided mentioning any of the writing. Brawley became enraged by the lack of skill in basic principles of poetics and the subject matter in the journal. "About this unique periodical the only thing to say is that if Uncle Sam finds out about it, it will be barred from the mails," Brawley sneered. "He who would be a poet in the new day must not only have a vision; but must labor unceasingly to give vision beautiful and enduring form."[3] Locke offered to serve as an editorial advisor, but the board of editors refused his assistance.

Thursman's lead editorial, "Fire Burns," suggests that the new direction for black writers would seek to prove Carl Van Vechten's controversial *Nigger Heaven* (1925) inaccurate as a portrayal of Harlem life because the author was ignorant of the people he sought to interpret. His novel was superficial but not insincere. Thurman stated that Harlem Negroes should build a statue to Van Vechten on the corner of 135th Street and Seventh Avenue, for his sentimental novel had popularized Harlem to the extent that cabarets were wearing out cash register keys and straining entertainers' throats and their instruments. Thurman placed Van Vechten alongside Jessie Fauset who, to him, had also failed in her fiction to interpret black people accurately. She was black but she wrote of the black upper class. Thurman wrote that the young writers wanted a less decorous art form and content than that of traditional black writing. "Putting the best foot forward" in ethnic literature defied truth and lowered the vitality of black art. Accordingly, the new journal was intended to reflect a "peoples' art," rendered by the sensitive interpreter among the masses of blacks.

Despite this goal, the creative writing in *Fire!!* was little different from that which the *Crisis* and *Opportunity* literary contests had generated. Cullen's "From the Dark Tower" and Hughes' "Elevator Boy" were not unusual poems for either of them. "Cordelia the Crude: A Harlem Sketch," is Wallace Thurman's description of the development of a sensitive, voluptuous girl into a prostitute. Gwendolyn Bennett contributed a poem about disappointing love between a black boxer and a prostitute in "Wedding Day." Hurston's "Sweat" concentrates on a black man who loses his wife and all his material possessions because he loves a fat, black woman. The only work that might suggest a freedom of subject matter not displayed in earlier works is the first part of "Smoke, Lilies, and Jade," a novel Bruce Nugent was writing about homosexual love.

Fire!! was a one-issue, narrowly circulated, expensive magazine that provided an outlet for some of the young writer's work. It has become a collector's item among black literary journals, but the editors were unable to publish a second issue. They were unsuccessful in finding sufficient financial backing for a sustained effort.

Notes

1. Wallace Thurman gives a fictional account of these meetings in "Thurman Manor" rooming house on 137th Street in Harlem during the summer of 1926 in his novel *Infants of the Spring* (New York, 1932). Hughes refers to the group and its discussions in one of his autobiographical novels, *The Big Sea* (New York, 1940). He suggests that most of the rebellion was expressed by Zora Neale Hurston.

2. In one of his columns, Cullen chastised black writers for portraying the seamy side of Harlem. *See* Walter C. Daniel, "Countee Cullen as Literary Critic," *College Language Association Journal* (March 1971): 281-90. Cullen was not a member of the editorial board of *Fire!!*, although he contributed a poem to it. He was preparing at the time to edit a special issue of *Palms* (1926-27).

3. Brawley, a Baptist minister and professor of English at Howard University, held a high position among the "old heads." He totally rejected the Harlem Renaissance writers, including the highly praised Jean Toomer whose *Cane* (1923) was, he wrote, "unpleasant and its impressionism often gross and its effect sometimes that of a shock rather than genuine power." See Brawley's "The Negro Literary Renaissance," *Southern Workman* (April 1927): 177-84 for his scathing denunciation of almost all of the writers who were gaining popularity with the reading public at the time. He accepted Charles Johnson's invitation to serve as a judge in *Opportunity*'s 1925 literary contest with the comment, "I am happy to note the progress being made by Mr. Cullen, Mr. Hughes and others."

Information Sources

BIBLIOGRAPHY:
Brawley, Benjamin. "The Negro in American Fiction." *Dial*, 11 May 1916, pp. 445-50.
————. "The Promise of Negro Literature." *Journal of Negro History*, January 1934, pp. 54-56.
Emanuel, James A. *Zora Neale Hurston: A Literary Biography*. Urbana, Ill., 1977.
Hughes, Langston. *The Big Sea*. New York, 1940.
Johnson, Abby Arthur, and Johnson, Ronald Maberry. *Propaganda and Aesthetics: The Literary Politics of Afro-American Magazines in the Twentieth Century*. Amherst, Mass., 1979.
Perkins, Huel D. "Wallace Thurman." *Black World*, February 1976, pp. 29-35.

Thurman, Wallace. *Infants of the Spring*. New York, 1932.
Waldron, Edward F. *Walter White and the Harlem Renaissance*. Port Washington, N.Y., 1978.
INDEX SOURCES: None.
LOCATION SOURCES: Atlanta Public Library; Fisk University Library; Hampton Institute Library; Norfolk State College; Greenwood Press Periodicals.

Publication History

MAGAZINE TITLE AND TITLE CHANGES: *Fire!!: Devoted to Younger Negro Artists*.
VOLUME AND ISSUE DATA: Vol. 1, no. 1 (November 1926), one issue.
PUBLISHER AND PLACE OF PUBLICATION: Board of Editors, New York.
EDITOR: Wallace Thurman (1926).
CIRCULATION: 500 estimate.

FIRST WORLD: AN INTERNATIONAL JOURNAL OF BLACK THOUGHT

Hoyt W. Fuller brought his extensive and successful experience as editor of *Negro Digest** and *Black World** to the new journal *First World: An International Journal of Black Thought*. Its January/February 1977 issue was its first. It resembled its predecessors. *First World's* editorial policy called for "reasoned, understandably written articles or commentary from all sectors of the Black community on any subject felt to be of interest to our readers." The journal also solicited original, not previously published fiction, poetry, plays, and cartoons, and the editors promised to "give the same consideration to work by new artists as it does to work by those with more established reputations."[1] The format contained articles on international and national affairs; culture and the arts including fiction, a book excerpt, and poetry; and various departments including "Editor's Page," "In Perspective," and "Books Reviewed." "Editorial Advisors" listed fifty of the best-known and most popular black scholars and creative writers.

In "Editor's Page," Fuller restated the theme most closely associated with his writing in *Black World*. After tracing the turbulent history of the post-world War II period and the end of "Western hegemony over the other peoples of the world," he expressed his impatience with the cycles of hope and despair he found in human affairs from one generation to another. "We do learn," he agreed, however slowly. Thus, a guiding aim of *First World* was

> . . . to make available to those Blacks who want to learn—then to act—the ideas of thinkers and activists throughout the black world. And undergirding that aim is the belief that racial reconstruction is a prerequisite for the attainment of genuine power in Africa, and that the destiny of Black men everywhere is ultimately, in some measure, dependent upon a genuinely

powerful Black Africa. And, finally, to focus on Africa and its regenera-
tion is not to descend to that ugly racism of which Africans for so many
years have been victims. Rather, it is to take first things first, to build
among African people a sense of unity, a pride of heritage and the firm
basis for an unfettered future. In pursuit of these goals, there is no automatic conflict with any other people or nation; indeed, in affirming our
own particular identity and direction we give tangible support to the universal idea of respect and self-determination for all people and all nations.[2]

That editorial suggested that *First World* would be largely concerned with
African affairs, but the journal had arisen from the voluntary efforts of persons
from around the United States who had banded together and contributed their
money, time, influence, and resources to create the First World Foundation. It
was mandated to confront the issues and events of the world from a black
perspective; to focus on blacks who achieved "firsts"; to provide a platform for
thinkers and activists of the black world who deserved an audience; and to keep
Afro-Americans aware of their political and economic state in the richest and
most technologically advanced nation in the world.

Articles on black arts in the first issues included Addison Gayle's "Blueprint
of Black Criticism," Horace C. Boyer's "Contemporary Gospel Music—Sacred
or Secular?" and Peter A. Bailey's "Spotlight on the Black Theatre Alliance."
Clearly, the dialogue about the black arts and the proper function of black
writing would become a part of the new magazine's concern. Other issues
concentrated, however, on economic policies of the Carter administration in
Africa. But literary criticism and creative writing prevailed. Toni Cade Bambara,
John O. Killens, and Chester Himes contributed short stories.

Through its editorials and articles *First World* repudiated conventional attitudes
toward black leaders and their image among the black masses of the American
population. Fuller wrote that an open confrontation between blacks and Jews was
long overdue. For Jews and their public organizations were, in the 1970s, no
longer sensitive to racism and historic discrimination in American society. Many
of them, sensing they had been accepted by white America, had adopted white
America's ethics and values with a vengeance. Fuller claimed that blacks who
sought to express national bias in education, the media, politics, government,
and the arts found their grievances discredited—if not silenced—by a telephone
call to or a conference with some black spokesman who reported that the complaint did not represent the view of "decent" members of the black community.
The inevitable confrontation between blacks and Jews had come not because of
Jewish activism against such crucial "Black-favored projects and programs as
Black Studies, affirmative action, community concerns about schools, fair political representation and open housing," but because Jews used their power to
pressure black elitist Andrew Young out of his prestigious position as U.S.
ambassador to the United Nations. The editor ridiculed Jesse Jackson's immedi-

ate call for a "summit" meeting of blacks following Young's dismissal and the impotence of the National Black Leadership forum, many of whose members had never given serious thought to the Arab-Israeli impasse and could not locate Lebanon, Israel, or the Sinai on a map. And he was equally critical of members of the Black Americans to Support Israel committee. Bayard Rustin, the well-known member of the black elite, had aggressively recruited blacks for that cause and had convinced many of them to reject the legitimate claims of the Arabs and Palestinians in the Middle East struggles. According to Fuller, Rustin had openly embraced the Jewish stance against affirmative action. The Anti-Defamation League of B'nai Brith quoted Rustin as terming affirmative action for equal opportunity in employment and education a gimmick that in no way contributed to the fundamental development of the black community.

Conventional modes of black leadership no longer served an important purpose, an article reported. Just one day after the rebellion broke out among black people in Miami, "at least four national Black leaders rushed to Miami in a vain and arrogant attempt to seize control of the outbreak."[3] The mayor had invited them. The article claimed that Jesse Jackson, Benjamin Hooks, Andrew Young, and Joseph Lowery would have gone without an invitation, for they had built their public reputations on claims that they could shape and influence the direction of blacks even in times of social upheaval and widespread violence. Miami blacks repudiated them, and that reaction exposed the "glaring weakness of national Black leadership." Its hold on the general population was diminishing. The reason was simple: Black leadership "anointed and legitimated by whites could no longer deliver the Black masses—or any significant portion thereof—to the satisfaction of the white power structure" largely because it had built its reputation on nonviolent appeals and actions.[4] *Black Enterprise** magazine had found in a recent survey of some 5,000 respondents that 73.3 percent of them doubted whether black America had any current, effective leadership.

Margaret Bush Wilson's endorsement of the industrial energy program espoused by most corporations only compounded *First World*'s attack on black leadership. Moreover, in her role as chairman of the board of the NAACP, Wilson had been only half right about racial nuances of the congressional assessment of the all-volunteer armed forces. She rejected "subtle racist forces" for suggesting blacks would not fight in certain parts of the world on the theory that no historical data supporting that expressed fear could be found. Fuller agreed with Wilson. He cited racial motives of congressmen like John Stennis of Mississippi and Sam Nunn of Georgia who, he wrote, had conducted deliberate campaigns to challenge the effectiveness and efficiency of military forces that were 28 percent black. The problem lay in Wilson's prediction that blacks would fight for the United States in any part of the world. Fuller's thoughts on that matter were different from Wilson's.

There may be no "historical evidence" that Blacks in the military will not fight wherever the war is, but that does not prejudge the future. So far,

Blacks have never been asked to fight against other blacks in Africa or the Caribbean, but there is a distinct likelihood that they could be asked to do so. U.S. interests support the racist regime in South Africa because of the natural resources controlled by that regime; and units at Ft. Bragg already have been alerted for possible combat in Angola. The growing preoccupation with the "leftist drift" in the Caribbean could very well propel the U.S. Army into invading Jamaica or some other Caribbean nation as it once did in the Dominican Republic and in Haiti. The consciousness of young blacks in 1980 is not as deficient as Mrs. Wilson assumes. But then, like most Black leaders, Mrs. Wilson operates as if the Sixties never happened. That blindness can have grave repercussions.[5]

First World is a black activist journal that focused on the impetus of the black movement of the sixties and seventies in public affairs and creative arts. The new journal appeared at a time that is not hospitable to new periodicals. The mortality rate has been extremely high in the last fifteen years, owing to losses of paid advertising to television and significant changes in the taste of readers.

Notes

1. "Why?" *First World* (Winter 1977): 63.
2. *First World* (January/February 1977): 3.
3. Francis Ward, "Days Are Numbered: The Black Leadership Elite," *First World* (Winter 1980): 4.
4. Ibid.
5. "Margaret Bush Wilson Rides Again," *First World* (Winter 1980): 5.

Information Sources

BIBLIOGRAPHY:
Baraka, Amiri. "Black Nationalism and Socialist Revolution." *Black World*, July 1975, pp. 30-42.
Fuller, Hoyt W. "Editor's Page." *First World*, January/February 1977, p. 3.
———. "Margaret Bush Wilson Rides Again." *First World*, Winter 1980, p. 5.
Joyce, Donald Franklin. "Magazines of Afro-American Thought on the Market: Can They Survive?" *American Libraries*, December 1976, pp. 678-83.
Nathan, Hare. "What Happened to the Black Movement?" *Black World*, January 1976, pp. 21-33.
Ward, Francis. "Days Are Numbered: The Black Leadership Elite." *First World*, July 1980, pp. 4-5.
INDEX SOURCES: None.
LOCATION SOURCE: University Microfilms International.

Publication History

MAGAZINE TITLE AND TITLE CHANGES: *First World: An International Journal of Black Thought.*

VOLUME AND ISSUE DATA: Vols. I-IV (January/February 1977 to present), bimonthly.
PUBLISHER AND PLACE OF PUBLICATION: First World Foundation, Atlanta, Georgia.
EDITORS: Hoyt W. Fuller, executive editor; Carole A. Parks, managing editor (1977).
CIRCULATION: 25,000.

FLASH: A NEWSPICTURE MAGAZINE

The general-purpose news magazine *Flash: A Newspicture Magazine* began publication in June 1937 in Washington, D.C. Its editors intended it to be a weekly journal of Negro affairs carrying information in words and pictures. During its first year of publication, the magazine published a wide range of news items covering practically every aspect of black American life, including current events in New York and other major American cities and news of the black colleges, sports, and entertainment. Beginning in 1938, the editors announced a specific emphasis for the future. *Flash*, they wrote, would stand out as a journal of Negro affairs in Washington, New York, and Chicago. It would carry news and pictures of black events omitted from the daily press; conduct art contests in the schools to encourage study and understanding of black ethnology; explain advancements Negroes were making in science, aviation, agriculture, and the healing arts; set forth the leading motion pictures of the day; and highlight black sports and athletes. "*Flash* will herald the brilliance of Negro American life against a background of darkness and sophisticated blues," the magazine promised.[1]

These editorial aspirations were magnanimous. *Flash* intended to achieve them by securing the assistance of a national advisory board of black educators, business men and women, military personnel, politicians, and entertainers. With their help, *Flash* proposed to become a significant institution that could command a wide base of respect among Negroes. Advertising itself as "America's Only Colored News-Picture Publication," it reported on a somewhat broader range of news items than appeared in earlier issues. Contents for the 1 April 1939 edition included "Art in Its Finer Sense," "Charm," "America to Train Colored Aviators," "The Famous Tenth Cavalry," "National Negro Health Week," "Virginia Inter-Racial Commission Conference," "Social Caravan," "Chicago News Flashes," and "Parade of Personalities," The brief editorial comment which never became a distinct feature of the magazine was titled "Undertone."

Flash was published for little more than two years. Its editors made a valiant effort to create a viable magazine. The photographs were numerous and the features covered many subjects. But the periodical was unattractive. It appeared at a critical time in the nation's history. The United States was gearing for the war that had already begun in Europe, and military preparedness was the watchword of the day. Agitation over the proper use of black men in the military forces engaged a large part of most of the Negro press. The crucial need for pilots for the Army Air Force lay heavily upon a nation that had not taken well to using air power at all. Black political leaders insisted upon including black youth in the training programs for the growing aviation sector of the military forces. Yet *Flash* presented pictures of personalities in the news for the most part. Its editorial comment was minimal.

The magazine was unable to compete successfully with the powerful black weekly national newspapers published in New York, Chicago and Pittsburgh and circulated throughout the nation. In October, the owners of *Flash* decided to change from a weekly publication schedule to monthly. This modification was ineffective. After 26 months, *Flash* ceased publication. Its chief significance is that it was one of the first black "newspicture" magazines.

Note

1. "The New Year's Forecast," *Flash* (3 January 1938): 6.

<h3 style="text-align:center">Information Sources</h3>

BIBLIOGRAPHY:
Boone, Dorothy Deloris. "A Historical Review and a Bibliography of Selected Negro Magazines 1910-1969." Ph.D. dissertation, University of Michigan, 1970, pp. 47-48, 109.
"Undertone." *Flash*, 1 October 1938, p. 3.
"Undertone." *Flash*, 3 January 1939, p. 3.
INDEX SOURCES: None
LOCATION SOURCE: Schomberg Collection, New York Public Library, New York, New York.

<h3 style="text-align:center">Publication History</h3>

MAGAZINE TITLE AND TITLE CHANGES: *Flash: A Newspicture Magazine*.
VOLUME AND ISSUE DATA: Vols. I-II (21 June 1937-31 August 1939), weekly until Vol. II, no. 65 (1 October 1938); monthly to 31 August 1939.
PUBLISHER AND PLACE OF PUBLICATION: Flash Publishing Company, Washington, D.C.
EDITOR: Dutton Ferguson (1937-1939).
CIRCULATION: 58,000.

Charles E. Holmes

<h1 style="text-align:center">FREEDOM'S JOURNAL</h1>

In 1827 John Brown Russwurm and Samuel E. Cornish founded the first journal edited by and for black Americans. *Freedom's Journal* appeared in New York City in March of the year that slavery was legally abolished in the state of New York on Independence Day. The two freeborn pioneer journalists were educated blacks. Russwurm was a graduate of Bowdoin College in Brunswick,

Maine, where one of his classmates was Henry Wadsworth Longfellow. Cornish had studied at the New York African Free School and at Princeton University. Before he was thirty years old he had founded and pastored the African Presbyterian Church, the first black church of that denomination in New York. Both Russwurm and Cornish joined an organization of blacks who set out to defend themselves against spiraling attacks New York newspapers were making on blacks who aspired to positions of leadership. Mordecai Noah, editor of the *New York Enquirer*, was proslavery. His editorials ridiculed blacks as raucous and rambunctious no matter how cultured they tried to be. Vivian Coleman, editor of the *Evening Star*, was equally hostile. The "Negro Question" was a subject for debate in colleges and universities. Denmark Vesey's infamous insurrection plot had been uncovered in Charleston, South Carolina, just three years earlier. The first editorial in *Freedom's Journal* expressed the weekly's purpose:

> We wish to plead our own case. Too long have others spoken for us. Too long has the public been deceived by misrepresentations in things which concern us dearly, though in the estimation of some mere trifles; for although there are many in society who exercise toward us benevolent feelings, still (with sorrow we confess it) there are others who enlarge upon that which tends to the discredit of any person of color.[1]

New York had passed a law outlawing slavery, but white slaveholders still pursued their ex-slaves into New York. Slavery was still legal across the Hudson River in New Jersey, which had 200 slaveholding families and 236 slaves as late as 1850. But *Freedom's Journal* was not an abolitionist paper in the strict sense of the term. It was among the early weeklies published in New York; 843 newspapers were being published in the United States in 1828, 161 of which were in New York State. Benjamin H. Day's *New York Sun*, the first successful penny daily, did not begin publication until 1833. James Gordon Bennett's *New York Herald* arrived on the scene in 1835, six years before Horace Greeley's *New York Tribune* appeared in 1841. Henry J. Raymond's *New York Times* did not come out until 1851.

Lionel C. Barrow, Jr., has described the format of the *Journal*:

> *Freedom's Journal* had originally a four-page, four column format. Its one-column headlines, typical of the papers of the day, had captions such as "To Our Patrons," "Memoirs of Paul Cuffee," "Common Schools in New York" and "The Effects of Slavery." This was changed with the start of Volume 2 (April 4, 1828) to a three-column makeup with eight pages. There were obviously no pictures in the paper, but drawings started to appear in the September 21, 1827, issue.[2]

News in the first issue was about Haiti and Sierra Leone. There was also the first installment of "Memoirs of Captain Paul Cuffee," a black Boston shipper; a sixteen stanza poem, "The African Chief," and an advertisement for the B. F. Hughes' School of Colored Children of Both Sexes.

The editor of the *New York Enquirer* was attacked in a subsequent issue as one "whose object is to keep alive the prejudice of the whites against the coloured communities of New York City."[3] Other articles disagreed with the platform of the American Colonization Society which advocated returning Afro-Americans to Africa and reported on lynching. Russwurm believed in universal education as a critical need for blacks who would be respected by white Americans. He often wrote that, without education, the next generation of blacks would advance no further than their fathers had.

> While other members of the community are daily advancing from the present improved modes of instruction, our children have been altogether excluded from a participation of them. So prejudiced are the minds of some, that they think a little reading and spelling is all that is necessary for them, while others care not whether they acquire even these.[4]

Russwurm withdrew from the partnership on 28 March, 1828, and Samuel Cornish became editor of the new paper, whose name became *Rights For All*, 28 May, 1828.

Freedom's Journal gave American blacks their own voice in the tradition of the institution of the American press. It arose out of a need for racial self-expression. It was a complement, not a supplement, to the white press, addressed to a special audience. It was designed to be a major newspaper for blacks. It provided news, information, entertainment, culture, and editorial comment. Most significantly, the journal devoted a good portion of its feature material to building up a positive image of black people and to describing progress individuals and communities were making. It published biographical sketches of blacks, including the eighteenth century New England poet Phillis Wheatley and the Haitian hero Toussaint L'Ouverture. *Freedom's Journal* established the pattern black periodicals have followed since 1827. It is the fountainhead of an Afro-American press. Further, it provides one of the most unimpeachable resources for black American life in the urban North in the first half of the nineteenth century.

Notes

1. "To Our Patrons," *Freedom's Journal* (16 March 1827): 1.
2. See Lionel C. Barrow Jr., "Our Own Case: *Freedom's Journal* and the Beginnings of the Black Press," *Journalism History* (Winter 1977-78): 188.
3. "Mordecai," *Freedom's Journal* (17 August 1827): 3.
4. *Freedom's Journal* (18 May, 1827): 3.

Information Sources

BIBLIOGRAPHY:
Dann, Martin E., *The Black Press: 1827-1890*. New York, 1971.

Fortenberry, Lawrence. *"Freedom's Journal*: The First Black Medium." *Black Scholar*, November 1974, pp. 33-37.

Joyce, Donald Franklin. "Magazines of Afro-American Thought." *American Libraries*, December 1976, pp. 678-83.

Penn, I. Garland. *The Afro-American Press and its Editors*. Springfield, Mass., 1891.

Pride, Armistead S. *"Rights For All*: Second Step in Development of Black Journalism." *Journalism History* (Winter 1977-78): 129-31.

Sagarin, Mary. *John Brown Russwurm: The Story of Freedom's Journal*. New York, 1970.

INDEX SOURCE: *Antebellum Black Newspapers: Indices to New York Freedom's Journal (1827-1829), The Rights of All (1829), The Weekly Advocate (1837), The Colored American (1837-1841)* (Westport, Connecticut, 1976).

LOCATION SOURCES: Library of Congress; Schomberg Collection, New York Public Library, New York, New York.

Publication History

MAGAZINE TITLE AND TITLE CHANGES: *Freedom's Journal* (16 March 1827-March 1828). The magazine then changed its title to *Rights for All* with a different emphasis and editor.

VOLUME AND ISSUE DATA: Vol. 1, weekly.

EDITORS: Samuel Cornish (1827) and John Russwurm (1827-1828). With Vol. 1, No. 27 4 September 1827 Russwurm became sole editor until the 28 March 1828 issue.

CIRCULATION: 1,000.

FREEDOMWAYS: A QUARTERLY REVIEW OF THE NEGRO FREEDOM MOVEMENT

Freedomways: A Quarterly Review of the Negro Freedom Movement is the full title of the journal which was first published in the spring of 1961 and is still being published. The overall purpose of *Freedomways* was explicitly stated in its first editorial, entitled "Three To Make Ready: It's a Journal."[1] The editor notes that there have been three calls for black freedom; the awakening to the call for freedom; the organization of the freedom movement itself; and, at present, the "make ready" effort to prepare blacks for their new freedom. Therefore, *Freedomways* will attempt to act as an organ for those voices and movements shaping the future course of action toward freedom unrestrained and ultimately triumphant. The editorial ends with the stirring rhetoric, "With this issue, *Freedomways* begins its examination of the objective, means, and methods to the good of Negro freedom as reflected in the programs an ideologies of foremost exponents in organizing the final sprint.[2]

The "Make Ready" prospectus clearly defines a broad editorial approach to the selection and content arrangement" of material selected for *Freedomways*. This material may include separatist views along with mainstream ones, with neither given precedent over the other. This position is stated more clearly in the lead editorial: "It is our view that, historically, the main force of the Negro people's freedom movement, and the main currents of Negro thought and leadership, have projected programs on the premise that Negroes, individually and as a people, are Americans no less than any other claimants; and that they have ever sought to identify their aspirations for freedom and equality of citizenship with the broadest national interest of the country."[3] With this ambitious goal, the editors launched a major and influential journal.

"It's a Journal" was another editorial declaration by the founders of *Freedomways*, which enumerated five distinct platforms: (1) The journal will be a forum addressing *all* problems confronting Negroes in America; (2) It will endeavor to strengthen ties between individuals of African descent here and throughout the world and will provide "accurate" information on the Third World; (3) Without bias, *Freedomways* will explore new economic, political, and social systems; (4) It will provide a medium of expression for any serious and gifted writer; and (5) It will speak for no special interest group, specifically disavowing any political, organizational, or institutional ties. This series of goals for *Freedomways* was also ambitious and much of the success of the stated goals depended upon the editorial committee. Four individuals set the tenor of the journal: Shirley Graham, editor in chief; W. Alphaeus Hunton, associate editor; Margaret G. Burroughs, art editor; and Esther Merle Jackson, managing editor. Of these four editors, Mrs. Graham and Mrs. Jackson were quite prominent. Mrs. Graham was married to W.E.B. Du Bois and was a Communist. It is not surprising that the first issue included an article by Du Bois entitled "The Negro People in the United States," written when he was in his nineties. Mrs. Jackson's husband was James E. Jackson, who was also a Communist. This is not to imply that *Freedomways* was intended as a publication by and for those in sympathy with Communism. It is more accurate to state that Marxist ideology helped to shape the periodical. One significant clue to the political leanings of *Freedomways* was a one-page announcement in the first issue proclaiming "hail workers of all lands on the MAY DAY."

The first issue adhered to most of the plenary comments. The articles were varied and had a broad appeal. "The North Star" editorial by Frederick Douglass is a reprint of the 3 December 1847 editorial in the first issue of *North Star* edited by Douglass and Martin R. Delany. "J. C. Furnas, Mrs. Stowe, and American Racism" by Ernest Kaiser is a cogent and relevant scholarly article. "Journey to the Sierra Maestra" by John Henrik Clarke is a historical view of Cuba and its expanding influence. "The Negro People and American Art" by Elizabeth Cotlett Mora opened up a new sphere for the periodical. "Minority Peoples in China" by Shirley Graham adds a global dimension to the journal. Ten articles, one poem, one book review, and a "Quick Quotes" section are presented in addition to the editorials. The book review section was quickly expanded under the direction of Ernest Kaiser to become a major feature of the journal.

The individual who was probably the most influential in the planning and development of *Freedomways* was Shirley Graham Du Bois. She is best known for her biographies of prominent Negro Americans. These studies, written for the juvenile market, included biographies of George Washington Carver, Paul Robeson, Phillis Wheatley, and Benjamin Banneker.[4] Probably the most revealing comments concerning her relationship with *Freedomways* are those made by Mrs. Du Bois herself after she had been away from the journal for many years.[5]

Freedomways became a solid and successful journal. The second issue, Summer 1961, contained three pages of welcome from enthusiastic readers and sponsors. They included such luminaries as J. Saunders Redding, J. A. Rogers, John Simon, and George A. Singleton, editor of the *A.M.E. Church Review**[6] The common thread in their praise is that *Freedomways* helped to fill an intellectual vacuum. *Freedomways* appealed to intellectual, theoretical, and progressive readers without pandering to a sensational or thoroughly racist point of view. A typical appraisal was: "*Freedomways*, a quarterly review of the world wide freedom movement among colored people has appeared on the newsstands. . . . The publication unquestionably can help to fill a historic and cultural vacuum and merits the support of freedom lovers everywhere. We wish the editors well."[7]

Within five years, *Freedomways* had become one of the more influential Afro-American journals. The Spring 1966 issue contains a summary of the first five years of *Freedomways* compiled by Ernest Kaiser.[8] He notes that *Freedomways* now provided a public forum for the freedom movement; a platform for examining emerging economic, political, and social systems; and a medium for fresh, talented writers. Kaiser then proceeds to summarize the major issues and contributions of the first-five-year history of *Freedomways*. Some significant issues included: Fall 1962, devoted to emerging African nations; Winter 1963, entitled "The Emancipation Centennial Number"; Summer 1963, devoted to Harlem, and the first special number on that topic since the 1925 *Survey Graphic* entitled "Harlem: Mecca of the New Negro"; Winter 1964, a number that examined the southern freedom movement—and one of the early projections of the impact the movement would make on American civil rights movements; Winter 1965, a tribute to W.E.B. Du Bois; Spring 1965, a formalized exposé entitled "Mississippi: Opening the Closed Society"; and Summer 1965, a Paul Robeson special number. Finally, the Winter 1966 issue was highlighted by articles about Afro-American women in American literature. The Harlem and Paul Robeson numbers, with a few minor changes, were published in book form by the *Freedomways* press.[9]

The Kaiser summary is revealing. Issue after issue, *Freedomways* examined a whole spectrum of controversial topics, individuals, and relevant movements. These topics were carefully chosen, researched, and the articles became recognized as major contributions to the documentation of the 1960s. Very few journals can make the same claim. The quality of the contributors and the journal itself continued to improve. The tenor and scope of *Freedomways* remained remarkably stable despite the difficulty of the subject matter examined and the economic difficulties being experienced by all scholarly journals during that period.

During the next decade, from 1965 to 1975, *Freedomways* continued to exert a steady and significant influence on race relations in the United States and the growth of economic awareness on the part of minorities, and it remained a beacon for the enlightenment of its readership about Caribbean and Third World concerns. The first quarter 1976 issue of *Freedomways* contained an editorial entitled "Fifteen Years of *Freedomways* (1961-1976)." It was a general summary of the original editorial stance of *Freedomways* and an evaluation of the success of that vision. The undeniable conclusion was that *Freedomways* had reached maturity but was by no means resting on its laurels because "today more than ever before, the Afro-American liberation movement needs a serious no compromise journal to mirror and help guide its struggles. In the face of a mounting domestic crisis from which Afro-Americans and poor people receive the sharpest blows, *Freedomways* will continue its contributions to the economic, political, social, and cultural battles for equality and social progress."[10] This recommitment to the original concepts of editors Shirley Graham Du Bois et al. further substantiated the lofty aspirations of its present editorial staff.

From 1976 to the present, *Freedomways* has maintained a standard of excellence and quality unmatched by most journals of the same general nature. Moreover, *Freedomways* is now considered to be a journal of ideas rather than a journal exploring controversy.

Notes

1. "Three to Make Ready: It's a Journal," *Freedomways* (Spring 1961): 7-10.
2. Ibid., p. 10.
3. Ibid., p. 10.
4. *See Current Biography*, 1946: 221-22 and *Living Black American Authors: A Biographical Directory*, edited by Ann Schockley and Sue Chandler (New York, 1973), p. 59.
5. Shirley Graham Du Bois, "Return After Ten Years," *Freedomways* 11 (1971): 158-67.
6. *Freedomways* (Summer 1961): 224-27.
7. Ibid., p. 226.
8. *Freedomways* (Spring 1966): 103-17.
9. *Paul Robeson: The Great Forerunner* (New York, 1978).
10. *Freedomways* (Spring 1976): 5.

Information Sources

BIBLIOGRAPHY:
Cruse, Harold. *The Crisis of the Negro Intellectual* New York: William Morrow and Company, 1967, pp. 242-49, 337-40.
"Fifteen Years of Freedomways" (1961-1975)." *Freedomways*, First Quarter 1976, p. 5.

Hughes, Langston. "My Early Days in Harlem." *Freedomways*, Summer 1963, pp. 312-14.

"It's A Journal!" *Freedomways*, Spring 1961, pp. 7-9.

Kaiser, Ernest. "Five Years of *Freedomways*." *Freedomways*, May 1966, pp. 103-17.

———. "With An Eye to the Future." *Freedomways*, Spring 1963, pp. 133.

Mitchell, Lofton. "Harlem Reconsidered—Memories of My Native Land." *Freedomways*, Fourth Quarter 1964, pp. 465-78.

Wolseley, Roland E. *Negro Press in the United States*. Ames: Iowa State University Press, 1971, pp. 140-44.

INDEX SOURCES: *American History; History Abstracts; Index of Periodical Articles by and about Negroes; Social Science Index.*

LOCATION SOURCES: Most academic and public libraries; University Microfilms International.

Publication History

MAGAZINE TITLE AND TITLE CHANGES: *Freedomways: A Quarterly Review of the Negro Freedom Movement* (Spring 1961 to present).

VOLUME AND ISSUE DATA: Vols. I- (Spring 1961 to present), quarterly.

PUBLISHER AND PLACE OF PUBLICATION: Freedomways Associates, Inc., New York.

EDITOR: Esther Jackson (1961-   ).

CIRCULATION: 8,500.

Brian Joseph Benson

—————— H ——————

HALF-CENTURY MAGAZINE

When Kathryn E. Williams introduced *Half-Century Magazine*, her new magazine, in Chicago in August 1916, she wrote in the first editorial that the periodical would not become a "literary gem" to suit the fancy of highbrows.[1] It would present facts in plain, commonsense language, so that the masses might read and understand its contents. It would chronicle such doings as might interest the majority of its readers. Editorials would discuss "the eternal race problem," but they would relate comments to the economic and industrial context of the current age. For the new environment required unity, cooperation, and race patronage as the essence of racial uplift. The editor praised men and women whose thought, sacrifice, and action were advancing the aspirations of the race. She criticized those who had been selected as leaders of the race by whites because of their willingness to advocate inferiority and to practice submission. To her, their assumed leadership was based on falsification, gall, treachery, bigotry, egotism, and borrowed oratory. Most race journals celebrated these "tired old aces," she claimed, but *Half-Century* would not use its precious pages to "gleam before the public" those persons who had assumed false virtues and accomplishments. The latest books by black authors and about black Americans and the latest songs, music, and talking-machine records would be noted and reviewed. Departments of domestic science and beauty hints would serve the special interests of women. William asked for short stories with plots and settings dealing with Negro life, and she promised she would "reserve the right to discuss fairly and impartially men and measures as they may come to affect the welfare of the race." These lofty words expressed the editorial purposes of the new magazine that appeared in black Chicago, already the setting of rising black business, social, and political activity uncommon in any other location in the United States except Harlem. The weekly newspaper the *Chicago Defender* had focused the attention of Afro-Americans on the growing power of special purpose journalism.

The first issue of *Half-Century* reported on the Centennial General Conference of the African Methodist Episcopal Church, the Republican National Convention, and the annual meeting of the National Association of Colored Women. It contained a music and drama column, two poems, and one short story. Despite the editor's relatively radical pronouncements about the character of her new journal, *Half-Century* was basically conservative. Williams planned to attract 50,000 paid subscribers by the end of the first year of publication. To that end, she initiated promotional projects, including one that published photographs of the two most popular black women in the United States, chosen through nomination on ballots appearing in each number of the magazine. Within less than two years votes were coming from readers in Illinois, Kansas, Oklahoma, the District of Columbia, Pennsylvania, Maryland, Missouri, Georgia, Texas, and California. In the seven years of its continuous publication, *Half-Century* became a national forum and platform for the concerns of black Americans in the World War I era. It was unique because it was published and edited by a black woman in a costly and competitive business area.

The magazine's comments on national politics were largely limited to the presidential elections of 1916 and 1920. Most black publications violently opposed President Woodrow Wilson for reelection in 1916 and favored Charles Evans Hughes. Williams, however, agreed with the *Chicago Daily Tribune*'s position that Wilson's election might prove a blessing in disguise for Negroes, inasmuch as it could force the Republican party to realize it could offset the strength of the Democratic party only by reaching accommodation with Negro voters in the West and the North. Most black national leaders wanted to reverse the growing erosion of voting rights for Negroes by realigning the electoral college to reflect parity within the two major parties. They argued that southern states that disfranchised blacks should lose an appropriate number of national electors. Republicans in Congress showed little enthusiasm for the plan, although they realized it would strengthen their party's numbers.

Half-Century's editorials did not raise the question of whether black Americans should fight in World War I as President Wilson moved the nation closer toward the conflict in Europe. Williams advised Americans to do their part to make the world so safe for democracy that "entrenched prejudice, caste, injustice, hate, oppression and all forms of wickedness in high places" would vanish from the nation.[2] She considered such a battle cry, conducted along "scientifically wise and intelligent lines," the best way for Negroes to take stock of their political powers. She believed the black press should play a significant role in that pursuit. As the war progressed Williams lost some of her idealistic expectation that patriotism would gain self-respect for black Americans. She reported that the 100,000 Negroes who had been inducted into the army by November 1917 had been assigned largely menial tasks to perform and suffered jim crowism in their own military force, mocking their wartime purpose. When the War Department initiated officers' training for blacks at Fort Des Moines, Iowa, editorials in *Half-Century* praised the promise of new opportunities for Negro military men.

By the end of the war, few black leaders felt the race had moved forward as a result of its loyalty to the nation at war. Agents of the Central Powers had sought unsuccessfully to cultivate subversion among Negroes. After the armistice, American Communists used disillusionment among blacks to attempt to recruit party members. Williams violently opposed these efforts. She called the Communists' efforts "Red Flagism." She attacked disfranchisement, lynching, squalor, and the high cost of living as the germ elements of the "Red Flag" doctrine. *Half-Century*'s editorials feared the possibility that widespread Communism would precipitate strife and open class struggle. They held that bloodshed would appeal only to that element of both races that had a horror of work and nothing to lose in such a conflict.[3] There was a better option, Williams wrote—the NAACP. That organization's philosophy and projects provided a viable mechanism for black and white Americans to pool their strength to solve the nation's problems. The editor asked the magazine's 75,000 readers to join the NAACP in order to "rally to the call of the greatest organization dedicated to a great cause, almost holy in its nature, ably led, and full of vigor."[4]

As the 1920 presidential campaign began, Williams did not discuss the qualifications of the major candidates. She simply declared that "few sane Colored men will support the Democratic party, not because the past Republican administrations have been perfect, but because the Democratic party does not offer even a ray of hope to the Colored voter."[5] Black men had sent a questionnaire to some candidates for the Republican nomination in order to make them "show their colors" on matters critical to black voters. Williams wrote that little good could come from the plan, for any document it would produce might prove embarrassing to potential candidates. One friendly to Negroes would hardly want to commit himself because to do so might lessen his chances of ever reaching the White House. It seemed far more feasible to ask contenders how they felt about legislation that might be introduced in Congress, including a federal law against lynching; reapportionment of Congress to reflect the lack of complete representation in states where Negroes could not vote in the primaries; abolition of jim crow practices in public carriers and public service facilities; apportionment of Negro soldiers in the army according to their percentage of the national population; and prohibition of racial segregation in the civil service.

The journal's editorials asked readers to support candidates who could bring an end to "Democratic extravagance" in terms of Negro rights and aspirations, without endorsing any contender for the Republican nomination. Williams once wrote that William Hale Thompson, mayor of Chicago, was probably one of the best-loved and most-hated citizens in the country. Black and poor people loved him for his fairness and southerners hated him for the same reason. He favored women's suffrage, he denounced profiteering, and he insisted that the federal government should keep its attention and resources trained on the nation rather than on Europe. The comments were not intended as a serious endorsement for Thompson but indicate what issues the editor considered most important.[6]

Williams did not comment extensively on the outcome of the 1920 election, nor did she express any expectations of Warren G. Harding, the new president. But such was the nature of most political editorials in *Half-Century*. They categorically denounced Democrats and espoused anything that would mean racial advancement without expressing any unusual insight or strong support for particular political personalities or issues. Williams usually did not engage national black figures to write about specific domestic or foreign affairs. She wanted to make readers of what she liked to call her "home magazine" aware of the need to vote, but never wrote an editorial about political activities in Chicago.

Half-Century carried news about black Americans in all parts of the country, especially those whose names and activities would attract wide attention. It is an unusual source of information about choral music concerts, musical recitals, and artistic development among black musicians. It also provided stories about black professional baseball teams. Its reviews of early motion pictures made by black producers provide a wealth of data about this unique aspect of Afro-American culture.

Although Williams tried hard to attract creative writers to the magazine and included in each issue some fiction and poetry, the works are uniformly undistinguished, except that the magazine had the curious distinction of publishing James Weldon Johnson's single novel, *Autobiography of an Ex-Colored Man* in serial form beginning November 1919 and ending December 1920. Johnson, who at the time was well known as managing editor of the *New York Age*, a published poet, a former diplomat who had served the State Department in Latin American posts, and a leading New York Republican, had released the novel anonymously in 1912. Fifteen years later he reissued it and accepted responsibility for its authorship. *Half-Century* published the entire novel without comment. No literary historian has noted that Williams published the work, using Johnson's name, before he publicly admitted it was his. No reference to the serialization in *Half-Century* appears in Johnson's autobiography, *Along This Way*.

Half-Century began to suffer from severe financial straits at the rise of the "New Negro" movement and the beginning of political activism among Chicago blacks. Throughout its life, the journal contained advertisements for cosmetics and insurance, and it enjoyed the patronage of several active members of Booker T. Washington's National Negro Business League. *Half-Century* was not an impressive publication. But it stands among those general-purpose magazines that reflected and guided, to some extent, the newly developing ethos of black Americans caught up in the drama of the new century, the world war, and migration from the South into the industrial, urban Midwest.

Notes

1. "Our First Issue," *Half-Century Magazine* (August 1916): 3.
2. "Do Your Bit," *Half-Century Magazine* (August 1917): 3.

3. "Waving the Red Flag in America," *Half-Century Magazine* (March 1919): 3; and "Trying to Turn Black Men Red," *Half-Century Magazine* (January 1921): 3, 10.
4. Ibid.
5. "Watch the Democratic Party Die," *Half-Century Magazine* (September 1919): 3.
6. "The *Half-Century*'s Choice for President," *Half-Century Magazine* (June 1920): 3.

Information Sources

BIBLIOGRAPHY:
Boone, Dorothy Delores, "A Historical Review and Bibliography of Selected Negro Magazines, 1910-1969" Ph.D. dissertation, University of Michigan, 1970.
Dann, Martin E., ed. *The Black Press, 1827-1890*. New York, 1971.
Johnson, Charles S. "Rise of the Negro Magazine" *Journal of Negro History*, January 1928, pp. 7-21.
Logan, Rayford W. *The Negro in American Life and Thought: 1877-1901*. New York, 1954.
Martin, Charles H. "Negro Leaders, the Republican Party, and the Election of 1932." *Phylon*, Fall 1971, pp. 85-93.
Meier, August. "The Negro and the Democratic Party, 1875-1915." *Phylon*, Spring 1956, pp. 173-91.
Strickland, Arvarh E. and Reich, Jerome R. *The Black American Experience: From Reconstruction to Present*. New York, 1974.
INDEX SOURCES: None
LOCATION SOURCES: Most college and university libraries; Greenwood Press periodicals for total available publication.

Publication History

MAGAZINE TITLE AND TITLE CHANGES: *Half-Century Magazine* (August 1916-May/June 1923).
VOLUME AND ISSUE DATA: Vols. 1-12 (August 1916-April 1922), monthly; vols. 3-14 (May/June 1922 to May/June 1923), bi-monthly.
PUBLISHER AND PLACE OF PUBLICATION: Kathryn E. Williams, owner, publisher, and editor in chief, Half-Century Publication Company, Chicago, Illinois.
EDITOR: Kathryn E. Williams (1916-1922).
CIRCULATION: Highest estimate 16,000.

HAMPTON INSTITUTE JOURNAL OF ETHNIC STUDIES, THE

The *Journal of Afro-American Studies*[1] originated in the Afro-American Lecture Series Program, which was implemented during the 1970-1971 academic year among several Virginia colleges. With Hampton Institute serving as the host institution, professors from Old Dominion, Norfolk State, Virginia Commonwealth and Virginia Union universities were engaged in this interinstitutional, interdisciplinary lecture series. Each of the twenty-five selected professors, drawn from various academic disciplines, prepared lectures which were revised and adopted into a research article or a position paper. Some of these articles formed the material for the first publication of the *Journal of Afro-American Studies*.

The *Journal*'s appearance in July 1971 was the beginning of the realization of a dream by H. I. Fontellio-Nanton, who was then serving as the director of the Division of the Social Sciences, and who was head of the African-American Studies Program, the latter of which he established at the institute. Professor Fontellio-Nanton viewed the *Journal* as the first step toward the realization of his dream—the establishment of a Center for the Study of African-American Life and Culture at the Hampton Institute.

Professors and students who participated in the lecture series "asked for this publication to which to make future reference and to continue this dialogue in Afro-American studies," wrote Alvin F. Anderson, the *Journal*'s first editor. Its central purpose was to serve as a "medium for the intellectual airing of expressions and research of faculty members."[2]

The first volume, 245 pages printed and spiral-bound by the Hampton Institute Press, consisted of articles dealing with a range of topics, including the social psychology of Afro-Americans, black education and the "disadvantaged" student, black identity and stereotypes, historiography of race, ghetto economy, African cultural traits in black Americans, Nat Turner's insurrection, blacks in the antebellum economy, Ernest Gaines' status as a writer, pathology of racism, aspects of the Harlem Renaissance, the effects of urbanization, and other similar topics. Each of the articles that appeared in the initial volume reflected good scholarship, with careful documentation and lucid style.

The second volume—consisting of 89 pages—continued to draw upon the productivity of those professors participating in the lecture series, but included for the first time an article written by an undergraduate student. Among the topics explored in this volume are the nature of Afro-American studies programs, slavery in Virginia before the American Revolution, W.E.B. Du Bois as sociologist, libraries and the black community, and plantation psychology.

For several reasons the third volume did not appear until some four years later. First, several professors, including the retiring director of the African-American Studies Program, resigned from Hampton Institute. Second, the central administration of the institute was undergoing considerable change and seems to have reduced its commitment to financing the publication of the *Journal*. And, third, the Afro-American Lecture Series Program, lacking continued financial support from cooperating institutions, was discontinued.

Under the direction of Patrick A. Lewis, not only was the interdisciplinary program's name changed to the Ethnic Studies Program, which reflected a broader interest than the name African-American Studies suggested, but also the publication was given a new title: the *Hampton Institute Journal of Ethnic Studies*. Consisting of articles and essays on Du Bois' philosophy of education, African heritage, American foreign policy, riots in the British West Indies, slave narratives, and Alain Locke, the contents of the third volume reflect a more international perspective than that of the previous volumes.

Beginning with the fourth volume and continuing until the present, the *Hampton Institute Journal*, published by the H. C. Young Press in Norfolk, Virginia, has included articles covering a range of topics, including the role of historically black colleges, politics in the Caribbean, blacks in politics in America and Africa, and the life and culture of American Indians, and it has included scholarly articles on such historical and literary figures as P. B. Young, Milton L. Randolph, Malcolm S. Maclean, A. Philip Randolph, and James Baldwin.

More recent volumes have included reviews of books, particularly those dealing with African, black American, and American Indian life and culture, and the magazine continues to include short poems. Volume IX includes for the first time an author-title index. To date, the *Hampton Institute Journal* is not indexed with any national publication of indices. Nevertheless, the publication continues to draw articles from colleges and universities across the United States and from some foreign countries.

Notes

1. *The Journal of Ethnic Studies*, which carries a similar title, is published by Western Washington University in Bellingham.
2. Editorial, *Journal of Afro-American Studies* (July 1971): 2.

Information Sources

INDEX SOURCES: None
LOCATION SOURCES: None

Publication History

MAGAZINE TITLE AND TITLE CHANGES: *Journal of Afro-American Studies* (July 1971-December 1972); *The Hampton Institute Journal of Ethnic Studies* (September 1976-present).

VOLUME AND ISSUE DATA: Vols. I-II, annually; Vols. III-IV, annually; Vols. V-VII (all published in 1978); Vol. VIII, no. 1 (November 1979); Vol. VIII, no. 2 (May 1980); Vol. IX (May 1981).

PUBLISHER AND PLACE OF PUBLICATION: Hampton Institute Press (published Vols. I-III); The H. C. Young Press, Hampton, Virginia (has published all subsequent volumes).

EDITORS: Alvin F. Anderson, editor, July 1971-August 1972; M. Barbee Pleasant, editor, September 1972-May 1973; Patrick A. Lewis, editor, September 1976-December 1980; Clayton G. Holloway, acting editor, January 1981-September 1981; Patrick A. Lewis, editor, September 1981-present.

CIRCULATION: Approximately 500 copies.

HARLEM QUARTERLY

Some of the political elements that had helped give rise to radical black magazines in the World War I era surfaced again in the 1940s. This time the organizations were visible and articulated a variety of ideological bases. Afro-American literary writing reflected conventional aesthetics in literature and at the same time carried the force of political activism. Ostensibly, journals of the World War II era would set forth and manifest their purposes more easily than the *Messenger,** the *Crusader,** and *Negro World* could a generation earlier when black radical journalism was a novel idea. *Harlem Quarterly* emerged in 1949 through a series of events beginning in the late 1940s when the Committee for the Negro in the Arts was organized as the cultural arm of the Harlem political left wing. Its antecedent, the Association of Artists for Freedom, included significant black writers—among them John Killens, Lorraine Hansberry, Ossie Davis—who fostered a special kind of literary and political stance apart from, but not opposed to, the civil rights and philosophers and activists of the old fighters for black equality.[1]

Benjamin Brown, a member of the Harlem Writers Club, launched the *Harlem Quarterly* as an independent black magazine devoted to cultural problems unattended by any other publication. It failed after four issues. But it represents group efforts among some Harlem black writers who believed political radicals could sustain a journal that sought to sublimate agitprop art. They had known the period when left-wing Harlemites customarily denounced the NAACP and the National Urban League as too deliberate in their approaches to black advancement. They were part of the group that would argue for the next decade what the relationship of art to politics should be. The Harlem Writers Club believed it could answer that question with a journal designed to bring its audience creative writing that met the dual requirements of aesthetics and social action.

Brown wrote in his "Prospectus of *Harlem Quarterly*" the purposes for the publication. It would include short stories, poetry, and articles on all aspects of Negro life and history, especially because "not enough portrayals of Negro life and interracial relations have been reaching the American people."[2] No magazine had given full expression to the needs and aspirations of the majority of the Negro reading public, Brown claimed. The new magazine would present "a broad cross-section of opinion on problems facing American Negroes, West Indians, Africans, and white allies." Brown wrote to writers in the United States, Africa, Europe, South America, and the West Indies to solicit contributions "on the struggle for racial equality, interracial relations, colonialism, humor, and other subjects" that would provide "wholesome, enlightening and stimulating reading."[3] The magazine would not publish stereotypes of the Negro or any other segment of the world's population. Shirley Graham, Langston Hughes, Alain Locke, and Herbert Aptheker would be among the contributing editors.

John Henrik Clarke contributed a short story, "The Bridge," to the first issue, which also included Brown's "Last Volume." Features included "Africa," written by Chuba Udokuu, a Nigerian living and working in the United States; "*Harlem Quarterly* Scope," a report of literary news about American blacks compiled by Ernest Kaiser; a brief essay on opinions youth had expressed on sex; and a sketch, "Return to the Inn," also written by Clarke. Langston Hughes furnished three poems under the title "The Corner Bar Speaks of War." Letters to the editor praised the announcement of the new publication. One was written in French and one in Spanish.

The magazine's beginning was less than auspicious despite its noble purposes; however, the Spring 1950 issue included some writing by an array of well-known black Americans. A symposium, "Should Negro Colleges be Perpetuated or Should There Be Integration in Education?" drew brief comments from Carl Foreman, John Haynes Holmes, Charles H. Houston, Benjamin E. Mays, Frederick D. Patterson, William J. Trent, and Doxey A. Wilkerson. Inasmuch as these comments were written four years before the Supreme Court decision in *Brown* v. *Topeka* declaring racially separate public schools unconstitutional, they may be the most valuable material in the magazine. The public figures who responded to the question represented a wide variety of opinion among black leaders. W.E.B. Du Bois contributed "Government and Freedom," and Langston Hughes wrote an obsequious essay titled "How to Be a Bad Writer" in which he enumerated ten prohibitions for the writer of the time. Apparently, he had the black writer in mind, for after listing his ten points he ended the piece:

If you are white, there are many more things I can advise in order to be a bad writer, but since this piece is for colored writers, there are some things I know a Negro just will not do, not even for writing's sake, so there is no use mentioning them.[4]

Shirley Graham wrote "82 Years Alive! W.E.B. Du Bois" to describe the elder statesman at that time of his life in the calm, dignified, yet busy setting of his penthouse study on Twenty-sixth Street in New York. The sketch emphasized Du Bois' world status following his confrontation with the Committee on Foreign Relations of the United States House of Representatives in August 1949 on charges of subversion.

The third and final issue of *Harlem Quarterly* contains a brief editorial that captured the national concern of the day.

"Peace, peace and more peace" is the cry heard around the world today, according to Secretary General Trygve Lie of the United Nations. On every tongue in every land the little people are asking, praying and fighting for peace.

Perhaps if it were up to the common people there would peace, for they have less to gain and more to lose by war than anyone else. Would that we common people could follow the suggestion of Clemenceau who said after the first World War, "Force the men who make the wars to fight the wars, and there will be no more wars."

Americans of all creeds are speaking out for peace.

We join our voices with all of the others who seek peace. How better can we sum up than through the words of Dr. Bunche: "To work for peace in these times is to work for the survival of mankind."[5]

Marguerite Cartwright, a faculty member at Hunter College in New York City, wrote "The U.N. and the Italian Colonies" for the final issue. There were some poetry, short fiction, and two book reviews in this final publication. Perhaps its most significant feature was a letter from the editor, "How to Lose Friends and Antangonize Negroes," addressed by Brown to "those white readers who for one reason or another take an interest in Negro life and Negro-white relations." Brown wrote that even if his advice was offensive, he felt his observations might assist his white associates to deal more effectively with Negroes. To him, the three most serious errors liberal whites could make in dealing with their black friends were paternalism, infantilism, and mimicry. Reading the letter, one can hardly avoid the keen disappointment the editor had experienced in his relationship with those white persons he had believed would work with him and black writers to make interracial relations a focus of his new magazine.

Clearly, *Harlem Quarterly* did not accomplish its editorial board's purpose. The Harlem Writers Club was unable to provide through this journal a sustained outlet for black writers. Financial problems alone did not bring on the collapse of the magazine. The founders did not anticipate the maze of serious problems, most of them political, that plagued their project as black and white Marxists debated the postures members of their factions should take.

Notes

1. Harold Cruse, chairman of the Harlem Writers Club, has written with careful detail of the tensions among New York City's political left-wing politicians in his *Crisis of the Negro Intellectual from Its Origins to the Present* (New York, 1967), parts I and II.

2. *Harlem Quarterly* (Winter 1949-50): 1.

3. Ibid.

4. *Harlem Quarterly* (Spring 1950): 14.

5. "The World Wants Peace," *Harlem Quarterly* (Fall/Winter 1950): 3.

Information Sources

BIBLIOGRAPHY:

Cruse, Harold. *The Crisis of the Negro Intellectual From Its Origins to the Present*. New York, 1967.

Johnson, Abby Arthur, and Johnson, Ronald Maberry. *Propaganda and Aesthetics: The Politics of Afro-American Magazines in the Twentieth Century*. Amherst, Mass., 1979.
INDEX SOURCES: None.
LOCATION SOURCES: New York Public Library; Greenwood Press Periodicals.

Publication History

MAGAZINE TITLE AND TITLE CHANGES: *Harlem Quarterly*
VOLUME AND ISSUE DATA: Vol. 1, no. 1 (Winter 1949-Spring 1950).
PUBLISHER AND PLACE OF PUBLICATION: Harlem Writers Club, New York, New York.
EDITOR: Benjamin Brown (1949-1950).
CIRCULATION: 3,000.

HARVARD JOURNAL OF AFRO-AMERICAN AFFAIRS

The Association of African and Afro-American Students at Harvard and Radcliffe started publishing the *Harvard Journal of Negro Affairs* as a semiannual series in 1965. Portions of the "Introduction" in the first issue gave the purpose or rationale for the journal:

> Two years ago, in the Spring, the distant noise of Birmingham aroused a sense of pressure among Negroes at Harvard, a sense which grew with every recurring shock wave from the South. From it some have emerged in a militant mood, some in a quest for common ground with Africa, some devoted to a new organization, the Association of African and Afro-American Students. But for some of us, as well, the time of pressure has become a time for reflection, a time to reconsider goals and individual positions. The journal you now hold was conceived as an aid in such thought, a means also to expand the exchange between Negro students and old Negro thinkers and teachers, an exchange which has become somewhat attenuated since the days of communion at Howard and Fisk and Negro History Week in the schools.[1]

By this statement, the association proposed to make a link between Harvard and Radcliffe and the students in the colleges of the South—all at historically black institutions—who were initiating and bearing the brunt of the victories and the pain of the student movement for integration of the races in public institutions and places of accommodation.

Articles contained in the first issue reflected the statement in the introduction. Sheila Rush, in "New Militants," attacked the in-place organizations devoted to interracial cooperation for their "invigorating security" from the real dynamics of social tension, their pathetic failure to formulate their purposes, and the reflection of a "seemingly ineradicable weakness of the civil rights movement in the North."

> In recent years, the North, stimulated by the activity in the South, has confronted anew the question of the Negro's right to equal rights. Groups and organizations in some way concerned with securing these rights have proliferated; demonstrations have been stated, leaders have emerged. To most of the groups, the unresponsiveness of the older, established leadership to the life needs of the Negro masses is patent and, necessarily, a factor in their emergence as activist groups.[2]

Her essay supports fully the rise of new militants who are critically and seriously committed to a new social order.

Most of the remainder of the articles in the first issue were similar to this one, including "A Dream Deferred," "A View from Further South in the Ivy League: A Negro Goes to Yale," "Martin Luther King at Oslo," and "Responses to Blackness: Negro Americans and Africa." Most articles were written by students.

By its second year, the staff of the *Journal* admitted that the issues generated from the "Negro Experience" and from the Negro community had become increasingly intricate as the civil rights agitation heated up. To be sure, the major news media had taken up publicizing the demonstrations and had printed some opinions of blacks alongside their own. But they had also omitted or overlooked some subtleties; differences of opinion and techniques that were important. Accordingly, the *Journal* felt that its responsibility included taking up these refinements.

An article in the second issue, "To Nat," related a series of events leading to the suicide of an expatriate South African Bantu journalist and generated enough controversy to produce a rejoinder. The *Journal* printed it, along with the original author's response to the rejoinder, in the form of a debate. "Olivier's Othello" took a swipe at liberal reactions to what has been called a "minstrel show-Othello," evaluating them as reactions to an internalized stereotype rather than a character.[3] "Black Judaism in New York" discussed a unique religious sect dealt with in Howard Brotz' book *The Black Jews in Harlem*, and their context with Black Nationalism. Other articles dealt with coups in Ghana and Nigeria and responses to the level of effectiveness of the governments in conducting their own affairs, and the rise of radicalism in postcolonial Africa.

Other articles into the late 1960s included "Mr. Monynihan in Bedford-Stuyvesant," "The Counterrevolutionary Reflex," "A Positive Agenda for Social Power," "Black Power: Anatomy of a Paradox," "SNCC's Call to Northern Black Students," "The Theme of Exile in Malcolm's Harvard Speeches," and the significant "Special Feature" of one issue, "The Black Press," which discussed the history of black journalism, black publishers today, the way urban press handle news about blacks in the ghetto, and law and freedom of the press.[4]

When it changed its title in 1971 to the *Harvard Journal of Afro-American Affairs* in keeping with the trend to reject the term "Negro," the lead editorial in the *Journal* explained:

> *The Harvard Journal of Afro-American Affairs* offers its pages as a vehicle for expression of their views, and as their sounding board for dialogue that is—and must continue taking place between Black students, intellectuals, and activists concerning the shape and direction of our struggle. Black people are undergoing a psychological revolution which demands the redefinition and restructuralization of fundamental premises governing our existence. We need programs for change based on the values of the Black community and the political realities of our situation in this world. Black students and other young Black people must aid in formulating, articulating, and implementing new concepts and programs for the liberation of our people.[5]

Because the *Journal* was published at Harvard by Harvard students, it gained respectful reading among black and white Americans. While that status symbol brought acceptance to the magazine and its contents, the circumstance represents one of the biases in the nation. Some other equally sincere and well-edited journals of opinion and creative writing by black students did not enjoy equal acceptance. As the "eye" of the civil rights activists' programs geared down and as the black students who had been at Harvard and Radcliffe in the middle 1960s graduated and took their places in American institutions of business, industry, law, and education, the need for the *Journal* subsided. Its essays were relevant to the times and well written. Perhaps the most effective function of the *Harvard Journal of Negro Affairs* was that it brought Harvard black students close to the realities of stringent racism their brothers and sisters were facing in black colleges in the South.

Notes

1. *Harvard Journal of Negro Affairs* 1, No. 1 (1965): iii-iv.
2. Ibid., p. 1.
3. Archie Epps, "Olivier's Othello," *Harvard Journal of Negro Affairs* 1, No. 3 (1967): 1-11. The article was written with regard to the performance of *Othello* that had been given by the National Theatre of Great Britain 2 February 1966 at Harvard Square Theatre, Cambridge, Massachusetts.
4. *Harvard Journal of Negro Affairs* 2, No. 1 (1968).
5. "Introduction," *Harvard Journal of Afro-American Affairs* 7, No. 1 (1971): i.

Information Sources

BIBLIOGRAPHY:
"Introduction." *Harvard Journal of Negro Affairs* 3, no. 2 (1968): iii-iv, 1.
Katz, Bill. *Magazines for Libraries*. 2d ed. New York, 1971, p. 110.

INDEX SOURCES: None
LOCATION SOURCES: Harvard University Libraries; Moorland-Spingarn Collection,
    Howard University, Washington, D.C.; University of California at Los Angeles
    Research Library.

Publication History

MAGAZINE TITLE AND TITLE CHANGES: *Harvard Journal of Negro Affairs* (Vol.
    1, No. 1, 1968-Vol. II, No. 2, 1971); *Harvard Journal of Afro-American Affairs*
    (Vol. II, No. 2, 1971-Vol. III, No. 2, 1972).
VOLUME AND ISSUE DATA: Vols. I-VII (January 1965-June 1971), semiannual.
PUBLISHER AND PLACE OF PUBLICATION: Association of African and Afro-American
    Students at Harvard and Radcliffe, Harvard University, Cambridge, Massachusetts.
EDITORS: Charles J. Beard; Henry C. Binford; Charles F. Lovell, Jr.; Lee A. Daniels
    (1968-1972). Student editors changed with volumes.
CIRCULATION: 3,000.

HEADLINES AND PICTURES

Headlines: A Monthly News Review, began publication in Detroit in July 1944.
Following the format of the news-photo magazines that sprang up in the country
in the thirties, *Headlines* considered itself the first digest of current news among
black periodicals. Appearing during the World War II period, the magazine had a
wide range of news sources from which to draw its contents. Its first issue
appeared just after United States armed forces invaded Europe to repel Adolf
Hitler's domination of the Western world.[1] *Headlines* published the full text of
President Franklin D. Roosevelt's "Invasion Prayer" inside the cover of the
premier number and fully supported the nation's defense efforts. Moreover, its
editorial comments aligned black Americans with the invasion and pointed to
their participation in it and their activities on the home front as well.

> Close to a million brown Americans are in uniform and a third of them are
> on a score of battlefields manfully meeting the exigencies of war in every
> sector. At home on the farm and in the factories ten times the number in
> uniform are working around the clock to sustain American and allied forces
> in foreign fields. In addition Anglo-Saxons are organizing their political
> strength in the South as well as in the North to a degree never before known
> in American history. Up-rooted from their peace-time "place" in society by
> the enormous demands of the war effort and by their growing urge for
> freedom and status, the Negro people are moving out of their obscure
> corner into the center of the nation's most important affairs. Heroics on the
> battlefield are being matched by brave deeds on the home front. Precedents
> are being shattered and new hope fills the heart of the oppressed people.[2]

The national agenda for Negroes was critically important, the comment continued; the conquest of German arms and the upcoming presidential election were the priorities. On the home front, and aside from the war effort, matters of interest to Afro-Americans were dynamic. The Supreme Court had outlawed the Texas white primary, a strategy that had excluded most black Americans from voting in state elections since the closing years of the nineteenth century and had practically nullified the voting rights granted by the Reconstruction amendments to the Constitution. Southern liberals were speaking up and working with black leaders through the newly organized Southern Regional Council. Lillian Smith, a southern author, had focused national attention on the human plight of Dixie with her best-selling novel *Strange Fruit*. Labor organizers had followed new war industries south, giving new status to black and white workers. The Committee on Industrial Organization's Political Action Committee was giving a new meaning to politics for industrial workers. Southern politicians had revolted against President Roosevelt and the social programs of his New Deal. Texas and South Carolina Democrats had named independent presidential electors who threatened to vote against Roosevelt in the electoral college regardless of the outcome of the popular vote in the election. Negroes had gained new political strength owing to their migration to the Pacific Coast to work in shipbuilding and aviation. They could form liaisons with Northern black voters to forge a new national coalition. No matter which candidate won the presidency in 1944, Chicago and Harlem would send black congressmen to Washington. There would be two of them for the first time since Reconstruction. Other portentous changes, as outlined by the editor of *Headlines*, were dramatic and significant.

> For the first time Negro women as well as men are getting a firm toehold in industry and together they are shattering traditional race concepts in a manner unparalleled even in the last war period. Hate strikes which reached their climax in the summer of 1943 have dwindled to negligible numbers. The Fair Employment Practice Committee can today justify its existence on the practical ground of increased production arising from a fuller use of minority manpower.[3]

These observations represent the principal emphasis of *Headlines*. Its format included, in most issues, an assortment of departments for news and commentary, including: "The Merry-Go-Round," "Political Trends," "The International Front," "Military Highlights," "Labor on the March," "The Educational World," "Religion in the News," "Meet the People," "The Round-Up of Sports," "Along Press Row," "Books and Art," "The Social Whirl," "Footlight Parade," and "Random Stars." "The Editor Speaks" carried quotations from black weekly newspapers, including the *Baltimore Afro-American, Pittsburgh Courier, Cleveland Call and Post, Los Angeles Sentinel, Norfolk Journal and Guide, Houston Informer*, and the *Chicago Defender*.

Frederick Douglass Patterson, then president of Tuskegee Institute, Robert C. Weaver, director of community services of the American Council on Race Relations, and Branch Rickey, head of the Brooklyn Dodgers baseball team were among the many contributors of articles, comment, or interviews to *Headlines*.

After the war, "State of the Nation," *Headlines'* editorial column, kept its audience aware of race relations in the nation. The Ku Klux Klan was trying to rise again, and senators Eastland and Ellander—arch-conservative Southerners with long tenures in the Senate—rebelled against President Harry Truman's nomination of Judge William Hastie, a Negro, as governor of the Virgin Islands. Black political leader A. Philip Randolph was organizing a third-party movement in Chicago. Veterans of World War II made front-page news with grievances and organizations they felt they needed to express their disillusionment with postwar employment and social opportunities. The United Negro College Fund was gearing up for significant fund raising for black private colleges that took the brunt of black war veterans returning from the war and seeking a college education.

Headlines contained news about black entertainers, and reviews of books and films. It highlighted black accomplishments in all areas of endeavor. It was highly illustrated after the fashion of the national news magazines. Photographs were logically wedded to news stories.[4] The magazine is an attractive, well-edited chronicle of public affairs in the nation in the war years. Its vitality lies in the editorial comments expressed from the black perspective. In effect, it was basically a newspaper for black Americans.

Notes

1. *Life* appeared in 1936; *Look*, its strongest competitor as a news-photo magazine, in 1937. *Flash**, the first black national "newspicture" periodical, began irregular publication March 1937 and ceased August 1939.

2. "Our War and Our Elections," *Headlines* (July 1944): 3.

3. Ibid., p. 4.

4. The magazine adopted a new layout with the July 1945 issue, adding more advertisement than had previously been included and increasing pictures by at least one-half.

Information Sources

BIBLIOGRAPHY:

Boone, Dorothy Deloris. "A Historical Review and a Bibliography of Selected Negro Magazines 1910-1969." Ph.D. dissertation, University of Michigan, 1970, p. 118.

Tebbel, John. *The American Magazine: A Compact History*. New York, 1969, pp. 231-33, 253.

Wolseley, Roland E. *Black Press U.S.A.* Ames: Iowa State University Press, 1971, p. 143.

INDEX SOURCES: None.

LOCATION SOURCES: Schomberg Collection, New York Public Library, New York, New York.

Publication History

MAGAZINE TITLE AND TITLE CHANGES: *Headlines: A Monthly News Review* (July 1944-January 1945); *Headlines and Pictures* (February 1945-September 1946).
VOLUME AND ISSUE DATA: Vols. I-III (July 1944-September 1946), monthly.
PUBLISHER AND PLACE OF PUBLICATION: Headline Publishing Company, Detroit, Michigan.
EDITOR: Louis Martin (1944-1946).
CIRCULATION: 5,000.

Charles E. Holmes

HORIZON: A JOURNAL OF THE COLOR LINE

Shortly after W.E.B. Du Bois began teaching at Atlanta University in 1897, he sought financial support for a black national journal that could reach an estimated 100,000 black readers. Charles Chesnutt, Paul Laurence Dunbar, and other respected black writers, he said, could lend editorial assistance. With an experienced printer and job-printing potential, Du Bois believed he could establish a publishing house and a journal along the lines of *Harper's Weekly*. He wanted money to produce a high-class journal to circulate among intelligent Negroes to tell them of the deeds of themselves and their neighbors and to interpret news of the world and inspire them toward infinite ideals. It would serve as the medium of communication for the Niagara movement which had been formed by Du Bois' call for "a few selected persons" to meet at Fort Erie, Ontario, in 1905 to organize a "thoughtful" and "dignified" membership that would avoid the masses and appeal to "the very best class of Negro Americans." The original conference of twenty-nine persons demanded, among other aspirations, an unfettered and unsubsidized press. They contended at the meeting that unless their own propaganda reached and aroused people, Negroes would remain a captive race. Claims that Booker T. Washington held much of the existing black press in fee provided an effective toxin for the gathering and their press for a new journal. *Horizon: A Journal of the Color Line*, published in Washington, D.C., beginning in January 1907, became the organ for the Niagara movement, although it was owned and edited by Du Bois, Freeman Murray, and La Fayette M. Henshaw, two federal employees in Washington. Henshaw, an attorney and worker in the Department of the Interior, was also head of the Niagara movement's District of Columbia branch.

Horizon's format was divided into three parts which were independently edited by Du Bois, Henshaw, and Murray. Each signed his own section. Du Bois used the organ as a platform against Booker T. Washington. His editorials and some creative writing formed the vitality of the small publication. The first issue appeared without a statement of purpose, although during the second year of publication, one editorial claimed:

> This is a radical paper. It stands for progress and advance. It advocates Negro equality and human equality; it stands for Universal suffrage, including votes for Women; it believes in the abolition of War, the taxation of monopoly values, the gradual socialization of capital and the overthrow of persecution and dogmatism in the name of religion. At the same time, our policy is ground in common-sense; it does not seek to force human brotherhood by act of legislature, it does not regard voting as a panacea for all ills; it honors marriage and motherhood, upholds the sometime piteous necessity of righteous self-defense, believes and maintains that what a man earns is his, and believes always in Good and God.[1]

The editors discussed contemporary issues in short articles under the column titles, "The Overlook" and "The Outlook." Du Bois' poem "The Song of the Smoke" and James Weldon Johnson's "O, Southland" appeared in the magazine, along with a few other notable literary works. Several unsigned poems appear to have been written by Du Bois.

The celebrated Brownsville affair, growing jim crowism in common carriers throughout the South, disproportionate congressional representation among Southerners, white immigration into the South, and support for the Democratic party in the presidential election of 1908 represented the radical tone for *Horizon*. Du Bois wrote that the Republican party had forfeited its claim to the Negro vote. It had betrayed the bright hope that followed Emancipation, and no longer deserved the loyalty black Americans had given it. He called for a new political focus born of performance and promise of individual candidates in lieu of automatic traditional allegiance. In "Separate Car Agitation" Henshaw blamed Booker T. Washington for jim crowism in public transportation on the assumption that he failed to use his influence with President Roosevelt to advance social equality and that his "Atlanta Compromise" address more than a decade earlier had adversely affected racial aspirations. All three editors wrote vigorous denunciations of the growing menace of lynching, after the fashion of other contemporary black periodicals. And they criticized Washington for seeming to suggest that Black Americans should be satisfied with the quality of their lives in the United States. *Horizon* was radical only in the sense that it attacked the social and educational philosophy of Booker T. Washington. It was not nearly so consistently a medium of agitprop as was William Monroe Trotter's Boston newspaper, the *Guardian*, and it never approached the level of "scientific socialism" that became the hallmark of the *Messenger** some years later.

Horizon fell considerably short of expectations Du Bois held for a successful national black journal. It failed to attract large numbers of blacks to the Niagara movement, although one has to remember that Du Bois wrote that he had not intended that effort to exceed more than 500 members. By the end of its first year of operation, the movement had established branches in seventeen states and some black newspapers were beginning to reflect its philosophy and promote its expansion. But Washington had retaliated against the radicals' attempts to nullify his influence. Black Americans had come to realize the power of an ethnic press within a nation. They imitated the white press in its contending state within the medium of national news and opinion. Even as most of the white newspapers and magazines divided along Democratic and Republican, or "liberal" and "conservative," lines in politics, society, and economics, the black press developed and exercised a measure of advocacy, too. Political party labels did not mark distinctions among these periodicals. Each remained fierce in promoting advancement of the race. Despite the plethora of writing about the so-called Washington-Du Bois controversy, the differences between the men lay in their methods of seeking racial edification. To a large extent the differences in their philosophies brought a healthy and enervating force to the black medium movement far more than a disadvantage.

The narrow audience Du Bois sought to address through *Horizon* proved a hindrance for the Niagara movement and for the magazine. In the July 1908 issue, Du Bois complained about the financial hazard inherent in publishing a black journal. He argued that *Horizon* should be enlarged and broadened so as in some measure to supply the need of a national monthly. He wanted the magazine to become self-supporting, but he had learned that although such a publication could struggle on appeals, campaign funds, and graft, it would take another five or ten years for Negroes to sustain a national magazine through subscription. Sufficient advertisement was even further in the future.

Financial straits led Du Bois to appeal for guarantors who would pay twenty-five dollars a year to support *Horizon* in return for becoming proprietors of the enterprise. He and his editorial associates led the list of subscribers, but they generated no more than twenty-one other investors. In November 1909 the editors enlarged the format of the magazine and began publishing it bimonthly rather than monthly. However, these innovations failed to save *Horizon*. It ceased publication within a year and a half of the changes.

Horizon has been called the precursor to the *Crisis*.* It was the second unsuccessful journalistic venture Du Bois undertook. Both the *Moon Illustrated Weekly** and *Horizon* led to the establishment of the *Crisis*, which Du Bois edited during the first quarter-century of its existence and its development into the premier black publication in the nation for its time. *Crisis* took responsibility for subscriptions to the defunct *Horizon* in 1910. Du Bois realized he could not generate resources to sustain an elitist magazine. His own standards of journalism and his insistence upon publishing a national black journal with characteristic addresses to his "Talented Tenth"[2] failed.

Notes

1. "Our Policy," *Horizon* (November 1909).
2. The "Talented Tenth" is the hallmark of Du Bois' elitist philosophy of education as opposed to Booker T. Washington's "common man" philosophy.

Information Sources

BIBLIOGRAPHY:
Aptheker, Herbert, ed. *The Correspondence of W.E.B. Du Bois*, Vol. 1. Amherst, Mass., 1973.
Green, Dan S. "W.E.B. Du Bois: His Journalistic Career." *Negro History Bulletin*, March-April 1977, pp. 672-77.
Johnson, James Weldon. *Along This Way*. New York, 1933.
Meier, August. "Booker T. Washington and the Negro Press." *Journal of Negro History*, January 1953, pp. 68-90.
Moon, Henry Lee. *The Emerging Thought of W.E.B. Du Bois*. New York, 1972.
Rudwick, Elliott M. *W.E.B. Du Bois: Propagandist of the Negro Protest*. New York, 1969.
INDEX SOURCES: None.
LOCATION SOURCES: Hampton Institute; New York Public Library; Library of Congress; Howard University.

Publication History

MAGAZINE TITLE AND TITLE CHANGES: *Horizon: A Journal of the Color Line* (January 1907-July 1910).
VOLUME AND ISSUE DATA: Vols. I-III, monthly; vols. III and IV (November 1909-July 1910), bimonthly. Final issue July 1910.
PUBLISHER AND PLACE OF PUBLICATION: W.E. Burghardt Du Bois, F.H.M. Murray and L.M. Hershaw, owners and editors, Washington, D.C.
EDITORS: W. E. Burghardt Du Bois; F.H.M. Murray; L. N. Henshaw (January 1907-July 1910).
CIRCULATION: 3,000 highest estimate.

I

INTERRACIAL REVIEW

Beginning in March 1928 as a medium of communication among parishioners of Saint Elizabeth's Catholic Church in Saint Louis, Missouri, *St. Elizabeth's Chronicle* devoted itself primarily to news of the church among blacks. Early issues limited their coverage to the Saint Louis area. Eventually, the periodical reported on general and religious news throughout the world. Its emphasis remained focused on black interests. The journal's editorial purpose may be seen in excerpts from an early editorial:

> Various conditions arising in the United States as a result of millions of Caucasians inhabiting the same land with millions of Negroes comprise a so-called inter-racial problem. . . . Seldom do we find a treatment of this important question emanating from a Catholic source. . . . I have yet to see a book dealing with this problem whose author is a Catholic. Catholics are ignorant of the inter-racial situation. For them the *St. Elizabeth's Chronicle* hopes to have a constructive message. Finally, Negroes have a great deal to learn about the eternal principles of right and wrong as enunciated by the Church. If colored people better realized the power, more or less dormant, in the Catholic slowly to crush and smooth out uneven and unfair conditions arising from the close juxtaposition of the two great races, they would make greater haste better to understand and make an ally of that power.[1]

The *Chronicle* devoted itself to articulating that power. It published religious articles, some poetry and fiction, and news of Saint Elizabeth's and other urban parishes. In "The Negro Viewpoint," William Markoe, the first editor of the magazine, wrote editorial comment on the Afro-American experience.

The periodical became the official organ of the Federated Colored Catholics of the United States in its second year of publication. It published proceedings of the meetings of that organization and news about black Catholics and public issues of the time. Its principal articles discussed attitudes of Negro Americans toward the Catholic Church; Pope Pius X and the Federated Colored Catholics; Bolshevism and the Negro; whether Communism would spread among Negroes as a result of the depression; the Scottsboro Case; and the controversy over a federal antilynching bill. In the 1930s the *Chronicle* published excellent articles on the Catholic Church's historic position on slavery, slum clearance, and the developing clout of organized labor in the United States. During that period, the journal became known as the *Interracial Review* and for more than a generation, under that title, presented its audience with a view of contemporary national and world social issues, primarily from the perspective of the black American Catholic. It is not a religious publication in the strict sense of the term. But it concerns itself with "Christian democracy" in the United States. To that extent, it is an unusual national publication.

Its articles and reports were always written by black and white Catholics—priests and laypersons—who discussed problems of race relations and black progress. The journal also always contained book, theater, and music reviews.

Note

1. *St. Elizabeth's Chronicle* (March 1928): 3.

Information Sources

BIBLIOGRAPHY:
Boone, Dorothy Delores. "A Historical Review and a Bibliography of Selected Negro Magazines, 1910-1969." Ph.D. dissertation, University of Michigan, 1970, p. 103.
Katz, Bill. *Magazines for Libraries*. New York, 1974, p. 110.
INDEX SOURCE: *Catholic Index*.
LOCATION SOURCES: Public libraries.

Publication History

MAGAZINE TITLE AND TITLE CHANGES: *St. Elizabeth's Chronicle* (March 1928-October 1929); *The Chronicle* (November 1929-September 1932); *Interracial Review* (October 1933-April 1971).
VOLUME AND ISSUE DATA: Vols. I-II, monthly; Vols. III-XXXVII, irregular, mostly monthly.
PUBLISHER AND PLACE OF PUBLICATION: Catholic Interracial Council, New York, New York.
EDITORS: William Markoe (March 1928-June 1933). Other editors who served for unspecified periods of time include George K. Hunton and Arthur Wright.
CIRCULATION: 5,000.

J

JET

The Johnson Publishing Company had enjoyed several years of dramatic success with its black journals when publisher John H. Johnson decided to convert *Negro Digest** into a pocket-size weekly magazine of news for and about black Americans.[1] In his "Backstage" editorial column, Johnson announced the new venture. he wrote that he made the decision "after more than a year's study of the Negro publication field both from the editorial and business points of view." *Jet*, first issued in October 1951, was not designed to replace or compete with any currently published weekly periodical. It was thought feasible to fill a need for a "a convenient-sized magazine that will summarize the week's biggest Negro news in a well-organized, easy-to-read format." Johnson believed that "the tempo and pulse of Negro life had been speeded up to a remarkable pace." Accordingly, *Jet* seemed an appropriate title. *Negro Digest* would, henceforth, become a quarterly journal intended to provide scholarly articles primarily for librarians and teachers. *Advertising Age* took note of the new publication with the following comment:

> The hard-driving Johnson Publishing Company, which has carved a pre-eminent niche for itself in the Negro magazine field, today introduced its fourth entry—*Jet*, a weekly pocket-size news and picture magazine selling for 15¢. . . . The company's other publications are *Ebony*, another picture magazine with a circulation of nearly 500,000; *Tan Confessions*, a romantic type monthly with a circulation of 300,000; and *Negro Digest*, with 100,000 circulation.[2]

Jet is a newsmagazine that resembles, in coverage, *Time* and *Newsweek*. It was designed, however, as a black response to *Quick*, a white pocket-size magazine, some observers have noted. Its popularity has clearly justified Johnson's belief that a small magazine could appeal to a wide audience. The format includes a few in-depth news stories. Most of the content is distributed among

214   JOURNAL OF AFRO-AMERICAN ISSUES

business, education, religion, health, medicine, journalism, politics, labor, poverty, and crime sections. "Ticker Tape, U.S.A." is a Walter Winchell-type feature of one-sentence news reports. "People Are Talking About" is a sophisticated gossip column about personalities and public affairs. A centerfold black bathing beauty is in most issues. A radio and television guide emphasizes performances in which blacks play principal parts. During football seasons, the magazine publishes the win-loss record of certain black college teams. Unlike *Ebony,** *Jet* contains no editorial comment. Its choice of news items allows editors to imply their social and political outlook. As a weekly illustrated report to black audiences on black life in the United States, *Jet* enjoys popularity among all levels of Afro-Americans.

Notes

1. Johnson's *Ebony* reached the newsstands in November 1945, after *Negro Digest*, begun in 1942, had launched John H. Johnson's phenomenal career as a black magazine publisher.
2. *Advertising Age* (29 October 1951): 27.

Information Sources

BIBLIOGRAPHY:
"Backstage." *Ebony*, December 1951, p. 12.
Boone, Dorothy Deloris. "A Historical Review and a Bibliography of Selected Negro Magazines, 1910-1969." Ph.D. dissertation, University of Michigan, 1970, p. 125.
"New Hue, New Color." *Newsweek*, 9 October 1953, p. 93.
Tebbel, John. *The American Magazine: A Composite History*. New York, 1969, p. 261.
Wolseley, Roland E. *The Changing Magazine: Trends in Readership and Management*. New York, 1973, pp. 104-5.
INDEX SOURCE: *Index to Periodicals by and about Negroes*.
LOCATION SOURCES: University Microfilms; most academic and public libraries.

Publication History

MAGAZINE TITLE AND TITLE CHANGES: *Jet* (29 October 1951 to present).
VOLUME AND ISSUE DATA: Vols. I-present, weekly.
PUBLISHER AND PLACE OF PUBLICATION: Johnson Publications, Inc., Chicago, Illinois.
EDITORS: John H. Johnson (1951-).
CIRCULATION: 718,000.

JOURNAL OF AFRO-AMERICAN ISSUES

Research in the behavioral sciences gave rise in the 1970s to publication of a scholarly journal devoted to increasing knowledge of the black American experience. The *Journal of Afro-American Issues*, first issued in 1972, aimed to provide articles with a theoretical and empirical approach to matters of immediate relevance within the black community. In 1975, black psychologists, educators, and social scientists who questioned the validity of standardized national intelligence and aptitude tests found a forum in the *Journal*. At other times, the *Journal* devoted entire issues to such topics as blacks and the criminal justice system, social and mental health, affirmative action and minority student development, dilemmas and prospects of black political dynamics, and black American literature as an expression of the black American experience.

While early issues of the *Journal* used an open format, it later became an entirely topic-oriented journal with each issue having its own guest editor(s). Robert L. Williams edited the Winter 1975 issue on "Testing, Measurements, and Afro-Americans." His editorial introduction, "The Politics of I.Q.: Racism and Power," highlighted the strong political implications that lay in uses made of IQ tests. He held that intelligence tests had precipitated a controversy that was largely political; hence, it was also a power issue. Other articles exploring the same subject discussed a multicultural perspective in educational testing, problems of "labeling" black children according to their scores on school tests, social-psychological implications of that practice, the assault on black culture that the labeling process permits, and variables as bases for testing black children.

During its later period of activity, the *Journal of Afro-American Issues* showed an especial interest in research on the black family. John Henrik Clarke assembled a series of essays and studies on "Black Families in the Economy" for a special double issue in 1975. Those essays and studies set forth the premise that the black family system and structure were most significantly threatened by current national economic policies and practices. Articles included studies of overviews of black families in North and South America as parts of national economies and the status of peoples who participated minimally in the governmental processes. Later, in the Spring 1976 and a subsequent special double issue, Dr. Alvin F. Poussaint brought together articles on "The Black Family: Black Child/Youth Development." The articles discussed theories of the black family, the influence of the African family heritage on black American family stability, the black matriarchy controversy, the development of black identity, and the causes and consequences of alcohol abuse among black youth.

The *Journal of Afro-American Issues* was not a general-purpose periodical; however, its contents did transcend narrow, academic subject matter. It sought to bring scientific relevance to the social and political thrusts that emanated from the civil rights movement.

Information Sources

INDEX SOURCE: *Abstracts in Anthropology.*
LOCATION SOURCES: Many college and university libraries.

Publication History

MAGAZINE TITLE AND TITLE CHANGES: *Journal of Afro-American Issues.*
VOLUME AND ISSUE DATA: Vols. I-V (Summer 1972-Summer 1977), quarterly.
PUBLISHER AND PLACE OF PUBLICATION: Roosevelt Johnson, Educational Com-
    munity Consultants Associates, Inc., Washington, D.C.
EDITORS: Clyde W. Franklin, Jr. (1972-1974); Roosevelt Johnson (1974-1977).
CIRCULATION: 5,000.

Mark A. Reger

JOURNAL OF BLACK POETRY

Joe Goncalves once wrote of the *Journal of Black Poetry* which he founded in 1966 and published in San Francisco, "The *Journal*, despite its name is not a 'poetry' magazine. It is a means of communication, and poetry is one of the ways to communicate."[1] He was referring to the view of blackness that he and his associates held and the way they expressed it in the new poetry of the 1960s.[2] His was one of the principal arts little magazines. These new journals expressed a trend widely different from that which the black press had followed from its beginnings. The long-lasting magazines—*Crisis,* Opportunity,* Phylon,** and *Negro Digest**—had been integrationist; however, the social unrest brought on by the assassinations of Malcolm X, Martin Luther King, and John and Robert Kennedy fostered a militant separatist stance among blacks. Black power advocates basically rejected King's passive resistance and search for civil rights by negotiation and demonstrations, as well as the NAACP's legalistic approaches. Beginning with the Harlem riots of July 1964 and other disturbances throughout most of the 1960s, new voices called for a revolutionary approach to social action. As had always been the case in the United States, creative writing among blacks reflected the tone and temper of prevailing group action toward first-class citizenship.

Young writers respected King's accomplishments at mid century, but they believed new techniques and attitudes were needed to further the struggle. Even as King had used the spoken word as a principal strategy for his purposes, these writers used the written word—poetry and drama—for theirs. The new literature resembled the Harlem literary renaissance of the 1920s, but its cadence was essentially different. Tone and purpose were equally significant in their poetry. They promoted blackness. And in doing so, they believed the media of communication for their literature should be owned and controlled by Afro-Americans. Walter Lowenfels wrote in *Liberator*:

The white poetry scene in the United States is in the control of a literary syndicate. It is divided up into different families, each of which has its favorite critics and anthologists, all of whom exclude nonwhite poets. . . to review anthologies of poetry for young people, the Times chose a critic who had written: "Until recently there hasn't been any Afro-American verse that was more than verse. . . . When I was editing anthologies in 1938 and again in 1946, I remember going through the complete works of Countee Cullen, Claude McKay, Langston Hughes, and the others, hoping desperately to find a *poem*, and falling back on the spirituals and the blues."[3]

This kind of statement and the attitude it represents caused leaders of the black arts movement to reject the popular national magazines as well as the little journals they considered white. Black publishing houses were developed largely by writers and other persons who joined with them in the business ventures.[4] They also attacked black studies journals that were not considered secure parts of the movement. John H. Johnson's commercially successful *Negro Digest** and *Ebony** were suspect, and *Essence,** published by an interracial conglomerate was, to them, a negative force.[5]

LeRoi Jones (Imamu Amiri Baraka) became a leader of the black arts movement through his drama, poetry, and fiction. He expressed the new aesthetic in an essay in the *Journal of Black Poetry*. The new leaders took their clues from Marcus Garvey and his emphasis on restoration of black Africa as the home of black Americans. Franz Fanon, who had predicted the decline and fall of Western civilization, Malcolm X, and Don L. Lee, the popular young poet, wrote:

We see the Sixties as a movement beyond the shadowiness of the Harlem Renaissance and the restrictiveness of the Negritude Movement. The poets of the Sixties and the Seventies move beyond mere rage and 'black is beautiful' to bring together a new set of values, emotions, historical perspectives and futuristic directions—a transformation from the lifestyle of the sayers to that of the doers.[6]

He held that literature produced by black hands is not necessarily black writing, as he delineated the embodiment of black art as a consciousness that reflects the true Afro-American experience. That art, he wrote, was functional, and it was committed to humanism, serving the community more than the individual.

Most issues of the *Journal of Black Poetry* published many poems, sometimes as many as forty or fifty. Gwendolyn Brooks, Ed Bullins, James Emanuel, Robert Hayden, Don L. Lee, and Sonia Sanchez were among the best known of the poets. Ishmael Reed's interviews are particularly important statements on literary criticism of the black arts movement.

This journal brought together most of the young black voices of the new arts effort. In addition to writers already mentioned, Clarence Major, Larry Neal, and Dudley Randall served at some time as associate editors and contributors.

When the journal faltered and ceased publication in the summer of 1973, Goncalves started another magazine, *Kitabu Cha Jua*, that survived for a brief time. All of them suffered from lack of proper funding. Their circulation was low and they carried little profitable advertisement. The *Journal of Black Poetry* is an important publication for its direct history of the black arts crusade—its principal participants, their theories of art, and their positions on society and politics.

Notes

1. *See* Goncalves' reviews of *Dynamite Voices* in *Journal of Black Poetry* (Summer/Fall 1969): 91.
2. Goncalves had been editor of *Black Dialogue* before he began publishing the *Journal of Black Poetry*.
3. "The White Literary Syndicate," *Liberator* (March 1970): 8.
4. These were Free Black Press of Chicago, Journal of Black Press of California, Black Dialogue Press of New York, Jihad Press of Newark, New Jersey, Broadside Press of Detroit, and Third World Press of Chicago.
5. *See* "Report on the *Essence* Magazine Affair," *Journal of Black Poetry* (Winter/Spring 1970): 108; and "Some Notes," *Journal of Black Poetry* (Summer 1972): 3.
6. "Black Writing," *Journal of Black Poetry* (Fall/Winter 1971): 95-96.

Information Sources

BIBLIOGRAPHY:
Anderson, S. E. "The Fragmented Movement." *Negro Digest*, September/October 1968, pp. 4-10.
Gayle, Addison, Jr. "Black Power: Existential Politics." *Liberator*, January 1969, pp. 4-7.
———. "Nationalism: The Black Novel and the City." *Liberator*, July 1969, pp. 14-17.
Johnson, Abby Arthur, and Johnson, Ronald Maberry. *Propaganda and Aesthetics: The Literary Politics of Afro-American Magazines in the Twentieth Century*. Amherst: University of Massachusetts Press, 1979, pp. 164-70.
Long, Richard A. "The Black Studies Boondoggle." *Liberator*, September 1970, p. 8.
Redmond, Eugene B. *Drumvoices: The Mission of Afro-American Poetry*. New York, 1976, pp. 294-308.
INDEX SOURCE: *Humanities Index*.
LOCATION SOURCES: Library of Congress; Moorland-Spingarn Collection, Howard University, Washington, D. C.; some university libraries.

Publication History

MAGAZINE TITLE AND TITLE CHANGES: *Journal of Black Poetry*.
VOLUME AND ISSUE DATA: Journal did not use volume designations. Published Spring 1966-Summer 1973, quarterly.
PUBLISHER AND PLACE OF PUBLICATION: Journal of Black Poetry, San Francisco, California.
EDITOR: Joe Goncalves (1966-1973).
CIRCULATION: 500.

JOURNAL OF BLACK STUDIES

The *Journal of Black Studies*, a journal of original research founded in 1970, rose on the crest of the popularity of black studies programs established in colleges and universities as a result of the black activism in the 1960s. The editorial policy set by its first editor, Molefi Kete Asante, director of the Afro-American Studies Center at the University of California at Los Angeles has remained constant. The journal seeks to sustain a full analytical discussion of issues relating to persons of African descent. Throughout the period of its publication it has also promoted black ethnic studies as an academic discipline, as well as the publication of significant research about the culture and concerns of people throughout the black diaspora. The journal's major focus has been on the United States and black Africa, but it has also included the Caribbean in its studies, as have the majority of similarly oriented publications.

The *Journal of Black Studies* contains book review essays of current publications in politics, literature, education, and the social sciences. During the mid and late seventies the journal published articles on comparative slave systems in the United States and Latin America; urban and plantation slave settings; an anthropological concept of race; group cohesiveness in the Black Panther party; the historical setting of Booker T. Washington and the rhetoric of his Atlanta Exposition Address in 1893; and the use of black models in advertising. Education was analyzed primarily through studies of college life as a source of black alienation and the status and problems of black faculty members at multiracial campuses. Caribbean studies included the relationship between African culture and contemporary Cuba.

From time to time the journal published issues devoted to single subjects. Some of these special series include: "The Black University: Assimilation or Survival?" "Locus of Control: Educational Implications for Blacks," "Modern Black Literature," "Facing North America: Caribbean Political and Cultural Definitions," "Nigeria: Problems of Development," "Ebonics (Black English): Implications for Education," and "Afro-Brazilian Experience and Proposals for Social Change." Articles in all of these issues were written by scholars well recognized in their respective fields. Some were faculty members at cooperating institutions that supported the journal—the State University of New York at Buffalo, Cornell, Fisk, and Northwestern universities, and the University of California at Los Angeles.

The *Journal of Black Studies* has enjoyed a level of financial security that has permitted it to sustain itself as a respected medium of scholarship on problems concerning the black experience. It is usually published without editorial comment. More strictly a collection of scholarly articles than *Black World**, this journal is a wealth of research on living black in the seventies and into the eighties in representative parts of the world whose populations include large numbers of black peoples.

Information Sources

INDEX SOURCES: *Ethnic Studies Bibliography*; *Black Information Index*; *Current Index to Journals in Education*; *Social Sciences Citation Index*; *Public Affairs Information Service*; *Index to Periodical Articles by and about Negroes*; *Current Contents*; *Social Sciences Index*; *United States Political Science Documents*.
LOCATION SOURCES: College and university libraries; major public libraries; University Microfilms.

Publication History

MAGAZINE TITLE AND TITLE CHANGES: *Journal of Black Studies*.
VOLUME AND ISSUE DATA: Vols. I-XII (Fall 1970 to present), quarterly.
PUBLISHER AND PLACE OF PUBLICATION: Sage Publications, Beverly Hills, California.
EDITORS: Molefi Kete Asante (formerly Arthur L. Smith) (1970-).
CIRCULATION: 1,500.

Mark A. Reger

JOURNAL OF HUMAN RELATIONS, THE

Central State University in Ohio began publication of the *Journal of Human Relations* in 1952 with purposes broader than those usually related to faculty research journals. Although its early issues contained articles written almost exclusively by faculty members at the home institution, the magazine, in its statement of editorial policy, offered to publish scientific findings and reasoned opinions and practical programs that should relate to the betterment of human living. Its first editorial stated: "The title of this periodical, *Journal of Human Relations*, defines itself. In the current chaotic state of our civilization the significance of such a journal is obvious. Any publication that emphasizes the existent problematical social conditions and seeks to contribute to their resolution, has a claim to significance."[1] Hence, the title. By implication, the emphasis would be on the behavioral sciences.

Beginning publication on the eve of the United States Supreme Court's landmark *Brown* v. *Topeka* decision on public school racial integration, the journal purported to contribute to social integration as that condition of growth in unity and harmony by which "our adolescent humanity may consciously progress to full maturity."[2] The magazine would not be a radical black voice. Nor would it reflect racial bias. Instead, it would testify to the truth that all men are one race—that which we call *human*. Scholars interested in participating in the enterprise, within and outside the university, were invited to submit contributions. The only editorial requirement with respect to philosophical orientation was that prospective contributors should share the concerns the journal intended to address.

Charles H. Wesley, the noted black historian and president of the university, wrote for the first issue. His "Three Basic Problems in Human Relations" laid a foundation for the areas of interest the new publication would address. They were relevant to the national milieu. Other articles included "Integration, the Chief Aim of Education," and "The Role of Intellectual Conflict in Human Relations." From the beginning, the magazine also included book reviews on subjects in human relations. The most useful feature was "Research Studies and Abstracts," a detailed report on investigation in the social sciences—published articles as well as a list of dissertations completed during each preceding school year. "Look at the Journals" was a group of abstracts of articles from other publications whose contents were similar to the *Journal of Human Relations'*.

In its earliest issues, this magazine sought to establish legitimacy for the term "human relations" as an academic subject. It published teaching aids and articles that discussed intergroup dynamics, unique dimensions of student personnel services at mid century, the sociology of adolescence, and attitudes of college students toward civil rights. Possibilities of *de jure* racial integration brought forth significant essays about labor organizations, black-Jewish relations, and stirrings of nationalism in colonial black Africa. Authorities in all of these areas wrote about the changing social order in these contexts.

The journal's articles and studies were focused on human psychology and sociology. Some interests are reflected in the titles of some contents over a period of several years: "Humanistic Consciousness and Student Activism," "Source of Problems Between Social Science Knowledge and Practice," "Interracial Communication Syndrome," "Drugs, Peace, and Freedom," "Ronald Reagan and Student Power Advocates," "America's New Anti-Police Sentiment," "Sociological Language and *1984*," "Pentagon Capitalism," "Color Line and Humanism: An Ethical Study of W.E.B. Du Bois," and "The Role of Social Intelligence in Literature and the Humanities."

Special editions were fairly common. The Winter 1961 edition was titled "Human Relations in the Communist World." Some of its articles included: "The Structure of Human Relations in Central-Eastern Europe," "Nationalism and the European Satellites in the USSR," "Recent Trends in Public Opinion in USSR," "Labor's Status Under the Communists," and "Religious Institutions in the Soviet Orbit." Other issues were devoted to "Glimpses of India in Village Life and Culture," Spring 1961; "Poverty in America," Fall 1972; and "Toward a Science of Value," First and Second quarters 1973.

As the journal moved into broad concepts of human relations, including theoretical approaches to the subject, a new statement of its purposes seemed necessary. It read in part:

Journal of Human Relations is committed to intelligent libertarian revolution, on the assumption that all life is a variant process, and is therefore being continuously revolutionized. In human society, when any variant way of living is organized and becomes dominant, it is used as a standard by which other variant ways are then perceived as dangerous deviants, which then require suppression. For this reason, we are in sympathy with the deep aspirations which are variously expressed through insurgency movements of the world. We also recognize that in most cases, the freedom that is being striven for is the freedom to reorganize society so that one's own way of life becomes dominant, and other ways are restricted. We therefore will both encourage and challenge all revolutionary and insurgency movements and ideas, seeking always to discriminate between the reactionary violence of blind revolt, which changes nothing, and the libertarian methods of conscious, nonviolent revolutionary change.[3]

A series of unfortunate incidents led to cessation of the publication of the journal. In 1971 the former editor was not replaced because the university, which subsidized the cost of the publication, faced severe straits. A tornado that struck the campus 3 April 1971 destroyed the building that housed the editorial offices. A year later the director of the college print shop who had supervised the camera-copy production of the magazine was killed in an accident. These problems caused the institution to suspend publication of the journal "until more secure financial and administrative arrangements could be made." It never resumed publication.

The *Journal of Human Relations* established a good reputation during its lifetime for the significant scholarship it published in the behavorial sciences with respect to human relations. Although literary studies were not its primary focus, occasionally the magazine contained discussions and analyses of writing by Afro-American authors. Several issues contained creative writing.

Notes

1. "Editorial Foreword," *Journal of Human Relations* (Spring 1952): 2.
2. Ibid.
3. "Foreword," *Journal of Human Relations* (Second Quarter 1973): ii.

Information Sources

BIBLIOGRAPHY:
Boone, Dorothy Deloris. "A Historical Review and a Bibliography of Selected Negro Magazines, 1910-1969." Ph.D. dissertation, University of Michigan, 1970, pp. 126-27.
Roland Wolseley, *Black Press, U.S.A.* (Ames: Iowa State University Press, 1971, pp. 142-43.
INDEX SOURCES: *Index to Selected Negro Periodicals*; *Public Affairs Information Service*; *Poverty and Human Resources Abstracts*; *Psychological Abstracts*.
LOCATION SOURCES: University Microfilms; many college and university libraries.

Publication History

MAGAZINE TITLE AND TITLE CHANGES: *The Journal of Human Relations*.
VOLUME AND ISSUE DATA: Vols. I-XXI (Spring 1952-Fourth Quarter 1973).
PUBLISHER AND PLACE OF PUBLICATION: Central State University, Wilberforce, Ohio.
EDITORS: Anne O'H. Williamson (Spring 1952-Autumn 1962); Ralph T. Templin (Winter 1963-Third Quarter 1968); Don Workhelser (Fourth Quarter 1968-Fourth Quarter 1971); Ralph T. Templin (First and Second Quarters 1972-Fourth Quarter 1973).
CIRCULATION: 1,500.

JOURNAL OF NEGRO EDUCATION, THE

One index of the significant development of Howard University as the capstone of black higher education in the United States lies in its establishment of the *Journal of Negro Education* and that journal's constant leadership among scholarly journals for blacks. It was first published in April 1932 at Howard University under the editorship of Charles H. Thompson, who served administratively as chairman of the Department of Education and as dean of the College of Liberal Arts. His personal prestige made the magazine a leader in its class. A fitting statement about his role in the development of the journal is seen in a portion of the editorial comment in the issue following his death.

Dean Thompson's obituary of January 23, 1980 in *The Washington Post*, C-4, stated that he left "no immediate survivors." But *The Journal of Negro Education* was his "baby." It was conceived by him, and born at Howard University in 1932. He was its Editor-in-Chief for 31 years, guiding it to maturity while simultaneously utilizing it as a major vehicle through which to provide ideas essential to change the unequal educational conditions guaranteed by the decision in *Plessy v. Ferguson*. The *Journal*, his offspring, will be 50 years old in 1981. It remains the major vehicle for distributing research data and other pertinent information about the education of Blacks in the U.S., as well as in developing nations. The *Journal* is pledged to carry on the tradition of excellence begun by its father/founder.[1]

The magazine was subsidized by the university and the editor was assisted by a board of editors, most of whom were members of the university Department of Education. A large contributing and advisory staff of prominent educators from around the nation also appeared on the masthead of the magazine. Thompson quickly established this publication as one of the most important vehicles for the study of "Problems Incident to the Education of Negroes." From its beginning until the present the journal has appeared quarterly. The annual yearbook issue within each volume is devoted to a rather comprehensive study of some particular aspects of problems of Negro education and has continued from its beginning to provide enduring and increasing value for the understanding of education among black Americans.

The first issue contained the lead editorial "Why a Journal of Negro Education?" which pointed out the threefold purpose of the journal. First, it would stimulate the collection and facilitate the dissemination of facts about the education of Negroes; second, it would present discussions involving critical appraisals of the proposals and practices relating to the education of Negroes; and third, it would stimulate and sponsor investigations of problems incident to the education of Negroes. These purposes were not being achieved adequately at the time by any other organ, the editorial claimed. Howard University's faculty could lead other black professions into providing, along with the resident faculty in Washington, such a needed resource. In the twenty-fifth anniversary issue of the *Journal of Negro Education*, editor Thompson could write with pride of the magazine's accomplishments.

> Perusal of the 24 volumes published to date. . . will reveal that there is scarcely a single problem in (these areas) which the *Journal* has not discussed; and it would be difficult to find a comprehensive study or critical discussion of any problem in these areas by other agencies which does not make reference to the *Journal* in some manner. In fact, if we can believe the overwhelming majority of our "fan mail," it would appear that the *Journal* has greatly surpassed our original expectations. And yet no one is more conscious of its shortcomings than we are.[2]

By mid twentieth century, the United States Supreme Court decision in *Brown v. Topeka* and other rulings concerning higher education and access to it by blacks who applied for admission to previously all-white state universities had seemed to eliminate the need for study of what was defined legally as "Negro education." Questions arose as to whether institutions and publications for blacks would be continued. Thompson had an answer. He argued that no one questioned whether the 300 or so Jewish publications listed in the *Union List of Serials* should cease. Nor whether the many women's organizations, the Japanese-Americans, or any other special interests groups, should end their periodicals. He concluded that the *Journal*'s purposes would remain the same, inasmuch as they were still valid concerns for scholarship. At the same time, he asked readers to advise him of their reactions to the question.

Although the *Journal* was devoted primarily to problems incident to the education of Negroes, it published articles relating to a wide variety of subjects about living black in the United States. Ralph J. Bunche, a young faculty member at Howard University during a part of the early history of the publication, contributed articles on national politics and the social order as they affected Negroes. He also wrote some studies on the emergence of educational policy and opportunities among natives of what were then the French colonies in Africa, suggesting early a direction of "Negritude," that later became a focus of several articles in the journal. Sterling Brown, a professor of English at Howard and renowned literary critic and poet, wrote about the American race problem as it is reflected in the nation's literature and Negro characters as seen by white authors. Ambrose Caliver, United States Department of Education specialist in Negro problems, wrote on a variety of problems dealing with the national involvement with public education among blacks.[3]

Nancy Bullock Woolridge, an English professor at Hampton Institute, wrote "The Slave Preacher—Portrait of Leader,"; Oliver C. Cox, a distinguished black sociologist who taught at Wiley College in Texas and Lincoln University in Missouri, wrote a score of articles on race relations, the black family, lynching, and graduate education in the black college. W.E.B. Du Bois, even when he was editor of the *Crisis** and director of research for the NAACP, contributed articles to the journal on social planning, racially separate schools, and one of his several pieces on Wilberforce University. E. Franklin Frazier, the sociologist, wrote about the social order, graduate education, and urbanization in Africa south of the Sahara. Other popular black scholars published in the magazine in its first decade, particularly Charles S. Johnson, Alain Locke, Rayford Logan, Benjamin Mays, and Martin Jenkins.

Accreditation of Negro high schools and colleges, the effects of World War II on Negro education, and admission of black students to the universities of Maryland, Missouri, Tennessee, and Texas as they wrestled in legal battles brought to force their integration remained a chief interest of the *Journal of Negro Education* during its first quarter-century of publication.

In 1963, Walter Green Daniel, a long-time member of the faculty of the School of Education at Howard University, became editor in chief when Charles H. Thompson became editor emeritus. In his first editorial, Daniel explored President John F. Kennedy's special message to Congress on civil rights delivered 28 February 1963. He devoted the Fall 1963 issue to a review of the progress of Negro civil rights since 1950. This kind of editorial policy was characteristic of the new editor's perspective of the role of the *Journal* in addition to citing needs for improvement in resources for American education at all levels and for both races; finding more opportunities to teach and practice democracy in institutions devoted to education; seeking new ways to assist minorities; and supporting minorities in self-help activities.

When Daniel became editor emeritus in 1973, an interim editor praised his work in an editorial comment that read in part:

Walter Green Daniel, Editor-in-Chief of the *Journal of Negro Education* since 1963, has been on the Editorial Board of the *Journal* since the first issue of April 1932. His retirement from Howard University in 1971 did not end his association with the *Journal*, for his contributions to its development continued. Walter Daniel was the second editor and a rightful successor to Charles H. Thompson, the founder and Editor-in-Chief Emeritus of the *Journal*. As new directions are being chartered for this publication, it is appropriate to review the accomplishments of Dr. Daniel, both in his contributions to the *Journal* and to the higher education of Blacks in the United States. His distinguished career has revealed an unusual pattern of competencies in many fields.[4]

Charles A. Martin, a newcomer to Howard from the University of Illinois, Chicago Circle, became the first editor in chief who was not a longtime faculty member of the university. He assumed office in July 1973. An announcement in the spring issue that year had told readers that the cover and format of the journal would be redesigned. The Winter 1974 issue bore a new subtitle, "A Howard University Quarterly Review of Issues Incident to the Education of Black People." The emphasis remained centered around the threefold purpose of previous editors.

The *Journal of Negro Education* served during certain periods of its publication as an eclectic magazine centering upon problems of black Americans, although it did not deviate from its special emphasis on education. However, in view of the extraordinarily small number of publications in which black scholars may report their studies and their essays about the black experience in America, the *Journal* served an unusual purpose in the nation's history. It still stands as perhaps the highest quality of material available for the study of black religion, schools, and family in the United States beginning in the early 1930s and continuing today. A large number of black scholars, no matter what their particular academic interest, published articles in the *Journal of Negro Education*. To this extent and in this respect, "Negro education," is practically synonymous with examination of the American black experience.

Notes

1. Faustine C. Jones, "In Memoriam: Dean Charles H. Thompson (1896-1980)," *Journal of Negro Education* (Spring 1980): 116.
2. "The Twenty-fifth Volume of the *Journal of Negro Education*," *Journal of Negro Education* (Winter 1956): 1.
3. Ibid., p. 2.
4. Carrall L. Miller, "Walter Green Daniel: Editor, Teacher, Scholar, Educational Administrator, Community Leader," *Journal of Negro Education* (Spring 1973): 102.

Information Sources

BIBLIOGRAPHY:
―――. "Black Studies in American Education." *Journal of Negro Education*, Summer 1970, pp. 189-90.

Daniel, Walter G. "A Priority for the Seventies." *Journal of Negro Education*, Spring 1970, pp. 107-8.

Jones, Faustine C. "The Ambiguities of Change." *Journal of Negro Education*, Fall 1980, pp. 361-62.

Logan, Rayford W., *Howard University: The First Hundred Years, 1867-1967*. New York University Press, 1969, p. 251.

Marshall, Albert P. "Racial Integration in Education in Missouri." *Journal of Negro Education*, Summer 1956, pp. 284-98.

Martin, Charles A. "Black English and Black History—Continuing Themes." *Journal of Negro Education*, Summer 1974, pp. 263-64.

West, Earl H. "Models in Education." *Journal of Negro Education*, February 1970, pp. 275-77.

INDEX SOURCES: *Education Index; Language and Language Behavior Abstracts; Psychological Abstracts; Sociological Abstracts; Current Index to Journals in Education; Abstracts for Social Workers; Chicorel Abstracts to Reading and Learning Disabilities.*

LOCATION SOURCES: University and college libraries; Kraus Reprints.

Publication History

MAGAZINE TITLE AND TITLE CHANGES: *The Journal of Negro Education.*
VOLUME AND ISSUE DATA: Vols. 1 to present (January 1932-).
PUBLISHER AND PLACE OF PUBLICATION: Howard University, Washington, D.C.
EDITORS: Charles H. Thompson (Winter 1932-Winter 1963); Walter Green Daniel (Spring 1963-Fall 1973); Carl H. West, acting editor (Winter and Spring 1973): Charles A. Martin (Summer 1973-Fall 1980); Faustine C. Jones (Winter 1980-).
CIRCULATION: 3,000.

JOURNAL OF NEGRO HISTORY

Carter G. Woodson organized the Association for the Study of Negro Life and History 9 September 1915 in Chicago for the purposes of collecting sociological and historical data bearing on the Negro and to publish books on Negro life and history. Through these activities he planned to promote the study of the Negro through clubs and schools and to bring about harmony between the white and black races by interpreting the one to the other. Beginning the next year, the association and its founder brought out the first issue of the *Journal of Negro History* which has been published regularly since that time as a quarterly. The publication quickly found favor with leading American scholars and was subscribed to by major university libraries. In 1922, the Laura Spelman Rockefeller Memorial Fund made a grant to the association to undertake systematic research on the Negro in the United States. That same year the organization established a department of research that was financially able to employ investigators whose work resulted in the publication of twenty-five monographs concerning a wide range of aspects of Afro-American life and culture. The majority of black academic historians and social scientists were involved in the association's research projects or contributed articles to the journal.

In 1926 the association initiated the celebration of Negro History Week, which focused on achievements of black Americans. Woodson envisioned the plan would engage the cooperation of ministers, teachers, and professional and business persons throughout the country. That project enjoyed success and led to the Extension Division of the association, which provided information about black Americans through public lectures and study by correspondence. To become a permanently organized branch required at least ten persons to pay the active membership fee and establish an organization. Each member received the *Journal of Negro History* for one year as part of the benefit of membership. This plan insured a nucleus of subscribers for the periodical.

Almost from its inception, the *Journal of Negro History* was highly respected among scholarly magazines. Its founder was the epitome of scholarship and personal achievement. Born of former slave parents in Virginia in 1875, Woodson was unable to attend school regularly before he was twenty years old, when he entered Douglass High School in Huntington, West Virginia. He received his diploma two years later and was admitted to Berea College in Kentucky. He eventually earned his bachelor's and master's degrees and taught in public schools during the next several years. He was granted a doctorate in history by Harvard University in 1912. As the second black American to become a trained historian, Woodson devoted his life to making the world familiar with the accomplishments of his race. He was convinced that if a race had no recorded history, its achievements would be forgotten and finally claimed by other groups. Thus, he devoted his talents and energies to research on Afro-American culture and ways to disseminate knowledge about it.

The first issue of the *Journal of Negro History* included historical articles written by Woodson, W. B. Hartgrove, Monroe N. Work and A. O. Stafford. Each dealt with some aspect of the history of black Americans. A section called "Documents" focused on what the Negro was thinking during the eighteenth century and presented a group of letters showing the rise and progress of the early black church in Georgia and in the West Indies. Book reviews, "Notes," and a news column completed the format.

The association and its journal were well established during the more than thirty years Woodson directed the activities of both. He died suddenly at his home in Washington, D.C., 3 April 1950, at the age of seventy-four. Friends took immediate steps to provide for continuation of the organization and the magazine. Mary McLeod Bethune, then president of the association, convinced Rayford W. Logan, professor of history at Howard University, to serve temporarily as editor. Within a year Logan could report to an annual meeting of the association that there had been no appreciable change in the number of subscribers as a result of Woodson's death and that considerable numbers of articles had been submitted by faculty members of some of the most prestigious universities in the United States. They were no longer only black, although the magazine continued its focus on scholarship about black people in the United States, as well as those in Latin America, the West Indies, and Africa.

The *Journal of Negro History* continues as a premier scholarly magazine concerned with black culture. It has retained the high quality Woodson set for it. Through the many changes of direction of black Americans and the shifting national and world pictures with respect to race and color, the journal has remained a source of significant scholarship. Well into its second half-century, its format contains three to five major articles, a section of documents on Afro-American history, book reviews, notes, and announcements. Some issues include "In Memoriam," obituaries of black scholars who have died within the recent past. Principal articles discuss Afro-American institutions, personalities, and historical events. Some recent issues have included: "Tuskegee Institute and Northern White Philanthropy: A Case Study in Fund Raising, 1900-1915," "Populism and Black Americans: Constructive or Destructive," "The Anti-Negro French Law of 1777," "Langston Hughes of Kansas," "Aspects of the Family and Public Life of Antoine Dubucet: Louisiana's Black State Treasurer, 1868-1878," "The Afro-Argentine Officers of Buenos Aires Province, 1800-1860," "Fugitive Slaves and Free Society: The Case of Brazil," "Communists and Blacks: The ILD and the Angelo Herndon Case," and "John Chavis, 1763-1838: A Social-Psychological Study."

Information Sources

BIBLIOGRAPHY:
Franklin, John Hope. *From Slavery to Freedom: A History of Negro Americans*. 3d ed. New York, 1967, p. 559.
Johnson, Charles S. "The Rise of the Negro Magazine." *Journal of Negro History*, January 1928, pp. 16-17.
Logan, Frenise A. "An Appraisal of Forty-One Years of the *Journal of Negro History*, 1916-1957," *Journal of Negro History*, January 1958, pp. 26-33.
Miller, M. Sammy. "The Sixtieth Anniversary of the *Journal of Negro History*: Letters from Dr. Carter G. Woodson to Mrs. Mary Church Terrell." *Journal of Negro History*, January 1978, pp. 26-53.
INDEX SOURCES: *Education Index*; *Humanities Index*; *Index of Periodical Articles by and about Negroes*; *Index of School Personnel*; *Social Science Citation Index*.
LOCATION SOURCES: Most university and public libraries; University Microforms International.

Publication History

MAGAZINE TITLE AND TITLE CHANGES: *Journal of Negro History*
VOLUME AND ISSUE DATA: Vols. I to present (January 1916-), quarterly.
PUBLISHER AND PLACE OF PUBLICATION: Association for the Study of Negro Life and History, Incorporated, Washington, D.C.

EDITORS: Carter G. Woodson (1916-1950); Rayford W. Logan (1950-1951); William M. Brewer (1952-1970); W. Augustus Low (1970-1974); Lorraine A. Williams (1974-1976); Alton Hornsby, Jr. (1976-).
CIRCULATION: 6,500.

Arvarh E. Strickland

L

LIBERATOR, THE

The *Liberator* began its life in New York City in 1961 as an information sheet of the Liberation Committee for Africa spawned by the death of Patrice Lumumba in Zaire. A May 1961 meeting of the committee announced a conference at which "Nationalism, Colonialism and the United States" would be the subject for discussion. Principal speakers were James Baldwin, James Higgins, and John O. Killens. The gathering was an outgrowth of a resolution passed at the Third Annual All-Africa Peoples Conference in Cairo earlier that year. Pan-Africanism as a vehicle for unity of black peoples throughout the world, expressed by creative writers, thus became the entente for the era that would give rise to a new generation of black journals—part literary and part political. The *Liberator*, first issued in May 1961, was the leader in that trend.

The name of Daniel H. Watts, editor in chief of the *Liberator* magazine, appeared on a list of sixty-five persons Congressman Richard Ichord of Missouri, chairman of the House Internal Security Committee, made available to the *New York Times* 14 October 1970. The list was of speakers who had appeared on college campuses as "radical rhetoricians of the New Left." Allegedly, they were affiliated with one or more of the twelve organizations Ichord's committee had determined were promoting violence and encouraging the destruction of the United States' system of government. A court order prohibited the committee from using official government printing and distributing facilities for disseminating the list. Watts accused the *New York Times* of playing hatchetman for the establishment by printing the notice without giving the "radicals" a chance to confirm or deny association with the discredited organizations. Ossie Davis, a black actor and playwright who had served on the advisory board of the magazine, wrote an open letter to Arthur O. Sulzberger, president and publisher of the *Times*, claiming the newspaper was out to punish Watts and to drive his magazine from existence. Davis continued, "*The Liberator* is the most important Black nationalist magazine in the country." He pointed out that it was the first journal to publish such black writers as LeRoi Jones, Nathan Hare, Eldridge Cleaver, Ed Bullins, Harold Cruse, Addison Gayle, Jr., Clayton Riley, Douglass Turner Ward, Toni Cade, and Malcolm X. These accolades were appropriate, for the *Liberator* had, indeed, been the premier black radical journal of the sixties. The names Davis mentioned were anathema to Ichord's committee, however. They were the most vociferous of the black revolutionists to their detractors. The *Liberator* had become a strong and loud voice for freedom that rang throughout the civil rights movement toward the federal legislation that granted once more in the nation's history first-class citizenship upon its black citizens.[1] In effect, placing the publication on the "blacklist" of the House committee ended its life.

Harold Cruse, intellectual historian of the "radical" movement in black America in the sixties, wrote that the *Liberator* never achieved its potential as an effective black journal. To him, it fell heir to the same unresolved historical conflicts and past mistakes that weighed down the activist branches of the Negro movement of the sixties, largely because it started off under the "incubus of having editorial elements in its directorship that were politically and ideologically incompatible."[2] The ownership and editorial directors were interracial. Its white members represented white liberals and pro-Marxist left-wingers. The editorial board was composed of American and West Indian Negroes. With these seeds of discontent bred into its structure, Cruse wrote, it was miraculous that the *Liberator* managed to hit the newsstands consistently.

It did live throughout the sixties, however. For the first two years—1961 to 1963—the *Liberator* managed a circulation of some 200 copies in Harlem. It took on a new life in October 1963, distributed 1200 copies monthly in a variety of large black communities, and became visible. The political affiliations of members of the advisory board probably did give writers some problems. Five members were Communists or pro-Communist, but their function in the publishing organization was not revealed to the editorial staff.[3]

These restrictions stifled some freedom on the *Liberator*, but for ten years the journal reflected critically the rise of black nationalism. It published good writers, old and new. But its vitality lay in its editorials and its observations about the black arts. To that extent, it was an important black journal that deserves examination in any definitive representation of the black magazine in the United States. As it began its second year of publication, *Liberator* editors attributed their growing success to three factors. "We are too poor to be sued; we are too small to be attacked; and too challenging to be ignored."[4] For the ensuing year the editors promised to remain too poor to be sued; to become too big to be attacked; and to remain too challenging to be ignored. Spokesmen reasoned the journal could reach its aspirations largely because it was one of a vanishing species of independent publications in the nation.

When the magazine first appeared, restive colonial areas of Africa found their nationalist aspirations articulated in the United States by Afro-Americans who associated themselves with black Africa. Integration at home and nationalism for the colonies stirred the black passions. Patrice Lumumba's name became the rallying cry for black Americans who considered the African struggle theirs. The civil rights activists had already shown their strength in the United States. Sit-ins had started in the South. Martin Luther King, Jr., still maintained the focus of the direction of action toward an unsegregated American society. The NAACP and the National Urban League took a "conservative" view of the young black college students who troubled their own campuses as well as the predominantly white ones at which blacks were enrolled. Black nationalism defined a course of action for social consciousness in the United States and a large part of the world that veered sharply from stances taken by King, Roy Wilkins, and Whitney Young.

Conventional civil rights organizations had come full circle. They were the "accommodationists" and the new vision encompassed a breadth and depth of human and civil rights that transcended any popular movement at any other time in the American experience. The emerging vein for the direction of black energies was "revolutionary." To its proponents this emphasis provided the only feasible response to the race's "colonial" status in its own native land. Proponents did not fear the label of "far-out" racial thinkers. Editor Watts, a promising young architect with a white New York firm, had willingly and enthusiastically turned to the perilous responsibility of supervising the publication of the *Liberator*. He was convinced that the only answer to the problem of meaningful black group self-realization lay in a final confrontation with the white power structure. He advocated in the United States the same kind of physical struggle that had taken place on the continent of Africa and said in a CBS documentary film that a similar showdown in this country would either bring meaningful negotiations, or else "the whites would march us off to concentration camps, led by Louis Armstrong playing "We Shall Overcome' and blessed by Martin Luther King as we go through the gates."[5]

This journalistic militancy seemed dramatic and reminiscent of the publications of Frederick Douglass a century earlier. Questions about the black movement that appeared and reappeared included: What is integration? What is nationalism? What is Marxist Communism and how does it relate to the first two ideas? The *Liberator* did not seek to provide definitive answers to these questions but it never wavered in its editorial support of the basic philosophy of the new black nationalism.

"Thoughts on the Emancipation Centennial," one of Watts' early editorials, expressed a revisionist approach to the history of the United States from the Afro-American perspective. It was to become the hallmark of the radical philosophy of the neocolonial black American. Noting that in September 1962 the National Civil War Centennial Commission had planned a major observance in Washington at the Lincoln Memorial that originally excluded any black participants, Watts reported that the noted historian, Allan Nevins, chair of the commission, had quipped that the roster of speakers selected by the commission had not been chosen by race and that no "outside" group was going to dictate to the commission. Watts wrote in response: "Just as today the granting of formal independence to our brothers in Africa has in many cases meant very little in the direction of achieving sovereignty and improving conditions, so the formal abolition of slavery one hundred years ago has remained more a symbol of hope than a significant change in status."[6]

The cultural revolution created and stressed new emphases. Negro History Week, studiously observed since Carter G. Woodson had inaugurated it a generation earlier, changed context. Watts wrote there was little reason for studying history as incidents of the past, for the present and the future were the contexts of the struggle. President John F. Kennedy was not praised for his "tea parties" for blacks at the White House but chided for not going south to give his personal endorsement to brave, young, black freedom fighters who risked their lives in the struggle for the dignity of man. Lorraine Hansberry, celebrated author of *Raisin in the Sun*, warned that "none of us should accept aesthetics which are not humanistic" and that "there is no art unless it has a moral base—not even in the Judeo-Christian tradition."[7] Once art loses its moral base, it is no longer art.

The Birmingham campaign of Martin Luther King, Jr., to desegregate public facilities became a *cause célèbre* for the *Liberator*, but not for the usual reasons. The editor saw broad implications in the confrontation.

> The real lesson of Birmingham is that the present leadership of the liberation movement is too far behind the people ever to catch up. Now that the end is in sight, mere "progress" is no longer acceptable. Total victory now—that must be the slogan. The brave people of Birmingham were fighting for much more than a promise of integrated lunch counters and interracial committees. It would be bitter fruit indeed to go through what they have endured and end up living in another hell like New York, Chicago or Los Angeles where every lunch counter is integrated and interracial committees are a virulent disease, but the black man's lot is still inferior jim crow schools, high-rent ghetto housing and an astronomical unemployment rate.[8]

Kennedy was attacked for wanting peace at home, lest a "revolutionary leadership" would develop out of the liberation movement and challenge the basis of American society. The school boycott in Harlem in 1964 proved that the NAACP and the National Urban League could no longer speak for or to restless natives. *Liberator* editorials claimed that so long as black leaders failed to realize that real political power could enable blacks to direct the affairs of their government with respect to their own public housing and public education, the accompanying evil of segregation would continue.

Malcolm X became the one leader the *Liberator*'s editorials could support from among the many black voices clamoring to be heard and heeded. But the editors realized that one man could not make a revolution. Watts wrote eloquently of his disappointment on the occasion of Malcolm X's death. He wrote that it was too early to assess Malcolm's contribution to the three-century struggle for freedom, but he knew his influence had been significant. And he warned at that time against self-destruction within the race, born of frustration and anger. He anticipated the growing tension within the ranks of radical black personalities and organizations that contributed to the decline of the magazine's public image.

While it lived, the *Liberator*'s editorials, feature articles, theater and book reviews, and letters to the editor captured significant portions of the turbulent sixties in the United States and on the continent of Africa. Watts, the journal's only editor in chief, interpreted and expressed the volatile nature of the civil rights direct-action period. No single spokesman received his full and constant approval. Yet his penetrating and challenging comments on all of them—King, Wilkins, Young, Malcolm X, Stokeley Carmichael, H. Rap Brown—represent an essential key to understanding the questions and issues raised by the black persons who sought to influence the responses to the dilemmas they faced.

Together with *Negro Digest*,* the *Liberator* went a long way toward shaping the black aesthetic that made arts an integral part of the political weapons activists used especially in the mid sixties. Its articles on the new black literature written by James Baldwin, LeRoi Jones, and Larry Neal, together with some of the revolutionary poetry of Langston Hughes, moved the *Liberator* into the vanguard of the new black journalism that served the artistic purposes of the traditional little magazine and, at the same time, was a communications medium for a new key in the response to the black American experience at a time of extraordinary unrest throughout the nation and black Africa.

Notes

1. See Rodney Carlisle, *The Roots of Black Nationalism* (Port Washington, N.Y., 1975), chapter 16, for a concise discussion of the rise of revolutionary nationalist thinking as an alternative to the legalistic tactics of the NAACP.

2. *The Crisis of the Negro Intellectual from Its Roots to the Present* (New York, 1967), p. 404.

3. Ibid.

4. "One Year After," *Liberator* (May 1962): 2.

5. This comment is recorded in William Brink and Louis Harris, *Black and White* (New York, 1966), pp. 57-58.

6. "The Brotherhood Conspiracy," *Liberator* (February 1963): 2.

7. "Rock the Boat," *Liberator* (March 1963): 2.

8. "Profiles in Courage," *Liberator* (June 1963): 2.

Information Sources

BIBLIOGRAPHY:
Brink, William, and Harris, Louis. *Black and White*. New York, 1966, pp. 57-58.

Cruse, Harold. *The Crisis of the Negro Intellectual*. New York, 1967, pp. 404-18.
Ford, Clebert. "Black Nationalism and the Arts." *Liberator*, January 1969, pp. 14-16.
Jones, LeRoi. "The Revolutionary Theatre." *Liberator*, July 1965, pp. 4-6.
Mayfield, Julian. "U.S.A. Journalist and His Troubles." *Ghana Evening News*, 11 May 1962, p. 13.
Russell, Carlos. "A New Breed in Politics." *Liberator*, January 1968, p. 9.
Watts, Daniel H. "Notes to Roy Wilkins, Executive Secretary, NAACP." *Liberator*, February 1962, p. 3.
————. "The Message." *Liberator*, June 1970, p. 13.
————. "Thoughts on the Emancipation Bicentennial." *Liberator*, October 1962, p. 7.
INDEX SOURCES: None.
LOCATION SOURCES: Many college and university libraries; University Microfilms.

Publication History

MAGAZINE TITLE AND TITLE CHANGES: *The Liberator* (May 1961-December 1970).
VOLUME AND ISSUE DATA: Vols. I-X (May 1961-December 1970), monthly.
PUBLISHER AND PLACE OF PUBLICATION: Afro-American Research Institute, New York, New York.
EDITOR: Daniel H. Watts (1961-1970).
CIRCULATION: 20,000.

LIVING BLUES: A JOURNAL OF THE BLACK AMERICAN BLUES TRADITION

In an early issue of *Living Blues*, an editor wrote: "We do not intend to explain, define, or confine the blues. We believe that the blues is a living tradition, and we hope to present some insight into this tradition." This statement has reflected the editorial policy of the magazine throughout its more than a decade of publication beginning in 1970. It has been a unique periodical devoted to illustrating and disseminating news and perceptions about the blues as a part of American culture. In this context, *Living Blues* extends its scope to history of the blues, and blues news from throughout the world. Book reviews, radio guides, and obituaries of musicians appear in each issue. The magazine maintains agents in Australia, England, Finland, France, Germany, Holland, Italy, and Japan. It has become the principal journal of the black American blues tradition.

Living Blues' editorials make no specific reference to LeRoi Jones's several books and articles about the blues as an integral expression of living black in the United States.[1] Jones wrote in *Blues People* that music is the result of thought. He held that Afro-American secular music flourished after slavery when masters were no longer on hand to censor music blacks created and performed. The editors of *Living Blues* assume validity for the blues. Their purpose has been to provide a medium of communication and education about the blues and blues musicians.

Living Blues has experienced the vicissitudes common to all black journals. In looking back over ten years of publication, one of the editors mused in a recent issue: "Starting *Living Blues* in 1970 was an exercise in naivete." She believed, she wrote, that everybody wanted to learn about the blues and what the editors thought and had to say about the blues. She learned that many people liked the subject matter only superficially. "They don't care beyond the immediacy of the boogie-high of a live performance to find out if the star on the stage has a record out," she complained. "They don't care enough to buy a record, if one exists. And they *really* don't care for reading about the blues." There are others, though, who are blues fans; those who can't wait for the next issue of the journal to come out and ask for the quarterly to become a monthly. It is these friends from countries around the world who "keep the spark of enthusiasm alive, the light of scholarship glowing, and—best of all—keep renewing their subscriptions."[2]

The editors want the public to consider the blues an entity unto itself—not merely a primitive form of jazz, or the roots of rock and roll. Blues music was, is, and will be a distinct manifestation of a certain part of the Afro-American struggle for existence and selfhood. This orientation to black music is the modus through which *Living Blues* becomes a serious journal of black culture. Its editorials can speak with authority about the singers of the past eighty-odd years as "manifestors of the blues" who have been indomitably stubborn and will not compromise their art because they know no other. These persons embody the living blues tradition. The magazine's poetic respect for these "keepers of the flame" makes its cultural statement.

As a matter of editorial policy, the editors do not like to duplicate coverage that is readily available in other magazines and newspapers. After ten years of publication, they can boast that *Living Blues* has rarely run two features on the same artist, other than to give an expanded view that enlarges upon the original one. Few of the photographs are used by any other source. The journal depends on its wide and deep network of contributors for "Blues News," a feature that covers one-third of the copy of a single issue. Contributors are not paid and most of them are not professional writers. The magazine calls them its "volunteer correspondence corps."

With its rather unusual approach to publication, *Living Blues* serves its chosen purposes well. Hardly any name known to followers of blues and jazz is omitted from some consideration in the magazine. In addition to news about musicians, interviews with them give in-depth coverage to their activities, their attitudes toward their art, and the state of that art throughout the world. Articles are well researched. Through its variety of media for exploring its subject, this journal maintains an excellent source of information on black popular musicians. Its discographies are uncommon. It celebrates the popular personalities and helps to popularize those who are only recently coming into prominence. Most of all,

Living Blues keeps the Afro-American blues tradition alive by respecting and nurturing it as a precious part of the black heritage.

Notes

1. Beginning in the mid 1960s, Le Roi Jones (Imamu Amiri Baraka) published three major works that set forth his own theories about the sociological dimensions of the blues: *Black Arts* (Newark, N.J., Jihad Productions, 1966); *Black Music* (New York: William Morrow and Company, 1967); and *Blues People: Negro Music in White America* (New York: William Morrow and Company, 1963).

2. "Ten Years of *Living Blues*," *Living Blues* (Spring 1980): 3.

Information Sources

BIBLIOGRAPHY:
Hudson, Theodore R. *From Le Roi Jones to Amiri Baraka: The Literary Works*. Durham, N.C.: Duke University Press, 1973; pp. 93-103.
"No Special Writer Here," *Living Blues* 45-46 (Spring 1980): 3.
O'Neal, Amy. "Ten Years of *Living Blues*." *Living Blues* 45-46 (Spring 1980): 4.
INDEX SOURCES: *Abstracts of Folklore Studies: Music Index: Popular Music Index: Xerox Microfilms*.
LOCATION SOURCES: Academic and public libraries: Xerox Microfilms.

Publication History

MAGAZINE TITLE AND TITLE CHANGES: *Living Blues: A Journal of the Black American Blues Tradition* (Spring 1970 to present).
VOLUME AND ISSUE DATA: Issues are numbered consecutively rather than by the traditional volume numbers; published quarterly.
EDITORS: Jim and Amy O'Neal (1970-   ).
PUBLISHERS AND PLACE OF PUBLICATION: Living Blues Publications, Chicago, Illinois.
CIRCULATION: 5,000.

___M___

McGIRT'S MAGAZINE

James Ephraim McGirt tried desperately to become an integral part of the black literary movement in the early days of the twentieth century. He established and operated a successful laundry and dray business in his native Greensboro, North Carolina, and wrote poetry and short fiction in his spare time. In 1898 he published *Avenging the Maine*, a volume of his poems. A year later he brought out an enlarged edition of that collection and added several new poems. By the turn of the century, he had met the leading black literary figures of the time, Charles Chesnutt and William Stanley Braithwaite, and had carried on correspondence with Thomas Nelson Page, another "plantation tradition" author of nationwide fame. In 1903, McGirt migrated north and established his own magazine and publishing house in Philadelphia, where he lived and conducted successful business ventures for six years before returning to Greensboro and investing his considerable earnings in real estate and a cosmetics manufacturing firm in partnership with his sister. Although *McGirt's Magazine* enjoyed uncommon financial success for publications of its kind, it fell short of McGirt's avowed purpose to publish a magazine for white and black readers that would keep them apprised of "what the race was doing and saying."

McGirt's Magazine imitated the format that had brought distinction to *Colored American** and *Voice of the Negro,** but it could not equal those competitors in the quality of its writing. McGirt invited creative writers to submit poetry and fiction to him, but Frances E. W. Harper was the only fairly well known poet who published in the journal. McGirt's own poems and short stories appeared in practically every issue. He also wrote lavish descriptions of his books in review-advertisements.

McGirt's latest book of poems, *For Your Sweet Sake*, has elicited a chorus of unstinted praise from leading papers of the country. The Preface of this book is made up of expressions of approval from periodicals and writers of national reputation, among which are: New York *American and Journal*, New York *Times*, New York *World*, Philadelphia *Enquirer*, and Washington *Post*; also the following authors: A.K. McClure, Julian Hawthorne, Kelly Miller, Thomas Nelson Page, Rebecca Harding Davis, Margaret Sangster, Mary Church Terrell, and Ella Wheeler Wilcox. It is estimated that during the coming Christmas holidays, the white people alone will use at least 10,000 of this book of poems for presents. This is the greatest tribute ever paid to the genius of a colored author.[1]

Like every other black periodical of the time, *McGirt's Magazine* entered the Booker T. Washington-W.E.B. Du Bois controversy over the appropriate philosophy and form of advancement for Negroes. Although McGirt was not an active member of Du Bois' Niagara movement and its "radical" approaches to educational and political activities for the race, the magazine leaned toward Du Bois' position. One long editorial praised Du Bois' *Souls of Black Folk*, a recent publication that had been reviewed by several leading American magazines and was the subject of vigorous discussion. Du Bois contributed an essay, "The Training of Negroes for Social Power," to *McGirt's* at the editor's request; and Kelly Miller's "Higher Education of Negroes" was reprinted without comment in another issue. A strong editorial, "Should the Negro Keep Out of Politics?" expressed McGirt's strong support of Du Bois and his associates in their fight for primacy of civil rights as a goal for black Americans. His position on the importance of voting is reflected in the following portion of one editorial:

Both friends and enemies of the Negro are advising to let politics alone. They say it is best for him to do so, but what is apparently best to man's dimmed eye, may not be right. The question is, is it Right? First, what does it mean for the Negro of his own accord to get out of politics? It means that he has come to the conclusion that he does not care who makes the laws that shall govern him; whether it be he who burns him at the stake or he who will give him justice. It means that these forty years of freedom have been a curse to him and that he does not care to have a voice in the selection of his needs, but is willing to entrust his whole being into the hands of his former master.[2]

McGirt's also took pride in reporting on black Americans who had broken into public positions and professions not normally available to them, and it celebrated those who, in the Booker T. Washington view of American life, had achieved distinction in the business world and had acquired property that brought them respect in their communities.

Largely because there was not a "yellow" line in it, Du Bois once recommended *McGirt's* in *Horizon*,* along with *Voice of the Negro*,* the *Boston Guardian*, and *Alexander's Monthly*.* That praise came primarily because McGirt allied himself with higher education and aggressive civil rights stances. Other than in its championing these positions for black Americans, there is little else to recommend *McGirt's Magazine*. Its value lies primarily in its publication during the period when blacks came to understand that strong newspapers and magazines could serve them in pursuing their aspirations.

Notes

1. *McGirt's Magazine* (September 1904): 12.
2. "An Appeal to Integrity," *McGirt's Magazine* (September 1903): 33.

Information Sources

BIBLIOGRAPHY:
Gloster, Hugh M. *Negro Voices in American Fiction*. New York, 1948.
Johnson, Abby Arthur, and Johnson, Ronald Maberry. *Propaganda and Aesthetics: The Literary Politics of Afro-American Magazines in the Twentieth Century*. Amherst, Mass., 1979.
Parker, John W. "James Ephraim McGirt: Poet of 'Hope Deferred,' " *Negro History Bulletin*, March 1953, pp. 123-27.
INDEX SOURCES: None.
LOCATION SOURCE: Moorland-Spingarn Collection, Howard University, Washington, D.C.

Publication History

MAGAZINE TITLE CHANGES: *McGirt's Magazine* (August 1903-October 1909).
VOLUME AND ISSUE DATA: Vols. I-VII, monthly.
PUBLISHER AND PLACE OF PUBLICATION: McGirt's Publishing Company, Philadelphia, Pennsylvania.
EDITOR: James Ephraim McGirt (August 1903-October 1909).
CIRCULATION: 1,500 highest estimate.

MESSENGER, THE: WORLD'S GREATEST MONTHLY

William White, president of the Headwaiters and Sidewaiters Society of Greater New York, engaged A. Philip Randolph and Chandler Owen to edit the *Hotel Messenger* for him early in 1917 in Harlem. That union periodical was the antecedent of the *Messenger* that was published for more than a decade during the World War I era and the period immediately thereafter. For four or five of those years it was the most vibrant and controversial black journal in the nation.

Randolph and Owen were Southerners who had joined the migration to New York City. Both were college-trained youth who planned to continue their education in the social sciences in the New York area. They met at City College of New York in discussion groups that were exploring the new socialism. Their radical orientation to politics led them to publish an exposé of White's exploitation of members of his union by overcharging them for uniforms. Enraged, White fired Randolph and Owen, ordered them out of the building that housed his offices, and gave them the furniture they had used for the *Hotel Messenger* as an expression of good riddance. Undaunted, the two young editors moved next door, organized the United Brotherhood of Elevator and Switchboard Operators of New York, became publicists for the Socialist party's campaign to elect Morris Hillquist mayor of New York, and, within a few weeks after their altercation with White, published the first issue of the *Messenger* in November 1917. They organized the Messenger Publishing Company with Randolph as president and Owen as secretary-treasurer. Each was an editor.

The time was especially fortuitous for the young black activists. They labeled their new periodical "The Only Radical Negro Magazine in America." With this identification, the editors could taunt the black leadership and the white establishment press. In addition to championing the rise of socialism in Harlem, the *Messenger* became the leader in the "New Negro" journalism, militant movement that began in 1917. Within a period of one year Marcus Garvey's weekly *Negro World*, Cyril Briggs' *Crusader*,* William Bridges' *Challenge*, and Hubert Harrison's *Negro Voice* all appeared in Harlem.

The *Messenger*'s vitality lies in its promulgation of the "New Negro" concept that permeated black politics and culture in that period. Randolph first sounded the emphasis with an editorial he titled "A New Crowd—A New Negro." He began by noting that throughout the world among all peoples and classes, "the cloak of social progress is striking the high noon of the Old Crowd." The new direction had come, he claimed, because of the "inability of the Old Crowd to adapt itself to the changed conditions and to recognize the consequences of the sudden and violent changes that were shaking the world." The Russian Revolution had overthrown a regime that had ruled for over three hundred years; the Hohenzollerns and the kaiser had been deposed in Germany; and the "shadow of Marx loomed in the distance."[1]

The black "Old Crowd" were the "reactionaries" in the colleges, the best-known political leaders, conservative black newspaper and magazine editors, and the leaders of the racial advancement organizations. Specifically, that designation included Kelly Miller, Robert Russa Moton, and William Pickens, educators at Howard University, Tuskegee Institute, and Talladega College in Alabama, respectively. In the press, they were W.E.B. Du Bois of the *Crisis** and James Weldon Johnson and Fred R. Moore of the *New York Age* weekly newspaper. The Republican politicians were Charles W. Anderson, W. J. Lewis, Ralph Tyler, Emmett Scott, and George E. Hayes. Editorials attacked conservative church pastors who were still preaching "the meek will inherit the earth" and "singing the old spirituals and preaching Old Testament sermons, totally oblivious that black men and women were being overworked and underpaid, lynched, jimcrowed, and disfranchised."[2]

The "New Crowd" were young, educated, radical, and fearless men. The time had come for their ascendency. They were, indeed, ushering in a new world. They were uncompromising. Their tactics were offensive rather than defensive. They would not send notes after a Negro was lynched. They would appeal to the plain working people everywhere to form a coalition that transcended race and nationality. "They would have no armistice with lynch-law; no truce with jimcrowism and disfranchisement; no peace until the Negro receives complete social, economic and political justice." Blacks would ally with white radicals such as the International Workers of the World, Socialists, and the Non-Partisan League to build a new society of equals, the *Messenger*'s editorial predicted.

Within the framework of these goals, the *Messenger* published Claude McKay's often-repeated poem "If We Must Die" September 1917. That issue of the *Messenger* was "more insolently offensive" than any other to Attorney General A. Mitchell Palmer.[3] The McKay poem was accompanied by an editorial written by W. A. Domingo, a Socialist West Indian importer of tropical products who later joined the Communist party. Race riots in Washington, D.C., and in Chicago had precipitated the outcry from blacks to fight against white agitation. The attorney general was convinced that the *Messenger* was the most dangerous of the radical black periodicals. Its offices were entered and ransacked at night on several occasions. Justice Department agents also visited the NAACP to inquire whether that organization was receiving funds from Bolshevik organizations.

The *Messenger* fought American officialdom and the "Old Crowd" among blacks that allied with them. It published cartoons that caricatured Du Bois, Johnson, and Moton. Du Bois, in particular, was a target. He was, to the editors of the *Messenger*, reactionary, opportunistic, and insensitive to class struggles among blacks and workers who opposed the establishment. In their zeal to dramatize their differences with Du Bois, Randolph and Owen pictured the editor of the *Crisis* as a vacillating idealist who considered himself radical without understanding the nature of revolution.[4]

Yet the *Messenger* did not embrace Marcus Garvey and his Universal Negro Improvement Association which captured Harlem's imagination during the years the journal was establishing itself there. The first direct attack on Garvey came with the editorial "The Garvey Movement: A Promise Or a Menace to Negroes?". Randolph admitted he had spoken from the same platform as Garvey, but that was because he was chiefly interested in educating people in the class-struggle nature of the Negro problem and wanted to convert members of the improvement association to the *Messenger*'s viewpoint. Randolph wrote that he could not agree with Garvey that the Negro's greatest needs could be achieved by an all-black movement. The *Messenger* and Garvey's *Negro World* competed for the same black audiences in Harlem. They came into existence about the same time. Claude McKay, who often criticized Garvey, wrote that *Negro World* was the best-edited colored weekly in New York.

When the Universal Negro Improvement Association's overwhelmingly ambitious programs became suspect because of their failure to pay expected dividends to investors, the black national press openly attacked Garvey. Friends of Negro

Freedom, organized by Randolph and Owen, launched a strong "Garvey Must Go" campaign. They were joined by William Pickens of the NAACP. George S. Schuyler, a columnist for the *Messenger* and later its editor, devoted many of his "Shafts and Darts" essays in the magazine to attacking Garvey.

Although the *Messenger* was not a promoter of the Harlem Renaissance per se, it was a significant force for the products of that literary movement. The first issue contained a short story, poems, and theater news. Langston Hughes published his first short fiction in the *Messenger*. Other writers of the renaissance period whose works appeared were Georgia Douglass Johnson, Angelina Grimke, Countee Cullen, Arna Bontemps, Bruce Nugent, Wallace Thurman, Dorothy West, and Zora Neale Hurston. Beginning in September 1923, Theophilus Lewis joined the staff as a part-time drama critic. He was not well educated, and he made his living working in the post office. But his sensitive essays on the drama provided an unusual value for the *Messenger* that no other black journal sustained at the time. Lewis joined the staff of the Catholic magazine *America* later and published his drama criticism there for more than twenty years.[5]

Randolph and Owen lost some of their interest in public affairs by 1922. Owen became disillusioned, he said, with white Socialists who turned their backs on him. He dropped out of the radical movement late in 1923 and settled in Chicago. There he continued to write some pieces for the *Messenger* and the magazine continued his name as a coeditor. But he worked primarily as a ghost writer for the *Bee*, a black Chicago newspaper. Randolph remained responsible for the *Messenger*, although he engaged George S. Schuyler to manage it. While he served as managing editor, Schuyler determined the literary works that would be published in the journal. He, together with Wallace Thurman, also a managing editor for a few months in the mid twenties, set the literary tone for the magazine. They could seldom pay for the works they published, but they kept the quality of their choices high and were almost never bereft of works from black authors. This was partly owing to the respect Schuyler and Thurman commanded among the young black writers and partly owing to the dearth of places black writers could find to publish their writing.

By 1925, all the political and labor groups Randolph and Owen had helped to found had faltered. The journal was faltering. For the next three years, until it ceased publication in 1928, it became more literary than political. Randolph turned to his significant work with the Brotherhood of Sleeping Car Porters which brought him international note. That union bore the costs of publishing the *Messenger* until it could no longer be responsible. A. Philip Randolph grew into the elder statesman of black activists, continuing his active role well into the civil rights struggles of the 1960s and 1970s.

Notes

1. *Messenger* (November 1917): 7.
2. Ibid.

3. For detailed discussion of the red scare and radicalism in black journalism, *see* Theodore Kornweibel, Jr., *No Crystal Stair: Black Life and the Messenger, 1917-1928* (Westport, Conn., 1975), chapters 2 and 3.

4. Ibid.

5. For some understanding of the significant role Theophilus Lewis played as drama critic for the *Messenger*, *see* "Interview with Theophilus Lewis," *Catholic World* (May 1941): 239; and Theodore Kornweibel, Jr., "Theophilus Lewis and the Theatre of the Harlem Renaissance," in *The Harlem Renaissance Remembered*, ed. Arna Bontemps (New York, 1972).

Information Sources

BIBLIOGRAPHY:

Anderson, Jervis. *A. Philip Randolph: A Biographical Portrait*. New York, 1973.
Cronon, E. David. *Black Moses: The Story of Marcus Garvey and the Universal Negro Improvement Association*. Madison, Wis., 1969.
Cruse, Harold. *The Crisis of the Negro Intellectual*. New York, 1967.
Garland, Phyl. "A. Philip Randolph: Labor's Grand Old Man." *Ebony*, May 1964, p. 31.
Kornweibel, Theodore, Jr. *No Crystal Stair: Black Life and the Messenger, 1917-1928*. Westport, Conn.: Greenwood Press, 1975.
Long, Richard A. "An Interview with George Schuyler." *Black World*, February 1976, pp. 68-78.
Nance, Ethel Ray. "The New York Arts Renaissance, 1924-26." *Negro History Bulletin*, April 1968, pp. 15-19.
Perkins, Huel D. "Wallace Thurman." *Black World*, February 1976, pp. 29-35.
Taylor, Clyde. "Garvey's Ghost: Revamping the Twenties." *Black World*, February 1976, pp. 54-67.
Thurman, Wallace. *Infants of the Spring*. Carbondale, Ill., 1979.
Vincent, Theodore G. *Black Power and the Garvey Movement*. New York, 1971.
INDEX SOURCES: None.
LOCATION SOURCES: Greenwood Press Periodicals; Universities Reprints; Atlanta Public Library; Fisk University; Library of Congress; New York Public Library; Tuskegee Institute.

Publication History

MAGAZINE TITLE AND TITLE CHANGES: *The Messenger: World's Greatest Monthly* (November 1917-May/June 1928).
VOLUME AND ISSUE DATA: Vols. I-X (November 1917-June 1928) monthly except last issues bimonthly.
PUBLISHER AND PLACE OF PUBLICATION: The Messenger Publishing Company, New York, New York.
EDITORS: A. Philip Randolph and Chandler Owen (November 1917-June 1923); A. Philip Randolph (July 1923-May/June 1928); George S. Schuyler, managing editor (April 1927-May/June 1928).
CIRCULATION: 18,000.

MIDWEST JOURNAL

The legislative faculty of Lincoln University, Jefferson City, Missouri, authorized publication of a research journal in 1947. It would be open to the instructional staff of the institution to serve them as a medium for disseminating articles reporting on their research, and it would be published at least twice a year. After one issue, that periodical became the *Midwest Journal* and broadened the base of the original plan. Its new editorial policy fostered a scholarly journal oriented toward the social sciences and the humanities, with some creative writing. The colleges of Arts and Science, Law, and Journalism voted to support costs of the new enterprise from their operating expenses. *Midwest Journal*'s first issue included articles on the future of the newly created United Nations' wartime, migration, and housing programs for Negroes; self-purchase of black slaves in Cole County, Missouri; race, caste, and class in Haiti; a biography of Horace Pippin, the first black to enjoy success as a "popular painter" during his lifetime; book reviews; and poems written by Carl Holman and Melvin B. Tolson.

Subsequently, the journal published articles on a wide variety of subjects including statehood for Hawaii, the Taft-Hartley Act, immigration restrictions, student movements in Chinese universities, mental health facilities in Missouri, American literature, social and religious life of American slaves, early stirrings of nationalism in Africa and the Caribbean in the post-World War II era, German communism, Nazi mobilization in South-West Africa, and Far Eastern economics.

Herbert Aptheker, Rayford Logan, August Meier, Benjamin Quarles, and Mabel and Hugh Smythe were among scholars outside the university's faculty who wrote on history, economics, and the broad spectrum of the social sciences. Among the resident faculty, Lorenzo J. Greene—who was also editor—Oliver Cox, and Armstead Pride wrote important articles in their academic fields. W.E.B. Du Bois contributed one of his significant essays to *Midwest Journal*, "The Freedom to Learn." In it, he urged American universities to offer courses about Lenin and Marx in their curricula in order to eliminate the current bias against "foreign ideology." His answer to the problem of academic provincialism was simple. He advised that the greatest disservice that this nation or any people could do to the United States would be to stop the study of economic change. His suggestion would, he claimed, ward off any threatened collapse of the civilization in which we live, not only by opposing war but by accepting a strong determination to keep the civil rights modern society had gained at so great a cost.

The journal also published a reprint of a British Broadcasting Corporation broadcast that presented valuable information about the University of Nigeria (now the University of Ibadan). In those early days of the focus on black Africa, this report was significant. It described the Nigerian educational enterprise as one designed to provide university education for Africa south of the Sahara in order that students there would have an alternative to going to Europe or North America for higher education. Also important in the journal's publication of matters pertaining to higher education was "The Supreme Court Decision on Education: What It Means to Missouri," a full reproduction of the transcript of a panel discussion sponsored by the West Central Division of the Missiouri Association for Social Welfare.[1]

During its life, *Midwest Journal* became one of the few black scholarly journals. It contained no news items or editorials. Its vitality lay totally in articles, historical documents, and creative writing. It is an important document of higher education in the era between the close of World War II and *Brown* v. *Topeka*.[2]

Notes

1. Sam Blair, judge of the Fourteenth Circuit District of Missouri who had earlier ordered the University of Missouri to admit blacks to graduate study in 1950, and State Commissioner of Education Hubert Wheeler participated in the panel with members of the Association for Social Welfare. The discussion explored white and black concerns and responsibilities that the *Gaines* v. *University of Missouri* decision had resolved in 1938 and which anticipated *Brown* v. *Topeka* of a few years later.

2. Ironically, the court actions ordering racial integration in higher education led indirectly to the demise of *Midwest Journal*. After May 1954, Lincoln University's status remained in doubt, inasmuch as blacks could then attend the state university. Fiscal restraints placed on Lincoln led to cessation of publication of the journal as an economy measure.

Information Sources

BIBLIOGRAPHY:
Greene, Lorenzo J., Kremer, Gary R., and Holland, Anthony F. *Missouri's Black Heritage*. Saint Louis, 1980, pp. 1-7, 83-87.
Research Journal 1, no. 1. Lincoln University, Jefferson City, Mo., 1947.
Savage, W. Sherman. *The History of Lincoln University*. Jefferson City, Mo., 1939, pp. 312-15.
INDEX SOURCES: None.
LOCATION SOURCES: Lincoln University Library; Atlanta University Library; Library of Congress; Microfilm Corporation of America.

Publication History

MAGAZINE TITLE AND TITLE CHANGES: *The Research Journal* (Spring 1947); *Midwest Journal* (Winter 1948-Spring/Fall 1956).
VOLUME AND ISSUE DATA: Vols. I-VIII (1948-1956). Spring 1948-Spring 1954, semiannual; Winter 1954-Spring/Fall 1956, quarterly.
PUBLISHER AND PLACE OF PUBLICATION: Lincoln University, Jefferson City, Missouri.
EDITOR: Lorenzo J. Greene (1947-1956).
CIRCULATION: 1,500.   *Noel Heermance*

MOON ILLUSTRATED WEEKLY, THE

W.E.B. Du Bois once wrote that he founded the *Moon Illustrated Weekly* in December 1905 in Memphis, Tennessee, to fulfill a boyhood dream and to climax an effort of several years to launch a black national magazine. Both these motivations did exist, but they are not the efficient cause leading to his undertaking to publish the *Moon*. In July 1905, the Niagara movement had been formed at Du Bois' invitation. His own keynote address had enunciated the platform. The movement would work through a selected cadre of black men to aggressively pursue an agenda for black Americans opposed to Booker T. Washington's accommodationism. Men oriented by training or imitation to the dream of a lifestyle a later generation would call "black bourgeois" needed a different polarization from Washington's. The "color line"—their metaphor for their frustration over racial discrimination—incensed them. It had to be dissolved. Du Bois had explained in *Souls of Black Folk* (1903) that the lure of education had given way to need for the ballot. One got the ballot only through consistently agitating for it. Participation in the government as a first class citizen alone led to American manhood. To give even the appearance of neglecting that fight disqualified anyone from leadership, even if he were a black Brahmin.

These sentiments led to the Niagara movement, a small but vociferous and energetic cross section of persons who considered themselves the black "thinking people," organized for concerted assault on the nation's perfidy toward its black citizens. Strangely, Booker T. Washington, a black man, would become the target of their crusade. To them, he represented white America's duplicity, yet he enjoyed the adoration of the masses of the black population. He was not one of Du Bois' "Talented Tenth."[1] He had acquired and maintained his favored position in the race through many techniques. One was his uncanny manipulation of the nation's pressure points of financial power. He molded opinion among people who did not vote. He "cloned" more and more persons like himself. He operated the "Tuskegee Machine." No other school, even those operated by whites for blacks, could divert to their causes the streams of money tycoons poured into Tuskegee Institute. Perhaps Washington could be stopped in the press by a counterweight intended to expose his subsidies to newspapers and magazines that held up his hand and espoused his assimilationist philosophy. Du Bois had claimed in his "Debits and Credits" column in the *Voice of the Negro** that Washington had used at least $3,000 during the preceding year to bribe black journalists into remaining silent about the evils of accommodationism. The exposé had made little impression. So the radical arm of black leadership needed a house organ that could serve as a medium of communication among the "classes" who were already converted to the "new gospel."

They, too, appealed to capitalists for subsidies to establish a journal to represent their purpose. Du Bois, as visible leader of the "new left" in black affairs, asked eastern financiers for funds to establish a journal. They equivocated and finally refused his request. Enraged, he claimed his efforts had been sabotaged by Washington and used his own meager funds to establish the *Moon Illustrated Weekly* as a foil to Washington. Ironically, he sought to transfer capitalist resources from Tuskegee to his own personal project. He chose to overlook the possibility that he would incur the same charges of subsidy and holding the press in fee that he made against Washington and his backers. With his own savings, Du Bois undertook to edit and publish a weekly black journal to present a "new race consciousness to the world" and to illustrate and explain "the inner meaning of the modern world to the merging masses." Edward L. Simon, a former student of his at Atlanta University, opened for Du Bois a small printing shop on Beale Street in Memphis. Another former student, Harry H. Pace, quit his teaching job at Haines Institute in Augusta, Georgia, and joined the enterprise as business manager. The three men pooled their personal resources and began publication with about $3,000. Du Bois was editor in chief. Pace and Simon managed the technical and business operations. Du Bois planned to continue teaching at Atlanta University and to secure funds for the *Moon* from his extensive speaking engagements around the country.

Black and white firms in Memphis and Atlanta advertised in the *Moon*. Washington's associates in the National Negro Business League welcomed the opportunity to advertise their products and services in a new black journal. The publication represented an alignment that, under normal circumstances, would have exhibited the allied strength of several factions in the race. A printer performed the technical services. Black and white businessmen bought ads. Du Bois wrote the editorials and selected the news items. The cooperation of industrial and higher education elements in the race might have proved fortuitous.

The *Moon*'s format included reprints from newspapers around the country, biographical sketches of prominent black Americans, Du Bois' trenchant editorials, and advertisements. Du Bois seldom mentioned the *Moon* later in his career. When he did, he spoke of it as the precursor of the *Crisis** in terms of time and content arrangement. But why did the *Moon* fail so quickly?

"Bookerites" attacked it, not for its content or its avowed role as spokespiece for the radical Niagara movement, but for Du Bois' vigorous efforts to seek subsidies for his project and for the poor physical appearance of the publication. The *New York Age* wrote superciliously to extend sympathy when the *Moon* failed. "We extend our sympathy to the editor in the necessity which forced him to suspend the newspaper, despite his brave pleas for Wall Street subsidy." *Alexander's Magazine** had complained earlier that the journal did not seem to represent the public image of Du Bois.

Dr. William E. Burghardt Du Bois has gone into journalism on his own account. He has started a weekly paper and he calls it "The Moon." The literary work on the Moon [sic] is somewhat disappointing to those who have read with a great deal of pleasures the addresses and splendid stories in "The Souls of Black Folk," and the mechanical features of "The Moon" are simply abominable. Dr. Du Bois is a man of splendid education, large experience and high ideals and we wonder how he could subscribe his name to a journal so carelessly put together as the one that comes from a print shop in Memphis, Tennessee.[2]

When the *Moon Illustrated Weekly* ceased publication, *Alexander's* quipped that it had "reached its zenith a few weeks ago and has fallen behind the veil."

Du Bois attributed the *Moon's* failure to Negroes' inability to pay the subscription rates he was forced to charge. Moreover, because he could not leave Atlanta University to give his full time to editing the journal, he was compelled to depend heavily upon his associates in Memphis. The periodical never attracted significant reader attention, even among members of the Niagara movement. It was started with little capital but did enjoy better than usual advertisement accounts for a black journal. Its demise can be attributed reasonably to the elite audience it addressed and its disappointing appearance. Obviously, Du Bois was not yet ready to edit a viable journal which served primarily as an organ for his essays. His views had not taken sufficient root for them to sustain a weekly magazine. Yet, the periodical merits some discussion as an early black little magazine that reflected some part of the black American experience in its time. Moreover, it affected an alliance between its three owners—two educated in industrial education and one the arch enemy of technical education—an accomplishment that has escaped the attention of most historians.

Notes

1. A reference to Du Bois' elitist philosophy of education.
2. *Alexander's Magazine* (February 1906): 16.

Information Sources

BIBLIOGRAPHY:
Aptheker, Herbert. *The Correspondence of W.E.B. Du Bois*, Vol. 1. Amherst, Mass., 1973.
Broderick, Frederick L. *W.E.B. Du Bois: Negro Leader in a Time of Crisis*. Stanford, Calif., 1959.
Du Bois, W.E.B. *The Autobiography of W.E.B. Du Bois*. New York, 1969.
———. "The Second Birthday." *Crisis*, November 1913, p. 27.
Green, Dan S. "W.E.B. Du Bois: His Journalistic Career." *Negro History Bulletin*, March/April 1977, pp. 672-77.
Hoffman, Frederick J., Allen, Charles, and Ulrich, Carolyn F. *The Little Magazine: A History and a Bibliography*. Princeton, N.J., 1946, pp. 1-17.
Partington, Paul. "*Moon Illustrated Weekly*: The Precursor of *The Crisis*." *Journal of Negro History*, July 1963, pp. 206-16.
INDEX SOURCES: None.

LOCATION SOURCES: Schomberg Collection; Moorland-Spingarn Collection, Howard University; Library of Congress.

Publication History

MAGAZINE TITLE AND TITLE CHANGES: *The Moon Illustrated Weekly* (December 1905-July 1906).
VOLUME AND ISSUE DATA: Vols. I and II, weekly; irregular June and July 1906.
PUBLISHER AND PLACE OF PUBLICATION: W.E.B. Du Bois, Memphis, Tennessee.
EDITOR: W.E.B. Du Bois (1905-1906).
CIRCULATION: 250 to 500.

------ N ------

NATIONAL EDUCATION OUTLOOK AMONG NEGROES

The black American Teachers Association began publishing its official organ, the *National Education Outlook Among Negroes*, in the fall of 1937 as a medium of communication among professional educators at all levels of schools. It never gained the stature of the prestigious *Journal of Negro Education*,* but it was popular for the three years of its existence. Its parent organization was a national federation of teachers before blacks were free to join the National Education Association and before the days of the American Council on Education and other national bodies for the free association of teachers.

Published monthly except July and August in Baltimore and distributed nationally, the journal contained articles on above-average school children, units of work for high school teaching, helps for librarians, child psychology, stories about Negroes holding executive positions in the federal government in Washington, teaching methods, and the growing field of student personnel services. The editor called repeatedly for fiction based on educational experiences, but little creative writing of note was printed in the *National Education Outlook among Negroes*.

In order to gain as wide a readership as possible, the association placed large numbers of its publicly prominent members on the editorial board of the journal and sought contributions of articles from them. Few black Americans could find easy entry to the columns of white national educational magazines at the time. Consequently, the journal served a significant purpose for black educators.

Guest editorials on a variety of subjects appeared in each issue. Some were written by Charles H. Wesley, then president of Wilberforce University in Ohio; Carter G. Woodson, the noted black historian and editor of the *Journal of Negro History*;* and Benjamin Mays, the distinguished black theologian and president of the highly respected Morehouse College in Atlanta, Georgia. Black schools and colleges contributed news about their activities and personnel to the magazine, making it a newspaper for blacks in education as well as a scholastic journal.

The magazine's value lies in the discussions of the land grant functions of the "1890" black colleges (segregated institutions for agricultural and industrial education); its articles about the history of black colleges, private and public; and federal government services for black education. It also provides a good perspective of the impact of the Works Progress Administration upon black education at the college level with respect to funding of physical facilities at the colleges and adult education programs.

National Education Outlook among Negroes is an excellent report on black education in the United States in the late 1930s. It is attractive and well edited. As the World War II years came, many organizations began to lose their strength on a national basis. Travel became difficult. Journals suffered because of the shortage of printing paper. These were some of the reasons that this magazine declined in popularity. It changed its publication from monthly to bimonthly before ceasing with the May/June 1940 issue.

Information Sources

BIBLIOGRAPHY:
Brunner, Henry S. "Land-Grant Colleges and Universities, 1920-1962." United States Department of Health, Education, and Welfare Publication, OE 50030, Bulletin 1962, no. 13.
Johnson, Charles S. *The Negro College Graduate*. Chapel Hill: University of North Carolina Press, 1938, pp. 274-75.
"Negro Education: Present Needs and Recent Advancements in Education." Department of the Interior, Bureau of Education, no. 38, 1916.
INDEX SOURCE: *Occupational Index*.
LOCATION SOURCES: Library of Congress; Moorland-Spingarn Collection, Howard University, Washington, D.C.

Publication History

MAGAZINE TITLE AND TITLE CHANGES: *National Education Outlook among Negroes.*
VOLUME AND ISSUE DATA: Vols. I-IV (September 1937-May/June 1940). Monthly until September 1939; bimonthly thereafter.
PUBLISHER AND PLACE OF PUBLICATION: American Teachers Association, Baltimore, Maryland.
EDITOR: T. Edward Davis (1937-1940).
CIRCULATION: 2,000.

NEGRO, THE:
A JOURNAL OF ESSENTIAL FACTS ABOUT THE NEGRO

Frederick W. Bond, who held a doctorate in speech and theater and had taught that discipline at a variety of black colleges, launched a magazine in Saint Louis in the winter of 1943-44. Its title varied from time to time.[1] Quite possibly it was an attempt to replicate John H. Johnson's success with *Negro Digest*,* which he had started a year earlier. The *Negro* called itself a journal of news about achievements among Negroes; however, it was a digest of magazine and newspaper stories on a wide range of subjects. It followed the format of *Reader's Digest*, as did Johnson's publication. Articles reprinted covered a variety of subjects, all relating in some way to race relations or the Afro-American experience. Some creative writing appeared in the journal, although it was a minor emphasis.

Profiles of black Americans and articles taken from white and black periodicals made up the general content of this journal. Some news items on accomplishments in these war years centered around national politics, the national defense effort, Federal Employment Practices Committee work, Afro-American and African arts and culture, and the activities of the Ku Klux Klan.

In the area of education, Bond expressed concern for the future of liberal education among Negroes. In his editorial "Is the Status of Liberal Arts Education Among Negroes Threatened?" he voiced his fear that the new importance given to the black state colleges—mostly land grant institutions—would diminish the long tradition of the liberal arts colleges that had provided education for leadership among black Americans.

In addition to church and social news and articles about religion and black society, the magazine contained many articles about blacks in the military and concerns for black veterans after the war. The resurgence of black literature in the 1940s brought forth articles on the new writers, including "Why Richard Wright Wrote *Black Boy*."[2]

The *Negro* is not a well-known journal, but it survived for nearly four years as an attractive magazine containing pertinent reprinted articles, some original discussions, and some strong editorial opinions. The respect that the magazine was able to command in its time may be shown through a listing of some of the Americans who contributed articles or comments in it from time to time. They include Zora Neale Hurston, Walter F. White, Earl Barnes, J. Saunders Redding, Charles Wesley, W.E.B. Du Bois, Langston Hughes, Roi Ottley, E. Franklin Frazier, Francis Cardinal Spellman, Margaret Walker, Mary McLeod Bethune, Adam Clayton Powell, Jr., Humphrey Bogart, and William Hastie.

As a digest type journal, the *Negro* is a valuable collection of contents from a variety of American publications in the 1940s. Finding these entries in one place is a convenience for scholars. Moreover, the range of reports and observations on black Americans and what others said and felt about them at a time when the nation was in peril is worthwhile. In the absence of specific information on reasons for the cessation of this magazine, one concludes that it suffered from a lack of sufficient financial revenue, especially inasmuch as it contained little advertisement. Further, *Negro Digest* cornered the audience among black Americans for a digest magazine at that time.

Notes

1. *The Negro* (May 1945): 12-13.
2. Richard Wright, who had gained unprecedented recognition as a black writer with *Native Song* (1940), the photo essay *Twelve Million Black Voices*, and his receiving the coveted Spingarn Medal—highest service award given by the NAACP—had become widely acclaimed among blacks in the United States. His accomplishments were a source of pride, and his newly published *Black Boy* (1945), a fictionalized autobiography of his childhood and youth in the South, made Wright a source of interest and discussion among black Americans.

Information Sources

BIBLIOGRAPHY:
Boone, Dorothy Deloris. "A Historical Review and a Bibliography of Selected Negro Magazines, 1910-1969." Ph.D. dissertation, University of Michigan, 1970, p. 115.
Wolseley, Roland E. *Black Press U.S.A.* Ames: Iowa State University Press, 1971, pp. 122-23.
INDEX SOURCES: None.
LOCATION SOURCES: Moorland-Spingarn Collection, Howard University, Washington, D.C.; Schomberg Collection, New York Public Library, New York, New York; Saint Louis Public Library.

Publication History

MAGAZINE TITLE AND TITLE CHANGES: *The Negro: A Journal of Essential Facts About the Negro.* The title varied. From time to time it was *Digest and Story*; *The Negro: Journal of Facts*; *The Negro: Journal of Essential Information*; and *Digest of Negro Achievement.*
VOLUME AND ISSUE DATA: Vols. I-VI (Winter 1943/44-November/December 1948). Quarterly for first two issues; Vols. III and VI, monthly; Vol. V, bimonthly.
PUBLISHER AND PLACE OF PUBLICATION: Thomas J. Bond, Publisher, Midwest Publishing House, Saint Louis, Missouri.
EDITOR: Frederick W. Bond (1943-1948).
CIRCULATION: 4,500.

NEGRO CHURCHMAN, THE

The African Orthodox Church founded the *Negro Churchman* in January 1923 as its official journal in the post-World War I era. The denomination had grown largely out of the personal ministry of George Alexander McGuire. Born in Antigua, British West Indies, McGuire had at first pastored a Moravian congregation after his graduation from a school sponsored by that fellowship. In 1893,

McGuire left his Frederiksted, Saint Croix, Virgin Islands, church, came to the United States and gained American citizenship. He first affiliated with the African Methodist Episcopal Church. Later he was ordained by the Protestant Episcopal Church in the United States and distinguished himself as archdeacon for colored work in the Arkansas diocese. Disillusioned with the slow progress in race relations of the Episcopal Church in Arkansas, McGuire moved to Cambridge, Massachusetts, to serve as pastor of a new congregation of West Indians who had been denied full participation in a white church. From 1911-13, he served as field secretary of the American Church Institute for Negroes with headquarters in New York City. After a brief period of work with the Episcopal Church in his native Antigua, McGuire returned to the United States and began his association with the Reformed Episcopal Church and the establishment of the African Orthodox Church. He was chosen that church's archbishop in the early 1920s. During that time, he also founded and edited the *Negro Churchman* for the first years of its existence.

McGuire is often associated with Marcus Garvey, the black West Indian best known for his Universal Negro Improvement Association which he initiated in New York. That organization attracted a level of support and of criticism unlike any that a movement among American blacks had experienced previously. The association and Garvey are an integral part of the Harlem Renaissance years. When Garvey arrived in the United States in 1916 and set about organizing his association, unrest among West Indian and American blacks led naturally to a common interest between Garvey and McGuire. There is no evidence that Garvey organized the African Orthodox Church as a part of his movement, however. McGuire had become disillusioned with the Protestant Episcopal Church and believed he should establish an independent or African Episcopal Church. He envisioned an amalgamation of Garvey's "racial vision" with a religious organization. It would not be limited to the United States but would include "Negroes everywhere." In effect, the African Orthodox Church would bring religious, political, and economic independence to blacks in North America and in Africa. Garvey established his newspaper, the *Negro World*, which enjoyed enormous popularity on both continents. McGuire founded the *Negro Churchman* to throw off forever the yoke of white ecclesiastical denomination. His journal has only recently become available for study in its entirety. Its copies confirm the often-repeated claim that the church and the press have played major roles in the Afro-American struggle for status.

McGuire was archbishop of the African Orthodox Church when he launched the magazine "*in tenebris lumen*"; as a beacon of light in the general social darkness. His first editorial was evangelical, as he asked for "Earnestness" to become the watchword of the Negro for 1923. His personal position was that "no people can build a permanent social, industrial, or political superstructure except upon a religious and spiritual foundation." Therefore, he called upon the Negro ministry of an awakened race to "stretch out their hands to the everlasting God and simultaneously exhort their brethren to righteousness, by which alone a nation is exalted." McGuire set the purposes of the magazine in the first issue.

While this purports to be a religious journal, we shall not lose sight of the fact that the material development of our Race is closely associated with the spiritual. In Harlem, a great Negro city within a city, business owned and managed by Negroes has met with unparalleled success during the year 1922. There have been some temporary set-backs as in the case of the Black Star Line, but these have served only as the spur to greater effort. The Negro has fairly well demonstrated his genius for big business in the real estate line and in the department store field. Without making invidious comparison, we select as evidence of the former the wonderful strides made by the Antillean Holding Company, and of the latter the expansion of the Department Store Business of A.I. Hart & Company, now located centrally in commodious quarters at Seventh Avenue and 138th Street. While we are pointing the way to leadership and independence in the religious affairs of our Race, we shall keep step and lock arms with our friends who are ambitious to be captains of industry and are reasonably certain that they will reciprocate our wish for "a very successful New Year."[1]

McGuire's aspirations for the race were compatible with the announced purposes of Garvey's association. Actually, he had already been elected chaplain-general of the association at its 1920 convention. McGuire and Garvey later became estranged, largely over the matter of whether members of the association should purchase and follow catechism and rituals McGuire prepared for the church and the movement. The Universal Negro Improvement Association captivated blacks as no other race-uplift organization could. And it engendered the wrath and ridicule of many blacks as its activities headed toward failure.[2] In the *Negro Churchman*, though, McGuire never forsook Garvey. He praised his fellow West Indian by writing that "this man has felt the pulse of the Negro masses in the Western world and inspired them with racial consciousness and hope more than any other leader since our forcible exile from our ancestral home." He particularly objected to those detractors of the improvement association who during Garvey's trial ridiculed the defense's claim that the movement was "spiritual."[3] After Garvey was imprisoned in "The Tombs" in New York City, McGuire published an impassioned support for Garvey, ending: "We venture to predict that Marcus Garvey who left The Tombs Monday, September 10th, will rise and ascend to higher leadership, and that Negroes everywhere will be the beneficiaries of the NEW IDEAS which he tells us he has gained during his vacation."[4]

McGuire was concerned about most public issues of social consciousness. He was enraged when President Charles Lowell at Harvard University announced that the institution would discriminate against black and Jewish students who applied to live in freshman dormitories. He complained that Harvard had undergone a metamorphosis. "She is no longer a friend to the Negro in his uphill struggle for justice and manhood rights, for in a cruelly frank manner she has slammed the door in his face and made him to understand his place," he stated in an editorial.[5] With Lowell's stand on racial segregation, the venerable American university had taken a place alongside "Vardaman, Williams, and Watson, with the framers of grandfather clauses, and with the enactors of Jim Crow laws," all that were, to McGuire, "assassins of Negro manhood."[6]

The journal contained news about the church in the United States and other parts of the world. Each issue published sermons and some aspects of church polity and rituals. McGuire used its columns to communicate with his communicants. From time to time, he wrote to explain his conception of the line of apostolic succession that gave validity to the African Orthodox Church as part of the Protestant tradition. When, as a result of the demands of his growing responsibilities as archbishop and primate for the denomination's principal cathedral McGuire relinquished the editorship of the *Negro Churchman*, the magazine lost some of its editorial vitality. It became largely a newspaper for activity among the churches of the denomination and a medium for publishing proceedings of the various meetings of the churches and the General Synod.

Notes

1. "Be Earnest," *Negro Churchman* (January 1923): 1.
2. Garvey's Universal Negro Improvement Association brought criticism from most middle class blacks and from the NAACP in particular. Although the *Messenger** magazine was primarily responsible for the "Garvey Must Go" movement that led to the West Indian's demise, W.E.B. Du Bois was severe in his criticism of the association and its leader. *See*, in *Crisis*: "Marcus Garvey" (December 1920): 58-59; "Marcus Garvey" (January 1921): 112-15; "The Black Star Line" (September 1922): 210-14; "Marcus Garvey and the NAACP" (February 1928): 51, for some of Du Bois' writing about Garvey.
3. January 1922 Garvey was arrested and charged with the use of the mails to defraud through selling stock and membership in false and fraudulent organizations and for selling passage to Africa on a "mythical" vessel. He was indicted by a federal grand jury on 16 February. Next year, 21 June 1923, Garvey was convicted and sentenced to five years in prison, fined $1,000 and required to pay court costs.
4. "Out of the Tombs," *Negro Churchman* (September/October 1923): 11.
5. "Et Tu Brute!" *Negro Churchman* (February 1923): 2.
6. Ibid.

Information Sources

BIBLIOGRAPHY:

Bergman, Peter M., and Bergman, Mort N. *The Chronological History of the Negro in America*. New York, 1969, pp. 402-3, 406-7.

Burkett, Randall K. *Garveyism as a Religious Movement*. Metuchen, N.J.: Scarecrow Press, 1978, pp. 71-110.

Cronon, E. David. *Black Moses: The Story of Marcus Garvey and the Universal Negro Improvement Association*. Madison, Wis.: University of Wisconsin Press, 1969, pp. 69, 103, 178-80.
————, ed. *Marcus Garvey*. Englewood Cliffs, N.J., 1973, pp. 107-11.
INDEX SOURCES: None.
LOCATION SOURCE: Kraus-Thompson, Ltd. Reprints.

Publication History

MAGAZINE TITLE AND TITLE CHANGES: *The Negro Churchman* (January 1923-November 1931).
VOLUME AND ISSUE DATA: Vols. I-IX (January 1923-November 1931), monthly but irregular.
PUBLISHER AND PLACE OF PUBLICATION: African Orthodox Church, New York, New York.
EDITORS: George Alexander McGuire (January 1923-August 1924); George Alexander (September 1924-November 1931).
CIRCULATION: 5,000 estimate.

NEGRO COLLEGE QUARTERLY, THE

Faculty at Wilberforce University in Ohio published a scholarly journal, *Wilberforce University Quarterly* that was the antecedent for the *Negro College Quarterly*. An editorial note in the first issue of the new periodical, first issued in March 1943, announced that the objectives of the two journals were the same, but that *Wilberforce University Quarterly* had come to seem to have a "clannish connotation" that did not describe the exact scope of the quarterly. The editorial board of the new organ would be intercollegiate, and the list of advisory and contributing editors had been enriched to include well-known educators. "It is our intention to improve the quality of material appearing in this *Quarterly*, and with this end in view we will send any article submitted to us to a specialist in the field concerned," the note continued. Unlike its predecessor, the *Negro College Quarterly* was not an instrument of Wilberforce University. Rather, the editorial board wanted it to serve as the university's contribution to the cause of higher education for Negroes.

In its expanded role, the *Negro College Quarterly* published in its first issue "College Notes and News," a department that carried brief news items about faculty and staff in black colleges. Walter R. Chivers, a professor of sociology at Morehouse College in Atlanta, contributed "The Negro Social Science Teacher in the Southern Rural Community" and Doxey Wilkerson, an associate professor of education at Howard University in Washington, published "The Role of the Negro College on the Economic Home Front." Another aspect of the wartime era and its impact on colleges was reflected in "The Crisis in Higher Education," written by Harry W. Greens, a professor of education at West Virginia State College, and in "A War-Time Negro Land-Grant College" by F. A. Williams, an instructor in rural economics at Southern University in Louisiana. Mollie E. Dunlap, a librarian at Wilberforce University, prepared "Suggested Readings on Higher Education." Thus, the scope of coverage for the *Quarterly* was set.

As World War II moved toward its end, the editorial board of the *Quarterly* sought ways to stimulate thinking and planning among black college faculty and administrators that would focus on the "Role of the Negro College in the Post-War World." A special issue devoted to that subject brought forth a symposium. Scholars wrote on functional programs for the liberal arts college, the Negro land grant college, and the state teachers college; graduate school and adult education, educational and social implications of the redirection of the Negro college; and the Negro college and the Negro veteran. Another special issue addressed innovations that were taking place in black colleges that were seeking to serve their constituents in the postwar period. "What the Negro Colleges Are Doing" became a regular feature of the journal as a result of this special issue. Other departments added included book reviews, educational events, college notes, special bibliographies and a Negro college directory.

Although the *Negro College Quarterly* concentrated primarily on articles that related to activities among black colleges, from time to time it published articles on a wider range of subjects, including: "Opportunities of Community Leadership in the Northern Metropolis," "Effects of Segregated Public Schools on Negro Youth," and "The Treatment of Education As a Phase of Reconstruction."

The most ambitious and useful project the *Quarterly* published was a compendium, "Institutions of Higher Learning among Negroes in the United States of America," that presented data taken from college catalogues and bulletins about their histories, organization, library holdings, degree offerings, accreditation, and control. This was the first time any systematic configuration of this kind had been undertaken by a black professional journal. Moreover, the study attempted to establish bases for drawing qualitative inferences about the colleges with respect to the competency of the faculties as represented by the degrees indicating extended academic preparation; adequacy of teaching personnel as seen in the student-faculty ratio; availability of library facilities as reflected in the number of volumes and the number of trained librarians; influence of the alumni as essential agents in the expansion of the colleges; contacts maintained by the institutions and the communities in which they were located; apparent duplication of colleges within the same or contiguous areas; and emergent graduate programs in terms of existing facilities in the college and the apparent capacity to extend their educational missions.

This evaluation project included nearly 100 black institutions of postsecondary education, both public and private. It came at a time when the majority of black colleges in the South were not full members of the regional accrediting associations. During this period these institutions were also experiencing enrollment increases that were taxing their resources, owing to the return of veterans. Further, pressure for graduate and professional education for black youth was mounting on the white, racially segregated colleges and universities of the South. For these reasons, particularly, the compendium was useful then and is interesting now for its historic value.

The *Negro College Quarterly* never gained the status among black educators that its competitors *Journal of Negro Education** at Howard University and the *Quarterly Review of Higher Education among Negroes** at Johnson C. Smith University achieved. It ceased publication in 1947 at a time when political tensions at Wilberforce University reached a critical stage.[1] Perhaps that problem led to the end of a reasonably significant journal of black education among colleges that were striving to come into a totally new experience with accreditation and enlarged graduate and professional missions for which they were ill prepared.[2] To that extent, the *Negro College Quarterly* is a valuable depository of news items about those institutions at that point in their development.

Notes

1. Wilberforce University operated at the time under the dual control of the African Methodist Episcopal Church and the state of Ohio. In 1947 the state of Ohio separated its resources from Wilberforce University and established Central State College at Wilberforce.

2. Accreditation for the black colleges in the South was limited to membership in an associate organization made up only of black schools. Colleges outside the South could become full members of the North Central Association of Colleges and Schools. Lincoln University in Missouri and Wilberforce University in Ohio held membership in that organization at the time. Lincoln University in Pennsylvania was a member of the Middle State Association of Colleges and Secondary Schools, the regional accreditation organization for that area.

Information Sources

BIBLIOGRAPHY:
Oak, V. V. "Editorial Note: Looking Ahead." *Negro College Quarterly*, March 1943, pp. 3-4.
Williamson, Anne O. H., and Dunlap, Mollie E., eds. "Introduction, Institutions of Higher Learning Among Negroes in the United States of America." *Negro College Quarterly*, June 1947, pp. ix-x.
INDEX SOURCES: None.
LOCATION SOURCES: Hallie Q. Brown Library, Wilberforce University, Wilberforce, Ohio; Krause Reprint.

Publication History

MAGAZINE TITLE AND TITLE CHANGES: *The Negro College Quarterly*.
VOLUME AND ISSUE DATA: Vols. I-V (March 1943-June 1947), quarterly.
PUBLISHER AND PLACE OF PUBLICATION: Wilberforce University; Wilberforce, Ohio.
EDITOR: Vishnu V. Oak (1943-1947).
CIRCULATION: 1,500.

NEGRO DIGEST

John H. Johnson, editor-publisher of *Negro Digest*, introduced that new journal late in 1942 as a response to demand for a publication "to summarize and condense leading articles and comment on the Negro now in the press in ever-increasing volume." The impact of World War II put a new emphasis on the ubiquitous "Negro Question" which had pervaded American society since Emancipation. What Negroes had been fighting for in the war had become a media focus, even as it had in the black press during World War I.

Johnson wrote that his editors read hundreds of magazines, newspapers, periodicals, books, and reports in order to select items for *Negro Digest*. Johnson dedicated *Negro Digest* to "the development of interracial understanding and the promotion of national unity." It stood "unqualifiedly for the winning of the war and the integration of all citizens into the democratic process." To this end, it published writing and comment from black and white Americans. It focused upon the black citizen through the materials it summarized, "Round Table" debates, book reviews, and special features. Its polls illustrate the purpose the magazine sought to serve. The first raised the question, "Is the Negro Demand for Full Equality Sabotaging the Nation's War Effort?" *Negro Digest* became a news and comment periodical that used its format ingeniously to bring before its audience a wider spectrum of expression about living black in the United States than any black or white publication had previously presented. Johnson called the first issue a sellout. He tripled the second printing.

The journal's appeal lay in its comprehensiveness. Its format permitted review of the widening opportunities for blacks to publish their observations about themselves, and the unusual mechanism for whites to comment pro and con on race relations in a magazine intended primarily for a black audience. *Negro Digest* included views on national and world affairs and preserved a compendium of black newspaper columnists' work that could not have been found easily elsewhere. Through the articles, the journal presented news and commentary on music, medicine, labor, the press, entertainment, government and politics, war and peace, and creative arts. Inasmuch as the editorial policy was eclectic, the magazine could include opinions of a wide range of well-known Americans. Some whose work appeared in early issues include: Carl Sandburg, Marquis Childs, Walter White, Horace Mann Bond, John Temple Graves, Roi Ottley, Bill Stern, Clare Boothe Luce, Pearl Buck, Richard Wright, Benjamin Appel, Eleanor Roosevelt, Ruth Benedict, Zora Neale Hurston, Erskine Caldwell, Rayford Logan, E. Franklin Frazier, H. L. Mencken, Adam Clayton Powell, Lillian Smith, W.E.B. Du Bois, and Benjamin Davis. No other American magazine has brought forth personal observations from so wide a range of black and white national public figures, especially at a time of strict racial segregation in at least one-third of the nation. Although the majority of its articles for summary were taken from *Newsweek*, *Saturday Evening Post*, *Collier's*, *This Month*, *News Story*, and other popular periodicals, such features as "If I Were a Negro" published reactions from Edward G. Robinson, H. V. Kaltenborn, Howard Fast, and Orson Welles, to name a few prominent personalities outside the regular areas of politics, media, and academe.

Negro Digest emerged from Johnson's experience with Supreme Life, a black insurance company based in Chicago for which he worked first as an office boy. When he got the opportunity to publish the firm's house organ which contained information about the insurance business and activities of the black community, Johnson prepared a monthly digest of news about Negroes that had appeared in national publications. This experience led him to consider publishing a monthly collection of articles that would interest Negroes. He mailed some 20,000 letters to Supreme Life's customers offering a charter subscription to *Negro Digest*. With 5,000 copies of the first issue of his new venture left on his hands because of the refusal of Chicago's principal magazine distributors to place *Negro Digest* on newsstands they controlled, Johnson convinced a group of his friends to go around Chicago asking for the magazine. As a result of that effort, the second issue required no unusual promotion scheme, and circulation quickly moved beyond Chicago.

Its editorial tone brought the digest phenomenal success early. Without political partisanship or provincial accommodationist or radical stances, Johnson's magazine brought a refreshing mode to the old American race problem discussions. He used the current popularity of *Readers' Digest* to build an audience for a novel "both sides of the question" approach to thinking about race. "My Most Humiliating Jim Crow Experience," patterned after *Readers' Digest*'s "Embarrassing Moments," projected the rage and helplessness well-known blacks experienced with American jim crowism. With this oblique method, *Negro Digest* carried out its purpose of developing interracial understanding and national unity from its beginning to the decade of the 1960s when the nation's social tensions relaxed considerably. In doing so, the journal moved away from the rigid philosophical dichotomy about race that had characterized black periodicals throughout much of the nation's history since, Johnson reflected in the early issues of *Negro Digest*, the dynamic black Robert S. Abbott had captured an earlier generation with his *Chicago Defender*. With the growing business acumen of the northern urban black, Johnson established the first financially secure black magazine that was freestanding as a black enterprise. Johnson's genius in adapting the *Readers' Digest* format to a black journal required a moderate tone on race, which came about through the contributors' expressions. The periodical was not narrowly black in perspective. At times, it would take entirely different approaches to communicating and analyzing tensions black writers would use to explore the black experience in several literary genres.

After an absence of nearly a decade, *Negro Digest* resumed publication in mid 1961. Johnson said he had revitalized it in response to strong requests from readers who had appreciated the magazine during its earlier life. For the first year of its reappearance, it followed the format and content of the original concept—summarizing articles from other magazines. But within a brief period of time, a different emphasis began to emerge. *Negro Digest* became revolutionary. Creative writing and literary criticism replaced digests and impressions. Slowly, managing editor Hoyt W. Fuller moved the digest into an active posture in the black arts movement that had begun to engage the talents and energies of a rising cadre of black writers. The militant civil rights impetus had affected the creative arts and in doing so had raised a new debate. *Negro Digest* was more than an outlet for black writing, as *Crisis** and *Opportunity** had been earlier. It was the principal journal of the growing coalescence between political and artistic activism. It was a medium for illustrating the black aesthetic that lay at the heart of the new renaissance and fostered conflict between followers of the Imamu Amiri Baraka wing of black artists and such established black writers as Ralph Ellison. *Negro Digest* saw the term "Negro" rejected by the prevailing political and artistic forces among blacks, who substituted "black" as the ethnic adjective for most movements. Accordingly, *Negro Digest* became *Black World** in the spring of 1970. Its direction had changed sufficiently for it to become essentially a new journal.

Information Sources

BIBLIOGRAPHY:
Cruse, Harold. *The Crisis of the Negro Intellectual: From the Origins to the Present*. New York, 1967.
Hudson, Theodore R. *From LeRoi Jones to Amiri Baraka: The Literary Works*. Durham, N.C., 1973.
Miles, Frank W. "Negro Magazines Come of Age." *Magazine World*, 1 June 1946, pp. 12-18, 21.
Reichley, A. James. "How Johnson Made It." *Fortune*, January 1968, pp. 152-53, 178-79.
Wolseley, Roland E. *The Black Press, U.S.A*. Ames: Iowa State University Press, 1971.
INDEX SOURCE: *Index to Selected Periodicals*; *Index to Periodical Articles by and about Negroes*.
LOCATION SOURCES: Moorland-Spingarn Collection, Howard University; Library of Congress; University of Colorado at Boulder.

Publication History

MAGAZINE TITLE AND TITLE CHANGES: *Negro Digest* (November 1942-November 1951; June 1961-April 1970).
VOLUME AND ISSUE DATA: Vols. I-X and XIX, monthly. Volume numbers continued consecutively with resumption of the new journal, *Black World*.
PUBLISHER AND PLACE OF PUBLICATION: Johnson Publishing Company, Chicago, Illinois.
EDITORS: John H. Johnson (November 1942-November 1951; June 1961); Hoyt W. Fuller (July 1961-April 1970).
CIRCULATION: 120,000.

NEGRO EDUCATIONAL REVIEW, THE

John Irving Scott, founder and editor-in-chief of the *Negro Educational Review* from its inception in 1950 until his death in 1981, was for many years associated with the public schools of Jacksonville, Florida. He had come to the United States from his native Jamaica and had earned degrees in chemistry from Lincoln University in Pennsylvania, in guidance from Wittenberg College, and in educational administration at the University of Pittsburgh. He served as principal at several elementary and secondary schools in Jacksonville, and as director of Negro education in that city before assuming positions in Negro colleges in Mississippi, South Carolina, and Texas. In 1949 Scott began to discuss seriously the need for a professional journal edited and published by Negroes. Unlike the *Journal of Negro Education** and the *Quarterly Review of Higher Education Among Negroes*,* established quarterly professional magazines intended for the special needs of black education, the publication that Scott envisioned would cover interests of persons engaged in all levels of education. His plans and discussions for such an enterprise resulted in the first issue of the *Negro Educational Review* that came off the press January 1950 from Alcorn State College in Mississippi, where Scott was a faculty member at the time. The journal became the official organization of the National Teachers' Research Association, which is a general-purpose medium for professional black educators that has reached a national audience throughout the three decades of its publication.

The lead editorial in the first issue expressed the founder's desire to provide a scholarly publication in "all fields of educational endeavor." Its statement of purpose included the following justification:

> For too long already Negro educators have not had sufficient media through which to make known the major findings of their research and experiments; their experiences, and re-interpretations; their practical needs and their realities in their classrooms.[1]

The *Review* proposed to offer space for articles, book reviews, problems of the profession, and news about black educators. Articles in the first issue included: "Errors in Teaching the Social Sciences," "Juvenile Delinquency in a Period of Tension," "Do Students Know What They Know?" "The Teacher's Role in Mental Health," "Negro Science Teachers' Status in Louisiana," "More Children's Literature," and "Secondary Schools and the Needs of Adolescents." Most of the articles were reports of research that had been carried on by members of the National Teachers' Research Association. Much of it was the essence of thesis and masters projects they had written in graduate schools of education. Throughout the years of its publication, the *Review* published detailed lists of thesis topics in education of black people in the universities of the nation.

The journal did not restrict its interest to educational research, however. From time to time it addressed larger concerns of black America. An editorial about the presidential campaign of 1952 admitted that the nation needed honest and capable men in government, but it warned against using "gutter politics" to get them. When the landmark decision against continued segregation in public school education was made in *Brown* v. *Topeka Board of Education*, Scott praised the Court's action, but he warned black educators against using it as an opiate of second class citizenship that might emerge from the integration of school systems at the expense of black leaders in school administration and faculties.

As late as 1960, the magazine reported on a meeting of the Southern Sociology Society at the Henry Grady Hotel in Atlanta that had announced on its agenda that a private and separate dining room for Negroes would be provided during the sessions. Negro members of the organization would be provided that facility in a basement locker room, one article predicted, lamenting that sociologists—of all people in the academic world—could hardly afford not to lead the way for others in showing progress in race relations at their annual convention. As the decade of the 1960s unfolded and the activities involving federal aid to education manifested themselves throughout the country, an editorial noted that it was becoming apparent that the nation would have the choice between a weak, inadequate educational system without federal aid or a satisfactory system with federal support. Regarding the sit-ins that took place on most black college campuses in the 1960s, the *Review* considered them significant in America for at least three reasons: (1) they were showing black students to be socially conscious and responsible; (2) they were revealing increasing sophistication in the secular thinking and techniques of organizations and action; and (3) they were proving that black college students were far more self-disciplined that many persons had believed them to be.

Although the journal approached most discussions of politics and education, except for the most obvious concerns felt among most black educators, it delineated the ramifications of the Eighty-ninth Congress in its attempt to have the Department of Health, Education and Welfare force Southern states to comply with the desegregation law of 1954. One service the *Review* rendered its audience was the listing in one issue of the several federal statutes that would impact upon educational opportunities for black Americans, including: The Elementary and Secondary Education Act of 1965, the National Defense Act, the Vocational Education Act of 1963, the Economic Opportunity Act, and the Civil Rights Act of 1964.[2] The editorial makes the significant point that those areas of the South that would most stubbornly resist implementing these federal actions could least afford to lose the federal funds that would be denied them for their refusals.

One significant article in a fairly recent issue of the journal explored the effects on white students of studying black history and culture in college courses. Praising the movement toward raising black consciousness that had been the impetus for demands for black studies courses in American colleges and universities, the author concluded from available studies that white students gained little social insight from taking courses in black studies. While they admired individual blacks, they still basically assumed that America was the product almost exclusively of whites, whether old-stock, ethnic or a combination of the two. There was a value, however, that the author praised—one that was a bit of a surprise to those who conducted studies to measure the extent of such courses on changing attitudes of white students.

A conclusion drawn by many whites was that racism, as social theory or actual discrimination, had been deeply injurious to Blacks. In many cases, a white student for the first time saw through the allegation that skin color has no bearing on economic advancement; in so doing he caught the tragedy of the color line. One white student vividly discovered the terrible implications of chattel slavery for the development of American race relations: "The white race from the very early meetings with the Africans, till even now, looked on this black-skinned individual as something of a mystery, and saw within this mysterious creature, deeply imbedded in the blackness, the unknown—from this came a fear, a fear of the unknown; to be conquered by retaliation, a retaliation leading to dominance, to superiority; a race to rule a race. . . . The implicit fear of a Negro's blackness, which has lurked long in American popular culture, became more evident to the eye trained by a careful reading of Afro-American history.[3]

The *Review*, like other journals of its kind, lost some momentum during the era of integration of public schools and colleges and universities in the South. Black educational associations were no longer so seriously needed to provide leadership roles for black educators and to make possible a place for publication of their studies. This journal adjusted itself to the new demands of its audience by moving into problems of the black professor on white campuses in public schools and postsecondary institutions, the merging image of the black college in the face of integration, the ghetto child as a challenge for American education, and compensatory education.

This periodical is not so well known as some others among black professional magazines, but it has maintained a balanced view of its purposes and has enjoyed a longevity that is respectable. It continues as a modest, but high-quality, black journal.

Notes

1. "Presenting *The Review*," *Negro Educational Review* (January 1950): 3.
2. "Politics and Education," *Negro Educational Review* (January 1969): 2-4.
3. Ronald M. Johnson, "Black History and White Students: Broadening Cultural Horizons," *Negro Educational Review* (January 1977): 13-14.

Information Sources

BIBLIOGRAPHY:
Lloyd, R. Grann. "Defining the Situation," *Negro Educational Review*, April 1981, pp. 2-5.

Wolseley, Roland E. *Black Press U.S.* Ames: Iowa State University Press, 1971, p. 146.
INDEX SOURCES: *Current Index to Journals in Education; Index to Periodical Articles by and about Negroes.*
LOCATION SOURCES: Library of Congress; Most college and university libraries.

Publication History

MAGAZINE TITLE AND TITLE CHANGES: *The Negro Educational Review* (January 1950-).
VOLUME AND ISSUE DATA: Vols. I- , quarterly.
PUBLISHER AND PLACE OF PUBLICATION: Negro Educational Review, Incorporated, Jacksonville, Florida.
EDITORS: John Irving Scott (January 1950-January 1981); R. Gann Lloyd (April 1981-).
CIRCULATION: 3,000.

NEGRO FARMER AND MESSENGER

Tuskegee Institute in Alabama published during the World War I era two periodicals—the *Negro Farmer* and the *Messenger*—which eventually merged in 1915 to form *Negro Farmer and Messenger.*[1] Together and separately, these organs focused on farming as a business and a profession. The merged journal amplified Tuskegee Institute's industrial education thrust by addressing itself to the large farm population among black Southerners, and promoting the institute. Throughout its publication, George Washington Carver, the black agricultural scientist, wrote advice for farmers in the Deep South. The magazine illustrates the shrewd sense of the use of communication media that Booker T. Washington possessed and used at Tuskegee Institute. Isaac Fisher, editor of the *Negro Farmer*, claimed that theirs was the "only racial publication, so far as we know, that has been started with a fully subscribed and paid-up capital sufficient to put it on a solid foundation."[2]

Tuskegee's philosophy of education provided the magazine's primary appeal. But it was more than a farm and home newspaper. It dignified farming and promoted the growth of scientific agriculture as the impending war was making serious impact upon the national economy. *Negro Farmer and Messenger* deserves attention that it has not previously received, for its content makes a significant statement about rural life for black Americans during a time when other journals focused largely upon urban life. The magazine served an agricultural extension function for its wide audience, teaching them to value and improve farming and homemaking activities; at the same time, it kept farmers abreast of national and international affairs through its feature articles, editorials, columns, and regular reports on the popular Tuskegee conferences. These communication purposes were performed with candor.

The journal was published in the interest of home, farm, and garden, especially devoted to Negro landowners and tenant farmers and to those who employed Negro labor. Its first issues contain greetings and words of encouragement from the United States Department of Agriculture and governors of several states that had already developed programs in agricultural education. From its beginning, the periodical viewed farming optimistically. It used statistics effectively. Negro farmers and agricultural laborers of all kinds numbered upward of 2 million, it reported before World War I started. Moreover, farmers owned $500 million of the estimated $700 million total wealth among black Americans. Twenty-eight percent of southern farmers were black. Tuskegee Institute had been a national leader in seeking federal legislation to aid the farmer in increasing his skill and making for himself a larger part of the national economy. Given the large investment black farmers had made, their interests were critical. *Negro Farmer and Messenger* helped them to realize they could not afford to lose ground in a nation growing increasingly complex. "Will the colored farmer hold his own in agriculture?" the editor asked. He sought to answer his question through instruction and exemplars.

"Winners from the Soil" contained vignettes of southern blacks who had succeeded in farming as a business and profession. Articles and simple statements relating to problems of animal husbandry, field crops, gardening, homemaking, and basic home economics brought Tuskegee Institute to the farmer. This process was the heart of agricultural extension, so important a part of the major public state college but neglected by black colleges that still agonized over whether agriculture was a proper subject for higher education.[3] Booker T. Washington has to be credited with initiating effective ways for the black college to relate to the working farmer. When George Washington Carver joined the faculty at Tuskegee after receiving his master's degree in agriculture from Iowa State College, Washington was able to persuade the Alabama state legislature in 1896 to pass a law setting up the Tuskegee Agricultural Experiment Station, which Carver headed. Its principal feature during the early years was the "Moveable School" from Tuskegee which was inaugurated in 1906 to demonstrate ways to improve their farming methods to farmers who most needed instruction. Carver and Washington noted that the church often served as the social center for blacks in rural communities. Accordingly, they placed their demonstration wagons on church grounds in order to reach the largest number of farmers. The United States Department of Agriculture and the General Education Board saw the merit in this novel concept in agriculture education and added their support.

Negro Farmer and Messenger effectively complemented and refined the extension philosophy by adding other dimensions of rural life enrichment to facts about farming and farm homemaking. Fisher wrote to governors of all states that practiced racial separation in education urging them to use their influence to have the provisions of the Smith-Lever Act fully implemented. In a strong editorial, he challenged black farmers to pursue this new fight. "There ought not to be any backwardness about asking for the money. Our Southern Congressmen promised the country they would do what is fair in the matter."[4]

With "Farmer's Dictionary," which began as a lexicon of terms relating to agriculture, Fisher kept his audience abreast of national and international affairs. The dictionary described the conflict between the United States and Mexico and the growing confrontation in Europe that would lead to World War I. The editor also explained the provisions of the several congressional acts designed to assist farmers and outlined provisions most southern states enacted in their constitutions for the purpose of limiting or preventing blacks from voting in state and local elections. While the issue of whether black Americans should enlist to serve in the war after the nation entered it divided the black press, Fisher wrote: "Since we are patriots, we must serve our country when she calls and follow her flag, reserving for times of peace our protests against all that is oppressive and unjust."[5]

Fisher was a graduate of Tuskegee Institute and totally devoted to Booker T. Washington's political, social, and educational policies for blacks. He remained above the often bitter controversy between "Bookerites" and "radicals." When he did comment on the conflict, he urged readers to refrain from considering the radicals enemies. He promoted Washington's posture on piety. He was adamant on prohibition. His "What We Have Learned about Rum—the Liquor Question" won the first prize of $500 among 900 entrants in an essay contest sponsored by *Everybody's Magazine*. To him, "a sober race is a powerful race."

The merger of *Negro Farmer* with the *Messenger* allowed the chief thrusts of the two publications to continue. Rural schools, churches, and community development received particular attention. Julius Rosenwald, a Chicago philanthropist associated with Sears, Roebuck Company, had been persuaded by Washington to establish a fund and a procedure for building schools and supervising their construction. Fisher advised local school boards on the procedures for applying for money to build schoolhouses and ways to gain full community participation in operating them. This service comported well with the sense of community Tuskegee's agricultural extension programs had already established.

In a special issue published when Washington died, Fisher wrote: "Every time I have wanted to say something in this paper about him [Washington], he said, 'It is very kind of you, Mr. Fisher, but I am afraid it would not be best for you to write it, since you are at Tuskegee and people might feel that you were asked to do it.'"[6] To critics who complained that Washington had not pursued goals of the race after the abolitionist fashion of Frederick Douglass, Fisher replied: "Dr. Washington did not try to be Frederick Douglass. He simply took the love of his race and added it to his own vision of work to be done for the world; and he died not as the second Frederick Douglass but as Booker T. Washington, Master Statesman and builder of his times."[7]

Fisher pledged his full support to Washington's successor at Tuskegee, Robert Russa Moton. Editorials and news items in the journal continued to report on progress with implementing the Smith-Lever Act in the South, rural education, and Tuskegee's pride in establishing the first veterinary hospital at a black institution. When Fisher resigned his position at Tuskegee and became director of publications at Fisk University, "Farmer's Dictionary" no longer appeared in the publication. *Negro Farmer and Messenger* became largely an experimental station bulletin and institute newspaper. George Washington Carver's scientific articles and his question-and-answer column provided the most valuable content in the journal at that time.

While Fisher was editor of *Negro Farmer* and editor in chief of *Negro Farmer and Messenger*, the journal contained a verve that communicated agriculture education, public health, world and national affairs, and events at Tuskegee Institute to the rural South. Its advertisements suggest the scope of the journal's audience. Far more than farm equipment was advertised. Most black colleges, including those that focused upon liberal education, bought space in the magazine. Perhaps *Negro Farmer and Messenger* serves the student of the black experience in the United States best with its comprehensive coverage of the rural South and Tuskegee's commitment to refining the quality of life there. Given current scholarship relating to the influence of Booker T. Washington and his alleged attempts to control the black press as organs for his own educational and business enterprises at the expense of blacks who followed a different approach to racial advancement, these journals merit consideration as an alternative viewpoint. Although there is little direct information on reasons for cessation of publication of *Negro Farmer and Messenger*, it appears that its preeminence as part of Tuskegee's mission declined with the passage of the leadership of the school from Booker T. Washington to Robert Russa Moton.

Notes

1. The profile on the two publications treats the two as one except for source citations. The emphasis and content of the two are discussed under the general rubric *Negro Farmer and Messenger*.

2. "An Evidence of Racial Unity," *Negro Farmer* (31 January 1919): 4.

3. The Smith-Lever Act of 1914 strengthened Tuskegee's resources for agricultural extension. Short course schools were conducted on farmers' land to teach seed selection, crop rotation, care of farm animals, pasture making, home gardening, and tool repair. The Smith-Hughes Act provided for home demonstration agents to assist with homemaking. *See also* "Alabama to Give Her Farmers 30 Percent of Smith-Lever Funds," *Negro Farmer* (15 August 1914): 4.

4. Ibid.

5. "We Are Patriots," *Negro Farmer and Messenger* (7 May 1917): 4.

6. "Say It Now," *Negro Farmer and Messenger*" (20 November 1915): 1.

7. Ibid.

Information Sources

BIBLIOGRAPHY:
Bullock, Henry Allen. *A History of Negro Education in the South from 1619 to the Present*. Cambridge, Mass., 1967.
Du Bois, W.E.B. "The Hampton Idea." *Voice of the Negro*, September 1906, pp. 391-92.
Hall, Clyde W., *Black Vocational Technical and Industrial Arts Education*. Chicago, 1973.
Jones, Allen W., "The Role of Tuskegee Institute in the Education of Black Farmers." *Journal of Negro History*, April 1975, pp. 252-67.
McCormick, J. Scott. "The Julius Rosenwald Fund." *Journal of Negro Education*, October 1934, pp. 605-26.
Reid, Herbert O., and Nabrit, James M., Jr. "Remedies Under Statutes Granting Federal Aid to Land-grant Colleges." *Journal of Negro Education*, Summer 1948, pp. 410-25.
INDEX SOURCES: None.
LOCATION SOURCES: Greenwood Press Periodicals; Tuskegee Institute Library; Booker T. Washington Papers, Library of Congress.

Publication History

MAGAZINE TITLE AND TITLE CHANGES: *The Negro Farmer* (January 1914-November 1915); *Negro Farmer and Messenger* (November 1915-November 1917).
VOLUME AND ISSUE DATA: Vols. I-V (January, 1914-November 1917), Published biweekly until 11 August 1917; resumed publication October 1917, monthly.
PUBLISHER AND PLACE OF PUBLICATION: Negro Farmer Corporation, Tuskegee Institute, Alabama.
EDITORS: *The Negro Farmer*: Isaac Fisher (January 1914-November 1915); *Negro Farmer and Messenger:* Isaac Fisher (November 6, 1915-July 1, 1916); Vernon W. Barnett (July 15, 1916-November 1917).
CIRCULATION: 10,000 estimate.

NEGRO HERITAGE/BLACK HERITAGE

Negro Heritage, renamed *Black Heritage* in 1977, was a small publication founded by Sylvester C. Watkins, Sr., in 1961 in Chicago. Originally published biweekly as an informal newsletter planned to inform, instruct, and stimulate further interest in the story of Negro contributions to mankind, many of its early concerns were fairly typical of those found in other black periodicals of the period. However, both in its early and later stages, *Negro Heritage/Black Heritage* has had several interesting and unique emphases.

The lead article of the first issue, written by Watkins, is entitled "Negro Cultural Contributions to America" and focuses on the early achievements of

American blacks. Responding to the facts that "historians have established the time of entry for Negroes into the New World on a day sometime in the year 1619" and that one of the legacies of slavery in America has been "the desire," largely of whites, "to ignore some incontrovertible facts, or treat them as being without sufficient basis for belief," Watkins pointedly informs us that "anthropologists believe that members of African tribes either lived and/or visited the North American continent even before the days of Columbus," and that "the carvings and handiwork of the Indian Mound Builders and the work found in Mexican temples clearly show Negro facial structure."[1] Watkins goes on to cite "a Negro colony in Mexico...who may have been instrumental in establishing the city of Mexico," to note that "the expedition of such famous explorers as Pizarro, Balboa, Cortes, and Velas included Negroes in their company," and finally to focus a fairly lengthy discussion on Estevanico, "the most interesting Negro figure of the period," who was involved in searching for the "Seven Cities of Cibola." The article continues by citing various black explorers who accompanied Lewis and Clark's expedition in 1804 and John C. Frémont's expedition in 1842 and concludes with the mention of "William Alexander Leisdorff, distinguished Negro pioneer of California," and "owner of the first steamship sailing in San Francisco Bay."

A bibliographic section lists books—some current and some older—that the editor wants to call to his readers' attention. The first "Heritage Calendar" was Chicago-oriented. 4 March 1815 is marked as the birthdate of Myrtilla Minor, founder of Minor Teachers College, and 13 March 1773 is the birthday of Jean Baptiste Point de Saible, the first Negro to come to Peoria and the first permanent settler in Chicago. From the Reconstruction period, 1 March 1841 marks the birth of Blanche K. Bruce, senator from Mississippi, and 5 March 1855 marks the birth of Frederick Douglass. Contemporary issues of greatest importance that the calendar notes are the sit-ins among civil rights activists in eight Florida cities, the date the mayor of Nashville, Tennessee, appointed a commission to work out racial problems, and when 350 student protesters were arrested and put in a stockade at Orangeburg, South Carolina.

"Heritage Calendar" was meant to be both a history lesson and a journalistic prod to contemporary blacks to recognize the evolving world around them. Taken in terms of the first year publication of the magazine, the calendar represented a living history. After the first full year (1961), the calendar was replaced by more active, contemporary, and thoroughly discussed materials as well as civil rights activities. The magazine went from a small four-page, biweekly format to a more extensive and discursive eight-page monthly structure.

Inasmuch as the magazine has remained the personal journalistic enterprise of the same man from its inception, many of the emphases have remained the same. When Watkins moved from Chicago to Reston, Virginia, the Chicago orientation diminished. For a while he moved into some international areas of interest, such as a reprint of the 17 August 1980 address by Alejandro Orfilia, secretary-general of the Organization of American States, entitled "Marcus Garvey: Hero of the Americas," and fequent reprinting of African recipes.

By the early 1970s, the coverage of the magazine had expanded considerably. The cover of one such issue is a picture of Vernon Jordan, executive director of the National Urban League. The first seven pages are devoted to reprinting part 1 of Jordan's "Blueprint for the Seventies," an address he delivered at the Equal Opportunity Day Banquet in New York on 18 November 1971. That address is followed by an 18 March 1853 quotation from Frederick Douglass to the effect that Negroes must become mechanics and build as well as use bridges, houses, and furniture; for before they can properly live, they must be respected by their fellow men. This quotation is followed in turn by a facsimile reprint of a "Steam-Trap" designed by Henry Creamer and awarded two patents, in 1891 and 1893—an obvious response to Douglass' call for skilled engineers, inventors, and artisans, and a clear continuation of one of Watkins' major emphases throughout *Negro Heritage/Black Heritage*'s existence. Following the facsimile is the full recipe ("Courtesy Embassy of Ghana") for "Fish Stew" and "Joloff Rice." The last page of the issue contains a picture of Cynthia Jean Murray, a "Receptionist-secretary of Loyola University," courtesy of the Chicago "Employee of the Week" program.

A list of special series undertaken by Watkins in the early years is also rather interesting and revealing. Many of them continue in today's issues. The first of these concerns the role of the black soldier in America's history. Beginning with a cover story on "The Negro Soldier," this interest led to a cover story on "The Negro in the Military Service," which began the second year of publication and became a series which was still being printed thirteen years later. This military interest persists even today in such diverse articles as "Hidden Heritage: the Tuskegee Airmen, the First Black Pilots and Air-Crewmen in the United States Air Force" and "Seminole Negro-Indian Scouts. After a brief, two-part series on "Emotional Aspects of School Desegregation," the next extensive series dealt with "The Heirs of Chicago's First Settler" (a "French-speaking Negro" named Jean Baptiste Point de Saible).

After another minor, three-part series on "The Negro in History," merely "a suggested outline . . . for a short course in Negro history," which had been requested by "quite a number of subscribers," Watkins began his second really huge—and enduring—series: "Historic Sites and Monuments," a "new feature that will run in every issue" in order to list, by state and "with some descriptive information about each" site, "monuments, statues, locations, and plaques" of interest to black Americans. Treating the sites by state and in alphabetical order, the first article dealt with several Tuskegee items of interest. Though the original name of this series eventually died out, Watkins' interest in historical sites, especially accompanied by photographs, has been a continuous emphasis of *Negro Heritage/Black Heritage*, so that the newsletter's pages have been a major source of black American geographic and architectural history throughout the last twenty years. Indeed, Watkins' interest in this vein has recently broadened.

A recent cover story is devoted to "An Archeological Perspective" (complete with numerous pictures) of "An Enduring Afro-American Neighborhood" in Alexandria, Virginia.

The magazine has been a veritable storehouse of information about black American explorers and inventors. Watkins has been most scrupulous in providing specifications for the inventions that interest him. They distinguish *Negro Heritage/Black Heritage* from other black journals. It is quasi-scientific and historical at the same time. And it is a newspaper. Watkins has also been interested in blacks in the postal service and in integration in housing, employment, and public accommodations. Most times he has approached those subjects with historical studies. Occasionally, he has published short, one-page series on blacks in aviation, space exploration, medicine, and other aspects of accomplishment in contemporary endeavors.

There has been a subtle and gradual shift in the tone of the magazine, even in its spirit. Perhaps the most enlightening way of tracing this evolution of *Negro Heritage/Black Heritage*—and perhaps the whole Civil Rights movement over the last two decades—is by noting its changing mastheads. It began with the strong—almost regal—assertiveness and promise of Carter G. Woodson's statement that "the achievements of the Negro properly set forth will crown him as a factor in early human progress and a maker of modern civilization." The year was 1961, and the civil rights movement was obviously asserting itself, promising "Freedom Now" and forever. By 1971 the masthead's outlook was less optimistic:

> We ain't what we ought to be, and we ain't what we want to be, and we ain't what we're going to be, but Thank God, we ain't where we was.
>
> (From an Old Negro Slave Preacher)

Two years after this emotional stepback, the magazine seemed to be in as much trouble as the waning civil rights movement, and Watkins dispensed with his philosophical mastheads altogether, devoting that space to the self-promotional printing of endorsements by various satisfied school librarians, from Chicago to North Bend, Nebraska, to Newark, New Jersey, all praising *Negro Heritage/Black Heritage*'s "up-to-date authentic presentation of Black person's and their accomplishments" and its "educational information for students and adults as well." Finally, as *Negro Heritage/Black Heritage*'s economic crisis presumably passed, the "Old Negro Slave Preacher" returned to the masthead and has remained there ever since.

Note

1. *Negro Heritage* 1, no. 1 (September 1961): 1.

Information Sources

BIBLIOGRAPHY:

Boone, Dorothy, Deloris, "A Historical Review and a Bibliography of Selected Negro Magazines, 1910-1969." Ph.D. dissertation, University of Michigan, 1970, p. 132.

Katz, Bill, and Richards, Berry G. *Magazines for Libraries.* 3d ed. New York, 1970, p. 46.

Wolseley, Roland R. *The Changing Magazine: Trends in Readership and Management.* Hastings House, 1973, pp. 110-14.

INDEX SOURCES: None.

LOCATION SOURCES: Library of Congress; Moorland-Spingarn Collection, Howard University, Washington, D.C.; most college and university libraries; University Microfilms.

Publication History

MAGAZINE TITLE AND TITLE CHANGES: *Negro Heritage* (January 1961-June 1977); *Black Heritage* (July 1977-).

VOLUME AND ISSUE DATA: Vol. I, no. 1 to present (January 1961-), bimonthly.

PUBLISHER AND PLACE OF PUBLICATION: Sylvester C. Watkins, Reston, Virginia.

EDITOR: Sylvester C. Watkins (1961-).

CIRCULATION: 5,000.

Noel Heermance

NEGRO HISTORY BULLETIN

Carter G. Woodson, who founded the prestigious Association for the Study of Negro Life and History and its *Journal of Negro History,** established in 1937 the *Negro History Bulletin.* Woodson served as managing editor of the new publication until his death in 1950. The *Bulletin* was oriented toward black education and black children's urgent need to learn about their cultural heritage. It sought to offset the practice of excluding educational material about Africans and Afro-Americans from most textbooks. The first issue contained an article on Africa that made the salient point that although Africa is the home of black people, sometimes called Negroes, meaning black, all Africans are not black. The journal implemented the goals of Negro History Week and Negro History clubs which Woodson had initiated throughout most of the country as part of the association. Celebration of events, accomplishments, and personalities among blacks was observed from time to time; the centennial anniversary of the death of Aleksandr Pushkin, the famous black Russian poet, was one such item. An early *Negro History Bulletin* book-of-the-month selection was Helen A. Whiting's *Negro Folk Tales.* Stories about contemporary life in black Africa were included in most issues.

The magazine was designed primarily to supplement Woodson's *Negro in Our History* which was used as a textbook in black schools and colleges that could choose their own teaching materials. In the years immediately preceding, including, and following World War II, the *Bulletin* pioneered in raising the consciousness of black Americans about their countrymen and other blacks. One lead article discussed Felix Ebové, first Negro governor of French Equitorial Africa at a time when few Afro-Americans held public office in the United States. Other articles in the same issue, published in 1949, included one on Egypt written by Woodson, "Education in Haiti," "The Negro Little Theatre Movement," and "The Canterbury Tale," concerning Prudence Crandall, a Quaker schoolteacher from Connecticut who dared to enroll a black girl in her private school. In recalling those early years of the *Negro History Bulletin*, one of its editors wrote:

> Every issue of the *Bulletin* included a Children's Page. These pages varied from one issue to another but they always contained questions which required the best efforts of the pupils. Following are two illustrations: (1) in what capacities are most of the Negroes in the United States employed? Account for their concentration in these particular fields. Has there appeared recently any tendency to change for the better? (2) How are the Natives used in the African dependencies of the British Empire? Do you consider the present economy in those parts conducive to the best interests of all concerned?[1]

Most early issues contained news about Negro History Week observations in schools and clubs around the country. Resource features for those purposes included biographies of white persons who had aided black slaves before Emancipation, non-American noted blacks in other parts of the world, and black Americans who had achieved distinction in a variety of endeavors. Personalities were presented in a column that made their biographies coincide with their birth months. Members of the editorial board wrote articles on Afro-American culture as well as on history and personal achievement. Material for school children covered the past and contemporary status of black American writing. Lesson plans defined poetry and drama and presented accompanying essays on the lives and works of the writers. Through this method children were taught biographies and some works of Charles Chesnutt, Claude McKay, Rudolph Fisher, Jessie Fauset, William Wells Brown, Zora Neale Hurston, and Arna Bontemps. One year, units of study included "Negro History Week to Feature Musicians and Their Music," "Negro Art from Africa to America," "Painters In Spite of Those of African Blood," "Negro Beginnings of Science," and "Philosophy in Every Man's Thought." These articles represent an especially useful and comprehensive study of Afro-American culture. As the years passed, lessons and articles on the professions, business, labor, and politics brought readers into current emphases in American life.

The *Negro History Bulletin* became popular early in its publication life. Its goals to inculcate appreciation of the Negro past and an understanding of his present elicited interest from a broad spectrum of Americans. With the beginning of inclusion of black personalities and Afro-American interest in textbooks and national media, the direction of the magazine's content changed. Classroom instructional units gave way to brief articles written by scholars on many phases of black American life. During the sixties and seventies the *Bulletin* responded effectively to rising nationalism in black Africa, black studies in American colleges and universities, and the International Women's Year. A special Bicentennial issue, Spring 1975, emphasized black Americans' participation in the nation's 200-year history. The *Bulletin* has continued its close alliance with the association that founded it. A report of the executive director of that organization stated recently:

> The *Negro History Bulletin* has the potential of being one of the most popular magazines of black life in America.
>
> To reach the stage of high volume in subscriptions will require an extended campaign. There is ample reason to believe that the *Bulletin* can reach thousands or more subscribers, but frankly, the funds to mount such a subscription drive have just not been available.[2]

This journal has faced the same problems common to most American scholarly periodicals. Its strength has been maintained, however, and it continues as a significant medium of communication about the black men and women in the world and the accomplishments of the black race.

Notes

1. Thelma D. Perry, *"The Bulletin—A Concept in Education," Negro History Bulletin* (October 1971): 124.
2. *Report of the ASALH Executive Director for 1974, 1975, and 1976* (Washington, D.C., 1977): 6.

Information Sources

BIBLIOGRAPHY:

Logan, Frenise A. "An Appraisal of Forty-One Years of the *Journal of Negro History*, 1916-1957." *Journal of Negro History*, January 1958, pp. 26-33.

Perry, Thelma D. *"The Bulletin—A Concept in Education." Negro History Bulletin*, October 1971, p. 124-26.

Report of the ASALH Executive Director for 1974, 1975, and 1976. Washington, D.C., 1977, pp. 6-7.

Wolseley, Roland E. *Black Press U.S.A*. Ames: Iowa State University Press, 1971, p. 147.

INDEX SOURCES: *Index to Periodical Articles by and about Negroes; Biography Index; Readers Guide to Periodical Literature; Book Review Index.*
LOCATION SOURCES: Most college and university libraries.

Publication History

MAGAZINE TITLE AND TITLE CHANGES: *Negro History Bulletin.*
VOLUME AND ISSUE DATA: Vols. I to present (October 1937-), monthly except June, July, August, and September.
PUBLISHER AND PLACE OF PUBLICATION: Association for Afro-American Life and History, Washington, D.C.
EDITORS: Carter G. Woodson: (October 1937-May 1950); Rayford W. Logan, (June 1950-December 1951); Albert N. Brooks (January 1952-May 1964); Charles Walter Thomas (October 1964-December 1966); Charles Wesley (January 1967-May 1973); J. Rupert Picott (October 1973-).
CIRCULATION: 8,500.

Arvarh E. Strickland

NEGRO JOURNAL OF RELIGION, THE: AN INTERDENOMINATIONAL REVIEW

Although the *Negro Journal of Religion* was published from 1935-39 at Wilberforce University in Ohio, the principal institution for the African Methodist Episcopal Church in the United States, it was not a denominational periodical. Its editor, Lendell Charles Ridley, was a minister of that church, but the list of contributing editors included Methodists, Baptists, and Episcopalians. All were pastors of churches in nearby Dayton, Ohio. The interdenominational review invited manuscripts on religion and ethical topics from scholars of any religious faith, but it was basically a newspaper for black churches and churchmen in the nation.

Each issue contained the lead column, "Our Churches and Their Workers," which reported on activities in the churches, often detailing some regional conference, a particularly successful project a congregation had experienced, or news about clergymen. Although the journal was not articulate about racial matters in the political sense, it did publish articles from time to time that indicated encouraging signs of improvement in black and white tensions. One, "When Race Relations Have Disappeared," was written by a white minister of the First Baptist Church in Dayton, Ohio.[1] He claimed that within the next forty years there would not be any race relations problem. There would be people belonging to different races, he admitted, but their relations one to another would be on the basis of persons with persons and not race with race. He predicted that within forty years cultural and diversional opportunities would be available to all people everywhere without discrimination; that the occupational fields would be open to all with regard only for pertinent qualifications; and that interracial Sundays and services would be fewer because meeting and worshipping together would be so well accepted that special occasions would not be required. This was the nature of the social idealism found in many of the journal's articles.

At the same time, Ridley wrote an editorial reacting to the attitude shown toward racial mixing by the president of the International Christian Endeavor Society, a churchwide organization of the Methodist Church. During a national broadcast question period, someone had asked the president whether mixed marriages should be approved and he had said no. The editorial judged that, with his answer, the speaker "stepped down from the pinnacle of a militant defender of right and became a grovelling American nationalist, a Nordic purist."[2]

On several occasions, the periodical took notice of changing practices of religion among blacks during the 1930s. The storefront church was discussed. In an editorial, the editor admitted he had been biased against these depression era churchhouses at one time. He had felt that there was an abundance of churches of the conventional type that could minister to the religious needs of black people, in particular. He had changed his opinion, he confessed. For he had come to realize that the storefront church reaches a type of people that should, by all means, be reached by someone; that few of the larger churches with their stilted services could do the work of these churches. He also concluded that the Christian church had started as a "storefront movement" and that few churches started off with great crowds.[3]

Contemporary black religion during the 1930s could hardly be considered without some reference to Father Divine.[4] The journal published a series of articles under the caption, "A Man They Called God," based on a Court of Common Pleas case in Newark, New Jersey. The black religious leader had been charged with disturbing the peace with his spiritual meetings. The complaint had attracted unusual attention to Divine's movement and had motivated the City of Newark to commission a study of the cult. The journal published articles about the organization in its March, April, and May 1935 issues. In response to requests from readers, the magazine published the full text of the court's formal appointment of the commission to study Divine's organization. Interestingly, the document shows that Father Divine concurred fully in the request.

In other editorials and reports, the *Negro Journal of Religion* gave some attention to the gathering Nazi movement in Germany in the mid 1930s, to the distress of the African Republic of Liberia, and to the developing ghettos in large American cities. It also published some poetry from time to time.

Notes

1. Charles Lyon Seashores, *Negro Journal of Religion* (May 1936): 2.
2. "Dr. Poling, Shame," *Negro Journal of Religion* (August 1937): 3.
3. "Store Front Churches," ibid.
4. Father Divine, born George Baker near Savannah, Georgia, in 1882, moved to Baltimore in 1907 and became a "God in Sonship" with a cult leader named Father

Jehovah. In 1919 he moved to Sayville, Long Island, and proclaimed himself God, establishing at the same time his Peace Mission movement. It was interracial and interdenominational and used a theme of universal peace. In 1931, Father Divine and some eighty of his followers were arrested on a disorderly conduct charge stemming from a noisy singing session. Divine was sentenced to a prison term, but shortly after that sentencing the judge died of a heart attack. That incident gave new strength to the movement and served as a rallying point for poor blacks and whites who needed a haven at the height of the depression.

Information Sources

BIBLIOGRAPHY:
Bergman, Peter M., and Bergman, Mort N. *The Chronological History of the Negro in America*. New York, 1969, pp. 293-93.
Nelsen, Hart M., Yokley, Raytha L., and Nelsen, Anne K., *The Black Church in America*. New York, 1971, pp. 175-78, 185-88.
INDEX SOURCES: None.
LOCATION SOURCES: Hallie Q. Brown Library, Wilberforce University, Wilberforce, Ohio; Schomberg Collection, New York Public Library.

Publication History

MAGAZINE TITLE AND TITLE CHANGES: *The Negro Journal of Religion: An Interdenominational Review*.
VOLUME AND ISSUE DATA: Vols. I-IV (January 1935-January 1939), monthly.
PUBLISHER AND PLACE OF PUBLICATION: Negro Journal of Religion, Wilberforce, Ohio.
EDITOR: Lendell Charles Ridley (1935-1939).
CIRCULATION: 1,000.

Charles E. Holmes

NEGRO MUSIC JOURNAL

J. Hillary Taylor, an elementary school teacher and instructor of music in Washington, D.C., began publishing the *Negro Music Journal* in Washington in 1902 for the express purpose of helping Negroes "toward a better knowledge and appreciation of the musical arts" and to perform a special service for his fellow music teachers and their associates.[1] Taylor asked, in his first issue, for information about black composers and musicians whose works had been published and featured articles on various themes in music education, especially those that discussed some successful approaches to teaching. The journal provided publication possibilities for teachers who wanted to write about pedagogy and performance, news about musical events among the black community, and biographies of classical musicians. Taylor's purposes were noble. For his was one of the first black periodicals that sought to compile facts about black artists and to make known their works.

Reading the journal gives insight into some of the personal and professional problems of the black artist in the early years of the twentieth century. Taylor once made a plea for patronage of black music teachers—an expression of a part of the distress black music teachers felt as they sought to hold on to students in their communities.

If we desire a white teacher on his merit, that is all right; but if we desire him on his color or nationality, then we are surely wrong. Yet many of our people engage a teacher on this basis. I have repeatedly heard the expression: "My child is studying with a German teacher," or "My child has a white teacher." Well, this would not be so unfortunate if these teachers had been engaged on their merits as teachers rather than on account of color or nationality. And in most cases of this kind, I have observed that the teacher was an inferior one. I plead with parents, give our teachers a chance and if you do hire a white one, hire him because he is a good tutor. If the colored teacher cannot get pupils, how do you expect him to prove to you his pedagogical ability?[2]

Taylor was often placed in the position of defending teaching European music to black children in order to give them the best musical education. He argued that black teachers should teach it. The apparent contradiction in his position reflects the limited opportunities black musicians found for making a living in American society and the elitist standards of art the black educated classes promulgated. The journal patterned its format and content after *Masters in Music*, *Musical Record and Review*, and *Etude*.[3] Black musicians associated with Taylor who were sympathetic to his cultural "accommodationist" attitude toward black culture formed the Washington Conservatory of Music for which the *Negro Music Journal* became the official organ in its last year of publication.

Interest in the rising popularity of Samuel Coleridge-Taylor, the London-born son of a native of Sierra Leone and an Englishwoman, drew special attention in the *Journal*. The Coleridge-Taylor Choral Society had been formed by the Treble Clef Club, an organization made up largely of the wives of black Washington professional men. In March 1903 the society performed Coleridge-Taylor's *Trilogy* to a standing room only audience at Washington's fashionable Metropolitan A.M.E. Church. "Hiawatha's Wedding Feast," a part of the trilogy, had been performed first in the United States in 1899 by the Temple Baptist Church choir in Brooklyn. John T. Layton, a local public school teacher, directed the Washington presentation. It was reviewed favorably in the *New York Times* and *Washington Post*. Taylor devoted an editorial to the production. The best-known black soloists had participated in it, including the internationally famous baritone, Harry T. Burleigh. Taylor praised the interracial cooperation the performance had fostered by commenting upon the support "the best white music teachers and music lovers of the city had shown by attending."[4] Black musicians were interested in Coleridge-Taylor because of his black heritage and took particular pride in his accomplishments as a composer. Moreover, his *Trilogy* was based on American folk traditions relating to the romances about Hiawatha. The "Hiawatha Overture" was based on the major melodic theme in the Negro Spiritual, "Nobody Knows the Trouble I See." Some of the basic elements of the music Coleridge-Taylor had composed identified black Americans with the Englishman. But the *Journal*'s editor was impressed because the music was "classical" and had been presented in the elitist tradition of many of the black musicians.

The *Negro Music Journal* was equally generous in its praise for Theodore Drury's New York opera company's production of *Aida* and *Faust*. Its news items followed the activities of black classical musicians, including Clarence Cameron White, Azalia Hackley, Flora Batson, Sidney Woodward, J. Rosamond Johnson, Melville Charlton, and Will Marion Cook, all graduates of the premier musical conservatories of the United States. Some had studied in Europe. "Blind Tom," a prodigy who could imitate any piano performance he had heard once, was praised as a musical phenomenon whose triumphs in the United States and abroad had brought him wide notice and a great deal of money. Taylor had no praise for ragtime music. He wrote that it degraded Negroes, who were not wholly responsible for creating it or keeping it popular. He urged black music teachers to oppose all music that was not of a healthy nature, which, to him meant, classical.

Taylor joined with other musicians in the black community of Washington to establish the Washington Conservatory of Music. In an editorial published in the journal's second year, Taylor wrote:

It gives the *Negro Music Journal* an inexpressible amount of pleasure to announce to the world that there exists in Washington, D.C., a conservatory of music. It has been the heart's wish of the *Negro Music Journal* to see our people stretch forth their arms and take widespread interest in the uplifting of their communities.[5]

From that time, the periodical carried on its masthead: "The Official Organ of the Washington Conservatory of Music." It seemed particularly fortuitous for the enterprise that it could advertise in its own magazine. However, the promise did not materialize. Reasons for the journal's demise are not clear, but it ceased publication after little more than a year and soon after it became a part of the conservatory.

Notes

1. "Editorial," *Negro Music Journal* (September 1902): 4.
2. "Editorial," *Negro Music Journal* (May 1903): 3.
3. Music magazines of the period, inclusive of the *Negro Music Journal*, were essentially devoted to the music of Europe and to those composers in the United States who

worked in the European tradition. *Etude*, one of the most popular of the group in the United States, included complete compositions in each issue.

4. *Negro Music Journal* (April 1903): 4.

5. Quoted in Doris E. McGinty, "The Washington Conservatory of Music and School of Expression," *Black Perspective in Music* (Spring 1979): 63.

Information Sources

BIBLIOGRAPHY:

Coleridge-Taylor, Avril. *The Heritage of Samuel Coleridge-Taylor*. London, 1979.

Janffer, Ellsworth. "Samuel Coleridge-Taylor in Washington." *Phylon*, Spring 1967, pp. 185-96.

Simms, L. Moody, Jr. "Clarence Cameron White: Violinist, Composer, Teacher." *Negro History Bulletin*, October/November/December 1980, pp. 95-96.

Terry, William E. *"The Negro Music Journal*: An Appraisal." *Black Perspective in Music*, Fall 1977, pp. 146-60.

INDEX SOURCES: None.

LOCATION SOURCES: Greenwood Press Periodicals; Moorland-Spingarn Collection, Howard University, Washington, D.C.

Publication History

MAGAZINE TITLE AND TITLE CHANGES: *Negro Music Journal.*

VOLUME AND ISSUE DATA: Vols. I-II (September 1902-November 1903), monthly.

PUBLISHER AND PLACE OF PUBLICATION: J. Hillary Taylor, Washington, D.C.

EDITOR: J. Hillary Taylor (1902-1903).

CIRCULATION: 500 estimate.

Addison W. Reed

NEGRO SOUTH, THE

The *Negro South* superseded *Sepia Socialite*, a weekly newspaper published in New Orleans about its Negro population, beginning in 1937. In 1946, Alonzo B. Willis, Jr., its editor-publisher, converted *Sepia Socialite* into a monthly news and opinion magazine that extended its coverage to national black institutions, personalities, and issues. It also focused on Negro figures in Louisiana history, particularly during the Reconstruction period. The magazine was a strong supporter of the NAACP and other black advancement movements, although its tone was conservative in terms of most black general-purpose periodicals. Willis reflected his attitude toward the South, the Negro and the post-World War II American scene in the first editorial he wrote for the magazine.

The Negro South comes into being under the inspiration of a South-wide awakening among Negroes that is everywhere evident. Negro business, coming into its own on a basis of competitive merit and a "buy from me because I'm black" sentimentality, is a definite step ahead. The prosperous war years and government's subsidies have lifted the standard of living among us to the extent that small Negro businesses, having accumulated a little capital, have invested in better facilities, improved and enlarged stocks, cafes, barber shops or what have you, have brightened their corner into needed perspicuity. Gone are the "hole in the wall" excuses for businesses of the pre-war years. Systems and organizations have supplanted the hit-and-miss, try-if-you-can uncertainty of a few years past....Negroes have in the prosperity period indulged a passion for home-owning. Thousands throughout the South bought a piece of ground and are now building and equipping homes, no longer to be at the mercies of the landlord....These are the fundamental things that make for mass progress and respect.[1]

The *Negro South* was a part of that "rising tide of Negro progress in the South," the editor explained. This was the essence of life in the South at the close of World War II. The new magazine promised to seek to interpret and portray this new and upward trend. It would do so with the support of fair-minded blacks and whites who had become ashamed "of the political, economic and social disgraces heaped upon the glorious, sunny South by sundry forces of ill-will." The editor promised that the *Negro South* would reflect the positive nature of the South. This editorial position did not exclude cogent observations about some dilemmas facing blacks in the 1940s. Hazel Scott, the boogie-woogie pianist who moved from night clubs to concert halls as an artist, pleased the editor when she announced that she would not perform before segregated audiences. And Lena Horne won his praise for refusing to play the role of a prostitute in *St. Louis Woman*, which was written by two black authors, Arna Bontemps and Countee Cullen.[2] Another editorial attributed a race riot in Columbia, Tennessee, to "long-prevailing, cankerous social and economic disparities that must be resolved in democratic equality if we would end not only race riots but race wars." The editor quoted Lester B. Granger, executive secretary of the National Urban League, who had warned recently that social disharmony in America was more acute than at any time since the Civil War.[3]

Despite the South's social problems, the periodical's editorials did not advocate wholesale migration North as a solution. It took issue with Harlem's colorful, militant Adam Clayton Powell, who, in his own *People's Voice* newspaper had advised southern blacks to move to the urban North. The editorial called Powell's argument "a labyrinth of inconsistencies and poor logic."[4] Publishing Powell's comments in *Negro South* drew attention from black and white readers. One wrote:

I think your article on Rev. Powell is terrible. You do not understand him....I am from the South and I had never seen a library until I came here. I did not know about a park to rest or relax in nor a nice free school.... You are jealous or have no race pride.... There is no need to get mad but do something to help the Negroes who are suffering on the farms. In New York I know how he (Powell) worked to get us jobs and a Negro should be the last person to try to pull him down. Shame on you. I expect to visit your city and talk to you face to face.[5]

But that response was atypical. Some fifty newspapers—black and white—in the North and in the South reprinted the editorial. *Reader's Digest* considered using it. Most periodicals supported *Negro South*'s positions that southern Negroes had every right to remain in their birthplace if they wished to do so. The editor reported that his "Stay South, Work, Save, and Own" campaign brought an increase of 5,000 to the circulation of the journal. Ideologically, *Negro South* was compatible with Booker T. Washington's "Cast down your buckets where you are" philosophy. The editor used Washington's slogan often and made for himself and his magazine a similar catchword: "If you live in the South, boost the South—the Negro South."[6]

Although the magazine was not militant after the fashion of Congressman Powell, it was in no way passive about social injustice. Its editorials and feature articles never ceased to expose and attack racial injustice. It served as a newspaper for many blacks who had migrated from the New Orleans area into the North and West. It also carried news about social and religious activities throughout Louisiana. Editor and publisher Alonzo H. Willis had been a high school teacher in Monroe, Louisiana, and coeditor of the *Monroe Broadcast* and the *Negro in Louisiana* before he and his wife established the New Orleans periodicals. He was reasonably successful, especially in securing articles from time to time written for his journal by such leading black personalities as Mary McLeod Bethune, George S. Schuyler, and Charles S. Thompson. Although the magazine published some fiction, it was not distinctive. Willis died in December 1946. His wife continued publication of the *Negro South* throughout the following year, but it became clear that its founder had been its vital force. It ceased publication a year after his death.

Notes

1. *Negro South* (January 1946): 2.
2. *Negro South* (May 1946): 4. *St. Louis Woman* is a musical adaptation of Arna Bontemps' novel *God Send Sunday* (1931), the story of a black jockey. Randolph Edmonds, a professor of drama at Dillard University in New Orleans, wrote "Should Artists Become Race Leaders?" for *Negro South* (February 1946): 7-9. He noted that in refusing to play the role of Della Green, the prostitute in the musical, Lena Horne followed the advice of the NAACP, whose leadership believed the part would demean her and the race. The musical drama is built upon the actions of carefree primitive blacks whose lifestyle was felt to be antithetical to racial uplift activities. Cullen died before he could witness a performance of the play.
3. *Negro South* (March 1946): 4.

4. "Negro Labor, the Race Problem and Our Editorial Policy," *The Negro South* (April 19467): 4.

5. "Pros and Cons on Negro Migration North," *Negro South* (May 1946): 4.

6. "In Conclusion," *Negro South* (July 1946): 4, 23.

Information Sources

BIBLIOGRAPHY:
Boone, Dorothy Deloris. "A Historical Review and a Bibliography of Selected Negro Magazines, 1910-1969." Ph.D. dissertation, University of Michigan, 1970, pp. 109-10.

Editorials in the *Negro South* without specific titles: January 1946, pp. 2, 6; March 1946, pp. 4, 35; April 1946, pp. 4, 42; May 1946, pp. 4, 16.

"Getting Along." *Negro South*, November 1946, p. 33.

"How to Destroy Prejudice." *Negro South*, December 1946, pp. 4, 33.

INDEX SOURCES: None.

LOCATION SOURCE: Schomberg Collection, New York Public Library.

Publication History

MAGAZINE TITLE AND TITLE CHANGES: *The Negro South*

VOLUME AND ISSUE DATA: Vols. I-X (July 1937-December 1947), monthly. Volume numbers carried over from *Sepia Socialite*.

PUBLISHER AND PLACE OF PUBLICATION: Alonzo B. Willis, Jr., New Orleans, Louisiana.

EDITORS: Alonzo B. Willis, Jr., editor and publisher (July 1937-December 1946); Alden W. Bynum (January 1947-February 1947); Leon L. Lewis (March 1947-July 1947).

CIRCULATION: 8,500 estimate.

Charles E. Holmes

NEGRO STORY: A MAGAZINE FOR ALL AMERICANS

In 1944 Alice C. Browning placed in the first issue of *Negro Story*—a black "little" magazine that was numbered among the many literary publications of the forties—"A Letter to Our Readers." She and her coeditor, Fern Gayden, had been attempting to improve their writing techniques and to express themselves through the short story for a long time. They became aware that many black Americans needed a market for their efforts at creative writing. "At this point, *Negro Story* was conceived," she wrote, "and quickly the machinery was started which would bring it to you." Like so many of its predecessors and contemporaries, *Negro Story* was born to provide a publishing outlet for black writers and to fill the needs of readers who, the editor claimed, were hungering for stories about Negroes who are real people "rather than the types usually seen in print." She reported that black servicemen overseas had written to request this kind of reading material. Moreover, the editors noted that the black writer had not achieved the same degree of maturity black artists enjoyed in other fields such as music and the fine arts. *Negro Story* did not wish to restrict its content to works written by blacks. It welcomed contributions from the increasing number of white fiction writers who portrayed the Negro sympathetically and honestly. The editors also felt a strong responsibility to contribute to racial integration and the realization of the national purposes in World War II. From Chicago, then, came a black literary magazine that was almost totally dedicated to publishing the short story.

The first issue represents an impressive successful response to the editors' call for manuscripts. Some writers had already gained national reputations. Gwendolyn Brooks, who had won the Midwestern Writers Award for poetry a year earlier, submitted a short sketch titled "Chicago Portraits." Richard Wright, at the time easily the most important name in the circle of black fiction writers by virtue of his *Native Son*, permitted *Negro Story* to publish a reprint of his "Almos' a Man." Nick Aaron Ford, author of the *Contemporary Novel* and editor of the *Southwestern Journal* published at Langston University in Oklahoma, contributed a poem, as did Lieutenant William Couch from "Somewhere in the Pacific." Lillian Smith, George Schuyler, Vernon Loggins, J. Saunders Redding, and Roi Ottley—all well-known figures in the American literary and intellectual world—joined editors of *Opportunity** and *Phylon** in expressing best wishes and promising cooperation with the new venture.

In their "Letter to the Readers" published in the second issue of *Negro Story*, the editors became explicit in describing the kinds of fiction they wanted for the magazine. They called for stories that would help to eradicate some of the stereotypes in American thinking concerning the Negro. They recognized the large problems of focus the writer faced who attempted to write about the black American, and they urged young writers to study story techniques in order to present effectively the wealth of dramatic material available to them.

Beginning with the second issue of *Negro Story*, Chester Himes began publishing his fiction in the journal and continued to do so throughout most of its life. He had already contributed short fiction to *Abbott's Monthly*,* the *Chicago Defender*, *Esquire*, *Coronet*, *Crossroad*, and *Crisis*,* and had recently won a Rosenwald Fellowship to assist in writing a novel.[1] Ralph Ellison—then in the Merchant Marine—had already been managing editor of *Harlem Quarterly** and had published stories in *Common Ground*, *New Masses*, *American Stuff*, and *Negro Digest*.*[2] Langston Hughes' poems, some short fiction, and a short play, *Private Jim Crow*, appeared in the journal. Margaret Walker and Gwendolyn Brooks, destined to become household names in American letters, wrote poetry for *Negro Story*. Hughes, Ellison, Himes, and Ford were appointed directors of the magazine as a strategy for encouraging them to permit reprints of their works from other magazines, or to submit stories for first printing.

Through its literary contests, *Negro Story* generated some short fiction from students in American colleges and universities that was suitable for publication. Its policy of including American writing by white and black authors during the World War II years contributed to the success of the short-lived but vital *Negro Story*. Much of the writing focuses on the war and the nation's crisis of conscience, particular with respect to its posture on race relations. An excerpt from a letter included in the final issue probably reflects some reasons for the cessation of the journal as well as for its appeal.

> I am sorry I am unable to give substantial donation to your valiant effort to publish *Negro Story*. I have been in the magazine publishing business, and I know what a difficult task it is. However, I hope *Negro Story* all the success in the world. Plug away! Your magazine is an oasis in the desert. I also like it because it *avoids propaganda* and recognizes that art transcends race, creed and dogma.[3]

Negro Story was an integrationist journal that began publication at a time when more and more black creative writers were placing their work in white periodicals. Their editors wanted "light, entertaining" fiction that did not explore tensions of the black American experience. *Negro Story* sought to attract and publish stories by and about Negroes that were incompatible with the general American taste for "local color" and sentimentality. World War II had enjoyed the interests and talents of black writers. Some new voices joined those remaining from the Harlem Renaissance period. The journal published works of both. It introduced short stories and poetry written by Richard Bentley, Frank Marshall Davis, Margaret Burroughs, and Shirley Graham. Langston Hughes contributed several poems, including "Madamme to You" and "The Queer Duck." Like many little magazines that had preceeded it, *Negro Story* existed briefly. It is, however, a representation of the early work of some black writers who became prominent in American letters.

Notes

1. Chester Himes did not write his popular novels until several years later. He placed in *Negro Story* a number of short stories: "He Seen It in the Stars," (July August 1944): 5-9; "Let Me at the Enemy—an' George Brown," (December-January 1944-45): 9-18; "A Penny for Your Thoughts," (March-April 1945): 14-17; "My But the Rats are Terrible," (May-June 1945): 24-32; "Make with the Shape," (August-September 1945): 3-6; "A Night of New Roses," (December-January 1945-46): 10-14; and "One Way to Die," (April-May 1946): 10-14.

2. Ralph Ellison was developing his skill as a short story writer at the time he contributed works to *Negro Story*. Several were reprinted from other publications. During his association with the journal, he contributed the following short stories: "Mister Toussan," (July-August 1944): 37-41; "Mr. Toussaint," (October-November 1944): 3-11; "Afternoon," (March-April 1943): 3-8; and "The Birthmark," (May-June 1945): 20-23.

3. The excerpt is from a letter written by Fenton Johnson, a minor black poet who published The *Champion Magazine: A Monthly Survey of Negro Achievement* in Chicago from September 1916 to April 1917.

Information Sources

BIBLIOGRAPHY:
Boone, Dorothy Delores. "A Historical Review and a Bibliography of Selected Negro Magazines, 1910-1969." Ph.D. dissertation, University of Michigan, 1970.
Browning, Alice C. "A Letter to Our Readers." *Negro Story*, May-June 1944, p. 1.
Milliken, Stephen F. *Chester Himes: A Critical Appraisal*. Columbia, Mo., 1976.
INDEX SOURCES: None.
LOCATION SOURCES: Atlanta Public Library; Fisk University Library; Greenwood Press Periodicals.

Publication History

MAGAZINE TITLE AND TITLE CHANGES: *Negro Story: A Magazine for all Americans*.
VOLUME AND ISSUE DATA: Vols. I-II, no. 3 (May-June 1944-April-May 1946), bimonthly.
PUBLISHER AND PLACE OF PUBLICATION: Negro Story Magazine, Chicago, Illinois.
EDITOR: Alice C. Browning (1944-1946).
CIRCULATION: 1,000 estimate.

NEW DAY, THE

George Baker, better known as Father Divine, began publication and distribution of the *New Day* as the weekly periodical of his Peace Mission Movement 3 January 1937. It continued publication in Harlem until 21 January 1943, serving as the sacred text for followers of the movement. In this respect, the *New Day* is unique among black periodicals. Members of the cult referred to the magazine rather than to the Bible when they wished to speak with authority about the world and the work of Father Divine. The *New Day* was read at all meetings of the groups throughout the nation. It contained the many speeches delivered by Father Divine and many facts and announcements for his followers. It superseded the *Spoken Word*, a pamphlet that carried Divine's speeches and a few advertisements for various small businesses operated by members.[1] By 1940, *New Day* issues carried as many as 125 to 130 pages and some 350 advertisements from such firms as F. W. Woolworth, Loft Candy, Fuller Brush, McCrory Five and Ten Cent Stores, and Lerner Shops. Every advertisement includes within its text the injunction, "Peace!" Frequently "Thank you, Father," was added. For some of the nationally established firms mentioned above to cast their advertisement in terms of the language of the Peace Mission Movement indicates the strength of Father Divine and his following in the major cities of the United States.

Although the Divine movement was basically religious, contents of the *New Day* were socially dynamic and repeatedly attacked racial discrimination. Father Divine refused to use racial designations in any of his speeches, but the *New Day* abounds with headlines to the effect that the American Red Cross announced that only white doctors were eligible for the Doctors-for-Britain project at the height of the London blitz by the German Luftwaffe; that the United States Navy would only accept black applicants for mess attendants; and that Curtiss Wright, one of the largest aircraft industries at the time, would not employ blacks.[2]

The *New Day*'s authority came from the unquestioned belief among his followers that Father Divine was God and that his word was binding and sacred. A common aspect of the rationale his followers used as the basis of their allegiance may be found in a comment made by one of the members of the cult.

> People have been talking about God for many years, but today, a God whom you can't see or never have any personal contact with just doesn't fill the bill. The promise of some home far beyond the clouds, with milk and honey flowing freely, really isn't what it takes to keep going down here, on terra firma. If God can't take care of me here and now, then how can I know or even believe He'll do so very much after I'm dead and gone. . . . Now, all in all, I ask you, what more of a God do you want, than one who'll give you shelter, food to eat, clothes to wear and freedom from sickness, worry and fear? Now isn't that wonderful![3]

This concept of religion and the God upon whose strength and promise it is built was the essence of the *New Day* and the many speeches Father Divine published. The depression had ravished the land. Unemployment and hunger abounded. The Peace Mission Movement offered a positive self-image, necessary creature comforts, and—above all—a kind of spiritual religion which held that God was everywhere, everything, and everyone. It appealed to millions of black and white Americans. Their faith gave the *New Day* its high standing in the nation.

Aside from Divine's religious messages, the journal carried business reports of the movement's various enterprises. It did not neglect national and international affairs. "Righteous Government News" reported on members of the cult and their accomplishments as examples of rectitude and the rewards of thrift, cleanliness, and high morality that Divine demanded of his followers.

In January 1938, Senator Allan J. Ellander of Louisiana launched a vicious attack on the antilynching bill that was before the Congress. He made references to Father Divine as an example of disruptive forces among blacks in the United States that had to be curbed and would run rampant if the states did not exercise some rights of community control. Divine responded in the *New Day* with his "Righteous Government Platform for Peace Mission." It was a simple affirmation of the rights of men to live peacefully in a democracy.

The Peace Mission was able to combine religious ferver with a sense of community to attend to the social ills of the depression era in a way not possible previously or since in American society. Father Divine succeeded, to a large measure, where Marcus Garvey had failed just a few years earlier.[4]

Father Divine had many encounters with the federal government and with law enforcement officers. As the Great Depression waned and the efficient cause for the Peace Mission Movement and its social service work gave way to a wartime prosperity in the wake of the United States' involvement in World War II, the *New Day* ceased publication. It served during its life as one seminal set of records of pragmatic religious cultism in the United States and of official attempts to curb the influence of a nonconventional religious-political force among blacks. The magazine, by serving almost exclusively as Divine's medium of expression, gives the essence of his movement and the unique style of his leadership.

Notes

1. The *World-Herald* and the *New Day* were the movement's weekly magazines after the semiweekly *Spoken Word* was discontinued. The kingdom's newspaper, the *New York News*, was published thereafter every Saturday.

2. Announcements of this kind were considered typical of Divine's comments in the *Spoken Word*, and the *New Day*. *See* Hart M. Nelsen, Raytha L. Yokley, and Anne K. Nelsen, eds., *The Black Church in America* (New York, 1971), pp. 175-93 for other examples.

3. Ibid., p. 178.

4. Garvey's Universal Negro Improvement Association had captured Harlem and many black Americans in other parts of the nation in the early 1920s. Garvey had emphasized black beauty and strength rather than inferiority, but he advised Afro-Americans to flee the United States and return to Africa. He was deported to his native Jamaica in 1927 as an undesirable alien after having served part of a prison term received for mail fraud. President Calvin Coolidge pardoned him in 1927. Divine, just a few weeks later, advocated first-class citizenship for Negroes in the United States and interracial peace and goodwill. *See* John Hope Franklin, *From Slavery to Freedom: A History of Negro Americans*, 3d ed. (New York, 1969), pp. 490-93, for some details of the contrast between the two black leaders.

Information Sources

BIBLIOGRAPHY:

Cantril, Hadley, and Sherif, Muzefer. "The Kingdom of Father Divine." *Journal of Abnormal and Social Psychology* 3 (1938): 147-67.

Fauset, Arthur Huff. *Black Gods of the Metropolis: Negro Religious Cults in the Urban North*. Philadelphia: University of Pennsylvania Press, 1944, pp. 52-67.

"5,000 Divinites Throng Meeting of Righteous Government." *New York Age*, 18 January 1936, p. 1.

Hashor, John. *God in A Rolls Royce: The Rise of Father Divine—Madman, Menace, or Messiah*. Freeport, N.Y.: Books for Libraries Press, 1971, pp. 68-70.

Parker, Robert Allerton. *The Incredible Messiah: The Deification of Father Divine.*
    Boston: Little, Brown, and Company, 1937, pp. 3-14.
INDEX SOURCES: None.
LOCATION SOURCES: Library of Congress; Tuskegee Institute, Tuskegee, Alabama.

Publication History

MAGAZINE TITLE AND CHANGES: *The New Day.*
VOLUME AND ISSUE DATA: Vols. I-VII, no. 3 (3 January 1937-21 January 1943).
PUBLISHER AND PLACE OF PUBLICATION: David Kiad, publisher and manager,
    New York, New York.
EDITOR: David Kiad (1937-1943).
CIRCULATION: 100,000 estimate.

NEW DAY: THE PEOPLE'S MAGAZINE

W. D. Dunlap began publishing *New Day: The People's Magazine* in Kansas
City, Missouri, in August 1947 with what he called a dedication to the proposi-
tion that each day was a new creation, and that the individual and the community
could be integrated into a national being that was international in planning and
action. Two premises were evident: war is inevitable, and peace is possible. This
post-World War II stance recognized that the world was not at peace, although
the military conflict had ended. "Peace or war is in man's everyday contact with
men," the lead editorial in the first issue stated. *New Day* would use for a
hallmark the symbol of a new beginning of desirable human relations. As a
general-purpose journal, *New Day* pursued the need and the status of community
improvement throughout the years of its publication. It was not unusually vociferous in setting forth any particular political position, although its editor did not
hesitate to comment on the 1948 presidential campaign. Its editorials were liberal
to the extent that they rejected extreme conservative or radical political philosophies and activities. As a black periodical, it championed the causes of Afro-
Americans, both in editorial analysis and in its features. It was not politically
partisan; yet it was not a bland publication.[1]

"The Lunatic Fringe" raised essential questions about high postwar prices of
goods and services. It agreed that wartime production needed inflated prices, but
it called for some economic plan that would be geared to an increasingly technolog-
ical civilization. "Like other good Americans, we would abhor the regimentation
and discipline of Communism, but we believe that with our literate populace and
our wealth of national resources we can work out some democratic system that
would guarantee almost every American a comfortable living in a fairly stabi-
lized economy," Dunlap wrote to further explain his thesis.[2] He ridiculed Congress for its failure to bring the Federal Employment Practices Commission Act
to the floor and argued that such a law was enforceable and essential for the

general welfare. He challenged the government to show the same concern for relief of its own needy that it had shown in establishing and executing the Marshall Plan to rehabilitate Europe at the close of the war. Dunlap related domestic inflation which had outlasted the war economy to the nation's responsibility to insure the highest level of employment possible to its citizens. He wrote that elected officials whose duty it is to know when to shift from the foreign to the domestic scene should do so since it is they who say how, where, and when the American dollar is spent. These national priorities seemed more important to Dunlap than the ideological struggle between elements of the Democratic party that were dividing themselves along conservative and liberal lines, resulting in the organization of Henry Wallace's Progressive party which sought to wrest the White House from incumbent Democrat Harry Truman.

In "Henry Wallace and the Third Party," a *New Day* editorial provided an impressively sound summary of conditions that gave rise to third parties in American history and how their candidates fared at the polls. The editor praised Wallace, the Progressive party nominee in the presidential campaign of 1948, and severely criticized those who called him a Communist. "Almost anyone who believes that Negroes are entitled to equality and first-class citizenship, that labor's rights should be protected, that friendly relations might be established with Russia is called a Red or a Fellow Traveler," he wrote.[3] And he agreed that Wallace could not possibly win the election, largely because influential sources would prevent him from doing so. But the *New Day* did not consider a vote for Wallace a wasted vote. Instead, his supporters typified serious signs of the times. They were registering the protest vote of the minority and establishing a safeguard against future dangers. Each action was necessary.

Dunlap's editorials consistently delineated superficial understanding of communism as a national menace to the country and the need for a social consciousness that would initiate for Americans certain creative social innovations. He wrote that the issue of communism had done the United States irreparable injury by setting back "the hands of social and economic progress for, perhaps, two decades." Race relations, interdenominational understandings, progressive labor legislation, and public health and housing had suffered because of the Red Scare, and the United States as a whole was the loser. Through this provocative approach, the *New Day* complained bitterly about the "Red" label that was used to frustrate advancement of social progress that arose in the war years.[4] Ironically, this attempt to maintain the status quo permitted the real Communists to go about their "regimented, rigidly planned, terrible disciplined affairs," while perpetrators of the scare tactics remained blissfully unaware of the harm the country was suffering.

Dunlap accused both Harry Truman and Thomas Dewey, candidates for president on the Democratic and Republican tickets, respectively, of "beating the Red tom-tom." They seemed to him to believe that being against communism was all the country needed. "Nobody wants Communism except Communists, and, by liberal estimate, there is only one Communist for every 104 thousand persons in the United States," the editor estimated. But by urging hatred of Communists through propositions like the Mundt-Nixon bill, the United States's policymakers were, whether they knew it or not, doing what Hitler did to Germany. The real issues were prices of goods, housing, and fair employment. No smoke screens could hide them.[5]

New Day editorials supported Harry Truman in his confrontation with General Douglas MacArthur and attacked James Byrnes of South Carolina and Eugene Talmadge of Georgia for their threats to abolish public schools rather than integrate them. In its indictment of Democrats and Republicans for failing to support civil rights proposals beyond election campaign speeches, the *New Day* urged its audience to separate Truman's good decisions from his bad ones. In doing so, one would conclude that the president had been consistent in his fight for a fair deal for Negroes. Even though none of his civil rights programs had yet been enacted into law, Truman had called attention regularly to the need to insure first-class citizenship for all Americans. "We predict," an editorial read, "that when the political clouds have been cleared away and an unbiased evaluation of Harry Truman's administration has been made, he will take his niche in the history of our nation beside such men as Washington, Lincoln, and Jackson."[6]

Dunlap anticipated the breakthrough into improved opportunities and general citizenship status for blacks. He called for direct action to advance these goals. He rebuked northern Negroes for not voting when they had the opportunity, and supported A. Philip Randolph for his insistence upon nonsegregated armed forces. He chided blacks who believed their progress had been dramatic by reminding them that during the last decade Negroes had been thoroughly integrated into big league baseball and there was partial integration in some colleges and universities. But these minor advances were no cause for rejoicing. Dunlap used his magazine to remind blacks that despite the Supreme court ruling against restrictive covenants in housing and closed political primaries, housing, voting, travel, and accommodation in public enterprises remained unavailable to many of them.

The *New Day* reported regularly on national and international affairs; however, it focused its attention on black interests. "Stage and Screen" contained a wealth of news items, impressions, and vignettes about motion pictures featuring black actors and black plots. This feature also provided a valuable source of information on blacks in films. Stories about collegiate and professional athletes and athletic competition also appeared regularly. "Sports and Sportsmen" included unusually significant data on the Kansas City Monarchs, an all-black baseball team that employed players including Jackie Robinson and Sachel Page. Sherman D. Savage, a history professor at Lincoln University in Jefferson City, Missouri, contributed several articles growing out of his research on the Negro in the West. The magazine included in each issue some creative writing. Among works contributed were some by Octavia B. Wynbush, a Kansas City public schoolteacher, who also published short fiction in the *Crisis** and *Opportunity.**

The *New Day* never became a national magazine. Its audience was limited primarily to Missouri and the surrounding area, and its advertisements promoted Kansas City businesses.

Notes

1. "The American Way," *New Dawn* (June 1951): 34.
2. *New Day* (November 1947): 26.
3. *New Day* (March 1948): 30.
4. "Smoke Screens," *New Day* (September 1945): 27.
5. Ibid.
6. "Harry Truman Consistent in His Fight for Fair Deal to Negro," *New Dawn* (July 1952): 33.

Information Sources

INDEX SOURCES: None.
LOCATION SOURCES: Some college and university libraries.

Publication History

MAGAZINE TITLE AND TITLE CHANGES: *New Day* (August 1947-November 1949); *New Dawn* (December 1949/January 1950-July 1953).
VOLUME AND ISSUE DATA: *New Day*, Vols. I-II (August 1947-November 1949); *New Dawn*, Vols. II-III (December 1949-July 1953). Monthly; bimonthly, July/ August 1948 and December 1949/1950.
PUBLISHER AND PLACE OF PUBLICATION: W. D. Dunlap, Kansas City, Missouri.
EDITOR: W. D. Dunlap (1947-1953).
CIRCULATION: 1,000 estimate.

NEW NEGRO TRAVELER AND CONVENTIONEER, THE

Urgent necessity gave rise to Clarence M. Markham, Jr.'s, establishing a guide for black American travelers in 1942. Its present title, *New Negro Traveler and Conventioneer*, was established in 1944 in Chicago and continues to the present. Markham was a steward on a New York Central Railroad parlor car in 1944 when he began to publish *Negro Traveler*. He had been a railroad news agency manager and came to feel that a monthly publication about the problems and experiences of black Americans working in the transportation industry would be profitable. Within a short time, his original publication gained strong recognition. It had over 70,000 controlled circulation monthly and was received by black travel agencies, organizations and offices planning conventions and conferences, and restaurants and taverns.

The success of the venture was the result of hard work on the part of the Markham family, but the social conditions of the nation affected the need for such a publication more than any one single factor. Blacks who traveled about the country by automobile were routinely discriminated against in hotel and motel accommodation in the South and other portions of the United States. Black boarding houses and menial hotels existed in some areas but they were restricted largely to the larger cities. Private travelers needed some guidance with respect to places to find lodging and food as they traveled about the country. Railroad crews, in particular, needed places to sleep and eat as they spent time between train services in towns away from their homes. The convention arrangement function of the magazine was secondary, although today it is a large part of the emphasis. Black social, religious, professional, and fraternal organizations have tended to use the few black travel agencies in the nation whenever possible, largely out of painful memories of the days when accommodations were hardly possible and never assured anywhere.

Interestingly, journalism historians seem to consider that the *New Negro Traveler and Conventioneer* has always been principally a travel agency publication. Markham has enlarged upon his original purpose. The Civil Rights Act of 1964 was the most far-reaching and comprehensive law in support of racial equality ever enacted by Congress.[1] It gave the attorney general additional power to protect citizens against discrimination and segregation in voting, education, and the use of public facilities. It forbade discrimination in most places of public accommodation and established a federal Community Relations Service to help individuals and communities solve civil rights problems. Until that time black Americans had little comfort in traveling by personal conveyance about the country. *Negro Traveler* and other publications like it were practically a necessity. It is fortuitous that Markham's magazine has led to an unusual and highly successful black business enterprise that has maintained the publication, which has changed its function somewhat as public accommodation has become available for black and white Americans.

Largely because the *New Negro Traveler and Conventioneer* relates to the multimillion dollar travel and convention and leisure activities of black Americans, it has attracted a high percentage of advertisement from such firms as Chrysler Corporation and Encyclopedia Brittanica. The advertising world believes that the magazine serves a public untouched by white publications. A fairly recent study reported on a black marketing company's calculation that nearly half a billion dollars of the income of black Americans is annually spent on travel, and that half of that amount is spent by the more than three-quarters of a million blacks who attend at least one convention a year.[2] While there are other black travel agencies and travel guides, the *New Negro Traveler and Conventioneer* is the most popular and most successful of them all.

The magazine contains excellent material on the history of black men in American railroading, particularly the pullman porters, and waiters and porters on passenger boats. The journal covers the history of railroad work in general; the nostalgia as well as details of problems and economics. Markham wrote in the May/June 1979 issue of his magazine that American railroads and the United States Postal Service and federal government did more to bring about improvement in the black American's social condition and personal income than any other source of employment.

Six issues of the *New Negro Traveler and Conventioneer* in 1978-79 presented the history of the impact of the transportation industry on black economics and social standing.[3] "My Train, the Century," by Markham in the May/June 1978 issue is an excellent piece of American railroad romance that details his own experiences as a pullman car porter on the famed Twentieth Century Limited train, which ran from Chicago to the West Coast.

Other features in each issue view American cities from the perspective of black tourists. These pieces gave insight into places of interest and special convenience for black travelers. Editorials, titled "Foreword," cover a variety of subjects, including the status and future status of black Americans and the fate of the railroads. The magazine publishes some creative writing. It is a vital and comprehensive black journal which represents well the ingenuity of Clarence Markham and his family.

Notes

1. When Lyndon B. Johnson became the thirty-sixth president of the United States on 22 November 1963, he was quick to make known his strong support of civil rights legislation that his predecessor, John F. Kennedy, had projected. Five days after he took office he told Congress he wanted a civil rights bill passed at the earliest possible date. Unprecedented social unrest and agitation for first-class citizenship for Afro-Americans had been high on the nation's agenda since the late 1950s.

2. *See* Paul J. C. Friedlander, "Blacks are Ready to Travel, But—," *New York Times* (26 April 1970): 39, for discussion of these statistics.

3. A. Philip Randolph, one of the most capable and strongest black leaders of the twentieth century, rose to prominence primarily through his organization of the Brotherhood of Sleeping Car Porters which became a forceful political organization for civil rights as well as advances in working conditions for black Americans. *See* Jervis Anderson, *A. Philip Randolph: A Biographical Portrait* (New York, 1974) for pertinent facts about Randolph's life and career; and Theodore Kornweibel, Jr., *No Crystal Stair: Black Life and the Messenger, 1917-1928* (Westport, Conn.: Greenwood Press, 1975) for Randolph's involvement with the *Messenger*, a radical black magazine of the Harlem Renaissance years.

Information Sources

BIBLIOGRAPHY:

Franklin, John Hope. *From Slavery to Freedom: A History of Negro Americans*. 3d ed. New York, 1969, pp. 635-36.

Katz, Bill. and Richards, Berry G. *Magazines for Libraries*. 3d ed. New York, 1978, pp. 49-50.

Miles, Frank W. "Negro Magazines Come of Age." *Magazine World*, 2 July 1946, p. 12.

Wolseley, Roland E. *Black Press, U.S.A.* Ames: Iowa State University Press, 1971, pp. 148-49.

INDEX SOURCES: None.
LOCATION SOURCES: Moorland-Spingarn Collection, Howard University, Washington, D.C.: Library of Congress; University Microfilm International.

Publication History

MAGAZINE TITLE AND TITLE CHANGES: *The New Negro Traveler and Conventioneer.* Formerly *Negro Traveler: A Monthly Magazine of the Negro Transportation and Hotel World.*
VOLUME AND ISSUE DATA: Vols. I to present (November 1942-), monthly.
PUBLISHER AND PLACE OF PUBLICATION: Travelers Research Publishing Company, Incorporated, Chicago, Illinois.
EDITOR: Clarence M. Markham, Jr. (1942-).
CIRCULATION: 72,000.

NEW SOUTH

The Southern Regional Council was formed during the closing years of World War II by Southerners who wanted to practice the ideals Americans had fought for abroad. White and black leaders joined in the enterprise. Their organ of communication was the *Southern Frontier,** the precursor of *New South.* In 1946 the council launched a broader and more intensifed program for the South. The premier issue of *New South* expressed the council's new direction.

The change lies in this: that SRC will from now on strive to study and solve the problems implicit in those goals as parts—symptoms, if you like—of the overall problem of the South, which is the region's need to develop fuller use of its resources, both natural and human, through achieving a healthy balance between agriculture and industry in the region. The democratic corollary to this, of course, lies in the duty of every Southerner to see to it that such development, as it is achieved, is used wisely and shared fairly by all, for all. It is to this development and democratic shaping of the South's growth that SRC will give most of its effort.[1]

This cautious language is the way an interracial organization expressed its objectives at mid twentieth century. *New South* was not, strictly speaking, a black journal; however, it addressed interracial problems, cooperation between the races, and approaches to solutions. Its contributors included some of the best-known public figures among white and black Southerners. Black scholars and other leaders who wrote for the periodical and served on its editorial board from time to time included: Ira DeA. Reid, a popular sociologist at Morehouse College in Atlanta; Carter G. Woodson, founder of the Association for the Study of Negro Life and History; Harold Trigg when he was associate executive director of the Southern Regional Council; John H. Wheeler, president of the Farmers and Mechanics Bank in Durham, North Carolina; Albert W. Dent, president of Dillard University in New Orleans; and Rufus E. Clement, president of Atlanta University.

The first issue of the magazine carried two documents that were integral in the organization of the council. One was "The Durham Conference Statement," drawn up by a group of black leaders. It stated that "compulsory segregation is unjust," and it delineated specifics of reform in areas of political and civil rights, jobs, education, agriculture, military service, social welfare, and health. A group of white leaders met to respond to the Durham statement and issued the "Atlanta Statement." At Richmond, a committee of both groups was empowered to organize the Southern Regional Council. They set forth the following reason for its existence and published it in the journal.

> For the improvement of economic, civic and racial conditions in the South in all efforts toward regional and racial development; to attain through research and action programs the ideals and practices of equal opportunity for all peoples in the region; to reduce race tension, the basis of racial tension, racial misunderstanding and racial distrust; to develop and integrate leadership in the South on new levels of regional development and fellowship; and to cooperate with local, state and regional agencies on all levels in the attainment of the desired objectives.[2]

These efforts were the focus of *The New South.*

Inasmuch as many black members of the council were educators, the role of colleges in improving race relations was a frequent subject of articles. "How Negro Colleges Can Develop Racial Cooperation in the South" is unusual among discussions on this subject. In 1947, this article highlighted the unique nature of the black college with respect to interracial relations. The author wrote that the responsibility for discovering an interest that brings white and Negro Southerners together as coworkers rests mainly on the shoulders of educated southern Negroes. Whites in the region, the article noted, had already shown they were unwilling and incapable of developing this interest. Negro colleges were the only place in which the interest could be implemented. Whites and blacks had always worked together in educational enterprise at these institutions. Most had been founded by white missionaries, and even as blacks had come to staff and operate their own colleges, these institutions had always been integrated. Their faculties and students, alone among Southerners, had experienced working together in a common endeavor. Further, black persons who pursued graduate studies had gone afield of necessity to integrated northern universities and had been in interracial environments there. The author reasoned that these were reasons to expect black colleges to take the lead in fostering cooperation between the races in the South.

Other articles about the South address areas of industry, voting patterns, Negro history, the church, health, and veterans' affairs. These post-World War II emphases reflected the council's studies of the South and its place in the future of the nation. A special issue "Race and Suffrage in the South Since 1940," edited by Luther P. Jackson, a black professor of history at Virginia State College, explained poll tax, voter registration, and white party primaries with candor. Court decisions on integrating all-white graduate and professional schools in Arkansas, Delaware, Florida, Kentucky, Louisiana, Maryland, and Missouri appeared in the journal.

As social tensions grew in the late 1950s and early 1960s, *New South* became a reliable, comprehensive source of news and attitudes toward the national race problem and organized efforts to include blacks in the public fiber of the nation. The essential value of the magazine lies in its chronicle of that dramatic movement. One example among many of this focus is a report on a 1947 hearing before the Atlanta City Council on a resolution providing for the appointment of eight Negro policemen on a trial basis.

> On the evening of November 26, approximately one thousand persons crowded into a large courtroom in the police station on Decatur Street. On the dais at the front of the room sat the members of the Police Committee and the Mayor. The Chief of Police had taken his stand at one end of the platform, and policemen were stationed about the room. Negroes, who made up about one-fourth of the audience, occupied the rear section of the courtroom. On the whole, they were the quietest and most attentive of the spectators. White persons filled the other benches and the space along the walls. Some of them were there to support the resolution, but many more, easily a majority, were there to oppose it. There could be little claim that the white spectators formed a cross-section of Atlanta's white population. Most of them were residents of those sections of Atlanta where white and colored citizens have been in fierce competition for housing, and flare-ups of race tension were fresh in their minds.[3]

The article went on to describe the atmosphere of expectancy in the hearing. The chairman rapped for order and the hearing got under way. The first white spokesman for the resolution made his way to the front of the room. Amid loud jeering and calls of "What's his name? Make him tell his name!" the first of several witnesses described the record of Negro police in other southern cities.

This incident represents the kind of action through investigation, testimony, and group cooperation that the Southern Regional Council supported. It was a case of people coming together to hear facts about a possible approach to a public problem the community was facing. Urban communities in the South with large black populations were no longer content to leave law enforcement in the hands of white policemen. Conflict between the police and black Americans was clearly a widespread problem. The resolution brought before the Atlanta City Council was one of many that worked to integrate police forces with the practical goal of lowering the potential for confrontation with law enforcement officers in black communities. At the same time, these efforts brought blacks a sense of responsibility for the promotion of the general welfare and for finding meaningful employment.

This article and many like it bring into clear focus some part of the race hatred Southerners experienced in the late 1940s. The public posture and attitudes were a prelude for the civil rights activities that covered the nation a decade later. *New South* was no dramatic activist publication. Its purpose was study and report and discussion.

New South merged with the monthly *South Today* into a bimonthly, general-interest magazine with the title *Southern Voices*, beginning publication with the March/April 1974 issue. During the more than quarter of a century of its life, *New South* was a highly valuable depository of interracial views of the changing South throughout some of the most dynamic periods of the nation's history. Articles and studies in the 1960s discuss and describe the integration of white public and private colleges and universities in the South from the standpoint of both black and white educators and social scientists.

Notes

1. "Introduction," *New South* (January 1946): 1.
2. Ibid.
3. "Race Hatred Gets a Hearing," *New South* (December/January 1947-48): 7.

Information Sources

BIBLIOGRAPHY:
Bergman, Peter M. and Bergman, Mort N. *The Chronological History of the Negro in America*. New York, 1969, pp. 490, 514.
Franklin, John Hope. *From Slavery to Freedom: A History of Negro Americans*. 3d ed. New York, 1967, pp. 557, 569.
Neal, Ernest E. "How Negro Colleges Can Develop Racial Cooperation in the South." *New South*, December/January 1947-48, pp. 3-6, 12-14.
Wilkins, Josephine. "The Origin of the Southern Regional Council." *New South*, January 1964, pp. 22-26.
INDEX SOURCES: *Index to Selected Periodicals Decennial Cumulation 1950-1959; Public Affairs Information Service.*
LOCATION SOURCES: Atlanta University Library; Fisk University Library; Moorland-Spingarn Collection, Howard University, Washington, D.C.; Tuskegee Institute Library; Schomberg Collection, New York Public Library; Kraus-Thompson Reprints.

Publication History

MAGAZINE TITLE AND TITLE CHANGES: *New South* (January 1946-Fall 1973).

VOLUME AND ISSUE DATA: Vols. I-IV (January 1946-December 1949), monthly; vols. V-XXIII (January/February 1950-July/August 1968), bi-monthly; vol. XXVII, nos. 3 and 4 (Fall 1968-Fall 1973), quarterly.

PUBLISHER AND PLACE OF PUBLICATION: Southern Regional Council, Atlanta, Georgia.

EDITORS: No designated editor January 1946-May/June 1961; Margaret Lay (July/August 1961-Fall 1968); Robert E. Anderson (Winter 1968-Fall 1973).

CIRCULATION: 3,000.

─── O ───

OPPORTUNITY: A JOURNAL OF NEGRO LIFE

John T. Clark, the energetic and imaginative member of the Saint Louis branch of the National Urban League who later became its executive secretary, deserves unusual credit for founding *Opportunity*, the league's official magazine. Often called "the dean of Urban League men," Clark persistently called for such a publication. The *Urban League Bulletin* appeared in December 1921 with Charles S. Johnson, director of the Research and Investigation Department, as editor. The *Bulletin* served a limited purpose, but Clark and others pressed their demand for a formal publication with advertisements and second-class mailing privileges. The next year, at the organization's national conference in Pittsburgh, *Opportunity* was founded. Its first volume was issued 19 January 1923.[1] Johnson was its editor. The masthead carried the names of the league's officers: L. Hollingsworth Wood, Eugene Kinkle Jones, William H. Baldwin, and A. S. Prezell. The price was fifteen cents, and appearing directly under the title was the League's slogan, "Not Alms but Opportunity." Johnson's qualification to edit the social service organization's journal lay primarily in his having recently published his study of causes of the Chicago race riots, including recommendations for improving race relations.

Executive Secretary Eugene Kinkle Jones wrote the lead editorial, "Cooperation and Opportunity," for the first issue. He noted that the National Urban League sought to provide information on the Negro for white people in order to clear up mooted questions about the race and establish amicable working relations between the two groups. He wrote that the organization needed a formal publication, for although newspapers and magazines had provided generous space for the league's causes, reports on its investigations and research called for considerably more space than was available. Jones asked for *Opportunity* "wholehearted support and encouragement of all white and colored people who are interested in the scientific treatment of 'the problem' and who wish to see more 'cooperation' between the races."

The magazine's course had been set within a year. "It was a development of a small experimental project," wrote Johnson five years later, intended to present the league's research in readable articles that had not been available to the public before, and, at the same time, to provide a journal for black scholars who could not easily publish their works in general organs.[2]

But *Opportunity* was more than that. It pursued several basic functions: to publish studies and surveys the league commissioned in its Research and Investigation Department; to report to the nation and to its members the activities of the National Urban League; to foster a high quality of cultural production among "New Negroes"; and to provide, through invited articles and comprehensive news features, an intelligent awareness of black experiences in the United States and other parts of the world. The Carnegie Corporation contributed $8,000 for each of three years to help launch *Opportunity* and added funds to sustain the magazine for an additional two and a half years.

Articles appearing in the first issue suggested the scope of the League's focus. Their authors included S. Parkes Cadman, pastor of Center Congregational Church in Brooklyn; Edith Sampson, an investigator for the Illinois Children's Home and Aid Society; A. Clayton Powell, Sr., pastor of Harlem's Abyssinian Baptist Church; W. F. McClellan, a personnel manager at Westinghouse Electric and Manufacturing Company in Pittsburgh; J. O. Houze, a personnel manager at Malleable and Iron Castings Company of Cleveland; and Horace J. Bridges, leader of the Chicago Society for Ethical Culture. These names represented a wide scope of American business and industrial leaders, social workers, and clergymen. All these writers, black and white, participated in the intercultural purposes of the league; and *Opportunity*'s interracial character, as the organization's spokespiece, provided a breadth of viewpoint.

Opportunity's impact during Charles S. Johnson's tenure as editor lies primarily in its having served as a foster parent for the literary movement of the day. From the beginning it published book reviews, literary columns, and creative writing. Its writers' contest, begun in 1925, together with a similar project carried on by the *Crisis** (the official publication of the NAACP) literally made the writers of the "New Negro" period. Langston Hughes, Claude McKay, Angelina W. Grimke, and Eric D. Walrond contributed creative writing to early volumes of the magazine. Johnson's influence on the flowering of the literary renaissance began with his remarks at a meeting of the Writers' Guild 21 May 1924. A selected group of young black writers met to honor the appearance of Jessie Fauset's first novel, *There Is Confusion*. James Weldon Johnson, who had recently published his anthology of Negro verse; W.E.B. Du Bois, who was introduced as a representative of the "older school"; Walter F. White, whose *Fire in the Flint* had just been accepted for publication; Carol Van Doren, editor of *Century Magazine*; Alain Locke, "dean of the movement"; Countee Cullen; and Gwendolyn Bennett were among those who attended. Charles S. Johnson gave a brief interpretation of the guild's object.[3]

A few months later, editor Johnson announced the magazine's first literary contest.

> To stimulate creative expression among Negroes and to direct attention to the rich and unexploited sources of materials for literature in Negro life, *Opportunity* will offer prizes for short stories, poetry, plays, essays, and personal experience sketches to the amount of five hundred dollars. There will be three awards for each division. Further particulars about the contest and an announcement of the judges will appear in the September issue of this magazine.[4]

"There is an extreme usefulness for the cause of interracial goodwill as well as racial culture and American literature in interpreting the life and longings and emotional experiences of Negro people," Johnson wrote in a special editorial setting forth his own black aesthetic. The spirit of the New Negro lay at the heart of the form and substance of the magazine's literary effort. For, as Johnson continued, the old romantic Negro characters of fiction were admittedly passé, and the forward movement of the rest of the world had presented to the Negro writer a chance to replace the outworn "representations in fiction faithfully and, incidentally, to make themselves better understood."

General and particular purposes came into focus in the contest. It hoped to stimulate and encourage creative literary effort among Negroes; to locate and orient Negro writers of ability; to stimulate and encourage the reading of literature by both Negro and white authors about Negro life, not merely because they were Negro topics but because what they wrote *was* literature. It would foster a market for Negro writers and for literature for and about Negroes, and it would bring these writers into contact with the general world of letters to which they had been for the most part timid and inarticulate strangers. It would promote a type of writing that would shake itself free of deliberate propaganda and protest.[5]

This "aesthetic manifesto," seldom attributed to Johnson, comported well with the National Urban League's reason for being. Only such an organization could promote the aspirations of young writers effectively. Its interracial membership made possible personal contact for prize money, judges for the contests, and publication of young writers' work.[6] But it would not replicate restrictions of previous periods. It would, instead, mirror current Negro life accurately, and it would do no more than make a social statement. It would adhere to the conventions of literature. It would add a new, needed, and valid dimension to the literature of the United States. Black and white persons active and respected in the literary world would insure quality in the works. Surely, a contest conducted by such a publication and judged by persons of such caliber—offering not unsubstantial prizes in money and publication possibilities—provided validation for a thrust in the literary phase of the renaissance.

More than 700 single entries came in to the judges that first year. In the short story category, first prize went to John Matheus, a teacher of Romance languages at West Virginia State College; second prize to Zora Neale Hurston, already a contributor of fiction to *Opportunity* and a student of anthropology at Hunter College in New York; and third place to Eric D. Waldron, a free-lance writer whose work had appeared in *New Republic*, *Current History*, and *National Interpreter*. Perhaps the most interest centered upon the poetry competition. Langston Hughes, the rising young writer who became America's best-known black poet, took first prize; Countee Cullen second; and the two of them tied for third-rank honors. In the fall of the same year, Harper Brothers published Cullen's first collection of poems, *Color*.

In the November 1926 issue, Cullen began a brief but significant tenure as literary editor of the magazine. He was twenty-three years old at the time and had acquired an uncommon reputation for his poetry, which had appeared in several magazines, including earlier issues of *Opportunity*. When Johnson announced Cullen's appointment to the post, he wrote of the young writer and his role:

> Mr. Cullen is not merely a leading Negro poet, but ranks in the first magnitude of the younger American poets. His coming to *Opportunity* we regard as both fortunate and significant, a step virtually decreed by the demands of that awakening generation to which this magazine, in many of its interests, has consistently addressed itself. Mr. Cullen will select the poetry, and, in his office as assistant to the editor, counsel with that large and growing group of young writers of verse whose work is gradually breaking into light. His opinions on books and events of literary significance will appear regularly as a special new department, and there will be occasional articles and poetry from his pen.[7]

Cullen used "Dark Tower" as the title for his monthly column, and in it he wrote of current literary and musical works, particularly those that related to American blacks. He performed as literary critic.

Gwendolyn Bennett, a member of the art faculty at Howard University, wrote "Ebony Flute," a feature she referred to as "literary chit-chat," beginning with the August 1926 issue. It provides the only source for many notes on the history of literary events and persons during the late 1920s.

In September 1929 Charles S. Johnson left the editorship of *Opportunity* to become director of the Department of Social Science at Fisk University. He was succeeded by Elmer Anderson Carter, who had been executive secretary of National Urban League branches in Columbus, Ohio, Louisville, Kentucky, and Saint Paul, Minnesota. In his first editorial, the new editor pledged the same standards of excellence that had prevailed under Johnson, and he particularly promised to keep his charge "to the younger Negro artists who have freed themselves from a slave psychology and are striving to depict their race and its environment in fine drawings and paintings and in enduring sculpture and with beautiful words." He wrote that the artistic renaissance of the Negro was not a "transitory phenomenon induced by the superlative flattery of a bored and jaded white intelligentsia." It was, to him, the beginning of a mighty effort that would enrich the cultural life of the nation.[8]

Shortly after Johnson left *Opportunity*, "Ebony Flute" and "Dark Tower" disappeared. Sterling Brown, professor of English at Howard University and a regular contributor of reviews and some poems to *Opportunity*, became principal literary critic. His "Literary Scene: Chronicle and Comment" first appeared in January 1932 and continued with minor interruption for the next six years. Like Cullen, Brown had won a prize from *Opportunity*, for his essay "Roland Hayes." It had taken second prize in 1925. Brown became one of the most respected men of letters among the young black writers of the early twentieth century. His essays on the history of American literature and the black presence in it might well have been motivated by the training ground that *Opportunity* provided for him. E. Simms Campbell, a black cartoonist and illustrator who was associated with *Esquire Magazine* almost from its first issue until his death some thirty years later, also first came to the national public's attention through his work for *Opportunity*.[9]

During the depression of the 1930s, *Opportunity* concerned itself with the United States' involvement in Haiti, but its main interest lay in unemployment and labor. Several editorials noted unique aspects of the effect of the economic crisis upon Negroes. Because Negroes were largely unskilled workers, they lay on the critical fringes of national wage earners and had to compete unfairly with white persons who also migrated to the cities searching for jobs. The intensified racial conditions, brought about because of growing unemployment, mitigated against the Negro worker. T. Arnold Hill, who wrote a labor column for *Opportunity*, advocated picketing as a means of securing some advantage for the black worker during the Great Depression. He noted that in Chicago Negroes had begun systematically boycotting merchants who did not hire them. He believed they should extend the practice to quasi-public corporations as well. And to the claim that white employers failed to hire black workers because their customers would object to being served by them, Hill retorted, "If corporations listen to prejudice from white workers, is it not logical to ask that they respect the prejudice of Negroes?"[10] A few months later he was able to report that since friendly methods had failed to secure employment, blacks had resorted to intimidation, boycotts, and threats which had caused some white employers to capitulate for fear of losing business.

"Slowly even the most obtuse politicians are becoming aware of the potentiality of the Negro vote in the North," an *Opportunity* editorial observed as the presidential election of 1932 approached.[11] Census returns from Ohio, Michigan, New York, Pennsylvania, Missouri, New Jersey, Maryland, Indiana, and Illinois indicated that in the event of a fairly close election, the Negro vote could easily determine the outcome. The Negro was breaking away from his traditional loyalty to the Republican party, but the direction his vote would take in the future was not at all certain. In an attempt to determine that trend, the magazine conducted a poll of its readers and other Negroes throughout the country. Preliminary tabulation of 2,680 responses from four states indicated that Democratic party candidates would receive substantial support from Negro voters. Negroes would vote for Franklin D. Roosevelt for president largely because they knew he was a liberal on politics and economics. They reasoned he would be liberal in his racial views as well.

Opportunity gave more than passing interest to Communist party activities that were intended to gain support from Negroes. Kelly Miller thundered his opposition to any relationship between Negroes and communism. Loren Miller, a Los Angeles lawyer and sometime editor of the *California Eagle*, advocated significant alignment between Negroes and Communism:

Let's quit kidding ourselves. The good old days are gone. There is no security for the Negro intellectual. America had no place for him and his own people are too weak to provide for his welfare. He must make a choice. On one hand there is the outside possibility that he may get a sinecure in return for support of a system that is worse than bankrupt and rapidly reducing its own people to beggars. On the other hand there is the certainty that he can throw in his lot with the working class and aid in the battle for a new social order in which the Negro can control his own economic, and hence political destiny.[12]

Opportunity did not state an editorial position on communism, perhaps because the league's sources of support from national industrialists would hardly countenance one. Too, the magazine held high hopes that Roosevelt, if elected, would promulgate the National Urban League's social purposes. When President Roosevelt signed the Industrial Recovery Act of 1933, *Opportunity* hailed the legislation as significant because it conceded labor's right to collective bargaining and forbade coercing employees to sign "yellow dog" contracts in order to affiliate with company unions. Black workers, comprising 11 percent of the workers of the nation, could benefit immeasurably from the minimum wage and maximum work hours which the act regulated.

Opportunity did not consider the Harlem riots in the spring of 1935 racial disturbances in the strict sense of the term. Negroes, it claimed, living in so densely populated an area as Harlem, attacked merchants and their establishments along 125th Street largely in frustration. As hiring policies increasingly limited their employment opportunities, black persons living in the shadow of white-owned businesses realized that employers in their neighborhoods merely reflected strictures that prevailed throughout the city. When their attempts to redress their grievances through boycotts failed, Negroes resorted to destruction and damage to establishments that they believed frustrated their employment aspirations.

But other causes contributed to the unrest. By the time the Mayor's Commission on conditions in Harlem made its report, *Opportunity* was able to point out the unsatisfactory condition of public education in Harlem. Most public schools held two and even three sessions daily, beginning in some cases as early as 8:00 A.M. and running until 5:00 P.M. Forty to forty-five students were enrolled in the average elementary school class. Most physical plants were old, shabby, and unsanitary. Through its new school construction program, the federal government had planned to build 163 new schools in New York City, but of the $120,747,000 allocated for this purpose only $800,000 would be spent in Harlem.

New York City had devised a plan for implementing the new federal low-income housing projects that *Opportunity* considered good for Harlem and Brooklyn. However, about 1,500 families had applied for housing facilities that would accommodate only 500. Moreover, not all of those applying could qualify under the low-income formula. The promise of improved housing conditions was welcomed, but the editor lamented what he called the "heartbreaking sacrifice" Negroes were making in order to live under fairly sanitary conditions and rear their families amid decent surroundings. The aspiration to break the Negro's cycle of despair occupied research reports and editorials as the New Deal moved into social consciousness in national legislation and projects.

The antilynching bill, problems of the Negro farmer, and the imminent menace of World War II interested *Opportunity* in the waning years of the 1930s. Carter wrote of the "shameful and unnecessary restrictions which are placed on Negro citizens who are desiring to enter the Army and Navy." He could not understand the stubborn opposition to granting Negro citizens the right to enter freely branches of the armed forces. A willingness to face death on behalf of one's country was the highest expression of patriotism. Yet in World War I Negroes had been humiliated by high United States Army officers under whom they served in France. The magazine reminded its readers that Negroes had fought in all the nation's wars, and as the country moved closer toward active involvement in the new world conflict, *Opportunity* highlighted in each issue contributions Negroes were making to the war effort on the military and home fronts. Special attention kept readers aware of the critical need for nurses in the armed forces and for technicians for the war industries.

By carefully managing its resources and bringing to its cause increasing numbers of persons who were sympathetic to the work of the organization, the National Urban League was able to survive the rigors of the Great Depression. At times the editor asked readers to make special contributions of money so the magazine could continue publication. With the January 1943 issue, *Opportunity* became a quarterly, due, in part, to wartime restrictions on paper, printing, and personnel. During those years, Elmer Carter relinquished his editorial duties to Madeline L. Aldridge, who had been his editorial assistant for a number of years.

Dutton Ferguson became editor in January 1947 and published the magazine as an organ of the league's department of Promotion and Publicity. A twenty-fifth anniversary issue released in the fall of 1947 recalled the accomplishments of *Opportunity*.

Board President William H. Baldwin wrote in the Winter 1949 issue: "Rather than continue it as just another magazine among all those in which the Negro writers and poets of ability are now at home and in which issues involving interracial relations are now accorded attention they merit, the Executive Board of the National Urban League has voted to discontinue publication." That was the magazine's final appearance. Baldwin's epitaph highlights, even at its demise, the dual purposes that stood at the forefront of the magazine—providing a respectable publication source for aspiring black writers and researchers, and placing before the reading public interracial issues of importance.

Notes

1. "Well Done," *Opportunity* (Winter 1949): 3.
2. "Rise of the Negro Magazine," *Journal of Negro History* (January 1928): 15.
3. "The Debut of the Younger School of Negro Writers," *Opportunity* (May 1924): 243-44.
4. *Opportunity* (August 1924): 228.
5. "An Opportunity for Negro Writers," *Opportunity* (September 1924): 258.
6. "The Donor of the Contest Prizes," *Opportunity* (January 1925): 3.
7. *Opportunity* (August 1924): 228. *See also* Walter C. Daniel, "Countee Cullen as Literary Critic," *College Language Association Journal* (March 1971): 281-90.
8. "A Charge to Keep I Have," *Opportunity* (October 1928): 293.
9. *See* Elmer A. Carter, "E. Simms Campbell—Caricaturist," *Opportunity* (March 1932): 82-85.
10. "Picketing for Jobs," *Opportunity* (February 1932): 5.
11. "The Negro Vote in November," *Opportunity* (February 1932): 5.
12. "One Way Out—Communism," *Opportunity* (July 1943): 214-17.

Information Sources

BIBLIOGRAPHY:

Bell, Roseann P. "*Crisis* and *Opportunity* Magazines: Reflections of Black Culture." Ph.D. dissertation, Emory University, 1974.

Carter, Elmer Anderson. "A Charge to Keep I Have." *Opportunity*, October 1928, p. 293.

Daniel, Walter C. "Countee Cullen As Literary Critic." *College Language Association Journal*, March 1971, pp. 281-90.

Ikonné, Chidi. "*Opportunity* and Black Literature, 1923-1933." *Phylon*, Spring 1979, pp. 86-93.

Johnson, Charles S. "Rise of the Negro Magazine." *Journal of Negro History*, January 1928, p. 15.

Miles, Frank W. "Negro Magazines Come of Age." *Magazine World*, 1 June 1946, pp. 12-13.

Pride, Armistead S. "The Black Press to 1968: A Bibliography." *Journalism History*, Winter 1977-1978, pp. 148-54.
INDEX SOURCES: None.
LOCATION SOURCES: Greenwood Press Periodicals; many college and university libraries.

Publication History

MAGAZINE TITLE AND TITLE CHANGES: *Opportunity: A Journal of Negro Life* (January 1923-Winter/January-March 1949).
VOLUME AND ISSUE DATA: Vols. I-XXII (January 1923-1944), monthly; vols. XXII-XXV (January/March 1945-Summer/July-September 1948), quarterly; vol. XXVII (Winter 1949), special issue.
PUBLISHER AND PLACE OF PUBLICATION: Research and Investigation Department, National Urban League, New York, New York.
EDITORS: Charles Spurgeon Johnson (January 1923-September 1928); Elmer Anderson Carter (October 1928-January 1945); Madeline L. Aldridge, editorial chairman (January 1945-June 1947); Dutton Ferguson (July 1947-January 1949).
CIRCULATION: 10,000 highest estimate.

OUR WORLD: A PICTURE MAGAZINE FOR THE WHOLE FAMILY

Less than a year after the Johnson Publishing Company launched *Ebony** from its Chicago base, in the spring of 1946 *Our World* appeared in New York.[1] Both publications endeavored to capitalize upon the extraordinary popularity of the giants in American photojournalism and create for black audiences a picture news magazine that would highlight black accomplishments. *Life* magazine had established a new relationship between pictures and news text when it appeared in November 1936, offering ninety-six pages of photographs with a minimal amount of text. *Our World* was comparable to *Life* in size and orientation of material. John P. Davis, its editor and founder, announced a circulation guarantee of 125,000 copies for the first issue and confidently fixed the basic page-rate for advertisement at $450. Although the magazine sought to imitate the appearance and the general format of the white news photograph periodicals, its content was unique. It focused on the black Americans' dilemma in a white-controlled world. Social problems of the day were presented. Stories about housing, court cases involving race, advances in science and education, the press, religion, government, entertainment, fashion, children, and the home were parts of the several departments. Humorous cartoons on a variety of subjects appeared in each issue. *Our World* considered itself "A Picture Magazine for the Whole Family."

Coming close upon the close of World War II, *Our World* devoted attention to the experiences of black veterans of that conflict. In the second issue, the editor called for stories from ex-servicemen about their reminiscences of serving in the armed forces. The first contest for such features resulted in "My Favorite Tan Yank," written by the newsman Oliver W. Harrington about a black pilot in the 332nd Fighter Group which was attached to the 15th Air Force in Italy. This type of material was particularly interesting to black readers. For despite the critical need for airmen in the war, only stringent efforts on the part of black politicians, educators, and public figures made it possible for black youth to offer themselves for pilot training. Black Americans were especially proud of the 96th Pursuit Squadron and the 332nd Fighter Group.

Beginning with its third issue, *Our World* settled into the format it would use throughout its publication. "Exclusive Picture Stories" illustrated black life in the United States with short news stories and photographs. "Swing Streets in the United States" is an ingenious presentation of the principal centers of black social life in a variety of American cities. These features discuss music and entertainment among blacks, and at the same time, show graphically the slum conditions of the black quarters of the cities. The Liberty Ship *Booker T. Washington* had caught the imagination of black readers. They were pleased with the recognition the Merchant Marine had given to black personalities. Understandably, a story about the ship at peacetime with several photographs of its crew at work made an attractive feature. The Broadway musical *Call Me Madam* used black entertainers. *Our World* published a picture review of the show. In the area of sports, Sugar Ray Robinson was making a name for himself in boxing, and the National Baseball League had signed Jackie Robinson and John Wright to play with a farm team. What the future status of the National Negro Baseball League would be was an appropriate subject for *Our World*.

News about popular personalities was always welcome. Jackie Robinson's wedding and Nat "King" Cole's rise as a performer in the affluent night clubs of the nation were well reported. The earliest stirrings of nationalism in colonial Africa were noted and discussed. Mary McLeod Bethune, W.E.B. Du Bois, Adam Clayton Powell, Jr., and Paul Robeson were quoted on their feelings about African aspirations for nationhood. While the magazine did not use the direct editorial approach of the editor's comment on current affairs, the picture stories advocated black advancement through exposés of social problems and reports of individual accomplishments.

Our World provides a comprehensive view of black American life in the cities from the mid 1940s through the mid 1950s including the period just before the beginnings of the dynamic social revolution of the 1960s. It was more than a newspaper. It was the first black periodical to conduct a series of studies on the urban Negro market. *Advertising Age* wrote of the first study:

Although undertaken primarily to determine the position of Negro magazines in the market, the survey also provides up-to-date information on the buying habits and brand preferences of this country's Negro population.

The data are now being processed and will be released later by John P. Davis, publisher of *Our World*. Nearly 3,500 families, representing 15 northern and 13 southern states, were questioned in the study, which was conducted by Dr. Raymond Franzen under the supervision of the Media Audience Group. Breakdowns will be made geographically and by sex. Competitively, the figures measure *Our World* on the basis of "confirmed reading" against *Ebony*, *Color* and against eight leading mass magazines.[2]

After nine years of publication, *Our World* filed a petition of bankruptcy listing debts of nearly $350,000. Among the company's creditors were more than twenty advertising agencies, most of which had applied for rebates arising out of the magazine's failure to meet its circulation guarantee. The periodical extended itself beyond reasonable expectation of sustained success. It was a leader among magazines of its type, however, and is a landmark in the development of black magazine journalism in the United States.

Notes

1. John H. Johnson's *Ebony* is considered the dramatic breakthrough for black commercial magazine journalism. *Our World* might be considered the first black magazine to succeed for nearly a decade in New York, the city that had been the home of *Crisis**, *Opportunity**, and a host of little literary journals.
2. "*Our World* Readies Study of Negro Market," *Advertising Age* (26 November 1951): 29.

Information Sources

BIBLIOGRAPHY:
Miles, Frank W. "Negro Magazines Come of Age." *Magazine World*, July 1946, p. 19.
"*Our World* Goes Bankrupt Owing 20 Ad Agencies." *Advertising Age*, 5 December 1955, p. 109.
"*Our World* Readies Study of Negro Market." *Advertising Age*, 26 November 1951, p. 29.
INDEX SOURCE: *Negro Periodical Index*.
LOCATION SOURCES: Library of Congress; Schomberg Collection, New York Public Library; Moorland-Spingarn Collection, Howard University, Washington, D.C.

Publication History

MAGAZINE TITLE AND TITLE CHANGES: *Our World: A Picture Magazine for the Whole Family*.
VOLUME AND ISSUE DATA: Vols. I-X (April 1946-November 1955).
PUBLISHER AND PLACE OF PUBLICATION: Our World Publishing Company, New York, New York.
EDITOR: John P. Davis (1946-1955).
CIRCULATION: 175,000.

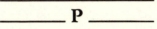

P

PHYLON: A REVIEW OF RACE AND CULTURE

Phylon: A Review of Race and Culture was founded by W.E.B. Du Bois in 1940. A decade after its founding, *Phylon* had become one of the most respected black scholarly publications in the country. This success stemmed, in large measure, from the focus and purpose of the journal. In its tenth anniversary issue, Mozell C. Hill, who was editor at that time, explained *Phylon*'s meaning and mission.

> PHYLON comes from the Greek and means a tribe, race or a genetically-related group; it was chosen (for this organ) not only because it was appropriate but also because it was considered to be thought-provoking and easily remembered. This title was not selected for its pedantic connotations; on the contrary, the founder and subsequent editors have seen in it a striking symbol well-adapted to a journal that purports to examine and report on racial and cultural relations everywhere.[1]

The journal's connection with Atlanta University was also important to its success. Horace Bumstead, one of the university's white presidents, invited W.E.B. Du Bois to join the faculty at Atlanta in 1897 as professor of economics and history and to direct the sociological studies already known as the Atlanta University Publications on the Negro.

During his service at Atlanta, Du Bois became one of the nation's preeminent black scholars and a recognized leader of black protest. He published his seminal *Souls of Black Folk*, led in organizing the Niagara movement, and launched and edited the *Moon Illustrated Weekly** and *Horizon.** In 1910 he accepted the position of director of Research and publicity for the newly formed National Association for the Advancement of Colored People. He founded its magazine, The *Crisis,** and edited it for nearly a quarter of a century. In 1933, shortly after the newly reorganized Atlanta University began to offer graduate and professional work, Du Bois returned to Atlanta for a series of lectures. John Hope, his friend and colleague when he was teaching at the undergraduate university in the old days and an associate in organizing the Niagara movement, had been named president of a consortium of colleges.[2] Du Bois believed that he and John Hope could build in the Deep South a university equal to if not superior to anything that the former seat of Negro slavery ever saw. Ironically, Du Bois had left Atlanta University the first time because he felt that his militant civil rights stance had caused some white philanthropists to decrease their financial support. Now, with John Hope in charge of the enterprise and with the new educational challenge, Du Bois relished in the new position a "certain poetic justification" for his long fight with supporters of industrial education to the exclusion of "higher education," and the emphasis on black American social studies he had advocated for the NAACP. He wanted to be able to write, to continue at Atlanta University the systematic study of Negro problems he had advanced with its *Publications*, and to establish a scholarly journal of comment and research on world issues.

John Hope's untimely death in 1936 delayed realization of these plans. Florence M. Read, president of Spelman College, one of the colleges comprising the university consortium, was named acting president of Atlanta University.[3] Du Bois believed that she had been placed in the position to placate the white South and guard the university from radical influences. President Read hesitated to approve the proposal for a journal. Du Bois wrote that Read's opposition to him postponed the starting of *Phylon* from 1934 to 1940. Rufus E. Clement, of Louisville Municipal College, eventually succeeded to the presidency of Atlanta University, and Du Bois asked him to recommend the establishment of the journal to the trustees.[4] In August 1939, Clement and Du Bois reached an agreement. Production and publication were to cost no more than $2,000 a year. Irene Diggs, who was working with Du Bois on a project financed by the Phelps-Stokes Fund, would be editorial assistant. Thus, under the auspices of Atlanta University and largely with funds provided by the university, *Phylon* first appeared 26 January 1940. Although Du Bois continued to teach sociology and to serve as principal investigator for several other funded studies, he devoted most of his energies to editing the new magazine.

Phylon enjoyed immediate success. The editorial board of university personnel named to assist Du Bois included Ira DeA. Reid, professor of sociology, who served as managing editor; Mercer Cook, professor of Romance languages; Rushton Caulborn, professor of history; William H. Dean, professor of economics; Oran W. Eagleson, professor of psychology; and William Stanley Braithwaite, poet, anthologist, and librarian. Contributing editors outside Atlanta University included Horace Mann Bond, president of Fort Valley State College in Georgia; Dantes Bellegarde, director of the Ecole Normale des Instituteurs, Port-au-Prince, Haiti; Ruth Anna Fisher, representative in England of the Library of Congress, Division of Manuscripts; Rayford W. Logan, professor of history at Howard University; and Allison Davis, professor of anthropology at Dillard University in

New Orleans. The editorial board, together with creative writers and scholars around the nation and in the Caribbean area, became regular contributors. Articles centered upon sociology, history, and *belles lettres*. A few poems appeared in each early issue, some written by well-established black poets. Portraits of black persons, American and foreign, became a part of the general format. Other features included "A Chronical of Race Relations," "Books and Race," and "Race in Periodicals." The magazine was published quarterly.

In November 1940, Du Bois reported to a university trustee that institutional appropriations and income from sales had paid the total cost of publishing *Phylon*. On that date, the publication was free from debt and about 650 copies had been circulated in thirty-nine states, as well as in parts of Europe, Asia, Africa, and the West Indies. "We have on our list 50 libraries, including many of the leading institutions of learning," Du Bois' report continued. The journal had received unsolicited commendation from "persons of distinction in many parts of the country."[5]

Phylon's issue for the second quarter of 1942, commemorating the seventy-fifth anniversary of the founding of Atlanta University, is a significant historical document. Two photographs featured Georgia Swift King, oldest living holder of an Atlanta University diploma (1874) and a color print of the Hinks Memorial Window. This window was designed and constructed by Tiffany Studios in 1909 for the university's sociology department in honor of the dean and first professor of sociology, John Howard Hinks. In an article entitled "The Cultural Missions of Atlanta University," Du Bois expressed his own ideas about a university. He also lauded Atlanta's efforts to continue the accomplishments of the past into the future.

Poems written by two well-know graduates—James Weldon Johnson (1894) and Georgia Douglass Johnson (1893)—and an engaging discussion of "The Sources of the Tradition of Atlanta University" by George A. Towns added interest. The black artist Hale Woodruff drew pen sketches of Edmund Asa Ware and Horace Bumstead, the first and second presidents of the university, respectively. There were also memorials to former administrators, faculty members, and students. The emphasis throughout this special issue was upon Atlanta University during its days as the premier undergraduate college providing higher education to Negroes in the Deep South.

Throughout Du Bois' editorship the journal featured scholarly work of a high order in the areas of social issues and literary criticism. Du Bois also published some creative writing. Although *Phylon* followed the tradition of the Atlanta University *Publications* on the Negro that Du Bois had edited during his earlier employment at the institution, the new journal was more broadly based than the more narrowly focused research publications. It stood among the best university journals in the nation and was the fulfillment of the old scholar's dream of a financially viable and academically respectable publication with him as its editor in chief. The establishment of the journal was made possible because of Du Bois' scholarly achievements and his personal relationship with John Hope. Although Rufus Clement cooperated with Du Bois in bringing *Phylon* into existence, the two men never developed a warm friendship. In fact, their relationship was characterized by acrimonious disagreement. Clement brought an end to this by getting rid of Du Bois. In a letter dated 23 November 1943, the president informed Du Bois that the Board of Trustees at its meeting in New York on 16 November had voted to retire Du Bois from the active faculty when his contract expired the following June. "The Board wishes you to know that it has appreciated your services to Atlanta University, and as a token of this appreciation you are to be retired as Professor Emeritus," the letter continued. Du Bois' old nemesis Florence Read offered the motion at the board meeting.

Du Bois did not take the decision easily. He wrote back that he would have followed a different course if he had been consulted on the matter. He wanted to continue to edit *Phylon* and to complete the social problems projects he had already planned for the Negro Land-Grant Colleges Association. He could have continued these duties with the assistance of an assistant and a secretary until 30 June 1946, at which time he could have retired with what he considered to be a salary sufficient for his living expenses. He would then be nearly seventy-five years old.[6]

Appeals to the president did not change the decision of the trustees; thus, Du Bois' editorship of *Phylon* ended with the second quarter issue for 1944. An editorial in the tenth volume perhaps best summarizes *Phylon* under Du Bois' editorship:

Despite the many intellectual lights who were in on its birth, *Phylon* took on to a great extent the personality of Du Bois, the intellectual race leader and social philosopher. The impact of Du Bois has been indelible: the identification of the journal with his name, the basic tone, and his essential objectives persist. It is fair to say that during the four years of his editorship, Du Bois "ran" the magazine; in terms of the time, the setting, and his broad powers and abilities, he was able to do it largely, as the artist-genius, "by ear."[7]

Ira DeA. Reid, who had been managing editor and a member of the editorial board from the beginning, now was named editor in chief. Du Bois had pointed out in one of his many letters to president Clement that Reid did little more than proofread certain articles. When Du Bois was retired, Reid inherited a magazine and a mission that had already been established. Like Du Bois, he taught courses and was engaged in commitments to several government agencies; consequently, Reid sought help to carry out his responsibilities to the journal. He chose Nathaniel P. Tillman, a professor of English at Morehouse College, within the university complex, as managing editor.

Reid had some ideas of his own about how *Phylon* should be managed and edited, but the nation was engaged in World War II and the national emergency hampered the new editor in making any sweeping changes he might have desired. He did make some changes, however, that were in keeping with the times. Articles began appearing, for example, that concentrated on the black participation in World War II and Reid added his own column, "Persons and Places." Through the two years of his editorship he discussed many subjects of general interest to black Americans. One item, "Sectional Inequality," vigorously attacked an article that Virginius Dabney wrote for *Saturday Review of Literature*, "Is the South That Bad?" Dabney considered himself a "liberal," and Reid considered him well qualified to speak about the South, especially inasmuch as he was editor of the *Richmond* (Virginia) *Time Dispatch* and had been a correspondent for the *New York Times*. But Dabney's approach to race problems, as expressed in the *Saturday Review* article, disappointed Reid.

> He admits everything, well, almost everything, that has been said critically about the South, but while doing so finds either answers to the criticisms and reasons for the facts underlying them or reasonable exceptions to the rules set down. It is a spirited circle, one calculated to cause people to see the South in a different light either through their emotions or their reason, chiefly, I fear, the former.[8]

It was this appeal to emotions that Reid found unfortunate. And the misfortune was all the greater because Dabney was "one of the few Southerners capable of making people think anew of the South and its problems." Reid lamented the fact that even this unusually well qualified spokesman resorted to the jargon of the "proud Southerner" who will not be driven into social change. In response to that argument, Reid asked: Who are the proud Southerners? White Southerners? All classes? How is it possible to persuade people with whom one has no contact—physical, intellectual, or cultural? At the end of the editorial he wondered whether the South must continue to alibi its deficiencies or strain toward decency by carrying upon itself the excess weight of neurotic sectionalism.

This trenchant retort exemplified the role and purpose of *Phylon* as a black periodical that reflected race and culture through its articles, reports, editorials, and *belles lettres* while at the same time focusing its commentary upon the black American experience. Reid's response to Dabney also showed that he had not changed the tone Du Bois set for *Phylon*.

In 1948 Reid gave up the editorship to join the faculty of Haverford College. Mozell C. Hill, who had served as visiting professor of sociology at Atlanta University on leave from his home position at Langston University in Oklahoma, where he was editor of the *Southwestern Journal*,* became editor in chief of *Phylon* in September 1948. Hill wrote in a preface to the December 1950 issue that he did not intend to rehash the "Negro Renaissance" and its literary milieu.

One of Hill's first undertakings was to plan a special issue on the Negro writer. Contributions came from a librarian, four college presidents, four academic deans, five professors, two creative writers, one student, one government official, and one educational executive in regional education. Their comments covered history, background, and supporting values of higher education for Negroes; differentiation of educational practices and forms; dilemmas and consequences of education for minorities; and the effects of segregation and discrimination on educational institutions and persons who worked and studied in them. Professional educators discussed their roles, and Langston Hughes' story "Simple Discusses College and Culture" provided some biting but subtle observations on schools for Negroes and what students expected from them. In organizing the issue from this frame of reference, the editor wrote that *Phylon* was carrying out its purpose as a journal of race and culture edited at a black American university; one that would remain vital and relevant only so long as its direction comported with its social environment.

Following the United States Supreme Court's decision in *Brown* v. *Board of Education of Topeka*, the second quarter issue for 1956 was devoted almost entirely to a series of articles intended to describe and analyze sociological and cultural balance in American society. One editorial commented on the climate of the times and chided those who saw grave consequences resulting from the Brown decision.

> Even before the Court decisions of May 1954 and May 1955 the increasing incidence of desegregation and the continuing prospects of rapid, though, uneven changes in race relations in the United States were taken for granted almost universally, even though they were welcomed by some and feared or resisted by others. In the two years since the May 1954 decision, and particularly during the past few months, the Cassandras seemed to have taken over. If much of the public media and many of the politicians and numbers of well-meaning but anxious observers are to be believed, tension and fear are virulently dominant.[9]

One person who held this view was Nobel Prize winner William Faulkner. Writing "in Olympian anguish," Faulkner warned the nation to "Go slow!" *Phylon*'s editor dismissed Faulkner and those who shared his views by asserting that talk of tension and moderation were so self-serving that any thinking person would have to ask: Who is tense? Which whites and which Negroes? And about what, specifically? The editor concluded that moderation could be a "virtue or a necessity," depending upon how one viewed the rate and means by which the real values and guarantees of the constitutional systems could be achieved.

John Hope II, industrial relations director of the Institute of Race Relations at Fisk University and associate director of programs for the Southern Regional Council, looked at the question of segregation from another angle. In an article

entitled "Trends in Patterns of Race Relations in the South since May 17, 1954,"
he said that bodily separation of the races had never been essential to the stability
and integrity of the southern system. Only Negro-white association or communication in terms of equal status had been the taboo. Hope said that the problem
was not and had never been whether communication between the races exists.
The critical question was who communicates with whom and who is willing to or
can afford to listen to the insistent voice of democracy everywhere in the nation
and in the world.

Other scholars and leaders wrote about desegregation and the South's future;
white citizens and the Supreme Court; consensus in the changing South; and
boycotts of public conveyances at the turn of the century, when another forward
thrust for civil rights had captured the energies of black Americans. Martin
Luther King, Jr., contributed "Facing the Challenge of the New Age," the
essential portion of an address he had delivered at the First Annual Institute on
Non-Violence and Social Change.

Another special feature was a forum on "The Negro in Literature: The Current
Scene." Hill posed a series of questions and asked a group of literary figures to
respond to them. Era Bell Thompson, Langston Hughes, Gwendolyn Brooks,
Thomas D. Jarrett, Sterling Brown, Ulysees Lee, Blyden Jackson, Margaret
Walker, Arna Bontemps, George Schuyler, Hugh Gloster, Nick Aaron Ford,
L. D. Riddick, and Nathaniel P. Tillman were among those who participated.
Their comments represent a significant contribution to American literature and
anticipated questions that would be raised during the black arts movement of the
1960s, when a strong emphasis was placed on writing as a political force in the
crusade for civil rights. As world conditions changed during the 1950s and
1960s, *Phylon*'s editors broadened its scope to include what would come to be
called the Third World. Hill commented on this enlarged purpose in an editorial.

It must be reiterated and stressed that *Phylon* not only looks at all peoples
but it also provides an organ of expression of views and comments of all
peoples. Concretely, the editors will continue to seek out high-quality
contributions—scientific articles, essays, humane letters, short stories, poems,
photographs, selected reviews, and appropriate art forms—that describe
and analyze the factors that affect societal balance and cultural integration.[10]

To a large extent, *Phylon* also continued studies in conditions of the black
experience in America after the fashion of the old Atlanta University *Publications* which had established Du Bois as a sociologist and brought recognition to
Atlanta University as a center for the discipline of sociology. The Regional
Housing Clinic on Urban Renewal which began with a formal symposium at the
university in November 1957 provided significant papers on urbanism and its
demands upon the "old city" that sought to be turned into the "new city." These
papers provide a unique body of information on the subject. The issues raised in

the symposium remained a focus of social thinking through the next two decades, and *Phylon* was a major organ for the dissemination of these documents.

From time to time, editorial responsibilities for *Phylon* changed during the 1950s and 1960s. A committee headed by Lucy Griggsby of the university's English department and Tillman C. Cothran of the History department kept the organ alive in unsettled times. Articles continued to center around civil rights, racial integration, and literary criticism. *Phylon* joined the black nationalism movement early in the 1970s. It adopted a red and black logo and stated on its title page that it had been founded by W.E.B. Du Bois. That addition seems entirely appropriate but also somewhat ironic, given the extraordinary difficulties Du Bois experienced in establishing and editing the journal. By the late 1960s and 1970s, however, Du Bois had again become a racial hero and an inspiration for scholarly investigation.

Du Bois was a man of many talents. Although he remained editor in chief of *Phylon* for only four years, the journal stands as a fitting memorial to his editorial and scholarly ambitions and aspirations. Even during the years that his name was seldom mentioned in the publication, it remained the embodiment of his dream for a scholarly publication from Atlanta bringing deserved honor and prestige to men and women who labored there to make its colleges and university a special source of pride for black Americans.

Notes

1. "Re-View of the Review," *Phylon* (Fourth Quarter 1940): 297.
2. On 1 April 1929, the governing boards of Morehouse College, Spelman College, and Atlanta University entered a contract to establish, with the help of the General Education Board, an academic center. Atlanta University would offer instruction in graduate and professional education and serve as the coordinating unit. A university administration building and library would be erected on the Morehouse property. Clark College would move from the southeastern portion of the city to property directly across the street from the new buildings. The Contract of Affiliation would preserve the identity of the constituent colleges. This bold new step in higher education for black Americans represented, in principle, the zenith of the aspirations of many persons who had championed the private liberal arts college for Negroes. Early discussions along these lines had gone back as far as the days when John Hope was a young faculty member at Atlanta Baptist College and Du Bois a professor at Atlanta University.
3. Florence M. Read had been appointed president of Spelman College in 1927. Laura Spelman, who endowed the college and for whom it was named, was a member of the Rockefeller family, which has to be given most credit for sustaining the institution almost from its founding. Read served as Spelman College's president for twenty-six years, retiring in 1953. When she served as interim president of Atlanta University after John Hope's death, Du Bois said that she exercised strong influence on the university's policies and kept it within the tradition its donors wanted it to serve.
4. Rufus E. Clement, a native Atlantan, received a bachelor's degree from Livingstone College, the African Methodist Episcopal Zion Church college in Salisbury, North

Carolina. He took his theological training at Garrett Biblical Institute in Evanston, Illinois. As a preacher and teacher working in Louisville, Kentucky, he helped to establish Louisville Municipal College, and he headed this institution at the time he was elected president of Atlanta University. *See* Du Bois' *Autobiography* and *Correspondence* for discussion of the relationship between him and Clement.

5. "Phylon," *Phylon* (Fourth Quarter 1940): frontispiece.
6. *See* Du Bois, *Correspondence.*
7. "Re-view."
8. "Persons and Places," *Phylon* (First Quarter 1946): 197.
9. "This Quarter," *Phylon* (Second Quarter 1956): 101.
10. "This Quarter," *Phylon* (Second Quarter 1958): 323.

Information Sources

BIBLIOGRAPHY:
Aptheker, Herbert, ed. *The Correspondence of W.E.B. Du Bois.* International Publishers, 1968.
Du Bois, W.E.B. *The Autobiography of W.E.B. Du Bois.* International Publishers, 1968.
Green, Dan S. "W.E.B. Du Bois: His Journalistic Career." *Negro History Bulletin*, March-April 1977, pp. 672-77.
Hill, Mozell, C. "The Formative Years of *Phylon* Magazine." in *Black Titan: W.E.B. Du Bois*, edited by John Henrik Clarke et al. Boston, 1970, pp. 115-19.
Logan, Rayford W. *The Betrayal of the Negro: From Rutherford B. Hayes to Woodrow Wilson.* New York, 1965.
Torrence, Ridgely. *The Story of John Hope.* New York, 1948.
INDEX SOURCES: *Current Index to Journals in Education; Psychological Abstracts; Public Affairs Information Service; Social Sciences and Humanities Index; Index to Periodical Articles by and about Negroes, Annotated, 1960-70; Guide to Negro Periodical Literature; Index to Selected Periodicals Decennial Cumulation, 1950-1959.*
LOCATION SOURCES: University Microfilms; Kraus Reprints; most university and college libraries.

Publication History

MAGAZINE TITLE AND TITLE CHANGES: *Phylon: A Review of Race and Culture.*
VOLUME AND ISSUE DATA: Vols. I to present (1940-), quarterly.
PUBLISHER AND PLACE OF PUBLICATION: Atlanta University, Atlanta, Georgia.
EDITORS: W.E.B. Du Bois (first quarter 1940-second quarter 1944); Ira DeA. Reid (third quarter 1944-third quarter 1948); interim editorial committee; Mozell C. Hill (fourth quarter 1948-second quarter 1958); Tillman C. Cothran (fourth quarter 1959-third quarter 1970); editorial committee (fourth quarter 1970-second quarter 1971); John D. Reid (third quarter 1971-second quarter 1978); Lucy C. Griggsby, acting editor (fourth quarter 1977-second quarter 1978); Charles F. Duncan, acting editor (third quarter 1978-second quarter 1980); Wilbur H. Watson (third quarter 1980-).
CIRCULATION: 2,200.

PROUD

Community and city magazines first arose in the United States in the 1960s. The earliest were published in San Diego, Philadelphia, and San Francisco. What had been the organ for communication of the local Chamber of Commerce traditionally became an independent alternative for local newspapers. Saint Louis' *Proud* is an example of this medium in the black community of that city.[1] It began publication in 1970 and drew attention to itself with a promotion plan to provide in-service training in basic journalism for black youth. The first year the group published the Black Cultural Edition, with an emphasis on black history, local and national. *Proud* is a consumers' magazine directed toward a regional audience. Advertisement comes from local establishments. *Proud* is different from black weekly city newspapers which report on social, personal, and institutional news that would hardly appear in the regular dailies. Their editorials concentrate on and advocate positions favorable to black citizens. Opinion columns explore local and national problems, but the treatment is usually superficial. Community magazines like *Proud* that are intended for local black audiences are published monthly or bimonthly. They contain researched articles on a variety of subjects together with regular features on politics and the arts.

Proud's basic format includes "Personality Profile" that features community personalities who are celebrated for some uncommon accomplishment or dedication to a social cause. "Black Studies" usually contains essays written by black faculty members of local colleges and universities. "The Black Woman, Man, Family in the Struggle for Liberation", written by an assistant professor of social work at Saint Louis' Washington University, is one example. "Education" may take a number of directions. One feature in the early seventies, "Lincoln University Must Survive," traced the history of Missouri's single historically black university and its need to overcome the ravages of student unrest, and the state legislature's concern for whether the institution was any longer needed after integration of all public post-secondary education.

"The Negro Spiritual," a brief history of this black folk art; "The Alpha of Liberation or the Omega of America," an argument for strong black political power, and several articles on the need for reform in the Missouri State Penitentiary for Men, community health problems, black businesses, and black sports represent the areas of interest the magazine explores. It seldom expresses a distinct editorial position. The Bicentennial issue centered on "Missouri Law: A Black Perspective." Each year *Proud* publishes a career opportunity issue for black youth in the Saint Louis area.

Note

1. Philadelphia's *Pride* was best known of the black group of these publications. *Philly Talk* also published in Philadelphia, and magazines of the type in Dayton, Milwaukee,

Rochester, and Syracuse represent some of the most successful ones among blacks. Some reported 20-30,000 circulation in the early seventies, with about half the printing going to regular subscribers.

Information Sources

BIBLIOGRAPHY:
Wolseley, Roland E. *The Black Press, U.S.A.* Ames: Iowa State University Press, 1971, pp. 159-60.
INDEX SOURCES: None.
LOCATION SOURCES: Newsstands; Saint Louis Public Library.

Publication History

MAGAZINE TITLE AND TITLE CHANGES: *Proud.*
VOLUME AND ISSUE DATA: Vols. I to present (January 1970-).
PUBLISHER AND PLACE OF PUBLICATION: Ernie McMillan, publisher, Proud, Incorporated, Saint Louis, Missouri.
EDITOR: Betty J. Lee (1970-).
CIRCULATION: 10,000.

PULSE

Pulse, first issued in February 1943, did not acquire its name until the fifth issue of the monthly periodical. Its editor and publisher conducted a contest they hoped would produce an appropriate name for the magazine. The journal set forth its purpose: to present "a magazine offering an opportunity for creative expression to talented persons whose dreams might be gathering dust for want of an audience." The editors promised to "welcome a diversity of ideas and opinions in politics, race relations, education, science, religion, literature and the arts." *Pulse* could not possibly meet so broad a coverage. It became a general-purpose news magazine with a strong religious orientation, although it was not related to any particular church or denomination. It reported on black Washington, including news about social, cultural and religious activities. As a wartime publication, its features discussed the Negro and the postwar economy, USO clubs, and the need for a second military front for Allied forces fighting in Europe.

Pulse's vitality lay in its collection of features and news stories rather than in any strong editorial positions. Doxey A. Wilkerson, an associate professor of education at Howard University, wrote about labor problems Negroes faced with the Capital Transit Company. That union firm's refusal to hire black streetcar and bus operators provided the magazine the opportunity to point out some of the ironies of racial discrimination during the war. The company was advertising nationwide for operators due to a scarcity of persons for the growing needs of the company, but when a single black was accepted for on-the-job training as an operator, public transportation in Washington was halted for two hours by white drivers who refused to operate their vehicles while the black would-be apprentice was in the terminal. *Pulse* used the incident to dramatize part of the nation's duplicity in using manpower in the national emergency. Transportation was a critical industry, but the Capital Transit Company, among other firms, was subverting the necessary strength of the national purpose because of entrenched racial discrimination.

Wartime accomplishments of blacks and recognition of their increasing importance in the nation also appeared in the magazine. It covered Liberian President William S. Tubman's visit to President Franklin D. Roosevelt, ostensibly to reach agreement on cooperation in the war effort between the two governments. War training programs, acceptance of the first black volunteer into the United States Marines, the creation of the separate black squadrons in the Army Air Corps, and the christening of Liberty Ships named for black Americans provided news highlights for the magazine.[1] Other stories and comments related to the introduction of the controversial Fair Employment Practices Act which sought to guarantee blacks economic partnership in their nation's war effort; the intransigence of labor unions responding to the NAACP's attempts to bring blacks into the main channel of the labor force; and the 1944 presidential election.

Pulse supported the reelection of President Roosevelt because he had been forthright in championing rights for all minority groups. An editorial stated that "the present administration has done more for the Negro than all the Republican administrations put together." The editor warned her audience about the new coalition in Congress between Republicans and southern Democrats. She wrote that Wendell Willkie, Roosevelt's opponent in the presidential campaign, was trying to please all factions of the electorate. The journal clearly preferred the Democratic party in the election, but it carried a statement by Perry W. Howard, black Republican National Committee member from Mississippi and probably the best-known Negro Republican, who argued against both major parties. To him, Republicans had given the Negro the vote and the Democrats had taken it away from him. Neither deserved the race's support.

Editors of *Pulse* noted the rising number of black voters and predicted the Republican party would never regain the automatic allegiance it had once received from blacks. The election of thirty-five-year-old Adam Clayton Powell, Jr., to Congress from New York's twenty-second district presaged a new political vitality for the urban black.[2] *Pulse* editorials expressed the idea that black members of Congress would increase and would earn influential positions in the legislative body through the seniority system.

The journal closely resembled black newspapers in its content. It did not seek to attract scholarly articles, and its creative writing was negligible. But to the extent that *Pulse* represents Washington, D.C., at wartime from the black perspective, it is a valuable document of the black American experience.

Notes

1. Liberty Ships (merchant vessels built to transport wartime material) were named for some black Americans including Leonard Roy Harmon, Frederick Douglass, George Washington Carver, Robert L. Vann, Paul Laurence Dunbar, and James Weldon Johnson.

2. Powell was part of Harlem's Abyssinian Baptist Church when he was elected to Congress as a Democrat. He had been elected to the New York City Council in 1941 and had been a major civil rights activist in Harlem during the depression.

Information Sources

BIBLIOGRAPHY:
Bergman, Peter M. *Chronological History of the Negro in America*. New York, 1969.
Boone, Dorothy Delores. "A Historical Review and a Bibliography of Selected Negro Magazines, 1910-1969." Ph.D. dissertation, University of Michigan, 1970.
Miles, Frank W. "Negro Magazines Come of Age." *Magazine World*, 1 June 1946, pp. 12-21.
INDEX SOURCES: None.
LOCATION SOURCES: Moorland-Spingarn Collection, Howard University Washington, D.C.; Atlanta University; Fisk University.

Publication History

MAGAZINE TITLE AND TITLE CHANGES: *Pulse*.
VOLUME AND ISSUE DATA: Vols. I and II (February 1943-January 1945), monthly.
PUBLISHER AND PLACE OF PUBLICATION: James C. Mason, Washington, D.C.
EDITOR: Helen S. Mason (1943-1945).
CIRCULATION: 2,500.

——— Q ———

QUARTERLY REVIEW OF HIGHER EDUCATION AMONG NEGROES

At the height of the Great Depression, in January 1933, Johnson C. Smith University in Charlotte, North Carolina, launched a new journal, the *Quarterly Review of Higher Education Among Negroes*. Its editorial board included Henry Lawrence McCrorey, president of the university , as editor; Theophilus E. McKinney, dean of the College of Liberal Arts, as managing editor; and six members of the faculty. Contributing editors included administrators from several black colleges as well as the executive agent for the Association of Colleges and Secondary Schools for Southern States and the director of the Division of Negro Education for the State of North Carolina.

The first editorial pointed out that higher education among Negroes was developing rapidly and since little formal reporting of this development was in progress, a review was needed to provide a continuing source of information on new movements, activities, and facilities of instruction. The review, then, would seek to provide a forum for discussing problems of colleges and universities for Negroes; it would present scientific studies through which instructional and administrative techniques could be studied with increasing exactness. It would report news of particular interest to workers in higher education for Negroes; review books and monographs bearing directly upon that phase of national education, and provide a special service for teachers and other workers who sought employment in black colleges. The *Quarterly Review* clearly perceived its special role within a firmly segregated professional society. It sought to perform for Negro educators a service that many existing journals provided for white institutions and their faculties.

"*The Quarterly Review* will be national in scope and treatment," the first editorial stated. The editor invited authorities and interested persons to write for the magazine. Others who wished to present manuscripts for consideration were invited to do so if their submissions dealt with problems of Negro colleges and universities "with some genuinely contributed view to their possible solutions."[1]

That particular school year, 1933, Johnson C. Smith University enrolled, according to its own figures, 250 students in its four-year liberal arts program and its professional school of theology. Given the financial stringencies of the depression, the institution's small enrollment and faculty, and the large number of magazines—popular and professional—that ceased publication at that time for financial reasons, initiation of the *Quarterly Review* was a bold move. State-operated black colleges and universities were not at all popular. Practically every postsecondary institution was supported by church and philanthropic bodies, mostly white Protestant church groups. Johnson C. Smith University had only recently started its rise as a leading black private college. However, the small institution was enjoying prosperity beyond that of most other black colleges. Some ten years earlier, its name had been changed from Biddle University in recognition of a benefactress, Mrs. Johnson C. Smith of Pennsylvania, whose generous financial support had practically rebuilt the campus of the Presbyterian school which had begun operation among those many black schools founded by church efforts immediately following the Civil War. James B. Duke, the North Carolina tobacco magnate, added to the university's endowment. With these new resources, the school attracted strong, young black faculty members who set a new course for the institution. No doubt, the *Quarterly Review* was initiated as part of the university's new vitality.

McKinney, who was in his early thirties when he began editing the magazine, had degrees in political science from Morehouse College and Boston University. He had already served a brief tenure as dean of the College of Education and General Studies at North Carolina Agricultural and Technical College at Greensboro. He was the moving force behind the establishment of the *Quarterly Review*. He secured wide and significant cooperation from the faculty of his home institution, from white and black educators around the nation, and from other national public figures. His lead article for the first issue of the magazine, "A Summary of Findings and Policies Bearing on Problems of Administration in Institutions of Higher Education," detailed the principal functions of boards of control, internal administration, and officers of administration. It also discussed college curricula, necessary articulation between high schools and colleges, and general efforts intended to improve the quality of Negro higher education. That first article, together with the first editorial, set the pattern of emphasis McKinney would reflect throughout his editorship of the publication.

For nearly thirty years the journal served the purposes set forth in these first statements. It responded to changes in its time, however; and in doing so provided a significant resource for observing the development of black public and private colleges in the United States at mid twentieth century in at least four important areas; (1) inclusion of black colleges in the Southern Association of Colleges and Secondary Schools, the regional accrediting agency for the South, where most of these institutions were located; (2) the rise and development of several academic professional organizations that black educators established for their intellectual camaraderie in a racially segregated South and a surprisingly rigid racially segregated profession; (3) the responsibilities for accommodating new and increasing education demands promulgated by legal action taken to desegregate public colleges and universities in the United States between 1936 and 1954; and (4) the impact of World War II upon the black college.

Before 1929, the Association of Colleges for Negro Youth existed as a voluntary confederation for rating black colleges and assisting them to upgrade the quality of education they provided. That year J. Henry Highsmith of the North Carolina State Department of Education, largely through McKinney's efforts, led a move toward separate accreditation of black colleges by the all-white Southern Association of Colleges and Secondary Schools. Most black educators supported the trend toward systematic accreditation among black and white colleges for the simple reason that they found the existing procedure burdensome. North Carolina, for example, had earlier certified all prospective public school teachers on the basis of their college work rather than by examination. "A" and "B" grade certificates could be granted to persons holding teacher training degrees from four-year colleges affiliated with the accrediting agencies. Because Negro colleges did not belong to the association, their graduates could not qualify for preferred certificates. Few professions were open to Negro college graduates. Teaching was one choice, largely because the racially separate schools had to be staffed. The penalty was clear. Leaders in black colleges understood and accepted the need for some system of rating the institutions their students attended, and they favored the accrediting method. They did not approve of its exclusion of black students, and there were no blacks in white schools.

In 1936 the Commission on Higher Education for the Association of Colleges and Secondary Schools for Negroes, a black counterpart for the regional accrediting body, asked the United States Office of Education to conduct a study of certain phases of the programs in southern black colleges with a view toward comparing their quality to white college and university programs. With an appropriation of $40,000 a survey was undertaken in 1940 to be carried out in a selected group of black colleges to study their curricula, organization, and administration. McKinney later wrote on this significant step toward improving the quality of higher education among Negroes in an "Editorial Comment" in the *Quarterly Review*:

> Practically all of the colleges are very much concerned over this whole matter of improving the quality of instruction. It is hoped that this committee will be able to work out some plan whereby work-shops might be established for teachers in Negro colleges.[2]

By 1933, Johnson C. Smith University and similar institutions had formed an accrediting association which adopted the standards of the white southern association and at the same time affected an alliance with that organization through a special commission for articulation with black colleges in the region. The *Quarterly Review*'s January 1935 issue carried the full transcript of the Negro association's meeting in Atlanta 5 and 6 December 1934. It provides an unusual insight into the manner in which members of that group directed their efforts toward self-improvement and formal accreditation at a time when no signs yet pointed to the gradual racial integration of white colleges and universities that would take place in the latter half of the century.

Some twenty years later, McKinney was able to look back over these early efforts with a definite sense of accomplishment. When, at the fifty-sixth annual meeting of the Southern Association of Colleges and Secondary Schools at Saint Petersburg, Florida, December 1951, action was taken to approve the formal alignment of the black and white associations, McKinney praised those persons— black and white—who had worked strenuously for the improvement and strengthening of Negro schools and colleges in the South.

Toward the end of its second year of publication, the *Quarterly Review* began to report sessions, proceedings, and papers read at a variety of professional academic organizations established and maintained to stimulate scholarship among faculty and administrators in black colleges and to provide them with a forum for discussing their unique problems. These organizations included the Conference on Social Science Teaching in Black Colleges, the College Section of the North Carolina Teachers Association, the Negro Land-Grant Colleges Association, the North Carolina Negro College Conference, the Commission to Study Public Schools and Colleges for Colored People in North Carolina, the Southern Association of Teachers of Dramatic and Speech Arts, the Association of Teachers of English in Negro Colleges, and Alpha Kappa Mu National Honor Society.

The influence of McKinney, the *Quarterly Review*, and Johnson C. Smith University can be seen clearly in the titles of many of these organizations. Each was concerned with improving the quality and environment for education in black colleges. The *Quarterly Review* reported on each in detail, often publishing full transcripts of sessions and complete texts of formal papers read at the gatherings. The journal served as a periodical of news about the profession for black educators and as a scholarly publication for faculty members and administrators who had little opportunity to publish in white professional magazines. The only commonality in the several reports was that they all related to some phase of Negro education. In serving this purpose, the magazine not only lent significant support to communication among scholars who shared common interests, but assembled, at the same time, a most complete chronicle of the rise of several professional educational associations among faculties of black colleges. McKinney saw this responsibility as paramount for the magazine he founded and edited.

The historic Supreme Court decision ordering the State of Missouri to admit Lloyd Gaines, a black applicant, to its law school at Columbia or to provide one for him came in 1938. That court action placed a new and different focus upon higher education in the nation. By and large those states that had maintained racially separate colleges and universities agreed hastily to establish graduate and professional degree programs in existing black state colleges. In many cases, the result was simply to reorganize the black institutions into patterns intended to parallel major state universities. Tennessee Agricultural and Industrial College at Nashville, for example, organized six undergraduate divisions to correspond to the colleges of the University of Tennessee. Most states increased funds allocated to their black colleges as they broadened their focus. This new direction and responsibility for black colleges became a critical consideration for their faculties and administrators.

W. Sherman Savage, a professor of sociology at Lincoln University in Missouri, wrote in the *Quarterly Review* on the impact the Gaines case could have on white state universities: admit Negroes to state universities already in existence; reduce the quality of white universities to the level of Negro land grant colleges; sit back and wait; or provide scholarships for Negroes to study outside their home states. He added that there was also a great deal of discussion about establishing regional universities for Negroes. The Gaines case and similar litigation involving admission of Negroes to graduate and professional schools in the South and in border states occupied a large part of the *Quarterly Review* at the time, just as they remained a focus of interest for black educators at that period.[3]

As the nation entered into World War II, the *Quarterly Review* turned its attention to ways white and black colleges could adjust to the new demands of the national emergency. Some significant articles prepared for the American Council of Education's publication of proceedings of a national conference on reorganizing education for national defense were reproduced in the journal. Other articles were about Negro labor in the wartime economy, social aspects of the selective service, and the special role of the black college in the war effort.

When large numbers of students returned to college after the war to resume their interrupted education, the magazine discussed housing for black students, the institutions' part in mobilization for peace, and problems of black graduate schools. The latter issue was serious and demanded attention, for the courts had ruled that southern and border states must provide graduate and professional education within their borders but little progress had been made in determining ways to implement the court mandates. The *Quarterly Review* recognized the magnitude of the new problems the postwar period placed on higher education for blacks. Inasmuch as larger numbers of students were applying for admission to black colleges than ever before, McKinney wrote that the new pressure could provide a positive measure for improving the quality of students admitted to black schools. Those schools which had competed among themselves for students and had been "charitable" in their admissions and retention policies in order to survive could benefit if they used their new resource wisely. In an editorial, he expressed a novel attitude toward the new responsibility:

The plain truth is that democracy does not prescribe that one has a right to waste society's resources in pretending to do what he is neither interested in doing nor capable of doing.... So long as there are those who wish to use fully society's resources for developing intelligence and are capable of doing so, democracy requires careful selection of the fit and capable and rejection of those who are unfit or incapable, or both.[4]

Johnson C. Smith University and Theophilus E. McKinney had launched the *Quarterly Review* in order to seek to explore problems peculiar to Negroes in higher education at a time when the nation's black colleges related minimally to white colleges. McKinney wanted to report activities which, to him, represented improvement in the quality of education delivered by the black college. He anticipated some degree of racial assimilation in higher education but did not look forward to the day of the decline of the separate black college as a result of full integration of faculties and students into the major public white universities. He was too practical to believe that day would come soon. But he was particularly pleased with the progress toward regional accreditation that he was able to foster and see come to fruition among the black colleges.

At the meeting of the Southern Association of Colleges and Secondary Schools in Dallas, Texas, 6 December 1956, that organization approved a recommendation to continue for the next five years to accredit colleges for Negro youth, as it had done in the past. After five years the separate list of colleges would be abolished. During those years, reports of standards beginning December 1957 would be filed with the commission. That special body would recommend for membership in the parent organization any black colleges that met the association's standards. After 1961, applications from colleges for Negro youth would be considered by the regular Committee on Admissions to Membership. "It has taken 32 years... to achieve a goal which from the outset appeared so simple and easy to attain," McKinney wrote of the Dallas convention's recommendation. The decision, he continued, "reflects the perseverance and patience of many able white and Negro educators in the South."[5] The editorial seemed a valedictory for McKinney, for the struggle toward full accreditation for the black college had engaged the energies of the magazine and its editor throughout the *Quarterly Review*'s publication life.

Although the final issue of the journal—October 1960—gives no indication that it will be the last, the editor does list some problems he believed called for urgent attention during the decade of the sixties. General in nature, they express the strain of interest the journal had espoused throughout its life: (1) abolition of the system of segregation and discrimination; (2) the need for leadership to instill a spirit of service in students; (3) the training of youth in responsibilities and purposes of family life; and (4) the need for greater understanding of other cultures, especially of the nonwhite areas of the world.

The Quarterly Review of Higher Education among Negroes was a professional journal which limited itself to education. Through its policy of carrying proceedings of organizations established for individual disciplines and school administrators, and providing editorials and news comment on education in general, the journal served as a medium of communication. It was not subsidized by any foundation grants; it was published solely by Johnson C. Smith University. The institution owned a printing press, a holdover from the days of teaching vocational education that helped the school to launch and publish the journal.

During its life, W.E.B. Du Bois, Rayford W. Logan, Sterling Brown, Ralph Bunche, Charles Wesley, and Mary McLeod Bethune all contributed articles to the journal. Its vitality came, however, from the professional papers it included and its editorial comments, written primarily by Theophilus McKinney and occasionally by other members of the editorial board.

Notes

1. "Editorial Comment," *Quarterly Review of Higher Education among Negroes* (January 1933): i.
2. "Accrediting of Negro Schools and Colleges, 1929-1952," *Quarterly Review of Higher Education among Negroes* (January 1952): 42-43.
3. "The Influences of the Gaines Case on Negro Education in the Post-War Period," *Quarterly Review of Higher Education among Negroes* (July 1943): 3.
4. "Final Break, We Hope," *Quarterly Review of Higher Education among Negroes* (January 1957): 67.
5. Ibid.

Information Sources

BIBLIOGRAPHY:
Campbell, E. Fay. "The Politics and Rationale Governing Support of Negro Private Colleges Maintained by the United Presbyterian Church." *Journal of Negro Education*, Summer 1960, pp. 260-63.
Holmes, Dwight Oliver Wendell. "Seventy Years of the Negro College: 1860-1930." *Phylon*, Fourth Quarter 1949, pp. 307-13.
McCrorey, Henry Lawrence. "A Brief History of John C. Smith University." *Quarterly Review of Higher Education among Negroes*, April 1933, pp. 85-94.
McCuiston, Fred. *Graduate Instruction for Negroes in the United States.* Nashville, Tenn., 1939.
INDEX SOURCES: Lytle, Charlotte W. ed. *Index to Selected Periodicals Received in the Hallie Q. Brown Library: Decennial Cumulation 1950-1959.* New York, 1961.
LOCATION SOURCE: Greenwood Press Periodicals.

Publication History

MAGAZINE TITLE AND TITLE CHANGES: *Quarterly Review of Higher Education Among Negroes.*

VOLUME AND ISSUE DATA: Vols. I-XXVIII (January 1933-October 1960), quarterly. One special issue April 1933.

PUBLISHER AND PLACE OF PUBLICATION: Johnson C. Smith University, Charlotte, North Carolina.

EDITORS: Henry Lawrence McCrorey and Hardy Liston served as editors while presidents of the university (1933-1947; 1948-1956); Theophilus E. McKinney, managing editor (1957-1960).

CIRCULATION: 1,000.

R

RACE: DEVOTED TO SOCIAL, POLITICAL, AND ECONOMIC EQUALITY

Participants in the Conference on Social and Economic Aspects of the Race Problem formed in 1934 initiated their own journal, *Race*, in 1935. The interracial group of educators, social workers, and labor leaders believed that no purely academic journal of anthropology or moderate race periodical such as the *Crisis** or *Opportunity** met their needs. Hence the group, meeting in 1934 at Shaw University in Raleigh, North Carolina, formed their organization, agreed on some aims, and decided to launch a journal that would amplify and explore several purposes, based on their accords:

That there is need of scientific analysis of the so-called race question; that this is like-wise need for a relentless intellectual war against the pseudo-anthropology and the dangerous myths that serve as apologetics for imperialism, fascism, race prejudice and discrimination.

That there is no "solution" of the "race problem" short of an organized, uncompromising struggle based on the mass organizations of black and white workers and poor farmers and other sections of the population most interested—an uncompromising struggle for complete equality, economic, political and social, of Negroes and whites and the end of all discrimination, legal or social, based upon "race," "color," "national origin," or "blood."

That the special system of discrimination against the Negro in America is so deeply rooted in the very foundations of the present social order and the vested interests of dominant capitalism that there is no complete "solution" of this basic problem of American life short of a fundamental reconstruction of society, a social upheaval which will plow up our institutions to their very roots and substitute a socialist order for the present capitalist-imperialist order.

While the struggle for race quality (like charity) must begin at home, we cannot remain indifferent to the questions of Ethiopia and Africa, the Japanese aggression in China, anti-semitism in Germany and related problems throughout the world. And while in America the "Negro question" overshadows all others, the treatment of the Japanese, Chinese and Hindus in California, the rapid and widespread growth of anti-semitism, the spread of fascist tendencies and doctrines, all indicates that *Race* must cover a wider field as well.[1]

The objectives were not novel, and the decision to publish a journal was commonplace for the time. An impressive editorial board was assembled to work under the direction of a managing editor to publish *Race*.

Their enterprise was short-lived, as were practically all of the little magazines in the development of Afro-American journalism. But the two issues are interesting illustrations of dissent against the prevailing tone and purpose of the two leading black journals, the NAACP, and leading Harlem black newspapers. The first editorial in *Race* commented on William Pickens, an NAACP official, and his complaint against strikers among the editorial employees of the *Amsterdam News*. Pickens was quoted as having said that "colored workers should not join labor unions if they are in the employ of colored business establishments."[2]

The editorial disagreed vigorously. It made the point that labor problems created a new dilemma for black employers.

In large cities the question of labor organization has begun to plague...Negro employers. Almost to the man they have taken the stand that has been attributed to Mr. Pickens. The argument that they cannot compete with white business is basically unsound; for most Negroes operate in fields where there is practically no competition from the "white world.". . .In many of these establishments labor is kept on a near starvation wage, and the till is well nigh drained by executive salaries. Failure in recent months of Negro banks and insurance companies has revealed in many cases extraordinarily good salaries in the top brackets and merely pittances for the wage earners. The salary scales of many of our Negro "uplift" societies are in much the same state.[3]

E. Franklin Frazier, then head of the Department of Sociology at Howard University, contributed a Socialist's perspective to W.E.B. Du Bois. Frazier claimed that the black leader had failed, as surely as Booker T. Washington, to understand the essence of American social and economic forces as they related to the Negro. For all his artistry with words, Du Bois was, to Frazier, a "cultural hybrid" whose New England upbringing had led him to think and write of the elitist educational concept of the so-called Talented Tenth and to describe himself in his celebrated *Souls of Black Folk*. But he had never understood socialism or Marxism. He had never advocated revolution; he had posed romantic solutions to class problems without coming to grips with workable solutions. George Streater, a former managing editor of the *Crisis* who was then working in the South as a field organizer for the Amalgamated Clothing Workers Union, wrote about the dearth of black leaders in his "In Search of Leadership," and concluded that little could be gained by continuing to investigate the Negro masses and to sell out to the parties of big business. "The only friend of the working man under capitalism is his organized collective strength," Streater wrote.

All articles in *Race* were "radical" in a new key. The writers found the old black leaders totally inadequate for a time of economic depression and rising fascism all over most of the Western world. Alain Locke, a perennial voice in most of the statements about cultural emphases for black creative artists, wrote on the lingering problem, "Propaganda—Or Poetry." He held that "as the articulate voices of an oppressed minority, one could naturally expect the work of Negro poets to reflect a strongly emphasized social consciousness."[4] And he lamented the relatively weak "generalized social-mindedness" that had been seen in black poetry. Ralph Bunche, an associate professor of political science at Howard University, wrote that the race was forming too many organizations and that labor problems for black Americans could only be solved through national labor organizations. Langston Hughes also contributed a poem and a piece of prose fiction.

Race experienced financial problems after the first issue. A call for help from the editorial board provided enough money for a second number, but after that the journal ceased publication. It contains some early thinking of some of the best-known names among black thinkers during the thirties, forties, and fifties. Its rejection of Frederick Douglass, Washington, and Du Bois illustrates the essence of the black intellectual's flirtation with political and economic radicalism in its search for solutions to the eternal race problem.

Notes

1. "Our Aims," *Race* (Winter 1935-36): 3.
2. Henry Lee Moon, "The *Amsterdam News* Lockout," *Race* (Winter 1935-36): 41-42.
3. Ibid.
4. *Race* (Summer 1936): 70.

Information Sources

INDEX SOURCES: None
LOCATION SOURCES: Greenwood Press Periodicals; Schomberg Collection; Library of Congress.

Publication History

MAGAZINE TITLE AND TITLE CHANGES: *Race: Devoted to Social, Political, and Economic Equality* (Winter 1935/36-Summer 1936).

VOLUME AND ISSUE DATA: Vol. I, nos. 1 and 2 (Winter 1935/36 to Spring 1936), quarterly.
PUBLISHER AND PLACE OF PUBLICATION: Conference on Social and Economic Aspects of the Race Problem, New York, New York.
EDITOR: Genevieve Schneider, managing editor (1935-1936).
CIRCULATION: 500 estimate.

REVIEW OF BLACK POLITICAL ECONOMY, THE

An editorial in the 1970 inaugural issue of the *Review of Black Political Economy* explained reasons for creating the publication.

The phrase "black economic development" is very much in fashion at this particular moment, and while the term may quickly fade away, the underlying task of erasing the economic disparity between black and white communities seems destined to be with us for quite some time yet. Increasingly, black people are taking it upon themselves to explore what steps seem to be the most promising ones for achievement of their developmental goals, and while the vast majority of the literature pouring forth on this subject is coming from whites, a nucleus of black economists and social theorists are beginning to make themselves heard.[1]

Accordingly, a growing number of economists among blacks felt the need for a journal that would stimulate and encourage other blacks to subject their own ideas to rigorous analysis and to share them with the reading public. "We hope that the articles which we publish will spark lively and well-presented responses from readers, and we shall print them," the editorial continued.[2] Seven years later, the editor of the *Review of Black Political Economy* wrote that the magazine had fulfilled those original expectations to a reasonable degree. He admitted that economic problems of blacks were essentially the same as they had been in 1970. But the number of blacks pursuing advanced study in economics had expanded considerably. Many of those persons had found the *Review* a sympathetic forum in which to air their views. And the collection of articles had gained a respectful audience.

Throughout its life the magazine published articles that addressed current aspects of the economic status of blacks in various parts of the world. An editorial comment in the mid seventies observed that all of the journal's contents deal with a specific racial group and unavoidably they often have a social and political aspect as well as an economic one. Its editors have always realized that a magazine with a specialized and scholarly focus could hardly be a financial success. The format has been constant almost throughout. Without photographs or art, the *Review of Black Political Economy* has published eight to ten in-depth studies of problems relating to economics of black people in each issue. They have covered blacks in the United States, most countries in black Africa, and the Caribbean. The journal's circulation has remained small. Its publishers have subsidized all of the earlier issues.

The scope of the *Review*'s articles has always been broad. They have explored the extent of black ownership of enterprises that make up the basic American economy; specific sectors of black economic activity; the inner-city economic status of blacks relative to suburban affluence in special geographic areas; and methods of measuring employment change over designated periods of time. Emphasis on the behavior of economics in the United States moved into efforts at business development in newly developed nations of Africa. Other articles encompass a range of interdisciplinary studies, including "Black Officeholding and Political Development in the Rural South," "The Black Stake in Globe Interdependence," "The Sociology of Oppressed Cultures," "Affirmative Action and the Quest for Job Security," and "An Urban Service Corps for Unemployment of Ghetto Youth."

Editorial reply is revolutionary only to the degree that a focus on the critical study of economics of black Americans was a new subject as the sole content of a journal. Nevertheless, the *Review of Black Political Economy* reflected the thinking of the Black Political Convention that demanded reparation for blacks as part of its platform. The *Review*'s staff agreed with the premise that the impoverishment of blacks in America was traceable to slavery. Therefore, an "incalculable social indebtedness" was owed to black people by the general American society which had built much of its wealth upon their exploitation. The same circumstance was true of blacks in Africa and the Caribbean. The magazine published its first special issue on reparations. Others centered upon "The Countries and Peoples of Africa," "Political Economy of United States Policy in Southern Africa," "Historical Patterns of Black-White Political Economic Inequity," and "Planning and Plan Implementation in Nigeria." Recent special issues have included papers presented at a symposium on "Black Community Revitalization" and proceedings of the National Economics Association meeting held in conjunction with the Allied Social Science Association.

Notes

    1. "Publisher's Foreword", *Review of Black Political Economy* (Fall 1972).
    2. Ibid.

Information Sources

BIBLIOGRAPHY:
Bobo, Benjamin F., and Osborne, Alfred E., Jr. *Emerging Issues in Black Economic Development*. Lexington, Mass. 1976, pp. ix-xi.

Browne, Robert S. "Publisher's Foreword." *Review of Black Political Economy*, Spring
    1976, pp. 336-37, Spring 1977, pp. 339-40.
Davis, Frank G. *The Economics of Black Community Development*. Chicago, 1972, p. 4.
INDEX SOURCES: *Social Science Index; Social Science Citation Index; Work Related
    Abstracts.*
LOCATION SOURCES: Many college and university libraries.

Publication History

MAGAZINE TITLE AND TITLE CHANGES: *The Review of Black Political Economy.*
VOLUME AND ISSUE DATA: Vols. I to present (Spring/Summer 1970-), quarterly.
PUBLISHER AND PLACE OF PUBLICATION: National Economics Association and
    Atlanta University Center; issued by Black Economic Research Center, New
    York, N.Y.
EDITORS: Alvin N. Puryear (Spring/Summer 1970-Winter 1972); Joseph F. Brooks
    (Fall 1972); Lloyd L. Hogan (Fall 1973-).
CIRCULATION: 1,200.

S

SATURDAY EVENING QUILL, THE

Boston's black literary community's "Renaissance" periodical was the *Saturday Evening Quill*. Its three issues were essentially annuals, published in 1928, 1929, and 1930. Material in the journals was written largely by Bostonians, but some authors outside that area also contributed. Waring Cuning, Helene Johnson, and Dorothy West were best known among the writers whose works appeared in the *Quill*. Each of them had won prizes in the *Crisis** and *Opportunity** literary contests. Eugene Gordon, editor of the *Quill*, was a member of the editorial staff of the *Boston Post*. He also wrote articles on a variety of subjects for *Opportunity* and the *Messenger*.*[1]

Gordon's "Statement to the Reader" that appeared in the first issue of *Quill* made clear the unique goals of the magazine. It was the organ of the Boston Quill Club, a group of black writers who had no interest in participating in a revolution in Afro-American letters. They pooled their own money to publish their own writing. They did not want to attract a particularly wide audience. Their statement admitted candidly that they did not consider themselves "extraordinary writers." They simply wanted to share their work with their friends after the tradition of a genteel literary club.

Members published fiction, drama, poetry, essays, and a few illustrations in their journal. Although the fiction and some essays addressed social issues among blacks that their contemporary little magazines explored, writers for the *Saturday Evening Quill* used standard English in all their works. Gordon was considered conservative among black literary editors. At a time when one emphasis in the "New Negro" focus reflected African heritage in black American writing, Gordon resolutely maintained a decorous distance from that strain. He did not attack it. Instead, he wrote that Afro-Americans could find in their own land rich sources "unavailable to whites." At the same time, he required black writers to observe the traditional conventions of literary art, irrespective of their subject matter. In the controversy over the proper subject and form for black writing that raged throughout the 1930s, Gordon's position was clear. His ethnoaesthetic held that black writers should "reach out to all people, black and white." Their literature should be "at once profoundly racial and still universal in its appeal."

W.E.B. Du Bois praised the *Quill* in *Crisis*, making the subtle point that it was "by far the most interesting and best of the booklets" issued by young writers in New York, Philadelphia, and elsewhere. Charles Johnson of *Opportunity* wrote in the same vein, singling out the *Saturday Evening Quill* as "the best evidence of a substantial departure from the feverish activity of the last few years."[2]

Notes

1. Some of Gordon's articles about the black press include: "The Negro Press," *American Mercury* (June 1926): 207-15; "The Negro Press," *Annals of the American Academy of Political and Social Sciences* (November 1928): 246-56; "Outstanding Negro Newspapers," *Opportunity* (December 1924): 358-63; and "A Survey of the Negro Press," *Opportunity* (January 1927): 7-11, 32.

2. Both Du Bois and Johnson had been targets of the "radical" young writers who launched *Fire!!** as their organ for free and unfettered expression.

Information Sources

BIBLIOGRAPHY:
"Browsing Reader, The." *Crisis*, September 1928, p. 301; and November 1929, p. 377.
Gordon, Eugene. "The Negro's Literary Tradition." *Saturday Evening Quill*, June 1930, pp. 6-8.
Johnson, Abby Arthur, and Johnson, Ronald Maberry. *Propaganda and Aesthetics: The Literary Politics of Afro-American Magazines in the Twentieth Century*. Amherst: University of Massachusetts Press, 1979, pp. 92-94.
Robinson, William H. Introduction to *The Living Is Easy*, by Dorothy West. Boston, 1948. Arno Press reprint, 1969.
INDEX SOURCES: None.
LOCATION SOURCES: Schomberg Collection, New York Public Library; Moorland-Spingarn Collection, Howard University, Washington, D.C.; Yale University.

Publication History

MAGAZINE TITLE AND TITLE CHANGES: *The Saturday Evening Quill*.
VOLUME AND ISSUE DATA: Vols. I-III (June 1928, April 1929, June 1930), annual.
PUBLISHER AND PLACE OF PUBLICATION: Saturday Evening Quill Club, Boston, Massachusetts.
EDITOR: Eugene Gordon (1928-1930).
CIRCULATION: 500 estimate.

SEPIA

Following the format of *Life* magazine and hoping for a share of the unprecedented popularity that periodical enjoyed with the American white and black reading public, *Sepia*, first published in 1947, has developed into a successful general-purpose publication directed to a black audience. In the *Life* tradition, *Sepia* usually runs an average of 80 to 100 pages per issue, with many photographs accompanying the various articles. The content consists of eight to ten feature articles, news items about black achievement throughout the country, and several regular departments. The magazine enjoys good advertising accounts that tend toward personal improvement products.

In-depth articles in recent issues have covered a wide range of subjects of interest to black readers. "Willie Brown: California's Sassy New Speaker," for instance, chronicles the rise of the speaker of California's state assembly from poverty in his native Mineola, Texas, to his powerful position in the most populous state in the Union. "The Busy Back-Up Singers" tells the story of black singers who have moved up from vocal accompaniment to become stars and headliners in their own right. Like most other black periodicals, *Sepia* emphasizes achievement within the race. Throughout the more than a generation in which it has been continuously published (originally under the title *Negro Achievement*—at which time it was a tabloid newspaper with a magazine format), *Sepia* has highlighted and celebrated black Americans in many fields of endeavor. At the same time, it has detailed the difficulties of living black in the United States. The first issue reported a lynching in South Carolina; a more recent issue noted the mysterious murders of black children in Atlanta and called attention to the Ku Klux Klan training camps in several southern communities.

Sepia also has maintained an interest in the black church. The magazine has referred to the church as the preserver of black culture, the guardian of humanity, and the incubator in the development of black leaders. The church is also the seedbed of black solidarity, the genesis of the black school, the creator of black political ascendency, and the headquarters of community concern and action. So seminal an institution in an American subculture is a rich focus for journalism at any time. A particular report in *Sepia* attempts to describe the importance of the black church to the present status of several black religious denominations and the black Jewish fellowship. The central point of the piece is that the church must change with the times, notwithstanding its historic position in the black community. Whether it is relevant at any moment in history depends on the decisions of its members. Churches that seem to promote civil rights and education at home and in other lands in which black people live, the report concludes, are by far the most popular.

Another area in which *Sepia* has been outspoken and consistently aggressive is in support of historically black colleges and universities at a time when statewide educational systems have brought conventionally black colleges into a common configuration that, to *Sepia* editors, diminishes one area of black leadership. Causes of this kind indicate that *Sepia* is a magazine that publishes serious articles on racial concerns.

Because of its format, *Sepia* has been compared to *Ebony*.* The two magazines are similar as instances of successful black photojournalism. *Sepia*, however, remains basically a newspaper with a focus on black achievement. Its
articles and reports are seldom so fully researched as are *Ebony*'s. Both publications capture the public's interest with the use of many fine photographs that also
attract advertisers. They subsequently enjoy a large circulation such as black
periodicals had not formerly known. They have proven more successful over a
longer period of time than many white and black efforts to publish a general-
purpose picture magazine.

Information Sources

BIBLIOGRAPHY:
Ploski, Harry A., and Marr, Warren II. *The Negro Almanac: A Reference Work on the
    Afro-American*. 3d ed. New York, 1976, p. 929.
Pringle, Beatrice. "We've Come A Long Way." *Sepia*, March 1981, p. 8.
Trebbell, John. *The American Magazine: A Compact History*. New York, 1969, p. 261.
INDEX SOURCE: *Index to Periodical Articles by and about Negroes*.
LOCATION SOURCES: Many college and university libraries; University Microfilms.

Publication History

MAGAZINE TITLE AND TITLE CHANGES: *Negro Achievements* (March 1947-December
    1951); *Sepia* (January 1952 to present).
VOLUME AND ISSUE DATA: Vols. I-(*Sepia* began its own volume series), monthly.
PUBLISHER AND PLACE OF PUBLICATION: Beatrice Pringle, publisher, Sepia Pub-
    lishing Company, Fort Worth, Texas.
EDITORS: Editorial board, including, at one time or another, Bill Lane; Edna Turner;
    Eunice Wilson; Val Holmes; Jeanette Barrett; Rose-Mary H. Carson; Vickie L.
    Hardnett.
CIRCULATION: 160,000.

Mark A. Reger

SOUTHERN FRONTIER, THE

The Commission on Interracial Cooperation, Incorporated, an Atlanta-based
organization of educators, civic leaders, and social scientists, began publication
of the *Southern Frontier* as its house organ in January 1940. In its first issue,
Howard W. Odum, a distinguished sociologist at the University of North Carolina at Chapel Hill and president of the commission, related the title of the
magazine to the commission's work.

We hear a great deal these days about New Frontiers. Sometimes we call
them educational frontiers, social frontiers, political frontiers, economic

frontiers, and many others. What we are all trying to say is apparently the fact that in our attempt to approach the new American frontiers, we assume that having mastered all the physical frontiers of land and rivers and mountains and plains, our next pioneering will be primarily on social and cultural frontiers.[1]

Frederick Jackson Turner's classic definition of the frontier became a frame of reference for the writer who noted that the term suggests advancement, progress, movement, change, high motivation, and horizons. The *Southern Frontier* provided commentary on principal events of the time and their effect upon established mores, particularly in the South. It sought to provide a positive interracial focus through its membership in southern states, including prominent white and black personalities whose gathering of news items, feature articles, and editorials made the slight publication more than a house organ. It chronicled significant movements in education and the broader society at the time, and, in doing so, created a valuable resource for observing some of the major concerns of the professional men and women in the nation during the busy World War II years.

The *Southern Frontier*'s emphasis on higher education was natural. The 1938 landmark decision in *Lloyd Gaines* v. *Missouri* ruled that states that operated racially separate systems of public higher education must either admit blacks to their professional or graduate schools or provide "separate but equal" institutions in those states for black residents who qualified for such services. That Supreme Court decision awakened wide interest and tension among educators and legislators. The Southern University Conference, meeting in Atlanta, pondered the "practical solutions" states could take to meet the new requirement. Few white educators advocated opening their universities to blacks. They preferred to find ways to provide acceptable separate education in the areas that had not been previously available to blacks. President Harmon W. Caldwell of the University of Georgia advised that states should expand their black public colleges into graduate and professional schools and make allocations for that purpose to their private institutions as a way of implementing the court edict.

A *Southern Frontier* article explained in detail the way Texas had met the needs of its black citizens who sought education not available at the segregated colleges designed for them. That State's legislature had appropriated $25,000 for each of two years following 1940 to support an out-of-state tuition program to keep its universities white. A detailed report showed that 53 or 180 applicants had received grants covering basic costs for matriculation in most professional curricula. Moreover, the legislature had appropriated monies for graduate work at Texas' black Prairie View State College. This choice of operating "separate but equal" professional and graduate education or contracting it to unsegregated universities found favor with most southern educators, including those who wrote for the *Southern Frontier*. Texas was not alone in funding plans like that described above. Each of the states that segregated students in higher education followed some form of the practice.

The "progressive view" taken by Texas was due in no small degree to the interest the Interracial Commission and Woman's Missionary Society of the Methodist Church took in pushing Negro higher education in the legislature. The *Southern Frontier* saw this trend to upgrade educational opportunities for blacks as a good sign of improvement in social relations in the country. One editorial quoted a Dallas newspaper editor who, after noting that a recent conference at Texas A. and M. College had determined that Prairie View was a substandard institution, wrote that the several Texas plans to improve black education were "in the common interest of the state." For the higher the level to which the black standard of living and training could be brought, the more constructive would be the black American contribution to the general welfare. The Dallas editor and the *Southern Frontier* agreed, in this respect, with "far-sighted" Henry Grady, who was recalled to have said: "Meanwhile we treat the Negro fairly, reassuring to him justice and the fullness that the strong should extend to the weak."

The journal was hearty in its praise of Judge John J. Parker of the Fourth Circuit Court of Appeals, who overturned a lower-court ruling and supported Melvin O. Alston, a Negro schoolteacher, in his suit to be paid a salary equal to white teachers in the Norfolk, Virginia, public schools. The jurist wrote of the case: "This is as clear a case of discrimination on the ground of race as could well be imagined and falls squarely within the inhibition of both the due process and the equal protection clauses of the Fourteenth Amendment." Parker was the same judge whose appointment to the Supreme Court had been recommended by President Calvin Coolidge earlier and had been successfully opposed by the NAACP and organized labor. The *Southern Frontier* thought the ruling progressive and significant.

From that time on, the journal became more politically active. It gave special attention to the presidential campaign of 1940. After Franklin D. Roosevelt had been reelected by a comfortable margin of votes, an editorial observed:

> The recent political campaign divided the race into two camps. Some stayed with the party of Abraham Lincoln, some remained in the party of "white supremacy." But this division on party affiliation has not been so deep as to divide the race on the question of their rights and privileges as citizens. They want no barriers placed against the exercise of the franchise; they want to serve their country on a basis equal with that of all other citizens; they want all discrimination set up by governmental agencies removed.[2]

This statement marked a movement toward advocacy of racial advancement rather than one of reporting on encouraging interracial cooperation. Members of the editorial board wrote to remind their audience of the magazine's responsibility to present the mind of the southern Negro to its readers, and the political activities of the race elsewhere which bore directly upon southern conditions. The magazine also began to reprint editorials from southern daily newspapers that commented upon the growing influence of Negroes in the Democratic party; their concern about enjoying benefits that should come from the nation's impending involvement in World War II; the continuing menace of lynching; advances in higher education; and economic problems of minority groups.

The growing strength of the black press drew praise from the *Southern Frontier*. An editorial noted that by early 1941 Negroes no longer were dependent upon white newspapers for knowledge about themselves; for "nowadays there are enough Negro newspapers—North, South, East and West—to support an Associated Negro Press, and enough local correspondents to furnish a mass of newsstories of Negro achievements and entertainment and of white injustice that roll off the press everyday."[3] The magazine joined other black journals that responded vigorously to Westbrook Pegler's attack on the black press in the *New York World-Telegram* for its insistence upon keeping civil rights for Negroes before the public. The *Southern Frontier* reprinted the response that Lester B. Granger, secretary of the National Urban League, wrote for the *Pittsburgh Courier*.

If Negro newspapers over-emphasize racial discrimination as practiced against their readers, it is because the white press generally shirks its own responsibility by keeping silent. Not a dozen important dailies in the United States even pretend to report honestly and fairly the aggressions of America's white majority against the citizenship rights of Negroes. If the Negro editor seems sometimes to try to extenuate a Negro's infraction of the law, it is because the white press almost invariably magnifies, distorts or ignores the real facts.

If a Negro newspaper, hard-pressed for advertisers, accepts contracts from business houses of doubtful repute, its sin is hardly as serious as that of the white daily carrying a full-page strike-breaking ad from an anti-union employer or a help wanted ad marked "white Christians only." If the effect of "lucky stone" advertisements contradicts the Negro editor's appeal to the intelligence and racial pride of his readers, this by no means matches the impotence of a Westbrook Pegler pretending to have any concern for or misunderstanding of the unbearable problems which confront and confuse Negro citizens in any imperfect American democracy.[4]

Inasmuch as *Southern Frontier* was primarily an organ of the Commission on Interracial Cooperation, a great deal of its content concentrated upon social aspects of American life. World War II focused particular attention on the black worker and women in the war effort and the expectations of the race following their participation in the national emergency at home and abroad. It was subscribed to by colleges, libraries, and private citizens throughout much of the nation. The journal received strong financial support and carried articles written by significant American personalities including sociologists Howard W. Odum, Charles S. Johnson, Ira DeA. Reid, and Walter Shivers; educator Frederick D. Patterson and poet Langston Hughes. During the first two years of publication, state issues were edited by persons living in Georgia, South Carolina, Mississippi, and Texas. Thereafter, the news activities came from the entire region covering the area from the Eastern Seaboard to Texas.

One irony of the black experience in the United States during the early years of the *Southern Frontier*'s publication is evidenced in the comment of Mrs. Henry A. Hunt, president of the Georgia Federation of Colored Women's Clubs.

Just as one is making up one's mind that the South is really undergoing a change in its feelings racially—that the spirit of justice and fair play are on the upward trend—something arises to take the joy out of life.

There are those of us who bought copies of *Gone With the Wind* and put them in our libraries. We read eagerly the newspaper accounts when the play was in the making in Hollywood, and felt so proud that Miss Myrick of Macon was making such a grand hit and that the colored artist, Hattie MacDaniel, was cited as being second to Miss Myrick in nearly stealing the show from Clark Gable and Vivien Leigh when the premier was given in Atlanta. And now right in the midst of our rejoicing comes the news that the colored people of Macon are asked to go to the second balcony by way of the open fire escape if they wish to see *Gone With the Wind*. No white theatre in that city admits colored people. The city auditorium doors are open on special occasions jointly to both groups. This was demonstrated in January when Cab Calloway appeared with his orchestra. The patronage of the white people was surprisingly large, especially on such a cold night.[5]

The *Southern Frontier*, published throughout the first half of the 1940s serves as a significant depository of news of interracial cooperation in the period immediately preceding and including the United States' entry into World War II. The greatest concerns of that time lay in the matters of the courts and higher education, the presidential election of 1940, race and the war effort, and general aspects of the growing strength of the Negro in the Democratic party in the United States.

Notes

1. "On the Southern Frontier," *Southern Frontier* (January 1940): 1.
2. "What Negroes Are Saying About Democracy and the White Primary," *Southern Frontier* (December 1940): 2.
3. "Negroes Have Their Own News Sources," *Southern Frontier* (March 1941): 2.
4. Ibid.
5. "Some Day the Veil Will Be Lifted," *Southern Frontier* (February 1940): 3.

Information Sources

INDEX SOURCES: None
LOCATION SOURCE: Greenwood Press Periodicals.

Publication History

MAGAZINE TITLE AND TITLE CHANGES: *The Southern Frontier*.
VOLUME AND ISSUE DATA: Vols. I-VI (January 1940-December 1945), monthly.
PUBLISHER AND PLACE OF PUBLICATION: Commission on Interracial Cooperation, Incorporated, Atlanta, Georgia.
EDITORS: Vol. I, no. 1-6, editorial board; beginning with Vol. I, no. 7, Jessie Daniel Ames.
CIRCULATION: 1,000 estimate.

SOUTHERN WORKMAN, THE

General Samuel C. Armstrong, a Union army officer in the Civil War, went South when the war was ended and joined in the work of assisting the freedmen.[1] The American Missionary Association, a New England-based philanthropic organization, gave him the job of starting Hampton Institute in Virginia in 1868. He established in the town of Hampton, Virginia, an early and important black school. Armstrong set the educational ideas that the institute carried out. He also established the *Southern Workman*, the publicity medium for the school. Its first issue appeared in January 1872 and it continued in publication until July 1939.

Throughout most of the publication history of the *Southern Workman*, the chief executive officer of Hampton Institute was chairman of the publicity committee that edited the magazine. The journal was the promotional organ for the school and the mouthpiece of the principal. As a private institution, Hampton depended on wealthy white Americans—North and South—for its maintenance. Armstrong was a northerner who worked diligently to make Hampton successful. He succeeded in his project. Two of his successors—Hollis Burke Frissell and James Edgar Gregg, the former a southerner and the latter a northerner—followed Armstrong's example in using the *Workman* to communicate the activities of the institute and to articulate its needs.

The *Southern Workman* was published regularly longer than any other black journal with the exception of the *Crisis*. It is an excellent source of details on the history of education for black Americans from the post-Civil War period to the depression, the racial tensions that accompanied movements for education and social and political advancement for Afro-Americans and Indians, American folklore, and some of the develeoping emphases toward social awareness of black Americans with respect to their growing role as first-class Americans. The journal published some creative writing, but that was not one of its emphases. Some essays about the rise of the Harlem Renaissance as a literary and cultural movement appear in the magazine, and many prominent Americans—black and white—contributed articles to *Southern Workman* over the many decades of its publication.

Clearly, Armstrong looked upon himself as a missionary to the American interior when he came to Hampton. His role was his philanthropy to black education. The "natives" to whom he ministered were the black freedmen in the Tidewater area of Virginia and neighboring states. As an outsider to that area, Armstrong felt a strong need to communicate the nature and worth of his work and his aspirations to northerners who might contribute to his cause and, at the same time, to secure the necessary cooperation of southerners in whose midst he worked. His was a delicate task, inasmuch as he was required to reconcile white northern and southern attitudes toward one another while operating a school for the education of black Americans who had recently been freed from physical slavery. In the tradition of most missionaries of the period, Armstrong felt industrial education and strict moral instruction were the priorities for black education.

Armstrong explained the uniqueness of the setting of Hampton in the first issue of his journal. With accompanying illustrations, he described Hampton as the birthplace of English civilization in North America:

> When the doughty Captain John Smith in 1607 was on his exploring voyage up the Potomac in search of a fit place for a settlement, he was met by five natives of the country, who invited his party to their town Kecoughtan, feasted them with cake made of Indian corn, and regaled them with tobacco and a dance. On the site of this Indian village stands the town of Hampton. It was founded three years after the visit of Captain Smith and is said to be the oldest continuous English settlement in North America.[2]

The institute occupied 125 acres formerly known as the Wood Farm that was the site of a Union army hospital, Armstrong wrote. The school was organized to prepare youth of the South for organizing and instructing in schools in southern states that would be devoted to "the industrial classes." The students would be black (later Indians were added) and they would be taught to serve the agricultural and industrial needs of the South in order to assist that section of the nation in returning to economic stability after the war. "Each number [of the magazine] will contain not less than three illustrations and will furnish a variety of choices of reading that tell what is going on in the world and will aim to please and profit both the old and the young," Armstrong promised.[3]

Armstrong's delicate balance between white northerner and southern philanthropists engaged in education for black freedmen caused editorial and feature articles in the *Southern Workman* to studiously avoid the controversial issues that interested most black Americans. It commented on the labor problem in Virginia, the presidential campaign of 1872, the Freedmen's Bank, agriculture in the South, and successful activities of black graduates of Hampton during the Reconstruction period but refrained from partisan comments. An editorial in 1877 summed up the journal's emphases in its first few years:

> *The Southern Workman* has entered upon its sixth year and has become one of the longest-lived of the periodicals published in the interest of the colored race. It has not been supported by nor represented any denomination or political party. The ideas it has advocated have not always been popular, yet have commended themselves to thoughtful men of both sections and races. It has sought for common ground on which good men, without regard to party, could work together for the well-being of our country ravaged by ignorance, prejudice, corruption and violence.[4]

The journal had preached the gospel of salvation by hard work, the editorial continued, warning freedmen of the "slippery tenure and great temptations of political position and the uncertainty of continued external support"; and had, instead, advocated industrial education as the panacea for the needs of recently enfranchised black Americans. The journal followed this editorial policy throughout the late years of the nineteenth century. It never commented on *Plessy* v. *Ferguson*,[5] the growing violations of the guarantees of the Fourteenth and Fifteenth Amendments to the Constitution that had been enacted during Reconstruction, and the growing restrictions on Negroes imposed by jim crow laws in southern states and the white political primaries. Armstrong was a primary author of the creed usually associated with Booker T. Washington—that hard work and scrupulous morality were preferable to seeking political participation on the part of black Americans. *Southern Workman* projected and supported this philosophy with its contents and the implications of those issues that it failed to discuss.

Commenting on President James Garfield's inaugural address in which he promised that "full devotion of the Negro race from slavery to the full right of citizenship" would be a hallmark of his administration, Armstrong wrote: "Making voters out of slaves and not fitting them to vote shows scant wisdom and weak patriotism."[6]

Hampton Institute became in the nineteenth century a principal school for the education of American Indians. *Southern Workman* established an Indian department as a supplement in 1886. It contained news about Indian students at Hampton and reports on the Bureau of Indian Affairs in various parts of the West and Southwest for the next two decades. During the same period, the journal instituted a feature, "The Southern Press," that contained comments on Negro affairs, pro and con, from mostly white newspapers.

Armstrong seldom mentioned the black press. In one issue, however, his editorials gave special attention to the A.M.E. Church's *Christian Recorder*, the

New York Age, and the *Indianapolis Freeman*, all leading black newspapers. The reason for mentioning them lay in an incident that had irked Armstrong. He had presented an essay to students at Yale University entitled "Missionary Work for the Negro." Armstrong seemed surprised that the *Freeman*'s editor was aware of the essay, and he was obviously offended by that newspaper's editorial on the talk. "It is charged that the estimate there made of the present status of the Southern Negro is incorrect," Armstrong wrote of the black paper's editorial, "and the deduction is made that the writer is not sufficiently familiar with his subject, and in plain language, does not know what he is talking about."[7] Armstrong protested that he could hardly be called prejudiced, given his long work with freedman; but for the first time in his journal, he made mention of opinions of blacks about their own affairs. Previously, he had been a chief exponent of the position that white philanthropy knew what was best for freedmen's education, their social status, and their future as American citizens. Further, inasmuch as philanthropic money paid for the education of the freedmen, they had the privilege and the responsibility of determining the content and format of that education.

Stung by the criticism of this very philosophy, Armstrong wrote:

> The colored journals of the country afford one of the best tests of the rate of development of the race in whose interest they are published. In this case, however, it is the direct testimony which is of value rather than the indirect; that is, it is not so much that the editors of these journals make certain statements or claims, as it is that the typical errors are fewer, the paper better, the English is more correct, the advertisements of a different character, the personalities less coarse, the whole thing better balanced, than of old. They claim, as a rule, much less, they admit much more, and by their willingness to accept facts, even when they count against themselves, are gradually winning the respect and confidence of their white readers. A few years ago there was hardly a colored journal in this country whose editorials were worthy of consideration. Today, there are several which are not merely worth reading, but are factors in the situation, having real and growing influence among whites as well as blacks.[8]

The growing influence of black journals seemed to give Armstrong concern, despite the patronizing tone of the editorial. Elsewhere in the same issue, another item in the column "Southern Press: Both Sides" calls the *New York Age* and the *Indianapolis Freeman* the "two ablest Negro papers now published in the country," whose editorials "[are] thoughtful, often eloquent and usually well balanced."[9] At no other time during Armstrong's administration did the *Southern Workman* take any notice of black newspapers.

Hollis Burke Frissell, Armstrong's long-time chief assistant in the administration of Hampton Institute, assumed the presidency and the responsibility for the *Southern Workman* upon the death of the founder. A southerner, Frissell stressed a new approach to education at Hampton. His was called the "Hampton Idea." It reversed Armstrong's original purpose. With Frissell, the academic department became the stepping stone to industrial and trade work, rather than the other way around as had been Armstrong's philosophy. Frissell reasoned that his new emphasis would ingratiate Hampton to those who were willing to pay for a system that would keep blacks in subservient positions in American society. And he was spectacularly successful. By 1925 Hampton was first among black schools and seventeenth among 176 American colleges listed according to the value of their endowment funds.[10]

By 1899, the format of the journal had changed considerably. Contributed articles began to appear. Paul Laurence Dunbar, the leading black poet of the day, published "A Southern Silhouette," one of his prose fiction pieces. Although the magazine had begun earlier to carry items of folklore, the content was broadened. Apparently in response to criticism W.E.B. Du Bois and other black leaders directed toward the "Hampton Idea," the *Southern Workman* began to resemble a black scholarly journal. Articles on race, including "A Comparative Study of the Negro Problem," comprehensive book reviews, and articles about American society in general appeared. Those included discussions of the educated colored woman, black wage-earners, the Negro in fiction, the Negro pulpit and its responsibilities, Negro business enterprises, and black Americans as army officers. Editorials centered on race relations. This new editorial policy brought forth articles written by popular black American leaders, including: George Washington Carver, William S. Scarborough, Lucy Laney, Robert R. Moton, R. R. Wright, Kelly Miller, and Booker T. Washington. Book reviews covered works written by Washington, Du Bois, and Charles W. Chesnutt. Articles about blacks in the Caribbean also appeared. On the death of Paul Laurence Dunbar in 1906, an editorial noted:

> In the death of Paul Laurence Dunbar, the Negro race has lost its foremost poet and *Southern Workman* a valued contributor. Mr. Dunbar has been pleasantly associated with Hampton Institute, not only through his contributions to its magazine, but also in other ways. Mr. Dunbar's recital before the school several years ago of some of his poems was greatly enjoyed.... As a sympathetic author in lyrical form of the quaintness, the foibles, and virtues of his race, he was unsurpassed.[11]

When Booker T. Washington died in 1915, the *Southern Workman* paid high praise to him as the institute's most illustrious alumnus and one who had carried the "Hampton Idea" into the "Tuskegee Idea." The January 1916 issue was dedicated to Washington and his work in education.

Although the *Southern Workman* was not primarily a literary magazine and seldom contained creative writing, some of its feature articles took cognizance of the Harlem Renaissance and its literary dimensions. Robert T. Kerlin, a white

American who had published an anthology of black poetry, wrote an essay, "Conquest of Poetry," that was his reaction to the literary contests conducted by the *Crisis** and *Opporunity** in the 1920s. He wrote that the American Negro poet was "plainly in the vestibule of the Hall of Fame," and expressed his surprise at the high quality of the eighty or so poems that had been in those literary contests.[12]

Benjamin Brawley, professor of English at Shaw University in Raleigh, North Carolina, at the time, wrote the most important article on the Harlem Renaissance to appear in the *Southern Workman*. In it, he attacked the superficiality of the literary works produced by this movement. He wrote of the authors:

> The recent literary striving on the part of young Negro people throughout the country really began in the throes of the World War. After all discount is made, after all the tinsel is brushed away, the fact remains that the grandiose schemes of Marcus Garvey gave to the race a consciousness such as it had never possessed before. The dream of a united Africa, not less than a trip to France, challenged the imagination; and the soul of the Negro experienced a new sense of freedom. To be black ceased to be a matter for explanation or apology; instead it became something to be advertised and exploited: thus the changed point of view made for increased racial self-respect.[13]

After detailing many works that had been submitted to the *Crisis* and *Opportunity*, Brawley attacked the vulgarity of much of them. He concluded: "He who would be a poet in the new day must not only have a vision; he must labor unceasingly to give the vision beautiful and enduring form."[14]

Alice Dunbar-Nelson, widow of Paul Laurence Dunbar and an author in her own right, attacked the "New Negro" concept for its reliance on the content and interpretation of world history used by white scholars and authors. She rejected a cultural trend based on winning wars and the economic emphases for the race as espoused by the black historians, Carter G. Woodson and W.E.B. Du Bois. They talked about the "gifts" of the race in terms of material matters, she complained. To her, the strength of black people in America lay in their natural inclination toward peace and the strength of Christianity rather than military and economic conquests. "If it were not for the black man in this country," she wrote, "the Christian religion would be a low point in the graph." She did not consider her repudiation of war a sentiment of disloyalty; instead, she wrote that "in an age of skepticism toward conventions," a break-down of tradition had brought with it an attitude of analysis of the clinging to outworn tradition.[15] While Dunbar-Nelson did not prescribe precisely the kind of literary works she would like to see represent the "New Negro" and the celebrated renaissance in Afro-American letters, like Brawley she sensed that some element other than the new freedom of expression was necessary to develop a lasting new art for a people who were striving desperately to express themselves with self-respect.

That "New Negro" concept, a hallmark of the 1920s, was the focus of distressing problems for Hampton Institute, although little discussion of those tensions and controversies appeared in the *Southern Workman*. James Edgar Gregg became Hampton's third white principal in 1918 at a time when Du Bois and other black leaders were criticizing the institute for the inability of its leading administrators to understand the black people it was educating and sending out into America. Gregg was educated at Yale and Harvard and had served pastorates in Massachusetts. He came to Hampton when the influence of the "New Negro" philosophy was making itself manifest throughout the nation, particularly in schools of black youth that had been headed and staffed by white "missionaries." The best known of these institutions—Howard, Fisk, Shaw, Lincoln (Pennsylvania)—were facing a recalcitrant student body and often a disillusioned alumni who contended that inferior education intended to keep black youth in subservient work and schools for blacks staffed by whites had run their course. Even as the years following World War I found new expectations and new strategies for achieving them present in American cities among black people, private philanthropy and missionary schools witnessed a siege of rebellions.[16]

Gregg liberalized Hampton considerably and added some twenty black members to the academic faculty. Armstrong's faculties had been all white. But he had serious problems, such as dealing with the demands of white people around Hampton for racially segregated seating arrangements at concerts at the institute. Moreover, while students held high appreciation for Negro spirituals and "plantation songs" as folk material, they resented singing them for visiting whites. The songs reminded students of the slavery they hated. They felt they were romanticizing the memory of the dehumanizing institution of slavery when they performed the music. R. Nathaniel Dett, the popular and talented director of music at the institute, wanted to use black folk music not for singing spirituals to visitors and donors but as the basis for creative works for voices and instruments. Dett was eventually relieved of his position at Hampton.

Student resistance to singing spirituals along with rigid standards of student dress and social conduct led to open rebellion against Gregg. At he same time, Gregg was seeking to respond to strong pressures from students and Hampton alumni to upgrade the institute's academic standards and to move away from his predecessor's philosophy that academic subjects should only support industrial education. Programs in education and in library science were attempts to respond to these demands. Gregg was also forced to appease philanthropists who held that Hampton never was intended to be a liberal arts college; they would not support such a school for Negroes. Du Bois in the *Crisis* and the editors of the *New York Age* attacked Gregg for suspending students who struck against his administration.

Throughout the height of these controversies, the *Southern Workman* seldom carried editorials or articles that dealt directly with the problems. Gregg used his editorials most often to convince philanthropists that Hampton's endowment drive was a worthy cause. The journal never responded directly to the continuous criticism of the "Hampton Idea" that the black press kept alive. When Gregg decided to resign in May of 1929, Hampton had undergone a remarkable metamorphosis since its founding some fifty years earlier. It was still administered and supported by whites, but its faculty was racially mixed and it offered baccalaureate and masters degrees. It maintained its technology, but it was also consonant—at least in curriculum—with the other black colleges that were becoming stronger with the passing of the years.

The *Southern Workman*, despite its role during much of its existence as a promotion medium for Hampton Institute, represents a significant document of black private education in the United States. It is also a treasure trove of black American folklore, of Indian lore and education, and of educational developments in Africa and the Caribbean and Hawaii, and a compendium of scholarly articles and research on American social problems as they relate particularly to race. It declined in scope and significance in the 1930s, finally ending publication in July 1939. *Southern Workman* is far more than an institutional periodical. Its longevity and the changing forces that scored that long period of sixty-eight years make it a significant document of American social, political, and cultural history.

Notes

1. Samuel Chapman Armstrong was born in the Hawaiian Islands, 30 January 1839. He graduated from Williams College in Massachusetts in 1862. After graduation, he entered the Union Army and eventually became commander of the Ninth and Eighth regiments of the United States Negro troops. In 1866 he was appointed an officer in the Freedmen's Bureau with responsibility for a section of eastern Viriginia. He founded Hampton Institute in April 1868. See L. P. Jackson, "The Origin of Hampton Institute," *Journal of Negro History* (April 1925): 131-49 for a succinct account of the conditions of the founding of Hampton Institute.

2. "Hampton and Its Surroundings," *Southern Workman* (January 1872): 1.

3. Ibid., p. 3.

4. Editorial, *Southern Workman* (February 1877): 4.

5. In 1896, the United States Supreme Court decided in the case of *Plessy* v. *Ferguson* that creation of "separate but equal" public accommodations is a "reasonable" use of state police power. Homer Plessy, a New Orleans Negro, had challenged the new jim crow Louisiana law that permitted segregated railroad carriages. Black Americans were outraged by the ruling. The black press complained bitterly about the decision that was essentially the basis for segregation in public facilities and accommodations until *Brown* v. *Topeka* in 1954.

6. "Report on President Garfield's Inaugural Address," editorial, *Southern Workman* (April 1881): 39.

7. Editorial, *Southern Workman* (April 1889): 4.

8. Ibid.

9. Ibid.

10. This estimate is reported in Raymond Wolters, *The New Negro on Campus: Black College Rebellions of the 1920s* (Princeton, N.J.: Princeton University Press, 1975), p. 231.

11. "Paul Laurence Dunbar," *Southern Workman* (March 1906): 136-37.

12. Robert T. Kerlin, "A Pair of Youthful Negro Poets," *Southern Workman* (June 1927): 282.

13. "The Negro Literary Renaissance," *Southern Workman* (April 1927): 177.

14. Ibid., 184.

15. "The Negro Looks at an Outworn Tradition," *Southern Workman* (May 1928): 196.

16. See Walters, pp. 262-75, for details of this matter.

Information Sources

BIBLIOGRAPHY:

Du Bois, W.E.B. "Advice." *Crisis*, March 1918, p. 215.

————, "Hampton." *Crisis*, November 1917, pp. 20-21.

————, "Social Equality at Hampton." *Crisis*, June 1925, pp. 59-60.

Jackson, L. P. "The Origin of Hampton Institute." *Journal of Negro History*, April 1925, pp. 131-49.

McBrier, Vivan Flagg. *R. Nathaniel Dett: His Life and Works (1882-1943)*. Washington, D.C.: The Associated Publisher, 1977.

Wolters, Raymond. *The New Negro on Campus: Black College Rebellion of the 1920s*. Princeton, N.J.: Princeton University Press, 1975.

INDEX SOURCES: None

LOCATION SOURCES: Hampton Institute Library; New York Public Library; Tuskegee Institute Library; Moorland-Spingarn Research Center, Howard University, Washington, D.C.; International Microfilm.

Publication History

MAGAZINE TITLE AND TITLE CHANGES: *The Southern Workman* (January 1868-July 1939).

VOLUME AND ISSUE DATA: Vols. I-LXVIII (January 1872-July 1939), monthly.

PUBLISHER AND PLACE OF PUBLICATION: Hampton Institute, Hampton, Virginia.

EDITORS: Samuel C. Armstrong, chairman of editorial board, January 1872-June 1893; Hollis B. Frissell, chairman of editorial board, July 1893-October 1917; Helen W. Ludlow, editor, November 1917-December 1918; James E. Gregg, chairman of editorial board, January 1919-December 1926; Allen B. Doggett, Jr., editor, January 1927-December 1930; Bessie L. Drew, managing editor, January 1934; George Adrian Kuyper, chairman of editorial board, February 1934-December 1934; Isaac Fisher, editor, January 1935-July 1939.

CIRCULATION: 4,000 (highest).

Brian Joseph Benson

SOUTHWESTERN JOURNAL

Few black scholars and educators published their scholarship and opinions in American professional journals before the establishment of faculty research publications in black colleges. Booker T. Washington, W.E.B. Du Bois, Kelly Miller, and a few others placed articles in "liberal" magazines. This limited opportunity led to the appearance of a large number of magazines for black scholars, particularly after World War II. *Southwestern Journal* was begun in 1944 to serve the unique need of black educators. Its editor expressed in the first issue the threefold purpose: (1) to present reports of research projects originating in or dealing with southwestern life; (2) to present scholarly discussions of historical, educational, economic, and cultural problems calculated both to interpret the Southwest to the nation and the nation to the Southwest; and (3) to emphasize those aspects of national life and thought which tend toward the integration of all races into the dominant culture pattern of the region and the nation. These goals were especially meaningful in black education. At Langston University in Oklahoma the need was clear and strong. For land-grant colleges were afterthoughts for black education. They emerged as a result of a stipulation in the Second Morrill Act that required a new wave of institutions supported by state and federal funds to offer education in the "practical arts" to black and white Americans.[1] Most border states gained public black colleges through this legislation. Land-grant colleges had the legal responsibility for teaching, research, and service.

The new black colleges engaged in little scientific research. They resembled liberal arts and teacher training institutions. All of them offered some courses in agriculture, home economics, and technology. Many were battlegrounds for adaptations of the classical argument between industrial and classical education. The post-World War II years found these institutions struggling to improve the educational level of their faculties and seeking to make themselves visible in a society that, forced with the beginnings of growing pressure to provide equal education opportunity for white and black youth, pondered whether to close their public black colleges or to integrate white universities. This peculiar milieu spawned faculty research journals.

Despite these social and historical imperatives, its editors wrote that *Southwestern Journal* did not intend to foster sectionalism or racialism. On the contrary, it aimed to assist in creating national unity through better understanding. To a degree, it would emphasize sectionalism, inasmuch as the Southwest was not a "fixed concept." For the journal, the term included Missouri, Oklahoma, Texas, Arkansas, and Louisiana. The journal offered to consider papers written by persons living outside the region and dealing with problems of national significance, although it preferred material from scholars and thinkers in the Southwest. In the traditional format of scholarly journals this one covered three major areas: articles of research and scholarly discussion; reports on authors and books; and reports on significant events. Melvin B. Tolson, an associate editor and a faculty member of Langston University who had gained some national notice as a published poet, served as the principal book reviewer.

"Humanizing scholarship" is the term the editors used to label some of their most significant articles. "A Song, A Dance, and A Play," a condensation of

Leslie M. Collins' doctoral dissertation for Western Reserve University, is a prime example of this emphasis. Collins, who earned that university's first Ph.D. in American Culture, wrote a study of the lives of Marian Anderson, Katherine Dunham, and Paul Robeson. These three black artists—a singer, a dancer, and an actor—used their artistic gifts in the service of social protest, overtly or unconsciously, Collins claimed. The universality these black Americans found in pursuing their art seemed compatible with *Southwestern Journal*'s editorial purposes. Other articles exploring the humanities were "Samuel Coleridge-Taylor," a biographical study of the black English musician that describes and analyzes several of his vocal and instrumental works. A socioaesthetic article, "Old-Time Negro Preaching: Its Purposes and an Interpretation," explored the subject matter and modes of persuasion used by the black preacher in America. The journal also published the text of a lecture on "Poetry and Life" that Langston Hughes delivered at Langston.

The journal was established primarily to serve as a research publication for the faculty of Langston University. But it transcended the original southwestern regionalism. It did limit its contents, primarily, to research about and by blacks. As was the case with most scholarly journals initiated by black colleges, *Southwestern Journal* favored publication of papers dealing with the humanities and teacher education. Limited resources, common to the "1890 land-grant colleges," seldom encouraged significant scientific research. The magazines published by those colleges reflected this impact.

Note

1. The First Morrill Act, approved by President Abraham Lincoln in 1862, established the first group of colleges and universities for these purposes. In 1890 the Second Morrill Act made possible assignment of the land-grant function to black colleges that were already in existence and, in some cases, establishment of others to serve those ends. The original act had been used by some states to provide some education for blacks. Virginia allocated one-third of its federal grant to Hampton Institute. Claflin College in South Carolina and Alcorn State University in Mississippi also received funds. Most black colleges arose as a result of the Second Morrill Act.

Information Sources

BIBLIOGRAPHY:
Brunner, Henry S. "Land-Grant Colleges and Universities, 1862-1962." United States Department of Health, Education and Welfare Bulletin no. 13. Washington, D.C., 1962, pp. 3-7.
Ford, Nick Aaron. "Aims and Methods of *Southwestern Journal*." *Southwestern Journal*, May 1944, pp. 1-4.
Holmes, Dwight Oliver Wendell. "Seventy Years of the Negro College, 1860 to 1930." *Phylon*, Spring 1949, pp. 307-13.
Hubbell, John T. "Some Reactions to the Desegregation of the University of Oklahoma, 1946-1950." *Phylon*, June 1973, pp. 187-96.
INDEX SOURCE: *Index to Selected Periodicals Decennial Cumulation 1950-1959.*

LOCATION SOURCES: Langston University; Lincoln University, Jefferson City, Missouri; Moorland-Spingarn Collection, Howard University, Washington, D.C.

Publication History

MAGAZINE TITLE AND TITLE CHANGES: *Southwestern Journal*.
VOLUME AND ISSUE DATA: Vols. I-V (May 1944-Winter 1951).
PUBLISHER AND PLACE OF PUBLICATION: Langston University, Langston, Oklahoma.
EDITORS: Nick Aaron Ford (May 1944-Fall 1945); Mozell C. Hill (Winter 1946-Summer 1949); Youra Qualls (Fall 1949-Winter 1951).
CIRCULATION: 1,500 estimate.

SPOKESMAN, THE

Its first editorial suggested that the *Spokesman* would be a militant publication, "condemning and opposing wrong" and "defending right in spite of results." It seemed compatible with the other periodicals growing up at the time. Georgia Douglass Johnson, Angelina Grimké, and James Weldon Johnson—all respected poets of the black Establishment—published poems in the *Spokesman*. As would be expected of a New York-based black magazine in the mid 1920s, the journal's editorials attacked lynching, denials of voting rights for blacks, and racial discrimination in public places. Articles discussed black history, African affairs, and higher education in the United States. But the *Spokesman* was not attuned to the prevailing "New Negro" theme of the Harlem Renaissance period in which it appeared. It did not become a well-known magazine. It had to compete with the *Crisis,** *Opportunity,** and the *Messenger,** together with the black weekly newspapers published in Harlem—the *Amsterdam News, New York Age,* and Marcus Garvey's *Black World*.

Like other black periodicals, the *Spokesman* commented broadly on the problem of black leadership wherein a vacuum had been created with the death of Booker T. Washington and the emergence of the NAACP. Garvey, the Jamaican-born leader of the dramatic and temporarily successful Universal Negro Improvement Association (UNIA), engaged the interest of most Americans. A. Philip Randolph of the *Messenger* and W.E.B. Du Bois of the *Crisis* rejected Garvey's leadership. His efforts sounded strikingly similar to those propounded by black Nationalists a generation later. But most Afro-Americans at that time considered the United States the home they had helped to build. To them, Garvey's plan to build a black world in Africa was impractical and fantastic, although blacks had discussed migration "back to Africa" throughout several decades before UNIA was organized. The *Spokesman*'s editorials were more in favor of the movement than was most of the black press. They praised Garvey for having "performed a spiritual miracle in getting colored people together and inculcating race pride." The general problem of leadership among blacks led the *Spokesman* to develop a regular feature that presented biographies of black leaders in history. When Frederick Douglass was nominated for a niche in the New York University Hall of Fame, the journal carried an essay on his life and public accomplishments.

The *Spokesman* was basically a "conservative" black journal. It played a brief role as a literary magazine during the Harlem Renaissance, though, during the four months in 1925 when Zora Neale Hurston served as its editor.[1] She published one of her short stories, "Magnolia Flower," in the *Spokesman*. Mary Fair Burks, one of the few literary historians to research and write about black little magazines wrote of Hurston's involvement with this journal during the renaissance.

> *The Spokesman*, under Miss Hurston, became a pilot journal for the little journals that were to follow. It replaced themes about the Black Gentility and the spurious black captain-of-industry with material about black people whose lives more nearly approximated reality and although the victims of the urban ghetto were consciously absent, the plight of the Southern sharecropper was dramatized and the race-proud black man appeared.[2]

Hurston was a serious student of anthropology at Barnard College at the time when she worked with this magazine briefly. She had begun her long and significant interest in using southern black folklore of the rural communities she knew well to provide characters and plots for her dramas and short stories. Later she was to write a significant novel, *Jonah's Gourdvine*, which captures the essence of the black preacher as a cultural icon. While she was editor of the *Spokesman*, Hurston published a short play, *The Release*, by Rudella Edythe Gordon, which used creative writing to portray the life of black sharecroppers in the South. This drama, together with Hurston's own short story, brought at least two pieces of literature to the magazine that can be counted, among tensions and portrayals of black folkways, one of the hallmarks of the un-self-conscious thrust of black writers during the 1920s.

When William H. Ferris followed Hurston as editor of the journal, he returned its emphasis to the earlier old-line black leadership mold. In the final issue, he wrote "The Myth of the New Negro," which was his refutation of the thesis of Alain Locke's *The New Negro* (1925). To him, whites were merely beginning to recognize black talent which had existed all along. Their acceptance, he held, was the dynamic some blacks misread as a new ethnic direction of thought and creative art.

Unfortunately, the format of the *Spokesman* seems at times to be little more than an advertisement for Herman's Herb Garden, a Harlem enterprise specializing in medicinal herbs. "Black Herman," president and treasurer of the *Spokesman*, financed the publication. More sophisticated black publications frowned upon advertisements for love potions and patent health medicines. The *Spokes-*

man, then, becomes an anomaly among black journals. Its features resemble other general-purpose magazines', despite the distracting huckstering for the Herb Garden that often appeared at the bottom of each page of text.

Notes

1. Zora Neale Hurston, the significant black woman author who rose to prominence in the mid 1920s, had published in Howard University's *Stylist Magazine* while she was a student there, and, before becoming associated with the *Spokesman*, had contributed two short stories to *Opportunity*. Both pieces won prizes in the latter's literary contests.

2. Mary Fair Burks, "A Survey of Black Literary Magazines in the United States: 1859-1940" (Ph.D. diss., Columbia University, 1975), p. 203. In making this observation, Professor Burks probably gives the impression that the *Spokesman* under Hurston was more important in the literary renaissance than it really was. *Opportunity* and *Crisis* preceded it as providers of literary contests for black artists and places of publication for their works. The *Spokesman*'s importance in their vein was extremely short-lived.

Information Sources

BIBLIOGRAPHY:
Burks, Mary Fair. "A Survey of Black Literary Magazines in the United States: 1859-1940." Ph.D. dissertation, Columbia University 1975, pp. 202-8.
Hemenway, Robert E. *Zora Neale Hurston: A Literary Biography*. Urbana, Ill. 1977, pp. 60-65.
INDEX SOURCES: None
LOCATION SOURCES: Moorland-Spingarn Collection, Howard University, Washington, D.C.; Library of Congress.

Publication History

MAGAZINE TITLE AND TITLE CHANGES: *The Spokesman.*
VOLUME AND ISSUE DATA: Vols. I-III (December 1924-July 1927).
PUBLISHER AND PLACE OF PUBLICATION: Herman's Herb Garden, New York, New York.
EDITORS: Thomas W. Anderson (December 1924-May 1925); Zora Neale Hurston (March 1925-June 1925); William H. Ferris (July 1925-July 1927).
CIRCULATION: 1,000 estimate.

STUDIES IN BLACK LITERATURE

The English Department at Martha Washington College, Fredericksburg, Virginia, began publishing *Studies in Black Literature* in the spring of 1970. It was one of a succession of black literary journals that appeared first in the 1960s. The trend continued into the mid 1970s. Black studies programs in American colleges and universities spawned these journals. They joined with new black publishing enterprises such as Free Black Press and Third World Press in Chicago, Black

Dialogue Press in New York, Jihan Press in Newark, and Broadside Press in Detroit to provide publishing outlets for black writers. Most of the journals were "revolutionary."[1] They projected a type of black nationalism reminiscent of the efforts and philosophies of W.E.B. Du Bois and his use of the black press for his Niagara movement, and Marcus Garvey's publications as part of the activities of his Universal Negro Improvement Association.[2]

During the Harlem literary renaissance, black authors published their works primarily in the *Crisis,** the *Messenger,** and *Opportunity.** In the 1960s they sought to tackle the "racial mountain" that lay between writing and publishing by establishing the little magazines and the black presses. Black studies programs in colleges and universities added to the new communication resources and necessities. Black colleges had taught Negro history and literature for decades. But in the widespread unrest experienced anew by traditionally white colleges at mid century, black students demanded courses about their own culture. Black colleges, too, were forced to expand their own Afro-American courses. As one black scholar put it, "Here in these first years of the Black Academic Revolution we have a literal explosion in course offerings and programs from Puget Sound to the Florida Keys."[3] In many cases they were placebos. Some universities hired black faculty to teach black studies. They were not Afro-Americans, however. From these programs several scholarly journals, conferences and newsletters sprang. *Studies in Black Literature* was one of them.

Studies in Black Literature was an anomaly in the view of some black authors and academicians. They called it the "Imperialistic approach" to black studies. Hoyt W. Fuller, editor of the prestigious *Negro Digest,** wrote about the irony of Martha Washington College's establishing a black studies journal. Its editor was a native of India. Fuller wrote that the Fredericksburg, Virginia, college—located in what he called the "cradle of the Confederacy," represented the very "symbol of inaccessibility to Black People." Thus, to him, it was an act of presumption for that college to attempt to preempt the field of journalism in Black Studies.[4] Many other black scholars found a journal coming out of Martha Washington College hard to accept.

Despite their objections, *Studies in Black Literature* became a reasonably significant publication. It attracted manuscripts from black and white scholars who explored black American and African writing. Some illustrations of the scope and nature of its offerings include "Black Jesus: A Study of Kelly's *A Different Drummer*," "*Lawd Today*: Richard Wright's Apprenticeship," "Gwendolyn Brooks: The Heroic Voice of Prophecy," "Black Literature and American Innocence," "The Novels of Zora Neale Hurston," "William Attaway's Unaccommodated Antagonists," "Ante-Bellum Slave Narratives: Their Place in American Literary History," and "The Link Between Tradition and Modern Experience— The Nigerian Novel." A special issue features works of Chinua Achebe, the Nigerian author whose lecture "The Writer and the African Revolution" created high interest in the United State at the time of the rise of African nationalism.

The journal published some poetry. Its most valuable feature is the cumulative author and subject index to *Studies in Black Literature* 1970-75, which is a useful bibliographic tool for students of Afro-American and black African writing. The magazine offers a worthy collection of literary studies. Like most similar publications, it ceased publication during the period of the late 1970s when interest in black studies waned considerably. During its life, however, the journal provided one of the best literary magazines of its type, largely because of the scope of its coverage and because its articles were of the highest literary quality.

Notes

1. Richard A. Long, "The Black Studies Boondoggle," *Liberator* (September 1970): 7.
2. The *Crisis*, the journal of the NAACP edited from 1910-34 by W.E.B. Du Bois, represented the new militancy of his time, at least at its beginning. Marcus Garvey, a West Indian living in Harlem, opened the national convention of his Universal Negro Movement Association in 1920. His *Negro World* was a leading black weekly newspaper for his movement.
3. See "Perspective," *Negro Digest* (November 1969): 50.
4. Ibid.

Information Sources

BIBLIOGRAPHY:
Fuller, Hoyt. "Perspective." *Negro Digest*, November 1969, p. 50.
Katz, Bill. *Magazines for Libraries.* 2d ed. New York, 1971, p. 114.
Randall, Dudley. "Broadside Press: A Personal Chronicle." In *The Black Seventies*, edited by Floyd B. Barbour. Boston: Porter Sargent, 1970, pp. 138-48.
INDEX SOURCE: *Humanities Index.*
LOCATION SOURCES: Vanderbilt University Library, Nashville, Tennessee; some college and university libraries.

Publication History

MAGAZINE TITLE AND TITLE CHANGES: *Studies in Black Literature.*
VOLUME AND ISSUE DATA: Vols. I-VIII (Spring 1970-Spring 1977), quarterly.
PUBLISHER AND PLACE OF PUBLICATION: Department of English, Martha Washington College, Fredericksburg, Virginia.
EDITOR: Ramon K. Singh (1970-1977).
CIRCULATION: 500.

STYLUS MAGAZINE, THE: A MAGAZINE TO ENCOURAGE ORIGINAL LITERARY EXPRESSION AT HOWARD UNIVERSITY

Students and faculty members at Howard University in Washington, D.C., the "capstone" of black education in the United States, established the Stylus Society in 1916. They envisioned an organization that could study the forms of literary composition and practice them under more favorable conditions than the classroom could offer. Members hoped to initiate at Howard a parallel to the purposes the "Hartford Wits" served at Yale in creating a distinguishable American Literature. The Stylus Society believed a Negro literature would promote progress for the race and would aspire "to sow the seed of a larger issue in the field of letters among the younger generation of our race, with the hope that the work so splendidly done by Dunbar, Du Bois, Chesnutt, and Braithwaite may be completely continued by the young men and women who follow them."[1] The *Stylus Magazine* became their journal. Montgomery Gregory, a Howard English professor, wrote the foreword to the first issue. In addition to the purpose noted above, Gregory wrote that the *Stylus* was the first literary magazine to be published by students at any Negro college. The club's members were elected on the basis of biannual competition. Alain Locke, distinguished black philosopher and art critic of the Harlem Renaissance, joined his faculty colleague, Gregory, in establishing the society. Its sentiments were essentially those Locke would set forth in his significant anthology *The New Negro* (1925).

The *Stylus Magazine* proposed to publish at regular intervals throughout the college year.[2] Faculty members and students who initiated the project believed they were establishing a new literary trend which Gregory explained as follows:

Heretofore there has been too little encouragement given in our schools to the students gifted with creative imagination and the possibilities of its artistic expression. The result is that our schools are often the graveyards of undiscovered and undeveloped talents. Instead of encouraging our trained students to go into the arena of authorship, we have permitted well-meaning but ignorant writers to represent or, better still, to *mis*represent us.[3]

In addition to its faculty and student members, the Stylus Society elected the following persons to honorary membership the first year: William Stanley Braithwaite, John Edward Bruce, W.E.B. Du Bois, Charles W. Chesnutt, Alice Moore Dunbar, James Weldon Johnson, Kelly Miller, Lenwood Morris, Arthur A. Schomberg, and William Sinclair.[4]

Campbell Johnson, a student member, wrote "Our Opportunity in Literature," an essay, for the first issue. He noted that the completion of half a century of freedom had begun a new era for Negro literature; that Negro youth were developing "a race consciousness which rises above the slowly dissipating mists of physical and political oppression and struggles for a voice." Johnson expressed a new direction for Afro-American letters that one would hear throughout the first half of the century. He wrote that there were storehouses of material for the Negro writer to use to create literature, such as "the beautiful tales of simple plantation life that have been told to him at his parents' knees; the sad stories of the separation of parents and children, husbands and wives, at the auction block;

the secret prayer meetings of slavery times; and the simple love stories as beauti-ful as any in the literature of the world."[5] The essay anticipates a black aesthetic. The issue also contained some poems—three contributed by Braithwaite—and a short story that had won first prize of ten dollars for the best work on the theme of race by a member of the Stylus Society. Benjamin Brawley, then a young poet and professor of English at Atlanta Baptist College and later a member of the English faculty at Howard University, contributed a short essay, "War and Literature." A bibliography of Negro fiction compiled by Locke was the first of his annual listings of writing by black authors.

The second issue was published five years after the first. Its "Foreword" stated that the world war had interrupted the society's work. Gregory was especially pleased to see the *Stylus* in print again. In the postwar period he saw an emerging role for black writers.

> It becomes clearer daily that it must be through the things of the Spirit that we shall ultimately restore Ethiopia to her seat of honor among the races of the world. The Germans have amply demonstrated the futility of force to secure a place in the sun. Any individual or people must depend upon the universal appeal of art, literature, painting, music—to secure the real re-spect and recognition of mankind. *Stylus* is on the right track although like all bearers of Truth they are in the minority for a day. Theirs are the future years, rich with the promise of a fulfillment of the visions of those whose love for their race embraces humanity.[6]

That second issue is significant especially for its inclusion of Zora Neale Hurston's "John Redding Goes to Sea." Hurston, who became a leading black writer of the Harlem Renaissance, was a member of the Stylus Society during her brief time as a student at Howard. She claimed later that that publication launched her literary career. Charles S. Johnson, who was then planning *Opportunity** as the official publication of the National Urban League, saw Hurston's story in the *Stylus* and asked her to send him a piece for *Opportunity*.* Subsequently, she published two short stories in that journal. Johnson encouraged Hurston to move to Harlem, which was becoming the center for black literary activity. Alain Locke's experience with the *Stylus* began as a faculty member of the Stylus Society. No doubt the Howard University publication led him toward his long and significant association with young writers of the Harlem Renaissance period.[7]

The *Stylus Magazine* is important primarily because it was the first of many literary magazines to be published at black colleges and because of the collection of black literary figures it brought together.

Notes

1. "Foreword," *Stylus* (June 1916): 3.
2. It actually was published sporadically between 1916 and 1941.

3. "Foreword," *Stylus* (June 1916): 3.

4. Chesnutt, the foremost black author at the time, wrote to *Stylus*: "You and your fellow students are quite correct in your assumption that I will be sympathetically interested in the objects of your Society. Literary composition is the best means of voicing the ideals, the aspirations and the genius of a race—at least the best way to reach the mind and heart of the world—and a race without such means of expression is under a handicap. The effort, therefore, of your Society is worthy of the highest commendation, and I feel honored by my designation as one of its honorary members."

5. Campbell Johnson, "Our Opportunity in Literature," *Stylus* (June 1916):5.

6. *Stylus* (May 1921): 6.

7. Locke wrote several essays for *Opportunity* and was editor for the issue of *Survey Graphic* magazine titled "Harlem: Mecca of he New Negro" (1925), which has been considered the hallmark of the Harlem Renaissance literary tradition.

Information Sources

BIBLIOGRAPHY:

Brawley, Benjamin. *The Negro Genius: A New Appraisal of the Achievement of the American Negro in Literature and the Fine Arts*. New York, 1966, pp. 264-65.

Burks, Mary Fair. "A Survey of Black Literary Magazines in the United States: 1859-1940." Ph.D. dissertation, Columbia University, 1975, pp. 193-95.

Hemenway, Robert E. *Zora Neale Hurston: A Literary Biography*. Urbana: University of Illinois Press, 1977, pp. 18-19, 64-65.

Johnson, Abby Arthur, and Ronald Maberry Johnson. *Propaganda and Aesthetics: The Literary Politics of Afro-American Magazines in the Twentieth Century*. Amherst: University of Massachusetts Press, 1979, pp. 68-69, 94-95.

INDEX SOURCES: None

LOCATION SOURCE: Moorland-Spingarn Collection, Howard University, Washington, D.C.

Publication History

MAGAZINE TITLE AND TITLE CHANGES: *The Stylus Magazine: A Magazine to Encourage Original Literary Expression at Howard University*.

VOLUME AND ISSUE DATA: Vol. I, no. 1 (June 1916); Vol. I, no. 2 (May 1921). Other issues published irregularly and without volume numbers: June 1929, June 1934, May 1937, June 1938, June 1941.

PUBLISHER AND PLACE OF PUBLICATION: The Stylus Society, Howard University, Washington, D.C.

EDITORS: Montgomery Gregory, (June 1916 and May 1921); Walter E. Merrick (June 1929); Benjamin Brawley (June 1934); Kenneth Clarke (June 1935); Victor Lawson (May 1937); Mamie K. Phipps (June 1938); Vivian I. Edwards (June 1941).

CIRCULATION: 750 highest estimate.

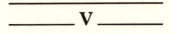

V

VOICE OF THE NEGRO, THE

During the fall of 1903, officials of the Atlanta branch of Illinois-based Hertel, Jenkins, and Company Publishing House completed plans with local black citizens to begin publication of the *Voice of the Negro*, a monthly journal of general readership interest. Austin N. Jenkins, manager of the Atlanta office, conceived the idea that a newspaper or magazine would be a desirable adjunct to the publishing company's rather extensive southern activities. It had issued books by and about Negroes, including Booker T. Washington's *Story of My Life and Work* (1900) and D. W. Culp's *Twentieth Century Negro Literature* (1902). After a series of conferences among interested persons, John Wesley Edward Bowen, president of Gammon Theological Seminary in Atlanta; Emmett J. Scott, private secretary to Tuskegee Institute's principal; Booker T. Washington; and Jesse Max Barber, a recent graduate of Virginia Union University in Richmond and editor of that institution's promotions organ, became leading figures on the editorial board of the new journal. Barber, as managing editor, began his brief but significant career with what was soon to become the most prestigious black periodical in the nation.

Atlanta seemed an unusually appropriate home for such a publication at the turn of the century. It contained the largest number of private black colleges and preparatory schools in the nation. The three religious denominations claiming the largest number of black communicants—Baptist, African Methodist Episcopal, and Methodist Episcopal—exercised strong influence in Atlanta.[1] The city had emerged as the center for black activities in politics, education, religion, and commerce. It was the focus of the "New South." The *Voice of the Negro*'s editorial purposes comported well with the developing local ethos. The new journal became the vehicle for a variety of expressions of the black American experience in race relations, state and national politics, and education in particular. Barber's vigorous editorials quickly set the pace and the tone of the magazine. Other members of the editorial staff exercised little influence on the journal's contents.

Barber wrote in his first editorial that the *Voice of the Negro* would not become a political magazine or "the tomb of dead men's bones, whether these bones are found to be the ancient sermonic literature of the ministry or in the bombastic fire-eating speeches of the disappointed politicians of the day." He promised that the journal would steer clear of the "prophets, seers, and visionaries who dream dreams and prophesy out of their lurid imaginations and unreasoning hopes." To Barber, magazines, newspapers, and books were "the products of civilization." Launching the *Voice of the Negro*, then, offered an uncommon "force for race elevation" that could reflect society's concerns so accurately and vividly that the new journal could become a "kind of documentation for coming generations, although often its commentary would rip open the conventional veil of optimism and drag into view conditions that shock."[2]

Originally, Barber sought to use the new journal to coalesce the growing dissonance among black leaders. Booker T. Washington had become the acknowledged spokesman for the race to philanthropists and national politicians. He had delivered a conciliatory address as part of the Atlanta Cotton States Exposition in 1895. His speech received almost unanimous sanction from the white press, but it enraged the increasing number of black academicians and some editors who eschewed piety, puritanical ethics, and capitalism as an approved direction for the race in the coming century. They labeled Washington "accommodationist" and rejected his failure to agitate for restored citizenship rights and an end to lynching. Both "accommodationists" and "radicals" wrote for the *Voice of the Negro*. At one time Barber ridiculed "the constant hub-bub and agitation and mud-slinging" over who is the greatest leader and which one policy of advancement the race should adopt. He considered much of the conflict "sophomoric" and warned that the race needed "downright hard thinkers and workers along all lines" rather than declaimers, orators, and essayists. He promised to furnish an open forum for "thinking men and women to deliver themselves upon all public concerns," and he understood well the growing power of the black press in the affairs of the race.

For the first months of publication, the *Voice of the Negro* remained true to Barber's promise. Toward the end of the year, the journal joined the "radicals," although it occasionally carried articles written by persons from other sides of the ideological race question. Barber became a personal adversary of Booker T. Washington through his dissension with Emmett J. Scott and, apparently, at the instigation of W.E.B. Du Bois and the "radicals."[3] One portrayal of Washington and what Barber considered the Tuskegee Institute principal's attitude toward his race may be seen in portions of an editorial titled "Good Negro."

> . . . one who says he does not want the ballot. He orates before his people and advises them against going into politics. He says to them "Keep out of politics. Go to the farms; keep quiet and let the whites handle the government. . . . [He] is one who says his race does not need the higher

learning; that what they need is industrial education, pure and simple. He stands up before his people and murders the truth and the King's English in trying to enforce upon them the evils of a College Education and the beauties of the plow.[4]

Emmett J. Scott resigned his post as associate editor of the journal within a few months of its appearance as a result of a bitter dispute with Barber. An editorial had reported on "reliable information" proving that Booker T. Washington owned controlling interest in *Colored American,** a competing journal published in New York City. Both Washington and Scott denied the claim, but publishers Jenkins and Hertel supported Barber. Scott complained to the owners against Barber's "malevolent spirit," his "nagging propensities," his "studied affectation of superiority," and his "overweening egotism and acceptance of everything as an insult." These personal characteristics in Barber, rather than any conflict of business interest, made working on the journal unbearable for him, Scott wrote.

Washington's forces had no official link to the magazine after Scott resigned his position on the editorial staff, although from time to time news of Tuskegee Institute appeared in the journal. With Barber's clear alignment with the "radical" black leaders, Du Bois emerged as a regular contributor to the *Voice of the Negro*. He used the publication as a significant medium for promoting his call for certain black leaders to meet 11-13 July 1905 at Niagara Falls, New York, to consider forming a national organization that would foster a more militant expression for the race than Washington's. The call anticipated launching a force diametrically opposed to Washington and his representation of the black American cause.[5] Du Bois wanted concerted action to "oppose firmly the present method of strangling honest criticism"; to organize intelligent Negroes for the purpose of insisting on manhood rights; and to establish and support organs of news and opinion. Twenty-nine ministers, editors, and teachers from various parts of the country came together and formed the Niagara movement.

Next year, the magazine announced the movement's second meeting and commented on its progress:

General Secretary W.E.B. Du Bois of the Niagara Movement begs to announce that the second annual meeting of that organization will be held at Harper's Ferry, West Virginia, Wednesday, October 18, 1906. The meeting will be held on historic grounds. Harper's Ferry will always be associated with the martyred John Brown...The Niagara Movement is now an incorporated body with 170 members in 34 states. During the year, a number of meetings have been had; more than 10,000 pamphlets have been sent out, and in many ways the Movement has used its influence to better the condition of the race.[6]

Barber was among the more than 100 prominent black Americans who met at Harper's Ferry and heard Du Bois state the movement's objectives in his keynote address. They included the following:

> We want full manhood suffrage and we want it now.... We want discrimination in public accommodations to cease. We claim the right of freedom to walk, talk, and be with those that wish to be with us. We want our children educated.[7]

These goals for the race coincided with Barber's, which he had expressed repeatedly in the *Voice of the Negro*. When he returned from the meeting at Harper's Ferry he wrote "The Niagara Movement at Harper's Ferry" for the journal. The physical setting, purpose, and tone of the proceedings fired his imagination and his resolve: "Because of the fact that John Brown laved the altar of freedom with his life-blood at Harper's Ferry, it is highly fitting that those who were freed by his death should reverence the man and the place where he dared to die."[8] He admitted that some Negroes doubted the wisdom of such fearless agitation as that promulgated by the movement. They were, to him, those persons who were paid to "place a hiatus on any ambition for racial equality." That same issue of the journal carried Reverdy C. Ransom's dramatic essay "The Spirit of John Brown." Ransom, an African Methodist Episcopal Church pastor in Boston who later edited his denomination's *A.M.E. Church Review*,* had already established a reputation as a political activist and Socialist. He prevailed upon black Americans to unite for their own advancement and attacked those leaders that "believe in money, property, the gospel of work, and industrial efficiency."

Most black leaders and scholars remained loyal to the Republican party in the presidential election of 1904. The *Voice of the Negro* entered vigorously into that campaign. It reported on the minor political parties and their conventions, candidates, and platforms. But it focused upon the two parties most likely to gain the White House and Congress. William Scarborough, president of Wilberforce University in Ohio, and Kelly Miller, dean of the college of liberal arts at Howard University in Washington, D.C., strongly recommended Theodore Roosevelt to black voters. Their articles, together with Barber's editorials, summarily dismissed William Jennings Bryan and the Democratic party because of their racial posture. To them, Roosevelt's position was clear and acceptable. He had shown "he stands for equality before the law for every man without regard to creed, race or birthplace." He had taken a strong stand against lynching. The black press expected Roosevelt to extend the hope for improved social and civil status that the race believed William McKinley had established. Most blacks failed to understand fully that Republicans had forged an alliance designed to insure the party's national success. That plan included Booker T. Washington. Washington, in turn, used the president and the party to gain resources for

Tuskegee Institute, his other projects, and his prominent role as official White House advisor on matters pertaining to Negroes.

After Roosevelt won the election handily, Barber praised a wide range of policies the president expressed in his first message to Congress. When Roosevelt proposed touring the South to seek to unify the nation, Barber expressed some apprehension, but he convinced himself that the president would maintain his liberal ideas on race no matter how long he remained in the South. However, when Roosevelt began his circuit of southern states, Barber fretted over the tone of his speeches which seemed to placate the South and omitted any remonstrance against the growing menace of lynching. Barber took particular umbrage at the educational philosophy for Negroes that the president advocated before audiences at Tuskegee Institute and Florida Baptist Academy.

> At Tuskegee he preached a doctrine that is not novel but preposterous. He advised our people to go into the mechanical and agricultural arts for the reason that the "professional and mercantile avenues to success are overcrowded." If Mr. Roosevelt knows anything about conditions in the South, he knows that the time is fast approaching when the Negro has got to have his own professional and mercantile men. The white man will not give the Negro the respectful service his money demands. It is becoming so in some sections of the South that a colored man is told that he can buy, but not try on, a hat. There is need for a great host of capable Negro doctors, teachers, preachers and lawyers. There is a great need for mercantile establishments among our people.[9]

Roosevelt's position on black education echoed Washington's. It became anathema to the growing ranks of the "radicals." The president's popularity reached its nadir, however, when he supported recommendations that black soldiers accused of rioting in Brownsville, Texas, should be discharged from the service and barred from subsequent enlistment in any branch of the armed forces.[10] *Voice of the Negro* editorials condemned the president for this action as vigorously as they had supported his candidacy during the election campaign.

Black editors and publishers took seriously their responsibility to provide black voice of outrage against lynching. They believed a free black press was indispensible as a vehicle for keeping the growing evils of mob rule before the public. Many black leaders criticized Booker T. Washington for his restrained complaints against lynching and for attributing the practice to punishment of sexual attacks by black men upon white women. Barber's diligence in this purpose led to his expulsion from Atlanta in an exceptional violation of freedom of the press. His dedication to making public at least another side of the reasons for the Atlanta race riot in 1906 led to the demise of the vitality of the *Voice of the Negro*.

The morning following the riot—25 September 1906—John Temple Graves, editor of the *Atlanta Constitution*, wired the *New York World* that "a carnival of rapes" in and around Atlanta by Negro men against white women had led to the riots. "When I read the letter that had gone out to the four corners of the world, I shivered with rage," Barber wrote. Over his own signature he wired the *World* begging the editor to publish an answer to Graves' letter—one written by a black man. The *World* requested Barber to send a telegram of 200 words at the newspaper's expense, giving his side of the matter. In his wire, Barber wrote there was no carnival of rapes, but a "carnival of newspaper lies" that had issued from the *Georgian* and the *Atlanta News*; that for eighteen months preceding the disturbance, Hoke Smith, the front-running candidate for governor, had fanned the fires of racial hate throughout the state in his campaign speeches. Barber also claimed that white men had blackened their faces and simulated attacks on white women in order to enflame white citizens of Atlanta. The day the riot broke out, he wrote, was one of fear and trembling as white women screamed they had been "insulted" by black men who had done nothing more than pass them on the street. Charles Daniel, editor of the *Atlanta News*, had for more than a month sought "by every hellish device to precipitate a race war." He had called for reorganization of the Ku Klux Klan and had offered rewards to lynchers. His paper had carried daily fire-eating and reckless editorials against Negroes.[11]

The wire to the *New York World* was signed "A Colored Citizen." Its text appeared in the *World* in the form of a letter. Next day, Captain James English, president of the Fourth National Bank of Atlanta and a member of the Board of Police Commissioners, sent for Barber and told him the origin of the letter had been traced to his office; that he had made a vile slander on Atlanta which he must retract in writing at once, or leave town immediately. Knowing full well that he would be indicted by a grand jury for slander and sentenced to serve some period of time on the chain gang, Barber left Atlanta. As soon as it was known he had fled the city, reporters from the daily press and detectives swarmed over the offices of the *Voice of the Negro*. Within a few days, the *Atlanta News* published a story which read in part:

> The authorship of the infamous communication published in the New York *World*, of the 27th, under an Atlanta date, and signed "A Colored Citizen," has been traced by officials of this county. They know the name of the man who wrote the card saying bloodhounds had trailed an assailant to a white man's house and he was not arrested; that white men blacked their faces and attacked white women; and that all the talk of assaults was a campaign trick in the interest of Hoke Smith.... The Negro who sent this article to the New York *World* has been quietly notified to leave the city. His name has been withheld from the public because if it were generally known he would be dealt with summarily and the officers are doing their utmost to prevent further outbreaks. The Negro could not be found yesterday in his accustomed haunts and it is supposed he has left the city. If he returns there is no doubt that he will be at once arrested and vigorously prosecuted.[12]

Barber opened temporary editorial offices in Chicago when he left Atlanta. Despite the major inconvenience of having to dismantle his magazine's established headquarters on such short notice, the October 1906 issue appeared only a few weeks later than its scheduled publication date. Some sense of the practical difficulties Barber experienced in the transition may be seen in a portion of an editorial he wrote for that first issue.

> When we left Atlanta, we brought with us some of the proofs for the October magazine. They were read here in Chicago and returned to the printers. We have never had an opportunity to see some of the proofs. To save the enormous expense of having the entire magazine reset here in Chicago we had to undertake to try to have the October *Voice* issued from Atlanta. A white friend there agreed to look after the work. He could not have done so openly. It would have ruined his Atlanta business had it been known generally that he was helping us. Our printers, for reasons best known to themselves—probably because they were afraid to print *The Voice* so soon after the riots—took their own good time to print the magazine. And when they were through with it, they had murdered almost every article therein. The magazines were hauled in a lump to the office of this good white friend. He in turn took time to have every one wrapped before he mailed any of them, so that when it got noised abroad that the October *Voice* was being issued in Atlanta, they had all been mailed.[13]

The original financial backers of the journal withdrew from the enterprise after Barber left Atlanta. He changed the name of the periodical, shortening it to the *Voice* on the theory that in the Chicago environment he could secure needed advertisements more easily with a title that did not suggest the narrowness of a black magazine for black readers. Chicago was not nearly so compatible as Atlanta for the kind of magazine Barber had made of *The Voice*. Atlanta was, in many ways, the natural habitat for a magazine with its orientation. Within a few months, the *Voice* ceased publication.

During the nearly three years it was published in Atlanta, the *Voice of the Negro* vigorously opposed racial discrimination, lynching, and unsavory Georgia politics. Barber did not consider his journal a "muckraker," although at one time he wrote that he was more concerned with "those who made the muck" than with those who raked it. Well-known black scholars and public figures contributed to the journal. Their voices were not unanimous in praise or condemnation of any single vein of racial philosophy.

The managing editor's decision to move from his original purpose of providing a variegated voice for black expression to alignment with the "radical" faction in the so-called Washington-Du Bois controversy contributed to the failure of the magazine. The most important cause, though, lay in Barber's confrontation with the power structure of Atlanta.

Although the *Voice of the Negro* became an activist publication from the standpoint of movements toward social advancement within the race, it served as a significant chronicle of other areas of activity in its time. Most issues discussed some phase of education for Negroes, including exposés of the conditions of public schools in urban and rural settings. It took appropriate note of the passing of Paul Laurence Dunbar, the best-known and best-loved poet among black Americans. And it provided its readers an opportunity to come to know the works of Samuel Coleridge-Taylor, a black English-born musician, and Henry O. Tanner, whose paintings won signal honors in European art competition. The journal remained basically conservative toward organized labor, largely because the rising movement often barred blacks from membership.

Barber enjoyed too much freedom in setting directions and emphases for the *Voice of the Negro*, especially inasmuch as the publication was a cooperative financial enterprise. He was, admittedly, a talented writer who represented well the responsibility of the black press to keep alive the aspirations of black Americans. Unfortunately, he irritated certain black scholars and leaders whose cooperation he needed in order to provide for the race a stable journal published in the South reflecting the spectrum of opinion arising from this center of black population but capturing the interest of blacks throughout the nation. For its weaknesses as well as its strengths, the *Voice of the Negro* is a significant document of American culture from the black perspective.

Notes

1. The Baptists operated Atlanta Baptist (later Morehouse) College and Spelman Seminary; the Methodists, Clark College; and the African Methodist Episcopal Church, Morris Brown College.

2. *Voice of the Negro* (January 1904): 4.

3. Letters relating to the conflict between Emmett J. Scott and Jesse Max Barber on this matter appear in Louis R. Harlan and Raymond W. Smith, eds., *Booker T. Washington Papers*, vol. 8, 1904-1906 (Urbana, Ill.: University of Illinois Press, 1977): 38-46.

4. *Voice of the Negro* (November 1905): 3.

5. *See* Langston Hughes, *Fight for Freedom: Story of the NAACP* (New York, 1966): chap. 1.

6. "The Niagara Movement," *Voice of the Negro* (July 1906): 476.

7. Hughes, Fight for Freedom.

8. "The Niagara Movement at Harper's Ferry," *Voice of the Negro* (September 1906): 669-70.

9. "The President and the South," *Voice of the Negro* (January 1905): 652.

10. A detailed account of this national incident and its repercussions in politics and in the black press appears in Ann J. Lane, *The Brownsville Affair: National Crisis and Black Reaction* (Port Washington, N.Y., 1971).

11. Barber's accounts of his confrontation with the power structure in Atlanta are found in "Shall the Press Be Free?", *Voice of the Negro* (October 1906): 391-92; and "Why Mr. Barber Left Atlanta" and "The Atlanta Tragedy," *Voice* (November 1906): 470-72 and 473-79. *See* the following for a comprehensive account of the Atlanta riot of

1906: "The Atlanta Riot," *Alexander's Magazine* (November 1906): 39-41; "The Atlanta Riot," *Outlook* (3 November 1906): 557-67; "Tragedy of Atlanta," *World Today*, (November, 1906): 1169-75; Charles H. Bacote, "Negro Officeholders in Georgia under President McKinley," *Journal of Negro History* (July 1959): 217-39; Ray Stannard Baker, "The Atlanta Riots," *Voice of the Negro* (June 1907): 222-24; Ray Stannard Baker, "A Race Riot and After," *American Magazine* (April 1907): 553-68; and J. Max Barber, "The Atlanta Tragedy," *Voice of the Negro* (November 1906): 473-79.

   12. *Atlanta News*, 28 October 1906, p. 4.

   13. Barber, editorial, *Voice of the Negro* (October 1906): 394.

Information Sources

BIBLIOGRAPHY:
Harlan, Louis R. "Booker T. Washington and the *Voice of the Negro*, 1904-1907." *Journal of Southern History*, February 1979, pp. 45-62.
Johnson, Abby Arthur and Johnson, Ronald M. "Away from Accommodation: Radical Editors and Protest Journalism, 1900-1910." *Journal of Negro History*, October 1977; pp. 325-38.
Johnson, Charles S. "Rise of the Negro Magazine." *Journal of Negro History*, January 1928; pp. 7-21.
INDEX SOURCE: *Analytical Guide and Indexes to "The Voice of the Negro," 1904-1907* (Westport, Conn. 1974).
LOCATION SOURCES: Most college and university libraries; Greenwood Press Periodicals available for total publication.

Publication History

MAGAZINE TITLE AND TITLE CHANGES: *The Voice of the Negro* (January 1904-July 1906); *The Voice* (August 1906-October 1907).
VOLUME AND ISSUE DATA: Vols. I-IV (January 1904-October 1907). Covering both titles.
PUBLISHER AND PLACE OF PUBLICATION: J. L. Nichols and Company, Atlanta, Georgia (January 1904-April 1904); Hertel, Jenkins and Company, Atlanta, Georgia (May 1904-July 1906); Voice Publishing Company, Chicago, Illinois (August 1906-October 1907).
EDITORS: J.W.E. Bowen and J. Max Barber (January 1904-October 1906); J. Max Barber (November 1906-October 1907).
CIRCULATION: 15,000 maximum.

W

WESTERN JOURNAL OF BLACK STUDIES, THE

The *Western Journal of Black Studies* is one of the most recent black journals. Its charter issue was March 1977 and it is a quarterly publication of the Washington State University Black Studies Program and the Washington State University Press. The journal was founded by and developed in cooperation with a number of individuals. *"The Western Journal of Black Studies* owes its creation to the individuals whose names appear as the Editorial Board, Regional Editors, and Contributing Editors, who by their expression of the need for and active support in the initial efforts contributed to its realization and success."[1] Their involvement reflects the pluralistic nature of the journal.

The most significant document concerning the editorial policy of the journal is its first editorial, written by Talmadge Anderson and entitled "Foreword: New Dimensions." Anderson notes that the wave of literature by and about civil rights activism has subsided but that the problems of the movement still exist. He further states that there will always be a need to study and research the experience of black peoples throughout the world. The overriding need for the *Western Journal of Black Studies* lies in the fact that the "cultural, social, and political concepts of Blacks from the southeastern, southwestern, central, and northeastern states have been dominant in the characterization and study of all Afro-Americans." A journal is needed to fill the gap in serious scholarly and philosophical studies of blacks in the western portion of the United states. *"The Western Journal of Black Studies* is designed as a forum for the presentation of the perspectives of both western and eastern writers who are concerned with the Black experience in the west but not exclusive of the experience in the eastern United States, Africa, or the world. The journal will provide innovative and progressive theories directed toward the growth and development of interdisciplinary courses and programs in Black Studies. In addition, the journal should serve as a medium to bridge the communciations gap between eastern and western Afro-American scholars. Finally, it is hoped that the journal, through its writers, will contribute in some manner toward the enhancement of the status of people of African descent all over the world."[2]

The format of the first issue is not unusual. It consists of five sections: History; Community, Economics, and Leadership; Black Art; Black Studies; and Inside Africa. A brief selection of book reviews follows. What is unique about this issue is the quality of the graphics. It was printed on expensive glossy paper with color photos generously distributed. Moreover, there is a photo of each contributor, generally on the first page of the appropriate article. The aim was to identify contributors as well as to demonstrate a high quality, expensively produced periodical. It was quite successful, and numerous individuals commented on the quality of the first issue.[3]

The second issue began a trend which continues. One aspect of Afro-Americana is emphasized with a cover theme and appropriate graphic cover illustrations. The second issue stressed "The Black Family" with three major articles on the subject. This theme-oriented approach adds a sense of continuity to the journal and deemphasizes the "special issue" approach employed by many of its competitors. The third issue stressed "Busing and Desegregation," with six major articles on the subject. In his foreword entitled "School Desegregation: Academics, Politics, and Culture," Anderson notes that "the time has come for Blacks and whites to examine the motives for school desegregation and weigh the social costs and social benefits of its implementation."[4] The result is a thorough examination of the issues with viable alternatives offered. Some of these concepts have since been implemented in major school districts throughout the country.

The December 1977 issue stresses "Black Enterprise and Economics" and is still useful as a source for economic planning by blacks. The first anniversary issue in the spring of 1978 is its most controversial because much of it is devoted to the subject of reverse discrimination. The uniqueness of the *Western Journal of Black Studies* becomes apparent with this issue. Instead of addressing topics months or even years after they are in the public's mind, the journal successfully manages to be current, relevant, and intellectually sound simultaneously. The anniversary message confirms such a commitment: "*The Western Journal of Black Studies* endeavors to publish articles, empirical studies, essays, and other literary items which are relevant to the past experience, present condition, and future promise of people of African descent throughout the world. In fulfilling these objectives the *Journal* provides a communications link between the Black intellectual, the Black masses, and other races and cultures of the world."[5] The pursuit of excellence was self-evident, and the journal pledged to continue its mission.

Since 1978, the journal had addressed such varied topics as "The Black Community," "Black Colleges and Universities in the United States," "Blacks and Criminal Justice," and "Racism and Higher Education." In each issue, superficiality is avoided. Rather, the topic at hand is examined thoroughly and objectively. The *Western Journal of Black Studies* has achieved the status of one of the leading journals of its kind in the United States.

Notes

1. "Acknowledgments," *Western Journal of Black Studies* (March 1977): 67.
2. Ibid., 2.
3. Ibid., 67.
4. *Western Journal of Black Studies* (September 1977): 15.
5. *Western Journal of Black Studies* (Spring 1978): 2.

Information Sources

INDEX SOURCES: *American Humanities Index; Reader's Guide to Periodical Literature.*
LOCATION SOURCES: Many college and university libraries.

Publication History

MAGAZINE TITLE AND TITLE CHANGES: *The Western Journal of Black Studies.*
VOLUME AND ISSUE DATA: Vols. I to present (Spring 1977).
PUBLISHER AND PLACE OF PUBLICATION: Washington State University, Pullman, Washington.
EDITOR: Talmadge Anderson (1977).
CIRCULATION: 1,000.

Brian Joseph Benson

Selected Chronology of Events in Black History as Related to Founding of Black Journals

YEAR	*JOURNAL*	*SIGNIFICANT EVENTS*
1619		First Negroes in the English North American colonies came to the Jamestown settlement in Virginia.
1706		Statutes enacted in New York and Virginia established that baptism did not alter the condition of slaves.
1709		Slavery was made legal in French Canada.
1770		Crispus Attucks, a slave who had escaped from his master in 1750, was one of three men killed during an attack on British soldiers in Boston.
1785		New York banned slavery.
1787		Richard Allen and Absolom Jones organized other Philadelphia Negroes in the Free American Society, which eventually became an "African church," affiliated with the Protestant Episcopal Church. Prince Hall and other Boston Negroes petitioned the Massachusetts Legislature for equal school facilities for Negroes.
1796		A grand jury in Charlotte, North Carolina, blamed the Quakers for slave unrest and cited as proof the unrest and the frequency of arson in North Carolina.
1802		All states north of the Mason-Dixon line, except New Jersey, had by this date passed antislavery laws or measures for gradual emancipation.

YEAR	JOURNAL	SIGNIFICANT EVENTS
1805		Frederick Ira Aldridge, the first great Negro actor, was born in New York City.
1807		The British Parliament abolished the slave trade on 25 March. The first schoolhouse for Negroes in Washington, D.C., was built by three Negroes, George Bell, Nicholas Franklin, and Moses Liverpool.
1809		Thirteen Negroes established the first African Baptist church in Philadelphia.
1812		The General Conference of the Methodist Church met in New York and adopted a resolution that no slave owner, if he lived in area where he could legally manumit his slaves, was eligible to be an elder in any Methodist church.
1819		A Missouri law forbade assembling of slaves or free Negroes, and forbade teaching slaves to read.
1820		The Missouri Compromise admitted Missouri as a slave state, but prohibited slavery in future states north of the 36° 30′ line.
1821		Lott Cary and Collin Teague formed the First Baptist Church of Monrovia and left Norfolk, Virginia, for Liberia as missionaries of the Baptist Triennial Convention.
1822		Free Negro Denmark Vesey plotted an insurrection on 16 July in Charleston, South Carolina, that failed, and as a result he was executed with his conspirators.
1827	*Freedom's Journal* (New York, N.Y.)	New York State emancipated approximately 10,000 slaves. The New York Abolition Society and the Dorcas Society of Colored Women arranged to minister to the needs of recently emancipated slaves. There were 130 abolition societies in existence in the United States at this time. The American Colonization Society sought congressional appropriation for colonization of American blacks in Liberia, West Africa. Most new states in the Northwest Territory—particularly Illinois, Indiana, the Michigan Territory, and the Iowa Territory—either barred Negroes as settlers or required certificate of proof of freedom and bond guaranteeing good behavior.

YEAR	JOURNAL
1828	

SIGNIFICANT EVENTS

1828 William Lloyd Garrison, editor of the *Journal of the Times* in Bennington, Vermont, began his antislavery career. The *Free Press*, an antislavery journal, began publication in Bennington, and the *Liberalist*, another antislavery journal, began publication in New Orleans. Philadelphia Negro William Whipper helped found a Reading Room Society in Philadelphia for educating Negroes and developing antislavery sentiment.

1829 Cincinnati riot caused 1,200 Negroes to leave the city for Canada. Antislavery pamphlet *Walker's Appeal, in Four Articles* by Boston Negro David Walker called upon slaves to revolt against their oppressors. Robert Alexander Young published *An Ethiopian Manifesto*, which condemned slavery in biblical language, and prophesied the coming of a black Messiah who would forcibly liberate his people. Daniel A. Payne opened a school for Negro children which soon became "the most successful institution of its kind in Charleston, South Carolina." The African Free School for boys was established in Baltimore and taught between 150 and 175 students every Sunday.

1830 James Forten helped to assemble a national convention of Negroes to consider the free Negro, to plan his social redemption, and to strike again at the colonization idea.

1831 The first Annual Convention of the People of Color was held in Philadelphia in June at Wesleyan Church. The *Liberator*, edited by William Lloyd Garrison, began publication on New Year's day in Boston. Slave rebellion broke out under the leadership of Nat Turner, a literate Virginia slave.

1833 The American Anti-Slavery Society was formed in Philadelphia by Negroes and whites. Mormons were driven out of Independence, Missouri, because local inhabitants thought the Mormons were trying to free the slaves. Oberlin College, which admitted both black and white students, was founded.

YEAR	JOURNAL	SIGNIFICANT EVENTS
1835		The Michigan Constitution limited the franchise to whites.
1837		Elijah Lovejoy was murdered in Alton, Illinois, for defending a newsman's right to oppose slavery.
1838		Frederick Douglass escaped from slavery in Maryland. The periodical *The National Reformer* was begun by William Whipper and other Negroes. *The Mirror of Liberty*, a quarterly magazine, was edited by David Ruggles.
1839		A group of Africans led by Cinque revolted, killed the captain, and seized their Spanish slave ship *L'Amistad* in July off the coast of Cuba.
1840		Boston Negro William C. Nell headed a list of signers of the petition to the Massachusetts Legislature asking that public schools be opened to Negroes.
1841		The *African Methodist Episcopal Church Magazine* was edited by George Hogarth. James W. C. Pennington published *Textbook on the Origin and History of the Colored People*.
1847		Frederick Douglass was elected president of the New England Anti-Slavery Society. The Prince Hall Lodge of Masons in Massachusetts, the First Independent African Grand Lodge in Pennsylvania, and the Hiram Grand Lodge in Pennsylvania formed a National Grand Lodge of Negroes. The A.M.E. Church began publication of the *Christian Herald*, a weekly magazine, whose name was changed to the *Christian Recorder* in 1852.
1849		Harriet Tubman escaped from slavery in Maryland and subsequently returned to the South nineteen times, rescuing over 300 slaves. Martin R. Delany, a Pittsburgh Negro, was admitted to Harvard Medical School.
1851		Myrtilla Miner, a young white woman of New York, went to Washington to establish an academy for Negro girls.
1852		Harriet Beecher Stowe's *Uncle Tom's Cabin*, which portrayed the plight of the slave in

YEAR	JOURNAL	SIGNIFICANT EVENTS
		highly emotional language, was published. William C. Nell's *Services of Colored Americans in Wars of 1775 and 1812* was published. William Wells Brown published a description of his travels, *Three Years in Europe*. Martin R. Delany published *The Condition, Elevation, Emigration and Destiny of the Colored People of the U.S., Politically Considered*, in Philadelphia.
1853		*Clotel, or the President's Daughter*, by William Wells Brown, was published in London.
1854		The Republican party was created to oppose the Kansas-Nebraska Act's opening of the West to slavery. Ashmun Institute, later Lincoln University in Pennsylvania, was founded by Presbyterians.
1855		Brigham Young declared that one drop of Negro blood prevented a man from entering the Mormon priesthood, thus making a distinction between white and Negro male members of the faith.
1857		In *Dred Scott* v. *Sanford*, Chief Justice Roger B. Taney declared that Negroes were not citizens and that Congress had no power to exclude slavery from the territories, thus making the Missouri Compromise unconstitutional.
1859	*The Anglo-African Magazine* (New York, N.Y.); *Douglass' Monthly* (Rochester, N.Y.)	John Brown raided the federal arsenal at Harper's Ferry, Virginia, to seize arms to free slaves in an insurrection. The African Supply Association was organized in Vicksburg, Mississippi to reopen the slave trade. Mulattos in Philadelphia and in Cincinnati brought suit for discrimination and assault against streetcar conductors. *Blake, or the Huts of America*, a novel written by Martin R. Delany, was published serially during the year in *Anglo-African Magazine*.
1861		In February, Jefferson Davis became the president of the Confederate States of America and endorsed slavery as necessary to "self-preservation." William C. Nell, appointed a post office clerk in Boston, became the first Negro to hold a civilian job under the federal government.

YEAR	JOURNAL	SIGNIFICANT EVENTS
1863		The Emancipation Proclamation was announced on 1 January, in which President Lincoln freed all slaves except those in states or parts of states that were not in rebellion.
1865		The Ku Klux Klan was formed in Tennessee.
1866		On 20 August President Johnson officially declared the Civil War to be ended.
1867		Howard University was chartered by the federal government and established in Washington, D.C.
1870		Senator Charles Sumner introduced a bill providing equal rights in transportation, hotels, theaters, schools, churches, cemeteries, and juries.
1872	*The Southern Workman* (Hampton, Va.)	Charlotte E. Ray became the first Negro woman graduate of any law school in the United States.
1875		B. K. Bruce of Mississippi served in the U.S. Senate from 1875-1881, and was the only Negro during Reconstruction to serve a regular term in the Senate.
1876		In August, ex-U.S. Senator H. R. Revels was reappointed president of Alcorn College by the Democratic governor of Mississippi.
1877		Henry O. Flipper became the first Negro graduate of West Point.
1881		In his first message to Congress, President Arthur implied that until Negroes became literate, they might rightly be disenfranchised.
1883		In the Civil Rights cases, the Republican-dominated U.S. Supreme Court declared the Civil Rights Act of 1875 unconstitutional.
1884	*The A.M.E. Church Review* (Philadelphia, Pa., original place of publication)	Fifty Negroes were lynched. The Methodist Episcopal Church, South, founded Paine College in Augusta, Georgia, for Negro youth. Ex-Senator Blanche K. Bruce was placed in charge of the World's Cotton Exhibition held in New Orleans, November 1884-May 1885.
1887		Charles Chestnutt's short story, "The Goophered Grapevice," was published in the *Atlantic Monthly*; this was the first time a Negro work of fiction reached a large white audience.

YEAR	JOURNAL	SIGNIFICANT EVENTS

YEAR   JOURNAL

SIGNIFICANT EVENTS

1890 — Susie Elizabeth Frazier became the first Negro woman appointed to teach in the New York City public schools.

1891 — Dr. Daniel Hale Williams, a Negro, incorporated Provident Hospital, the first training hospital for Negro doctors and nurses in Chicago.

1893 — Paul Laurence Dunbar published his first collection of poetry, *Oak and Ivy*.

1894 — Harvard University awarded its first Ph.D. to a Negro, W.E.B. Du Bois, the only Negro to receive a doctorate between 1890 and 1894, compared with 876 whites.

1895 — Booker T. Washington, in his Atlanta Compromise speech, renounced equality for the time being, urged the acceptance of a subordinate position for southern Negroes in politics, and advocated education for the practical end of gaining a livelihood.

1896 — In *Plessy* v. *Ferguson*, the creation of "separate but equal" was ruled on Homer Plessy, a New Orleans Negro who attempted to ride in a white railroad car.

1900   *The Colored American* (Boston, Mass.) — Negroes outnumbered whites in Charleston, South Carolina; Savannah, Georgia; Jacksonville, Florida; Montgomery, Alabama; Shreveport and Baton Rouge, Louisiana; and Vicksburg, Mississippi. The American Federation of Labor adopted a policy of establishing Negro locals where the situation warranted it; 32,069 Negroes were members of labor unions. Charles P. Graves, president of the Gold Leaf Consolidated Company of Montana and Illinois, a mining company, was the first black American millionaire. Booker T. Washington organized the National Negro Business League. Virginia, Arkansas, Georgia, and Delaware had established black state colleges by this year. George H. White, Negro representative in Congress from North Carolina, introduced the first bill to make lynching a federal crime.

1901 — W.E.B. Du Bois stated that there were many Negro intellectuals who refuted Booker T.

YEAR   JOURNAL

SIGNIFICANT EVENTS

Washington as a popular leader, refusing to accept his position that the Negro was to give up social equality for the time being. President Roosevelt invited Booker T. Washington to the White House for an interview and dinner, outraging southerners and pleasing many Negroes.

1902   *Negro Music Journal*
       (Washington, D.C.)

John D. Rockefeller pledged one million dollars to an agency to promote education without discrimination as to race, sex, or creed. Louisiana instituted a jim crow streetcar law. Alabama and Mississippi Democrats adopted white political primaries. Paul Laurence Dunbar published the novel, *The Sport of the Gods.* "In Dahomey," a musical with lyrics and book by Dunbar and Will Mercer Cook, opened a successful run at the Globe Theatre in Boston.

1903

Du Bois' collected short works were published under the title *Souls of Black Folk,* a collection that contained attacks against Booker T. Washington's ideas of work and money, his lack of emphasis on dignity and manhood, and his failure to oppose discrimination. Paul Laurence Dunbar published a collection of prose titled *Lyrics of Love and Laughter* and a book of verse, *In Old Plantation Days.*

1904   *The Voice of the Negro*
       (Atlanta, Ga.)

Andrew Carnegie financed a meeting of Negro leaders called by Booker T. Washington. Mississippi, Maryland, and South Carolina instituted segregation of public conveyances. Kentucky passed a law establishing segregation in public and private schools. Charlotte Hawkins Brown opened Palmer Memorial Institute in Sedalia, North Carolina.

1905   *The Moon Illustrated*
       (Memphis, Tenn.)

W.E.B. Du Bois called a conference of black leaders to meet at Niagara Falls, Canada. The organization they formed became known as the Niagara Movement. The Committee for Improving Industrial Conditions of Negroes in New York City and the National League for Protection of Colored Women were formed in New York. Anna T. Jeanes, a wealthy Philadelphia Quaker, gave

YEAR	JOURNAL	SIGNIFICANT EVENTS

SIGNIFICANT EVENTS
$200,000 to the General Education Fund to help improve Negro schools in the South. The *Voice of the Negro* began to criticize Booker T. Washington's philosophy.

1906
The biggest of the southern race riots between 1900 and 1910 occurred in Atlanta, Georgia, during the week of 24 September. Days before the riot there was talk of disenfranchising Negroes. Several hundred Negroes met at a state convention in Macon, Georgia, under the leadership of William Jefferson White, and formed an Equal Rights Association, rejecting Booker T. Washington's philosophy.

1907 *Horizon* (Washington, D.C.)
President Theodore Roosevelt revoked the civil disabilities of black soldiers engaged in race riots in Brownsville, Texas. Du Bois' Niagara Movement met in Boston. The Negro Business League had 320 branches. Philanthropists and southern boards of education made farm demonstration agents available to help improve rural living conditions.

1908
A riot in Springfield, Illinois, on 14 and 15 August became so violent that the governor called in 4,200 militiamen. Because of Theodore Roosevelt's actions in the Brownsville, Texas, incident, and encouraged by the big city Democratic machines in the North, a large number of Negroes gave their support to the Democratic party.

1909 *McGirt's Magazine* (Philadelphia, Pa.);

Alexander's Magazine (Boston, Mass.)
A biracial group of Americans began a meeting that led to the founding of the National Association for the Advancement of Colored People (NAACP) as a response to race riots in Springfield, Illinois. President Charles W. Eliot of Harvard University denounced any mixture of racial stock at the university and supported the South's demand for separation of the races. Booker T. Washington's *Story of the Negro* was published.

1910 *The Crisis* (New York, N.Y.)
As a result of Abraham Flexner's critical study of medical education in the United States, three black medical colleges were discontinued for deficiencies in resources to provide high-quality medical education. There were 100 colleges for Negroes in the

YEAR	JOURNAL	SIGNIFICANT EVENTS
		United States by this year. Julius Rosenwald made the first of several contributions to build YMCA facilities for Negroes. Jack Johnson, a black fighter, defeated James Jeffries for the heavyweight boxing championship of the world. Despite many complications, the formal organization of the NAACP was completed, primarily through the efforts of Oswald Garrison Villard.
1911		The National Urban League was founded. Marcus Garvey began the Universal Negro Improvement Association in Jamaica, whose purpose, among others, was to promote unity among all Negroes regardless of nationality.
1912		James Weldon Johnson published *The Autobiography of an Ex-Coloured Man*, the first novel by a Negro to become a permanent part of American literature.
1914	*Negro Farmer and Messenger* (Tuskegee Institute, Ala.)	NAACP reached membership of over 6,000 with fifty branches. A delegation headed by Monroe Trotter, Boston black journalist, secured an audience with President Woodrow Wilson to protest growing racial segregation in the country. The Lafayette Stock Company was formed in Harlem for promotion of Negro theatre. "Darktown Jubilee," the first motion picture to star a Negro, Bert Williams, caused a race riot in Brooklyn.
1915		Booker T. Washington died. Scott Joplin composed a ragtime opera, *Treemonisha*.
1916	*Journal of Negro History* (Washington, D.C.);	An antilynching committee of the NAACP was established to serve as an agency for investigation and gathering information on lynching. W.E.B. Du Bois, disappointed in Woodrow Wilson's administration, supported Charles Evans Hughes, the Republican candidate for president. James Weldon Johnson was appointed field secretary for the NAACP in the South.
	Champion Magazine (Chicago, Ill.);	
	Half-Century Magazine (Chicago, Ill.);	
	The Stylus Magazine (Washington, D.C.)	
1917	*The Messenger* (New York, N.Y.)	Marcus Garvey came to New York and founded the *Negro World*, a newspaper. Ten thousand black and white Americans marched through New York in a silent pro-

YEAR   JOURNAL   *SIGNIFICANT EVENTS*
                                              test against a race riot in East St. Louis,
                                              Illinois. Joel Spingarn convinced the War
                                              Department to establish an officers' train-
                                              ing camp for Negroes to serve in World
                                              War I. President Wilson declared war on
                                              Germany amidst controversy over whether
                                              Negroes would be recruited. The Selective
                                              Service Act was passed providing for en-
                                              listment of all able-bodied men from twenty-
                                              one to thirty-one; more than 700,000 Ne-
                                              groes registered. James Weldon Johnson's
                                              50 Years and Other Poems was published.
                                              Paul Robeson was named to the all-American
                                              collegiate football team.
1918   *The Crusader*   World War I ended and some 367,000 Ne-
       (New York, N.Y.)   groes had been drafted, although the major-
                                              ity were used in service battalions. Most
                                              combat troops were assigned to the Ninety-
                                              second and Ninety-third Infantry Divisions.
                                              The American Federation of Labor invited
                                              black leaders to a conference to discuss
                                              participation of Negroes in labor unions. A
                                              civil rights law was passed in New York
                                              State covering services in places of public
                                              accommodation. Fifty-eight Negroes were
                                              lynched. For publishing an article, "Pro-
                                              Germanism Amongst the Negroes," in the
                                              Messenger, one of the few magazines not
                                              to support the war wholeheartedly, publishers
                                              A. Philip Randolph and Chandler Owen
                                              were sentenced to jail for one to two and
                                              one-half years, and the *Messenger* was de-
                                              nied second-class mailing privileges. The
                                              AFL invited Robert Moton, head of Tuskegee
                                              Institute, Emmet Scott of the War Depart-
                                              ment, Eugene K. Jones of the National Urban
                                              League, and Fred Moore of the *New York
                                              Age* to discuss the "unionization of Negroes."
1920   *The Brownies' Book*   Marcus Garvey opened the national conven-
       (New York, N.Y.);   tion of his Universal Negro Improvement
                                              Association in Liberty Hall in Harlem. The
       The Competitor   Ku Klux Klan revived with reported mem-
       (Pittsburgh, Pa.)   bership of 100,000 in twenty-seven states.
                                              W.E.B. Du Bois published *Dark Waters*.
                                              The Harlem "Literary Renaissance" began
                                              as a new cultural movement. "Emperor

YEAR   JOURNAL

SIGNIFICANT EVENTS

Jones," Eugene O'Neill's first successful drama, opened at the Provincetown Theatre in Greenwich, starring a Negro, Charles Gilpin, in the title role. Gilpin also starred in "Ten Nights in a Barroom," made by the Colored Players Film Corporation of Philadelphia. The National Negro Baseball League was organized.

1923 *The Negro Churchman*
      (New York, N.Y.);

      Opportunity
      (New York, N.Y.)

Marcus Garvey was convicted of using the mails to defraud and sentenced to five years in prison, fined $1,000, and required to pay court costs. President A. Lawrence Lowell's ruling that Negro freshmen could not reside in the freshman dormitories was rescinded by the Harvard Corporation. Jean Toomer published *Cane*. "King" Oliver's Band was the first Negro jazz orchestra to record on a major record label.

1924 *The Spokesman*
      (New York, N.Y.)

The Negro Sanhedrin or All-Race Sanhedrin Conferences opened in Chicago with Kelly Miller, professor at Howard University and newspaper columnist, as its leader; some fifty of the sixty-one black organizations attended and held discussions bearing on one comprehensive organization for racial advancement. The largest number of Negroes to this date attended the Democratic National Convention meeting in New York City. Walter White published *The Fire in the Flint*, the only novel of the 1920s to concern itself with Negro-white relations in the South during the height of the KKK revival.

1925

Countee Cullen published his first collection of poetry, *Color*. Edited by Alain Locke, *The New Negro* was published, which defined the aims of the Harlem Renaissance movement.

1926 *The American Life Magazine*
      (Chicago, Ill.);

      Fire!!
      (New York, N.Y.)

The *Chicago Defender*, the black Chicago newspaper, launched a campaign to open all trade unions to Negroes, appoint a Negro to the president's cabinet, and include Negroes in police departments. In Chicago, 100 Negro women struck against the Moran Stuffed Date factory because of wage cuts and were fully supported by the International

YEAR   JOURNAL

SIGNIFICANT EVENTS

Workers Aid organization. Some 1,000 students attending the meeting of the Interdenominational Students Conference in Evanston, Illinois, found many were denied
accommodation at hotels, theatres, and restaurants. Roland Hayes, leading Negro tenor,
refused to go on the stage for a concert at
the Lyric Theatre in Baltimore until segregated seating had ended. Negro History Week
was introduced by Carter G. Woodson of
the Association for the Study of Negro Life
and History in Washington, D.C. The New
York Public Library purchased Arthur A.
Schomberg's private collection of history
and Negro literature. James Stanley Durkee,
white president of Howard University, announced his resignation following a series
of student riots against him.

1927   *Black Opals*
(Philadelphia, Pa.)

The NAACP sued the Democratic party in
Texas for its exclusion of black citizens. In
Nixon v. *Herndon*, the Court ruled that the
Texas primary was an obvious infringement
of the Fourteenth Amendment. The Supreme
Court also ruled that same year that the
State of Louisiana and City of New Orleans
could not prohibit blacks from living in white
residential communities without having first
received permission of whites. Cases against
segregation were raised in Mississippi, Georgia, and Colorado. A. Philip Randolph led
the Brotherhood of Sleeping Car Porters in
a protest for wage increases and an end to
receiving tips for a living. The Chicago
Urban League initiated a boycott of white-
owned stores in black neighborhoods that
would not hire black clerks. John Davis, a
state assemblyman from St. Louis County,
introduced an antilynching bill in the Missouri legislature.

1928   *Interracial Review*
(started in St. Louis, Mo.);

The Saturday Evening Quill
(Boston, Mass.)

Paul Laurence Dunbar Apartments opened
in Harlem as the first low-rent housing; this
project was financed largely by John D.
Rockefeller, who also backed the Dunbar
National Bank that opened in Harlem the
same year. The National Urban League and
the Fellowship of Reconciliation joined with

YEAR   JOURNAL

SIGNIFICANT EVENTS

other black leaders to persuade proprietors of large department stores in Harlem to hire black salespersons. The Harlem riot occurred, in which some 2,000 people fought with police. Claude McKay published *Home to Harlem*. W.E.B. Du Bois published *Dark Princess*.

1929   *The Bronzeman*
(New York, N.Y.);

Abbott's Monthly
(Chicago, Ill.)

Oscar De Priest, Republican representative from Chicago's First Congressional District, was elected the first black congressman since 1901 and the first to be elected from a northern state. The United Colored Socialists of America was established in Harlem. The American Federation of Labor granted temporary admission to the Brotherhood of Sleeping Car Porters. The International Ladies Garment Workers Union planned to organize 4,000 workers in dress shops in New York City. The Chicago NAACP started a campaign against bus companies that practiced segregation of passengers. Richard B. Harrison, a drama instructor at North Carolina A. and T. College, was chosen to play a lead in Marc Connelly's "The Green Pastures."

1932   *The Journal of Negro Education*
(Washington, D.C.)

The Communist party appealed for the Negro vote on the promise that their party championed the oppressed masses of the people. Franklin D. Roosevelt received only 23 percent of the Negro vote. John W. Ford, a Negro, was Communist party candidate for vice president. The NAACP published 10,000 copies of *Mississippi River Slavery—1932*, an investigation Roy Wilkins and George Schuyler conducted into conditions on Federal flood-control projects. White employees of the Illinois Central Railroad fought Negro workers to keep them out of railroad jobs. Rudolph Fisher, a Harlem physician and author, published *The Conjure-Man Dies*, the first Negro detective novel. Wallace Thurman published *Infants of the Spring*, the last important novel of the Harlem Renaissance period.

YEAR	JOURNAL	SIGNIFICANT EVENTS

1933   *The Quarterly Review of Higher Education Among Negroes* (Charlotte, N.C.);

The Black Man (New York, N.Y.)

Elder Solomon Lightfoot Michaux' Good Neighbor League that was founded this year fed a quarter of a million unemployed persons in its Happy News Cafe in Washington, D.C. Angelo Herndon, a nineteen-year-old black youth from Cincinnati, was sentenced to twenty years on a southern chain gang for bringing Communist literature into the South. The Works Progress Administration, a part of President Roosevelt's New Deal, employed teachers in adult education projects that taught some 400,000 black adults to read. Approximately 200,000 Negro boys worked in Civilian Conservation Corps camps.

1934   *Challenge* (Boston, Mass.)

Arthur Mitchell, a Negro Democrat, replaced Oscar De Priest, Republican, in Congress. Senator Costigan of Colorado and Senator Wagner of New York proposed an anti-lynching bill. W.E.B. Du Bois resigned as editor of the *Crisis* because his policies of desegregation conflicted with the NAACP Board's. Roy Wilkins succeeded Du Bois as editor of the *Crisis*. The Louisiana legislature repealed the poll tax. *Negro Folk Symphony* no. 1, written by William L. Dawson, a Negro composer, was performed by the Philadelphia Symphony Orchestra at Carnegie Hall in New York under the direction of the famous conductor, Leopold Stokowski.

1935   *The Negro Journal of Religion* (Wilberforce, Ohio);

Race (New York, N.Y.);

Education (Corona, N.Y.)

The Social Security Act discriminated against Negroes by excluding agricultural and domestic workers from its benefits. The Committee on Industrial Organization (CIO) created interracial unions in steel, automobile, rubber, and packing house plants and factories. The National Council of Negro Women was established in New York City with Mary McLeod, president of Bethune-Cookman College in Daytona Beach, Florida, serving as its first president. A Harlem riot caused more than $200 million in damages, largely to stores that refused to hire black salespersons. The Federal Theatre, a part of the Works Progress Administration

YEAR   JOURNAL

SIGNIFICANT EVENTS
(WPA) brought a project to Harlem that became significant in development of black drama.

1936   *The Brown American*
(Philadelphia, Pa.)

Faculty members at Howard University formed the National Negro Congress to create a coalition of leaders from religious, fraternal, and civic groups. Negroes objected to platforms of both major political parties for the presidential campaign. At the Democratic National Convention, Senator "Cotton Ed" Smith of South Carolina and Mayor Burnet Maybank of Charleston walked out when a Negro minister rose to offer the opening prayer. William Grant Still was the first Negro to lead a major symphony orchestra as guest conductor of the Los Angeles Symphony Orchestra in Hollywood Bowl. Jesse Owens, Ralph Metcalfe, Archie Williams, and John Woodruff—all Negro athletes—won medals at the Berlin Olympics.

1937   *New Day*
(New York, N.Y.);

Flash
(Washington, D.C.);

National Education Outlook Among Negroes
(Baltimore, Md.);

Negro History Bulletin
(Washington, D.C.);

The Negro South
(New Orleans, La.)

The Supreme Court declared that the picketing of firms which refused to hire Negroes was a legal technique for securing redressment. White teachers in Maryland were paid almost twice as much as Negro teachers of the same grade. Thurgood Marshall argued for equalization of public school teachers' salaries before the Maryland Board of Education. The NAACP successfully challenged the attempted exclusion of Negro Boy Scouts from the Scout Jamboree in Washington, D.C. Negro Federal Judge William H. Hastie was confirmed for the Federal Court in the Virgin Islands. Waters Edward Turpin published *These Low Grounds*, the first Negro attempt at a family chronicle novel. Negro novelist Zora Neale Hurston published her second and most successful novel, *Their Eyes Were Watching God*. Warner Brothers released the movie version of *The Green Pastures*, with an all-Negro cast. Joe Louis defeated James A. Braddock to become the world's heavyweight boxing champion. Henry Arm-

YEAR	JOURNAL	SIGNIFICANT EVENTS

YEAR   JOURNAL

SIGNIFICANT EVENTS

strong, the Negro prize fighter, became featherweight boxing champion.

1938

In the case of *Missouri Ex Rel Gains* v. *Canada Registrar of the University et al.*, the Supreme Court ruled that a state was required to allow Negro admission at the state university if equal educational facilities were not available. A *Fortune* magazine poll showed that 84.7 percent of the Negroes supported President Franklin D. Roosevelt. *Uncle Tom's Children*, by Richard Wright, was published.

**1939   *The Black Politician*
(Los Angeles, Calif.)**

The Greater New York Coordinating Committee for Employment, led by Adam Clayton Powell, Jr., demonstrated at the offices of the World's Fair in the Empire State Building, and opened up several hundred jobs for Negroes. The Ku Klux Klan in Greenville, South Carolina, issued a statement warning: "The Klan will ride again if Greenville Negroes continue to register and vote." In April, Mississippi Senator Theodore C. Bilbo introduced a back-to-Africa bill in the Senate. Jane Matilda Bolin became the first Negro woman judge when she was appointed to the Court of Domestic Relations in New York City. Marian Anderson gave her Easter concert on the steps of the Lincoln Memorial when the Daughters of the American Revolution prevented her appearance at Constitution Hall, which they owned.

**1940   *Phylon*
(Atlanta, Ga.);**

***The Southern Frontier*
(Atlanta, Ga.).**

Through efforts by the NAACP in *Alston* v. *School Board of the City of Norfolk*, a Federal Circuit Court of Appeals declared that under the Fourteenth Amendment, Negro teachers could not be denied pay equal to that of white teachers. In *Hansberry* v. *Lee*, the Supreme Court overthrew an Illinois Supreme Court verdict by ruling that Hansberry was not bound by a restrictive covenant and could sell his house to a Negro if he desired. There were 210 Negro newspapers, most with local circulation, and 120 Negro magazines in existence. The *Pittsburgh Courier* had the largest circulation,

398   APPENDIX A

YEAR   JOURNAL

SIGNIFICANT EVENTS

followed by the *Chicago Defender*. Atlanta passed a city ordinance requiring jim crow taxes, with different colored signs to indicate the race served. Richard Wright published his novel *Native Son*. The American Negro Theater was founded. Negro actress Hattie McDaniel received an Academy Award as best supporting actress for her role in "Gone with the Wind."

1941

The NAACP gave its approval and support to A. Philip Randolph's plan for a march of 100,000 Negroes on Washington, D.C. Robert Weaver was appointed director of integration of Negroes into the National Defense Program in the Office of Production Management. After a four-week boycott of buses by New York City Negroes, local bus companies agreed to hire Negro drivers.

1942   *Negro Digest* (Chicago, Ill.);

The New Negro Traveler and Conventioneer (Chicago, Ill.)

On 28 February, 1,200 persons in Detroit armed with knives, clubs, rifles, and shotguns gathered to prevent three Negro families from moving into the 200-unit Sojourner Truth settlement, designated by the U.S. Housing Authority as Negro housing. The Congress of Racial Equality (CORE) was founded by James Farmer and a group of University of Chicago students and soon achieved national prominence and participation. The first U.S. merchant ship with a Negro captain (Hugh Mulzac), the *Booker T. Washington*, was launched at Wilmington, Delaware. Margaret Walker won the Yale University Younger Poets Award for *My People*, a collection of poems. Walter White, NAACP leader, conferred with the film industry about the undignified stereotyping of Negroes in films.

1943   *The Negro* (St. Louis, Mo.);

The Negro College Quarterly (Wilberforce, Ohio);

Pulse (Washington, D.C.)

A Harlem riot in August required 9,000 state guard troops to quell. The Ninety-ninth Pursuit Squadron, a Negro Air Force unit, flew its first combat mission in the Mediterranean theater. William L. Dawson, a Chicago Negro and Democrat, became a member of the House of Representatives. Benjamin J. Davis, Jr., a Negro and a member of the National Committee of the Commu-

YEAR   JOURNAL

SIGNIFICANT EVENTS

nist Party, was elected to the New York City council and was reelected in 1945. Paul Robeson played Othello at the Shubert Theater in New York for 296 performances, a record for Shakespeare on Broadway. An all-Negro musical film "Stormy Weather" was released by 20th Century Fox and starred Lena Horne, Bill Robinson, and many other Negro stars.

1944   *Headlines and Pictures*
(Detroit, Mich.);

Negro Story
(Chicago, Ill.);

Southwestern Journal,
(Langston, Okla.)

Approximately 500 Negroes were among the U.S. soldiers at Omaha Beach on D-Day. The War Department announced the end of racial segregation in recreation and transportation facilities in all Army posts. Gunnar Myrdal wrote in his book, *American Dilemma*, "Segregation is now becoming so complete that the white southerner practically never sees a Negro except as his servant and in other standardized and formalized caste situations." The United Negro College Fund (UNCF) was chartered, with the aid of the Julius Rosenwald Fund and the General Education Board.

1945   *The African*
(New York, N.Y.);

Ebony
(Chicago, Ill.)

Colonel Benjamin O. Davis, Jr. was named commander of Godman Field in Kentucky. The NAACP was invited to send a representative to the United Nations Conference in San Francisco. Congress killed the Fair Employment Practices Commission by refusing to vote funds for it. Adam Clayton Powell, Jr. became a member of the House of Representatives. Richard Wright's largely autobiographical *Black Boy* was published.

1946   *Color Line*
(Mt. Vernon, N.Y.);

New South
(Atlanta, Ga.);

Our World
(New York, N.Y.)

President Truman issued Executive Order 9808 creating the Presidential Committee on Civil Rights to study existing federal protection of civil rights and ways to improve it. The American Nurses Association removed its barrier to Negro membership by allowing qualified nurses to join the association directly if their local societies refused to admit them. Charles S. Johnson, a Negro, was a member of the U.S. National Commission at the first meeting of UNESCO in Paris. William H. Hastie became governor of the Virgin Islands.

YEAR	JOURNAL	SIGNIFICANT EVENTS

YEAR   JOURNAL

1947   *New Day*
(Kansas City, Mo.);

Sepia
(Fort Worth, Tex.);

Midwest Journal
(Jefferson City, Mo.)

1948

1949   *Harlem Quarterly*
(New York, N.Y.)

1950   *The Negro Educational Review*
(Lorman, Miss.)

1951   *Jet*
(Chicago, Ill.)

SIGNIFICANT EVENTS

CORE sent the first Freedom Ride group into the South in April. Langston Hughes wrote the lyrics to Kurt Weill's score for "Street Scene." Jackie Robinson became the first Negro to play on a major baseball team, the Brooklyn Dodgers.

In July, President Truman's Executive Order 9981 barred segregation in the armed forces and created the President's Committee on Equality of Treatment and Opportunity in the Armed Services, to end discrimination in military facilities and units.

In *Johnson* v. *Board of Trustees*, the University of Kentucky was ordered to open its graduate school to Negroes. WERD in Atlanta, the first Negro-owned radio station, went on the air. Congressman William L. Dawson became chairman of the House Expenditures Committee; he was the first Negro to head a standing committee of Congress. William H. Hastie became judge of the Third U.S. Circuit Court of Appeals. Joe Louis retired as world heavyweight boxing champion after holding the title for eleven years and eight months, a record length of time.

A state court decision opened the University of Missouri to Negroes. The American Medical Association seated its first Negro delegate.

In *McKissick* v. *Carmichael*, the University of North Carolina Law School was opened to Negroes by court order. A Washington, D.C., municipal court of appeals ruled segregation in restaurants illegal. President Truman established the Committee on Government Contract Compliance to combat discrimination against Negroes in private companies doing business with the federal government. Ralph Bunche, the American Negro diplomat, was appointed under secretary for the United Nations. Carver National Monument, the first national park honoring a Negro, was opened near Joplin, Missouri.

YEAR	JOURNAL	SIGNIFICANT EVENTS

YEAR   JOURNAL

SIGNIFICANT EVENTS

1952   *The Journal of Human Relations*
(Wilberforce, Ohio)

In *Gray* v. *University of Tennessee*, the University of Tennessee was ordered to admit Negroes to its graduate, professional, and special schools. The NAACP succeeded in gaining admission of Negroes into the Nursing School of Louisiana State University, but legal attempts to desegregate the University of Florida graduate schools failed. Through legal action, the NAACP opened certain public housing projects in Detroit, San Francisco, Long Branch, New Jersey, Sacramento, and Richmond, California. Tuskegee Institute reported that for the first time in the 71 years records had been kept, there were no lynchings. Charlotta A. Bass, a Negro editor and publisher of the *California Eagle*, received the nomination of the Progressive party for vice president. Ralph Ellison's *The Invisible Man* was published.

1953

President Eisenhower's administration ended segregation in schools on military bases, and of civilian employees in the Navy shore establishments. The NAACP tried unsuccessfully to have civil rights put on the agenda of a top-level conference between President Eisenhower and Republican congressional leaders.

1954

On May 17, in *Brown* v. *The Board of Education*, the Supreme Court ruled that school segregation was unconstitutional since "separate educational facilities are inherently unequal." The AFL Convention endorsed the 1954 Supreme Court decision on desegregation.

1955

Walter White, executive secretary of the NAACP since 1931, died, and Roy Wilkins was chosen as White's successor. Marian Anderson, the first Negro to sing at the Metropolitan Opera House in New York City, appeared in Verdi's *The Masked Ball*.

1956

Martin Luther King, Jr. and almost 100 other Negroes were indicted on a charge of conspiring to conduct an illegal boycott in Montgomery, Alabama.

1957   *College Language Association
Journal*
(Atlanta, Ga.)

North Carolina began token desegregation in the Greensboro, Winston-Salem, and Charlotte schools. Tennessee announced that

YEAR   JOURNAL

SIGNIFICANT EVENTS

desegregation of its six state colleges was to take effect in the fall of 1958. As a result of the Montgomery bus boycott, the Southern Christian Leadership Conference (SCLC) was organized by Dr. Martin Luther King, Jr., Bayard Rustin, and Stanley Levinson. Negroes were admitted into the International Brotherhood of Electrical Workers in Cleveland and the Bricklayers, Masons and Marble Masons Protective Association in Milwaukee, Wisconsin. White city officials of Tuskegee, Alabama, redrew the city lines to exclude all but 10 of the 400 registered Negro voters.

1958

The U.S. Civil Rights Commission, when they conducted an investigation in Macon County, Alabama, found the county, home of Tuskegee Institute and a literate Negro population which comprised 85 percent of the total county population, had only 28 percent of the Negroes registered to vote. As a result of NAACP campaigns, public housing projects were desegregated in Erie, Pennsylvania, and Trenton, New Jersey.

1961   *Freedomways*
       (New York, N.Y.);

       The Liberator
       (New York, N.Y.);

       Negro Heritage/Black Heritage
       (Reston, Va.)

President John F. Kennedy created the President's Committee on Equal Employment Opportunity and appointed Vice-President Lyndon B. Johnson chairman. The Supreme Court reversed convictions of sixteen sit-in demonstrators arrested in Baton Rouge, Louisiana. A Freedom Ride campaign was begun by thirteen CORE members, headed by James Farmer, and later joined by SNCC. On 4 May an integrated group set out from Washington, D.C., for a bus ride through the South to test compliance with integration orders of the Interstate Commerce Commission and federal courts.

1962

The President's Committee on Equal Employment Opportunity ordered desegregation of southern paper mills. Marjorie Lawson, Negro lawyer and federal adviser, was appointed a judge for the District of Columbia by President Kennedy. In the Albany movement, Martin Luther King, Jr. and SNCC, CORE, and NAACP members

YEAR	JOURNAL	SIGNIFICANT EVENTS
		joined in a campaign against segregation and discrimination in the Georgia city of Albany.
1963		In his inaugural address, Governor George Wallace of Alabama said, "I draw the line in the dust and toss the gauntlet before the feet of tyranny and I say segregation now, segregation tomorrow, segregation forever." President John F. Kennedy was assassinated in Dallas, Texas.
1964		The Civil Rights Act of 1964 forbade discrimination in public accommodations and employment. It allowed the attorney general to institute suits and to deny federal funds to local agencies which practiced discrimination. In a riot in Harlem in July, 1 person was killed, 140 injured, and 500 arrested, all set off by the killing of a fifteen-year-old Negro boy by an off-duty policeman.
1965		A massive march from Selma to Montgomery, Alabama, was held on 7 March and led by Martin Luther King, Jr. and John Lewis of SNCC. Major General Benjamin O. Davis, Jr. was named lieutenant general in the U.S. Air Force, the highest rank yet obtained by a Negro in the armed services. Malcolm X, black nationalist leader, was shot to death in New York City.
1966	*Journal of Black Poetry* (San Francisco, Calif.)	Stokely Carmichael of SNCC and Floyd McKissick of CORE began to champion "Black Power." Julian Bond, a Negro, was denied his seat in the Georgia House of Representatives because of his opposition to the war in Vietnam. In an open housing march in Chicago, Dr. Martin Luther King, Jr. was stoned by white Chicagoans. Edward W. Brooke from Massachusetts was elected the first Negro senator since Reconstruction. Robert Weaver, secretary of Housing and Urban Development, was the first Negro cabinet member. Constance Baker Motley was appointed the first woman federal judge.
1967	*Black American Literature Forum* (Terre Haute, Ind.)	President Johnson asked Congress in February to pass a civil rights bill to bar discrimination in the sale and rental of housing, to stop interference with the exercise of civil

YEAR	JOURNAL

SIGNIFICANT EVENTS

rights, and to end discrimination in the selection of juries. Dr. Martin Luther King, Jr. announced he would work against the Vietnam war because he believed it had become the major obstacle to progress in the area of civil rights. President Johnson named Thurgood Marshall to the Supreme Court; he was the first Negro to ever serve on the Court. Carl B. Stokes, a Negro Democrat, was elected mayor of Cleveland, Ohio. Vice-President Humphrey, in a speech in Detroit on 2 August, called for a "Marshall Plan" of aid for the impoverished areas of cities.

1968 *Black Politics*
      (Berkeley, Calif.);

      Black Theatre
      (New York, N.Y.);

      *Harvard Journal of Afro-
      American Affairs*
      (Cambridge, Mass.)

Several hundred Negro students of South Carolina State College and Claflin College marched through the streets on 5 February after protesting the segregation of a bowling alley. Dr. Martin Luther King, Jr. was assassinated in Memphis on 4 April. *Fortune* Magazine reported the Negro market represented $30 billion a year before taxes. Combined circulation of the Negro press and magazines was 3 million; the leading magazine was *Ebony*, with a subscription of a million copies per month.

1969 *Black Scholar*
      (Sausalito, Calif.)

The House of Representatives voted to seat Adam Clayton Powell after a long and entangled debate concerning his qualifications and conduct. The confessed murderer of Dr. Martin Luther King, Jr., James Earl Ray, was sentenced to ninety-nine years. Student members of the campus Afro-American Society seized a student center at Cornell University, protesting the alleged harassment of black coeds and the burning of a cross on campus. The Justice Department filed suit against the state of Georgia to end segregation in its schools in the first desegregation suit against an entire state. A 105-page report by the U.S. Commission on Civil Rights, chaired by Father Theodore Hesburgh, president of Notre Dame University, charged the Nixon administration with choosing the wrong school desegregation policy and with covering its actions

YEAR   JOURNAL

1970   *Black Academy Review*
       (Buffalo, N.Y.);

       Black Business Digest
       (Philadelphia, Pa.);

       Black Collegian
       (New Orleans, La.);

       Black Creation
       (New York, N.Y.);

       Black Enterprise
       (New York, N.Y.);

       Black Sports
       (New York, N.Y.);

       Black World
       (Chicago, Ill.);

       Essence
       (Boulder, Col.);

       Journal of Black Studies
       (Beverly Hills, Calif.);

       Living Blues
       (Chicago, Ill.);

       Proud
       (St. Louis, Mo.);

       *Review of Black Political
       Economy*
       (New York, N.Y.);

       Studies in Black Literature
       (Fredericksburg, Va.)

SIGNIFICANT EVENTS
with overly optimistic statistics. Dr. Clifton Reginald Wharton, Jr., a black economist from New York City, was elected president of Michigan State University, becoming the first black to head a major public and predominantly white university.
Nomination of G. Harold Carswell to the Supreme Court drew immediate fire from civil rights associates. Senators John Stennis and Strom Thurmond demanded that northern school districts be obliged to observe federal desegregation guidelines in the same way as their southern counterparts. Self-imposed exile Stokely Carmichael testified before a closed session of the Senate Internal Subcommittee in Washington, D.C. A student strike was called at Yale in support of the eight Black Panthers awaiting trial in New Haven. Two black students were shot and killed after a night of violence outside a women's dormitory at Jackson State College in Mississippi. California's Governor Reagan signed a bill forbidding busing of school children without the written consent of their parents or guardians.

YEAR	JOURNAL
1971	*Amistad* (New York, N.Y.);
	Black Careers (Philadelphia, Pa.);
	Black Review (New York, N.Y.)
	Hampton Institute Journal of Ethnic Studies (Norfolk, Va.)
1972	*The Black Church* (Boston, Mass.);
	Encore American and Worldwide News (New York, N.Y.);
	Journal of Afro-American Issues (Washington, D.C.)
1973	*About Time* (Rochester, N.Y.);

SIGNIFICANT EVENTS

James A. Floyd, a black man, was appointed mayor of Princeton, New Jersey, an affluent university town. The Reverend Leon Howard Sullivan was elected to the board of directors of General Motors, the first black man to participate in the direction of a U.S. auto company. The Supreme Court ruled by a vote of 5-4 that a community can close publicly owned recreational facilities rather than desegregate them. Addressing the annual convention of the NAACP, Executive Director Roy Wilkins stated that young black activists differed most markedly from their predecessors in their distrust of whites. Black youth, he added, may have repudiated NAACP's "slow and careful methods," but not its basic philosophy. President Nixon proposed a moratorium until July 1973 on all court-ordered busing and diversion of $1.5 billion for "impoverished" schools. Representing a wide spectrum of political views, 8,000 blacks attended the first National Black Political Convention in Gary, Indiana. Frank Wills, a black security guard in Washington, D.C.'s Watergate office complex, detected and detained a group of men installing surveillance equipment in the Democratic party national headquarters. Senator George McGovern of South Dakota obtained the Democratic nomination for the presidency at a convention in which 400 blacks, or 15 percent of the total, were delegates. The number of black congressmen increased from twelve to fifteen. Andrew Young from Atlanta and Barbara Jordan from Houston were elected the first black congressmen from the South since the days of Reconstruction. Republican Senator Edward Brooke in Massachusetts won reelection by a landslide victory, even though Massachusetts was the only state to be carried by George McGovern.

Paul Robeson was honored on his seventy-fifth birthday by Rutgers University, his alma mater. Thomas Bradley, son of a share-

YEAR   JOURNAL
The Afro-American Journal
(Indianapolis, Ind.);

The Black Perspective in Music
(Cambria Heights, N.Y.);

Ebony Jr.
(Chicago, Ill.)
1974

1975

1975

1977   *Callaloo*
(Lexington, Ky.);

First-World
(Atlanta, Ga.);

*The Western Journal of Black
Studies*
(Pullman, Wash.)

SIGNIFICANT EVENTS
cropper, was elected mayor of Los Angeles. The number of black elected officials
in the United States rose from 370 to 2,991,
in an election held mostly for municipal and
county offices.

President Richard M. Nixon resigned from
office in August. Riots against integration
of public schools in Boston peaked as police struggled to restrain violence which
wrenched much of the city.

General Daniel "Chappie" James, Jr. became commander-in-chief of the North
American Air Defense Command (NORAD),
becoming the first black four-star general
in U.S. history.

Governor Jimmy Carter said his presidential campaign would include commitments
to guarantee civil rights and end racial discrimination, even if it cost him votes. Black
conservative Thomas Sowell said evidence
did not support assumptions that busing benefits schoolchildren. Ronald Reagan, candidate for Republican nomination for president, said government was correct in
eliminating discrimination at the start, but
he attacked reverse discrimination.

Vernon Jordan, executive director of the
National Urban League, charged that President Jimmy Carter's administration had forgotten black voters. A *New York Times* survey showed southern blacks had shifted from
civil rights activism in the 1960s to political and economic activity in the 1970s. Fewer
rural blacks headed for northern cities. On
the eve of their annual convention, NAACP
officials bitterly accused northern legislations
of opposing civil rights in recent years. Black
Panther party founder Huey Newton urged
an end to racism as a preventive to national
disasters. U.N. Ambassador Andrew Young
in a British Broadcasting Corporation interview compared the racial situation in Rho-

YEAR	JOURNAL	SIGNIFICANT EVENTS

YEAR   JOURNAL

SIGNIFICANT EVENTS

desia and South Africa to that in the South in the days before civil rights gains. A National Urban League survey showed 44.6 percent of those polled believed that although integration was desirable, blacks should first have equal voice in control of schools and housing. More than 300 black American artists, writers, and dancers participated in the Second World Black and African Festival of Arts and Culture in Lagos, Nigeria.

1978

New NAACP Executive Director Benjamin Hooks told local chapters to seek 2 million new members to help fight recent setbacks for black people. The Reverend Jesse Jackson told the Republican National Convention that blacks would vote Republican if that party sought their votes and espoused their causes. A *New York Times* survey found Detroit blacks had mixed feelings about President Carter.

**1979   *Black Odyssey*
(Jamaica, West Indies)**

The top leadership of the NAACP and the NAACP Legal, Defense and Education Fund met in Washington, D.C., to discuss problems growing out of their competition for funds. The National Association of Black Social Workers vowed to end use of the term "minority" to describe black Americans. A. Philip Randolph, black civil rights labor leader and founder of the *Messenger*, died at age 90. President Carter chided black Americans for failing to exercise their voting rights to conquer the "cancer of racial injustice." The U.S. Supreme Court ruled 5-2 that private employers could legally give special preference to black workers to eliminate a manifest imbalance in traditionally white-only jobs. Ambassador Andrew Young resigned from his position in the United Nations organization. The House of Representatives voted 408-11 to place a bust of Dr. Martin Luther King, Jr. in the Capitol. Civil rights activists troubled over repercussions of the recent killing of five Communist Workers party members by the Ku Klux Klan in Greensboro, North Carolina.

| YEAR | JOURNAL | SIGNIFICANT EVENTS |

YEAR   JOURNAL

1980   *Buffalo*
       (Fayetteville, N.C.)

1981

SIGNIFICANT EVENTS

Rosa Parks, a black woman who helped start the national civil rights movement by her refusal to give up her bus seat in 1955 to a white man in Montgomery, Alabama, was awarded the Martin Luther King, Jr. Nonviolent Peace Prize. Benjamin Hooks, executive secretary of the NAACP, said he expected blacks to continue their tradition of voting for Democratic presidential candidates because they do not believe that Republican politics will bring them into the economic mainstream. President Carter and Ronald Reagan discussed the issue of strained race relations on a nationally televised debate. President-elect Ronald Reagan said he was "heart and soul" in favor of things that have been done in the name of civil rights and desegregation. The Presidential Commission on National Agenda for the Eighties opposed any reduction in a federal role in enforcing civil rights. A Justice Department report revealed that FBI agents knew about and apparently covered up involvement of the FBI's chief paid informer Gary Thomas Rowe, Jr. in attacks on blacks, civil rights activists, and newsmen in the early 1960s.

Vice-President Bush, seeking to allay concerns among blacks about the attitude of the Reagan Administration toward civil rights, said at Tuskegee Institute that Reagan was committed to improving the quality of life for all who have suffered bigotry and discrimination in the past. A tribute was given by black show business celebrities in honor of the twenty-fifth anniversary of Rosa Parks' "refusal," one incident that gave rise to the movement for civil rights. Five thousand demonstrators, led by the Reverend Jesse L. Jackson, reenacted the 1965 Selma to Montgomery civil rights march in honor of the thirteenth anniversary of the death of Martin Luther King, Jr.

Geographical Distribution of Black Journals

East

About Time
African, The: Journal of African Affairs
Alexander's Magazine
Amistad
Anglo-African Magazine, The
Black Academy Review
Black Business Digest
Black Careers
Black Church, The
Black Creation
Black Enterprise
Black Opals
Black Perspective in Music, The
Black Review
Black Sports
Black Theatre
Brown American, The
Brownies' Book, The
Challenge/New Challenge
Colored American
Color Line
Competitor: The National Magazine
Crisis, The
Crusader, The
Douglass' Monthly
Education: A Journal of Reputation
Encore American and Worldwide News
Fire!!: Devoted to Younger Negro Artists
Flash: A Newspicture Magazine
Freedom's Journal

Freedomways
Harlem Quarterly
Harvard Journal of Afro-American Affairs
Horizon: A Journal of the Color Line
Interracial Review
Journal of Afro-American Issues
Journal of Negro Education, The
Journal of Negro History
Liberator, The
McGirt's Magazine
Messenger, The: World's Greatest Monthly
National Education Outlook Among Negroes
Negro Churchman, The
Negro Heritage/Black Heritage
Negro History Bulletin
Negro Music Journal
New Day, The
Opportunity: A Journal of Negro Life
Our World: A Picture Magazine for the Whole Family
Pulse
Race: Devoted to Social, Political, and Economic Equality
Review of Black Political History, The
Saturday Evening Quill, The
Spokesman, The
Studies in Black Literature
Stylus Magazine, The: A Magazine to Encourage Original Literary Expression at
    Howard University

Midwest

Abbott's Monthly
Afro-American Journal, The
American Life Magazine, The: A Magazine of Timely Features and Good Fiction
Black American Literature Forum
Black World
Bronzeman, The
Champion Magazine: A Monthly Survey of Negro Achievement
Ebony
Ebony Jr.
Half-Century Magazine
Headlines and Pictures
Jet
Journal of Human Relations, The
Living Blues: A Journal of the Black American Blues Tradition
Midwest Journal
Negro, The: A Journal of Essential Facts about the Negro
Negro College Quarterly, The
Negro Digest

Negro Journal of Religion, The: An Interdenominational Review
Negro Story: A Magazine for All Americans
New Day: The People's Magazine
New Negro Traveler and Conventioneer, The
Proud

South

A.M.E. Church Review, The
Black Collegian, The: The National Magazine of Black College Students
Buffalo
Callaloo: A Black South Journal of Arts and Letters
College Language Association Journal
First World: An International Journal of Black Thought
Hampton Institute Journal of Ethnic Studies
Moon Illustrated Weekly, The
Negro Educational Review, The
Negro Farmer and Messenger
Negro South, The
New South
Phylon: A Review of Race and Culture
Quarterly Review of Higher Education Among Negroes, The
Southern Frontier, The
Southern Workman, The
Voice of the Negro, The

Southwest

Essence: The Magazine for Today's Black Woman
Sepia
Southwestern Journal

West

Black Politician, The: A Quarterly Journal of Current Political Thought
Black Politics: A Journal of Liberation
Black Scholar: Journal of Black Studies and Research
Journal of Black Poetry
Journal of Black Studies
Western Journal of Black Studies, The

West Indies

Black Man, The: A Monthly Magazine of Negro Thought and Opinion
Black Odyssey: A Magazine on Travel and Leisure

Index

Abbott, Robert S., 3, 170; and the Republican party, 5

Abbott's Monthly, 3-9; Afro-American authors, 7; goals of the *Chicago Defender*, 3; interest in African culture, 4; politics, 5-6

Abdul, Raoul, 172

Abolition, 152-153

About Time, 9-11; political issues, 9-10

African, The: Journal of African Affairs, 12-16; African affairs, 13-14; Afro-American authors, 14-15

African Biblical Review, 50

African Blood Brotherhood, 148, 149

African history, interest in, 29, 36-37, 54, 85, 93-94, 95, 184-185, 189, 196-197, 198, 215, 231-232, 233, 246, 256-257, 273, 276, 326

African Methodist Episcopal Church: founding, 28-29; significant in forming a black nation, 51

African Students' Association, 12

Afro-American Journal, The, 16-20, African heritage, 17; Institute of Afro-American Studies, 18-19; political issues, 18

Alexander, Charles, 20, 26

Alexander's Magazine, 20-27, 248-250; Atlanta riot, 22-23; black life in Boston, 21; Brownsville incident, 23-24; Niagara movement, 24-25; politics, 25-26

Allen, Robert L., 88

A.M.E. Church Review, The, 27-32; church history, 28; civil rights, 28; race pride, 29

American Life Magazine, The: A Magazine of Timely Features and Good Fiction, 32-34; black participation in World War I, 33; "Chicago Renaissance," 32; migration North in World War I era, 32

American Teachers' Association, 252

Ames, Jessie Daniel, 350

Amistad: Writings of Black History and Culture, 34-38; Afro-American authors, 34-36; European colonialism, 36-37; popular American culture, 37

Amistad Mutiny, 38

Anderson, Charles W., 242

Anderson, Talmadge, 378, 380

Anderson, Robert E., 303

Anderson, Thomas W., 363

Angelou, Maya, 87, 172

Anglo-African Magazine, The, 38-41; Afro-American authors, 39-40; anti-slavery movement, 39; Civil War, 39

Anti-slavery movement, 39-40, 154-155, 156

Appel, Benjamin, 115, 262

Appleton, Clyde, 75

Aptheker, Herbert, 198, 246

Armstrong, Samuel C., 350, 351-352, 353

Asante, Molefi Kete, 219

Black press, 352-353
Black Review, 81-84; Afro-American
authors, 81-82; popular American music,
82
Black Scholar, The: Journal of Black
Studies and Research, 84-88;
African liberation, 85; black authors,
87; black studies, 86-87; Du
Bois and the government of the United
States, 85; revolutionary black
ideology, 84
Black separatism, 216
Black Sports, 88-90; Jackie Robinson's
entry into major league baseball,
88-89
Black studies, 43, 86-87
Black Theatre, 90-92; black theatre,
89-91; Ed Bullins, 90; Free
Southern Theatre Workshop, 91; New
Lafayette Theatre, 90; Third
Annual Black Power Conference, 91
Black World, 93-96; black theatre, 94;
Negro Digest, 93
Black World Foundation, 84
Bland, James A., 103
Blount, Carolyn S., 11
Blount, Jonathan, 170
Blount, Mildred, 103
Blyden, Edward W., 39
Bogart, Humphrey, 253
Bond, Frederick W., 253
Bond, Horace Mann, 262, 316
Bonner, Marita, 97
Bontemps, Arna, 44, 114, 242, 277,
285, 321
Booker, Simeon, 162
Boone, Dorothy Deloris, ix
Bowen, John Wesley Edward, 23, 369
Boyer, Horace C., 179
Bradley, Ed, 11
Braithwaite, E. R., 56
Braithwaite, William S., 139, 366
Brawley, Benjamin, 175, 176, 355, 367,
368
Briggs, Cyril V., 148, 149, 150
Bright, Nellie R., 71
Brimmer, Andrew F., 47, 76

British colonialism, and black nationalism,
13-14
Bronzeman, The, 96-100; black higher
education, 97; Communism among
blacks, 98; politics, 98-99; social,
religious and cultural life in Chicago,
96-97; World War I, 97-98
Brooke, Edward, 11, 76
Brooks, Albert N., 279
Brooks, Gwendolyn, 87, 97, 217, 288,
321
Brooks, Joseph F., 341
Brotherhood of Sleeping Car Porters, 244
Brown American, The, 100-105; and
Afro-American authors, 103;
communism, 101; politics, 100, 101,
102; Scottsboro case, 101;
Washington-Du Bois controversy,
100-101; World War II, 102,
104
Brown, Benjamin, 198, 201
Brown, Cecil, 81, 82, 87
Brown, H. Rap, 235
Brown, Sterling, 225, 308, 321
Brown, William Wells, 39, 40, 277
Brown v. Topeka, 220, 224, 266, 320
Brownies' Book, The, 106-108, 164; Du
Bois' interest in children, 106; "The
Crow" as Du Bois' personna for
commenting on world affairs, 107
Browning, Alice C., 287
Brownsville incident, 23-25, 208, 373
Bruce, John Edward, 366
Bruce, Richard, 176
Bryan, William Jennings, 25
Buck, Pearl, 262
Buell, Raymond Leslie, 4
Buffalo, 108-110; black military history,
108-109; Ninth and Tenth United
States Cavalry, 108
Bullins, Ed, 81, 87, 90, 91, 217, 231
Bumstead, Horace, 315
Bunche, Ralph, 224, 338
Burk, Mary Fair, ix
Burleigh, Harry T., 114, 282
Burns, Haywood, 36
Burroughs, Margaret G., 187

Race: Devoted to Social, Political, and Economical Equality, 336-339
Race riots, 22-23, 136-139, 150, 165-166, 216, 309-310
Ramsey, Andrew, 19
Randall, Dudley, 43, 58, 172, 217
Randolph, A. Philip, 11, 149, 197, 241-242, 243, 244, 245, 361
Ransom, Reverdy C.: associated with Niagara movement, 30; attacks "Gospel of Work," 372; on the death of Booker T. Washington, 30; editor of *A.M.E. Review*, 30; as Socialist, 21; supports NAACP, 30
Raspberry, William, 109
Read, Florence M., 322
Reagan, Ronald, 9-10
Redding, J. Saunders, 7, 188, 253, 288
Reed, Addison W., 73, 76, 284
Reed, Ishmael, 34, 172, 217
Reger, Mark A., 50, 70, 216, 220, 345
Reid, Ira DeA., 299, 316, 318, 319, 323, 349
Reid, John D., 323
Republican party and causes of black Americans, 5-6, 26, 127-128, 137, 142, 191, 193
Review of Black Political Economy, 339-341; black economic development, 339; black enterprise and business ownership, 340
Richardson, Willis, 107
Rickey, Branch, 88, 206
Ridley, Charles, 279, 280
Robeson, Paul, 188
Robinson, Jackie, 88, 295, 313
Robinson, Sugar Ray, 313
Rochester, N.Y., 9
Rockefeller, Nelson, 11
Rogers, J. A., 15, 188
Rogers, Jefferson P., 55
Rollins, Charlene, 44, 97
Roosevelt, Eleanor, 262
Roosevelt, Franklin D., and blacks, 5, 6, 101, 146, 205, 309, 326, 347, 373
Roosevelt, Theodore, on black issues, 23-24, 25, 372-375

Rosenberg, Fred, 132
Rosenwald, Julius, 270
Rowan, Carl, 109
Rowell, Charles H., 111
Rudwick, Elliott M., 143
Rush, Sheila, 201
Russell, Charles Edward, 139
Russwurm, John Brown, ix, 183-184, 185
Rustin, Bayard, 180

Salaam, Kalamajyal, 55
Sampson, Edith, 305
Sanchez, Sonia, 54, 87, 217
Sandburg, Carl, 262
Sanders, Tom, 80
Saturday Evening Quill, 341-343; Boston "literary renaissance," 341-342
Savage, Sherman D., 295, 332
Scarborough, William S., 126, 138, 354
Schneider, Genevieve, 339
Schomberg, Arthur, 166
Schuyler, George S., 15, 65, 244, 285, 288, 321; conflict with Marcus Garvey, 65
Scott, Emmett J., 138, 242, 369, 371
Scott, Hazel, 285
Scott, John Irving, 265
Scottsboro case, 13, 166
Selassie, Haile, 12
Sepia, 343-345; black church, 344; black colleges and universities, 344
Sepia Socialite (newspaper), 284
Shaw, Beverly, 33
Shaw University, 336
Simms, Paul R., 133
Simon, Edward L., 349
Singh, Ramon K., 365
Singleton, George A., 188
Singleton, Walter S., 136
Smith, James McCune, 40
Smith, Lillian, 205, 262, 288
Smith-Lever Act, 269
Smythe, Hugh, 246
Smythe, Mabel, 246
Socialism, and blacks, 21, 243
South African Students Liberal League, 13

Contributors

BRIAN JOSEPH BENSON is Director of Graduate Studies in English and Professor of English at North Carolina A & T University. He has published in *Studies in Short Fiction* and *CLA Journal*; contributed to *Richard Wright: The Critical Reception*, edited by John M. Reilly, and *A Biographical Guide to the Study of Southern Literature*, edited by Louis Rubin et al.; and is assisting in the completion of *Richard Wright: An International Bibliography* with Keneth Kinnamon and Michael Fabre.

J. NOEL HEERMANCE is Professor of English at Lincoln University (Mo.). His writings in the area of black American literature include "The Modern Negro Novel," *William Wells Brown and Clotelle*, and *Charles W. Chesnutt*. Pursuing his other major commitment, to prison improvement, reform, and abolition, he is the founder and editor of the *Missouri Corrections Newsletter* and cofounder and coordinator of the Missouri Coalition for Correctional Justice.

CHARLES E. HOLMES is a psychiatric social worker and civic activist in New York City. Prior to retirement, he was an operations analyst in New York's Human Resources Administration and also Psychotherapist for the Mayor's Office for the Handicapped. His civic activities have included directorship of a social organization for teenagers, school social work, and chairmanship of an organization for mental health practitioners. He has contributed authoritative articles to *Science of Mind* and related magazines. Currently, he is in the private practice of psychotherapy and is Adjunct Instructor of English at the Spanish-American Institute in New York City.

TOM QUIRK is Assistant Professor of English at the University of Missouri. He has published essays on a variety of American authors, including Jean Toomer, Mark Twain, Herman Melville, and Joyce Carol Oates, in such journals as *Nineteenth-Century Fiction, Studies in Short Fiction* and *CLA Journal*. He is currently preparing a book on Herman Melville.

ADDISON W. REED, a musicologist, is Chairman of the Division of Humanities and Professor of Music at Saint Augustine's College in Raleigh, N.C. He has published articles and reviews in the *Piano Quarterly*, the *Black Perspective in Music*, and the *New Grove's Dictionary of Music and Musicians*. An article on

Scott Joplin by Reed will appear in the forthcoming *Ragtime: Its History, Composers and Music*, edited by John Hasse.

MARK REGER is a Teaching Fellow in English at the University of Missouri-Columbia. He has catalogued the University of Missouri library holdings in periodicals for the *North American Union List of Victorian Serials*. At present, he is preparing a study of Leslie Stephen and the practice of mid-Victorian journalism.

ARVARH E. STRICKLAND, Professor and Chairman of the Department of History at the University of Missouri-Columbia, teaches courses in both Afro-American history and American history. In addition, he has taught history at Tuskegee Institute in Alabama and at Chicago State University. In 1973, he was one of five historians appointed to a special advisory committee on the publication of papers of black Americans. He is author of a *History of the Chicago Urban League* and is coauthor of *Building the United States* and *The Black American Experience*. He has contributed articles and book reviews to the *Missouri Historical Review*, *Encyclopaedia Britannica*, the *Journal of Negro History*, the *Journal of American History* and other professional journals.

About the Author

WALTER C. DANIEL is Director of the College of General Studies and Professor of English at the University of Missouri, Columbia. He is the author of *Some Images of the Preacher in Afro-American Literature*, and of numerous articles which have appeared in such scholarly publications as the *Negro History Bulletin*, the *College Language Association Journal*, and *The Crisis*.